CHRISTIANITY

CHRISTIANITY

A Global History

DAVID CHIDESTER

HarperSanFrancisco
A Division of HarperCollins*Publishers*

HarperCollins books may be purchased for educational, business, or sales promotional use. For information please write: Special Markets Department, HarperCollins Publishers, 10 East 53rd Street, New York, NY 10022.

HarperCollins Web site: http://www.harpercollins.com
HarperCollins®, ♣®, and HarperSanFrancisco™ are trademarks of HarperCollins Publishers, Inc.

FIRST PUBLISHED IN GREAT BRITAIN IN 2000 BY PENGUIN BOOKS LIMITED.
FIRST U.S. EDITION.

Library of Congress Cataloging-in-Publication Data
Chidester, David.
Christianity: a global history/ David Chidester. —1st US ed.
p. cm.
Includes bibliographical references and index.
ISBN 0–06–251708–2 (cloth)
1. Church history. I. Title
BR145.2 C435 2001
270—dc21
00-037006

00 01 02 03 04 ❖/RRDH 10 9 8 7 6 5 4 3 2 1

Contents

PART III
GLOBAL TRANSFORMATIONS

Preface

At the beginning of a new Christian millennium, I am writing this preface in Cape Town, South Africa. By birth, I am an American. By virtue of having lived for the past fifteen years as a permanent resident in South Africa, I am an African. Under contract with Penguin Books Limited, I have been working for a distinguished publishing house in England. America, Africa, England—this book was already global even before I started to write. As the product of these international relations, my account of Christianity could be nothing other than a worldwide story.

In taking up that global challenge, I present the story of Christianity as a sweeping epic that moves from ancient origins, through the historical transitions of the medieval and Byzantine periods, to the religious transformations of the modern world. As we begin a new Christian millennium, the global character of Christianity has dramatically expanded through new forms of travel, communication, economic exchange, and political relations. More than ever, we need a global understanding of Christianity.

But this history of Christianity is also local. Extending throughout the entire world, the Christian religious tradition displays distinctive local features in different times and places. This book dwells in local detail. Concentrating on specific beliefs and practices, the book explores the textures and rhythms, the spirituality and materiality, the creativity and conflicts that have arisen within the rich variety of local forms of Christianity. Although I provide a broad, comprehensive overview, I hope that I have lingered long enough over individual cases to give a sense of depth and dimension to our understanding of the many distinctive locations of Christianity in the world.

Often this attention to specific location produces surprises. For example, where is the Church of England? In England, of course, but the global history of the Anglican communion has resulted in a church that is predominantly African. With nearly 18 million members in Nigeria and 8 million in Uganda representing the largest concentrations of Anglicans in the world, Anglicans in England—approximately 2 million—form a church that is roughly the same size as Anglican communities in Kenya and South Africa. These statistics suggest that the Church of England is by numerical majority an African church. But the Church of England is also an Indian church, with about the same number of Anglicans living in southern India as in England. As the Indian and cosmopolitan novelist Salman Rushdie once remarked, the English do not know their own history because it happened elsewhere. In this history of Christianity, I have looked elsewhere. Although no separate chapter on the Church of England appears in this book, Anglicans definitely appear—in America, Africa, India, China, the Pacific Islands, and even in Great Britain—in locations that might be unexpected but nevertheless have been crucial for the global history of Christianity. In similar ways, I have sought out other surprises in retelling the Christian story.

Since this book is not an encyclopedia, many things, perhaps most things, have had to be left out. Certainly, readers will find their own favorite omissions. What is included, however, is intended to provide engaging and challenging occasions for thinking about Christianity as a religion. Over the past two thousand years, Christianity has emerged as a religion among religions and as a religion in relation to other religions. As I try to show in this book, Christianity is a religion that has been thoroughly interreligious in its historical formation. Christianity has been shaped by contacts, relations, and exchanges that have taken place between and among religions. Although my primary subject is Christianity, which carries the challenge of bringing to life Christian beliefs, practices, experiences, and social formations throughout the history of the tradition, I also want to understand Christianity as a religion in a world of religious diversity. In a profound sense, the historical character of Christianity can be illuminated from the perspective of those who do not regard themselves as Christians. Obviously, Muslim perspectives on the Crusades or Jewish perspectives on the Holocaust are critical for our understanding of Christian involvement in events that shaped the history of Christianity. The perspectives of "outsiders," therefore, can be very important for thinking about the internal dynamics and external impact of the Christian tradition. Accordingly, I offer a history of Christianity that is also a history of religions.

Now, I have to admit that I have also tried to make the history of Christianity interesting, entertaining, and fun. Although I have made every effort to get the facts straight, I have undertaken that historical responsibility with the ethics of a novelist rather than with those of a theologian, suspending the normative requirements of systematic, dogmatic, or practical theology for the narrative demands of telling a good story. Recognizing that many different stories might be told, I have assumed the responsibility of telling stories that stimulate creative and critical thinking not only about Christianity, but also about religion, religions, and religious diversity. In that spirit, I offer this global history of Christianity as an occasion for thinking something new.

Many years ago, when I first met Archbishop Desmond Tutu, he asked me what I did at the university. "Comparative religion," I replied. "Ah, comparative religion," he observed with a mischievous glint in his eye. "That is religion for the comparatively religious." I laughed, even though I had heard that joke before and even though it is not particularly funny, especially if you have been working to develop a study of religion that is not about being religious, comparatively or otherwise, but is dedicated to creating a free, open space for the imaginative and disciplined exploration of religion in all its diversity. As I understand it, comparative religion is not involved in comparing religions, judging their strengths and weaknesses, and picking the best. Rather, comparative religion is engaged in developing resources for understanding religion in all its global variety and local specificity that can in principle be applied to the study of any form of religion. In this book, I have followed that comparative path in exploring the many forms of Christianity in the world.

I would never have written a book on Christianity at all if it had not been for the intervention of John Hinnells, series editor for religion at Penguin U.K., who recruited this book. "Why me?" I asked. As I recall, he said that he wanted an author who came from outside of the familiar academic circles in the study of Christianity in Britain and North America, who could work quickly, and who was not afraid of taking risks. Apparently, I fit the bill. For the tangible signs of trust, broad mandate, and interactive readings, I will always be grateful to John Hinnells.

Other debts incurred in writing this book can only be briefly mentioned here: I thank Ninian Smart for telling John Hinnells that I could write a book on Christianity; Charles Long for pointing me away from the land and toward the oceans in our understanding of Christianity;

W. Richard Comstock, my mentor in Santa Barbara, for reading the entire manuscript and finding nothing wrong except for one typographical error; Phillip Dexter, my political adviser in South Africa, for reading the entire manuscript and deciding it was actually a detective novel; and Judy Tobler, senior researcher at the Institute for Comparative Religion in Southern Africa, for research, collaboration, editing, and care in the painful task of cutting thirty thousand words—"cutting with compassion," we called it—out of the original manuscript. Further debts should be clear from the references, although cutting with compassion has eliminated a body of referencing that would have run to nearly a hundred pages. Too much. In this regard, as in many other aspects of production, I have been guided by the excellent editorial advice of Caroline Pretty. As always, I acknowledge the Board of Directors, now for over twenty years, for existing and Careen, my wife, now for over ten years, for sharing a life.

PART I
ANCIENT ORIGINS

I

Beginnings

During the last year of his reign over the Roman province of Judea, King Herod the Great (73–4 B.C.E.) erected a magnificent statue of a golden eagle above the main gate of the temple in Jerusalem. In a dramatic act of defiance, two religious teachers, Judas and Matthias, along with forty of their students, went to the temple and pulled down the golden eagle. They were arrested and tried before King Herod. "Who ordered you?" the king demanded. "The law of our fathers," they confidently replied. "And why so exultant," Herod asked, "when you will shortly be put to death?" As the teachers explained, they had defied the king's authority, even under threat of execution, "Because after our death we shall enjoy greater felicity." If they were faithful to their ancestral religion, they asserted, they would be rewarded after death. At the conclusion of their trial, Herod had the teachers and their students executed by burning them alive.[1]

Christianity began in the first-century Roman provinces of Galilee and Judea. There Jesus of Nazareth lived, taught, and was executed. The incident of the golden eagle illustrates some of the characteristic features of religion in the time and place of Christian beginnings. Religion operated in different spheres—political, priestly, and popular—which intersected in the emergence of Christianity. First, political religion, which was ultimately located in the extensive power and administrative scope of the Roman Empire, was also localized in the province of Judea through the rule of King Herod. Under imperial authority, Herod not only ruled Judea as a Roman surrogate, but he also engaged in ceremonial projects—constructing a theater in Jerusalem, building an amphitheater outside the city, holding athletic contests—that were all familiar forms of Roman imperial religion. When he placed the statue of the golden eagle at the gates of the temple as a votive offering to the divine Caesar, Herod indicated the lengths to which he was prepared to go in accommodating the city of Jerusalem to the religion of the empire.

Second, a priestly religion was dedicated to maintaining the religious life of the temple. Throughout the ancient world, priests and other attendants at temples officiated at the sacrifices, feasts, and festivals that enacted a regular cycle of religious ritual. In Jerusalem, an organized priesthood was responsible for preserving the temple as a sacred space—the center of the world—by observing a ritual cycle of sacrifices and festivals. According to Judas and Matthias, however, the priests had conspired with Herod to defile the purity of that sacred space by introducing an alien symbol of a foreign imperial religion into it. Not only symbolizing Jerusalem's political domination by Rome, therefore, the golden eagle represented a violation of the purity of the sacred center of the city.

Third, an ancestral religion, embodied in written and oral traditions, provided popular religious resources that were in principle independent of either the political or the priestly spheres. For example, in their opposition to foreign domination and spiritual defilement, Judas and Matthias did not appeal to the Judean king or to the Jerusalem priests. Rather, they invoked the authority of the "law of our fathers," which they felt had been betrayed by both. According to these teachers, ancestral religion provided resources that could be mobilized against both political and religious injustice. In this conviction, Judas and Matthias echoed the terms in which resistance to political oppression and religious defilement had been advanced during the Maccabean revolt between 168 and 167 B.C.E. against foreign imperial rule. As one Maccabean leader had declared, "We are ready to die rather than transgress the laws of our fathers" (2 Macc. 7:2). Ancestral religion, therefore, was a way of life that could be valued more than life itself. Like the Maccabees, Judas and Matthias even asserted that adherence to the ancestral law in the face of execution promised a transcendence of death in which they would "enjoy greater felicity" or experience an "everlasting renewal of life" (2 Macc. 7:9).

For the most part, however, ancestral religion did not depend upon promises of personal salvation after death. It was a way of life that was anchored in the patriarchal household, modeled on village-based society, and tied to the agricultural cycles of the land. Preserving an ancient covenant with God, ancestral religion established the terms and conditions for a life of piety and purity. However, in first-century Palestine that way of life was under enormous pressures from foreign domination, heavy taxation, and socioeconomic changes that were creating an impoverished peasantry. In response to this colonial situation, a series of movements led by bandits or brigands, by prophets or messiahs, gained popular followings for various political and religious objectives. This era of revolt against the Roman Empire, as well as against the priestly aristocracy that acted as imperial surrogates in Jerusalem, exploded in the Jewish War, which began in 66 C.E. As the culmination of that conflict, the destruction of the temple and the city by the Romans in the year 70 C.E. marked a dramatic turning point in the history of religion in the region. Out of that sudden destruction, Judaism and Christianity only gradually emerged as alternative and competing ways of being religious.

RELIGION OF THE EMPIRE

Conquered by Roman troops in 63 B.C.E., Judea and the entire eastern Mediterranean were brought within the imperial *pax Romana*. The Romans set up a system of indirect rule in Judea that relied upon the compliance of the Jerusalem ruling class and priestly aristocracy. Although a small military force was stationed at Caesarea on the coast, the Roman Empire asserted its political authority primarily through the collection of tribute and taxes. In the conduct of religion, Rome required daily sacrifices for the emperor in the Jerusalem temple, but otherwise did not directly interfere in the religious life of the region. Nevertheless, certain features of the religion of the Roman Empire were unavoidable. During the reign of the emperor Augustus (r. 27 B.C.E.–14 C.E.), key terms of an emerging imperial religion became part of the sacred vocabulary of the Greco-Roman world. Imperial temples, public inscriptions, and religious festivals proclaimed the "good news" *(euangelion)* of the deified emperor, who, as savior or son of God, had brought peace, faith, and justice into the world. Assuming the highest priestly office, that of *pontifex maximus,* the emperor himself became a divine being in Roman imperial religion.

Throughout the Roman Empire, temples provided the most visible manifestations of religion. In Corinth, on the Greek mainland, for example, the first-century Roman city featured temples to Aphrodite, the goddess of love; to Apollo, the god of wisdom and prophecy; to Asklepios, the god of healing; to Hera Argaea, the goddess of marriage and childbirth; to Tyche, the god of fate and good fortune; and to Demeter and Kore, goddesses of fertility, where the Eleusinian mysteries of Dionysius were celebrated in both public spectacles and secret rites. Each of these temples, with their priesthoods and attendants, their devoted patrons and adherents, contributed to a Greco-Roman religious life of processions, hymns, sacrifices, festivals, and feasts.

Feasting represented the most frequent and tangible form of participation in Roman religion. Patronized by a social elite, Roman sacrificial ritual was regarded as a civic duty necessary for upholding public order. But sacrificial ritual also presented opportunities for personal involvement in a sacred meal. Although ceremonial meals could be held in the private homes of the wealthy, the temple offered a public sacred site for eating and drinking together with friends in the presence of divinity. As the divine being of the temple served as host, master of ceremonies, or guest of honor, participants ate the sacrificial meat and drank the consecrated wine. However, as the Roman philosopher Plutarch (ca. 46–120 C.E.) explained, "It is not the abundance of wine or the roasting of meat that makes the joy of festivals, but the good hope and belief that the god is present in his kindness and graciously accepts what is offered."[2] Eating and drinking in the presence of a divine being, therefore, was a significant ritual event in Roman religion.

More portable than temples, however, were texts. Drawing upon traditions of ancient Greek theoretical reflection, Roman philosophical schools developed various text-based approaches to religion. In general, these philosophical schools developed essentially utopian ways of talking about divinity. From a Platonic perspective, for example, all the gods of the Greco-Roman pantheon could be explained as different names for the one God. According to Plutarch, that one God transcended name, space, and time. "Therefore," he concluded, "in our worship we ought to hail him and address him with the words 'Thou art.'"[3] Behind the display of temples, statues, festivals, and processions, therefore, philosophical reflection could discern a divinity that transcended all the conditions of the world.

At the beginning of the first century, the religion that revolved around the city of Jerusalem involved both temple and text. Religion was centered in the daily sacrifices and annual festivals of the temple; it was authorized by a sacred text—the Torah—that contained the model for religious, ritual, and ethical life. Like many other ancient religions within the Roman domain, the religion of Jerusalem had also been relocated to other parts of the empire, establishing diaspora communities in Syria, Egypt, Rome, Asia Minor, Babylonia, and elsewhere in the East. The institution of the synagogue emerged as the center of Jewish life in the diaspora. In that relocation, the transportability of the sacred text was crucial. The Hebrew text of the Torah was translated into the Greek text of the Septuagint; it was reinterpreted in terms of Platonic philosophical categories by religious thinkers such as Philo of Alexandria. However, the temple in Jerusalem remained a center of religious attention. Until its destruction in 70 C.E., the temple in Jerusalem was a fixed center of religious life in Roman Judea.

RELIGION OF THE TEMPLE

Originally built in 516 B.C.E. after the Babylonian exile, the Jerusalem temple, which is often referred to as the "second temple" because it succeeded the first sacred structure built by Solomon in 960–950 and destroyed by the Babylonians in 587, was substantially modified under the reign of King Herod. Retaining the temple's basic design, which divided its sacred space into a porch, an outer room, and an inner "holy of holies," Herod constructed a large compound around the temple and rebuilt the fortress at its northwest corner. As another indication of his accommodation to Roman rule, Herod renamed the fortress "Antonia" in honor of the Roman general Mark Antony. For most adherents, three annual pilgrimage festivals, especially the observance of Passover, provided the strongest connection to the temple in Jerusalem. In the first-century temple, sacrifices were performed as they were required by the Torah, while additional sacrifices in honor of Rome and the emperor were introduced. Certain tensions were evident, however, in the religious and political contradictions imposed on the temple by Roman domination. For example, since the annual Passover festival celebrated the liberation of the people of Israel from enslavement in Egypt, many people wondered how such a festival of liberation could be celebrated by those who were currently enslaved by the Roman Empire.

A variety of religious positions were adopted in relation to this contradiction. First, different styles of accommodation were advocated, not only by the priesthood in Jerusalem, but also by other adherents of the religion throughout Roman Palestine. Within the orbit of the official religion that was centered in Jerusalem, scribes, lawyers, and teachers found scope to extend the influence of the religion of the city, in different ways, to the surrounding cities, towns, and villages of the region. As officials of the temple, scribes were charged with maintaining regional outposts, or "stations," for the Jerusalem temple throughout Judea, Samaria, and Galilee.

Although they might assume responsibility for offering religious instruction, scribes were primarily responsible for collecting tithes and encouraging pilgrimage to the temple.

Less directly connected to the temple than the scribes, two other religious movements—the Sadducees and the Pharisees—also found ways to accommodate themselves to the imperial situation that dominated religious life in Jerusalem. Perhaps originating within the priestly aristocracy, the Sadducees formed a religious movement devoted to a strict, conservative, and literal interpretation of the Torah. In opposition, the Pharisees, perhaps emerging from the scribal class attached to the Jerusalem temple, developed standards of piety, purity, and religious observance that made them widely regarded as interpreters of the personal and social implications of the Torah. Although they respected the claims of the Jerusalem priesthood, the Pharisees placed greater emphasis on the covenant that they understood to be binding upon the lives of all the people of Israel.

Second, different styles of resistance to the religion of the Jerusalem temple were also evident during the first century. Within Judea, resistance could be demonstrated by a radical withdrawal from society. Retreating to the desert, the Essenes established an alternative society beyond the reach of Jerusalem. As reflected in the Dead Sea Scrolls, the community at Qumran acted out a new "exodus," leaving behind a Jerusalem priesthood that they regarded as corrupt to form a new "Israel" in the desert. In developing a dualistic worldview, the Qumran community understood the universe to be a battlefield between God and Satan, between the Prince of Light and the Angel of Darkness. Poised between these spirits of truth and falsehood, each person was engaged in a struggle between two opposing ways of life that was expected to continue until the end of the world. This apocalyptic expectation of a sudden end of the world promised the restoration of the old order of Israel. In earlier apocalyptic texts, visionaries had described the restoration of Israel as a unified nation (Ezek. 37:1–14; Hos. 6:1–3; Isa. 26:19) or the vindication of the nation's martyrs, as in the book of Daniel, when "one like a son of man" would appear through the clouds and join the "Ancient of Days" on his throne to judge the dead and identify the righteous who had died for Israel (Dan. 7:13–14). Within the Qumran community, however, apocalyptic visions of the end were directed explicitly against foreign imperial domination and the illegitimate priestly rulers who were established in Jerusalem. In Qumran, therefore, the dualism of good and evil and the apocalyptic promise of ultimate triumph provided a framework for locating one small community of light in the midst of a vast Roman darkness that had even darkened the temple.[4]

A more obvious form of resistance could be demonstrated by open revolt against the priesthood, the temple, and the foreign rulers. From the beginning of the first century, organized revolts against the prevailing political order periodically erupted. These revolts almost always revolved around the issue of taxation. Since the system of Roman indirect rule was supported by dual taxation—one tax for Rome, one tax for the priestly aristocracy—many people experienced the system as both a political and a religious problem. Although the Jerusalem priesthood advocated payment of taxes as a way of ensuring peace, there were many who resisted payment even at the risk of war. In such acts of resistance, popular support could be mobilized in the name of God against the religion of the temple.

RELIGION OF THE VILLAGE

In the villages of first-century Palestine, relations with the temple flowed in two directions. Agents of the temple came to the villages, and villagers were supposed to go on pilgrimage three times a year to the temple. Independent of the temple, however, village life sustained an ancestral religion centered in the patriarchal household. Interwoven with kinship relations, agricultural production, and ancestral claims to the land, that religion of the village reinforced the household as a domestic sacred space. Under the patriarchal authority of the father, the household was created as a religious space of piety and purity.

During the first century, however, the household was threatened by the social forces of economic exploitation and imperial domination. Under the pressure of double taxation, members of any household were increasingly at risk of going into debt and losing their ancestral land to large estates run by stewards on behalf of absentee landlords. In the religion of the village, land was regarded as sacred on the grounds that it was ultimately owned by God. Increasingly, however, ancestral lands were being lost through conquest or expropriation. Under these conditions, many entered wage labor, tenant farming, or debt slavery. This socioeconomic situation marked a profound crisis in the religious life of the village.[5]

Throughout the first century, a series of popular prophetic movements addressed this crisis by gaining village-based support for some alternative religious or political project. As the historian Josephus (ca. 37–100) complained, all of these prophets were nothing more than charlatans who "under the pretense of divine inspiration worked to bring about revolutionary changes and tried to persuade the multitude to act like madmen, leading them out into the desert under the belief that God would there give them tokens of deliverance." Even worse, from Josephus's perspective, popular leaders of such mass movements "aspire to the kingship." They desired to "be acclaimed king," the "anointed one," the "messiah" of Israel. For example, in the case of a leader by the name of Judas, the son of the brigand chief Hezekiah, his popular tax revolt in 4 B.C.E. inspired people of the town of Sepphoris, a few kilometers from Nazareth in Galilee, to proclaim him as their king. The Romans, however, responded by conquering the town, devastating the region, and selling the people into slavery. Other popular movements were similarly suppressed by the Roman army.[6]

The most devastating Roman exercise of military force, with the most serious consequences for the location of religion in first-century Palestine, occurred in response to widespread revolt that broke out in 66 C.E. Initially led by Zealots, the insurrection eventually involved both temple-based and village-based leadership. Under the Roman general Vespasian, imperial troops crushed the revolt in 70 by destroying the temple and the city of Jerusalem. Although the last fortress held out until 73, when the garrison at Masada chose to die by suicide rather than surrender, the destruction of Jerusalem had removed the heart of the revolt.

After 70 C.E., therefore, the religion of the temple ceased to have any location in the world. The political religion of divine kingship, royal priesthood, and temple worship had been effectively destroyed. In certifying that destruction, the Romans captured Simon bar Giora, who had been proclaimed king during the 70 revolt, took him to Rome, and executed him as the one who had operated during the war as the king of the Jews.[7] In response to the end of the religion of the temple, however, a group of religious scholars under the leadership of the sage Johanan ben Zakkai relocated the heart of religion from the temple to the text. Gathering in Yavneh around 90 C.E., this group of scholars began the work of reformulating traditional religious resources in ways that would result in the emergence of rabbinic Judaism. Based on the interpretation of sacred texts and the preservation of oral traditions, religious life could thereby continue without the temple. In this process of reformulation, the Pharisees emerged after 70 C.E. as the dominant group in Palestinian Judaism. Increasingly, however, they found themselves competing for Jewish loyalty with new religious movements that adhered to the memory of an earlier Galilean prophet named Jesus.

2

Jesus

Jesus was born in the Galilean village of Nazareth sometime between 6 and 4 B.C.E., shortly before the end of the reign of King Herod the Great. He was raised in a pious Jewish family, the eldest of five brothers and several sisters. His home language was Aramaic, but he knew some Greek and biblical Hebrew. He acquired basic literacy and learned the craft of a woodworker. In his early thirties Jesus was attracted to the religious movement of John, known as the Baptist, who was gaining a following at the Jordan River for his ritual of repentance and purification. Shortly after receiving John's baptism, Jesus embarked upon his own project of teaching. He traveled around the villages of Galilee and went to the city of Jerusalem during pilgrimage festivals. After less than three years of public activity, Jesus was arrested in Jerusalem, examined before officials of the priestly aristocracy, turned over to the Roman procurator, Pontius Pilate, and condemned to death by crucifixion. Suffering that torturous form of Roman execution reserved for traitors or rebels, Jesus died in his mid-thirties around the year 30 C.E.

Such is the bare outline of the life of Jesus of Nazareth as it might be reconstructed by a modern historian.[1] Every aspect of this account, however, has been subject to intense historical debate. The precise dates for Jesus' birth and death are uncertain. His family life, educational training, occupation, and marital status have all been questioned. His religious background, participation in the religion of the Jerusalem temple, and degree of involvement in the baptizing movement of John have been disputed. Most significantly for the history of religion, Jesus' brief public activity has been reconstructed in vastly different ways. Historians confront us with conflicting versions of that public project. In different accounts, Jesus has appeared as a Jewish preacher, a wandering sage, a magical healer, or a political revolutionary. The modern search for the "historical Jesus" has produced multiple images of the same man.

Ancient historians provide little help. Writing at the end of the first century, the Jewish historian Josephus (ca. 37–100) referred to Jesus as both a philosophical sage and a wonder-worker. Jesus was "a wise man" and a "doer of startling deeds." According to Josephus, Jesus was "a teacher of people who receive the truth with pleasure." Gaining a following among people of both Jewish and Greek origin, Jesus was accused by religious officials in Jerusalem and condemned to crucifixion by the Roman procurator, Pilate. After the death of Jesus, followers preserved his memory, so that, Josephus concluded, even at the end of the first century, the "tribe of Christians" named after him had not died out.

Although this brief mention of Jesus by a Jewish historian seems to provide contemporary verification, it was written over fifty years after the death of Jesus. By that point, Josephus could easily have been influenced by the proliferation of groups, which did attract people from Jewish and Greek backgrounds, that had fashioned a particular memory of Jesus not only as a teacher of wisdom or a worker of wonders, but as the Christ. Among this "tribe of Christians" at the end of the first century, Jesus was remembered as *christos,* the Greek term for the Hebrew *messiah,* the royal "anointed one" of God. History, therefore, even as it was told by a Jewish historian, could be shaped by that particular religious memory of Jesus as the Christ.[2]

Writing at roughly the same time, the Roman historian Tacitus (ca. 56–ca. 120) had little sympathy for the "tribe of Christians." In recalling the great fire that had swept through Rome during the reign of Emperor Nero in 64 C.E., Tacitus noted that the emperor had used the Christians of the city as scapegoats by accusing and punishing them for starting the conflagration. According to Tacitus, "Their name comes from Christus, who suffered the extreme penalty during the reign of Tiberius at the hands of one of our procurators, Pontius Pilate." As this brief reference indicates, the Roman historian had been influenced by the presence in Rome of groups that recalled Jesus as the Christ to assume that Christ was the personal name of their founder.

Although many Christians had been unjustly executed on the false charge of arson, Tacitus observed that they were nevertheless justifiably "hated for their abominable crimes." Their crimes, however, derived not from political subversion, but from what Tacitus identified as their superstition. Momentarily suppressed by the execution of Jesus, this "mischievous superstition again broke out not only in Judea, the first source of the evil, but even in Rome, where all things hideous and shameful from

every part of the world find their center and become popular." In defending the integrity of the city, Tacitus invoked the classic distinction between
religio, which reinforced public order through the practices and performances of civic ritual, and *superstitio,* disruptive practices based on ignorance, fear, or fraud. History, therefore, even as it was told by a Roman
historian, could be shaped by the religious interests of a particular social
formation.[3]

In the first century of the Christian era, images of Jesus were shaped at
the intersection of history, religious memory, and social interest. Images of
Jesus in the gospels that were eventually included in the Christian New
Testament are no exception. Although they contain earlier texts and traditions, these gospels were only composed after the destruction of the
Jerusalem temple in 70 C.E. The earliest text, the Gospel of Mark, was
written shortly after that event. By editing the Gospel of Mark and inter-
weaving material from a collection of sayings that scholars call Q (from
the German word *Quelle,* meaning "source") as well as from independent
traditions that scholars call M and L, the gospels of Matthew and Luke
were written sometime between 80 and 90 C.E. Although these three
gospels are referred to collectively as the Synoptic Gospels (from synopsis,
meaning "viewed together"), because they seem to adopt a common perspective on Jesus, they actually display considerable diversity of descrip-
tive detail, religious emphasis, and narrative organization.

As an alternative to the Synoptic depictions of Jesus, the Gospel of John
was probably written at the end of the first century. Other gospels, such as
the sayings collection the *Gospel of Thomas,* which many scholars date as
early as the 50s (but others place between 100 and 150 C.E.), did not find
their way into the authoritative collection—the canon—of the New
Testament. All of these accounts represent different ways of remembering
Jesus. Although the gospels reflect the social interests of different historical communities, they nevertheless provide evidence of some of the characteristic ways in which Jesus was remembered. They suggest that Jesus
was recalled as a teacher of wisdom, a worker of wonders, and a preacher
of the kingdom of God.

TEACHER OF WISDOM

According to the Gospel of Mark, Jesus was a teacher. Early in his public
work Jesus "entered the synagogue, and taught. And they were astonished

at his doctrines: for he taught them as one that had authority, and not as the scribes" (Mark 1:21–22). In the religious life of first-century Palestine, as already noted, scribes were stationed around the region as mediators between the priestly government in Jerusalem and the Jewish people of local towns and villages. As the historian Josephus observed, these representatives of the religion of the temple were known as "teachers."[4] However, if Jesus was a teacher, he certainly was not an official teacher of the people, such as a priest or scribe, who represented the interests of the temple establishment. Rather, Jesus appeared in the gospel traditions as a teacher of wisdom, as the transmitter of an alternative knowledge that carried a different kind of authority. He taught a wisdom in which knowledge merged with power. In Mark's account, people who heard Jesus teaching wondered "what wisdom is this which is given unto him, that even such mighty works are wrought by his hands?" (Mark 6:2). At a very early stage, therefore, Jesus was remembered as a powerful teacher of wisdom.

Modern historians, however, continue to wonder, "What wisdom is this?" Ancient wisdom certainly assumed many different forms. For example, in the Jewish literature produced after the return from Babylonian exile in 539 B.C.E., the wisdom of God was often personified. As a popular figure in Jewish poetry, wisdom—Hokmah in Hebrew, Sophia in Greek—increasingly assumed a divine female form. According to these poetic expressions, divine wisdom was crucial to the order of the world, the city, and the temple in Jerusalem. In the beginning, God and wisdom had created the world (Prov. 8:22–31); during times of crisis, wisdom appeared unrecognized at the city gates (Prov. 1:20–33); and wisdom finally found a home when the temple was rebuilt in Jerusalem (Ecclus. 24:1–34). Scribal traditions within Jewish literature, therefore, developed a foundation for stories about the power and presence of divine wisdom.

The image of divine wisdom was further developed during the first century. In the work of the Jewish philosopher Philo of Alexandria (ca. 10 B.C.E.–ca. 45 C.E.), wisdom was present at the beginning of creation not only in designing the order of the universe, but also in providing instruction to Adam, the first human. According to Philo, "The first man was wise with a wisdom learned from and taught by Wisdom's own lips."[5] In the Wisdom of Solomon, a Jewish text probably written around 40 C.E. in Alexandria, wisdom was represented as a divine guide who would lead the righteous into a relationship with God:

The beginning of wisdom is the most sincere desire for
    instruction
and concern for instruction is love of her,
and love of her is the keeping of her laws,
and giving heed to her laws is assurance of immortality,
and immortality brings one near to God.

(Wisd. of Sol. 6:17–19)

In apocalyptic texts, however, a perceived social, political, or religious crisis might be represented as the departure of divine wisdom from Jerusalem. Having left the world, she waited in the remote heavens, perhaps to return only after a period of cataclysmic judgment.[6]

All of these images of divine wisdom were available to those who remembered Jesus as a teacher of wisdom. Jesus could be imagined as the child of wisdom, who was taught by her own lips to teach others. In the earliest collections of his sayings, however, Jesus was presented as a teacher of wisdom in ways that did not necessarily depend upon such a mythic personification of divine wisdom. The *Gospel of Thomas,* which might represent an early collection of sayings of Jesus, recorded illustrations of his wisdom that were not placed in a narrative framework about his birth, miracles, or death. In other words, the wisdom of Jesus required no mythic support. Rather, the format of the collection was consistent with the practice of ancient wisdom literature in stringing together memorable "sayings of the sages" that might be characterized as insight. His often enigmatic aphorisms in that collection encouraged people to see the light of divine wisdom that was within them, among them, and all around them. As a quality of insight that was immediately available, divine wisdom was presented in the *Gospel of Thomas* as a liberating realization of the presence of God.

A similar collection of sayings, which was used in the composition of both Matthew and Luke, has been identified by scholars as Q, or the Sayings Source. As it has been carefully reconstructed, the Sayings Source emerges as a text initially containing instructions in practical wisdom. Here wisdom was less a matter of *sophia,* of gaining insight into the stable order of the world, than a matter of *metis,* cleverness in dealing with the practical challenges of specific situations. However, that practical wisdom seems to have had a distinctively unconventional, perhaps even countercultural, character in the context of the patriarchal household, the peasant village, and the social relations of first-century Palestine.

In the context of the household, for example, the wisdom of Jesus subverted its patriarchal authority by challenging all bonds of kinship. As recorded in the Sayings Source, Jesus said: "Whoever does not hate his father and mother will not be able to learn from me. Whoever does not hate his son and daughter cannot belong to my school" (Luke 14:26–27; 17:33; Matt. 10:37–38; *Gos. Thom.* 55; 101). By cutting these basic family ties, the student left home to learn the wisdom of Jesus. More than that, however, this demand to forsake the bonds of kinship undermined the domestic foundation of an ancestral religion. When a prospective student in the school of Jesus said, "Let me first go and bury my father," the teacher replied: "Leave the dead to bury their dead" (Luke 9:57–62). The wisdom of Jesus, therefore, required a renunciation of home, family, and the ancestral religion of the household.

Within the daily life of the village, the teachings of Jesus countered many of the conventions of human relations and social interactions. In the face-to-face relations of the village community, Jesus advocated mutual forgiveness, the cancellation of debts, and an ethical reciprocity based on treating other people as one would want to be treated (Luke 6:27–35; Matt. 7:12: *Gos. Thom.* 45; Luke 11:1–4). In a society that valued honor and sought to avoid the humiliation of shame, Jesus recommended humility. "Everyone who glorifies himself will be humiliated," he observed, "and the one who humbles himself will be praised" (Luke 14:11; 18:14; Matt. 23:12). In a society riddled with economic uncertainty, Jesus promised release from all anxiety, saying, "Do not worry about your life, what you will eat, or about your body, what you will wear. Isn't life more than food, and the body more than clothing?" (Luke 12:22–31; Matt. 6:25–34; *Gos. Thom.* 36). Certainly, this practical wisdom of Jesus defied many of the conventions of village life.

Most dramatically, perhaps, the wisdom of Jesus ran counter to common sense by exhorting people to love their enemies, to bless those who cursed them, and to pray for those who mistreated them. This must have seemed like a crazy kind of wisdom. However, some of the illustrations of loving enemies that appear in the Sayings Source suggest a playfully strategic approach to human conflict. "If someone slaps you on the cheek," Jesus advised, "offer your other cheek as well." In response to such an insult, which was a conventional manner of chastising inferiors, the student was advised to turn the other cheek as a challenge that denied the striker's superiority. "If anyone grabs your coat," Jesus recommended, "let him have your shirt as well" (Luke 6:27–35). Since villagers wore only two garments, removing the undershirt would result in nakedness and thereby bring shame upon the assailant. In these sayings, Jesus appeared as a subversive sage whose witty aphorisms provoked unexpected insights that undermined many of the standard assumptions about human relations.

Although the wisdom of Jesus intervened in the ordinary conventions of village life, it also demanded a special dedication from its most committed students. In the Sayings Source, the students of Jesus were required to give up family, home, and possessions for a life of wandering. Going from village to village, Jesus instructed these students, "Do not carry money, or bag, or sandals, or staff." When they entered a village, they were to stay at one house, eating and drinking whatever was offered to them. As they visited other houses in that village, they were to say, "Peace be to this house!" If a person of peace resided there, then that greeting would be received. If not, Jesus advised, "Let your peace return to you." While they remained in a village, they were instructed to pay attention to the sick and to announce to the people, "God's kingdom has come near to you." If they entered a town or village that did not receive them, they were to shake its dust from their feet and say, "Nevertheless, be sure of this, the realm of God has come to you" (Mark 6:8–11; Luke 9:3–5; 10:1–11; Matt. 10:7–14; *Gos. Thom.* 14:2).

This wandering lifestyle, renunciation of possessions, and disciplined begging, coupled with a provocative, unconventional wisdom, has caused many historians to recognize a parallel between the early students of Jesus and the ancient philosophical movement known as the Cynics. For over a thousand years from the fourth century B.C.E. to the sixth century C.E., Cynic philosophers sacrificed the comforts of the world for the sake of truth. Adopting a life of voluntary poverty, Cynics challenged the conventional values of acquiring and accumulating property. But they also attacked all social conventions that cast the natural integrity, virtue, and intelligence of human beings into artificial molds. As popular philosophers, Cynics taught in the marketplace, demonstrating their unconventional wisdom through aphorisms and riddles, through dialogue and argument, and through dramatic displays of themselves as living alternatives to the ordinary. For example, when asked why he was begging from a statue, the Cynic philosopher Diogenes of Sinope reportedly responded, "To get practice in being refused."[7] By living according to nature, many Cynics imagined they followed a divine way of life that transcended the social and political order. According to Epictetus, the Cynic philosopher was actually a sovereign who ruled over a divine kingdom of wisdom by telling and showing others how to live a natural life.

If Jesus was a teacher, therefore, his teachings conveyed a message and required a lifestyle that recalled the unconventional wisdom of the Cynics. Like those popular philosophers, Jesus apparently taught by example. According to the Sayings Source, Jesus exhorted his students to learn his divine wisdom by imitating him. "It is enough," he said, "for a student to be like his teacher." As they journeyed to the villages and towns of Palestine, conveying the peace of the kingdom of God, the students of Jesus were supposed to act just like the teacher. As recorded in the Sayings Source, they were required not only to proclaim an unconventional kingdom, but also to pay special attention to the sick. Therefore, healing seems to have been part of the wisdom taught by Jesus as that wisdom was remembered in the earliest collection of his sayings. As the memory of Jesus took shape in the first century, dramatic acts of healing, exorcism, and other wonders assumed prominence in accounts of his work. In some reports, therefore, Jesus was not merely a teacher; he was also a worker of wonders. Jesus was, as the historian Josephus put it, a "doer of startling deeds."

WORKER OF WONDERS

In the Gospel of Mark, Jesus clearly appeared as a worker of wonders. When that gospel introduced Jesus as a teacher of wisdom, it also identified him as "the Holy One of God" who exercised power over demons. "With authority," the people declared, "he commands even the unclean spirits" (Mark 1:27). By 70 C.E., therefore, Jesus was being remembered as an exorcist, as a holy man of spiritual power who traveled around Galilee not only teaching, but also "casting out demons" (Mark 1:39). Over one-third of the Gospel of Mark was devoted to depicting Jesus as a powerful worker of wonders. His power was recalled in stories about extraordinary acts of healing, of feeding the multitudes, of walking on water, and of raising the dead. In the gospels of the New Testament, these acts were termed signs, works, or deeds of power. They were strange, wonderful, or paradoxical things. They were miracles.

In very general terms, belief in miracles was commonplace in the Greco-Roman world. Miraculous healing was institutionalized in the temple of Asklepios at Epidauros; miraculous control over spirits and demons could be achieved through specific techniques; and miraculous deeds were credited to certain divine men, such as Apollonius of Tyana, who reportedly performed healings and other wonders. In the Greco-Roman context, miracles were understood as acts that demonstrated the power of a god or some other superhuman being. They were signs of an intersection between the human world and the sacred. The religion of ancient Israel also displayed an interest in miracles, most notably in accounts of the miraculous events associated with Moses—the manna in the wilderness, the crossing of the reed sea—that demonstrated the superhuman power of God to the children of Israel during the exodus from Egypt. The miracles of the prophets Elijah and Elisha were also remembered. Evidence from Palestine during the first century C.E. suggests that the wonder-worker was a recognizable religious role in the Jewish tradition.

Although the possibility of miraculous occurrences might have been widely accepted, people nevertheless struggled with the challenge of interpreting the meaning and significance of such displays of superhuman power in the world. As already noted, the very definition of religion, as legitimate access to superhuman power, depended upon its opposition to other forms of access alleged to be nothing more than illegitimate superstition. When interpreting extraordinary wonders, ancient thinkers invoked this basic opposition to distinguish between religious miracles and superstitious magic. Modern historians continue to live with the dilemma contained in that opposition: there is no substantial difference between what are called miracles and magic. Rather, the distinction implies a religious judgment holding that some exercises of superhuman power are legitimate and some are illegitimate. In the context of any religious community, the distinction between "religion" and "magic" depends upon the essentially religious discrimination between *our* real miracles and *their* fraudulent, deceptive, and illicit practices of magic. In other words, the distinction between miracle and magic is a mark of social difference in the context of interreligious relations.[8]

Conventionally, the distinction between religious miracles and superstitious magic has been defended on the basis that religion requires faithful submission to divine power while magic manipulates, seduces, or coerces supernatural forces. By implication, religion submits to divinity in order to build up a human community, while magic manipulates the supernatural to serve the selfish interest of individuals. However, since all these assumptions have been derived from the basic opposition between religion and superstition, the notion of magic as selfish manipulation is merely another way of stigmatizing certain claims on the ability to produce effects through access to superhuman power. By the second century, Jesus was being stigmatized on precisely those grounds. For example, around 177 C.E. the Platonic philosopher Celsus discredited Jesus by arguing that he had achieved his unwarranted notoriety by performing acts of magic. According to the Jewish philosopher Trypho, as recorded in the dialogue composed between 150 and 165 by the Christian philosopher Justin Martyr, Christianity had emerged only because a "godless and libertine heresy has arisen from a certain Jesus, a Galilean magician." In these ancient arguments, a magician was defined as someone responsible for "godless and lawless and unholy things." From various pagan and Jewish perspectives, Jesus was a magician.[9]

According to the gospels eventually included in the Christian New Testament, however, Jesus performed miracles rather than acts of magic. His extraordinary deeds of exorcism, healing, multiplying food, and defying basic laws of nature were all represented as authentic demonstrations of a legitimate access to superhuman power. According to Christians, therefore, these miracles were the opposite of magic. Behind the written accounts of the various miracles that finally appeared in those gospels, however, popular stories about Jesus as a wonder-worker might have circulated in oral and written traditions. Certainly, the depiction of Jesus as an exorcist was prominent. In fact, the exorcisms performed by Jesus were understood early in the tradition as decisive evidence of a new reign of God. "If by the finger of God I cast out demons," Jesus was remembered to have said, "then the kingdom of God has come upon you" (Luke 11:20; Matt. 12:28). Accordingly, Jesus was recalled as someone who engaged in battles with the evil forces of demons.

New Testament accounts of the exorcisms performed by Jesus, however, omit any reference to the use of prayers, incantations, or special religious objects. Rather, Jesus is described as driving out demons by rebuking or commanding them. As in his teaching, Jesus' words carried power, an authority that was even imagined to extend over the world of spirits. By the end of the first century, Jesus was remembered as someone who could drive out evil spirits and mobilize good spirits merely by speaking. If Jesus only said the word, the Gospel of Matthew reported, twelve legions of angels, a total of 72,000 angelic spirits, could be instantly deployed against the forces of evil (Matt. 26:53). As an exorcist, therefore, Jesus commanded demons and invoked angels through powerful speech.

Clearly, the practice of exorcism was based on a cosmic dualism in which the forces of darkness contended against the forces of light over the human world. During the first century, as already noted at Qumran, for example, good and evil could be understood not as abstract moral concepts, but as powerful supernatural forces engaged in combat. In the religion of ancient Israel, the figure of Satan only gradually emerged as the supreme personification of evil, as the supernatural accuser, tester, or tempter of human beings, who opposed God and his angels. By the first century, that evil being was firmly in place. Satan and his demons were part of the imaginative universe of the era. According to the gospels of the New Testament, Jesus was accused of working on behalf of Satan, Beelzebub, or the prince of demons, because he conversed with demons when he performed exorcisms (Mark 3:23–27; Matt. 12:25–30; Luke 11:17–23). Although Jesus' opponents might have accused him of magic, sorcery, or witchcraft, his supporters interpreted his power over demons as evidence that he was on the side of the angels in the battle between the supernatural forces of good and evil.

In the religion of ancient Israel, life and death, illness and healing were all attributed directly to God. According to the Torah, God said, "I kill, and I make alive; I have wounded and I heal" (Deut. 32:39). In the gospels, the dramatic acts of healing attributed to Jesus appeared as signs of the power of God. In healing the blind, the deaf, and the dumb, in curing the paralyzed, the lame, and the leper, a sociodrama was enacted that demonstrated before an audience the transcendent power of God. It is possible that Jesus' reputation as a healer brought him into conflict with the priestly authorities in Jerusalem. Since the power to declare people healed, clean, or forgiven was vested in the priesthood, independent acts of healing, such as those attributed to Jesus, challenged the religious authority of the temple. In this respect, Jesus' healings might have registered as a threat to the established religious order.

The students of Jesus were also supposed to demonstrate power over suffering, misfortune, and evil by healing the sick. As they went to a village, they were instructed to "heal the sick among them" (Luke 9:1–6; Matt. 10:8–14; *Gos. Thom.* 14:2). They would also have a special "authority over unclean spirits" that could be demonstrated through exorcism and healing (Mark 6:7). All of these wonders, according to the Christian gospels of the New Testament, demonstrated God's reign, a divine kingdom on earth. Healings and exorcisms, therefore, were interpreted as more than merely demonstrations of divine power over personal misfortune. They were signs of the divine power that was destined to rule the world.

PREACHER OF THE KINGDOM

As the Gospel of Mark observed, after John the Baptist had been imprisoned, "Jesus came into Galilee, preaching the gospel of the kingdom of God" (Mark 1:14). What kind of a kingdom is this? Although the "kingdom of God" echoed general ideas about God as a divine king in Jewish tradition, it also resonated with Greco-Roman debates about political rule, sovereignty, tyranny, and justice. As already noted, the philosopher, whether Platonic, Stoic, or Cynic, could claim sovereignty over a kingdom of divine wisdom. Nevertheless, the kingdom proclaimed by Jesus seems to have been primarily located in the Hebrew biblical traditions that represented God as king.

Although the precise expression "kingdom of God" *(basileia tou theou)* does not appear anywhere in the Hebrew Bible, the general notion of God's kingship or kingly rule can be found in the biblical myth of divine kingship that was important for the religion of the temple in Jerusalem. The ancient "Song of the Sea," for example, declared, "Yahweh will reign as king forever and ever" (Exod. 15:18). In the Psalms, hymns praising God as king appear to parallel praises of the Judean king as divine. "Yahweh has established his throne in the heavens," one psalm declares, "and his kingly power rules over all" (Ps. 103:19). Under God's supreme rule, the earthly king and the temple were established. When the expression "kingdom of God" does appear, it occurs in the first-century Greek text of the Wisdom of Solomon (10:10). Although adopting a Hellenistic philosophical approach to divine wisdom, the Wisdom of Solomon also anticipates a "kingdom of God" to be established with the inauguration of a new era of divine rule on earth. The kingdom of God, therefore, could also take on an apocalyptic character in expectation of a future restoration of divine order.

In preaching the divine rule of God, however, Jesus seems to have declared a kingdom that had already come. As we have seen, Jesus instructed his students to visit local villages for the purpose of teaching wisdom, healing the sick, and proclaiming the presence of the kingdom of God. Even those villages that rejected them were nevertheless to be told that "God's kingdom has come near to you" (Luke 10:11). In the New Testament gospels, this present reign of God was frequently emphasized. The kingdom of God "has come upon you" (Luke 11:20); it is "in the midst of you" (Luke 17:21). "The time is fulfilled," according to the Gospel of Mark, when Jesus began his public preaching, because "the kingdom of God is at hand" (Mark 1:15). However, the kingdom of God might also have been anticipated as a divine rule that was not entirely present. When Jesus instructed his students to pray, for example, he encouraged them to look to the future by addressing God, "May your rule take place" (Luke 11:1–4). Nevertheless, this anticipation of God's rule did not necessarily imply any expectation of a sudden, cataclysmic apocalypse. In fact, the Sayings Source recorded two of Jesus' metaphors for the kingdom of God—the growth of a mustard seed in the ground, the growth of leaven in bread—that suggested a gradual, natural process of development (Mark 4:30–32; Luke 13:18–21; Matt. 13:31–33; Gos. Thom. 20, 96). Apparently, according to the sayings of Jesus, the kingdom of God was a divine domain in the world that was present and growing.

The kingdom of God also appeared as an unconventional social experiment. "How fortunate are the poor," Jesus was recorded as saying; "they have God's kingdom" (Luke 6:20–23; Gos. Thom. 54). The village life of poverty, debt, heavy taxation, and foreign oppression was the primary location of the kingdom of God. Ordinary people living in the villages and small towns of Galilee, rather than the priestly aristocracy, scribal retainers, or wealthy landowners, were the "lost sheep of the house of Israel" that comprised that kingdom (Matt 10:6; 15:24). In response to their situation, the kingdom proclaimed by Jesus promised new social relations that were egalitarian, nonexploitative, and nonauthoritarian. In the context of their poverty, the kingdom of God was realized through abundant eating and drinking. Accordingly, the free, festive, and communal meal emerged as the central symbol of the kingdom.[10]

In contrast to the ascetic regimen of John the Baptist, who was described as surviving on a desert diet of locusts and honey, Jesus and his followers feasted on bread and wine. Their meals celebrated the presence of the kingdom of God that would be denied by fasting (Mark 2:19). As people ate and drank together, without concern for differences of social status, ethnic origin, or gender, they enacted the egalitarian character of the kingdom. Around those meals, stories eventually developed about miraculous feasts, at which food was mysteriously multiplied by Jesus for his followers just like Moses had found manna in the wilderness to feed the people of Israel during the exodus from Egypt. Like Elisha, who miraculously fed a hundred (2 Kings 4:42ff.), Jesus was also able to provide food and drink, but in quantities that satisfied thousands. Furthermore, out of those meals emerged the image of an ultimate banquet, a feast in which people would share bread and wine with the ancient ancestors of the people of Israel. "I tell you," Jesus was reported to have said, "many will come from east and west and sit at table with Abraham, Isaac, and Jacob in the kingdom of heaven" (Matt 8:11; see Luke 13:28–29). In these stories, Jesus replicated models from Israel's past, such as Moses, Elijah, and Elisha, and anticipated reunion with the original ancestors of Israel in the future. In the present, however, eating and drinking together, with the conversation, festivity, and sense of kinship supported by sharing the common meal, effectively enacted the kingdom of God. Irrespective of social conventions or religious rules of purity, anyone was included at the meal who wanted to eat and drink; only those who did not respond were excluded (Luke 14:16–24; Matt. 22:1–10; *Gos. Thom.* 64).

If the kingdom of God was a festive meal, how was that divine kingdom related to the sovereignty of the emperor in Rome or to the primacy of the temple in Jerusalem? Where did this kingdom of God fit in the context of the political and religious relations of power that dominated first-century Palestine? With respect to Rome, the kingdom proclaimed by Jesus had to somehow come to terms with the reality of foreign domination, especially as it was most immediately experienced by villagers through imperial taxation. As already noted, first-century Palestine experienced tax revolts against Rome. Religious leaders, such as Judas of Galilee in 6 C.E., argued that payment of taxes to Rome violated religious law. The Romans, however, viewed nonpayment as an act of rebellion. Where did Jesus stand?

By the end of the first century, Jesus was remembered as having opposed paying taxes either to Rome or to the priestly surrogates who served Roman interests in Jerusalem. As recorded in the Gospel of Luke, the priests accused Jesus of "perverting our nation" and "stirring up the people" by "forbidding us to give tribute to Caesar" (Luke 23:2–5). A tradition recounted in the Gospel of Mark, however, suggests on the surface that Jesus encouraged payment of imperial taxes. By distinguishing between the "things of God" and the "things of Caesar," Jesus reportedly addressed the issue of taxation by advocating, "Render unto Caesar what is Caesar's" (Mark 12:13–17). Writing shortly after the Roman destruction of Jerusalem, the author of the Gospel of Mark might have been trying to distance the followers of Jesus from the tax resisters who had been actively involved in the revolt against Rome. In the second century, the Christian philosopher Justin Martyr interpreted Jesus' response in this instance as advocating Christian obedience to the Roman order in the interests of maintaining good relations of peace and tranquillity.[11]

However, in the story related in the Gospel of Mark, Jesus responded to the issue of taxation by holding up a coin bearing the image of Caesar that had been accidentally discovered in the mouth of a fish. Although on the surface the account seems to advocate payment, it is possible to read this story as providing grounds for tax resistance: since tax was required by Rome on the produce of land, livestock, or trade, that story might imply that people should only pay taxes in coin acquired by accident, like money found in the mouth of a fish, rather than by their labor. An even more radical reading is possible: if God actually rules over everything, then the "things of Caesar" amount to nothing. At the very least, therefore, questions were raised about Jesus' position on imperial taxation.

In relation to the temple, the Christian gospels proclaimed Jesus' strong opposition. Written after the destruction of the temple, the gospels depicted Jesus as an adversary of the priestly aristocracy and ruling class in Jerusalem. They recounted his prophetic judgments against the entire temple complex. In the Gospel of Mark, for example, Jesus went to the Jerusalem temple, disrupted business in the courtyard, and threatened destruction: "I will destroy this temple that is made with hands" (Mark 14:58; see *Gos. Thom.* 71). The business in the temple courtyard—the buying and selling of animals, the exchanging of foreign currency—were legitimate activities of the temple and the financial basis for sustaining its priesthood and sacrificial system. If Jesus disrupted those activities, he acted out a symbolic destruction of the economic foundation of the temple. Combined with his alleged opposition to paying taxes, this attack on the temple could have provided sufficient grounds to arrest Jesus and try him for sedition against the political order of Roman Jerusalem.

According to the historian Josephus, John the Baptist had been executed by Herod Antipas because he feared that John's preaching would inspire revolt. Not a revolutionary, John the Baptist was described by Josephus as "a good man" who called Jews to join in baptism, provided that they were cultivating virtue and practicing justice toward one another and piety toward God. Nevertheless, fearing the potential of his persuasive ability, Herod arrested and killed John as a preemptive strike before the Baptist could spark a revolt.[12] Perhaps Jesus was executed as a similar potential threat. Certainly, his wisdom challenged many conventional social values, his reputed wonders looked like dangerous magic, and his preaching about the kingdom of God held political implications by announcing an alternative order of divine rule. In the end, Jesus was executed by the Romans, crucified as a traitor to the Roman state. After that execution, however, his followers found new ways of imagining that Jesus continued to live.

3

Christ

In the forty years following Jesus' death, different types of religious groups formed around his memory. Some adhered to the memory of Jesus as their founding teacher, collecting his sayings and recounting his deeds, while others remembered Jesus as a divine being, the Christ, whose death and resurrection promised salvation. These two types of groups—Jesus movements and Christ congregations—appeared in different geographical regions of the Roman Empire. They also developed different spiritual geographies to the extent that groups outside of his birthplace in Palestine increasingly understood Jesus as a deity who had descended into the world only to ascend to the heavens. In this respect, the Christ congregations followed a path that diverged from that of the Jesus movements, which had built their followings on recollections of the sayings and deeds of a teacher.[1]

Jesus movements developed in Palestine and southern Syria. Although evidence for these movements is scarce, historians have been able to identify some of the earliest formations. The "Pillars of Jerusalem," under the leadership of Peter, James, and John, who were later identified in the gospels as central disciples of Jesus, maintained the practice of eating and drinking together in the holy city. The "Family of Jesus," under the leadership of James, the brother of Jesus, built a small community across the Jordan River. The "Congregation of Israel," which was largely responsible for producing early accounts of the miracles of Jesus, understood Jesus in the context of ancient traditions of Moses and Elijah, but distinguished him from the religion of the temple. The "Synagogue Reform Movement" tried to introduce their particular celebration of a communal meal in or around established synagogues and came into conflict with synagogue leaders and Pharisees. Dedicated to the memory of Jesus, all of these movements positioned themselves within a changing Jewish tradition in Palestine and southern Syria. Although they might have revered the sayings and deeds of Jesus, they did not divorce themselves from a broadly Jewish environment.

For the history of Christianity, the most significant Jesus movement was the community based in Galilee that collected and edited the Sayings Source, which scholars call Q. During the 30s and 40s C.E., as historians have reconstructed that community, the people of the Sayings Source were wandering teachers in Galilee who were committed to preserving and communicating the unconventional wisdom of Jesus. Clearly they were outsiders, on the margins of Galilean society, adopting a countercultural way of life they called the kingdom of God.

By the 50s and 60s, however, this community seems to have become disillusioned by the lack of response to its new social experiment. The people of the Sayings Source began to attack all those they perceived as ignoring or rejecting them. They demanded repentance. They predicted divine judgment and eventual destruction of "this evil generation." They developed an apocalyptic orientation in which Jesus was reinterpreted as the precursor of the "Son of Man" who would come at the end of time to reward the righteous and condemn the wicked. By the time the Sayings Source was incorporated in the gospels of Matthew and Luke, the community it represented had come to stress Israel's rejection of all its prophets. In this respect, the death of Jesus was evidence of a more general blindness and wickedness that would eventually be punished.

Other communities emerged, however, outside of Palestine, in which the death of Jesus was regarded as more than merely the public rejection of a righteous teacher of wisdom. Jesus' death was understood as a redemptive event. Certainly, within diaspora Judaism, different ways were available to interpret the death of a righteous prophet. In the symbolism of martyrdom, for example, especially as it was developed during the Maccabean period, the righteous person might be killed by an oppressive authority, but would eventually be vindicated after death. As an extension of this vindication of the martyr, the righteous one might even be exalted or enthroned after death in a heavenly kingdom. If Jesus' death were interpreted as martyrdom, therefore, the power of redemption applied solely to whatever vindication Jesus could be expected to achieve after death.

However, in the Christ congregations, which developed in northern Syria, Asia Minor, and Greece, the redemption represented by Jesus' death promised a salvation for all who participated in that death and in the resurrection that followed. For these Greek-speaking groups, Jesus was a deity. He was the Christ who originally founded the community, the Lord who ruled over it, and the Son of God who supervised a divine plan of salvation for the world. For example, in an early song of praise to the Christ, Jesus was depicted as divine being, "in the form of God," who humbled himself by assuming "the form of a slave, born in the likeness of humankind." By descending from the form of God to the appearance of humanity, Jesus even submitted to death. Therefore, the hymn concluded, "God exalted him on high," raising Jesus to supreme power in the universe so "that at the name of Jesus every knee should bow, in heaven and on earth, and under the earth, and every tongue should confess that 'Jesus Christ is Lord,' to the glory of God the Father" (Phil. 2:6–11). In this formulation, dramatic oppositions—descending and rising, humiliated and exalted, enslaved and empowered—framed a celebration of Jesus Christ as sovereign lord of the entire cosmos.

Like the Jesus movements, the Christ congregations met together for meals, sharing bread and wine, but they transformed those events into ritual remembrances of Christ's death. The ritualized meal also provided an occasion for reading sacred texts, reciting poetry, singing hymns, and formulating statements of faith. For example, an early ritual creed proclaimed: "That Christ died for our sins according to the scriptures; that he was buried; that he was raised on the third day according to the scriptures; and that he appeared" (1 Cor. 15:3–5; see Mark 14:22–24).

How did the Christ appear? According to the gospels of the New Testament, Jesus appeared on the third day after his death to close followers, first to Mary Magdalene and other women and then to his circle of disciples. In an earlier account, however, Jesus appeared to his closest disciples, then to five hundred people, then to his brother, James, and finally to a highly educated, religiously trained, and committed Jew who came to play a crucial role in the emergence of Christianity, Paul the apostle of the Christ (ca. 3–62 C.E.). That earlier account of the appearances of Christ, which was provided by Paul himself, asserted Paul's direct connection to the Christ, maintaining that he was the last to have seen and heard Jesus, a man he had never known (1 Cor. 15:4–9). Although his claims to apostolic authority were contested throughout his lifetime, Paul nevertheless succeeded in creating a body of literature that defined the issues at stake in the development of Christ congregations outside of Palestine. As many historians have observed, Jesus might have been identified as the Christ, but Paul was the founder of Christianity.

Paul was a Jew, as he described himself, "circumcised on the eighth day, a member of the people of Israel, of the tribe of Benjamin, a Hebrew born of Hebrews" (Phil. 3:5). He had received a thorough education in both Greek literature and Hebrew scriptures. Identifying himself with the Jewish piety and purity of the Pharisees, Paul seems to have participated in the religious life of the diaspora synagogues in Syria, upholding a conservative approach to the ancestral religion. As he later recounted, he opposed the emerging Christ congregations as unwarranted Jewish innovations because he was "zealous for the traditions" (Gal. 1:14). In particular, he objected to the mixed communities—Jew and gentile, circumcised and uncircumcised—that were gradually forming around the ritual meals of the Christ. In response, Paul "preached circumcision" as the only authentic means by which a man might become part of the people of Israel (Gal. 5:11). At some point, however, Paul decided that the Christ congregations might have discovered a novel way of expanding the scope of the people of Israel by embracing both the circumcised and the uncircumcised within one spiritual family under the same God.[2]

FLESH AND SPIRIT

Around the year 48, Paul went to Jerusalem to meet with the "pillars" of the Jesus movement in the city, Peter, James, and John. According to Paul, they discussed the issue of circumcision (Gal. 1–2). Since the movement in Jerusalem had remained within a predominantly Jewish environment, its leaders had not seriously confronted the crucial question that Paul had found within the diaspora: Could Jews acknowledge uncircumcised men as brothers in the family of God? The issue of circumcision, however, raised a host of other questions: Could Jews share their meals, their homes, or their holy scriptures with gentiles? Could people who did not observe Jewish ritual practices have any place in the ancestral religion of the people of Israel? According to Paul, the leaders of the Jerusalem community had no answers to these questions because their movement operated within the orbit of first-century Judaism. Instead, they agreed upon a division of religious labor. Peter, James, and John would continue their mission to the circumcised, but Paul would conduct a mission to the uncircumcised, as "apostle to the gentiles," who would call all people of the Greco-Roman world to become part of the people of Israel.

In Paul's religious vocabulary, this disagreement with the leaders of the

Jerusalem community was over different understandings of the flesh. Human beings lived in the flesh, but the term—*sarx*, in Greek—was given a complex range of significance by Paul. First, the flesh was the penis, the male generative organ, which was circumcised on the eighth day as a sign of the ancestral covenant with God that originated with the patriarch Abraham. In the ritual of circumcision, the covenant was literally inscribed on the male member of the male members of the community of Israel. Circumcision, therefore, was a powerful marker of inclusion, a physical boundary line that distinguished those who were inside from those who stood outside of the people of God.[3]

In addition to the male ritual of circumcision, however, female participation in the formation of the people of Israel was also highly valued. To be born of a Jewish mother came to signify another definitive mark of inclusion within the community. Second, therefore, the flesh was understood as genealogy, as lineage that could be traced through mothers and fathers back to the founding events—the original ancestors, slavery in Egypt, deliverance under Moses, and entry into the promised land—that defined the religious formation of the people of Israel. By the flesh, in this sense, Israel was a genealogical inheritance that constituted a particular ethnic group in the Greco-Roman world.

In addition to circumcision and genealogy, Jewish religious life was formed and animated by observing the *torah*, the ritual and ethical teachings embodied in the Hebrew scriptures. The Ten Commandments, along with all the other injunctions and prohibitions contained in those scriptures, comprised an entire way of life that Paul reduced to a single term, the law. This reduction was a remarkable act of compression, trying to capture a religious way of life in one word. In another remarkable act of compression, however, Paul fused Jewish circumcision, genealogy, and law into his singular understanding of the flesh. According to Paul, Jewish law, from its highest spiritual aspirations, through its careful attention to ritual purity, to its most profound ethical considerations, was, like circumcision and genealogy, essentially a matter of the flesh.

In opposition to the flesh, Paul proposed the spirit of Christ. To a certain extent, Paul drew upon the philosophical resources of Platonic dualism, which distinguished between two separate realms—a spiritual realm of ideal forms and a physical realm of materiality—in working out his opposition between the spirit and the flesh. However, Paul's project was directed not merely toward rising above the limitations of the flesh, but also toward transforming those specific aspects of Jewish tradition—circumcision, genealogy, and law—that constituted the people of Israel. In the process, Paul sought to define the emerging communities devoted to Christ as the new Israel in the spirit.

Paul's project was certainly not unopposed. In fact, he worked out many of its details in vigorous arguments against Christian alternatives that he regarded as either too fleshly or too spiritual. Sometime between 52 and 54, for example, Paul wrote a letter to several communities in the Roman province of Galatia, in central Asia Minor, to counter the influence of Christian teachers, perhaps from Jerusalem and Antioch, who were advocating the observance of Jewish law as a necessary condition for being a Christian. They had succeeded in convincing gentile Christians in Galatia that they would have to be circumcised (Gal. 5:2–12; 6:13). Resorting to scathing invective, Paul responded, "I wish those who unsettle you would castrate themselves!" (Gal. 5:12). Paul insisted the ritual of circumcision was irrelevant. "For in Christ Jesus," he argued, "neither circumcision nor uncircumcision counts for anything" (Gal. 5:6). As Paul developed this opposition to circumcision in subsequent letters, he invoked the contrast between spirit and flesh to insist that Christians required not the physical ritual, but a spiritual circumcision of the heart. "He is a Jew who is one inwardly," Paul proposed, "and circumcision is a matter of the heart, spiritual and not literal" (Rom. 2:29). The "true circumcision," he insisted, was performed by those "who worship God in spirit, and glory in Christ Jesus, and put not confidence in the flesh" (Phil. 3:3). Therefore, the ritual of circumcision defined a persistent problem that Paul tried to resolve by distinguishing between the flesh and the spirit.

At stake in this controversy, however, was more than merely the relevance of an ancestral ritual practice of the people of Israel. The issue raised the fundamental question of how a person might be included among those who belonged to the God of Jesus Christ. In Galatia, gentile Christians had evidently become convinced it was necessary to be circumcised, to keep purity laws, and to observe the special feasts and fasts of Jewish tradition (Gal. 3:2; 4:10; 4:21). By becoming Jews, these Christians could claim the genealogy of Israel.

In response, Paul developed a second application for his distinction between flesh and spirit. He used it to reread the sacred scriptures of Jewish tradition on two levels of interpretation, literal and allegorical. Corresponding to the flesh in Paul's scheme, the literal meaning of the

sacred texts related the terms and conditions of a divine covenant with the
Jews. However, by reading the texts spiritually, Paul argued, a different
meaning was revealed, a hidden allegorical layer of significance that
applied directly to Christ and those who adhered to Christ. In his letter to
the Galatians, Paul worked out this allegorical method of reading Jewish
sacred scriptures to argue that Jesus Christ was the legitimate spiritual
heir of the patriarch Abraham. As the book of Genesis recounted, God
promised Abraham that his offspring, "his seed," would multiply and
that "all the nations would be blessed in him" (Gen. 12:1–3, 7; 15:5–7;
17:1–8; 18:17–19; 22:17–18). Paul insisted on an allegorical reading of
the promise as a matter not of physical descent, but of spiritual faith.
According to Paul, the promise to Abraham could not be fulfilled "until
the offspring would come to whom the promise had been made" (Gal.
3:19). As he insisted, that offspring was Jesus Christ, who fulfilled the
spiritual promise of faith and righteousness prefigured in Abraham so that
"all the nations would be blessed in him" (Gal. 3:8). By extension, Paul
concluded, this spiritual reading of the Jewish scripture revealed that
Christians actually owned the genealogy of the people of Israel, in a spiritual sense, because, he declared, "If you belong to Christ, then you are
Abraham's seed, heirs according to the promise" (Gal. 3:29).[4]

In between the promise to Abraham and its fulfillment in Christ,
according to Paul, the law of Moses had intervened to contain human sinfulness (Gal. 3:17–19). However, by following the law, Paul argued, no
one could achieve the righteousness that was only possible through spiritual faith. Accordingly, Paul applied his distinction between flesh and
spirit to identify the Jewish law as a matter of the flesh, which could even
become a kind of spiritual enslavement, and to proclaim by contrast the
spiritual "freedom we have in Christ" (Gal. 2:4). Certainly, as a Jew who
had once been "zealous for the traditions," Paul had a complex relationship with the Jewish *torah*. As he later argued in his letter to the Romans,
merely hearing and knowing the law were not sufficient for righteousness,
but the law itself was "holy and just and good" (Rom. 7:12) and doers of
the law would be counted as righteous before God (Rom. 2:13). In his
controversy with the Galatians, however, Paul stressed the freedom of the
spirit, a freedom that transcended circumcision, genealogy, and adherence
to the distinctive terms and conditions of the Mosaic covenant. "For freedom Christ has set you free," Paul declared; "stand fast, therefore, and do
not submit again to a yoke of slavery" (Gal. 5:1). Paul proclaimed a rad-

ical freedom that was universal because it erased all the particular distinctions of ethnicity, social class, and gender. In that spiritual freedom, Paul insisted, "There is no longer Jew or Greek, there is no longer slave or free, there is no longer male and female; for all of you are one in Christ Jesus" (Gal. 3:28).

DEATH AND RESURRECTION

A few years later, in the Greek city of Corinth, the limits of this spiritual freedom were tested when Paul entered into another controversy, this time with Christians who claimed a radical liberation from all ethical constraints on the basis of their "spiritual gifts and power" (1 Cor. 12–14). Members of the Corinthian community were reportedly engaging in extraordinary experiences—visions, prophecy, healings, miracles, and speaking in tongues—that they interpreted as evidence of their spiritual freedom. For some of these free spirits, this freedom apparently allowed them to disregard any prohibitions governing sexuality, marriage, or eating meat at pagan sacrifices. No rules applied, they argued, for those who were experiencing the spiritual power of Christ's resurrection from the dead. By assuming they had also acquired their own resurrection bodies just like Jesus Christ, Corinthian "spiritists" claimed a radical spiritual freedom from all laws by declaring, "All things are lawful for me" (1 Cor. 6:12).

Paul countered this claim by focusing on the human body. Describing the body as a temple of the Holy Spirit, Paul exhorted the Corinthians to "glorify God in your body" (1 Cor. 6:15–20). He advocated certain dispositions toward the body, self-restraint in sexuality, in eating, and in speaking, that represented new purity rules for a Christian community. In contrast to the freedom from the law that Paul recommended to the Galatians, he advised the Corinthians that "obeying the commandments of God is everything" (1 Cor. 7:19). By maintaining physical purity, Paul argued, the Christians of Corinth would not defile their community, the *ekklesia*, which he symbolized as one extended body, the body of Christ. Paul's concern for disciplining the physical body, therefore, reflected his interest in building up a disciplined Christian community, a social body in which there existed "no discord in the body, but that the members may have the same care for one another" (1 Cor. 12:25). Forgetting that they were still in the flesh, the Corinthian "spiritists," according to Paul, were acting in ways that defiled and disturbed the body of Christ.[5]

The contrast between Paul's messages to the Galatians and the Corinthians is striking: the spiritual freedom proclaimed in Galatia stands in tension with the discipline of the physical and social body advocated in Corinth. To the Galatians, Paul declared he was dead to the flesh. "I have been crucified with Christ," he wrote; "it is no longer I who live, but Christ who lives in me" (Gal. 2:19–20). Apparently, some of the followers of Christ in Corinth also claimed to have died to the world, achieving a radical liberation from the moral conventions of their social environment.

Furthermore, by assuming that they had already been spiritually transformed, the "spiritists" insisted that "there is no resurrection of the dead" (1 Cor. 15:12). Although they might have anticipated a spiritual immortality after death, they found the notion of an embodied afterlife, like the concept of a square circle, simply unthinkable. Certainly, from a Greek perspective, which often assumed a human being was an independent soul *(psuche)* in a body, any survival of death could only be spiritual. The prospect of an embodied resurrection, which had achieved prominence by the second century B.C.E. in Jewish reflections on death and afterlife, was based on an entirely different way of imagining what constituted a human being. Rather than a soul in a body, a human being was a mixture of materiality, symbolized by earth, clay, or dirt, and the animating breath of spirit. At death, that mixture was dissolved and the human person—as a *nephesh*, or living being—ceased to exist. Resurrection of the dead held out the prospect that those who had ceased to exist might eventually be restored as living beings.

For Paul, the Corinthian challenge to the resurrection of the dead went straight to the heart of his understanding of Christ. "If there is no resurrection of the dead," he argued, "then Christ has not been raised; if Christ has not been raised, then our preaching is in vain and your faith is in vain" (1 Cor. 15:13–14). Although Paul's distinction between flesh and spirit seemed to identify different spatial levels—higher and lower ways of being in the world, one descending away from God, the other ascending toward God—his symbolism of death and resurrection was clearly temporal, charting a progression from before to after, from old to new, from death to resurrected life. According to Paul, that temporal process was based on the model set by the death and resurrection of Christ. As Paul informed the Corinthians, "we preach Christ crucified" (1 Cor. 1:23). Paul's singular focus on the death of Christ permeated every aspect of his religious teachings, setting the pattern for his interpretation of baptism, the sacred meal, and the future resurrection of the dead.

Paul's understanding of the ritual of baptism, which marked the initiation of a person into the Christian community, was clearly informed by the death of Christ. "Do you not know," he demanded, "that all of us who have been baptized into Christ Jesus were baptized into his death?" As initiates entered the consecrated water, according to Paul, they died and were buried in the tomb with Christ. Emerging from the water, they rose like Christ from the dead to "walk in newness of life" (Rom. 6:3–4). The dying and rising of Christ, therefore, established Paul's basic model for interpreting the ritual of initiation into the Christian community. Accordingly, he rendered baptism a symbolic death and rebirth, an initiatory ritual that enacted not merely initiation, purification, and repentance as they might otherwise be understood, but the mythic drama of the crucifixion and resurrection of Jesus Christ. Apparently, Corinthian "spiritists" adopted a similar interpretation of baptism by assuming that the ritual had conferred upon them a new spiritual status. They had already been resurrected. In opposing this claim, Paul insisted that as long as they were in a body they remained entangled in the realm of death. They would have to wait for the resurrection. In the meantime, the regular ritual of the sacred meal, celebrating the body and blood of Christ, should focus their attention upon death.

Like baptism, the sacred meal of bread and wine, which came to be known as the Eucharist, or thanksgiving, was a ritualized meditation on death. As noted, the Christ congregations that emerged in northern Syria, Asia Minor, and Greece had begun to celebrate Jesus Christ as the patron deity of a communal meal, a love feast, in which the bread and wine, a shorthand phrase for food and drink, were reinterpreted as the body and blood of the deity. In a formula that Paul acknowledged he had received from those congregations, the entire ritual meal was regarded as a commemoration of the last supper Jesus had shared with his students. According to that formula, "The Lord Jesus on the night when he was betrayed took bread, and when he had given thanks, he broke it, and said, 'This is my body which is for you. Do this in remembrance of me.' In the same way also the cup, after supper, saying, 'This cup is the new covenant in my blood. Do this, as often as you drink it, in remembrance of me.'" In these terms, when Christians met for meals, they remembered and revered the life of their Lord. According to Paul, however, the ritual meal celebrated not the life, but the death, of Jesus Christ. "For as often as you eat this bread and drink this cup," Paul exhorted, "you proclaim the Lord's death until he comes" (1 Cor. 11:23–26).

According to Paul, some of the Corinthian Christians had failed to recognize that the sacred meal was essentially about death. The meal was a sacrifice, he insisted, "For Christ, our paschal lamb, has been sacrificed" (1 Cor. 5:7). Unworthy of that sacrificial offering due to their immorality, pride, or arrogance, many had been "guilty of profaning the body and blood of the Lord" (1 Cor. 11:27). They had desecrated this most sacred ritual, Paul insisted, because they had treated it as a celebration of life rather than as a memorial to the physical death of Jesus Christ. As a result of this ritual transgression, Paul argued, they had suffered misfortune, illness, and even death. "For any one who eats and drinks without discerning the body," he warned, "eats and drinks judgment upon himself. That is why many of you are weak and ill, and some have died" (1 Cor. 11:29–30).

What did Paul mean by "discerning the body"? Clearly, in his view, a failure to discern the body had brought divine judgment against many Christians in Corinth. They had suffered as a result. Therefore, the challenge of "discerning the body" must have been important for his understanding of what it meant to be a Christian. In Paul's religious discourse, the body was certainly a complex symbol: on the one hand, the body could refer to human physical life in the world, which Paul often represented as an existence entangled in desires and temptations, in bondage and ignorance, in the existential separation from God he tried to capture in the term "flesh." On the other hand, Paul used the body as a powerful metaphor to represent the Christian *ekklesia* as if it were a living organism, the body of Christ. In the end, however, "discerning the body" required accepting a novel concept, which Paul developed in his reflections on death, of a "spiritual body." Neither purely spirit nor purely body, this spiritual body was crucial to Paul's understanding of death and resurrection.

Like the rituals of baptism and the Eucharist, the resurrection of the dead, from Paul's perspective, was based on the model set by Jesus Christ. What kind of body, Paul asked, did Jesus have after his resurrection? Certainly, there are many kinds of bodies, he observed, because plants, animals, birds, and the sun, moon, and stars all have different bodies. Recognizing these different types of bodies, Paul nevertheless drew a somewhat strained analogy from the world of plants. Just as a seed is placed in the ground in order to sprout new life, the body must die in order to be resurrected as a spiritual body. "So is it with the resurrection of the dead," Paul proposed. "What is sown is perishable, what is raised is imperishable." Like planting seeds, therefore, the human being "is sown a physical body, it is raised a spiritual body" (1 Cor. 15:42–44).

A human body, however, was inherited from the original human, Adam, the first to have lived in a physical body. In a remarkable interpretative move, Paul linked Adam with Jesus, as the last Adam, to draw a dramatic contrast between the physical body and the spiritual body of the resurrection. In Paul's rendering, Adam was first, Jesus was last; Adam was physical, Jesus was spiritual; Adam was from the earth, Jesus from heaven. In the resurrection of the dead, Christians could expect to be transformed from the image of Adam to the image of Jesus. "Just as we have borne the image of the man of dust," Paul promised, "we shall also bear the image of the man of heaven" (1 Cor. 15:49). Like Jesus, Christians could expect to assume a spiritual body at the resurrection. In the end, however, the resurrection of the dead remained a mystery. "Lo!" Paul declared, "I tell you a mystery. We shall not all sleep, but we shall be changed, in the twinkling of an eye, at the last trumpet" (1 Cor. 15:51–52). The ultimate mystery, according to Paul, would only be revealed at the end of the world.

BEGINNING AND END

Paul worked hard to locate Christ within the broader narrative of Jewish epic history and religious myth. As we have seen, he placed Christ in continuity with Abraham, as the heir to the divine promise of the people of Israel, thereby providing new Christian communities with an ancient history. At the same time, by placing Christ in opposition to Adam, the first human, Paul used ancient myth to situate Christ in a drama that encompassed not only a single ethnic group, but also the entire scope of humanity. As the second Adam, according to Paul, Christ played a role in the human drama that could only be compared by stark contrast to that performed by the original human. Adam brought sin into the world, but Christ, by dramatic reversal, brought salvation. In these ways, therefore, Paul located the meaning and significance of Christ in relation to crucial points of origin—the beginning of humanity, the beginning of the people of Israel—in order to work out the details of a comprehensive Christ myth.

Ultimately, however, Paul identified Christ as the son of God who was born in human form to transform the human condition of sin, flesh, and death into the new life of a spiritual kingdom. In that transformative process, human beings could also become sons and daughters of God. As Paul wrote to the Galatians, "when the fullness of time had come, God sent his son, born of a woman, born under the law, in order to redeem those who were under the law, so that we might receive adoption as children" (Gal. 4:4–5). In these terms, the birth of Jesus was depicted as an original event, a point of beginning for a new humanity and a new Christian "Israel" that was redeemed from any of the conditions inherited from the sin of Adam or the lineage of Abraham. Christ, therefore, was the beginning of a new world.

For followers of Paul, it was a short step from understanding Christ as the beginning of a new world to depicting Christ as the beginning of the entire world. Sometime during the 70s or 80s, a Christian author who had been influenced by the teachings of Paul celebrated this cosmic Christ in an evocative hymn: "He is the image of the invisible God, the firstborn of all creation; for in him all things were created, in heaven and on earth, visible and invisible, whether thrones or dominions or principalities or authorities—all things were created through him and for him" (Col. 1:15–16). By placing Christ at the beginning of the cosmos, this hymn located the meaning and significance of Christ beyond the scope of the people of Israel or even of all humanity. Christ came to be celebrated as the original beginning of everything.

During the first century, Christians could draw upon certain resources of Greek philosophy to represent this vision of a cosmic Christ. For example, in the prologue to the Gospel of John, which historians date in the 90s C.E., the author could identify Christ with the *logos,* the eternal word, speech, or reason of God, which had been developed as a prominent theme within Greek schools of Platonic and Stoic philosophy. According to the Gospel of John, "In the beginning was the *logos,* and the *logos* was with God, and the *logos* was God. He was in the beginning with God; all things were made through him, and without him was not anything made that was made" (John 1:1–3). Not merely an abstract philosophical principle, however, this divine *logos,* which had existed from the beginning of the cosmos, became flesh in the person of Jesus. By assuming humanity, the word of God became the light of the world. In the Gospel of John, therefore, the cosmic Christ was depicted as the divine *logos* that represented both the word of God that created the universe and the light of God that initiated a new era "full of grace and truth" (John 1:14).

For those who imagined the universe as the domain of the cosmic Christ, an opposing evil force in the cosmos—Satan, the devil, or, in Paul's terms, the "ruler of this world"—became increasingly important. If Christ was at the beginning, the creator of the universe, they had to ask, why did sin, suffering, misfortune, and evil pervade so much of human experience in the world? As an independent, supernatural agent of evil, Satan assumed an increasingly important role in the Christian cosmic drama.[6]

According to Paul, human beings generally experienced evil as death, which he personified as the "last enemy." In his earliest surviving letter, written to the Christian community in Thessalonica, Paul addressed the issue of death by developing an apocalyptic scenario in which the forces of good would eventually defeat all the forces of evil at the end of the world. As Paul promised, at the end—the *eschaton,* in Greek—Christians would be saved by Jesus Christ "from the wrath that is coming" (1 Thess. 1:10). In advance of that unspecified destruction, Jesus was expected by Paul to arrive, unexpectedly, like a thief in the night, accompanied by military exhortations and angelic trumpets, to initiate a raising of the dead and the living from the earth to "meet the Lord in the clouds" (1 Thess. 4:16–5:3). There, in the heavens, all Christians, whether living or dead, would be "in the air" with Jesus Christ forever. In this formulation, Paul combined a Jewish expectation of a resurrection of the dead from the earth with a Greco-Roman hope of achieving immortality in the air, merging both, however, within a dramatic perspective in which Christians could see in the present that "the form of this world is passing away" (1 Cor. 7:31). To a certain extent, this anticipation of the imminent return, or second coming, of Christ influenced many of Paul's attitudes toward conditions in the world. For example, he advised Christians to remain slaves if they were enslaved and to obey the political authorities that ruled over them, because events were unfolding that would put an end to all of the old power relations that organized the social order (Rom. 13:1–7). Furthermore, he advised Christians not to seek vengeance against their enemies because the apocalypse would bring sufficient punishment (Rom. 12:14–21). In the end, Paul advised, the power relations of this world would be dissolved by the power of Christ. The end of the world, the "close of the age," became a persistent element in early Christian reflections on time and human destiny. If Christ was the beginning, Christ must also be the end.[7]

At the beginning of the second century, this Christian imagination of the end, an end that "must soon take place," was elaborated in the book of Revelation, the apocalypse of John of Patmos (Rev. 1:1). On the Greek island of Patmos, according to its author, John received a revelation that was seen and heard "in the spirit" about the end of the world in which the cosmic Christ, with legions of angels, would defeat all of the forces of evil in the universe. Like Paul, the author of the book of Revelation anticipated an ultimate victory of Christ over Satan and his demons. That victory would be realized in the heavens and on the earth. On the earth, however, in the most immediate social world of early Christianity, the Roman Empire still dominated the political life of the ancient Mediterranean. Although Satan, in Paul's terms, might be the "ruler of this world," the Roman Empire still exercised political power. Rome ruled the world.

The author of the book of Revelation, however, conflated Satan and Rome, producing a single image of evil in the power of domination, discrimination, and persecution that he saw being exercised by imperial authority. Rome was the evil beast, the alienating whore of Babylon, the enslaving power of oppression that stood as the Antichrist against the cosmic Christ that promised salvation. According to the book of Revelation, the *pax Romana,* the peace upheld by the Roman emperor and the Roman gods, was actually a regime of oppression from which people had to be liberated. The cosmic Christ held the key to that liberation. In the beginning, Christ had been present at the creation of the world. In the end, Christ would be active in the destruction of the Roman political, social, and economic order of the world. In between the glorious beginning and the violent end, Christians would have to await the return of Christ, the *parousia,* which promised to change everything in heaven and on earth. By the beginning of the second century, Christian hopes and fears became increasingly focused on the imperial center of Rome.

4

Christians

In 112 C.E. the Roman administrator Pliny, who was serving as governor of the Roman province of Bithynia, wrote a letter to Emperor Trajan in which he reported on the activities of the Christians under his jurisdiction. "They were in the habit of meeting on a certain fixed day before it was light," Pliny reported, "when they sang in alternate verses a hymn to Christ, as to a god, and bound themselves together by a solemn oath, not to any wicked deeds, but never to commit any fraud, theft, or adultery, never to falsify their word, nor deny a trust when they should be called upon to deliver it up; after which it was their custom to separate, and then reassemble to partake of food—but food of an ordinary and innocent kind." By this account, Christians formed a community based upon certain ritual practices—sharing a meal, singing a hymn, reciting an oath—that were all performed on a particular day of the week. Certainly, the fact that they addressed Christ in song as a god suggested that these rituals must have been attended by myths and doctrines about divinity. Nevertheless, it was ritual that constituted the Christian community, resulting, according to Pliny, however, in "nothing more than depraved and excessive superstition."[1]

Responding to this type of accusation, Christian intellectuals during the second century struggled to clarify the conceptual content of their religion. Although they were certainly a small minority in the emerging Christian communities of the Roman Empire, these intellectuals nevertheless assumed the challenge of defining the basic parameters of religious doctrine for Christians. As cultural innovators, they worked with materials at hand, with the intellectual resources they could appropriate from traditions current in the Roman world. Positioning themselves at the intersection of Hebraic and Hellenistic traditions, they claimed elements from both, taking those elements out of context, but rearranging them into new syntheses of religious doctrine. Christian intellectuals drew certain aspects from the Hebraic tradition of Judaism, such as the concepts of God, scripture, prophecy, wisdom, and apocalyptic, but also engaged in conversation with Hellenistic schools of Greco-Roman philosophy. As a result, a lively Christian discourse characterized by intellectual experiments, fervent defenses, and vigorous polemics emerged during the second century.

From the beginning, the development of Christian religious discourse was marked by conflict. Understandably, Jews objected to Christian attempts to appropriate their religious resources. How could such a small numerical minority as the Christians claim to be the legitimate heirs of the entire history of ancient Israel? During the second century, as the number of Christians increased from no more than 250,000 to as many as 1.5 million, constituting less than 2.5 percent of a total population of about 60 million in the Roman Empire, Jews outnumbered Christians by as much as four to one. In that context, from the perspective of rabbinic Judaism, Christians, like other heretics, had to be opposed in order to preserve the integrity of the Jewish tradition.[2]

In Roman imperial policy, Judaism was a legally protected religion, respected for its antiquity, but Christianity was under suspicion, as a recent innovation, of being an immoral, irreligious, and dangerous cult. As indicated by Pliny's correspondence with Emperor Trajan, by the beginning of the second century Christians had become subjected to official investigations. They were suspected of enormous crimes. They were accused of incest, cannibalism, and atheism. Christians were suspected of incest because they married their brothers and sisters in Christ; cannibalism because they consumed flesh and blood in their ritual; and atheism because they refused to pay the proper respect or share in the public sacrificial meals dedicated to the Roman gods. Although Trajan ruled that the Christian cult was illegal and that Christians should be punished, he nevertheless advised his governor in Bithynia that it was not necessary to search for them.[3]

Roman rulers did not have to search the provinces for Christians, however. They could find them at the imperial center in Rome. By the middle of the second century, the substantial Christian community in Rome had attracted Christian intellectuals from all over the empire. In particular, three prominent religious thinkers, Marcion, Valentinus, and Justin, converged on Rome from different directions—Marcion from the province of Pontus in Asia Minor, Valentinus from the Egyptian city of Alexandria,

and Justin from Samaria—to formulate the conceptual terms and conditions of Christian doctrine. However, they came up with dramatically different intellectual constructions of that doctrine. In the process, Marcion,
Valentinus, and Justin demonstrated that Christian religious discourse
was marked not only by conflicts with Jews and pagans, but also by the
intense intellectual battles that were waged among Christians. Although
all three regarded themselves as Christians, Marcion, Valentinus, and
Justin seemed to live in different intellectual worlds. Their careers suggest
the diversity of religious worldviews that could be signified by the term
"Christian" within second-century Christianity.

MARCION

Born in the port city of Sinope, on the shore of the Black Sea of modern
Turkey, Marcion (ca. 85–160 C.E.) became a wealthy shipowner and merchant. Although he was identified as the son of a Christian bishop, the
extent of his early involvement with Christianity is unknown. However,
Marcion must have been familiar with the Jewish community in Sinope,
which was developing literal approaches to reading the Hebrew scriptures
to counteract Christian allegorical claims on Jewish sacred texts.
Certainly, Marcion's understanding of Christianity was situated in that
contest over the authentic ownership of the Hebrew Bible. As we will see,
Marcion entered that religious contest not by defending the legitimacy of
Christian claims, but by rejecting the entire Hebrew Bible.

Moving to Rome sometime in the 130s or 140s, Marcion introduced
himself to the Christian community there by making a large donation of
money. Marcion tried to convince the leaders of the Roman church to
adopt his approach to Christian doctrine. Insisting that he was only continuing the teachings of Paul, Marcion formulated a doctrinal system with
several distinctive features.

First, Marcion proposed that two gods operated in the universe. One
God was the creator of the world, the other was the redeemer of humanity. Using the terms "flesh" and "spirit," which he had derived from the
letters of Paul, Marcion represented the creator deity as a God of the flesh,
a God who had created the material world, with all its imperfections, and
had given the law to the Jews. Although the creator God was not evil, that
deity was nevertheless temperamental and capricious, harsh and vengeful.
By reading the Jewish scriptures, Marcion argued, a picture could be

gained of the creator God who had produced the world. Although that creator God demanded righteousness according to his law, he had actually produced a strange, contradictory world. According to the book of Isaiah, for example, this creator God had declared: "I am the one who forms light and makes darkness, who makes peace and creates evil" (Isa. 45:7). Throughout the created world, Marcion found, similar confusions reigned: some places were too hot, other places were too cold. Some places suffered floods, others drought. In some regions people had abundant food, in other regions people starved. The world created by this God, therefore, was a strange, chaotic, and ultimately alienating environment for human beings.

As a result of living in such a world, people suffered not only physical hardship, but also spiritual blindness. As Paul had put it, "The God of this world has blinded the minds of the unbelievers, to keep them from seeing the light of the gospel of the glory of Christ who is the likeness of God" (2 Cor. 4:4). According to Marcion, Christ was the likeness not of the creator God, but of a superior God who promised salvation for humanity. In opposition to the creator God, who was the "God of this world," Marcion posed the redeemer God, the father of Jesus Christ, who had revealed the previously hidden existence of that good God.

Second, Marcion insisted Christians owed no worship to the creator God. Although human beings were entangled in the world made by that creator, they could achieve salvation only by detaching themselves from worldly pursuits and adhering to the savior, Jesus Christ, who had appeared on earth "in the likeness of human flesh" to reveal the love and mercy of the superior God. Marcion advocated an ascetic lifestyle for Christians, a disciplined denial of the body and its pleasures, as essential for salvation from the created world. By renouncing sexuality, even within marriage, Christians could begin to detach themselves from the domain of the inferior God. But the grace, mercy, and compassion of the superior God was ultimately necessary for human beings to achieve salvation. As revealed in Christ, the love of the supreme God promised liberation from the world in a spiritual kingdom.

According to Marcion, the appearance of Jesus in the world was an unprecedented revelation of the supreme God. Nothing in ancient Israelite history, whether in the promise to Abraham, the law of Moses, the lineage of David, or the visions of the prophets, hinted at the existence of this good, loving, and merciful God. Although Jesus only appeared to have assumed the form of human flesh, he nevertheless entered the world of the creator God in order to reveal the saving power of the good God of love.

Third, Marcion proposed that the road map to the Christian spiritual kingdom could be found in a collection of sacred texts consisting only of the letters of Paul and the Gospel of Luke. Although he demonstrated he had read and diligently interpreted a wide range of religious literature, Marcion insisted that all other sacred texts, whether traditionally Jewish or ostensibly Christian, effectively proclaimed the law and vengeance of the inferior God who had created the visible world. Even Paul and Luke, Marcion found, had to be carefully edited in order to recover what he regarded as their authentic revelation of the supreme God. But the Hebrew scriptures had to be utterly rejected. In the battle over the legitimate ownership of Jewish sacred texts, Marcion urged Christians to surrender, but only because he had determined that those texts were not worth owning, since, in his terms, they only led away from the supreme God of salvation uniquely revealed in Jesus Christ.

For all his intellectual brilliance, moral rigor, and total commitment to the Christian cause, Marcion was rejected by the established Christian community in Rome. Around 144, the leaders of the Roman church renounced his teachings and returned his donation. Until his death in 160, however, Marcion continued to proclaim his understanding of Christian doctrine. By that time, as his adversary Justin noted with some exaggeration, the teachings of Marcion had spread throughout the whole human race. Fifty years later, Tertullian of Carthage, in his *Adversus Marcionem*, was still arguing against proponents of the Christian doctrines of Marcion, who, he complained, had "filled the whole world." Three hundred years later, Theodoret of Cyrrhus was still debating with Marcionites who had established long-standing Christian communities in Syria. For many Christians in this era, therefore, Marcionite Christianity was nothing more or less than Christianity.[4]

What was at stake in this internal Christian controversy? Marcion had outlined a conceptual scheme for Christians in which the old God of creation, which was described in Jewish scriptures, had been displaced by the new God of redemption revealed in Christ. In this opposition between two Gods, Marcion tried to explain to Christians how the new had replaced the old. Although the old God of Israel was not evil, that God was nevertheless inferior to the God of love that promised redemption. For Marcion's opponents, however, Christians could only establish legitimacy in the Roman Empire if they were not just new, but also old. They had to carry with them the authenticity of ancient tradition, an antiquity they could only acquire by claiming an unbroken continuity with the sacred history preserved in Jewish sacred texts. For strategic reasons, they needed to represent themselves as a new religious order with an ancient sacral warrant contained in Jewish scriptures. Essentially, therefore, Marcion engaged his fellow Christians in a battle over the interpretation of the Hebrew Bible.

In this regard, although he denigrated the Jewish God as inferior to the Christian God, Marcion was content to respect Jews, Jewish texts, and Jewish religious practice as constituting a religion that was essentially independent of Christianity. As a Christian, Marcion made no attempt to appropriate Jewish scriptures. His opponents, however, wanted to claim the Jewish legacy as their own. Accordingly, they tried to erase Jews from the present, or at least to undermine the legitimacy of Jewish religion in the context of the Roman Empire, in order to appropriate a Jewish past. They needed to establish continuity with that epic history—from creation to the present—which Marcion had tried to break. While Marcion looked to a Christian future, his opponents insisted on linking any future to an ancient past stretching back through the history of Israel to the creation of the world.[5]

More than ancient history, however, was at stake in this controversy. Marcion had proposed an elegant and simple solution to the problem of evil, suffering, and misfortune in human experience. According to Marcion, evil resulted from the incompetent design of the created world. Although the creator God had no evil intent, the inadequate world he created resulted in all the suffering and misfortunes human beings had to endure. The redeemer God, as revealed through Jesus Christ, had nothing to do with causing human distress. Independent of all the evil, suffering, and misfortune of the world, that God alone could save human beings. In rejecting Marcion's solution, however, his opponents had to find different ways to explain the problem of evil that human beings inevitably encounter by living in the world.

Finally, through his detailed analysis of sacred texts, Marcion forced Christians to take their texts seriously, not only as inspiration for a religious life, but also as legitimation for a religious community. When Marcion drew a boundary around the writings of Paul and Luke, and thereby excluded all other religious texts, he introduced the notion of a

Christian canon—a measuring ruler, norm, or standard—that would determine the precise limitations of what should be included within the collection of Christian sacred literature. Although some texts remained controversial for centuries, Marcion's opponents were adamant that the Hebrew Bible must be included. Accordingly, they appropriated the texts of Jewish sacred scripture as an "old" testament that supplemented the "new" testament of gospels, histories, letters, and revelations that Christians had produced. In this respect, therefore, Marcion was instrumental in the production of the Christian Bible.

Nevertheless, Christian texts continued to be written, often claiming status as revelation. During the second century, anonymous Christian authors composed letters attributed to the apostle Paul or to the disciples Peter, John, or James. Some of these writings were included in the canon, the orthodox list of accepted Christian scriptures. Others, however, were excluded. In many cases, religious texts were excluded because they claimed special revelations that contradicted the authority of the leadership of established Christian communities. In particular, some texts were opposed because they claimed to be based upon a special knowledge not available to the ordinary Christian. That special knowledge—or *gnosis,* a knowledge that could only be derived from an intimate acquaintance with the divine—generated considerable controversy among Christians in Rome and elsewhere in the Roman Empire during the second century. While Marcion was defending a Christian doctrine of two Gods, his contemporary in Rome, Valentinus, was developing a form of Christianity that came to be known as Christian Gnosticism.

VALENTINUS

Born in an Egyptian seacoast village, Valentinus (ca. 100–ca. 175) was educated in rhetoric and philosophy in Alexandria, the center of learning in the Greco-Roman world. Although Valentinus moved to Rome around 140, his intellectual home remained Alexandria. During a time of dramatic social change, as the Roman imperial order threatened older social forms, loyalties, and allegiances, Alexandria survived as an island of Greek education and philosophical conversation. Although different schools of pagan, Jewish, and Christian thought developed in Alexandria, they all seemed to share a sense of being removed from the conflicts and seductions of the broader Roman world.

The ancient philosophy of Plato, in a phase of its development known as Middle Platonism, provided the basic framework for philosophical reflection. According to Plato's *Timaeus,* which became an influential text in Alexandria, the supreme God was not a being among other beings, a being with personal attributes such as thinking, feeling, or acting. Rather, God was transcendent being itself. As unchanging perfection—the good, the true, and the beautiful—the supreme God was entirely above and beyond the world.

Human aspirations for transcending the material world, developed in Platonic terms, could be found in both Jewish and Christian religious thinkers in Alexandria. Educated in that environment, Valentinus demonstrated a similar concern for achieving a radical transcendence of the world. He was influenced, however, not only by Platonic philosophical reflection, but also by the creative, imaginative currents of Gnostic thought—from *gnosis,* or knowledge—that were generating new myths of creation and redemption. Although the precise roots of Gnosticism remain obscure, the evidence suggests a panreligious interchange drawing upon ancient Egyptian, Greek, Persian, and Jewish resources that resulted in the formulation of a new mythic universe.

In basic outline, Gnostic myth proceeded through four stages. First, a purely spiritual realm, emanating from the highest God, was populated by divine beings of wisdom and power. All together, the supreme God and the divine beings constituted the perfection, fullness, or entirety of the spirit. Second, the material world was created by mistake, by some unexpected accident. As a result of that original error, which also included the accidental production of human beings, the material world was essentially imperfect. Human beings were entangled in that imperfect world. Third, by the mercy of one or more of the divine beings, a spark of light was placed in some of the human beings. Although they had to live in darkness, as if they were asleep even when awake, forgetting their spiritual gift, these human beings nevertheless carried the divine spark of light that had originated from the spiritual realm. Fourth, and finally, in order to awaken those who were spiritually asleep, a redeemer came from the spiritual realm to reveal the knowledge—the *gnosis*—that would remind those who responded to return home.[6]

By the time Valentinus was studying in Alexandria, a Gnostic Christianity had already taken shape. Moving to Rome, Valentinus developed it into a system. He proclaimed a supreme God, invisible, ineffable, and ultimately inconceivable, who existed before the beginning, in peace and stillness, as the "Primal Ground" of being. The emanation, emission, or seed of that original God, however, entered the womb of the Silence and began to produce further spiritual beings—Mind and Truth, Logos and Life—until a total of thirty *aeons*, or infinite spaces, occupied the infinity of the spiritual realm, which Valentinus called the *pleroma*, the fullness. As the emanation, or overflow, of the supreme God, the *pleroma* was a complex realm of spiritual reality.

However, when the last emanation, Sophia, tried to become a creator like the supreme God, she was expelled from the spiritual realm. Outside of the eternal *pleroma*, Sophia could only produce a monster, Hokmah. These two forms of wisdom—the one banished from the spiritual realm, the other produced by a monstrous mistake—together created the Demiurge, an ignorant, incompetent craftsman, who fashioned the material world and human beings to live in the world. Taking mercy on the human beings, Sophia and Hokmah were able to implant the spark of *gnosis*—knowledge, insight, or intimate acquaintance with the divine—into a few of them. In other human beings they were able to instill the capacity for faith and good works. For most human beings, however, Sophia and Hokmah were unable to do anything to relieve them from the darkness and ignorance in which they were enmeshed by living in the material world.

As a result of the inherent deficiency of creation, human beings were divided into three basic types—the spiritual humans who held a spark of divine light; the ensouled humans who were capable of faith and goodness; and the fleshly, earthly, or material humans who were entirely identified with the conditions of the world. All humans were subject to the passions and desires of the heart, through which evil spirits defiled and corrupted, distracted and ensnared everyone who lived in the material world. All were in need of redemption. Although many would be called to that redemption, only few would be chosen. Some would not be called at all because they were unable to hear. But others would hear the call and respond by faithfully believing what they heard. Living by faith, however, they would remain in ignorance. Only those who carried the spark of light would recognize the call as an awakening, as an occasion for remembering their divine origin and achieving liberation from the material world. For those who achieved that intimate knowledge of the divine, the Gnostics, "the knowledge of the All is sufficient for them, and this is the true redemption."[7]

In a material world based on accident, mistakes, error, and ignorance, spiritual redemption depended upon knowledge, a liberating insight into the "ineffable greatness" of the spiritual realm. In the Christian Gnosticism of Valentinus, that special knowledge was revealed by a redeemer, Jesus Christ, who entered the world to awaken spiritual human beings from their sleep. According to Valentinus, the redeemer was comprised of four aspects. First, the appearance of the redeemer in a physical body, the body of Jesus, which was "created with inexpressible skill," was produced by a special dispensation of time. When the time was right, Jesus was born. Second, the human soul of Jesus, his psychic aspect, which entered through his mother, Mary, "like water flowing through a pipe," came from the *demiourgos* who had imperfectly created the material world. Third, the spiritual seed of wisdom, given by Sophia, was implanted in Jesus at the time of his baptism, hovering over him like a dove. Finally, the spiritual power of salvation, which also descended on Jesus at his baptism, came from the entirety of the *pleroma,* deriving its spiritual knowledge and power from the original source of everything. In these four aspects, therefore, Jesus Christ encompassed the entire scope of the material world and the spiritual realm. Drawing light from above, he was able to awaken those who lived in ignorance in the material world below.

In these complex terms, Valentinus proclaimed Jesus as "the most perfect beauty and star of the Fullness, a perfect fruit, Jesus, who was also named Savior, Christ, and after his Father, Logos and All, because he is from the All." When he appeared in the material world, Jesus taught the hidden mysteries of the *pleroma* to a group of chosen initiates. According to Valentinus, "Jesus Christ shed light upon those who were, because of forgetfulness, in darkness. He enlightened them and gave them a way, and the way is the truth, about which he instructed them." However, the power of error, which dominated the material world, was angered by these teachings and the enlightenment they produced. Error persecuted and eventually crucified Jesus. Although the material and psychological aspects of Jesus suffered on the cross, his spiritual nature rose above the scene of the crucifixion. Only Gnostics, however, were able to perceive that spiritual nature through a profound quality of insight. Although Jesus was hung on the cross like a fruit on a tree, all those with insight were nourished by that fruit because they "discovered him within them— the inconceivable, uncontained, the father, who is perfect, who created the entirety." By looking within themselves, therefore, Gnostics were able to discern the truth of spiritual perfection that was revealed in Jesus Christ.[8]

Flourishing in the second century, Gnostic Christianity remained a significant variety of the Christian religion, even though it was vigorously opposed and eventually suppressed by Christian opponents. By their own account, Gnostics were always a minority, an enlightened elite, within the broader diversity of Christianity. Nevertheless, Gnostic Christianity stood as an important alternative that had to be opposed by those who were trying to establish the Christian religion as a broad-based, popular movement. From the second century, Gnosticism influenced their definition of Christianity in at least three respects.

First, like Marcion, Gnostics raised the question of defining an authoritative canon of Christian sacred texts. However, although Marcion scrupulously closed his canon by including only Paul and Luke, Gnostics opened the canon of relevant sacred literature by producing new gospels, histories, and revelations all claiming authoritative status because they were based on direct spiritual insight. For example, drawing inspiration from the early Gnostic text *The Secret Gospel of John,* Valentinus himself wrote a new gospel, *The Gospel of Truth,* that was regarded as sacred scripture within Gnostic Christian circles. Other Gnostic texts proliferated. During the second century, therefore, some Christians could position themselves as "centrists" by opposing both the strict limits placed around Christian sacred texts by Marcion and the potentially unlimited production of Christian sacred texts inspired by Valentinus. By trying to occupy that middle ground, they began the process of certifying a collection of Christian sacred scriptures that was broader than Marcion's but narrower than that of Valentinus.

Second, these centrists countered the Gnostics by claiming that they ultimately derived their religious authority not from direct spiritual insight, but from a historical lineage that could be traced back to the disciples of Jesus Christ. They insisted on the power of "apostolic authority" as if it represented an ancestral connection or legitimate inheritance they had derived from those who had actually been present at the founding events of the Christian era. Certainly, Marcion and Valentinus held the apostle Paul in great regard. While Marcion relied only upon Paul, Valentinus, according to his followers, had originally learned Christianity from one of Paul's students, Theudas. In opposition to Marcion and Valentinus, the centrists in Rome rejected Paul for Peter, asserting in the process that someone who had seen, heard, and touched Jesus in the flesh held greater apostolic authority than someone who had merely reported spiritual experiences of the Christ.

Third, although Gnostic Christians emphasized spiritual insight, they devalued the importance of Christian ritual practices. In Rome, for example, the students of Valentinus met in small study groups, interpreting texts, engaging in philosophical conversation, and cultivating an intimate knowledge of spiritual reality. Although Gnostic rituals were developed, they seem to have been occasions for affirming sacred knowledge rather than affirming a shared faith. Since they were intent upon gaining Christian knowledge, the Gnostics placed less importance on the saving power of faithful devotion or the rituals of Christian faith. Their opponents, however, stressed those rituals. Baptism, the Eucharist, and all the forms of Christian worship were essential ingredients of a Christian life that led to salvation.

However, with their different approaches to sacred texts, apostolic authority, and ritual practices, centrist Christians in Rome still had to participate in the same intellectual environment as Marcionites and Gnostics. While Marcion and Valentinus were teaching Christianity in Rome, a third Christian, Justin, who came to be known as Justin Martyr, also taught a version of Christianity at the imperial center. Like his adversaries, Justin also had to engage the intellectual challenges posed by Judaism and Greco-Roman philosophy if he was going to make the conceptual content of Christianity relevant. Although he might claim to represent a centrist position among different Christian options, Justin had to demonstrate to a broader Roman audience that his position should be taken seriously by any thinking person in the Roman Empire.

JUSTIN

Born in Flavia Neapolis, the modern town of Nablus, near Shechem in Samaria, Justin (ca. 100–165 C.E.) seems to have come from a Greco-Roman background. Certainly, he was thoroughly educated in Greek language, literature, and philosophy before he converted to Christianity. According to legend, Justin was walking by the seashore when he met a Samaritan peasant who raised questions about religion that Justin would pursue for the rest of his life. After consulting the books of Moses and reading Christian literature, Justin decided that the wisdom of Greek philosophy was fulfilled in Christianity. When he moved to Rome, however, Justin found that Christianity was not a single system of wisdom, but a diverse and vigorous conversation, an argument animated by discordant voices that included Marcion, Valentinus, and many others. If Christians were to establish themselves in Rome, Justin must have thought, they had to speak with a single voice. For the rest of his career, Justin tried to work out a single centrist or mainstream position for Christians in Rome—in conversation with Greek philosophy, in opposition to Judaism—that would establish a legitimate place for Christianity as a religion in the Roman Empire.

Against Marcion and Valentinus, Justin argued that the supreme God of Christians was the divine being who was ultimately responsible for creation. However, since that transcendent God was above and beyond the world, timeless and unknowable, the revelation of divine creativity was effected through the *logos,* the Word of God. The *logos* was the divine medium through which the supreme God acted. The created universe, therefore, reflected the rational order originally derived from the *logos.* In everything, according to Justin, the divine "seed-bearing" *logos*—the *logos spermatikos*—had planted traces of itself, sowing seeds of wisdom throughout the world. Endowed with reason, human beings also contained traces of the *logos spermatikos,* but by exercising free will the original humans, seduced by fallen angels, had introduced evil into the world. For Justin, the role of the fallen angels was particularly important in explaining the force of evil. It was not the result of an incompetent creator or of human ignorance. Rather, evil was a supernatural force promoted by wicked angels who had turned against God. Those evil angels caused "murders, wars, adulteries, all sorts of dissipation, and every species of sin." Disrupting the rational order of the *logos,* a host of demons had led humanity into the chaos of evil.[9]

With the birth of Jesus, the divine *logos* became incarnate in human form. As angel and revealer of the supreme God, the *logos* had been active throughout human history. As incarnated in Jesus, however, the *logos* had lived, suffered, died, and been raised from the dead. According to Justin, Jesus was not a good man who had been raised to divine status; he was the divine *logos*—the Word of God, the Son of God—who had assumed human form. Justin expected that Jesus would soon return in glory to judge human beings, conquer all the demons, and rule over a new world. Therefore, the ultimate Christian victory could only be expected in the apocalyptic return of Jesus Christ. In the meantime, however, human beings could follow Jesus Christ by uncovering the seeds of the *logos* that were planted within them. By conforming to the law of the *logos,* Justin promised, Christians could be liberated from the forces of evil. From Justin's perspective, the church was a gathering of those who were committed to learning and living the ways of God as revealed through the *logos.* Since the *logos* had become incarnate in Jesus Christ, the Christian church had become the location of the *logos.*

Having formulated his basic theory of the divine *logos,* Justin devoted much of his work to arguing that it belonged exclusively to Christians. Although the truth of the *logos* had always been available, especially in Greek philosophy and Hebrew revelation, Justin insisted that the *logos* had become Christian property. Within the context of a lively interreligious conversation in second-century Rome, many thinkers inquired about the nature of truth. However, Justin also asked: "Who owns the truth?" Since Justin had clearly drawn upon intellectual resources from ancient Greece and Israel, he had to answer that question on two fronts— in relation to philosophers who worked within various schools of Greek thought and in relation to Jews who lived within the heritage of ancient Israel. To assert Christian ownership of the truth, therefore, Justin had to counter the alternative claims, which were underwritten by superior numbers, long-standing history, and social convention, that had been established by pagans and Jews.

In relation to Greco-Roman pagans, Justin asserted bluntly that "whatever things were rightly said among all men are the property of us Christians." In other words, because the Christian *logos* was the original source of all truth, anything true was necessarily Christian. Since truth had been scattered throughout the world by the "seed-bearing" *logos,* any truth harvested by pagan philosophers now belonged to the Christian church, in which, according to Justin, the divine *logos* resided. Many pagan philosophers, therefore, had been Christians without knowing it. In making this observation, Justin might have intended a very broad and inclusive definition of what it meant to be a Christian that would have embraced all seekers of truth. Such a definition would have included under the designation "Christian" anyone who worked to uncover traces of the divine *logos* and endeavored to live accordingly. In this sense, therefore, any lover of truth would have counted as a Christian.[10]

However, Justin actually asserted a much more exclusive claim to ownership of the *logos* on behalf of the Christian church. Regarding the phi-losophy of Plato, for example, Justin maintained that Platonism con-tained truth only because Plato had drawn his insights from a Christian heritage that could be traced back to ancient Israel. Justin insisted that "it was from our teachers—we mean the account given through the prophets—that Plato borrowed his statement that God by shaping origi-nal matter made the world." According to Justin, Plato had actually stolen his account of creation from the revelation delivered by the divine *logos* to the prophet Moses of ancient Israel. In exposing this act of appro-priation, Justin depicted Plato not merely as Moses speaking Greek, as Philo had held, but as a plagiarist of the Christian *logos* revealed to Moses. Justin insisted that Plato had actually taken his imagery, insight, and access to truth from the revelation of the divine *logos* in Christ.[11]

Although Justin appropriated the truth of Plato for Christians, he demoted the gods of Greco-Roman paganism to the status of demons. Instead of dismissing the existence of pagan gods, Justin maintained that they were real and powerful forces in the universe, but they were forces of evil that Christians had to resist. The pagan gods, according to Justin, were actually the original fallen angels and their demonic offspring who prompted deception and evil in the world. They had disguised and dis-torted the *logos* in the myths and rituals of pagan religion. Anyone who participated in Greco-Roman religious life was unknowingly engaged in the worship of demons. Therefore, Justin not only incorporated the Greek philosophical concept of the *logos* into his Christian cosmology, but also incorporated the Greco-Roman gods into his Christian demonology.[12]

As Justin intervened in Greco-Roman paganism by appropriating and transposing its basic elements, he also engaged Judaism in a contest over the legitimate ownership of the truth. Although Judaism held the legal sta-tus of a religion in the Roman Empire, Jews had suffered a series of polit-ical disasters. As already noted, the destruction of the Jerusalem temple in 70 C.E. had devastating effects on religious life in Judea. While some Jewish leaders worked to reconstruct the religion in exile, others hoped to reclaim Jerusalem, restore the temple, and reestablish political indepen-dence in Judea. Under the leadership of Simon bar Kosiba—who was known as Bar Kokhba, "Son of the Star," perhaps referring to his mes-sianic status—a Jewish revolt was mounted in 132 C.E. against Roman political authority in Jerusalem. After suppressing the revolt in 135, the Roman emperor Hadrian ordered the city to be rebuilt as Aelia Capitolina

and the temple to be dedicated to the Roman god Jupiter. Jews were banished from the city and the surrounding region.

One response to this final separation from the temple and the sacred
city of Jerusalem appeared in the efforts of rabbis to formulate a religious
way of life based on the Torah, but was independent of the city, the temple,
and sacrificial ritual. By the end of the second century, the ethical standards and ritual purity of that way of life had been recorded in the
Mishnah. Exiled from Israel, the rabbis who compiled the Mishnah
defined the terms and conditions for the formation of a "New Israel."

According to Justin, however, the "New Israel" could only be found
among Christians. Christians rather than Jews legitimately claimed the
inheritance of the religion of ancient Israel. Like Paul, Justin differentiated
Jews from Christians by distinguishing between the circumcision of the
flesh, which marked Jews by a physical sign of difference, and the circumcision of the spirit claimed by Christians. In his anti-Jewish polemic, however, Justin pushed this distinction further than Paul did by insisting that
circumcision had marked Jews for divine punishment. Circumcision
marked Jews, as Justin informed the Jewish philosopher Trypho, "so that
you alone might suffer what you now rightly suffer; so that your land
might become desolate, and your cities burned, and strangers eat the fruits
of your land before you, and not one of you set foot in Jerusalem." All of
these punishments, according to Justin, had resulted from Jewish adherence to the ancestral religious practice of circumcision. However, Justin
also explained Jewish suffering as a direct result of rejecting the messianic
status of Jesus. "Therefore these things have rightly and justly come upon
you," Justin told Jews, "for you put the just one to death, and before him
his prophets, and now you deal treacherously with those who hope in
him, and with him who sent him, Almighty God, the Creator of all
things."[13]

Justin alleged that Jews had forsaken God, the prophets, and the
Messiah and thereby had lost any claim to their own sacred scriptures.
Certainly, Justin promoted a particular Christian reading of the ancient
texts. Insisting that the prophets of ancient Israel had been inspired by the
Christian *logos,* Justin concluded that the entire Hebrew Bible was actually a Christian text. According to Justin, Jews misunderstood the
Christian content of their own scriptures. "Jews who possessed the books
of the prophets did not understand," Justin argued, "and therefore did
not recognize Christ even when he came." Justin was not merely con-

cerned with the interpretation of biblical texts; he was determined to claim exclusive ownership of the Bible. In this battle over the legitimate ownership of sacred scripture, Justin contributed to the gradual transposition of the Hebrew Bible into the Christian "Old Testament." However, by casting polemical accusations against Jews he also contributed to the development of a Christian tradition of anti-Judaism and anti-Semitism.[14]

In defining a centrist position for Christians in Rome, Justin positioned his religion between Greco-Roman paganism and Judaism. Strategically, he appropriated some elements from the broader religious environment, such as the Greek *logos* and Jewish scriptures, while he inverted other elements, such as the pagan deities, which he transposed into demons, and the ritual of Jewish circumcision, which he transformed from a mark of divine covenant to a mark of divine punishment. Although they formed only a small minority in Rome, Christians could nevertheless claim to be at the center of religion in the Roman Empire because they owned the sacred symbols.

For the most part, however, that claim was only of interest to other Christians. During the second century in Rome, as we have seen, Marcion, Valentinus, and Justin represented different ways of conceptualizing what it meant to be a Christian. In the contest over ownership of sacred symbols, their intellectual struggles revealed different strategies for dealing with sacred texts. While Marcion rejected most sacred scriptures and Valentinus produced new ones, Justin proposed a strategy for appropriating the entire body of Jewish sacred texts as a product of the Christian *logos* and the property of Christians. Although Marcionites and Gnostics persisted into the fourth century, the position articulated by Justin eventually dominated. It defined the conceptual content of Christianity not only for a school of intellectuals, but also for a broader, diverse community of believers. "You can hear and learn these things," Justin observed, "from persons among us who do not even know the letters of the alphabet, who are uncultured and rude in speech, but wise and believing in mind."[15] As Justin suggested, Christian men and women from different social classes and ethnic backgrounds had gathered together to form a special institution, the church, in which wisdom merged with worship. According to Justin, the illumination of the *logos* appeared not only in creation, wisdom, and the sacred scriptures, but also in the rituals of the Christian church.

5

Churches

The Christian church emerged as a new type of organization. From Syria to Greece, North Africa to Rome, Spain to Gaul, and Persia to India, Christians developed a new social formation in the institution of the church. Although a small minority within the Roman Empire, Christians organized an alternative enclave of moral authority and ritual practice. New leadership roles, such as bishop, presbyter, and deacon, as well as new roles for teachers, healers, and exorcists, were established within the Christian church. As the institution of the church developed, Christians defined what it meant to be Christian less in terms of the kinds of philosophical speculations entertained by Marcion, Valentinus, and Justin than in terms of a shared way of life. The character of that common way of life registered in religious activities that drew people together as a church.

Until the third century, the Christian church, or *ekklesia,* referred not to a building, but to the act of gathering together for ritual. That gathering occurred for the most part in private homes. In the case of Justin's school in Rome, for example, the meeting of the *ekklesia* took place at his upstairs residence by a public bath. As Justin proposed, "The Christian's God is not circumscribed by place; invisible, he fills the heavens and the earth, and he is worshipped and glorified by believers anywhere."[1] In this utopian sense, therefore, the Christian church was not defined by space. It was not a sacred place set apart from the ordinary space of the city. Rather, the church was defined as a special time, a sacred day for coming together and celebrating the Christian God. As small groups gathered to sing and pray, to eat and drink, the act of meeting itself constituted the church. Therefore, the sacred day of Sunday, rather than the place of meeting, defined the Christian church.

The ritual observance of a sacred day of the week was certainly suggested to early Christians by the Jewish sabbath day of rest. Some first-century Christian groups, conforming to Jewish practice, observed the

Sabbath as a sacred day for refraining from work (Col. 2:16; Gal. 4:10). However, even in the first century, Christians had shifted the sacred day from Saturday to Sunday, the "day of the sun" in the Roman calendar, as Justin noted, on which "all who live in towns or in the country gather together in one place." In terms of the Jewish calendar, this shift from Saturday to Sunday meant that Christians observed not the last day but the first day of the week. The last day of the week, according to the book of Genesis, marked God's rest from the work of creation; the first day signified the beginning of the creation of the world. "We assemble on the day of the sun because it is the first day," Justin explained, "that on which God transformed the darkness and matter to create the world."

At the same time, however, Sunday signified the day of the week on which Jesus rose from the dead. For some Christians, that sacred day was so powerful it stood outside of the ordinary flow of time. It was the "eighth day," a day that transcended the pattern of the seven-day week, according to the author of the early second-century *Epistle of Barnabas*, because it was the day "on which God inaugurated a new world." This "new world" was not the old world of creation; it was the "world to come" that would be inherited by faithful Christians. By representing a time outside of time, therefore, Sunday could mark both the beginning and the end of the world. In coming together for collective worship on that sacred day, a day that signified the creation of the world, the resurrection of Christ, and the transcendence of ordinary time, Christians could imagine that they had already entered the new world promised at the end.[2]

Like the week, the year was also organized according to a Christian sacred calendar. Two annual festivals—Passover and Pentecost—were appropriated from the Jewish year and invested with specifically Christian significance. The most important of these holy days was Passover (Hebrew *Pesach*; Greek *Pascha*), which Christians transposed from the Jewish day for remembering the liberation of their ancestors from slavery in Egypt into an annual recollection of the suffering, death, and resurrection of Christ. Although Sunday was set apart as a sacred day of the week according to the Roman solar calendar, the Christian day of Pascha, or Easter, was calculated according to the Jewish lunar calendar. In the eastern churches of Asia Minor, Easter was observed on the 14th day of the Jewish month of Nisan, on whichever day of the week it happened to fall. In Rome and elsewhere, however, the sacred significance that Sunday had assumed in the week was combined with the Jewish lunar calendar to place Easter on the first Sunday after the 14th of Nisan. As a result of these different calculations, both claiming apostolic authority, Christians were divided over the correct date for celebrating Easter. This controversy over the dating of Easter continued to divide Christian communities in the Roman Empire.

The Christian festival of Pentecost was taken from the Jewish Feast of Weeks, part of an annual cycle that proceeded from the Feast of Un-leavened Bread to the Feast of First Fruits. Pentecost extended the sacred significance of Easter over the following fifty days. During that period, which was regarded as fifty days of Sundays, Christians commemorated the ascent of Christ into the heavens and the descent of the Holy Spirit onto the earliest Christian church.

For Christian participants, the beginning and the end of this annual cycle were both marked by keeping a night vigil. On the Saturday night before Easter Sunday, for example, Christians stayed awake to "watch all night in prayers, supplications, the reading of the prophets, of the gospel and of psalms in fear and trembling and continual supplication until three in the morning." By candlelight, small groups of Christians kept vigil in preparation for Easter. A similar vigil was observed on the last night of Pentecost. These late-night rituals were regarded as the most appropriate times in which to induct new members into the community. According to some early Christian authorities, these were the only occasions in which a convert might be initiated. After participating in the vigil, the convert was incorporated into the church through the dramatic ritual of baptism.[3]

BAPTISM

In the ancient Near East, especially in Persia and Babylonia, water rituals were commonly performed for purification or to celebrate new life. Ritual washing was also a familiar feature of ancient Israelite religion (Num. 19:1–22). Water rituals addressed various conditions of impurity or defilement. Israelite prophets occasionally drew on the symbolism involved in the ritual washing of the body to represent an inner spiritual cleansing (Isa. 1:16). During the first century, this link between ritual purification and moral purity appeared in the water rituals performed at Qumran. Confronted with an ethical choice between the "Two Ways," those who underwent water baptism at Qumran indicated they were committed to the good path. Similarly, the water ritual performed by John the Baptist was understood not only as a baptism of purification, but also as a moral cleansing, "a baptism of repentance for the forgiveness of sins" (Mark 1:4). Although rituals of water purification also appeared in some forms of Greco-Roman religion, the Christian significance of baptism emerged at this nexus of purification, repentance, and forgiveness of sins.

Early in the third century, Hippolytus (ca. 170–ca. 235), a Christian leader in Rome, described the ritual of baptism. The initiates were carefully prepared for the water ritual that would take place on Sunday morning. As much as three years earlier, the candidates for Christian conversion had appeared before the church, accompanied by character witnesses, and had submitted to a preliminary investigation. Following their years of instruction, or *catechises*, they were subjected to a second interrogation. Those who were chosen from the catechumens for baptism were then separated from the community. In addition to following strict rules of moral propriety, they were ritually exorcised by leaders of the church and then by the bishop, who "exorcises each one of them, so that he may be personally assured of their purity." If any impurity had been found at this point, the candidate would have been excluded from the ritual.[4]

Those found to be free of evil, however, were still in a dangerous state of transition in which they were neither pagan nor Christian. On the borderline of the community, they were neither inside nor outside the church. During the days preceding their baptism, therefore, they continued to be kept separate from the community, protecting the church from the danger of being contaminated by persons of such indeterminate status. As the Sunday of baptism approached, the candidates entered the final stages of ritual preparation. On Thursday they bathed; on Friday they fasted; and on Saturday they underwent one last exorcism in which the bishop blew on their faces and touched their foreheads, ears, and nostrils. Following the Saturday night vigil, they were ready for baptism.

As Hippolytus reported, baptism was performed at dawn. "At the moment when the cock crows," he reported, "first a prayer is said over the water." Moving water was preferred, what the late first-century text of the *Didache* called "living water," water that was running into a font or flowing from above. This emphasis on the power of moving water in rituals of purification was shared by Christians and Jews. As a guide to Jewish practice, the Mishnah distinguished three types of flowing water and assessed their varying powers of cleansing when used in ritual. The movement of the water, recalling the spirit of God moving over the deep at the beginning of the creation account in Genesis, increased its spiritual power. If it was not possible to find moving water, however, Hippolytus advised Christians to "use what water you can find." His contemporary in North Africa, Tertullian (ca. 160–ca. 220), agreed that any water could be used. In fact, according to Tertullian, any water would do because all water comes from the original deep that had received the spirit of God in the beginning:

> Therefore, in consequence of that ancient original privilege, all waters, when God is invoked, acquire the sacred significance of conveying sanctity: for at once the Spirit comes down from heaven and stays upon the waters, sanctifying them from within himself, and when thus sanctified they absorb the power of sanctifying.

In this formulation, Tertullian equated the role of water in both the myth of creation and the ritual of baptism. The water of baptism could be understood as the primordial water of creation. Having been sanctified by the powerful invocation of the breath, spirit, or word of God, any water held the power to sanctify in the ritual of baptism.[5]

After the blessing of the water, as Hippolytus continued, the initiates were instructed "to remove their clothes." They stood "naked and unashamed" (Gen. 2:25). Both initiates and priests stood naked. The bodies of the initiates were anointed with oil by a deacon of the church. Taking off their clothes, their "garments of shame," and treading them beneath their feet, the initiates symbolically cast off human mortality. By being anointed with oils, which signified that they were receiving the Christ, the "anointed one" of God, the initiates began to assume a new immortality. Standing naked before the gathering of the church, they were prepared to enter the waters of baptism.[6]

Nakedness was also an essential ingredient in the contemporary Jewish practice of baptizing converts. In the Jewish ritual, as in the Christian, no clothing could be allowed to intervene between the initiate's body and the water. Under ordinary circumstances, public nakedness was prohibited. As a custom associated with animals, barbarians, and Greco-Roman pagans who frequented the gymnasium and the baths, the public exposure of the naked body to the eyes of others was alien to Jewish thought. However, in the context of conversion, public nakedness was a necessary part of the baptism of Jewish proselytes. Although Christians displayed a similar "horror of nakedness" under ordinary conditions, they required public nakedness during the ritual of baptism. In that ritual context, nakedness signified the primordial state of Adam and Eve or the innocence of children. Nakedness was therefore an emblem of a new beginning.

In the Christian practice of anointing the naked body, a question of ritual propriety arose: Should a male deacon anoint the naked body of a woman? According to one authority, the third-century Syrian *Didascalia Apostolorum,* a woman ought to be anointed by a woman deacon. Although a male deacon might anoint her head, a female deacon should complete the anointing of the rest of her body. However, the text advised, "Where there is no woman at hand, especially a deaconess, he who baptizes must of necessity anoint her who is being baptized."[7] Although these guidelines show a concern for maintaining a certain standard of sexual propriety, they clearly indicate that such considerations are less important than the requirements of the ritual that all the initiates, male and female, must be naked and anointed with oil before entering the water. In fact, the nakedness of males and females together was occasionally interpreted as a radical freedom from gender differences and human sexuality. In this respect, ritual nakedness could be interpreted as acting out Paul's proposition that "there is no longer male and female; for all of you are one in Christ Jesus" (Gal. 3:28).

After the anointing, children were baptized first. "All those who can speak for themselves should do so," Hippolytus instructed; "if not, their parents or other relatives shall speak for them." The baptism of infants and children, therefore, was performed, but their adult sponsors assumed the responsibility of assuring that they lived as Christians. Next the men were baptized, and finally the women, but only after they "loosen their hair and put aside any gold or silver ornaments that they were wearing: let no one take any alien thing down into the water with them." As each child, man, or women entered the water of baptism, he or she was immersed three times in the name of the Father God, the Son of God, and the Holy Spirit. As Hippolytus explained:

> When he who is being baptized goes down into the water, he who baptizes him, putting his hand on him, shall say thus: "Do you believe in God, the Father Almighty?" And he who is being baptized shall say: "I believe."

Then holding his hand placed on his head, he shall baptize him once. And then he shall say: "Do you believe in Christ Jesus, the Son of God, who was born of the Holy Spirit of the Virgin Mary, and was crucified under Pontius Pilate, and was dead and buried, and rose again the third day, alive from the dead, and ascended into heaven, and sat at the right hand of the Father, and will come to judge the living and the dead"? And when he says, "I believe," he is baptized again. And again he shall say: "Do you believe in the Holy Spirit, and the holy church, and the resurrection of the flesh?" He who is being baptized shall say accordingly, "I believe," and so he is baptized a third time.[8]

Emerging from the water, each initiate was met by the bishop, who laid his hands on the person and prayed for the descent of the Holy Spirit. Having put on their clothing or in some cases special white garments, the initiates were given a drink of milk and honey before being admitted for the first time into the celebration of the Eucharist, the ritual meal of bread and wine.[9]

In addition to gaining access to the central ritual of Christian worship, the baptized made an ethical commitment to live a moral life. Having been exorcised of demons and cleansed of sin, they were bound by the ritual of baptism to avoid all forms of impurity or immorality in the future. Prebaptismal instruction provided moral guidance—based on the same kind of ethical dualism found in Jewish literature on the "Two Ways"— that set standards for Christian conduct. For example, Hippolytus noted that the catechitical instructions identified certain professions, such as operating a brothel, putting on plays, or being a schoolteacher in an educational system that required learning the pagan classics, as prohibited occupations for Christians because they led away from the light and down the path of darkness. A Christian man could only be a sculptor or a painter if he did not depict the pagan gods; he could only be a soldier if he did not kill; and he could only be a magistrate if he did not govern. In their occupations as well as in their daily lives, therefore, baptized Christians were bound to follow the right way.[10]

By breaking the hold of the old way of sin, evil, and Satan, baptism was freedom. But it also placed a heavy burden of responsibility on Christians because it was a ritual of repentance, purification, and forgiveness that could only be performed once. After baptism, therefore, Christians risked lapsing into sins that could not be washed away by the waters of forgiveness. Taking this risk into consideration, some Christians postponed baptism, even delaying their participation in the ritual until they experienced a life-threatening illness or reached an advanced age, so they would have less chance of defiling their purity.

Although baptism initiated Christians into the community of the church, the ritual also marked significant religious divisions among Christians. Those who had received baptism became full members of the church. As a result, they were entitled to participate in the entire spectrum of the religious life of the church, especially in the eucharistic meal of bread and wine, which celebrated the ultimate mystery of the Christian faith. Those who had been accepted for baptism, the catechumens, formed a second class of Christians. While they underwent the three-year period of religious instruction and moral training, they were excluded from the Eucharist. However, a third class of Christians, who were deemed to be not ready for or not worthy of baptism, yet who nevertheless expressed an interest in the religion of the church, were designated as "hearers." Lingering on the fringes of the community, they were only able to listen to the teachings of the church without joining in its most important rituals. Therefore, these three classes of Christians—baptized, catechumens, and hearers—were marked out by the ritual of baptism.

Finally, the ritual of baptism, which required three immersions of the initiate in the sanctified water, with each immersion accompanied by a different statement of faith in the Father, the Son, or the Holy Spirit, located Christian belief in a specific ritual context. As we have seen, baptism was not a single ritual event; it was a ritual process that unfolded only after a long period of preparation through various stages involving exorcisms, fasting, and staying awake until the process culminated at dawn when the initiate, naked before the community, was anointed in oil and immersed in water to be reborn as a new being. Responding to three questions, the initiate said, "I believe." In the ritual process, however, belief was not an abstract assent to a philosophical proposition about the nature of God. In other words, when initiates said, "I believe," they were not merely affirming an abstract Christian doctrine of God. They were entering and emerging from the water three times in a way that corresponded to the three aspects, dimensions, expressions, or personalities of the Christian God. Certainly, those three divine forces—Father, Son, and Spirit—could appear as if they were three different gods, each with its own personality, sphere of influence, and power in the universe. However, in baptism they were unified in a single ritual process that initiated people into the Christian church. By the fourth century, as the question of belief was abstracted from the ritual process of baptism, the triple nature of the Christian God became a serious point of contention among Christians. How could God be both one and three? In the ritual of baptism, however, initiates into the Christian mystery experienced a performative answer to that question by being immersed three times in the sanctified and sanctifying waters.

EUCHARIST

Having been baptized, Christians could participate in the central mystery of the church, the celebration of the Eucharist. From the Greek *eucharistein,* "to give thanks," the Eucharist was a thanksgiving ritual of bread and wine. As described by Justin in the second century, the Eucharist was celebrated at the culmination of an elaborate ritual process that came to be known as the liturgy. At the beginning of that ritual process, people assembled to listen to readings from the sacred scriptures and a homily delivered by the president of the church. After that stage of instruction, everyone stood to recite a prayer for the blessing of the church and the welfare of the emperor. At the end of that prayer, people kissed each other with the "kiss of peace." Then the bread and a cup of wine mixed with water were brought to the president of the church to be blessed by a special eucharistic prayer. Although the president was free to improvise, the eucharistic prayer was expected to follow a basic pattern.

In the early third century, Hippolytus provided a model for the prayer. First, the prayer opened with thanksgiving: "We give thanks to you, O God, through your beloved Child Jesus Christ whom you have sent us in these last days as Savior, Redeemer and Messenger of your plan." As in baptism, Christian beliefs were integrated within a ritual process, in this case, a ritual of eating and drinking. In the act of giving thanks, the eucharistic prayer recounted basic Christian beliefs. It affirmed that Jesus Christ was the *logos,* through whom God had created all things, and was incarnated in human flesh, born of the Holy Spirit and the Virgin, to suffer, but also to free human beings from suffering by destroying death, defeating the devil, and bringing the righteous to the light. More than statements of belief, however, these affirmations were a ritual litany of the mighty deeds of God. Addressed to God in thanksgiving, this litany opened up lines of communication between the congregation and God.

Second, the prayer centered on remembering the Last Supper of Jesus. At that occasion, Jesus, "taking bread, gave thanks to you and said, 'Take, eat; this is my Body which is broken for you'; likewise the cup, saying, 'This is my Blood which is shed for you. When you do this, do it in memory of me'" (1 Cor. 11:23–25). This ritual act of remembrance merged the Last Supper with the death of Jesus on the cross.

Third, the prayer focused on the Eucharist as an offering to God. Addressing God, the prayer specified that "we offer you this bread and this cup, giving thanks to you for accounting us worthy to stand before you and to minister to you as priests. And we ask you to send your Holy Spirit upon the offering of your holy Church." This part of the prayer suggested that the Eucharist was an exchange of gifts. Recalling that Jesus had given bread and wine to his followers, the prayer indicated that the Christians gathered at the Eucharist were giving an offering of bread and wine to God. Therefore, as the thanksgiving opened lines of communication, the offering opened relations of exchange between God and the church.

Finally, as servers prepared to dispense the sanctified bread and wine to the congregation, the prayer concluded with a petition for divine blessings on the church. "In gathering them together grant to all those who share in your holy mysteries that they may be filled with the Holy Spirit for the strengthening of their faith in truth; in order that we may praise you and glorify you through your Child Jesus Christ, through whom be to you glory and honor with the Holy Spirit in your holy Church now and throughout all ages."[11]

At the culmination of the prayer, the entire congregation intoned "Amen" as an expression of their collective participation in the ritual process of thanksgiving, memorializing, offering, and blessing. Justin stressed the importance of this ritual use of Hebrew, defining "Amen" by the Greek term *genoito,* "So be it," as a powerful expression of the collective solidarity of the church. Following the prayer, deacons distributed the bread and wine to those present, who could consume it there or take it home. Special provision was made for those who were absent. The celebration of the Eucharist concluded with a collection of money for the support of the church.

The Eucharist, therefore, was a sacred meal shared by all the participants in the presence of their God. In this respect, the Christian ritual recalled the Greco-Roman practice of sharing a sacred meal accompanied by songs, prayers, and sermons, as participants ate and drank together in the presence of a patron deity. It also recalled the thanksgiving blessings of bread and wine in the Jewish observance of a weekly Sabbath meal. An early Christian text, the *Didache*, which claimed to preserve the teachings of the apostles of Jesus, recorded prayers for the Eucharist similar to the *birkat ha-mazon*, the Jewish thanksgiving prayer at meals. As a sacred meal, therefore, the Eucharist brought Christians together as a unified community for a taste of the divine kingdom.[12]

As the ritual developed, however, two other layers of significance became prominent. In addition to being a thanksgiving meal, the Eucharist was a memorial ritual and a sacrificial ritual. As a memorial ritual, the Eucharist was an exercise in sacred memory, an occasion to remember the life and death of Jesus. In the service of memory, the Eucharist reenacted the Last Supper, as recounted in the gospels, in which Jesus had identified the wine with his blood and the bread with his body (Mark 14:22–25; Matt. 26:26–29; Luke 22:19–20; 1 Cor. 11:23–26). According to tradition, Jesus had instructed his disciples that when they met together for meals they were to "do this in remembrance of me" (Luke 22:19; 1 Cor. 11:24). Since the Last Supper was linked to the crucifixion, the Eucharist also served, according to Justin, as the "memorial of solid and liquid food in which the suffering of the Son of God is remembered." In this sense, the Eucharist was a living memorial to the death of Jesus Christ.[13]

However, the sacrificial character of the Eucharist became increasingly prominent in Christian reflections on the ritual. In Rome, Justin praised the Eucharist as the "pure sacrifice"; in North Africa, Tertullian maintained that the Eucharist was essentially a sacrificial ritual; and in Syria, Ignatius of Antioch, writing in the early second century, even defined the eucharistic assembly of the church as "the place of sacrifice."[14] Church leaders argued that pagan sacrifices were immoral because they were offered to demons. Christians were forbidden to participate. Jewish sacrifices were irrelevant because they had been superseded by the "new covenant" of Christianity. The only "pure sacrifice" was offered in the Christian church. What did it mean to identify the Eucharist as a sacrifice?

In their classic study of the ritual, French sociologists Henri Hubert and Marcel Mauss proposed that sacrifice "consists in establishing a means of communication between the sacred and the profane worlds through the mediation of a victim, that is, a thing that in the course of the ceremony is destroyed."[15] Clearly, the liturgy of the Eucharist was directed toward establishing lines of communication with God, thereby linking the church with the sacred. Mediation in that ritual relationship was provided by the symbolic elements of the bread and the wine, which were consecrated and consumed. But they were also offered as a gift to God. In the offering of bread and wine, Jesus Christ was the sacrificial victim.

Drawing upon the religious heritage of ancient Israel, Christians developed different ways of understanding Jesus Christ as a sacrificial victim. The rhetoric of sacrifice involved complex relations of exchange between God and the world. First, in the biblical story of the patriarch Abraham, who was commanded by God to sacrifice his son, Isaac, Christians found an ancient model for understanding the sacrifice of Jesus. Although Abraham had not actually killed Isaac, substituting a sheep instead, the ritual killing of a son by his father represented a precedent for God's sacrifice of his Son, Jesus Christ. By extending the model of Abraham, Christians could conclude that God had killed and offered his Son as a gift to the world.[16]

Second, the ancient Israelite festival of Passover, commemorating liberation from slavery in Egypt, provided another model for understanding the sacrificial death of Jesus. Prior to the destruction of the Jerusalem temple in 70 C.E., the festival involved the sacrifice of lambs in thanksgiving for liberation. By applying the model of Passover, Christians could understand the sacrificial offering of Jesus on the altar as an act of thanksgiving similar to the Passover offering of lambs. "For Christ our Passover lamb," as Paul declared, "has been sacrificed" (1 Cor. 5:7).

Third, in the ancient Israelite practice of sacrificing the first fruits of the field or the firstborn of a herd, they found yet another model. As the firstborn of creation, Jesus Christ was the perfect sacrificial victim to be killed and offered to God. According to Irenaeus, "We are bound, therefore, to offer to God the first fruits of his creation, as Moses also says, 'You shall not appear in the presence of the Lord your God empty.'" In the Eucharist, the Christian church symbolically killed and presented Jesus Christ, the firstborn of creation, as a sacrificial offering to God.[17]

This complex imagery of sacrifice pervaded the ritual of the Eucharist. Sacrificial imagery proliferated during the first four centuries, continuing to inform Christian understandings of the practice. That imagery continued to define the presence of Christ in the ritual. As Cyril of Jerusalem (ca.

315–87) observed, as Christ had been sacrificed by God and offered to the world, in the Eucharist Christians "offer up Christ, sacrificed for our sins."[18] Although these themes of sacrifice, presence, and exchange were not necessarily worked out in any systematic way, they nevertheless represented religious reflections on the larger economy of salvation enacted in the Eucharist.

At the same time, the ritual was still a sacred meal, a communal sharing of bread and wine within the assembly of the church. The bread of that meal, however, was not ordinary bread. As Tertullian insisted, it was "the Creator's bread by which he makes manifest his own body." By eating that bread, Christians were consuming the body of Christ. As a result, they could anticipate a transcendence of death derived from that spiritual nourishment. For example, according to Ignatius of Antioch, the bread of the Eucharist was "the drug of immortality, the remedy that we should not die." According to Irenaeus, "our bodies receiving the Eucharist are no more corruptible, having the hope of eternal resurrection." As many church authorities agreed, the most appropriate psalm to sing during Communion was Psalm 34:8: "O taste and see that the Lord is good."[19]

CEMETERY

Christians knew that the bread of the Eucharist did not work as a "drug of immortality" in the sense that it exempted them from undergoing physical death. Like brothers and sisters in Christ who had gone before, they would also have to undergo that transition. The living were faced with the challenge of keeping alive the relations of kinship, friendship, and love between the living and the dead. Although those relations were certainly threatened by death, they could be restored in ritual. Funeral inscriptions from the third century reveal some of the ways in which early Christians engaged the reality of death by keeping those relations alive.

Besides gathering together as a church for the weekly celebration of the Eucharist, Christians met at the cemetery for special religious activities that renewed relations with the dead. On the anniversary of the birthday or death day of the deceased, Christian friends and relatives celebrated a ritual meal, the *refrigerium,* held at the cemetery. Assembling at the burial site, they shared a meal of fish, bread, cakes, and wine. As part of the ritual, they poured a libation of wine over the tomb, inviting the deceased to share in the enjoyment of the meal. By eating and drinking with the dead, these Christians reaffirmed bonds of kinship and community that could not be broken by death. More than a memorial ritual, therefore, the *refrigerium* was an occasion for speaking with the dead, for offering prayers or requesting assistance, in ways that suggested the continuity of a relationship. The ritual meal in the cemetery was devoted not merely to the memory of the deceased friends and relatives, but to their ongoing presence in social life.

Both the living and the dead, therefore, comprised the Christian community. The inscriptions at cemeteries left by Christians after their ritual meals declared a confidence in the life, peace, and well-being of the dead. Frequently, they invoked the Roman drinking salutation *Vibas!* ("Live!") in addressing the dead. In the context of the ritual meal, this common expression, drawn from the festivity of drinking, enjoined the dead not to come back to life, but to share the wine offered by the living. Similarly, the familiar Roman drinking salutation *in pace* ("in peace") was used by Christians at cemeteries to exhort the dead to enjoy the food and wine of the ritual meal. In these expressions, Christians displayed a confidence that relations between the living and the dead could be maintained.[20]

In the light of the emphasis on the sacrificial death of Christ in the Eucharist, it is strange that the archaeological evidence from third-century cemeteries does not reveal any images or inscriptions suggesting the importance of the suffering and death of Jesus Christ. The cross does not appear. Instead, the religious imagery produced by Christians before 400 C.E. consists of symbols representing spiritual support, strength, peace, and prosperity. At cemeteries, Christians inscribed images of anchors, doves, boats, olive branches, palm trees, bread, fish, vines, and grapes. When they represented Jesus Christ, they depicted not the suffering savior on the cross, but the good shepherd, a youthful wonder worker and healer perhaps, but certainly not a sacrificial victim.

Since the eucharistic imagery of the crucified Christ was entirely absent from funeral inscriptions, a certain tension might have developed during the third century between the ritual life of the church, with its emphasis on salvation through the sacrificial death of Jesus Christ, and the rituals practiced at the cemetery. Although the church promised salvation from death, the cemetery provided a special location in which Christians could sanctify the enduring relations between the living and the dead.

During the course of the third century, however, the cemetery became an increasingly important religious site for Christians. Under intensified persecutions by Roman authorities, many Christians were executed for the capital crime of being a Christian. As a result, the cemetery held the bodies of those heroes—the martyrs—who had died bearing witness to their Christian faith. Martyrdom forged a bridge between the ritual of the church and the ritual of the cemetery. In the ritual language of the church, the martyrs, like Jesus Christ, were sacrificial victims whose violent sacrifices promised redemption from death. In the ritual language of the cemetery, however, the martyrs, like all the Christian dead, were embraced within the social network of ongoing relations sustained between the living and the dead. As Tertullian proposed, the Christian martyrs, although buried in the cemetery, were the seed of the church.[21]

6

Martyrs

The Christian church was constituted as a gathering—an *ekklesia*—through ritual. The initiation of baptism, the celebration of the Eucharist, and the ongoing attention to the dead defined a Christian community. The Latin term for these rituals, *sacramentum,* drew its meaning from both a legal context, in which it referred to a binding oath, such as the oath a soldier might take to his legion or an oath that might be taken in court, and a religious context, in which the term was used to refer to a sacred mystery. Christian sacraments therefore were mysteries that bound Christians by an oath of allegiance to the church. Unlike most religious associations in the Roman Empire, however, that binding oath was exclusive. It prohibited Christians from participating in any other forms of religious life. The sacraments erected a barrier against contemporary Judaism, distinguishing the religious practices of the church from the synagogue, and also prevented Christians from engaging in the ancestral, temple, or civic rituals of Greco-Roman paganism. As already noted, this refusal to participate in offerings to the gods exposed Christians to the accusation of atheism. However, since public sacrifice, especially for the emperors, was a significant aspect of civic life, Christian rejection of the gods registered as an attack on the city. In these terms, Christians were charged with committing crimes not only against the gods, but also against society.

The earliest mass persecution of Christians, which occurred when Nero blamed them in 64 C.E. for causing the fires in Rome, exploited Christians as scapegoats. Due to their marginal position in Roman society—living in society, but not being of society—Christians were particularly vulnerable to accusations of antisocial conduct. But Christians could also be identified as the cause of natural disasters. As Tertullian complained, many people considered Christians "the cause of every public defeat and every misfortune of the people. If the Tiber rises to the city walls, if the Nile does not rise to the fields, if the sky stays the same, if the earth moves, if there is a famine, a plague, straightaway the cry is heard, 'The Christians to the lions!'"[1] As a strange anomaly in the Greco-Roman world, Christians were associated with anomalous events in both nature and society. Although few in numbers, Christians nevertheless appeared as a dangerous disruption of order, an order that was understood to be simultaneously natural, public, and sacred.

Since they were suspected of crimes against humanity and the gods, Christians were occasionally brought before Roman courts of law to be confronted with a test that combined, like the sacraments, an oath and a mystery. They were required to share in a sacrificial ritual. Roman governors, who held the power to condemn them to prison, slavery, or death, were baffled at their refusal. How could anyone object to participating in the normal ritual life of the empire? Why would anyone refuse to show respect to the gods and recite an oath to the emperor? In many cases, Roman governors pleaded with Christians to perform these simple acts and set themselves free. Pagan critics, such as the second-century novelist Lucian, derided these conscientious objectors to Roman imperial religion. "The poor wretches have convinced themselves," Lucian observed, "that they are going to be immortal and live forever, in consequence of which they despise death and even willingly give themselves over for arrest."[2] From this perspective, Christians only brought their sufferings upon themselves by their stubborn, perverse, and deluded opposition to participating in public ritual.

Christians who resisted, however, were engaged in an interreligious battle over the meaning of sacrifice. As we have seen, Christians interpreted their weekly ritual in the gathering of the church as the "pure sacrifice." They denigrated the public sacrifices of Greco-Roman religion, whether directed to gods or emperors, as sacrificial offerings to demons. Therefore, Christians saw themselves as engaged in ritual warfare over the truth and power of sacrificial ritual. In Christian terms, the "pure sacrifice"—the execution of Jesus Christ on the cross, the death and rebirth of the initiate in baptism, and the ceremonial presentation, killing, and offering of Christ in the Eucharist—could only be found in the Christian church. Having been bound by a sacramental oath to the church, Christians could participate in no other mysteries.

However, for Christians who directly confronted Roman authority in a court of law, the ultimate sacrificial ritual could be performed by imitating the self-sacrifice of Jesus Christ. As Jesus had been recorded in the

Gospel of Mark, "If any man would come after me, let him deny himself and take up his cross and follow me, for whoever would save his life will lose it; and whoever loses his life for my sake and the gospel's will save it" (Mark 8:34–35). The ultimate sacrifice was performed by those Christians who bore witness—the martyrs, from the Greek word for witness, *martyrein*—to the "pure sacrifice" by dying for the Christian faith.

In 107 C.E., under the reign of the emperor Trajan, whose official policy made Christianity a criminal offense, but did not call for any measures to seek out Christians for prosecution, the bishop of Antioch, Ignatius, was arrested, probably on the basis of a public complaint, tried for treason, and condemned to death. As he was being escorted from Antioch to Rome to be killed by beasts, Ignatius wrote letters that reflected his thoughts as he faced the prospect of suffering a horrible death in the arena. In a letter to Christians in Rome, Ignatius begged them to do nothing that might interfere with his execution. "Allow me to follow," he entreated, "the example of the suffering of my God." By imitating the sacrificial death of Christ, Ignatius hoped, "I may be found a sacrifice." Out of the death of such martyrs, Christians forged a new definition of the "pure sacrifice."[3]

The most influential early history of martyrdom was the second-century account of the death of Polycarp (ca. 69–ca. 155), the bishop of Smyrna. Although the reasons for Polycarp's arrest were not specified, he was probably charged with the crimes of atheism and treason. Trying to avoid arrest, Polycarp went into hiding. One night he dreamed his pillow was on fire. When he awoke, he announced to his friends, "I must be burned alive." Although he anticipated his own death, Polycarp tried to evade the Roman authorities. Betrayed by two slaves, however, he was taken into custody. The Roman governor offered him a way out. "Take the oath," he said, "and I will let you go." Polycarp refused. Under interrogation, Polycarp steadfastly refused to betray his sacramental oath to the Christian religion. When his interrogators threatened him with death by fire, Polycarp responded, "The fire you threaten burns but an hour and is quenched after a little; for you do not know the fire of the coming judgment and everlasting punishment that is laid up for the impious." Polycarp challenged the court to condemn him to death. If the Roman authorities executed him, Polycarp declared, they would enable him to attain the "crown of immortality."

In the arena, Polycarp was burned at the stake. His dream was fulfilled. He was consumed by fire for his Christian faith. Drawing on the powerful religious imagery of sacrificial ritual, however, the account of his death described Polycarp as "a burnt offering ready and acceptable to God." His death was a sacrifice, the "pure sacrifice" that only the martyr could offer to God. While his body was in the flames, Polycarp was "not as burning flesh, but as bread baking or as gold and silver refined in a furnace." When his executioners saw that his body was not actually being consumed by the flames, they stabbed Polycarp with a dagger. As the blood flowed from his body, it extinguished the fire surrounding him. The crowd was said to have marveled at this miracle and to have been convinced of Polycarp's sanctity at the moment of his death.

The story of the martyrdom of Polycarp related a redemptive sacrifice. That sacrifice was understood as redeeming in two basic senses. First, the martyr achieved instant salvation by imitating the model of sacrificial suffering, torture, and death established by Jesus Christ. For the martyrs who followed Christ into death, as the narrator of Polycarp's martyrdom concluded, "the fire of their inhuman tortures was cold. They were no longer men, but already angels." Martyrdom therefore marked an immediate entry into the angelic company of Christ. Their deaths marked a direct entry into the realm of salvation. Second, in the process of imitating Jesus Christ, the martyr also set a model to be followed by other Christians who sought redemption in the face of adversity. The sacrificial death of Polycarp, for example, was widely regarded as a model to be followed by Christians. The day of his death, which was commemorated as his "birthday," and the "birthdays" of other martyrs were celebrated as sacred days "in memory of those athletes who have gone before, and to train and make ready those who are to come hereafter." The story of the sacrificial death of Polycarp, therefore, became a training manual for those Christian athletes, the martyrs, as they prepared to make their own redemptive sacrifices.[4]

DREAMS OF REDEMPTION

In 203 in Carthage, North Africa, a young woman, Vibia Perpetua, followed the example of Polycarp by entering into martyrdom. From an upper-class background and with a good education, she was twenty-two years old with an infant son. At the time of her arrest, Perpetua was a catechumen, undergoing preparation for baptism in the Christian church. A few days after her arrest, Perpetua was baptized, but while going through the ritual, she noted, "The Spirit told me I should seek nothing from the water other than the suffering of the flesh." She regarded the baptism of water, therefore, as a prelude to the baptism of blood in martyrdom. Appearing with other Christians before the governor's court, Perpetua was asked to offer a sacrifice for the welfare of the emperors. Her father, who was not a Christian, begged her to participate in the sacrifice. Perpetua refused. "Are you a Christian?" the governor asked. "I am a Christian," she replied. The governor condemned Perpetua and her companions to be killed by beasts in the festive games that would soon be held in honor of Geta, the emperor's younger son. The Christians were imprisoned to await their execution.

While in prison, Perpetua kept a diary that recorded her thoughts, dreams, and visions. The editor of that diary, who was most likely Tertullian, celebrated Perpetua as a martyr, a "new witness to the Grace of God." She was a revelation of the spirit in the flesh, a tangible incarnation of the spirit "which we have heard and touched." She was also a living sign of the end of the world, a "revelation of the last days," anticipating the reign of Christ on earth. Perpetua's suffering and death, therefore, displayed the spirit, grace, and ultimate power of the Christian God.

Perpetua recorded four visions she had in prison. In her first vision, which she beheld after praying to "talk with the Lord," she saw a bronze ladder surrounded on either side by instruments of torture. At the bottom of the ladder, a dragon lurked, but Perpetua stepped on the dragon's head to begin her ascent. At the top, she saw a white-haired shepherd who was milking a goat in the company of thousands of people dressed all in white. The shepherd gave her a "lump of the cheese he was milking." When she awoke from this vision, Perpetua found she was still chewing something in her mouth.

This first vision, therefore, anticipated Perpetua's ascent to martyrdom. Treading on the devil's head, she saw herself climbing through the tortures of her imprisonment to the paradise of Christ, the Good Shepherd. At the summit, however, she received a sacred meal that the shepherd had strangely milked as cheese. Recalling the baptismal meal of milk and honey, as well as the sacred meal of the Eucharist, this taste of paradise also resonated with Christian symbolism of Christ as the provider of heavenly milk. For example, the Christian philosopher Clement of Alexandria, writing about the same time as Perpetua's martyrdom, described

Christians as children who fed on the milk of Christ. "O Jesus Christ," he exclaimed, "heavenly milk from the sweet breasts of the bride, expressed from the favors of your wisdom, the infants, reared with tender lips, are filled with the tender spirit from the nipple of the Word."[5] During Perpetua's suffering in prison, her infant son lost desire for her milk. "By God's will," she noted, "the boy no longer hankered after the breast, and my breasts no longer gave me pain." Instead of providing milk, Perpetua drew spiritual nourishment during her imprisonment by receiving the milk of Christ.

In her second and third visions, Perpetua saw her young brother, Dinocrates, who had died at the age of seven, receiving the waters of salvation. One night during her prayers, she saw Dinocrates, who was hot, thirsty, and wearing dirty clothes, struggling to drink from a font of water with a rim that was too high for the boy to reach. Understanding that her brother was suffering, Perpetua prayed for his relief. "Day and night," she recorded, "I moaned and wept in prayer that what I asked be given." Perpetua's next vision revealed that her prayers had been answered. She saw the same place she had seen before, but now Dinocrates appeared refreshed, clean, and well clothed. The rim of the font had been lowered to the boy's waist. As Perpetua watched, he "took water from it endlessly." In addition to drinking from the font, Dinocrates drank from a golden bowl full of water that never ran dry. When not drinking from these sources of water, the boy played with childish abandon. "I woke up then," she recalled, "and understood that he had been taken from his pain."

These visions suggested the power of a martyr's prayers to intercede with God. Having climbed the ladder linking earth and heaven, martyrs were imagined to hold special power to effect God's judgment. In the case of Dinocrates, who had probably not been baptized before his early death, Perpetua's prayers enabled him to receive a spiritual baptism. With an infinite supply of holy water, the boy was cleansed and sustained. Perpetua's dream of redemption, therefore, extended beyond herself to those who became the focus of her prayers. In turn, the martyrs themselves became the focus of Christian prayers. Since their sacrificial sufferings for the faith had opened up a direct line of communication with God, Christians could engage the martyrs as intermediaries in their relations with the divine. As the second-century Christian philosopher Origen observed, martyrs were able to "grant forgiveness of sins to those who pray."[6]

On the day before she was to be executed, Perpetua beheld her fourth and final vision. She saw her deacon, Pomponius, dressed in white robes, escort her through narrow and windy paths to the center of the amphitheater. Assuring Perpetua he would be with her, Pomponius left the arena. She expected to encounter wild beasts, but was surprised to see she was scheduled to fight an Egyptian gladiator. As the Egyptian was prepared for combat by his helpers, Perpetua was also stripped and oiled. Standing naked in the arena, however, she discovered she was no longer a woman, but had become a man. As the umpire entered the arena, he held up a wooden rod and a green branch with golden apples. If the Egyptian won, he announced, the gladiator could kill his opponent. If Perpetua won, she could claim the branch of victory. After a brief battle, Perpetua killed the Egyptian by crushing his head under her heel. Taking the branch, she left the arena through the gate of triumph reserved for victorious gladiators. Awaking from this vision, Perpetua saw the meaning of her martyrdom. "I understood," she recorded, "that I was to fight against the devil, not with beasts; but I knew the fight was mine." Even in death, therefore, the martyr could claim victory over the forces of evil.

In Perpetua's last vision the act of martyrdom was revealed as a battle with the devil. Recalling the dragon she stepped on to ascend the ladder in her first vision, Perpetua crushed her opponent under her heel in her final vision of combat in the arena. The ordinary terms of victory, however, were dramatically reversed. In martyrdom, defeat was victory because death was life. The martyrs' willing embrace of torture, suffering, and death for the faith signified their ultimate freedom. As Perpetua insisted, "We came to this of our own free will that our freedom should not be violated." Similarly, Tertullian explained that the martyrs' free acceptance of death showed their power. A martyr's death, he proposed, announces to the Roman authorities that "your power against me is, unless I so will, no power at all; your power depends on my will, not on power in you."[7] By willingly consenting to their own deaths, therefore, martyrs demonstrated their supreme power over death, the devil, and the political authority of the Roman Empire.

As envisioned by Perpetua, martyrdom took on the character of a ritual. Like the ritual of baptism by water, the ritual of martyrdom in her final vision involved stripping off the "garments of shame," standing naked in public, and being anointed with oil. Perhaps Perpetua's discovery that she had become a man only suggested that she had acquired strength for combat, but it also recalled the blurring of gender differences in the public nakedness of baptism in which the initiates were "no longer male and female." Furthermore, by switching genders, Perpetua changed her ritual status. As a woman she was prohibited from presiding over the rituals of the church, but as a man she could officiate over the sacraments. Although women had limited roles in the ritual life of the church, they could nevertheless preside over the ritual of martyrdom, the "pure sacrifice" performed by offering their own lives for the Christian faith.

As reported by an eyewitness, Perpetua officiated at the ritual of her own death in the arena. When she was attacked and knocked down by wild beasts, Perpetua got up, adjusted her tunic out of modesty, and called for a pin to fasten her hair because it was "not right that a martyr should die with her hair in disorder, lest she seem to be mourning in her hour of triumph." As the crowd called for the Christians to be killed by a gladiator, the martyrs freely went to meet their executioner "and kissing one another sealed their martyrdom with the ritual kiss of peace." By enacting the ritual kiss of the Eucharist, they indicated they were offering themselves as a sacrifice. Perpetua presided over her own sacrificial death when "she took the hand of the young gladiator and guided it to her throat." Through that gesture, she presented herself as a willing sacrifice. "It was as though so great a woman," the eyewitness concluded, "could not be killed unless she herself was willing."

As an ardent proponent of martyrdom, Tertullian declared that the martyr's willing sacrifice was evidence of the truth of the Christian faith. "No one would want to be killed," he argued, "unless possessed of the truth."[8] The martyrs were filled with the truth of the Christian gospels and sacraments. According to Tertullian, their voluntary deaths witnessed to the validity and potency of that revealed truth. However, martyrs could also be regarded as sources of new revelations of truth. The visions of Perpetua, for example, provided fresh insights into the workings of Christian myth and ritual. She developed vivid imagery of ascent to the heavens, intercession through prayer, and combat with the forces of evil that amplified and expanded the scope of Christian truth.[9]

Tertullian eventually found a similar expansion of Christian revelation in the church of Montanus, a Christian movement that began in Phrygia during the second century, but was castigated as a heresy by Christians who objected that its women leaders were receiving new revelations. The visions of these women prophets might have developed distinctively feminine imagery of Christ. For example, according to one of the visionaries, "under the appearance of a woman, in a gorgeous dress, Christ came to me. He made me wise, and declared that this place was sacred, and that there the heavenly Jerusalem will come down from heaven." Although the hidden truths of the Montanist visionaries were generally rejected, the visions of the martyrs were embraced by those who regarded themselves as orthodox Christians. From their perspective, the martyrs revealed new truths by enacting a new sacrament, the "baptism of blood."[10]

BAPTISM OF BLOOD

Although martyrdom was widely honored, some Christians expressed reservations about the ritualized celebration of death. Christian Gnostics, for example, sometimes argued that martyrdom was unnecessary. The true Christian witness *(martyria)* was found not in sacrificial death, but in the intimate knowledge, or *gnosis,* of the supreme God. According to Basilides of Alexandria, Gnostic Christians had already transcended the world to such an extent that they could not be affected by participating in a pagan sacrifice or by renouncing any allegiance to the assembly of the Christian church. For Gnostics, he advised, "eating of meat offered to idols and the unguarded renunciation of the faith in times of persecution were matters of indifference." If such things actually caused no harm, then the martyr's stubborn refusal to sacrifice was in vain. As a result, the voluntary death of the martyr appeared to be nothing more than an act of suicide.

Other Christian Gnostics might have valued martyrdom, but they did not conclude that the martyr's faithful witness under interrogation necessarily ensured salvation. Heracleon, a student of Valentinus, distinguished between two confessions, one made verbally in court, the other made through the cultivation of a Christian way of life. "The confession that is made with the voice before the authorities," he observed, "is what many reckon the only confession. Not soundly: for the hypocrites also can confess with this confession." Only a genuine martyr, Heracleon concluded, "will confess rightly with his voice who has first confessed with his disposition."[11]

In early-third-century Alexandria, the Christian philosopher Clement (ca. 153–ca. 217) was sympathetic to this argument. Not all martyrs, he argued, followed the "divine call" when they went to their deaths. Some were Christians in name only, Clement argued, because they actually worshiped death. "Now we, too, blame those who have rushed to death," he observed, "for there are some who are really not ours, but share only the name, who are eager to hand themselves over in hatred against the creator." Although they might have been officially executed as Christians, these "athletes of death" did not bear true witness because they did not know the true God of Christian faith. Instead, Clement maintained, they "give themselves up to a futile death, as the Gymnosophists of the Indians to useless fire." As he imagined that Hindu yogis of India sometimes immolated themselves by fire, Clement concluded that false martyrs needlessly sacrificed themselves out of a suicidal love of death.

Clement acknowledged that genuine martyrs, whose lives bore witness to truth, might be called by God to undergo death. Without receiving such a divine call, however, Christians were required to hide from persecution and avoid confrontation with the authorities. Any Christian who does not protect himself or herself from being arrested, Clement warned, "becomes an accomplice in the crime of the persecutor." Perhaps Clement's reservations about the voluntary death of martyrdom reflected his own situation during the persecutions that broke out in Alexandria in 202. Avoiding arrest, Clement left the city and went into hiding. But it also reflected his conviction that martyrdom was a matter of life rather than death. The true witness of martyrdom, he insisted, was found not in the deaths, but in the lives of those who "bear witness [martyrousi] in each of their acts, by doing what [God] wills, consistently naming the Lord's name, and being witnesses [martyrountes] by deed to him whom they trust, crucifying the flesh with its desires and passions."[12]

One of Clement's students, Origen (ca. 185–ca. 254), whose father was killed in the persecutions in Alexandria, passionately embraced the prospect of martyrdom. Eager to expose himself to danger, Origen was only saved from a martyr's death when his mother prevented him from going outside by hiding his clothes. Origen survived that persecution to become a leading Christian teacher, Platonic philosopher, and biblical interpreter. Developing Paul's allegorical reading of the Bible into a system, Origen explored the literal and spiritual levels of meaning in Christian scripture. As a Platonist, he distinguished between an ideal realm and a material realm in the order of the cosmos; and he distinguished between the soul and the body in the composition of human beings. During life, Origen maintained, a Christian should strive to keep the soul as much as possible separate from the desires of the body. Death was not to be feared, he held, because it was the final liberation of the soul from the body. Death set the soul free from materiality so it could ascend into the higher heavens of the ideal world. Martyrdom promised such a liberation. "Why then do we hang back," Origen demanded, "and hesitate to put off the perishable body, the earthly tent that hinders us and weighs down the soul?" In these terms, Origen did not merely condone the voluntary death of martyrdom; he exhorted faithful Christians to become martyrs.

In response to the persecution of Christians in Caesarea during 235, Origen addressed his fervent *Exhortation to Martyrdom* to the local Christian community. Based on philosophical arguments, detailed readings of scripture, and an analysis of Christian sacraments, Origen deployed five basic arguments in defense of martyrdom. First, a Christian death under persecution guaranteed immediate salvation for the martyr. When martyrs realized that death would deliver them from bondage to the body, which Origen represented, in Platonic terms, as a prison or a tomb, they proclaimed, "Thanks be to God." All Christians, Origen insisted, should welcome such a liberation from the body. By witnessing to the faith through death, however, the martyr achieved both liberation from materiality and salvation in the heavens. Martyrs would ascend and not have to return to this earth. "You will not come down," Origen promised, "if you take up your cross and follow Jesus."

Second, the notion of taking up the cross meant that martyrdom was required if Christians were to follow the example of Jesus Christ. By imitating Christ in sacrificing family, possessions, and their lives, martyrs could anticipate the greater reward of salvation. Paraphrasing the instruction of Jesus, Origen urged Christians to lose their lives if they wanted to save their lives. "If you wish to save your life in order to get it back better than a life," he advised, "let us lose it by our martyrdom." Following the model of the sacrificial death of Christ, therefore, was the ultimate sign of a truly Christian life.

Third, by imitating Christ's death, the martyrs themselves became exemplary models for other Christians. In this regard, Origen cited with approval the last words of the Jewish scribe Eleazar, who had chosen voluntary death in response to persecution during the second century B.C.E. "By manfully giving up my life now," Eleazar had declared, "I will show myself worthy of my old age and leave to the young a noble example of how to die a good death willingly and nobly for the revered and holy laws" (2 Macc. 6:27–28). Although Eleazar was not a Christian, Origen found that his death nevertheless illustrated the way in which a martyr could serve as a model for future generations. The Christian martyr, Origen held, assumed a similar obligation to serve as a model of righteousness in the face of death to be emulated by other Christians.

Fourth, Origen argued that all human beings were indebted to God. Human beings had been given so much. What could they give in return? "What shall I give back to the Lord," the psalmist asked, "for all his bounty to me?" (Ps. 116:12). Origen proposed that martyrdom was the best way to repay that debt. "Nothing else can be given to God from a person of high purpose that will so balance his benefits," he maintained, "as perfection in martyrdom." In this sense, martyrdom was more than an imitation of the sacrificial model established by Jesus Christ. It was an act of repayment, the settling of a debt, that was transacted in the ongoing relations of exchange between God and the world.

Fifth, and finally, Origen found that martyrdom was necessary because it supplemented the Christian sacramental system. Although the sacrament of baptism washed away sins, it could not be repeated. Any further transgressions therefore adhered to Christians and weighed down their souls as they proceeded toward death. "It is impossible according to the laws of the gospel to be baptized again with water and the spirit for the forgiveness of sins," Origen observed. "And that is why the baptism of martyrdom has been given to us." As a second baptism—a baptism of blood, a baptism of fire—martyrdom was a sacramental ritual that achieved a final and absolute forgiveness for sins.

Origen persisted in his vigorous defense of the ritual of martyrdom. Addressing a council of bishops in Caesarea around 245, he continued to exhort Christians to enter the baptism of blood. "Come wild beasts, come crosses, come fire, come tortures!" he exclaimed. "I know that as soon as it is over, I depart from my body, I am in peace with Christ." Although not all Christians shared his Platonic philosophical assumptions or followed his subtle biblical interpretations, many identified with Origen's celebration of martyrdom as the royal road to salvation.[13]

That faith in martyrdom, however, was severely challenged in the 250s when the emperor Decius issued an edict requiring all his subjects to respect the religion of the empire and the cities by participating in public sacrifices. Although designed to renew the religion of the empire, this edict placed a special burden on Christians who refused to partake in the sacrificial ritual. Once again, from the perspective of Greco-Roman paganism, Christians were exposed as atheists in relation to the gods and traitors in relation to the political order of the Roman Empire.

Many Christians refused to sacrifice and were sentenced to death. Pionius, the bishop of Smyrna, where Polycarp had been martyred 150 years earlier, followed the example of Jesus and all the martyrs who had gone before by willingly embracing a martyr's death. In terms Origen would certainly have approved of, Pionius declared, "I am not rushing toward death, but toward life." As he was being prepared for execution, however, Pionius must have been briefly disappointed that his companion in martyrdom was a Marcionite, a heretic from his perspective, who did not deserve the crown of immortality. The Roman administration, however, did not make such subtle distinctions among Christians. Anyone who refused to perform civic sacrifices to the gods was a potential threat to the social order.[14]

During the persecutions of the 250s, many Christians followed Clement's advice by avoiding confrontation and hiding from the law. One prominent Christian leader, the bishop Cyprian, hid for years until he finally died a martyr's death in Carthage. Others gave in, or lapsed, and performed the required sacrifices to the gods and emperors. However, some Christians, through either wealth or influence, were able to secure immunity from prosecution by obtaining a certificate testifying to their participation in the sacrifice. Typically, the certificates read: "I have always sacrificed to the gods, and now in your presence in accordance with the edict I have made sacrifice and poured a libation and partaken of the sacred victims. I request you to certify this below." By acquiring that legal document, many Christians saved themselves from undergoing the "baptism of blood" that brought salvation.[15]

Nevertheless, the model of the martyrs continued to inform the conduct of Christian "athletes of death" under official persecution. Under the emperor Diocletian, beginning in 303, a new and even more violent era of persecution dawned on Christians. Over the following ten years, Christians were subjected to harassment, prosecution, and execution for crimes against the empire. Under those conditions, Christian martyrs revived the "baptism of blood" as both a defense of Christianity and a realization of the religion's highest aspiration for salvation.

In the city of Antioch in 303, for example, Christians succumbed to official pressure by agreeing to participate in public sacrifices. Visiting the city, a Christian from Palestine by the name of Romanus observed them "going up in crowds to the idols and sacrificing." Shocked by what he saw, Romanus tried to intervene in the public ritual by stopping the procession. Instead of preventing this violation of Christian faith, however, he was arrested and executed for creating a public disturbance during a sacrificial ritual. The martyrdom of Romanus, therefore, was a death in defense of the integrity of Christianity. Trying to prevent the apostasy of his fellow Christians, Romanus sacrificed his own life. In a similar instance during the same year, a Christian by the name of Alphaeus was arrested in Caesarea when he tried to intervene to prevent Christians from participating in public sacrifices. Arrested by Roman guards, Alphaeus refused to sacrifice and was beheaded. These martyrs, therefore, continued to represent exemplary models that other Christians could follow.[16]

At the same time, however, during the Diocletian persecutions at the beginning of the fourth century some Christians voluntarily embraced martyrdom as a death that promised personal salvation. In April 304, for example, a Christian by the name of Euplus stood outside the governor's home in Catania, Sicily, and shouted, "I want to die; I am a Christian." Complying with this wish, the governor had him tortured and executed. As the account of his martyrdom reported, "So it was that the blessed Euplus received the unfading crown." In Nicomedia, Christians willingly gave themselves to the fires of execution, as "men and women leaped upon the pyre with a divine and unspeakable fervor." In the process, as the fourth-century Christian historian Eusebius concluded, they "were perfected by fire." Baptism of blood, baptism by fire—the sacrificial death of martyrdom continued to represent a powerful Christian sacrament of salvation for a church under persecution.[17]

NEAR THE SAINTS

After Polycarp was executed, Roman guards took his corpse and disposed of it so Christians could not claim the body of their martyr. As the author of the account of the martyrdom of Polycarp complained, they "prevented us even from taking up the poor body, though so many were eager to do so and to have a share in his holy flesh." Sanctified by a sacrificial death, the flesh and bones of the martyr were holy artifacts of Christian redemption. They were tangible symbols of salvation. As such, they were worthy of veneration by the living. Fully aware of this sacrificial complex, Roman officials worried that the martyr would become the focus of deviant devotion. They were concerned, as one remarked, that the Christians "may abandon the Crucified and begin to worship this man." Having already demonstrated their devotion to one executed criminal, these Christians might transfer their religious allegiance to another. Therefore, the Roman officials kept the body of Polycarp from falling into the hands of these worshipers of the dead.[18]

As the followers of Polycarp suggested, the body of the martyr was significant for Christians. Although in the case of Polycarp the martyr's body could be imagined as baked bread or refined gold, it was also "holy flesh," a human body transformed into the sacred. The physical remains of the martyr, therefore, conveyed a religious aura that could benefit all Christians who came near it. The benefit gained by being close to the bodies of the martyrs could be experienced during the course of life as well as in death.

Generally, Christians imagined death as an entry into a period of sleep or waiting (1 Cor. 15:6, 20; 1 Thess. 4:13–15), a kind of suspended animation that would only end when Christ returned to supervise the general resurrection of the dead expected at the end of the world. In this way of imagining death, Christians assumed that all deceased human beings had to wait for the apocalyptic end of the world before they could come back to life to be judged by the supreme Lord of the universe. While awaiting the general resurrection of the dead, however, the best place for a corpse to be was in close proximity to the physical remains of a martyr. Accordingly, Christians tried in life as well as in death to position themselves close to the tombs of the martyrs, to be near to the holy remains of their "special dead."[19]

Following Roman practice, Christian martyrs, along with other Christian dead, were buried in the cemetery, or *necropolis*, outside the walls of a city. In that alternative city of the dead, the tombs of the martyrs assumed a crucial significance for faithful Christians. From a Christian perspective, the martyrs, who had been executed because they had refused to subscribe to the religion of the city, ruled over the city of the dead. Wearing the "crown of immortality," they reigned supreme as the most powerful forces in the cemetery. The tombs containing their sacred remains became a focal point of Christian religious attention.

By the fifth century, as Maximus of Turin explained, the practice of burying Christians near the remains of the martyrs was regarded as an ancient Christian custom. As Maximus observed, the martyrs watched over the lives and deaths of Christians. "The martyrs will keep guard over us, who live with our bodies," he noted, "and they will take us into their care when we have forsaken our bodies. Here they prevent us from falling into sinful ways, there they will protect us from the horrors of hell. That is why our ancestors were careful to unite our bodies with the bones of the martyrs." Certainly, this ritual attention to the sacred remains of the martyrs baffled pagan observers. Commenting on Christian practice in Egypt, one pagan educator complained about this strange worship of the dead: "For they collected the bones and skulls of criminals who had been put to death for numerous crimes . . . made them out to be gods, haunted their sepulchers, and thought they became better by defiling themselves at their graves." Reflecting a Greco-Roman aversion to contact with corpses, this account represented Christian veneration of martyrs as a defiling interchange with the dead.[20]

According to Maximus, however, Christians buried their dead near the bodies of the martyrs to gain protection in life and death. As close friends of God who, like Perpetua, could speak directly with the Lord, the martyrs had the power to intercede on behalf of the living. In that role, as intermediaries with God, the martyrs aided living Christians in fulfilling their faith. After death, however, Christians could continue to benefit from the sacred power of the martyrs by being buried in close proximity to their "holy flesh." Since the remains and relics of the martyrs were felt to emanate a special power, being buried near those saints placed Christians in a good position to await the resurrection of the dead. They could wait for the last judgment in confidence that they would benefit from the influence of the martyrs, those saints whose influence continued to radiate a sacred energy through the physical remains they had left behind.

7

Christian Empire

Although they were still a small minority at the beginning of the fourth century, probably comprising no more than 5 percent of the population, Christians continued to register as a serious threat to the political and religious order of the Roman Empire. Although the cities of the empire remained pagan with the support of the aristocracy, the military, and the intelligentsia, the peasantry maintained the countryside as a pagan domain by preserving ancestral rituals of the land, the seasons, and the hearth. For the most part, Christians lived in the major cities, such as Rome, Carthage, Alexandria, Ephesus, and Antioch, where despite their small numbers they nevertheless presented a serious problem. Their refusal to pay ritual respect to Roman gods and rulers was thought to bring divine wrath. War, civil unrest, crop failures, storms, and earthquakes were attributed to the impiety of Christians. Ironically, both pagans and Christians agreed that the sacrificial killing of Christians was necessary. However, although Christians celebrated the sacrifices of their martyrs as redemptive acts, many pagans regarded the execution of Christians as a sacrificial ritual required to appease the gods and restore the harmony of the divine order that sustained the Roman Empire.

During the course of the fourth century, the religious balance of power between Christianity and paganism dramatically shifted. Two imperial decrees only hint at the scope of this change: an edict of the emperor Constantine issued in 313—the Edict of Milan—made the Christian religion a legally recognized form of worship; an edict issued by the emperor Theodosius I in 381 made Christianity the only legal form of religious worship.[1] In between these two decrees, Christian bishops and emperors formed new alliances. After Constantine's edict, they began to redefine the position of Christianity in the empire as both a religious and a political force. They forged a merger of church and state in which Christianity eventually displaced pagan tradition as the established religion of the

Roman Empire. In the process, the Roman Empire became a Christian empire.

At the beginning of this historical transformation, the first Christian emperor, Constantine (ca. 273–337), initiated new measures in both church and state that would have wide-ranging consequences for the Christian religion. As a young officer, Constantine had served with distinction during the 290s in military campaigns in Persia and Gaul. While he was in Britain during 306, Constantine's army proclaimed him as emperor, but he accepted a subordinate position under Emperor Galerius as ruler over Britain, Gaul, and Spain. Six years later, after another victorious campaign in Gaul, Constantine led his army south toward Rome to confront the troops of the new emperor, Maxentius. On October 28, 312, Constantine defeated the forces of his rival at the Milvian bridge, outside of Rome, and proceeded into the city. There he established himself as emperor of the West.

Curiously, from a pagan perspective, Constantine neglected to go to the Capitol in Rome to celebrate his victory by offering sacrifices to the gods. Pagan commentators complained about this flagrant disregard for the conventions of Roman religion. They were surprised, because Constantine had been known as a devotee of the god Apollo under the god's auspices as *sol invictus,* the unconquerable divine sun.[2] When Constantine entered the city and refused to perform public sacrifices to Apollo, he indicated he had adopted a new divine patron. Certifying the religious authority of his victory, Constantine's new patron was the Christian God.

On the night before his victory at the Milvian bridge, another vision had caused Constantine to shift his allegiance to a new God. Looking at the sky, "he saw with his own eyes the trophy of a cross of light in the heavens, above the sun, and an inscription, 'Conquer by this' attached to it." Reportedly, his entire army witnessed this same miracle of the cross in the sky. While asleep that night, Constantine dreamed that "the Christ of God appeared to him with the sign which he had seen in the heavens." He saw he was "to use it as a safeguard in all engagements with his enemies." In the morning, the Christian bishop Osius of Córdova, who had been traveling with the army, assured Constantine that the symbol of the cross he had seen in the sky and in his dream signified the God of the Christian religion. Embracing that God as his new patron deity, Constantine ordered all pagan religious symbols to be removed from the standards carried by his army. As his vision had promised, they would conquer under the banner of the Christian cross.[3]

The conversion of Constantine to Christianity, therefore, appeared as a transfer of allegiance on the battlefield to a new divine patron. His Christian deity was a God of war. In a prayer Constantine gave to his soldiers to recite during Sunday worship, he indicated the military character of his religious devotion.

> We acknowledge you, the only God. We own you as our king and implore your aid. By your favor we have gained the victory. Through you we are mightier than our enemies. We give you thanks for your past benefits and trust you for future blessings. Together we pray to you and ask you long to preserve for us, safe and triumphant, the emperor Constantine and his pious sons.[4]

Once established as emperor of the West, ruling with Licinius, the emperor of the East, until he became sole emperor after 324, Constantine provided official support for the Christian religion. Not only permitting Christian worship, the emperor substantially advanced the religion by recognizing the authority of bishops and by financing the construction of churches, shrines, and other holy sites for the faith. Although Constantine postponed his own baptism until shortly before his death in 337, his intervention marked the beginning of a Christian empire.

CHRIST AND CAESAR

During the first three centuries, relations between the Christian religion and politics were characterized by profound ambivalence. According to the gospel account, Jesus had proposed a basic distinction between religion and politics when he advised Christians to render a different kind of allegiance to God than they would render to Caesar. Although that advice might be subject to different interpretations, Christians could conclude that religion and politics represented two distinct spheres, one devoted to the worship of God, the other dedicated to maintaining the public order of the state. Nevertheless, Christians adopted different strategies in working out the cooperative and conflictual relations between religion and the political order.

On the one hand, Christians could adopt a strategy of cooperation between religion and the state. Following Paul's instruction to the Romans,

Christians were to "be subject to the governing authorities. For there is no authority except from God, and those that exist have been instituted by God." Although religion and politics might still represent separate spheres, the authorities in the political realm were regarded as holding divinely ordained power to contain evil and maintain public order. Anyone who resisted the established political authorities was opposing an institution sanctioned by God (Rom. 13:1–2). From the beginning, therefore, Christians found religious reasons for cooperating with the Roman Empire.

On the other hand, Christians could develop a strategy of opposition between religion and the state. Although religious resistance to the political order was often forced upon Christians in the context of official persecution, opposition to the state was deeply embedded in the tradition. In the apocalyptic visions of the book of Revelation, Christians were encouraged to see the Roman Empire as the Antichrist. The political order of the empire disguised demonic forces that Christians were called upon to resist. From the beginning, therefore, Christians also found religious reasons for opposing the Roman Empire.

Under Constantine, however, this tension between cooperation and opposition assumed an entirely new character as the Christian religion merged with politics. As Christian religious interests entered the political arena, the conceptual distinction between religion and politics increasingly blurred. Of course, from an imperial perspective, religion had always been intertwined with politics. Public ritual brought divine blessings on the political order, and its neglect risked political disaster. When Constantine legitimated Christian worship, he affirmed the importance of religion for politics in terms that would have been familiar to any Roman emperor. Constantine declared that "great dangers to public affairs are brought about when divine worship, by which the greatest reverence for the most holy divinity is maintained, is set at naught, and that when it is legally restored and maintained it brings about the greatest good fortune to the Roman name and special prosperity to all human affairs, for divine beneficence bestows these blessings." Constantine's innovation, however, was the introduction of Christian worship into this political calculus of divine wrath and blessings. By embracing the Christian religion as his own, Constantine deployed it as the "divine worship" of his empire.[5]

Representing the churches in this new dispensation, many Christian bishops enthusiastically embraced the prospect of a new Christian empire. For the first time, the possibility of establishing a Christian state—a theocracy, based on the rule of God—actually seemed within reach. The emperor was the key to that Christian kingdom. One of Constantine's ardent supporters, Eusebius (ca. 260–ca. 339), the bishop of Caesarea, celebrated the emperor as the fulfillment of biblical prophecy. By establishing the foundation for a Christian empire, Constantine had fulfilled "the oracles of the holy prophets which long ago cried out, 'and the saints of the most high God shall receive the kingdom'" (Dan. 7:18). According to Eusebius, therefore, the promise of a Christian kingdom of God was realized on earth through the imperial rule of Constantine.

In making this claim, Eusebius drew an elaborate analogy between Christ and emperor. He established four points of comparison between the "Word of God" and the "Friend of God." First, they both displayed the power of sacred kingship. "The only-begotten Word of God," Eusebius explained, "co-reigns with his Father from ages without beginning to limitless, unending ages." In the name of Christ, therefore, the Christian emperor ruled on earth as a divine king just as the Word of God ruled over the heavenly realm.

Second, both maintained the divine order of the universe. As the Word of God had arranged all things in heaven and earth according to a beautiful sacred order, the Christian emperor brought his subjects into alignment with the order of the divine kingdom. As Eusebius proposed, the imperial Friend of God "leads his subjects on earth to the only-begotten and saving Word and makes them fit for his kingdom." By fitting his subjects into the pattern of the divine kingdom, the Christian emperor established a perfect harmony between the order of heaven and the order of the earth.

Third, both protected the divine order against dangerous forces of evil. By invisible power, Eusebius maintained, the Word of God protected humanity from "the rebellious powers which at times fly around in the air above the earth and attack men's souls." While the Word of God battled invisible demons, the Friend of God, "adorned by him from on high with his trophies against his enemies, chastens the visible enemies of truth whom he conquered by the law of war." Those visible demons, which from Eusebius's perspective included both pagans and heretics, were engaged in holy warfare against the Christian religion. As the defender of the Christian empire against all forces of evil, the Friend of God was charged by the law of God and the law of war with the sacred responsibility of conquering those enemies of the faith.

Finally, both provided human beings with the knowledge necessary for salvation. Like Justin, Eusebius understood Christ, the Word of God, as the seed-bearing *logos,* the divine agent who implanted the seeds of reason that sprouted into Christian salvation. As Eusebius explained, "The Word, who has existed before the world and is the Savior of all things, imparts the seeds of reason and salvation to his followers, and makes them both reasonable and possessing knowledge of his Father's kingdom." The Christian emperor, however, played a similar role in imparting the divine knowledge that led to salvation. The Friend of God, Eusebius held, was "an interpreter of the Word of God." In proclaiming Christian truth, therefore, the Christian emperor invested that religious knowledge with a new political power, providing it with a "mighty voice" that called all people to the worship of the "Mighty One" who ruled the universe.[6]

The merger between religion and politics celebrated by Eusebius had definite consequences for Christian churches under Constantine. Embracing his role as "an interpreter of the Word of God," the emperor intervened directly in controversies over church leadership and doctrine. If he was going to maintain the order of heaven on earth, the "Friend of God" had to establish a uniform system of belief and practice to be shared by all Christians. Under Constantine's rule, the Christian religion would be "catholic," or "universal," to the extent that imperial power reinforced uniformity in Christian beliefs, practices, and social organization.

Constantine occasionally intervened in church affairs by deposing or exiling bishops. For example, in 316 he arbitrated a dispute in Carthage between rival claimants to the office of bishop. After the end of official persecutions, churches in North Africa, as elsewhere in the empire, were faced with the dilemma of dealing with Christians who had lapsed from the faith by performing sacrifices or turning over copies of the scriptures to the Roman authorities. In the controversy in Carthage, one faction, with some popular support, advocated strict treatment of lapsed Christians by requiring them to be rebaptized if they wanted to be accepted again within the church. Claiming to be the church of the martyrs, this group advanced Donatus as its candidate for bishop of Carthage.

Most of the bishops in North Africa, however, adopted a more lenient approach to lapsed Christians by not requiring rebaptism. Following this line, a second faction in Carthage succeeded in getting its candidate, Caecilianus, who had himself been accused of betraying the faith under persecution, elected as bishop. Although Caecilianus was confirmed as bishop by several church councils, the conflict continued to divide Christians in North Africa. Finally, in November 316 Constantine intervened not only by confirming the decision against the supporters of Donatus, but also by ordering all their churches to be confiscated, thereby backing up a religious judgment with imperial force. Four months later, the Donatist Christians who resisted this repression gained their first martyrs when several were killed in Carthage by Roman soldiers and an angry mob of opposing Christians. Therefore, although the era of martyrdom had ended for most Christians, a new church of the martyrs, which saw itself persecuted by a Christian emperor, was emerging in the Donatist movement. Although Constantine had intervened in this dispute in the interest of Christian unity, the conflict between Donatists and "Catholics" continued to polarize Christians in North Africa for over a century.

In addition to a unified church organization, Constantine also desired unanimity among Christians in matters of religious belief. After he conquered the eastern empire in 324, Constantine's demand for uniformity in Christian doctrine embraced both East and West. As supreme ruler of the entire empire, he moved to suppress paganism and advance the interests of a "universal" Christianity. In an imperial letter circulated in 324, Constantine indicated his opposition to the traditional practices of pagan religion. Although pagan temples, shrines, and sacred groves could be maintained, his subjects were prohibited by law from performing sacrifices, practicing divination, or engaging in any other rituals to consecrate those holy places dedicated to the gods. By this ruling, pagans could continue to believe, but they could not practice their religion.

By enforcing an implicit distinction between belief and practice in his suppression of pagan religion, Constantine highlighted the importance of belief as a defining feature of the Christian religion. Unlike Greco-Roman paganism, which allowed for wide variation in religious opinions, convictions, and commitments, Christianity emphasized the crucial significance of belief. Regarded as more than personal opinion, belief was a social marker of inclusion in the Christian community, a creed that could be recited in unison by all those who joined in the Christian church. By emphasizing belief, therefore, Christians had already placed tremendous importance on religious doctrines that were always and everywhere embraced by adherents of the Christian faith. Accordingly, Constantine's interest in consolidating his political power intersected with his interest in establishing a single system of belief for all Christians. Clearly, however, Christians were not in fact agreed on matters of religious belief. In 325 Constantine presided over a major church council that brought together bishops from all over the empire to settle the question of orthodox belief for Christians.

CONTROVERSY AND CREED

Constantine selected Nicaea as the site of the church council so he could divide his time between participating in its deliberations and monitoring the construction of his new city, Constantinople, which the emperor declared to be the "New Rome" of a unified empire. Following his conquest of the East, Constantine drew out the perimeter for his new capital in November 324 on the site of the ancient Greek city of Byzantium. Constantinople was designed as an exclusively Christian city. The emperor prohibited the shrines or practices of any other religion within its precincts, consecrating his city to the "God of the martyrs."[7] As a new sacred center for the empire, the city contained numerous Christian churches, memorials, and shrines. The imperial palace featured a magnificent jeweled cross hanging in midair in its largest assembly hall. In its sacred architecture, pervasive Christian symbolism, and legal restrictions on pagan practices, Constantinople was constructed as a new center of political and religious power for a Christian empire.

Although the empire was ostensibly unified by revolving around a new imperial center, the churches of the Christian faith were divided. As we have seen, diversity characterized Christianity from the beginning. In the early fourth century, however, as the era of persecution ended, Christian leaders turned to internal disputes. In a Christian empire, the terrain of those conflicts had shifted. Provided with preferential treatment and financial support by the emperor, bishops in the major cities emerged as a new urban elite. With that social advancement, new rivalries broke out over status and prestige in the churches. In competition with each other, rival bishops often tried to gain mass support for their authority in the church. When conflicting popular factions developed, as in the Donatist controversy, the results could be violent. Although Constantine wanted to focus on converting pagans, he had to attend to these Christian conflicts in order to establish a united Christian church for his unified empire.

Constantine called the Council of Nicaea in 325 to deal precisely with such a conflict, which came to be known as the Arian controversy. This controversy divided bishops into two warring camps over a crucial question of doctrine: What is the nature of God? More specifically, in terms of Christian symbolism, the Arian controversy raised the problem of the relation between the Father God and the Son of God in a Christian understanding of divinity. Growing out of a rivalry in Alexandria between the bishop Alexander and the priest Arius, the controversy quickly spread throughout the churches of the empire. Although the debate was complex and intense, it can be reduced to two basic options. Either the Son was the same as the Father or the Son was different from the Father. As Christians took sides on this issue, the unity of the Christian empire was at stake.

Taking the first option, some Christian leaders held that Father and Son were essentially equal. They affirmed that the Father and the Son were the same in essence, in eternity, and in divinity. Both were God. Drawing on terms developed by Tertullian, Christians could understand their God, the Trinity, as one substance in three persons. In this formulation, Father, Son, and Spirit were all essentially equal. They all shared the same divine substance—*substantia* in Latin, *ousia* in Greek—that comprised the Christian divinity as three in one and one in three. In these terms, therefore, the Father and Son were substantially the same. Advocates of the equality of Father and Son could cite the authority of the Gospel of John, in which Jesus said, "He who has seen me has seen the Father" (John 14:7–9; 12:45; 17:21). Many Christians believed this scriptural passage confirmed that the Father was basically the same as the Son of God.

Adopting the second option, however, other Christian leaders insisted that Father and Son were essentially different. Although both were divine, the Father God held an essential priority. As the singular, eternal, unchanging, and unknowable deity, the Father was above and beyond the world. Born of the Father, the only-begotten Son of God, the divine *logos*, held a secondary position in the Christian divinity. Proponents of the difference between Father and Son could also cite the Gospel of John, recalling that Jesus had said, "I have not spoken on my own authority; the Father who sent me has himself given me commandment what to say and what to speak" (John 12:49). In this passage, as the Son of God spoke on behalf of the Father God, a substantial difference between Father and Son was established. Accordingly, some Christians insisted on maintaining that difference in their understanding of Christian divinity.

In Alexandria, the bishop Alexander championed the equality of the Father and the Son. Apparently, the controversy was initiated when the bishop delivered an ambitious sermon proclaiming "God eternal, the Son eternal." In response, the priest Arius objected to this identification of Father and Son on three basic grounds. First, Arius argued that the Christian symbolism of Father and Son, adapted from the model of human procreation, implied that the Father preceded the Son. According to Arius, "there was a time when the Son was not." Although the Son was the only-begotten offspring of the Father, the Son of God was not equal in eternity with the supreme God of Christian faith. Second, that supreme God was so far beyond the world that the Father could not be known by human beings. As mediator between God and the world, however, the Son of God was different from the Father because the Son entered into communication, exchanges, and interchanges with the world of human beings. Third, the Father was immutable, beyond change, and therefore incapable of suffering. As Arius put it, God could not be involved in suffering, not even, referring to his opponents, "with the suffering of insults." From an Arian perspective, those who equated the Father and the Son insulted God by proposing that the supreme deity could be born, suffer, and die. Affirming that the Son of God suffered, Arius insisted on the difference between the Son and the Father to protect the supreme God of Christian faith from such an entanglement with the created world.[8]

As Christians, therefore, in defense of the Christian God, Arians insisted on an essential difference between the Father and the Son. Although subordinate to the Father, the Son was nevertheless understood by Arians as being fully and completely God. The Arian message gained a wide popular following. The majority of bishops, however, objected to this differentiation between Father and Son. At the Council of Nicaea, they met under the authority of the emperor to decide the question.

At the beginning of June 325, the council opened in the judgment hall of the imperial palace. When the bishops had assembled, Constantine entered, with Christian attendants instead of military bodyguards, and assumed his seat at the front of the hall. After a welcoming speech, the emperor addressed the council. He told the bishops his victories in war would be complete only when Christians had resolved their religious warfare in peace and harmony. Since he intended to center his unified empire in a Christian city, Constantine needed a unified church. However, Constantine observed, the church was rent by violent disagreement. By fomenting internal conflicts, the emperor proposed, the devil had succeeded in damaging the Christian religion to an extent its persecutors could never have accomplished. Warning against that demonic influence of dissension, Constantine concluded by calling for Christian unity.

As its first order of business, the Council of Nicaea dealt with the Arian controversy. A defense of the Arian position was presented to the council; a lively debate ensued over the relation between the Father and the Son in a Christian understanding of God. Intervening in the debate, Constantine proposed that the bishops draft a creed, a statement of belief all could embrace, that would include the term *homoousios*—of the same substance—to capture the relation between Father and Son. Accordingly, the creed of Nicaea was adopted by the council as an affirmation of the unity of Father and Son and the divinity of the Son:

> We believe in one God, the Father Almighty, maker of all things visible and invisible; and in one Lord Jesus Christ, the Son of God, God, begotten from the Father, only-begotten, that is, from the substance of the Father, God from God, light from light, true God from true God, begotten not made, of one substance [*homoousios*] with the Father, through Whom all things came into being, things in heaven and on earth, Who because of us men and because of our salvation came down and became incarnate, becoming man, suffered and rose again on the third day, ascended to the heavens, and will come to judge the living and the dead; and in the Holy Spirit.[9]

Although this creed could be interpreted in different ways, it provided terms that most of the bishops at Nicaea could embrace. Clearly, the creed was formulated to counter the Arian understanding of the difference between Father and Son. This intent was underscored by the council's condemnation of anyone who held doctrines associated with the Arian position: that the Son of God was created in time, that the Son of God was subject to change, or that the Son of God had a different essence than the Father. Those who held such doctrines, the council decreed, "the catholic church anathematizes."

What was at stake in this controversy? Certainly, the council sought to affirm the unity of God. The term *homoousios* was the strongest statement of that unity, asserting that Father and Son, by sharing the same essence, were equally God. The Nicene Creed, however, was positioned between what the majority of bishops saw as two heretical extremes. On the one hand, the assertion that Father and Son were *homoousios* recalled the early third-century teachings of Sabellius, who had proposed that the Father, Son, and Spirit were three different modes, masks, or personalities through which the one God appeared. Just as the sun appeared in rays of light, Sabellius had held, God was one, but appeared in three modes. Because it denied the independent divinity of the Son of God, Sabellianism was condemned as a heresy.[10]

On the other hand, *homoousios* recalled the teachings of Paul of Samosata, bishop of Antioch in the middle of the third century, who had insisted on the unity of God by arguing that the Son was subordinate to the Father. Paul had distinguished between the Word of God, which he understood as the divine wisdom, and the Son of God who only appeared at the birth of Jesus. In Paul's account, the Son of God was not divine, but only shared the same substance as God by being infused with the divine wisdom of the Word of God. The *logos,* reason, or wisdom of God, Paul had held, was of the same substance—*homoousios*—as the Father, but was different from the Son, who had been adopted by the Father in the incarnation of Jesus Christ. Because Paul of Samosata had also denied the independent divinity of the Son of God, his teachings were condemned as heresy.[11]

By positioning its creed between these two heretical extremes, the Council of Nicaea tried to affirm the unity of God by emphasizing the coequal divinity of Jesus Christ, the Son of God. Although the creed could be defended on doctrinal grounds, it also reflected the new political situation posed by a Christian empire. The new place assumed by the emperor—as interpreter of the Word, as Friend of God, as mediator between God and the world—displaced the Son of God from performing those roles. According to Eusebius, the emperor acted in ways previously ascribed to the Son of God. The emperor exercised divine kingship, maintained a sacred order, combated evil, and disseminated knowledge that was necessary for salvation. If the emperor, the Friend of God, performed those Christlike functions on earth, then Christ, the Son of God, could easily be assigned to the heavens, above and beyond the world, transcendent, unchanging, and eternal, of the same essential substance as the supreme God, the Father. As the Christian emperor rose in importance, therefore, the Son of God rose even higher into the heavens. Although the creed affirmed that the Son of God had been incarnated on earth, it stressed the Son's divinity by emphasizing that the Son of God had descended from the heavens and had ascended back to the heavens to await the final judgment.

In addition to the unity of God, however, the council also tried to establish the unity of the church. The bishops dealt not only with doctrine, but also with ritual, discipline, and organization in their efforts to create a unified and universal ("Catholic") church. The council formulated rules—or canons—governing the ordination of clergy, the election of bishops, and the scope of authority of bishops in different cities in the Christian empire. Church unity, however, was also established by means of exclusion, by the excommunication of heretics and schismatics who disrupted the unified consensus of the Catholic church. For example, the council insisted that a bishop excommunicated in one province could not be accepted in another. Christian unity, therefore, was defined not only by inclusion, but also by exclusion.[12]

Although it affirmed universal principles of exclusion to be shared by all Christians, the council also created ritual regulations for the reincorporation of those who had been excluded. Schismatics, such as the Donatists, Novatians, or others who had set up their own churches because they felt that Catholics had betrayed the legacy of the martyrs, could be reincorporated through a ritual of laying on of hands. Heretics, however, those who followed the doctrines associated with Sabellius or Arius, could only be accepted in a Catholic church if they renounced their heresy and submitted to a second baptism. Those who refused to undergo these rituals of reincorporation, however, were anathematized. Backing up that religious condemnation with the force of law, Constantine specified that religious toleration of Christianity applied only to Catholic Christians.

With these terms, Constantine and the bishops at Nicaea tried to create a unified Christianity for a unified Christian empire. However, in spite of rulings on heretics, schismatics, and lapsed Christians, churches throughout the empire remained divided on matters of doctrine and ritual practice. The Arian controversy persisted throughout the fourth century, and diversity on other doctrinal matters remained a Christian fact of life. Likewise, variations in ritual practice also caused Christian disunity. For example, in some churches Sunday prayers were offered kneeling, while in others they were offered standing. In the interest of ritual uniformity, the Council of Nicaea insisted that prayers had to be offered in a standing position. Whether standing or kneeling, however, the crucial concern was that all Christians do the same thing, in the same way, at the same time. More seriously, perhaps, the sacred time of Easter was still calculated differently in various regions of the Christian empire. However, in addition to trying to establish a common sacred time, Constantine and the bishops turned their attention to promoting a new sense of Christian sacred space. By discovering, consecrating, and constructing holy places, the emperor produced a new sacred landscape for his unified Christian empire.

HOLY PLACES

Following the Council of Nicaea, Constantine embarked upon building projects in Jerusalem and Roman Palestine. Giving thanks for the agreement achieved at the council, he commissioned the construction of a magnificent basilica, the Church of the Holy Sepulchre, at a site in the city of Jerusalem determined to be ancient Golgotha, the place of the crucifixion, tomb, and resurrection of Jesus. Constantine also had churches built in Mamre, in Bethlehem, and on the Mount of Olives above the city of Jerusalem. His mother, Helena (ca. 248–ca. 328), was instrumental in the construction of these sacred sites. On pilgrimage in the Holy Land, Helena worked under imperial authority to identify Christian holy places. In some cases, she supervised the actual construction of churches on those sites. By claiming those places for Christianity, Constantine and Helena created a new sacred landscape for the empire. However, as in the production of any sacred space, the sites of this new Christian landscape were sites of conflict, contested by competing claims asserted by different religious groups. Accordingly, Constantine's Christian building projects in the Holy Land involved a struggle for the conquest of sacred space.

When the emperor Hadrian had reconsecrated the city of Jerusalem as Aelia Capitolina in 135 C.E., he had built temples to the Greco-Roman gods. According to Christian reports in the fourth and fifth centuries, Hadrian had built a temple to the goddess Venus on the exact site of the crucifixion of Jesus. Illegitimately occupying a Christian holy place, pagans had allegedly defiled the site simply by performing their rituals. Although there is no literary or archaeological evidence to suggest that Christians venerated Golgotha or other places in Jerusalem and Palestine before

Constantine, the emperor's defenders insisted that he was merely restoring the Christian sites that had been stolen and desecrated by pagans. According to this justification, Constantine's acts of appropriation were not theft, but the restoration of holy places to their rightful owners.[13]

Although the allegation that pagans had intentionally stolen and defiled Christian sites was problematic, the appropriation and desecration of pagan sacred sites was certainly a strategy deployed by Constantine. Under Constantine's order, many pagan shrines were destroyed and their locations were claimed for Christian use. When he destroyed the temple of Venus and built his basilica, Constantine asserted a Christian victory over the forces of Greco-Roman paganism. Under its foundations were found not only the places of the crucifixion, the tomb, and the resurrection of Jesus, but also the cross upon which Jesus had been crucified. Legend celebrated Helena's discovery of the true cross, which had been buried under the temple of Venus. Wood from the cross was distributed throughout the empire so widely that by 348 Cyril of Jerusalem observed that the "whole world" had been filled with pieces of the cross. Constantine seems to have been convinced that the discovery of the cross of Christ certified the sanctity of the site. When he built a Christian basilica on that location, therefore, Constantine dedicated it as a monument to the cross, a memorial in honor of the "saving sign" not only of Christian faith, but also of the military victory on the Milvian bridge that had initiated his imperial reign.[14]

In the struggle over the ownership of sacred space, Constantine continued to engage in symbolic warfare on behalf of his Christian empire. The contested character of sacred sites in Palestine can be suggested by the shrine of the sacred oak at Mamre, near Hebron. It was claimed by Jews, then by pagans, and eventually, under Constantine, by Christians. According to Eusebius, the local inhabitants identified the sacred tree of Mamre as the place in which three angelic visitors had appeared to the patriarch Abraham to inform him that his wife, Sarah, would bear a son (Gen. 18:1–22). For two thousand years, the site was venerated in ancient Israel by those who traced their ancestry back to Abraham. The antiquity of the shrine was so well established that the first-century Jewish historian Josephus imagined that its sacred tree had been alive since the creation of the world. Curiously, however, by the early fourth century, Mamre was primarily a pagan shrine. An annual festival brought people from all over Palestine, Phoenicia, and Arabia to worship at the pagan shrine of Abraham at Mamre.

Of course, Christians also claimed a spiritual lineage that went back to Abraham. In Christian interpretations of Abraham's angelic visitors, one of the visitors was consistently identified as Christ. From a Christian perspective, therefore, Mamre was significant as a sacred place in which Christ had appeared in the world. Furthermore, Constantine understood himself as the new Abraham, the new patriarch to many nations who would restore the true religion. When Constantine began claiming holy places in Palestine, he was outraged by the pagan practices at Mamre. His mother-in-law, Eutropia, visited the site and reported that the place in which "Abraham lived is defiled by some of the slaves of superstition in every possible way." Constantine ordered his officials to destroy the pagan altars and punish the priests of the shrine. Claiming the site for Christians, Constantine had a church built into the sacred enclosure. Nevertheless, although pagans were evicted from this new Christian holy place, Mamre continued to attract Jews, pagans, and Christians. According to a fifth-century church historian, at the annual festival of Mamre, Jews came because of the patriarch Abraham, Christians came on account of Christ, and pagans came out of reverence for "the angels." Placing burning lamps at Abraham's well, pagans "called upon the angels, poured out wine, burned incense, offered an ox, a he-goat, a sheep, or a cock." Although Constantine had asserted exclusive Christian ownership of Mamre, alternative claims on that sacred site continued to be advanced by Jews and pagans through such ritual actions.[15]

Under Helena's direct supervision, two other sites were consecrated as Christian holy places: Bethlehem, the place where Jesus first appeared in the world, and the Mount of Olives, the last place where Jesus appeared on earth before ascending into the heavens. At the end of the fourth century, Jerome reported that the cave in which Jesus was born in Bethlehem had been taken over by pagans as a shrine to the goddess Venus and her lover, Adonis, who according to pagan myth had died only to return to life once a year. Like the temple of Venus in Jerusalem, the sacred cave of Venus and Adonis at Bethlehem, with its grove of sacred trees, was destroyed and the site was claimed for exclusively Christian use. Helena directed the construction of "rare memorials" on the site and adorned the cave, in "all possible splendor," with gold, silver, and embroidered cloth donated by Constantine. With the dedication of the Basilica of the Nativity in 339, the Christian appropriation of another pagan site was complete.[16]

Although Helena appropriated a pagan site at the cave of Bethlehem, she consecrated a site with Gnostic significance when she built a church at the cave on the Mount of Olives. In contrast to the gospel accounts, only the book of Acts among the texts of the New Testament placed the ascension of Jesus into the heavens on the Mount of Olives (Acts 1:6–12; see Mark 16:19; Luke 24:50–53). However, an early third-century Gnostic text, the *Acts of John,* described a conversation between John and Jesus that took place in a cave on the Mount of Olives. According to that text, when Jesus appeared to John he illuminated the cave with divine light just as he illuminated his beloved disciple with the divine *gnosis* of salvation. After imparting that secret mystery, Jesus ascended into the heavens. A century later, Eusebius assumed that Jesus stood "upon the Mount of Olives at the cave that is shown there . . . and handed on to his disciples the mysteries of the end, and after this he made his ascension into Heaven." In memory of that event, as Eusebius recounted, Helena erected a church, because Jesus had "initiated his disciples into secret mysteries in this very cave."[17] As Catholic Christians appropriated the cave on the Mount of Olives as a sacred site, they also incorporated certain elements of Gnostic tradition into their understanding of the sanctity of that holy place. The conquest of holy places, therefore, was achieved not only against Jews and pagans, but also against Christians who were regarded by Catholics as heretical.

Under Constantine, a new Christian sense of sacred space was developed. Like any production of sacred space, the consecration of Christian holy places depended upon the practice of ritual. Obviously, the new churches constructed in Palestine became locations for Christian ritual. But another ritual practice—pilgrimage—certified the sanctity of Christian holy places. Although there is some evidence of Christians visiting Jerusalem and Palestine before Constantine, the explosion of popular interest in Christian pilgrimage during the fourth century was unprecedented. In one of the earliest accounts, Egeria, a pious woman from northwestern Spain, embarked in 381 on a three-year pilgrimage through the Holy Land. She visited places associated with the patriarchs and prophets of the Old Testament; she worshiped at the holy places that were identified with the life, death, resurrection, and ascension of Christ. By merging sacred story, ritual observance, and a specific place, pilgrimage gave precise location to Christian faith.

However, as Egeria observed, all ritual in Jerusalem was connected to sacred places. In the Jerusalem liturgy, the day of the year and the site for worship were carefully coordinated so that "all of the hymns and antiphons and readings they have and all the prayers the bishops say, are always relevant to the day which is being observed and to the place in which they are used." As the sacred calendar of the Christian year was coordinated with the holy places, all ritual in Jerusalem became a kind of pilgrimage requiring participants to move from site to site in a regular procession through Bethlehem, Golgotha, the Tomb, the Mount of Olives, and other holy places of the Christian story. Like the wood from the true cross, the ritual innovation of connecting the sacred time of the religious calendar with the sacred places of the Holy Land spread throughout the Christian world. Although many Christians went on pilgrimage to Jerusalem, many others stayed at home in their local churches and imaginatively visited the holy places through the annual sacred calendar of the liturgy. As a lasting legacy of the Christian empire, the emphasis on the importance of sacred places introduced under Constantine continued to inform the ritual life of Christian faith.[18]

8

Holiness

According to Paul, the Christian church was holy because it was the body
of Christ (1 Cor. 12; Rom. 12). Like the parts of the body, the members of
the church were coordinated to comprise a single organism with Christ as
its head. This symbol of the church as a single body was consistently
developed in Christian discourse to represent the unity, purity, or sanctity
of the Christian community. If the church could be a body, however, the
human body could also be a church, a temple for the living God. Paul
directed attention toward the physical body as a holy site. Although the
body could be corrupted by the flesh, it could also be maintained in holiness by conforming to the good order of the spirit. Freedom in the spirit,
as Paul understood it, required a discipline of the body.

Sometimes that body discipline involved detailed attention to modes of
dress, adornment, and hairstyle. For example, Paul insisted that a
Christian man had to cut his hair short. "Does not nature itself teach
you," Paul demanded, "that for a man to wear long hair is degrading to
him?" (1 Cor. 11:14). Although Paul assumed that short hair for men was
natural, he also regarded it as a spiritual disposition of the body. Long
hair on men was not only morally degrading, but also spiritually debili-
tating. As Paul advised, "a man ought not to cover his head, since he is the
image and glory of God" (1 Cor. 11:7). Since "the head of every man is
Christ" (1 Cor. 11:3), a man's head must remain uncovered by long hair
so it can be open to the head of Christ which is God. By the third century,
this standard of Christian holiness in hairstyle had become normative.
The *Didascalia Apostolorum,* for example, instructed all Christian men to
wear their hair short. "You shall not grow the hair of your head," men
were told, "but cut it off." In the fourth century, Jerome advised all
Christians, "Avoid men when you see them loaded with chains and wearing their hair long like women, contrary to the apostle's precept." Not
only going against the instructions of Paul, these fashion statements,

Jerome warned, were "tokens of the devil." For Christian men, therefore, short hair contributed to maintaining the holiness of the physical body.[1]

In the case of women, however, Paul required an entirely different hairstyle. A woman had to wear her hair long, he insisted, because "her hair is given to her for a covering" (1 Cor. 11:15). Although a man's head, as the embodied image of spiritual glory, had to be uncovered, a woman's head, according to Paul, had to be covered to maintain the holiness of the female body. Prevailing standards of female conduct, which required modesty, humility, and subservience to men, certainly influenced this insistence that a woman's head must be covered by long hair. "The head of every man is Christ," Paul held, but "the head of a woman is her husband" (1 Cor. 11:3). However, Paul was also concerned with controlling access to supernatural power within the community. From Paul's perspective, women were already open, in potentially dangerous ways, to demonic, defiling influences from outside the Christian gathering. Therefore, their heads had to be covered not only by long hair, but also by a veil when they participated in the spiritual power generated within the church. Although the tops of their heads were covered, their mouths were also closed, because, as Paul insisted, "it is shameful for a woman to speak in church" (1 Cor. 14:35). By closing the top of the head and the mouth, the openness of the female body to dangerous spiritual forces could in some measure come under male control. According to Paul, the holiness of the church as the body of Christ depended upon maintaining that control over the human body.

Different standards of holiness, therefore, were prescribed for men and women. Men became holy when their heads were open to Christ; women became holy when their heads were covered, their mouths closed in church, and their bodies enclosed within modest clothing. As a student of Paul put it, "Women should adorn themselves modestly and sensibly in seemly apparel, not with braided hair or gold or pearls or costly attire but by good deeds, as befits women who profess religion" (1 Tim. 2:9–10). At the beginning of the second century, Tertullian complained vehemently about the elaborate hairstyles and luxurious fashions favored by Christian women. Like Paul, Tertullian was also worried that a woman's body represented a dangerous opening through which demonic forces might invade the Christian community. As Tertullian interpreted the account of Adam and Eve in Genesis, the original woman had provided precisely such an opening through which evil had entered the world. Following the model set by Eve, Tertullian concluded, every woman "opened the door to the devil."[2] In this respect, the integrity of the church depended not merely on disciplining the body, but more specifically on maintaining male control over the opening in the walls of the church represented by the female body.

Although they were generally prohibited from teaching, preaching, or officiating over the liturgy, women assumed other Christian roles. As we have seen, women could be deacons in order to maintain propriety during the nakedness and anointing required by the ritual of baptism; they could become martyrs, imitating the example of Perpetua, and achieve saint-hood; or they could speak as prophets, like the visionaries of the Montanist movement, and be condemned as heretics by the orthodox church. In general, however, Christian roles for women were defined by marriage. Although Paul had shown some aversion to the institution of marriage by insisting that "it is good for a man not to touch a woman," he nevertheless held that "to avoid fornication, let each man have his own wife, and let each woman have her own husband" (1 Cor. 7:1–2). However, a Christian marriage required sexual discipline. Intercourse within marriage was only for procreation. In the 170s Athenagoras exhorted Christian husbands and wives to follow the model of a farmer who plants his seeds into the ground and then awaits the harvest. Having planted, a farmer does not keep sowing more seeds.[3]

As Justin reported in the second century, Christians adopted one of two lifestyles with respect to sexuality: "Either we do not marry except to rear children, or we refuse to marry and we exercise complete self-control." This second option emerged during the third century as a crucial demon-stration of Christian holiness. By renouncing sex, a Christian could main-tain the integrity of body and soul, gain in spiritual stature, and demonstrate mastery over the desires of the flesh. Tertullian argued that sexual continence kept the soul intact within the body. When experienc-ing orgasm, he asked, "in that very heat of extreme gratification, do we not feel that something of our soul has gone out from us?" Abstaining from sex not only retained the soul, it also increased the spirit. As Tertullian maintained, "By continence you will buy up a great stock of sanctity, by making savings on the flesh, you will be able to invest in the Spirit."[4]

At the same time, however, the renunciation of sex was part of a more general discipline of the body through which a Christian could exercise control over desire. Clement of Alexandria advised Christians to develop a rational discipline of the body in which they did not eat or drink too much, sleep too long, or laugh too loud. Clement allowed for sex within marriage, as long as both partners were conscious that the act was only being performed for the reproduction of children in accordance with God's plan. It was not done for pleasure. However, Christians sought to minimize pleasure, whether in sex or in any other pursuit, as a way of bringing all physical desire under rational control. Ultimately, Clement explained, "our ideal is not to experience desire at all."[5]

In the West, this ideal of spiritual freedom from desire gradually became the special responsibility of Christian clergy. At the beginning of the fourth century, the Council of Elvira, in southern Spain, declared that "bishops, priests, deacons, and all members of the clergy connected with the liturgy must abstain from their wives and must not beget sons." Although this rule was not binding in the East, where parish priests continued to be married, the distinction between celibate clergy and married householders came to represent the essential division of religious labor within Christian communities in the West. According to Eusebius of Caesarea, this division was part of the divine plan, since "Two ways of life were thus given by the Lord to his church." Although the celibate life could be observed by clergy, it was not their exclusive preserve. Widows, virgins, and even married men and women could aspire to that ideal of Christian holiness.[6]

BRIDES OF CHRIST

Celebrating their heroic life of sexual renunciation, Tertullian praised the "many virgins married to Christ." As brides of Christ, they had achieved a distinctive degree of holiness within the Christian community. They anticipated the time of the resurrection when, as Jesus had promised, there would be "neither marriage nor giving in marriage" (Luke 20:35). Accordingly, they lived like angels in human form. Supported by the charity of the church, the virgins were honored as living exemplars of a holy Christian life. In return for food, lodging, and other gifts, the virgins were expected to remain constant to their vows throughout their lives. Addressing the virgins in Carthage, Tertullian exhorted them to remember, "You married Christ, to him you gave over your flesh, to him you betrothed your maturity." If they had sex with a man, as Cyprian put it,

they would be committing "adultery to Christ." Keeping their faith, therefore, meant maintaining the fidelity of their marriage to Christ.[7]

This Christian veneration of virgins was widespread. Since the ideal of
virginity did not apply solely to women, in Syria male and female virgins
became "Sons and Daughters of the Covenant." Renouncing sex, family,
and home, they traveled from village to village, singing the beautiful,
rhythmic hymns of their Christian faith. In Syria, Mesopotamia, and elsewhere in the East, virginity became a common feature of Christian life.
Christians in the East and West celebrated virginity as a lifelong and total
religious commitment to Christ.

In addition to the example of Jesus, the mother of Jesus, Mary, became
a model for virginity. As Jerome observed in the fourth century, "The virgin Christ and the virgin Mary have consecrated the pattern of virginity
for both sexes." In following the example of Jesus, Christian men could
renounce sex, even if they were married, and thereby become "eunuchs
for the kingdom of heaven." Some men took this injunction to become
eunuchs literally. As Justin reported, a man in his church decided to be
castrated. However, since castration was illegal under Roman law, he had
to apply to the governor for permission. When that permission was
denied, the man decided to live a virginal life as if the operation had actually been performed. The Christian philosopher Origen, who excelled at
the allegorical interpretation of biblical texts, also reportedly took the
instruction to become a eunuch for Christ literally by having himself castrated. Disapproving of this practice, the Council of Nicaea ruled that
men who had been castrated could not become bishops, presbyters, or
priests in the church. The fact that the council ruled on this matter, however, suggests that there were Christian men in the fourth century who felt
it was necessary to physically ensure that they maintained the spiritual
status of virginity.[8]

As a role model for women, the Virgin Mary assumed increasing importance. Although the gospels referred to brothers of Jesus (Mark 3:31–5;
Luke 8:19; Matt 12:46–50), suggesting that perhaps Mary had given birth
to other children, by the second century she was celebrated as a perpetual
virgin. Widows who refused to remarry assumed a special status, like the
Virgin Mary, as "virgin mothers" in the church. They were honored for
recovering their virginity after having undergone marriage, sex, and childbirth. With other virgins, they were assigned special places to sit in the
church. But the example of Mary also demanded the perpetual defense of

virginity by young unmarried women. In a popular second-century text, the *Acts of Paul and Thecla*, the fictional heroine, Thecla, was so moved by the teachings of Paul on the virtue of virginity that she willingly risked martyrdom as a Christian to save herself from an arranged marriage. "Blessed are they who have kept the flesh pure, for they shall become a temple of God," Thecla learned. "Blessed are the continent, for to them will God speak." Although Thecla died a martyr's death like Perpetua, the fact that she did not enter prison with an infant at her breast suggested that she had died to preserve the holiness of her virginity. For that reason, Thecla, even though she was a fictional character, became a much more popular martyr than Perpetua. In the stories of the martyrs, countless women were similarly venerated as saints because they chose to die rather than surrender their virginity.[9]

Eventually, under the Christian empire, the holiness of the brides of Christ was enshrined in an imperial law of 354 that called for their protection as "most sacred persons." Writing two years later to the Christian emperor, Constantius II, Athanasius of Alexandria (ca. 293–373) maintained that Jesus Christ had bestowed upon the world, "in the state of virginity, a picture of the holiness of the angels." Athanasius reminded the emperor of the importance of this holy state:

> Such as have attained this virtue, the Catholic church has been accustomed to call the brides of Christ. And the heathen who see them express their admiration for them as the temples of the Word. For indeed this holy and heavenly profession is nowhere established, but only among us Christians, and it is a very strong argument that with us is to be found the genuine and true religion.

By the middle of the fourth century, therefore, the brides of Christ had become an important Christian institution. According to Athanasius, the virgins provided a foretaste of salvation for Christians and a proof of the validity of Christianity for pagans. In these terms, many Christian leaders asserted that the virgin was no longer a woman, but "a sacred vessel dedicated to the Lord."[10]

In principle, a young Christian woman might dedicate herself to a life of virginity at the age of sixteen or seventeen, but in some regions of the empire that vow was only taken at a later age. In any case, the vow was certified when a woman received a special veil that marked her consecration, covering, and enclosure within the Christian community as a perpetual bride of Christ. In addition to the spiritual benefits of achieving the status of a virgin in the church, material interests were also at stake. Some young women might have found the prospect of a spiritual marriage to Christ preferable to an arranged union, with the prevalent risk of death in childbirth that came with a conventional marriage. However, many young women had no choice in the matter, since they could find themselves bestowed upon the church as gifts. As one church leader complained, "Parents and brothers and other relatives bring forward many girls before the proper age, not because the girls have an inner impulse toward the celibate life, but in order that their relatives may gain some material advantage." Nevertheless, these women became consecrated as the "most sacred persons" of the Christian church.[11]

In Italy at the end of the fourth century, Ambrose (ca. 339–97), the bishop of Milan, took a special interest in maintaining the spiritual integrity of the virginal brides of Christ. However, although earlier defenders of the institution of virginity might have praised the virtue of the young women, Ambrose insisted that the virgins were necessary for the integrity of the entire Christian community. They were the walls, the barricades, the enclosure that protected the holiness of Christian faith. "What is virginal chastity," Ambrose asked, "but an integrity free of stain from outside?" In protecting the Christian church from any defilement from outside influences, Ambrose drew the line of defense at the virgins. Like the Virgin Mary, the virgins of the church represented an impenetrable boundary that made the Christian community a holy space that no defiling influence could enter. The integrity of the church, according to Ambrose, depended upon maintaining the virgins as its front line of defense.[12]

At the same time, another Christian leader, Jerome (ca. 347–ca. 420), celebrated the virgins of the church. Having traveled widely throughout the East establishing a reputation as a scholar, Jerome was in Rome in 385. There he addressed his Christian teachings almost exclusively to the women of the Roman church. "It often happened that I found myself surrounded by virgins," Jerome recounted, "and to some of these I expounded the Divine Books as best I could." Among the virgins of the Roman church, Jerome found educated women, some of wealth and influence, whose freedom from the world of marriage, family, and responsibility had enabled them to devote time to study and contemplation. The following year, when Jerome moved to Bethlehem, some of these women followed him there to become his students. The Roman noblewoman Paula, a recently widowed woman of wealth, financed the enterprise, providing resources for housing and a library.

Certainly, the early history of the church depended heavily on such donations from women of position and wealth. As Jerome recognized, women had thereby achieved not only Christian status, but also profound Christian learning and insight. His situation in Bethlehem, however, forced Jerome to defend his own holiness against accusations that he was cohabiting with Christian virgins. Although he defended himself against those charges, Jerome betrayed a sensitivity to human sexuality that differed from the orthodox ideal of mastering the passions. Only a heretic, he responded, would claim that although "crowds of women may surround me, I feel no stirring of desire." According to Jerome, however, only a heretic would suggest that virginity was not a higher state of holiness than marriage. Around 395, Jovinian, a celibate monk, made this suggestion by asserting that "virgins, widows, and married women, who have once gone through Christian baptism, if they are equal in other respects, are of equal merit." Jerome, Ambrose, and Augustine vehemently attacked Jovinian, declaring him to be a heretic because "he has dared to place marriage on an equal level with perpetual chastity."[13] In fashioning their arguments, these church leaders drew inspiration from the Christian renunciates, hermits, and monks who had left the world to establish new communities in Egypt. Far away from the settled life of the city or the village, they wrestled with temptation and confronted the intractability of human desire in search of holiness in the desert.

THE CITY OF THE DESERT

A new definition of holiness emerged among the renunciates, hermits, and monks of the desert. Although the holiness of the desert required celibacy and therefore built on earlier Christian assumptions about sacred virginity, it was more than merely a renunciation of sexuality. Holiness required a complete withdrawal from the world—*anachoresis*, in Greek—in which the anchorite abandoned the ties of home, family, friends, and possessions to retreat from the world and communicate with God. This new movement produced heroic Christian hermits. Antony in Egypt abandoned the human company of his village for a life of extreme self-denial in the desert.

Symeon in Syria, known as Symeon Stylites, avoided all human contact by sitting every day on the top of a sixty-foot column on the ridge of a mountain. With the end of the age of martyrdom, these renunciates worked out a different form of redemptive sacrifice, a type of social death. Like the martyrs, they died to the world in order to live with God.

Although these hermits sought to break all connections with the world, they nevertheless became the focus of popular religious attention. Crowds flocked to stand beneath Symeon's column, trying to be close to the sacred power that was generated by the hermit's solitary communion with God. During the fifteen years Antony spent living alone in the tombs outside his village, prospective followers, attracted by rumors of his spiritual power, invaded the privacy of his retreat. Their attention forced Antony to move deeper into the desert to be alone with God. Nevertheless, he continued to be the focus of popular reports about his power over demons, serpents, lions, and lack of food and water in the desert. Like the martyrs, these ascetics came to be regarded in the Christian imagination as special "friends of God." Living like angels in close contact with God, they were human exemplars of the intersection between the divine and the world.[14]

These heroes of the desert not only became objects of popular veneration, they also inspired emulation. The formation of hermit communities was undertaken by one of Antony's associates, Amun, who had been a successful farmer in the Nile Delta. Around 315 Amun left his wife, home, and land to organize small desert colonies, which came to be known as "cells," of Christian renunciates. These colonies combined the lifestyle of the hermit with a new sense of community in which "the desert was made a city by monks, who left their own people and registered themselves for the citizenship in the heavens." Located in the remote desert, these hermit communities occupied an unknown region, a kind of "outer space," that was beyond the human world. However, since they were only one or two days' journey from Alexandria, these colonies could be visited by Christian pilgrims, who came to admire the heroic self-denial and record the wisdom of the "desert fathers."[15]

Having embarked upon a life of celibacy, the hermits of the desert struggled with sexual temptation. They wrestled with the "demon of fornication." In their encounters with that demon, the hermits confronted sexual fantasies and alluring hallucinations. They subjected their desires to meticulous scrutiny and disciplined control in a lifelong battle against temptation. As Antony had advised, "The greatest thing that a man can do is to throw his faults before the Lord and to expect temptation to his last breath." However, although the "demon of fornication" tempted hermits to satisfy sexual desires, its greatest danger was that it led to the social entanglements of marriage, family, work, and other responsibilities of the world. An anecdote about one desert father illustrates this link between sexuality and the burden of responsibility:

> Abba Olympios of the Cells was tempted to fornication. His thoughts said to him, "Go, and take a wife." He got up, found some mud, made a woman, and said to himself, "There is your wife, now you must work hard in order to feed her." So he worked, giving himself a great deal of trouble. The next day, taking some mud again, he formed it into a girl and said to his thoughts, "Your wife has had a child; you must work harder so as to be able to feed her and clothe your child." So he wore himself out doing this and said to his thoughts, "I cannot bear this weariness any longer." They answered, "If you cannot bear such weariness, stop wanting a wife." God, seeing his efforts, took away the conflict from him and he was at peace.

In this respect, human sexuality had to be renounced because it led back to the social world from which the hermits had escaped. The "demon of fornication," therefore, tempted the renunciates not only to violate sexual purity, but also to return to the commitments, attachments, and distractions of ordinary life in the world.[16]

The desert was an arena, however, in which hermits battled many demons. As Antony advised a new hermit, "Behold, you have become a monk! Stay here by yourself in order that you may be tempted by demons." They fought the demons of greed, avarice, and gluttony by long periods of fasting. More than the triumph over sex, the victory over craving for food represented the hermit's liberation from the world. They fought the demons of anger, envy, and jealousy in their interpersonal relations within the desert communities. They guarded against harsh speech. An elder hermit was asked, "Why are the demons so frightened of you?" The old man responded, "Because I have practiced asceticism since the day I became a monk and not allowed anger to reach my lips." In fighting against these demons of sex, greed, and anger, the hermits engaged in constant holy warfare against supernatural forces of evil.

However, they also recognized that these dangerous enemies were projections of their own desires. When asked how the demons fight, Abba

Poemen observed, "Our own wills become the demons, and it is these which attack us in order that we may fulfill them." The awareness that demons were extensions of human thoughts and desires required intensive introspection. The renunciates of the desert searched their own hearts, as if they were texts, to interpret the spiritual signs of demonic desires and angelic guidance. Although they diligently read and interpreted the Christian scriptures, the hermits also became adept at reading the Bible of the heart. Its secret text could be translated into words through confession. By revealing their thoughts to their brothers and elders, hermits could bring their inner demons into the light and release them. In the process, as they gained insight into their own hearts and the hearts of others, the hermits cultivated a sense of peace (in Greek, *hesychia*) that transcended the ordinary conditions of life in the world.[17]

The desert hermits were credited with extraordinary spiritual power. However, in the interest of total renunciation, they also renounced any glory that might be gained by that power. According to one account, "Some say of Abba Antony that he became a bearer of the Holy Spirit, but he did not wish to speak of this because of men, for he could see all that passed in this world and could tell all that would come to pass." Abba Macarius was said to have become "a god upon earth." His divine power, however, was demonstrated in his ability to discern the fears, desires, and demons lurking in the human heart. Gained through the rigors of self-denial and a life of self-examination, this capacity to understand the language of the heart defined the city of the desert as an alternative social world.[18]

The organization of these ascetic impulses into a formal community was achieved under the direction of another Egyptian, Pachomius (ca. 292–346). While serving in the army, Pachomius had converted to Christianity. In about 320, he established an ascetic community in an abandoned village near the Nile. Those who joined this community, adopting its rough garment as their uniform, divided their time between manual labor in agriculture and crafts and the spiritual labor of study, prayer, and performing the liturgy. Within fifteen years, four associated villages had been established in the Egyptian desert.

Pachomius also gained a reputation for displaying supernatural power. His preaching could induce intense spiritual experiences in his listeners. As Pachomius spoke, according to one account, "All the brethren were like men drunk with wine, and saw the words coming forth from his mouth like birds of gold, silver and precious stones, which flew over the brethren in secret and went into the ears of many of those who listened well." In this intoxicating fusion of the senses, as the flying words were seen appearing in the forms of jeweled birds, the extraordinary speech of Pachomius seemed to fit the extraordinary situation in which the monks found themselves in the city of the desert. Outside of the ordinary world of social relations, they were able to develop remarkable faculties of seeing and hearing. More important than such supernatural experiences, however, was the ability to search the human heart. When a group of bishops questioned Pachomius, they inquired: "We confess that you are a man of God, and we know that you can see the demons. But on the issue of the searching of hearts, as this is a great matter, tell us more of that."[19]

By the end of the century, over five thousand renunciates had adopted this communal lifestyle of self-denial in Egypt. A similar development occurred in Syria, where Jacob Baradeus of Nisibis (ca. 500–78) founded communities to emulate the practices of local hermits. However, the Pachomian village, with its balance of manual and spiritual labor, as well as its intimate language of the desires and demons of the heart, established the basic pattern for Christian monasticism. Christian visitors to Egypt, such as Jerome, John Cassian, and Hilary of Poitiers, wrote enthusiastic reports about the monks of the desert. Inspired by their example, Martin of Tours (316–97) established the first Western monastery on the Pachomian model in northern Gaul. Although political turmoil and invasions eventually displaced the hermits and monks from the Egyptian desert, their example continued to sustain the development of monastic communities elsewhere in the Christian empire. The Pachomian model of manual labor and spiritual devotion set the standard for monastic orders dedicated to both the contemplation of God and the detailed inspection of the human heart.[20]

A NEW SONG

As the Roman administrator Pliny observed at the beginning of the second century, Christians could be distinguished by their practice of meeting once a week "to sing in alternate verses a hymn to Christ, as to a god." Weaving melodies into the words of the psalms, Christians came together to sing the holy music of their faith. Singing, therefore, was central to the religious life of the church. As voices harmonized, as words moved in rhythm, melody, and counterpoint, as the air filled with song, the church was consecrated by music. Christians were Christians because they sang together. As many Christian authors observed, the central significance of music in the Christian community was only fitting because the churches represented an alternative to the "old song" of pagan superstition and immorality. Christian churches sang Christ, the "New Song" (Rev. 5:9; 15:3–4).

Certainly, music was an integral part of Greco-Roman paganism. The hymns of priests, the harmonies of choirs, and the instrumental music of processions and festivals were all familiar features of pagan ritual. Although music was common in religious practice, it was also a topic for philosophical reflection. In his *Republic,* Plato specified two religious roles played by music. First, musical rhythms, melodies, and harmonies could produce moral effects. By resonating with the soul, certain musical movements developed a moral sensitivity in both performers and listeners.

Second, according to Plato, music orchestrated the entire universe. In the celestial music of the heavenly spheres, as each planet in the heavens, from the moon to Saturn, resounded with its own musical note, the order of the cosmos was established as a musical harmony. This insight into the music of the heavenly spheres, attributed to the ancient philosopher Pythagoras, who was credited with the ability to actually hear the celestial music, became a common theme in Greco-Roman reflections on the harmonious order of the universe. As the third-century Platonist Plotinus held, the divine One was the origin of all music in the heavens and on the earth. "All flows so to speak from one fount," Plotinus observed, "all melodies, every rhythm." Music, therefore, moved the soul and the cosmos.[21]

As already noted, in Syria the "Sons and Daughters of the Covenant" used music as a Christian medium for moving the soul. They were poets, singers, and musicians. As these Christian virgins wandered around the countryside, they were often mistaken for bands of traveling musicians. Occasionally, they were even hired to provide entertainment at pagan feasts or festivals, "singing the songs of the Lord in the strange land of the heathen." The Egyptian monks also integrated music into their religious practice not only in the liturgy, but also in the daily routines of manual labor. Around 375, Basil defended the monastic practice of men and women who "sing hymns to God continually while working with their own hands." Twenty-five years later, Augustine took this practice for

granted. In place of the scandalous love songs, bawdy ballads, and theatrical tales that workers usually sang, the psalms gave rhythm to repeti-
tive labor while also providing edifying moral and spiritual content. Just
as the rowers of a boat sang a rhythmic chant—in Latin, the *celeuma*—to
coordinate their efforts, the monks sang the psalms, the sacred music,
Augustine observed, of "the divine *celeuma*."[22]

Musical innovations, developed in the monastic contexts of Syria,
Egypt, and Jerusalem, had an impact in the West. In the 370s, the bishop
of Milan, Ambrose, introduced eastern musical styles for chanting psalms
in church. Some complained that he had corrupted the Catholics of Milan
with these new rhythms and melodies from the East. One member of his
community, however, recalled the evocative power of these sacred songs.
As Augustine remembered his days in Milan, he addressed himself to
God: "I wept at the beauty of your hymns and canticles, and was powerfully moved at the sweet sound of your church's singing. Those sounds
flowed into my ears, and the truth streamed into my heart: so that my feeling of devotion overflowed, and the tears ran from my eyes, and I was
happy in them." According to Augustine, however, the sound of sacred
songs stimulated both feeling and insight by opening the heart to
Christian truth.[23]

Beginning in the fourth century, Christian leaders showed an increasing
interest in making this sacred music spill out of the church and into the
world. Sacred singing not only consecrated the church as a holy place, it
could also sanctify the city and the countryside. As a way of extending the
domain of Christian holiness in the world, they hoped to replace the popular songs of laborers with the hymns, psalms, and sacred music of
Christian faith. In this musical effort, the self-professed orthodox and the
alleged heretic found common ground. Arius composed Christian work
songs for sailors, millers, and travelers; Athanasius recommended the
appropriate psalms to be sung by workers in vineyards. In the countryside, the adoption of Christian song promised to elevate workers from the
tedium of their labors into an angelic life. As in the monastery, manual
labor in the fields could be transformed into the melody of prayer. In the
city, although sacred music held the same potential to transform work
into prayer, it also signified membership in the Christian community.
Within the multireligious urban context, where Christians worked alongside pagans, Jews, and others, laborers who sang hymns while they
worked set themselves apart as Christians. As both sign and significance

of a worker's Christian life, therefore, sacred music was recommended as a way to make manual labor a holy instrument.[24]

Around 402, the pagan philosopher Synesius of Cyrene, who would later become a Christian bishop, described the music that featured prominently in country life. On his estate, Synesius reported, "Plucking the strings we often sing to the harp songs about the fig tree and the vine, but nothing as often as prayers: songs that ask for the well-being of people and crops and livestock." In this idealized rural scene, work songs and prayers flowed together to the tune of the harp. Some Christians tried to give specific religious content to a harmonious rural ideal based on the monastic model of work and prayer. The Roman noblewoman Paula, who supported Jerome in Bethlehem, wrote home to the city to describe such an idealized Christian farm. "Wherever you turn," she noted, "the farmer holding the plow sings alleluia, the sweating harvester distracts himself with psalms, and the vineyard worker pruning the vine with a curved sickle sings one of the songs of David. These are the songs of the country; these are, as they are commonly called, the love songs; these the shepherd whistles; these are a tool in cultivation." As tools of cultivation, Paula suggested, the sacred songs, hymns, psalms, and praises intoned by workers transformed the farm into a holy place.[25]

In the urban context, John Chrysostom called for the adoption of Christian work songs. Music, he observed, eases the heavy burden of manual labor in both the country and the city. The same musical effects experienced by travelers, farm workers, sailors, and weavers, he proposed, could be gained by workers in the city, "for the soul faces troubles and difficulties more easily when it hears tunes and songs." John Chrysostom recommended that sacred songs be adapted for their work by artisans, craftsmen, soldiers, and even judges. Not only easing the burden of labor, however, these sacred songs held the power to spiritually transform the worker's body, mind, and soul. The conventional work songs of the city, which John Chrysostom called "demonic" music, appealed only to the senses, desires, and lusts. Accordingly, they weakened and corrupted the mind. By adopting Christian work songs, however, the "sacred" music, sung with self-control, caused the Holy Spirit to descend upon the worker and "sanctify the mouth and soul."

According to John Chrysostom, Christian music had an inherent sacred power. Adapting elements of the Platonic philosophy of music, he held that the tunes and words of Christian song produced moral effects;

they carried a spiritual influence, with the descent of the Holy Spirit, that came from the harmony of the heavens. Christian music conveyed an intrinsic sacrality beyond human understanding. In fact, workers did not have to know what the songs meant in order to derive moral and spiritual benefit from singing them. "Even if you do not know the meaning of the words," John Chrysostom advised, "meanwhile teach your mouth to utter them." The sacred power of the songs themselves would sanctify the mouth and body, the mind and soul, in the harmony of Christian music.[26]

As he recalled his profound experience in Milan, Augustine had been moved by the sound of Christian music. Beyond words, his heart had been filled with divine truth by the sounds of singing. Years later, however, when Augustine had become the bishop of the small North African town of Hippo, he insisted that his congregation think about what they were singing. "Sing it with human reason," he insisted, "not like birds." Drawing a comparison similar to John Chrysostom's distinction between "demonic" and "sacred" music, Augustine asked his listeners to consider how those who delighted in singing obscene songs knew precisely what they were singing. "We know only too well the way bad, loose-living men sing, as suits their ears and hearts. They are all the worse for knowing only too well what they are singing about. They know they are singing dirty songs—but the dirtier they are, the more they enjoy it." If singers of obscene lyrics knew the words of their songs, Augustine exhorted, "we, who have learnt in the church to sing God's words, should be just as eager." In order to enter into the sacred music, it was not enough merely to sing. Sacred music required rational reflection on the words as they moved to the rhythms, melodies, and harmonies of song. "Now, my friends," Augustine concluded, "what we have all sung together with one voice—we should know and see it with a clear mind." The New Song of Christian faith, according to Augustine, had to be sung with the clarity of reason.[27]

9

Faith and Reason

The Roman philosopher, scientist, and medical doctor Galen probably expressed a common pagan criticism of Jews and Christians when he observed: "If I had been a follower of Moses or of Christ, I should not have given you a definition; I should have said, 'Just believe.'"[1] Trained in classical language and literature and conversant with ancient logic, science, and philosophy, many educated pagans assumed that Jews and Christians had simply forsaken reason for the authority of their religious faith. One Christian thinker, Augustine (354–430), who served as bishop of the small North African town of Hippo, directly addressed the challenge of defining the relation between faith and reason. They were necessarily related, Augustine insisted, because Christians were called not only to believe, as if belief were an end in itself, but they were called to believe in order that they might understand.[2] According to Augustine, therefore, the Christian faith was a faith in search of rational understanding. In the process of clarifying his understanding of Christian faith and reason, Augustine profoundly influenced the development of Christianity in the West.

Born in Tagaste, in a region of North Africa that became modern Algeria, Augustine grew up in a religiously mixed household. His Christian mother, Monica, established the religious atmosphere of the home. Although he was not baptized, Augustine nevertheless became familiar with the Christian faith of his mother. His pagan father, Patricius, financed Augustine's education, sending him to the metropolitan center of Carthage to be trained in the classical art of rhetoric. An education in rhetoric, which developed skills in verbal persuasion, prepared students for careers in teaching, law, or government. By immersing themselves in classical language and literature, students of rhetoric learned an art of eloquence that had many practical applications. Christians, however, tended to mistrust the verbal eloquence and persuasive appeal of classical rhetoric. As Gregory of Nazianzus (ca. 330–ca. 389) proposed, Christians required an education "which disregards rhetorical ornaments and glory." Augustine would later share that assessment of rhetoric by observing that his education in classical eloquence only led him to desire "that wealth which is poverty and the glory which is shame." Nevertheless, Augustine would apply what he had learned in the school of rhetoric in his persuasive appeals on behalf of the Christian faith.[3]

Between 373 and 382, Augustine was a professor of rhetoric in Carthage. Although unmarried, he lived with a woman with whom he had a son, Adeodatus. While his professional life was occupied with rhetoric, Augustine's religious interests were directed toward the teachings of the third-century Mesopotamian prophet Mani (ca. 216–ca. 276). Mesopotamia was noted for its extraordinary Christian visionaries. Around 100 C.E., the Mesopotamian prophet Elchesai had reported a vision of a male angel and his female companion who revealed themselves as the Son of God and the Holy Spirit. According to Elchesai, they explained that Christ had lived on earth before he had been born to the Virgin Mary and that Christ would be reborn periodically to remind human beings of the path to salvation. A community of Elchesaites developed in lower Mesopotamia. A century later, a twelve-year-old member of that community, Mani, had a vision of his divine double, his heavenly twin, who disclosed his special religious destiny. When he was twenty-four, his heavenly twin reappeared to announce Mani's divine status as the Apostle of Light.

After traveling for three years in India, Mani settled in Persia, where he proclaimed his "gospel of light," which wove together elements of Christianity, Buddhism, and the ancient Persian religion of Zarathustra, under the patronage of the Persian king, Shapur. Mani composed five books in Aramaic, along with a summary of his teachings in Persian, which became the sacred texts of Manichean religion. Mani proclaimed a dualism of good and evil, of light and darkness, in which two Gods operated in the universe. Far above the Kingdom of Darkness of this world, a world that had been created by the evil God, the Kingdom of Light was governed by the good God. Like Gnostics, Mani found salvation in a liberating knowledge of the supreme God. As the Apostle of Light, Mani worked to lead human beings to that supreme divine kingdom. After Shapur's death in 272, however, a new Persian regime placed Mani in prison, where he died three years later, a martyr for his new religion.

Persecuted in Persia, followers of Mani established themselves initially in Egypt and then spread throughout the Roman Empire. Manicheans were feared by both pagans and Christians. In his efforts to restore the purity of Roman religion, the emperor Diocletian legislated against the Manicheans because he saw them as a foreign incursion from the enemy territory of Persia. In 297, as a prelude to his mass persecution of Christians, Diocletian ordered the leaders of the Manichean community in Egypt to be arrested and burned at the stake along with their sacred texts. Under the Christian empire, Manicheans continued to suffer persecution. In support of banning the Manicheans from the empire, Eusebius condemned the movement as "a deadly poison that came from the land of the Persians." By the time Augustine joined the movement, therefore, Manicheans had suffered a long history of persecution.[4]

In spite of its foreign origin and illegal status, the Manichean movement gained a following. Its leaders, who were known as the "elect," traveled around the Roman Empire as apostles of the Kingdom of Light. Supporters of the movement, who were called "hearers," met in small groups to listen to a representative of the "elect" reading the sacred texts of Mani. In the process, as the teachings of Mani provided a window into the Kingdom of Light, the hearers, as Augustine later recalled, were "filled with light." By knowing the God of "unmeasured light" as a "vast luminous body," Manichean hearers learned that they had a soul of light, "a sort of piece broken off from this body." That realization prepared Manicheans for a journey back to the light, a salvation in which the "Light shall return to its place, the Darkness shall fall and not rise again." By identifying with Christ, who had descended into the realm of darkness to save the light that was captured in the world, Manicheans could recognize their own divine nature.[5]

Augustine was attracted to this radical dualism of light and darkness because it seemed to provide a rational explanation for the place of evil in the universe. As the product of an evil God, all evil, including the human experience of sin, suffering, and misfortune, could be explained. After nine years as a hearer, however, Augustine eventually decided that the Manichean insight into the light of God and the light of the soul only encouraged a false pride. Addressing God in his *Confessions*, Augustine complained that the Manicheans "will boast of their knowledge and will be praised for it, thus turning away from you in their evil pride and losing the light that comes from you." By assuming that they were light in themselves and therefore of the same spiritual essence as the supreme God, the Manicheans were alienated from the true light that Augustine was later convinced could only illuminate the soul, so that, he prayed to God, "having been sometime darkness, we may be light in Thee." Throughout his life, Augustine struggled to reconcile the light of reason with the demands of faith in Christ, the Word of God, the light of the world.[6]

CHRIST, THE TRUTH

In 383 Augustine left Carthage and established himself as a professor of rhetoric in the Italian city of Milan. Breaking with the Manicheans, Augustine joined a small group of intellectuals—mostly pagan, but a few Christian—who were intent on recovering the wisdom contained in the philosophy of Plato. They were guided by the teachings of Plotinus (205–70), an Egyptian Greek who had taught in Rome a century earlier, as they had been edited into a collection, the *Enneads,* by his student Porphyry. According to Augustine, Plotinus was "Plato born again," bringing the ancient philosophy back to life. However, although Plato had taught a dualism that distinguished between two levels of reality—an eternal realm of ideal forms and a changing world of illusions, sensory perceptions, and unstable opinions—Plotinus turned the Platonic dualism into a monism.[7]

According to Plotinus, there was one ultimate reality, which he called the One, and everything that existed emanated from the One. As the One radiated outward, like the rays of the sun, the order of the universe was produced through an ongoing process of emanation. The ideal forms of reality were located in the mind of God; the animating force of the universe was the soul of God; and the material world was the outer limit of divine emanation, a world of shadows that held only dim reflections of their origin in the One. Caught in that material world of shadows, the human soul was ensnared in ignorance. Plotinus called human beings to awaken from their ignorance by returning to the source, by turning inward to the divine reason within the soul and embarking upon a spiritual journey of the soul back to the eternal being of the One.

This imagery of the cosmic procession of the One and the soul's return provided Augustine with a new philosophical vocabulary. It pointed him toward reason, the intellect, or the *logos* as the power of the soul that mediated between God and the world. Like many of his educated contemporaries, Augustine found that the Platonic *logos* was the same Word of God that the Gospel of John had proclaimed when it declared, "In the beginning was the *logos,* and the *logos* was with God, and the *logos* was God" (John 1:1). Although they seemed to share this common ground in divine reason, Augustine was troubled by an apparent gap between Platonism and Christianity. Although it provided theoretical insight into the eternal Word of God, Platonism lacked what Augustine decided was the practical means of gaining access to the Word, the incarnation of Jesus Christ in which the Word was made flesh in the world. The story of the heroic Egyptian ascetic Antony, which Augustine learned at this time, represented a liberation from the flesh in the name of Christ, the Word of God that had become flesh. Following this new determination that Christ was the only way, Augustine had a dramatic conversion experience that convinced him to apply for baptism in the Christian church of Milan. Along with his mother, his son, and his close friend Alypius, Augustine retired to a country estate in Cassiciacum to devote himself to philosophical reflection on divine wisdom. Augustine spent the years 386–391 in Platonic and Christian philosophical contemplation of Christ, the Truth.

The object of his philosophical inquiry, Augustine insisted, was simple: "I desire to know God and the soul." Those simple terms, however, were complicated by the merger of Platonism and Christianity. In broadly Platonic terms, Augustine identified God as being. Rather than understanding God as a personal being, with personal attributes, Augustine understood God as supreme being. God was "true being." Unbound by space or time, God was everywhere. Above all, God was eternal, unchanging truth. "You do I invoke," Augustine prayed, "God, truth, in whom and by whom and through whom are all things true which are true." The *logos* of God determined the eternal forms of truth as well as the ability of human reason to discern the truth. In terms that any Platonist could embrace, Augustine described the *logos* of God as the "intelligible light" that enabled the human mind to recognize the eternal patterns of divine truth. At the same time, however, Augustine insisted on the Christian character of truth. According to the Gospel of John, followers of Jesus Christ were promised, "you shall know the truth, and the truth shall set you free" (John 8:32). By knowing Christ, the truth, Augustine concluded, human beings could be liberated from the ignorance that entangled them in the material world.[8]

In his early work, Augustine adopted a Platonic confidence in reason. Defining reason as the gaze of the soul, he proposed that the soul's eye could gain direct insight into truth and eventually achieve an intellectual vision of God. As a Christian, however, Augustine argued that the attainment of this liberating vision had to begin with faith. On the recommendation of Ambrose, Augustine adopted a biblical passage that captured the relation he wanted to establish between Christian faith and reason. "Unless you believe," the prophet Isaiah had advised, "you will not understand" (Isa. 7:9). On this model, the gaze of the soul had to be guided by the authority of Christian faith. Access to truth, on this account, could only be achieved by a belief in God that was directed by faith, informed by hope, and inspired by a love that motivated reason to look for the truth.[9]

Augustine occasionally proposed rational arguments for the existence of God. For example, in one early text he asked, "If we could find something existing and superior to reason, would you call it, whatever it may be, God?" In that analysis, he considered the five senses, the interior sense that processes perceptual information, and the faculty of reason that distinguishes among the different senses. Above and beyond all those faculties, however, was the eternal truth. "We must have no doubt," he wrote in another text on the true religion, "that the unchangeable substance which is above the rational mind is God." Instead of relying on such argumentation, however, Augustine celebrated an intellectual vision of God, guided by faith, hope, and love, that resulted in "a conjunction between seer and seen." Seeing God, therefore, was in some way to enter into the being of God.[10]

During this period of philosophical reflection, Augustine developed the outlines of a Christian theory of knowledge. He tried to clarify the process by which human beings learn and verify the truth. As a retired professor of rhetoric, Augustine remained interested in education. At this point, he believed that all the liberal arts of classical learning led to truth and were measured by truth. Since he held that truth was God, Augustine felt that these educational disciplines had an important place in the divine classroom of the world. While at Cassiciacum, Augustine wrote a book on education, De magistro, in the form of a dialogue with his son, Adeodatus, in which he argued that Christ, the truth, actually teaches within the human mind.

The dialogue began with a question: "What do you suppose is our purpose when we use words?" By verbal signs, Augustine suggested, we intend to convey information, or, in other words, to teach. However, words failed in this regard. Augustine argued, "By means of words, we learn nothing but words, in fact, only the sound and noise of words." Although words might point to objects of knowledge, learning only could be achieved by seeing directly the things to which the words referred. "I shall learn the thing I did not know," Augustine argued, "not by means of the words spoken, but by seeing it." The immediacy of vision, therefore, provided the key to learning about things in the world.

Likewise, in the realm of ideas, Augustine held that learning depended upon the insight that could only be gained by direct intellectual vision. By using words, a teacher, whom Augustine called an *exterior magister*, could not convey an insight into truth to someone who had not beheld "that interior light of truth which effects enlightenment and happiness in the so-called inner man." In order to see that inner light of truth, the mind required an inner teacher, the *interior magister*, who could display the truth directly to the eye of the mind. That light of truth, Augustine concluded, was the divine *logos*, the Word of God, that was at work in the learning process as "Christ teaches within the mind."[11]

When Augustine returned to North Africa in 391, hoping to establish a monastery near his old hometown, he was rapidly co-opted as a priest and then ordained four years later as the bishop of Hippo. Torn from the contemplative life of reason, Augustine was abruptly thrust into the difficult, complex, and often violent world of action. As bishop of a small-town church, Augustine found himself embroiled in local disputes over property and prestige. He had to deal with the illiterate faithful and the educated inquirers, the aspiring rich and the oppressed poor, and the recalcitrant and penitent sinners of his congregation. In this practical context in which he operated over the next forty years, Augustine gradually became less confident in the liberating power of the divine light of human reason.

From this new vantage point, Augustine asserted that anyone who thought that the human soul could attain a direct vision of God in this life did not understand either the soul or God. As Augustine put it, "Whoever thinks that in this mortal life a man may so disperse the mists of bodily and carnal imaginings as to possess the unclouded light of unchangeable Truth and cleave to it with an unswerving constancy understands neither what he seeks nor who he is that seeks it."[12] From this point, as he placed less confidence in the soul's access to the rational light of God, Augustine turned increasingly to the soul's dependence on the authoritative word of God. The context in which the word of God operated, however, was not confined to the comfortable conditions of a philosophical retreat from the world. The word of God operated in the city.

THE CITY OF GOD

In assuming the responsibilities of a Catholic bishop in North Africa, Augustine had to confront the fact that the region was not predominantly a Catholic domain. Besides noticing the survival of pagan practices and the continuing presence of the Manicheans, Augustine had to acknowledge that the dominant religious force in North Africa was the Donatist church, which claimed to represent the pure church of the martyrs. Against the Donatists, Augustine argued that because the Christian church had to be a mixed body combining saints and sinners, it could never claim to be spiritually pure. No church could set itself apart as the pure church. Insisting on Christian unity, Augustine advanced Catholic reasons for absorbing Donatist Christians into a common Christian community. As Christian emperors were drawn into this conflict, however, Catholic reason came to be supported by imperial force. Condemned as heretics, Donatist Christians were placed under legal proscriptions that denied their basic civil rights. Not only were Donatist churches confiscated, but Donatist Christians were prevented from protecting their personal property in the courts or passing it on to their heirs. Supported by imperial law, the Catholic church rapidly emerged as the dominant force in North Africa.

For their part, however, Donatists held fast to the ideal of religious purity. Turning to guerrilla warfare, militant adherents of the Donatist cause, who were known as Circumcelliones, roamed the countryside carrying wooden clubs they called "Israels" to engage in counteroffensives against Catholic churches. Courting martyrdom for their Donatist faith, the Circumcelliones gained a reputation for seeking violent confrontations in which they might prove the purity of their religion. It was better to die for their pure faith, they were convinced, than to be incorporated into the mixed body of Catholic Christians. Remaining true to the church of the martyrs, the Circumcelliones were prepared to die for their faith.[13]

In 394 Augustine entered this Christian conflict by composing a popular song, his "ABC Against the Donatists." In a jingle that moved to a

rhythmic beat and followed a structure in which each couplet started with
a different letter of the alphabet, the song repeated the refrain: "You who
take your joy in peace, now is the time to judge what's true." As this venture into popular propaganda should suggest, Augustine had moved from
the contemplative life to a new arena of Christian activism. As the
Donatist controversy intensified, he advanced arguments for using force
in compelling compliance with Catholic faith. Truth was less a matter of
insight than a question of judgment. Carrying the responsibility on behalf
of his congregation for judging what was true, Augustine the bishop had
to adjudicate among competing Christian interests. In fighting against the
Donatists, he learned that his own rational or faithful judgments about
truth carried little weight unless they were backed up by force. Under
these conditions, Augustine linked faith not only with reason, but also
with the coercive use of power.

Before returning to North Africa, Augustine had assumed that the
social order on earth could be a reflection of the cosmic order of the heavens. If it was organized according to the rationality of God's creation,
human society could be in harmony with the order of the universe. In a
Christian empire, both church and state could conform to that divine pattern of rational order. In his conflicts with the Donatists, however,
Augustine changed his mind about the nature of the Christian church.
Instead of standing as a separate enclave of order, or, as the Donatists
hoped, a pure vessel for the saved, the church in Augustine's mature
thought was a microcosm of the world, incorporating the mixed and
messy state of the human condition. Within the Catholic church,
Christians were called to be holy; but they were also required to coexist in
the same Christian community with sinners and to correct, rebuke, or
chastise them when necessary. Since he was convinced that no salvation
was possible outside of this mixed community of the Catholic church,
because that church alone owned the ritual sacraments, Augustine
increasingly justified the use of force against dissident Christians to "compel them to come in."[14]

Like the Catholic church, the larger society, even under the authority of
a Christian empire, appeared to Augustine as a mixed body of the saved
and the damned. Around 412, he began writing a monumental analysis of
Roman religion, society, and history, the *City of God*. By the time that
book was completed in 426, Augustine had developed a carefully reasoned account of the role of Christian faith in the world. That book was

occasioned by the turmoil surrounding the incursion of the Goths, the "barbarians" from the north, into Rome. Under the leadership of Alaric, who was an Arian Christian, the Goths had sacked the city in 410 and continued to represent a threatening foreign presence on the northern frontier. Although Rome soon recovered, this invasion of the city was an extremely disorienting event for both pagans and Christians. As Jerome declared, "If Rome be lost, where shall we look for help?" Pagan intellectuals blamed Christians for the disaster. By abandoning the ancient gods of the city, they argued, an increasingly Christianized Rome had exposed itself to destruction. Christians blamed pagans, who were reviving some of the moral values and ancestral rituals of Roman religion, for bringing down God's wrath on the city. The religious meaning of this catastrophe, therefore, was intensely contested.

Augustine provided an alternative interpretation of the religious significance of the sack of Rome. Rather than attributing it to the specific failings of pagans or Christians, he interpreted the disaster as a symptom of the suffering endemic to the human condition. The world, he proposed, was like an olive press. Sharing a deep, collective guilt, human beings were inevitably pressed by the world. They suffered hardships, turmoil, and disasters under the pressure of the world. By alienating human beings from God, the collective guilt of humanity was sufficient to account for any specific catastrophe that might occur. However, Augustine proposed that the suffering human beings endured under the pressure of the world was not only a punishment; it was also a corrective, disciplinary, and even educational process that could produce spiritual benefits. "The world reels under crushing blows," Augustine observed, "the old man is shaken out; the flesh is pressed, the spirit turns to clear flowing oil." Living in the world, human beings were necessarily subject to such painful, yet potentially refining, pressures.[15]

In his mature religious thought, Augustine increasingly emphasized the fundamentally flawed and fallen nature of the world, which was the result of sin. With the original sin of Adam and Eve, human nature, in its thinking, willing, and desiring, had become thoroughly and completely perverted. According to Augustine, that damage was collective, affecting all humanity. He used the metaphor of the city to capture that shared, collective character of human identity. Human desire, he argued, had social consequences. "Two loves," he proposed, "founded two cities."

In his *City of God*, Augustine analyzed the social effects of those two dispositions of desire, one that loved God, the other that loved the changing, imperfect, and sinful conditions of the world. The first ten books advanced a sustained critique of pagan religion, arguing that its myths and rituals actually celebrated evil demons. That critique, however, was designed not only to debunk pagan religious claims, but also to disconnect the ancestral religion from its historical role in providing sacred support for the social order. Instead of supporting the city of Rome, Augustine argued, pagan religion had entrenched the rule of the devil and his demons on earth. In the last twelve books, Augustine developed an alternative history in terms of the progress of two cities, the earthly and the heavenly. In the beginning, these two cities originated from two desires, the desire for the spirit and the desire for the flesh. During the course of human history, however, they had become mixed together in the world, as the spiritual city traveled through the realm of the flesh. Although it was ultimately above and beyond the world, the City of God nevertheless wandered through the world as a spiritual haven for those who directed their desire toward God. In the end, however, the City of God would emerge from its wanderings through the world to reign supreme as the divine "kingdom of which there is no end."[16]

Augustine analyzed human history in terms of binary oppositions—God and the devil, angels and demons, Abel and Cain, Jerusalem and Babylon, and so on—that represented the basic conflict between the city of the spirit and the city of the flesh. In this respect, a lingering Platonism informed his view of history. Two orders of reality, the spiritual and the material, could in principle be separated for purposes of analysis. In the *City of God*, however, Augustine abandoned this basic Platonic distinction between spiritual and material realms for a much more complex interpretation of the historical process as a process of struggle. Human nature, which was damaged from the beginning, was inevitably entangled not only in materiality, but also in desires beyond the control of human intellect or will. In this ongoing struggle, the faculty of reason, if properly guided by faith, could discern the causes and consequences of the damage, but it could do nothing to correct the situation. Only the grace of God, Augustine concluded, could bring human beings into the City of God. Mysterious, unfathomable, and ultimately beyond reason, that divine grace, which Augustine saw working through the church, the sacraments, and the Christian faith, was a gift of God that "makes his worshipers into gods."[17] In the end, he concluded, only the mysterious grace of God could undo the enormous, collective damage done to human nature at the beginning. The City of God, therefore, was a divine gift.

THE GIFT OF GRACE

In confronting the conflicts that arose in the Christian church and in the Roman state, Augustine developed a critical perspective on the inherent limits of both church and state. In both the Christian church and civil society, he decided, social order could never be established according to the rational principles of the good, the true, and the beautiful. Instead of providing a practical program, those Platonic ideals only represented utopian dreams that were beyond the capacity of human institutions. Order had to be maintained, he concluded, not merely by persuasive appeals to reason, but by authority, discipline, and, when necessary, the judicious exercise of coercive force. In the real world, Augustine found, church and state had to cooperate, even in the exercise of force, to secure the fabric of social order against conflict, disruption, and disintegration. By maintaining some measure of social stability, this exercise of force enabled church and state to constrain the forces of evil and protect the spiritual character of the city of God.

This linkage between Christian religious discourse and force made sense to Augustine because he had arrived at a new understanding of the pervasive and intractable nature of human sinfulness. Augustine reinforced this apparently pessimistic conclusion about human nature in the context of another religious controversy, this time by opposing the teachings of the British monk Pelagius and his followers, who celebrated the human ability to follow freely and conform perfectly to the practical requirements of Christian faith. Augustine was shocked by the arrogance of this claim. In arguing against the Pelagians, Augustine developed his mature analysis of the human will, original sin, and the mysterious workings of the grace of God. Although he ultimately concluded that divine grace was an inscrutable mystery, Augustine never abandoned the use of reason in the work of making sense out of the central mystery of Christian faith.

According to the Pelagians, human nature was essentially good. At birth, they held, "evil is not born with us, and we are begotten without fault or sin, and the only thing in man previous to the action of his own will is that which God created in him." Endowed with free will, human beings had the power to avoid sin and live according to the moral precepts of faith. As the followers of Pelagius argued, sin was "a fault, not of nature, but of human will." As infants, human beings were born, like Adam and Eve in the beginning, in a state of original innocence, with a will that was free to choose between right and wrong. Because they were able to choose, human beings, according to the Pelagians, were obligated to choose the right path. On the basis of that exercise of free will, as it could be measured in good or evil conduct, human beings would justly undergo the judgment of God. In calling upon Christians to employ their free will to love, fear, serve, and obey God, Pelagians could cite the Gospel of Matthew, "Be perfect, even as your Father in heaven is perfect" (Matt. 5:48).[18]

Augustine was concerned that the Pelagian doctrine of free will, human goodness, and moral perfectionism denied the central claim of Christian faith, the necessity of the grace of God, which was extended to human beings through the sacrificial death of Jesus Christ. If humans could be judged righteous on the basis of their own free will and conduct, then they had no need to receive divine grace. Through his reading of the New Testament letters of Paul, however, Augustine became increasingly convinced the human beings were nothing without God. As Paul had demanded, "What have you that you did not receive?" (1 Cor. 4:7). Not only did human beings receive life, reason, and will from God, but they also depended upon the power of God to exercise those faculties. In this respect, Augustine argued, a free will was not independent of the will of God.

By 396 Augustine had abandoned his earlier confidence in the inherent power of the human will. As he developed his analysis in controversy with the Pelagians, he distinguished between "the exercise of the will itself and the exercise of its power." In the exercise of the human will, people often will themselves to do what they cannot do and actually do things that they do not will. As Paul had found, the human will was inevitably caught in moral struggles that it often lost. Lacking the power to do what it ought to do, even a good will, with the best intentions, was unable to act well unless it received that power from God.[19]

As Augustine argued, human nature had been severely damaged in the beginning through the original sin committed by Adam and Eve. For their sin, the first ancestors of humanity had been driven from the paradise of the Garden of Eden. What was that sin? In general terms, early Christian thinkers defined it as disobedience, a turning away or alienation from God that disrupted the perfect order of creation. However, they also connected that sin with sexuality. Cast out of the garden, according to the book of Genesis, "Adam knew his wife, and she conceived, and bore Cain" (Gen. 4:1). As we have seen, Christian concerns about the carnal, material, or lustful nature of human sexuality supported the ideal of virginity. Accordingly, this ideal was read back into the biblical account of Adam and Eve to render their sin as a loss of virginity. According to Augustine, however, their sin was not to be found in the act of sexual intercourse, the relationship of marriage, or the reproduction of children. In fact, sin was not defined by any specific action. Rather, sin was a disposition of desire. Consistently, Augustine found that human sinfulness appeared not merely in specific acts against divine law, but in a pervasive corruption of desire.

If they had remained in paradise, Augustine argued, Adam and Eve would have had sexual relations, but they would have kept their physical desires under complete control. Without desire, lust, or even pleasure, the primordial sexuality of the Garden of Eden would have served only rational ends. Adding an intimate detail to this depiction of primordial sexuality, Augustine even proposed that Adam would have achieved an erection not from lust, but by making his physical organ respond by a conscious act of will. In this state of paradise, human reason and will were guided solely by desire for God. When Adam and Eve "conceived a desire for freedom," however, they lost that original harmony of desire between human and divine will. Asserting their personal autonomy, the first human ancestors turned away from God. This sinful disposition of desire, which Augustine saw as the root of pride, greed, lust, and all sin, alienated the original human beings from the divine will. As a result, Augustine recounted that Adam and Eve were cast out of paradise into a life of cruel and wretched slavery instead of the life of freedom they desired. By definition, therefore, the origin of all sin was a perversion of human desire.

According to Augustine, that perversion of desire was pervasive and collective. Every human being, simply by virtue of being born, was complicit in the collective guilt of the original sin. In response to Pelagius, who had argued that "Adam's sin injured only himself, and not the human race," Augustine insisted that all human beings had sinned in the original sin. Many of his Christian contemporaries, especially in the East, disagreed with this insistence on the collective character of original sin. According to Augustine, however, the guilt of that original sin had been inherited from Adam and Eve, transmitted in the semen through which the human race, with the exception of Christ, who was born of a virgin, had been propagated from the first ancestors. As a result, humanity was a corporate mass of sin. The fallen lump of humanity, with damaged wills, perverted dispositions of desire, and the heavy burden of guilt, could do nothing, Augustine concluded, without the saving gift of divine grace.

Augustine found that all human beings had sinned in the beginning; all continued to live in sin: "Nobody in this flesh, nobody in this corruptible body, nobody on the face of this earth, in this malevolent existence, in this life full of temptation—nobody can live without sin." Anyone who claimed to be exempt from the contamination of sin knew nothing about the pervasive and collective damage that had been done to human nature. They also were ignorant of the grace necessary for salvation within the community of Christians. Accordingly, Augustine exhorted, addressing anyone who claimed to have achieved moral or ritual purity, "Let them and their cleanliness be outside." Salvation, according to Augustine, was achieved not through purity, but through power, the power of grace that God extended to some human beings, the elect, in order to display divine mercy.[20]

Since all had sinned, Augustine argued, all deserved the harsh judgment of divine punishment. As a simple matter of justice, a question of balancing the scales, he felt that God would be completely justified in condemning every human being to eternal damnation. Tempering justice with mercy, however, God in Augustine's view had selected a few human beings to be transformed by the power of an undeserved divine gift, the grace that alone could empower those elect to believe, to develop a good will, and to act in accordance with divine will. Christian belief, will, and action, therefore, were all empowered not by human will, but by the divine gift of grace. As Augustine insisted, human beings received this grace "not because it is in the choice of man's free will to believe or not to believe, but because in the elect the will is prepared by God."

In a plan designed before the establishment of the world, God recognized that most human beings would fail to respond and would therefore receive the just punishment that all deserved on account of sin. Out of divine mercy, God destined a few to receive the grace that would lead to salvation. This entire drama of damnation and salvation, however, was being performed not for the sake of humanity, but for the ends of God. "As the Supreme Good," Augustine maintained, "he made good use of evil deeds for the damnation of those whom he had justly predestined to punishment and for the salvation of those he had mercifully predestined to grace." In this formula, which is sometimes called double predestination, Augustine concluded that God had mercifully called some humans to salvation and justly condemned the vast majority of humanity. Exhibiting their evil deeds as object lessons to the elect, God sent the damned to eternal punishment for the collective guilt of human sinfulness, which was shared by all human beings.[21]

During the last years of his life, Augustine concluded that the mysterious gift of grace was the foundation of Christian faith. Since he was profoundly convinced that human nature was irrecoverably damaged, Augustine maintained that only a divine infusion of a supernatural gift of healing could enable recovery. Without forsaking reason, however, he tried to explain the mystery of grace in terms of the relation between divine justice and mercy. As the Supreme Good, Augustine's God mercifully saved a few when he could have justly condemned all. In the economy of predestination, God's goodness was displayed, but his supreme, ultimate, and mysterious power over the entire scope of creation was emphasized. In his doctrine of predestination, therefore, Augustine tried to work out a rational account of the mystery of faith. The God of Augustine's Christian faith was affirmed as all-good and all-powerful. Mani's supreme God was good, but not all-powerful, because his influence over the world was constrained by an evil God. Plotinus's supreme God was good and was even identified as the Supreme Good, but was not all-powerful because its influence was diminished by human ignorance in the shadows of the material world. Augustine's God, however, was good in electing some for salvation and powerful in granting the undeserved gift of grace that enabled the elect to believe, act, and persevere in their salvation. Of course, Augustine's God was also powerful in justly consigning the fallen mass of humanity to the eternal punishment it deserved. Both grace and damnation demonstrated divine power. In his mature vision of salvation, therefore, Augustine determined that neither faith nor reason was sufficient. Everything depended upon the supreme power of God.

10

Power

By the end of the fourth century, the Christian religion had achieved unprecedented power in the Roman Empire. Emerging from humble peasant beginnings in Galilee, perhaps as a Jewish reform movement, Christianity had succeeded, at least in its establishment as the official religion of the empire, in conquering the entire Roman world. As we have seen, Christian power was initially understood as exclusively spiritual, as a power evoking an alternative kingdom of God that, with its unconventional wisdom, capacity for healing, and festive meals, might have had practical effects, but was ultimately not a kingdom of this world. Within the first century, however, the Jesus movements that grew up around their founder's preaching about this spiritual kingdom receded before the Christ congregations that celebrated Jesus as a deity, the supreme Lord to which "every knee should bow, in heaven and on earth, and under the earth" (Phil. 2:10). The Christ congregations merged the cosmic Christ and the human Jesus into a single divine sovereign who was destined to reign over the universe. At work in the creative process at the beginning, Jesus Christ was expected to be present at the end, judging the living and the dead, in a general resurrection that promised to establish an eternal Christian kingdom on earth.

Second-century Christians had to locate that eternal spiritual kingdom in relation to the temporal domain of power of the Roman Empire. Some advocated accommodation. As Justin insisted, Christians, although they ultimately belonged to a heavenly kingdom, were nevertheless good and faithful citizens of the empire. Other Christians, however, following the lead of the book of Revelation, identified the Roman Empire with the Antichrist, the violent, oppressive, and persecuting force of evil in the world. In the end, they anticipated, the descent of the heavenly Jerusalem would destroy the Roman beast and establish the angelic city of God. In that hope, many Christians suffered persecution in expectation of gaining future power. Some calculated the precise chronology, numbering the days that Christians would have to suffer Roman oppression before taking power.

At the beginning of the third century, for example, the Roman church leader Hippolytus referred to the four world empires described in the book of Daniel to understand the historical situation of Christianity in the context of the Roman Empire. Following the world empires of the Babylonians, the Persians, and the Greeks, he found, the last era, the iron age, had arrived with the Romans ruling the world. Applying imagery from the biblical text of Daniel, Hippolytus asserted that no other empire "will be raised up except that which possesses the domination in our own day and is solidly established: this is a fact evident to all. It has teeth of iron, because it kills, and tears to pieces the entire world by its own force, just like the iron." The end of the iron age, according to Hippolytus, would mark not only the end of the Roman Empire, but also the end of the world. Having determined that the world had a life span of 6,000 years, a calculation he based on correlating the six days of creation with a passage in the Psalms asserting that each divine day was 1,000 years (Ps. 90:4), Hippolytus had a rough idea of when the end of the world would come. Using biblical evidence, he calculated that Jesus Christ had been born 5,500 years after the creation of the world. Living about 200 years after that event, Hippolytus concluded that the world had approximately another 300 years to go before the end of human history. Although the precise timing of the end might be uncertain, the result was assured: in the end Christians would reign in power with Christ within a new kingdom of God on earth.[1]

As we have seen, Christians found ways to act in the present as if the end of the world had already occurred. The martyrs, according to the *Martyrdom of Polycarp*, were no longer merely human beings in the world; they were "already angels." Like the martyrs, Christian virgins, hermits, and ascetics had already entered the "holiness of angels." With the closing of the era of persecutions, monks generally assumed the place of martyrs in providing heroic demonstrations of this proleptic anticipation of the end of the world. Monks served as living exemplars that the promise of salvation for the future was already being fulfilled in the present. For ordinary Christians, however, this sense of living in the heavenly kingdom was supported by the ritual life of the church. Entering through baptism and nourished by the Eucharist, the Christian participated in that spiritual world as it was ritually enacted in the prayers and songs, the candlelight and imagery, the smell of incense, the taste of bread and wine, and all the gestures and motions of the liturgy. As Augustine declared, the Christian liturgy was performed in the service of the one true God who "makes his worshipers into gods." In the ritual life of the church, therefore, Christians anticipated their future deification as godlike beings in the kingdom of God on earth.[2]

With the advent of a Christian empire, the spiritual power of the church intersected with the political power of the Roman state. By the end of the fourth century, Christianity was not merely the preferred religion it had been under Constantine; it had become the official religion of the Roman Empire. This advancement of Christianity had been briefly resisted by the emperor Julian, who, during his brief reign between 361 and 363, attempted to revive the religious beliefs and practices of pagan Rome. After Julian's early death on the battlefield in a campaign against the Persians, however, his successors returned to Christianity for religious support. Beginning with Emperor Theodosius in 381, all other religions were proscribed by imperial legislation. Ironically, therefore, Christianity had gone from being a persecuted religion to a persecuting religion within the course of four centuries.

As we have seen, the power of the church was consolidated by prescribing uniformity of doctrine and practice within the domain of Christianity. Although protected by the emperor, the Christian church still derived its ultimate power from Jesus Christ. At the Council of Nicaea in 325, the bishops of the church had agreed upon a doctrinal formula—one God, three Persons—that clarified an orthodox understanding of the divinity of Christ. At a second general, or ecumenical, council, which was held in the imperial capital of Constantinople in 381, the bishops reaffirmed the Nicene Creed, which held that Jesus Christ shared the same divine essence as God the Father. Having established terms for orthodox belief in the divinity of Jesus Christ, however, the church was faced with further disputes over the precise relation between Christ's divinity and Christ's humanity. During the 250 years from the third ecumenical council, at Ephesus in 431, to the conclusion of the sixth ecumenical council, at Constantinople in 681, the Christian church was riddled with controversy over this question. Although all the disputants agreed on the divinity of Christ, they differed in their understandings of Christ's human nature. By insisting on uniformity of doctrine, these councils reinforced the power of the church.

THE RULE OF THE CHURCH

The council that met at Constantinople in 381 was not only concerned with religious doctrine. Like other councils, it ruled on ritual observances, the ordination of clergy, and other matters of church discipline. In addressing the territorial authority of the church, however, this council introduced an agreement that would have wide-ranging effects on the development of Christianity. The bishops who gathered in the imperial capital in 381 affirmed that the city should be elevated to a new status. The council specified: "The Bishop of Constantinople shall have the prerogatives of honor after the Bishop of Rome, because Constantinople is the New Rome." Although it did not replace the old Rome in prestige, Constantinople nevertheless assumed a new prominence as a leading Christian city. The bishop of Rome, however, refused to grant formal recognition to this claim. Representing the city of Peter and Paul, the pope in Rome insisted on exercising special authority over all the Christian churches of the empire. Apprehensive that the imperial capital might take over its supreme authority, Rome ignored the council's ruling on Constantinople.[3]

In the Eastern empire, however, the ecclesiastical elevation of Constantinople also caused apprehension. Among the leading Eastern cities, the Egyptian city of Alexandria had previously held the most prominent position of religious authority. The bishop of Alexandria, who like the bishop of Rome employed the title "pope," felt his authority dramatically undermined by the elevation of Constantinople. Over the next seventy years, Alexandria struggled against the new eminence of the imperial city. Within a few years, the bishop of Alexandria, Theophilus, succeeded in his campaign to depose the bishop of Constantinople, John Chrysostom (ca. 347–407), and force him into exile. At the third ecumenical council, held at Ephesus in 431, his successor, Cyril of Alexandria (d. 444), deposed another bishop of Constantinople, Nestorius. During the first half of the fifth century, as competition between Alexandria and Constantinople divided the church, these regional interests were articulated in an ongoing controversy over the relationship between divinity and humanity in Jesus Christ.

Trained in Antioch, with its more literal approach to biblical history and interpretation, Nestorius came to his position as bishop of Constantinople prepared to defend an orthodox affirmation of both the divinity and the humanity of Jesus Christ. Nestorius had studied with the leading biblical scholar in Antioch, Theodore of Mopsuestia, who had argued that the human and divine natures of Christ were essentially distinct and separate. According to Theodore, the divine nature of God had favored the human nature of Jesus by dwelling completely in him as the Son of God. In analyzing the relation between these two natures, Theodore proposed that "it is clear that the name 'mixture' is useless, inappropriate and unsuitable, since each of the natures remains undissolved from itself. It is also clear that the name 'union' is suitable, for through it the natures brought together produce one person according to the union." As a creative union, but not a confused mixture, therefore, was how, according to Theodore of Mopsuestia, both human and divine natures dwelt in one person, Jesus Christ.[4]

Nestorius adhered to this basic distinction between the two natures of Christ. As a result, he was unable to approve of the popular custom of praising the Virgin Mary as *theotokos,* "mother of God." Mary was the mother of Jesus Christ, Nestorius argued, and not the mother of God. By referring to Mary as the mother of God, he warned, Christians ran the risk of confusing the divine and human natures "within a single form of sonship." However, Nestorius's opposition to the phrase *theotokos* provided Cyril of Alexandria with an opportunity to attack the orthodoxy of the bishop of Constantinople. "If anyone in the one Christ divides the persons after the union," Cyril wrote to Nestorius, "and does not speak rather of a meeting according to a natural union, let him be anathema." With the support of a sympathetic emperor and empress and the blessing of the Roman pope Celestine I, Cyril was able to have Nestorius excommunicated at Ephesus in 431 on the grounds that he had divided the divine and human natures of Christ into two Persons instead of recognizing their union.[5]

Driven into exile, followers of Nestorius found a home in Persia, where the Church of the East—often referred to as the Nestorian church—flourished, even advancing missions into China. In those eastern regions, Nestorians defended a Christian doctrine distinguishing between the two natures of Christ—human and divine—which had appeared as a single presence in the incarnation. However, they argued that position against Christian adversaries who had also been excommunicated and exiled from the orthodox church. Known as Monophysites, because they held that Christ had a single nature (Gk. *phusis*), those Christians refused to separate the human nature of Christ from the nature of his divinity. From the perspective of the orthodox, the Monophysites emphasized the divine nature of Christ at the expense of his humanity. They made Christ's divinity absorb his humanity like a drop of water is absorbed in the ocean. In Syria, Egypt, and Ethiopia, however, the Monophysites gained a substantial following for their understanding of the single nature of Christ.

After the death of Cyril of Alexandria in 444, two of his followers, Dioscurus, the bishop, and his associate Eutyches, continued to pursue the battle against the Nestorians. They concluded that Jesus Christ actually had a single divine nature. Where Nestorius seemed to go too far in stressing the separate and distinct humanity of Christ, Dioscurus and Eutyches seemed to exceed the bounds of orthodoxy by emphasizing Christ's divinity. In retaliation, the new bishop of Constantinople, Flavian, issued a decree of excommunication against Eutyches. Referring the case to Rome, he inspired Pope Leo I (440–61) to formulate his *Tome*, which clarified the Roman position on Christ. For a brief time Dioscurus of Alexandria seemed to be in control of the controversy. In 449 he called a council at Ephesus that restored Eutyches, condemned Flavian, and ignored Pope Leo's *Tome*. Two years later, however, another council was convened under the new imperial authority of Empress Pulcheria that effectively reversed all those decisions. By deposing Dioscurus and adopting the guidelines set out by Pope Leo, that council, the fourth ecumenical council, at Chalcedon, arrived at the definitive orthodox formulation of the doctrine of Christ.

In drafting his *Tome*, Pope Leo had referred to the work of the third-century North African Tertullian, who had proposed that Christ should be understood as two natures—fully human, fully divine—in one Person. At the general council of Chalcedon in 451, the bishops adopted this formula by affirming that Christ was two natures in one Person. In adopting what they hoped would be a uniform Christian statement of faith, the bishops asserted their belief in "one and the same Son, perfect in Godhead and perfect in manhood, truly God and truly man." Therefore, the statement of faith devised by the council of Chalcedon was set out to refute the claims of Monophysites that Christ had one nature. However, the council of Chalcedon also intended to refute Nestorian claims that Christ's human and divine natures could be separated. Although the bishops at Chalcedon affirmed Christ's two natures, they insisted that humanity and divinity were joined "unconfusedly, unchangeably, indivisibly, inseparably" in the single Person of Christ. By steering a middle course between the Nestorians and the Monophysites, therefore, the council of Chalcedon tried to claim the middle ground of orthodoxy for their church.[6]

The rule of the church, therefore, depended upon finding and holding the middle ground. Certainly, the ecumenical councils arrived at formulas—God is one essence in three Persons, Christ is two natures in one Person—that reflected centuries of doctrinal debate. However, they also involved conflicts over the territorial authority of the church. As the question of Christ was being resolved at Chalcedon, the religious jurisdiction of different cities was also being adjudicated. Although it had briefly succeeded in advancing its cause, Alexandria succumbed at Chalcedon to the authority of Constantinople in the East and Rome in the West. From that point, as agreed at Chalcedon, Alexandria had to accept an ecumenical division of the Roman world into spheres of influence governed by Rome and the "New Rome," Constantinople. Following those two cities in prestige and influence, Alexandria, Antioch, and, by the middle of the fifth century, Jerusalem, due to its association with the birth of Christianity, formed the Pentarchy, the five Christian cities governing the orthodox Christian world. Although Rome was granted priority, the bishop of Rome was regarded in the East as the first among equals. Nevertheless, even from the perspective of Rome, these five cities represented the power of the Christian world.

The structure of power was consolidated by resolving internal differences. As the council at Chalcedon showed, Rome and Constantinople might disagree on many issues, but they could find common cause in ruling against the authority of Antioch and Alexandria. From the perspective of both Rome and Constantinople, the Nestorians, who emerged in Antioch, were too material because they stressed the humanity of Christ; the Monophysites, who originated in Alexandria, were too spiritual because they emphasized the divinity of Christ. Ruling against both of those extremes, Rome and Constantinople joined at Chalcedon to define the precise balance between human and divine that would constitute the middle ground of Christian orthodoxy in the Roman Empire. Within the politics of religious knowledge, they limited the range of possibilities for what might count as Christianity by capturing and controlling that middle ground of Christian doctrine.

However, the power of the church was also negotiated in relation to religious options that were clearly beyond the field of Christianity. Certainly, the suppression of Greco-Roman paganism, which continued to be resisted, remained a battlefield for the church. Within its jurisdiction, the church also persisted in placing legal restrictions on Judaism. Beyond the borders of the Roman Empire, however, orthodox Christians increasingly engaged people who held alternative religious commitments. To the West, they encountered Germanic groups, many of whom had adopted Arian Christianity, while many others had retained ancient Indo-European forms of religious life, who resisted Roman authority. To the East, with the rise of Islam in the middle of the seventh century, they encountered adherents of a faith that challenged the religious and political authority of Christianity in the world. In relation to those alternatives, the church tried to maintain its control over the middle ground by defining those outside of its orthodox orbit as Christian heretics.

The rule of the church depended upon the identification, suppression, and excommunication of heretics. The scope of Christian power, therefore, was based not only on including people through conversion, baptism, participation in the Eucharist, and subscription to an orthodox confession of the faith. Christian power was also reinforced through rituals of exclusion. Whether within the Roman polity or beyond its borders, religious difference posed a serious problem for the power of the Christian empire. When the emperor Theodosius proscribed all non-Christian religions in 381, he formulated the terms of this problem:

> We commend that those persons who follow this rule shall embrace the name Catholic Christians. The rest, however, whom We adjudge demented and insane, shall sustain the infamy of heretical dogmas, their meeting places shall not receive the name of churches, and they shall be smitten first by divine vengeance and secondly by the retribution of Our own initiative, which we shall assume in accordance with divine judgment.[7]

In establishing Catholic Christianity as the religious norm for the Roman Empire, Theodosius judged every alternative to be abnormal. Castigating other religious commitments as "demented and insane," the emperor ruled that they must suffer divine punishment. Because God would eventually condemn them to eternal damnation, the emperor was justified in subjecting heretics to judicial inquisition, punishment, exile, and even execution. As the middle ground of Christian orthodoxy was established by ecumenical councils, therefore, it was positioned over the abyss of hell.

THE PROSPECT OF HELL

In the fourteenth century, the Italian poet Dante Alighieri would place a sign over the entrance to hell that read: "Divine power made me." In this reading, the Christian God who ruled the universe had created a place of eternal punishment to reinforce his divine power. From the beginning, Christian visions of hell revealed a similar display of the transcendent power of God over his divine kingdom. Hell represented the ultimate degree of exclusion from the kingdom of God. In the texts of the Christian New Testament, Hades or Gehenna was the hellish place of eternal torment and punishment. It was the underground pit (Matt. 5:29; Luke 12:5); it was the place of fire (Matt. 5:22; 18:9; Mark 9:43; James 3:6); it was the place of torture for the damned (Luke 16:23). As the Gospel of Mark specified, hell was the place of eternal punishment "where the worm dieth not, and the fire is not quenched" (Mark 9:44). As the supreme demonstration of the power of God, hell represented the prospect of an ultimate Christian victory by ensuring the eternal suffering of the excluded.

At the beginning of the third century, Tertullian assumed that punishments in hell were eternal. At the end of time, when Christ would return to supervise the resurrection of the dead, the relegation of the damned to hell could only be expected to be confirmed. In the geography of the underworld, Tertullian imagined a location just above hell—the bosom of Abraham—that was an interim place of refreshment for the righteous while they awaited the resurrection. As Tertullian explained, "This place, the bosom of Abraham, though not in heaven, and yet above hell, offers the souls of the righteous an interim refreshment until the end of all things brings about the general resurrection and the final reward." Using the same term that referred to the ritual meals held in a cemetery, this interim place of waiting was also called the *refrigerium*. But hell was a region of eternal damnation. Throughout the ages, according to Tertullian, those condemned to hell would suffer torture, torment, and agony without end.[8]

Also during the third century, however, Origen argued against the eternity of hell. Influenced by Platonic assumptions about the inherent immortality of the soul, Origen proposed that all souls who were born in this world had existed in other worlds before their birth and would be reborn in other worlds after death in order to continue their ongoing process of spiritual refinement. The fires of hell did not merely exact retribution; they were purifying fires, or what Origen called "intelligent fires," that contributed to the afterlife education of the soul. According to Origen, therefore, hell was not a place of eternal punishment, but a process of educational suffering that purified the soul. The general councils of the church, however, consistently rejected this teaching of Origen; the fifth ecumenical council, at Constantinople in 553, condemned "whoever says or thinks that the punishment of demons and the wicked will not be eternal."[9]

For mainstream Christians, the eternity of hell certified divine power. The power of the Christian God was ultimately demonstrated in the divine capacity to judge, condemn, exclude, and punish. In their visions of hell, Christians imagined that God exercised that punitive power in two ways: through environmental punishments that separated people from the divine kingdom and through measure-for-measure punishments that exacted divine retribution for specific sins.

Environmental punishments were a form of retribution consigning people to a certain kind of place. They were punishments that relegated people to the biblical pit, the fire, or the dark recesses of the earth in which the worm never died. As the tradition developed, however, those biblical images were elaborated. In apocalyptic visions of hell, Christians imagined that the damned were punished by being enclosed in regions of dark fire. They were engulfed in fiery rivers that gave off an intensely burning heat, but shed no light. In the smoky fires of hell, those who had been condemned to punishment were immersed in boiling pitch, dazed by noxious fumes, and overwhelmed by the sulfurous smell of burning brimstone. The damned were not only tortured by demons, they were also tormented by worms, snakes, lions, dogs, panthers, dragons, and three-headed beasts that attacked them constantly. These environmental punishments were not directed at specific sins, but were features of the general condition of damnation that all sinful souls shared in hell.

In even greater detail, measure-for-measure punishments exacted retribution in hell for specific acts of sinful behavior. "An eye for an eye, a tooth for a tooth" provided the basic standard for these punishments in hell. Christians imagined that the damned would ultimately be punished in ways that corresponded directly to the sins they had committed while living in the world. As a kind of poetic justice, these measure-for-measure punishments displayed images of punishment that fit specific sinful acts. Besides being a place of eternal punishment, hell was also imagined as a place of revelation in which even the most secret sins would finally be disclosed for divine judgment. Among those secret sins, the sins of speech and sexuality received special attention in Christian visions of hell. For example, those who were damned for verbal sins of lying, slander, or blasphemy were punished by being hung from their tongues. Gossips might be hung by their ears. Sexual sins were punished by hanging men from their genitals and women by their hair. Just as thieves were hung by their hands, those sinners who violated Christian standards of speech and sexuality were hung by their offending organs in order to display the specific character of their sins in hell.[10]

Through environmental and measure-for-measure punishments, therefore, hell demonstrated divine power. Although the underworld was the dark realm of the devil, and administered by demons, it ultimately represented God's supreme power over evil in the power to punish. In the early Christian imagination, however, Jesus Christ held special power over hell. As related in the apocryphal *Gospel of Nicodemus,* Jesus descended into the abyss of hell to rescue righteous souls, such as the patriarchs and prophets of ancient Israel, who had not been able to avail themselves of Christian baptism.

The story of Christ's descent into hell raised the possibility that the condition of some souls might be changed after death. Early Christian rituals at the cemetery—the meal of the *refrigerium,* the drinking salutations to the deceased, the prayers for departed relatives and friends—all suggested that the living could maintain ongoing contact and communication with the dead. "We make offerings for the dead on the anniversary of their deaths," Tertullian observed, even though nothing in the New Testament suggested this practice of ritual veneration of the dead. "If you look in Scripture for a formal law governing these and similar practices," he admitted, "you will find none. It is tradition that justifies them, custom that confirms them, and faith that observes them." Offerings for the dead, therefore, indicated a Christian belief that the living could affect the condition of those who waited in the underworld for the resurrection.[11]

Although the bosom of Abraham was initially imagined as an underworld place of rest or sleep, it assumed a different character during the persecutions of the third century. As martyrs were thought to enter directly into heaven, those who lingered after death in the interim place of refreshment assumed an inferior status. Bishop Cyprian, for example, identified two different Christian experiences of the afterlife. At death, the martyrs entered heaven, arriving in glory, with all their sins forgiven, to receive their reward. Other Christians, however, had to await forgiveness as if they were "sent to prison to be let out only when the last farthing had been paid." While waiting for the resurrection of the dead, those Christians had to pay for their sins by undergoing "long suffering in fire." In the context of the official persecutions of the third century, Cyprian imagined that Christians who had lapsed and returned to the faith would have to submit to this afterlife purification by fire to be worthy of eventually entering heaven with the martyrs.[12]

The imagery of purifying fire, however, became a dominant feature of Christian reflections on life after death. According to the Christian philosopher Lactantius (ca. 240–ca. 320), all Christians could expect to undergo a trial by fire at the Last Judgment. Certainly, the wicked would be subjected to the flames. "The just also, when God shall judge them," Lactantius observed, "will be tried by Him with fire." For the righteous, however, that trial by fire would be a process of purification. Similarly, Ambrose held that all Christians would have to pass through a fiery ordeal in the final judgment of the living and the dead. "All shall be subjected to examination by fire," Ambrose promised, "for all who want to return to heaven must be tried by fire." In this expectation, Lactantius, Ambrose, and other Christian leaders adapted Origen's imagery of purifying, refining, or even educational fires of the afterlife and located it at the Last Judgment.[13]

Augustine also adopted this imagery of purifying fire, but he located it not only at the Last Judgment, but also in those afterlife places in which souls waited for the resurrection. Approving the Christian practice of praying for the dead, Augustine only cautioned that such prayers could do nothing for demons, infidels, or the godless. They could only help those Christian sinners who had been neither very good nor very bad during their lifetimes. Augustine imagined that those souls had to undergo "correctional fire." Therefore, some afterlife punishment could have an educational character, represented by the refining fire. However, the process of refinement in the afterlife involved all the tortures of hell. Many Christians could be expected to endure hellish torments in preparation for the prospect of eventual salvation.[14]

Out of this imagery of refining fire, the geography of the Christian afterlife was expanded to include a special location—purgatory—in which Christian souls underwent suffering in preparation for heaven.

Although the precise details of purgatory were not elaborated until the twelfth century, the symbolism of the correction, refinement, and purification of the dead suggested the possibility of a third place in the Christian afterlife between heaven and hell. The New Testament had promised a simple, absolute, and final separation of the damned from the saved. As the Gospel of Matthew promised, the evil "will go to eternal punishment, while the righteous will go to eternal life" (Matt. 25:34, 41–46). Positioned between those extremes, however, the purgatorial fires of the Christian afterlife defined a middle ground in the other world. Between eternal damnation and ultimate salvation, the refining fires of purgatory offered ordinary Christians both the torments of hell and the hope of heaven.

THE PROMISE OF HEAVEN

Early Christians imagined heaven as both a world above and a world of the future. As the realm of God above the world, heaven occupied the highest point in a cosmology of heavenly spheres that encircled the earth. In keeping with Greco-Roman assumptions, Christians generally pictured seven heavens, corresponding to the seven visible planets, rising above this world. Although these were properly the realms of God and angels, on rare occasions human beings could gain access to those heavenly spheres. In Jewish apocalyptic literature, visionaries ascended into the heavens to behold the angelic hierarchy, the celestial temple, and the throne of God. Christians beheld similar heavenly visions. Paul reported to the church in Corinth that he had personally been transported to the third heaven and also to paradise, perhaps the seventh heaven, where he "heard things that cannot be told, which man may not utter" (2 Cor. 12:4). Accounts of mysterious ascent into the heavens, therefore, did not always provide detailed descriptions of the celestial domain. Nevertheless, they suggested that even in this life human beings could rise above the world to gain a glimpse of heaven.

Although heaven was located far above this world, it was also placed in the near future through the expectation of the imminent return of Christ. In the book of Revelation, the Christian New Testament anticipated a heaven on earth that would arrive with the second coming of Christ. The author of that apocalypse was also a visionary who saw through "a door open in heaven" as he was instructed by an angel to "come up" in heavenly ascent. Rising above the world, the author described his vision of the heavenly throne, temple, and angelic company of God (Rev. 4:1–5:2). As he saw the future, the heavenly Jerusalem would descend upon the earth, transforming the world into a new heaven and a new earth. Revolving around God's throne, the heavenly city of the New Jerusalem would finally establish divine order in the world.

The book of Revelation, therefore, promised an urban apocalypse, a vision of the end in which heaven appeared as a new city, the New Jerusalem. In the end, heaven was a well-ordered city in which all heavenly citizens, from the angels to the righteous, lived in peace and harmony under the supreme sovereignty of God. Embracing this urban vision of heaven, Justin articulated a Christian hope of heaven in the second century by anticipating the imminent return of Christ in royal glory to establish his reign of a thousand years in the New Jerusalem, the heavenly city on earth. As already noted, Hippolytus, writing at the beginning of the third century, also imagined heaven not only as an urban revolution, but also as an imperial conquest of the Roman Empire, the last beast that would rule the world before the establishment of God's kingdom would be centered in the urban power base of the New Jerusalem. Therefore, although the original paradise had been a garden, in the end paradise would be a heavenly city.[15]

Most early Christians imagined heaven in terms of urban order, governance, and political power. In part, this preference was dictated by the conditions of persecution under which many Christians suffered in the urban centers of the Roman Empire. Their battlefield was the city. For example, Bishop Irenaeus, who had lived through the persecutions between 175 and 177 in Lyons, focused his hopes on a heaven that would ultimately compensate for the sufferings and deaths of Christian martyrs in his city. The current era of persecutions, Irenaeus promised, would be followed by the thousand-year kingdom of the Messiah and then the eternal kingdom of God. In a new city, the martyrs who had died for Christ would be revived under the sovereignty of God to live forever in a heavenly "communion with the holy angels." The vision of heaven as a new city, therefore, reflected the urban situation of Christians within the context of the Roman Empire.[16]

However, this emphasis on an urban heaven displayed a more general Christian concern with identifying the location of political power in the world. If the temporal power of the Roman Empire was urban, then the supreme power of God must assume a corresponding form capable of ultimately dominating the city. As Augustine argued in the early fifth century, heaven was an urban order, the "City of God." During his years of Neoplatonic exploration of divine truth, Augustine had also undergone an extraordinary personal ascent into the heavens. As he later described this event in his *Confessions*, he had risen out of his body, leaving the material world behind and entering into the dazzling splendor of the divine light of the heavens. If only he could have remained in that state permanently, Augustine concluded, it "would be something not of this world, not of this life." However, returning to his body, Augustine was left with the dilemma of defining a Christian life in this world that would lead not merely to a brief glimpse of heaven, but to gaining a permanent heavenly home.[17]

The metaphor of the city provided Augustine and other Christian thinkers with an image of permanence. It also reinforced the corporate or collective character of heaven. As a city, heaven might contain extraordinary individuals, the martyrs, saints, and visionaries of Christian faith. But it was also a heavenly *polis* or *civitas* of citizens who were distinguished not by their personal accomplishments, but by their commitment to upholding the middle ground of civic order. As Aristotle had proposed, the order of the city was negotiated as a human space between beasts and gods.[18] In Augustine's terms, the City of God was similarly organized as a human space that Christian citizens of heaven could occupy between the sinners who suffered like beasts in hell and the supreme glory of God. Between animals and divinity, therefore, the City of God was a heaven for human beings.

Within this celestial urban environment, with its sense of sovereignty, governance, order, and collective citizenship, the Christian heaven still allowed a certain scope for personal experiences. In the Christian imagination, heaven promised three personal features—the vision of God, reunion with loved ones, and deification—which would be further developed in the tradition.

First, the vision of God emerged as a defining feature of heavenly life. As Paul had suggested, human beings see everything in the present in the distortions of shadows and mirrors. In heaven, however, they will see "face to face" (1 Cor. 13:12). This clarity of vision in heaven, as interpreted by Irenaeus, for example, meant that Christians would behold a direct vision of God. They "shall see God, that they may live, being made immortal by that sight." Similarly, Augustine imagined the fulfillment of heaven as the vision of God. In heaven, he promised, "there we shall rest and see, see and love, love and praise. This is what shall be in the end without end." The vision of God, therefore, implied an immediacy of human presence before divinity in the afterlife that would transform Christians in heaven into immortal beings.[19]

Second, the meeting with loved ones characterized heavenly life. The Christian vision of heaven did not suggest that all human souls would eventually be absorbed into an impersonal ocean of divinity. Cyprian proposed, for example, that the reunion with friends and relatives after death was one of the primary attractions of heaven. As Cyprian asked, "Why do we not hasten and run that we may see our country, that we may greet our relatives? A great number of those who are dear to us is awaiting us there. A dense and abundant crowd of parents, brothers, and children is longing for us." The city of heaven, therefore, was imagined as a place in which souls were reunited with loved ones.[20]

Third, heaven promised an ultimate deification of human beings. Living forever in a state of divine grace, that gift from God, as Augustine observed, "that makes his worshipers into gods," human beings became divine in heaven. In the economy of Christian salvation, Jesus Christ was the nexus between humanity and divinity. Certainly, Christ performed many functions in Christian religious life. He was teacher, healer, role model, sacrificial offering, and divine agent in the battle against the forces of evil. By assuming humanity, however, Jesus Christ had opened a way for human beings to become divine. During the first four centuries, this interchange between humanity and divinity represented a sacred formula of deification: Jesus Christ became human so humans could become divine. As Irenaeus maintained, Jesus Christ "became as we are that we might become as he is." Similarly, Athanasius proposed that "He was made man that we might be made God." This promise of deification was developed to a greater extent among Christians of the Greek-speaking East, where divinization, or *theosis,* became a central doctrine of the Orthodox church, than it was in the Latin-speaking West, which came to emphasize the redemption rather than the deification of human beings in heaven. Nevertheless, the interchange between humanity and divinity that Christians found in the incarnation, the sacraments, and the gift of divine grace culminated in a heavenly kingdom in which human beings became godlike citizens of the City of God.[21]

PART II
HISTORICAL TRANSITIONS

11

Christendom

Poised between heaven and hell, Christians waited for the appearance of the apocalyptic city, the New Jerusalem. In the meantime, however, they could imagine the earthly city of Jerusalem as the center of the world. As the site of foundational events of the Christian story—the crucifixion, burial, resurrection, and ascension of Jesus—Jerusalem represented the point at which salvation had entered the world. Under the authority of Emperor Constantine in the fourth century, the Christian holy places associated with those events had been restored; the True Cross had been discovered; and Jerusalem had been transformed into a Christian city, not only in myth and imagination, but also through sacred architecture and rituals of pilgrimage. For Christians in the Greek-speaking East who accepted the authority of the Byzantine emperor and the Orthodox patriarch in Constantinople, Jerusalem was one of five patriarchal cities that preserved Christian orthodoxy in the world. From the perspective of Christians in the Latin-speaking West, where the bishop of Rome, as pope, asserted primacy in the name of St. Peter over the Christian world, Jerusalem was the principal destination for Catholic pilgrims. Although divisions arose between East and West over matters of language, doctrine, liturgy, and authority, the city of Jerusalem continued to represent the spiritual center of a religious world that Christians eventually came to view as Christendom.

During the reign of the Byzantine emperor Heraclius (r. 610–41), however, the city of Jerusalem was forcibly removed from the political control of any Christian ruler. In 614 the forces of the Persian Empire, which had adopted as its state religion Zoroastrianism—or Mazdaism, the religion of the prophet Zarathustra—captured Jerusalem, sacked the city, and confiscated the True Cross. Although Heraclius finally succeeded in 628 in defeating the Persians, recovering the True Cross, and returning it to Jerusalem, the city and the cross were soon under the control of Arab con-

querors, adherents of Islam, the religion of submission to the one God as
revealed in the sacred text of the Qur'an to the prophet Muhammad.
Having already conquered Syria and Persia before taking Jerusalem in
638, Arab forces proceeded to achieve rapid military victories over Egypt
and North Africa. Along with Jerusalem, therefore, the patriarchal cities
of Antioch and Alexandria also came under Muslim control. Increasingly,
in both the East and West, the unity of Christendom came to be seen in
opposition to Islam.

For Muslims, Jerusalem, known in Arabic as *al-Quds*, "the Holy," was
also a sacred city. Although the Islamic world located its most sacred center in Mecca, the "sacred sanctuary" that Muslims faced five times a day
in prayer, Jerusalem was the "Remote House of Worship" to which the
Prophet had been miraculously transported one night by God (Surah
17:1). Following the death of the Prophet in 632, his followers sent an
embassy to Heraclius, declaring:

> God has given this land as an inheritance to our father Abraham and to his
> posterity after him. We are the children of Abraham. You have held our
> country long enough. Give it up peacefully, and we will not invade your
> country. If not, we will retake with interest what you have withheld from us.[1]

After capturing the city, its new Muslim rulers intervened in the sacred
geography of Jerusalem. On the ruins of the ancient Temple Mount, they
established a mosque, al-Masjid al Aqsa, and a shrine, the Dome of the
Rock. By appropriating this sacred site of the religion of ancient Israel,
Muslims certified their claims on a sacred history that went back to
Abraham, who, as the Qur'an taught, was neither Jew nor Christian.
While respecting the earlier revelations of Jews and Christians—the Torah
of Moses, the gospel of Jesus—Muslims embraced the Qur'an as the ultimate revelation disclosed to the prophet, messenger, and servant of God,
Muhammad. Under Muslim rule, Jews and Christians were in principle
tolerated as "people of the Book." Having been denied access to the city
for nearly five hundred years, Jews were permitted to return to Jerusalem
in 638 and reestablish their major *yeshiva* for training rabbis. Like Jews,
Christians were allowed to practice their religion under Muslim authority,
but both were subject to special taxes. By contrast, Emperor Heraclius
marked the loss of Jerusalem by ordering every Jew within his shrinking
empire to be baptized. A policy of religious toleration enshrined in the

Qur'an, however, promised to maintain peaceful interreligious relations among Muslims, Jews, and Christians within the world of Islam.

Nevertheless, the conflicts that arose between Christians and Muslims were suggested by the different orientations of their sacred geographies. Muslims living in Jerusalem, like Muslims elsewhere in the world of Islam, faced Mecca in their daily prayers; Christians in both the East and the West participated in a liturgy that at crucial points symbolically looked toward Jerusalem. The ceremony of the liturgy invoked the holy city through its hymns, prayers, and symbolic reenactment of the sacrificial death of Jesus in Jerusalem. Furthermore, within the religious practice of both East and West, the entire Christian sacred calendar revolved around the holy day of Easter, which caused all Christians to think of Jerusalem in recalling the death and resurrection of Christ. In these most important rituals of the Christian week and year, therefore, religious attention was constantly being directed toward the holy city of Jerusalem. With the holy city under Muslim control, however, Christians of both the East and the West came to perceive Islam as the primary threat—not only a religious dilemma, but also a social, political, and military challenge—to the integrity of Christianity in the world.

UNITY

Although the world of Christianity has never presented a unified front, the estrangement between East and West emerged as the most basic division of Christendom. Ironically, both the Greek East and the Latin West developed religious terms for representing the global unity of Christianity. Put simply, the ideal of Christian unity in the East revolved around the person of the emperor in Constantinople, while in the West it centered on the authority of the pope in Rome. In different ways, both emperors and popes stood for the political, religious, and cultural unity of Christendom. Certainly, conflicts arose between East and West long before the formal break between Greek Orthodoxy and Roman Catholicism was ratified in 1054. Besides the question of whether ultimate religious authority resided in the emperor or the pope, the Eastern and Western churches were divided over the language to use in worship, the precise interpretation of the doctrine of the Trinity, the calculation of the date of Easter, and many other matters of Christian belief, ritual practice, and church organization.

In the context of the broader sacred geography and sacred history of

Christianity, however, East and West came into conflict over which city—Constantinople or Rome—would stand in the Christian world as heir to the holy city of Jerusalem. For its part, the city of Constantinople could claim a spatial connection with Jerusalem not only while it ruled over Palestine, but even after the Muslim conquests, because a fragment of the True Cross had been rescued and transported from Jerusalem to Constantinople. This relocation of the holy power of the cross on which Jesus had been crucified certified the claim of Constantinople as the spiritual heir to Jerusalem. By contrast, Rome asserted a temporal connection, relying on an unbroken historical succession of bishops of the city who could trace their lineage back to the legendary founding of the church of Rome by the apostle Peter. In this sacred history, Rome was the heir to Jerusalem not because it held the cross upon which Jesus had been crucified, but because it represented the rock upon which Jesus had built his church. In these calculations of sacred space and sacred time, therefore, Christians in the East and West produced different images of the unity of Christianity. The images of a unified Christianity they represented, however, were contradicted not only by the division between East and West, but also by the obvious diversity that could be observed among Eastern Christians and Western Christians. Although emperors and popes asserted Christian unity, they faced a Christian world that from the sixth to the tenth century produced a diverse range of "micro-Christendoms."[2]

In the East, Christian unity was represented as a harmony of the human and divine that was administered by the emperor. As the emperor Justinian (527–65) declared in 535, God had displayed his love for humanity by bestowing the two greatest gifts, "the priesthood and the imperial dignity." Through the offices of patriarchs, bishops, priests, deacons, monks, and nuns, the priesthood of the Christian church, according to Justinian, "serves divine things." By means of prayer and sacraments, the priesthood maintains "access to God." However, the second divine gift, the "imperial dignity," was also understood by Justinian as a power flowing directly from God. Under divine authority, the Christian emperor "directs and administers human affairs." The two greatest gifts of God, therefore, enabled a harmony between the divine and the human. While Christian priests prayed for the welfare of the emperor, the emperor guaranteed the support, dignity, and order of the priesthood in the world.[3]

Justinian's vision of divine and human harmony, however, should not be understood as cooperation between two independent spheres, the

Christian church and the imperial state. Since he understood the imperial dignity to be a power from God to administer all human affairs, Justinian assumed that imperial power extended over the management of the "human affairs" of the church. Although the holy mysteries of prayer, sacraments, and liturgy belonged to the priesthood, everything else to do with the administration of the church fell under the jurisdiction of the emperor. Accordingly, Justinian prescribed legislation governing the ownership and disposition of church property, the residence of bishops, the legal status of clergy, the question of marriage for priests, and many other matters of church organization and discipline, because according to his vision of general harmony these matters fell within the "human affairs" that God had entrusted to the management of the imperial state.

As the centerpiece of this vision of Christian imperial unity, Justinian sponsored the construction of the great church of Constantinople, the Hagia Sophia. Built between 532 and 537, the magnificent church of "Holy Wisdom" was designed as both the central meeting point of heaven and earth, with its architectural elevation, radiant light, and holy images, and as the center of a vast Christian empire in the East. However, the Monophysite (or "single nature") movement, so named because it rejected the Chalcedonian doctrine of Christ's two natures, produced such churches as the Coptic church in Egypt and the Jacobite church in Syria, which emerged during the sixth century with independent patriarchs, church hierarchies, and regional alliances. In Persia, the Nestorian church flourished, extending its missions into India and China. Therefore, Justinian's vision of a unified Christian empire was an unrealized ideal. Even his own household was divided, since his powerful and influential wife, the empress Theodora, was devoted to the Monophysite faith. A century after the death of Justinian and Theodora, the Monophysite and Nestorian churches were permanently lost to the Christian empire anchored in the sacred center of the Hagia Sophia by the Muslim conquests of Egypt, Syria, and Persia. Nevertheless, Justinian's successors, who ruled over a contracted Byzantine empire, continued to dream of Christian imperial unity.

In the West, Christian unity was represented as adherence to an unbroken apostolic succession, anchored in Rome, extending back to St. Peter. Embodying that apostolic continuity and authority, the pope was the "Vicar of St. Peter" on earth, the head of the Catholic, or "universal," church of Christ. Like the emperor in Constantinople, the bishop of Rome asserted an authority over both divine and human affairs. For example, building upon the theory of papal primacy asserted by Pope Leo I, Pope Gelasius I (492–96) announced that his priestly authority was greater than the temporal power of any king. In practice, however, the pope had to engage in complex diplomatic negotiations with various rulers to exert any political influence over a bewildering diversity of kingdoms. Gradually, however, Roman Catholic authority grew. The baptism of King Clovis and three thousand of his subjects on Christmas Day in 496 brought the kingdom of the Franks within the Roman orbit; the missions initiated by St. Columba (b. 521) in the 560s established monastic outposts in Ireland and Scotland loyal to Rome; and the last Arian Christian kingdom, the Visigoths of Spain, came under Roman Catholic authority in 589. Nevertheless, at the end of the sixth century, the role of the pope was largely limited to what Emperor Justinian had identified as matters of the priesthood.

During the papacy of Gregory I (590–604), who became known as Gregory the Great, the church's administration of the "human affairs" of Rome increased. As a wealthy Christian layman and lawyer from a senatorial family, who had served for a time as the prefect of Rome, Gregory had extensive experience in dealing with the public life of the city. Although he had renounced that public responsibility by turning his father's estate into a monastery, living there in a small, secluded community under the spiritual direction of an abbot, Gregory was later drawn into the administration of the church, first as a deacon representing the interests of Rome at the imperial court in Constantinople, then as the bishop of Rome. As pope, Gregory quickly assumed many of the same administrative functions he had performed as prefect of Rome, managing Roman territories, securing food and water supplies, supervising military commanders and troops, and negotiating treaties. In the model of Pope Gregory, therefore, subsequent popes could find a precedent for asserting the authority of the church over the state.

While dealing with such practical matters of state, however, Gregory maintained his interest in spirituality. As reflected in his massive biblical commentaries, Gregory developed Christian spirituality according to the Augustinian distinction between action and contemplation. He worked out the details of a formula that became conventional in the Christian West: "There are two lives in which Almighty God by His holy word instructs us—the active and the contemplative." The contemplative life, which was best pursued in a monastic context, was devoted to the care of the self. Aloof from the desires, activities, and practical concerns of the world, the contemplative life directed the mind and heart toward God. As an anticipation of heaven, the contemplative life prepared the soul "to join the hymn-singing choirs of angels, to mingle with the heavenly citizens, and to rejoice at its everlasting incorruption in the sight of God." In the active life, however, Christians were called to exercise pastoral care, the quality of care shown by a good shepherd, in supporting the well-being of others. As Gregory observed, the active life meant "to give bread to the hungry, to teach the ignorant the word of wisdom, to correct the erring, to recall to the path of humility our neighbor when he waxes proud, to tend the sick, to dispense to all what they need, and to provide those entrusted to us with the means of subsistence." Although the contemplative life of monks and nuns anticipated heaven, the active life of pastoral care for others was exemplified by priests, deacons, bishops, and even Christian kings for the good of the world.

When he reflected on the exercise of political authority, Gregory found that the same model of pastoral care applied. "The government of souls," he observed, "is the art of arts!" By contrast with a model of imperial power that directed, legislated, and administered human society under divine authority, Gregory's model of pastoral power sought to coordinate religious and political resources in supporting the development of souls. Certainly, from Gregory's perspective, pastoral care occasionally required coercion. Just as the abbot had to enforce discipline over the monastery, the political ruler was mandated to exercise force to establish order within his domain. In both the monastery and the kingdom, however, the force of coercion was only justified to the extent that it served the interests of cultivating souls for salvation. According to Gregory, the ultimate pastoral responsibility, resting equally on Christian clergy and Christian kings, was to gather souls into the church to prepare them with the sacrament of baptism to face the final judgment at the end of the world.[4]

EXPANSION

Until the seventh century, the growth of Christianity in the Mediterranean world had resulted from gradual diffusion rather than from a concerted missionary program designed to convert others. Certainly, official support of Christianity by the Roman state aided the process of diffusion, a process reinforced in Europe with the emergence of the king of the Franks as the new Holy Roman Emperor of the West. In the East, however, state support of Christianity became increasingly irrelevant to its expansion, as the Nestorians of Persia and the Monophysites of Syria and Egypt were cut off from Constantinople by the seventh-century Arab conquests. Some actually welcomed this situation as a divine punishment of the Chalcedonian church of Constantinople for its years of persecuting the "true churches," which could now go their own way, developing their own Christian doctrines, liturgies, and missions, under the general policy of religious toleration in the world of Islam.

At the initiative of Pope Gregory I in 596, a Christian mission went out from Rome, led by monks from Gregory's own monastery, to pursue the conversion of the English. From Gregory's perspective, this mission was necessary to fulfill the biblical mandate to extend Christianity to all the nations of the world before the world came to its end. As Pope Gregory wrote to King Aethelbert of Kent, "We have learned from the words of Almighty God in holy Scripture, that the end of this present world is at hand and the everlasting kingdom of the Saints is approaching." Settling in the kingdom of Kent, which would emerge as the Christian center of Canterbury, Gregory's emissaries of the kingdom of the Saints, who were themselves credited with performing great miracles of spiritual power, confronted an indigenous religion in England that located spiritual power in the natural environment. Gregory complained that "the English, placed in a corner of the world, remained until now in the false worship of stocks and stones." Although the Christian missionaries attacked this religion as the "false worship" of animals, rocks, trees, and other features of nature, the indigenous religion of England, as elsewhere in pre-Christian Europe, continued the ritual observances of ancient Indo-European tradition.[5]

As Christian missions expanded throughout Europe, Christians confronted the persistence of this indigenous European religion. The historical record only hints at the continuing vitality of this European paganism, with its sacred sanctuaries, ritual sacrifices, and popular feasts. In Saxony, sacrifices were regularly performed in forest sanctuaries. In Poitiers, sacrifices were offered on certain days of the year to a mountain lake, as people threw fabrics, cheese, wax, and bread into the water and feasted for three days. On the border between Frisia and Denmark, sacrifices were performed at a spring regarded as so sacred that nothing around it could be touched. From Spain to England, the Christians complained, European pagans "venerated trees as gods."[6]

On the front lines of the encounter with European paganism, Gregory's missionaries in England looked to the pope for guidance. In developing a missionary policy for Europe, Gregory first advocated the destruction of local religion. He advised the missionaries among the English to "make their conversion your first concern; suppress the worship of idols, and destroy their shrines." As an accomplished biblical commentator, Pope Gregory knew that this policy of destruction was consistent with the divine instruction to the ancient Israelites to attack the indigenous religion of Canaan by destroying their altars, stone pillars, and sacred trees. Furthermore, the destruction of paganism was consistent with Roman imperial policy since the edict of Theodosius in the fourth century.

However, Gregory soon changed his mind about this missionary policy of destroying the altars, pillars, and trees of pagan England. Sending new instructions to his missionaries, Gregory advised that "the temples of the idols among the people should on no account be destroyed." Although the sacred stones, trees, or statues within the temples had to be removed, Gregory instructed that "the temples themselves are to be aspersed with holy water, altars set up in them, and relics deposited there." According to some historians, this new policy advocated a certain measure of accommodation with pagan religion. But Gregory's missionary policy is better understood not as accommodation, but as appropriation, as an effort to claim existing pagan sacred sites for Christianity. By claiming these sites, Gregory hoped for a translation of pagan practices into a new Christian idiom, replacing the sacrifice of oxen with the sacrifice of Christ, the veneration of idols with the veneration of relics, and the feasts of European paganism with the festivals of Christian saints. Of course, translation could work both ways. Many features of European paganism, such as rituals for ancestors, concern with the fertility of the earth, and the celebration of heroism in war, were incorporated into the fabric of an emerging European Christianity.[7]

Although Roman Catholic missions into Europe confronted these persisting pagan religious interests, they also engaged the diversity of Christianity within open frontier zones. Originally from southern Britain, the missionary Boniface (675–754) was commissioned by the pope to serve as an apostle to Germany, to act "for the enlightenment of the people of Germany sitting in the shadow of death, steeped in error." What Boniface found, however, was a complex religious frontier along which Christians and pagans had negotiated new forms of religious life. Pointing to new mergers of Christianity and paganism, the "sacrilegious worship of idols," Boniface complained, was being conducted "under the cloak of Christianity." In the 730s, Boniface entered this fluid religious zone, not only by preaching, teaching, and enforcing church discipline, but also by attacking European paganism. In one dramatic incident, Boniface cut down the Oak of Thunor, a sacred tree revered by Saxons, who regarded it as the center of their religious world, and used its wood to build a chapel for St. Peter where the oak tree had stood. However, this religious intervention, which combined the policies of destruction and appropriation, was performed by Boniface not merely to attack European paganism, but to break an alliance that had formed between pagan Saxons and another political grouping, the Hesse, who regarded themselves as Christians. Therefore, Boniface understood his mission as the challenge of converting both pagans and Christians.[8]

For some Christian leaders in Europe, it was possible to work out an accommodation with the pagan past. In the case of a church leader by the name of Clement, for example, pagan concerns about the fate of their ancestors, who might have led blameless, shameless, and even heroic lives before the recent appearance of Christianity, were addressed by a promise of universal salvation through Christ. When Jesus Christ descended into hell, Clement taught, he saved the souls of all human beings, "believers and unbelievers, those who praised god and those who worshiped idols." Other Christian leaders in Europe, however, developed innovations in Christian authority. For example, describing himself as a bishop not by ordination from any church, but "by the grace of God," a charismatic figure by the name of Aldebert gained a considerable following among the Saxons. In his Christian ministry, Aldebert set up chapels in fields and by springs where he preached his gospel, which was based not only on the texts of the Bible, but also on a letter in his possession said to be written by Jesus Christ and to have miraculously dropped from heaven. Credited with performing healings and other miracles, Aldebert also claimed a kind of clairvoyance by knowing the sins of his followers before they confessed them. For many Christians of Francia, Aldebert was regarded as "a most holy Apostle, a patron-saint, a man of prayer, a worker of miracles."[9]

Opposing Clement's accommodations with paganism and Aldebert's innovations in Christianity, Boniface succeeded in having both condemned by a church council convened in 745 by the pope in Rome. As Boniface understood his Christian mission to Europe, Christianization depended not on adapting to pagan interests or performing Christian miracles, but on a long, slow, and gradual process of education defined by the authority of Rome. Committed to educating Europeans in the school of Rome, Boniface even insisted that Christian priests had to observe the rules of Latin grammar and pronounce the language in the Roman style if they expected God to recognize their liturgy. Roman sacred authority, however, was an ideal standard by which even the actual city of Rome could be found wanting. In the attempt to convert pagans and Christians to the religion of Rome, Boniface complained, some of them had visited the city, where "in the neighborhood of St. Peter's church by day or night, they have seen bands of singers parading the streets in pagan fashion." Even Rome, from Boniface's perspective, could be seen to deviate from the ideal Christian order represented by Rome. Nevertheless, attacking not only pagans but also Christians he regarded as pagans, Boniface pursued a mission designed to educate Europeans in conformity to a Roman Catholic model.[10]

Nevertheless, the religious practices of European paganism persisted. They were evident in the continuing ritual attention to sacred trees, groves, mountains, and springs. The scandal of their persistence caused Roman Christians to revitalize the term "superstition"—as *superstare,* that which "stands over"—for these remnants of European paganism. In the *Index of Superstitions and Pagan Practices* of 743, for example, the Roman Catholic Church attacked the sacred sites, the holy fires, the priests, and the priestesses of this indigenous European religious life. By using the term "superstition," the *Index* presumed that European paganism had actually ceased to exist; its beliefs and practices supposedly only survived as the "leftovers" of a dead religious world.[11] In practice, however, European paganism survived in different ways—by resisting Christian colonization, by negotiating with Christians, and by translating into explicitly Christian terms pagan religious interests in revering ancestors, physical healing, agricultural fertility, military heroism, and the sacred power of special persons and special places.

The reign of Charles the Great—Charlemagne, king of the Franks (ca. 768–814)—ultimately unified coercion and education in Christian missions to Europe. As successor to the Frankish Christian king Clovis, King Charles in 772 led his warriors into Saxony, where Boniface had

developed his Christian mission, and destroyed the Saxon pagan sanctuary of the Irminsul, the sacred tree believed to support the entire world.
In these military, political, and religious maneuvers, King Charles succeeded in closing the Saxon frontier by bringing the region under the
control of the Franks. No rituals other than those authorized by the
Roman Catholic Church and its supreme defender, the Holy Roman
Emperor, Charles the Great, would be permitted. In his imperial decree
to the Saxons, Charles declared, "If there is anyone of the Saxon people
lurking among them unbaptized, and if he scorns to come to baptism and
wishes to absent himself and stay a pagan, let him die." Within the terms
and conditions established by this new Holy Roman Empire of the West,
therefore, the choice posed to Europeans was not a choice between
Christianity and paganism, but between Christianity and death.[12]

OPPOSITION

While Christian emperors were delivering ultimatums to European pagans,
the expansion of Islam in the Mediterranean world was also driven by this
tension between religious choice and military threat. As the sacred text of
the Qur'an advised, the infidels—all those who did not recognize the true
religion of submission to the will of God—must first be presented with a
choice. "We would never chastise [any community for the wrong they may
do] ere We have sent an apostle [to them]" (Surah 17:15). The ultimate
apostle or messenger of God, the prophet Muhammad, had taught and
warned. After his death, his successors in the religion of Islam carried that
responsibility. Translating the term *jihad,* which simply means "struggle"
on behalf of the faith, on to the battlefield, Muslim forces engaged in struggle not only for territory and tribute, but also for the expansion of Islam.
Like Christian expansion, Muslim territorial conquest was fueled by religious interest. Although Jews, Christians, and, in some cases, Zoroastrians
might be tolerated as *dhimmi,* as "people of the Book," all unbelievers,
especially polytheists, were confronted with both the choice and the threat
of Islam. Failing to submit to the true faith and pay tribute to its representatives, unbelievers could be exposed to total war. "O you who have
attained to faith," God advised in the text of the Qur'an, "when you meet
a host in battle, be firm, and remember God often, so you might attain to
a happy state" (Surah 8:45). In this religious and military mandate,
Muslim forces were charged with the responsibility of meeting the aggres-

sion of idolaters with force. In the midst of battle, the Qur'an exhorted, "Slay those who ascribe divinity to anything beside God wherever you may come upon them" (Surah 9:5). In spite of their religious differences, therefore, early medieval Christianity and Islam both embraced a military mission.

Conflict between Christians and Muslims, however, was not only waged over territory, tribute, and taxes. A sacred history was also at stake. Just as Christians had appropriated the sacred history of Israel by claiming to be the legitimate heirs to the lineage of Abraham, Muslims asserted their rightful inheritance from Abraham as the spiritual successors of both Jews and Christians. Based on revelations received by the prophet Muhammad (570–632) from the One God (in Arabic, *Allah*), which were collected in the text of the Holy Qur'an, Muslims could understand themselves as "children of Abraham." Although principally calling Arab pagans, idolaters, or unbelievers to submit to the will of the One God and adopt the religion of Islam, from the Arabic root *slm* "to surrender," the Qur'an also held implications for Jews and Christians. As disclosed to Muhammad, the Qur'an transcended the Torah of the Jews and the gospels of the Christians, the sacred texts revealed through previous messengers of God, Moses and Jesus. Since these sacred texts had allegedly been corrupted and distorted over the centuries, the revelation of the Qur'an was necessary, not only for the conversion of unbelievers, but also to call believing Jews and Christians back to the pure faith of Islam, which had been revealed to Abraham, Moses, and Jesus.

As Jesus was incorporated into the religion of Islam as a revered prophet rather than a deity, the Qur'an reinforced belief in one God. "There is no God but God," Muslims affirmed. Although Muhammad was God's final prophet, Jesus had proclaimed the same faith in one God. According to the Qur'an, God said, "O Jesus, son of Mary! Didst thou say unto men, 'Worship me and my mother as deities beside God'?" In this question, the Qur'an challenged Christians with the serious error of *shirk,* the heresy of adding to God, assuming partners for God, or multiplying Gods. From a Muslim perspective, the Christian doctrine of the Trinity, in which Jesus Christ operates as the second "Person" of God, and the Christian practice of venerating Mary as bearer or mother of God violated faith in one God. As recorded in the Qur'an, Jesus denied ever teaching the divinity of himself or his mother. Jesus answered, "Limitless art Thou in Thy glory! It would not have been possible for me to say what I had no right to [say]! . . . Nothing did I tell them beyond what Thou didst

bid me [to say]: "Worship God, [who is] my Sustainer as well as your
Sustainer" (Surah 5:116–17). According to the Qur'an, therefore, Jesus
was not "Son of God," but "Son of Mary," the messenger of God.
Although Jesus bore the title Messiah and performed miracles, he was celebrated in the Qur'an as an inspired prophet who had preceded the
prophet Muhammad in the unfolding revelation of the one God.

The Qur'an credited Jesus with being born of a virgin, thus continuing
the gospel tradition that gave a special role to Mary and paid tribute to
Mary's purity of faith. However, that miraculous conception did not
imply that God was the father of the son of Mary. Although denying the
divinity of Jesus Christ, which was central to the Christian doctrine of
the Trinity, the Qur'an nevertheless affirmed a close relationship between
Jesus and the one God. Not only was Jesus the product of a miraculous
birth, but he also underwent a miraculous death—or transition from this
world—through divine intervention. According to the Qur'an, the Jews
rejected the messenger of God and tried to have him executed. However,
"they did not slay him, and neither did they crucify him, but it only
seemed to them [as if it had been] so." Whether or not Judas was actually
substituted for Jesus on the cross, as some Muslim commentators have
held, the Qur'an revealed that Jesus was not actually crucified because
"God exalted him unto Himself" (Surah 4:157–58). As the Qur'an
engaged Christianity by denying the triune God, the divine sonship of
Jesus Christ, the divinity of Mary, and the reality of the crucifixion,
Muslims understood these interventions as necessary for correcting the
distortions that had entered the Christian tradition. Accordingly, Muslims
could view Islam as both the restoration of the original Christian gospel
and the fulfillment of the promise of Christianity.[13]

Christians of the East and West, however, were quick to define Islam as
a Christian heresy. Although occasionally recognizing that the Islamic
faith in one God was an advance over Arab idolatry, defenders of
Christianity attacked Islam as a deviation from, rather than a fulfillment
of, Christian faith. In the Muslim Syria of the eighth century, for example,
John of Damascus (675–749) provided an account of Islam as a Christian
heresy. Employed within the Muslim administration of the city of
Damascus, John worked closely with Muslims. Although he gained some
knowledge of Islam, he represented the religion in his writings only to
the extent that it affected Christianity. Summarizing the teachings of the
prophet Muhammad, for example, John asserted:

He says that there exists one God, maker of all, who was neither begotten nor has he begotten. He says that Christ is the Word of God, and his spirit, created and a servant, and that he was born without a seed from Mary, the sister of Moses and Aaron. . . . And that the Jews, having themselves violated the Law, wanted to crucify him and after they arrested him they crucified his shadow, but Christ himself, they say, was not crucified nor did he die; for God took him up to himself into heaven because he loved him.[14]

Accordingly, John of Damascus depicted Islam as a perversion of Christianity. He developed a new literary genre, the dialogue between a Christian and a Muslim, in his text *Discussion Between a Christian and a Saracen*. That "dialogue," however, was not a real conversation, but a series of questions that might be posed by a Muslim to which were given Christian answers. Attacking and answering Islam in terms that would be further developed in Christian polemic, John of Damascus represented Islam as a Christian heresy, as a revival of Arabic paganism, and as the product of a false prophet.

First, John of Damascus identified Islam as the heresy of Arianism. Without any historical basis, he maintained that the Prophet's inspiration had come not from God, but from meeting an Arian monk who had introduced him to the heretical denial of the divinity of Christ. As a Christian heresy, therefore, Islam had to be attacked not as another religion, but as if it were an internal Christian problem.

Second, despite the Qur'an's obvious opposition to all forms of pagan idolatry, John of Damascus asserted that Islam had actually revived the pagan Arab worship of idols. Pointing to the annual pilgrimage to Mecca, where the ancient shrine of the sacred black stone in the Ka'bah had been appropriated for the religion of Islam, he accused Muslims of the idolatrous worship of a rock. Pushing this argument further, John of Damascus insisted that the black stone of the Ka'bah was dedicated to Aphrodite, the goddess of the moon, love, and sexuality. Although the Qur'an clearly identified the Ka'bah in Mecca as the site of Abraham's original sacrifice to the one God, and therefore as the point of origin for the prophetic faith of Islam, this accusation of idolatry stuck in the Christian imagination and frequently appeared in polemics against Islam.

Third, John of Damascus countered Islam by attacking the Prophet, accusing Muhammad of creating a false religion so he could indulge his personal sexual desires. Certainly, the Qur'an permitted a man to marry as many as four wives, provided they were all treated equally and with justice, and the Prophet himself had many wives in his household. By rendering the religion as merely a cover for Muhammad's sexual indulgence, Christians attacked the person of the Prophet, depicting him not only as a sexually obsessed deviant, but also as an epileptic, a madman, and a violent tyrant. Muslims denied the divinity of Jesus, but Christian attacks on Islam went so far as to deny the normal humanity of Muhammad.

For most of the Christian West, the impact of Islam was less immediately felt than it was in the conquered regions of Syria, Persia, Palestine, and Egypt or in the besieged Greek Orthodox empire of the East. By the eighth century, Constantinople had become accustomed to almost constant attacks from Muslim military forces. In the West, however, Muslim advances were stopped in 732 by the king of the Franks, Charles Martel, but not before the Muslim conquest of Visigothic Spain in 711. As elsewhere in the world of Islam, the rulers of Muslim Spain, who were based in Córdoba, established a policy of religious toleration in which Jews and Christians were allowed to practice their religions, but not to convert others, especially Muslims, since the penalty for apostasy from Islam was prescribed as death. Nevertheless, some Spanish Christians experienced Muslim rule, even with its policy of religious toleration, as an intolerable situation. For example, in 851 a Spanish monk by the name of Isaac left his mountain monastery, walked eight miles to the city of Córdoba, and sought out a Muslim judge, or *qadi,* to confront. In front of this Muslim authority and in the public space of the Muslim palace, Isaac denounced Muhammad and declared the divinity of Jesus Christ. Following a trial for this blasphemy, Isaac was beheaded. His execution, however, inspired other Christians, particularly monks, to confront their Muslim rulers, resulting in the deaths of as many as fifty Christians over the next ten years. Recalling the intentional martyrdoms sought by Christians under the rule of Roman paganism, the Córdoba martyrs' movement directly embraced death rather than submission to the authority of Islam.

Although nearly 150 years of Muslim rule in Spain had resulted in a relatively peaceful coexistence between Muslims and Christians, the Córdoba martyrs revitalized Christian polemic against the religion of Islam. Sometime before his death in 859, for example, Eulogius published a defense of the Spanish Christian martyrs. Arguing against his fellow Christians in Spain who assumed that Isaac and his followers could not be regarded as martyrs because they had been judged by Muslims "who venerated both God and a law," Eulogius set out to attack the God, the law, and the religion of Islam. Recalling the basic thrust of the arguments of John of Damascus in Syria, Eulogius in Spain discounted the Islamic prophet as a "demoniac full of lies" and attacked the Islamic doctrine of God as a Christian heresy, like Arianism, in which the prophet Muhammad "teaches with his blasphemous mouth that Christ is the Word of God, and the Spirit of God, and indeed a great prophet, but bestowed with none of the power of deity." This Muslim denial of the divinity of Christ could not be tolerated, Eulogius insisted, by Christians who followed a universal religion that had "penetrated every corner of the world and traversed every nation on earth" (Gal. 1:9). By implication, if Christianity was everywhere, it was certainly in Spain, where Christians directly confronted Islam. On that interreligious frontier, Eulogius attacked Islam as the ultimate heresy. Moreover, he introduced three new features into the anti-Muslim debate by being the first Christian to recognize Islam as a separate religion, to attribute the origin of that separate religion to the devil, and to label the prophet Muhammad as the Antichrist who was anticipated by the book of Revelation. In these highly charged terms, therefore, Islam began to appear to Christians not merely as an error, deception, or heresy, but as a manifestation of the supernatural forces of evil in the world.[15]

In November of 1095, Pope Urban II journeyed from Rome to Clermont, in the kingdom of the Franks, to deliver a sermon about the evil of Islam. Adherents of the religion of Islam, he asserted, were "an accursed race, a race utterly alienated from God." Although the Roman Catholic Church had also pursued a policy of destruction and appropriation against other religions, Pope Urban II argued that Christians could not stand by while Muslims conquered Christian territory, sanctuaries, and shrines, especially since they had appropriated the most sacred place in Christian geography, Jerusalem. Addressing the Franks, Urban appealed to both their Christian conscience and military prowess to call them to avenge these Muslim conquests. "On whom, therefore, is the task of avenging these wrongs and of recovering this territory incumbent," the pope asked, "if not upon you? You, upon whom above other nations God has conferred remarkable glory in arms, great courage, bodily energy, and the strength to humble the hairy scalp of those who resist you." As the new "people of God," the new chosen people, who were under the ruler of a new Holy Roman Emperor, the Franks were singled out by the pope as divine agents called to enter into battle against the Muslim forces of evil.

Celebrating the military, religious, and spiritual strength of the Franks and demonizing Muslims, Pope Urban II tried to work out a dual strategy that would reinforce the unity of Christendom by promoting peace within its borders and committing Christians to conducting an ongoing war outside of its domain. The pope insisted a truce had to be declared, the "Truce of God," among all Christians. Under the terms of this peace, Christians in Europe were called to deflect any conflicts, animosities, or aggressions that might arise among themselves onto an external enemy, the Muslims. Therefore, any internal violence that might have arisen among Christians was directed by Pope Urban II against the Muslims who controlled Jerusalem. Although Muslim control over the sacred city of Jerusalem had been established for more than four hundred years, Pope Urban II treated the situation as if it were a recent event that had to be immediately redressed. "Enter upon the road to the Holy Sepulchre, wrest that land from the wicked race, and subject it to yourselves," he exhorted. "The land which, as the Scripture says, 'flows with milk and honey,' was given by God into the possession of the Children of Israel."

At the Frankish town of Clermont in 1095, therefore, Pope Urban II called Christians to certify their unity by opposing Islam. In terms of the sacred history of Israel being contested by Jews, Muslims, and Christians, Christians could certify their inheritance to the legacy of the "Children of Israel" by conquering Jerusalem. At the same time, the sacred geography of Christianity, revolving around a promised land that "flows with milk and honey," was also at stake in this conflict. As Pope Urban II recalled, "Jerusalem is the navel of the world," the *axis mundi* that had been sanctified by the presence, suffering, death, burial, resurrection, and ascension into heaven of Jesus Christ, where he ruled over the living and the dead. In terms of this sacred geography of Christianity, therefore, Jerusalem was the city of Christ the King. However, as Pope Urban II observed, "This royal city, situated at the center of the world, is now held captive by his enemies." Maneuvering within this sacred history and sacred geography, Pope Urban II called upon Christians to achieve their personal salvation through a collective assault against Muslims.[16]

As Pope Urban II called Christians to battle against Muslims, he did not announce a "crusade," a term that was only much later applied to these adventures. Rather, he called Christians to embark upon a pilgrimage, a "pilgrims' war," in which each warrior could achieve personal salvation on the journey to the sacred center of the world. Whether killing or being killed, armed Christian pilgrims to the sacred city of Jerusalem reinforced the unity of Christendom on earth and in heaven by enacting the central Christian ritual of redemptive sacrifice. The Christian Crusades, as they became known to history, might not have fulfilled Pope Urban's vision of creating a reign of divine peace in Europe by deflecting European aggression against Muslims in the East. Nevertheless, the military ethos of the Crusades, which idealized the role of Christian soldiers, emerged as the defining feature of a unified Christendom in the West.

12

Hierarchy

During the sixth century an unknown author wrote a series of books in Greek on God, the heavens, the church, and spirituality under the name of Dionysius the Areopagite. The adoption of the name of an Athenian who had been converted in the first century by the apostle Paul (Acts 17:34) made his writings appear as if they had come from the biblical era, giving them an aura of ancient authority. In the Christian East, Dionysius was praised as *Theophantor*, the "revealer of God." His texts were cited as apostolic and incorporated into the thinking of leading Orthodox theologians such as Maximos the Confessor and John of Damascus. Around the year 832, these Greek texts were translated into Latin by a French monk who mistakenly identified the author not only with the biblical Dionysius, but also with St. Denis, the first Catholic bishop of Paris, who eventually became the patron saint of France. Accordingly, the texts of Dionysius the Areopagite assumed an even greater significance in the Christianity of the Latin West than in the Greek East by combining the ancient authority of a convert of Paul with the local authority of a European saint. Although modern scholars have exposed the sixth-century origin of these texts, referring to their author as the "Pseudo-Dionysius," medieval Christian theologians in the West and Byzantine theologians in the East regarded these writings as similar in authority to the canon of the New Testament.

Under the influence of Neoplatonism, the texts of Dionysius the Areopagite depicted the order of the universe as a cosmic harmony. In his treatise *Celestial Hierarchy*, the author outlined the "sacred order" of the heavens as a harmony of three ranks of angelic beings. The highest rank was comprised of the seraphim, cherubim, and thrones, those manifestations of spiritual intelligence that most closely approached divine perfection in their union with God. These expressions of spiritual intelligence manifested divine order, knowledge, and presence. In the middle rank, the dominions, virtues, and powers transmitted the perfection of the highest spiritual beings by extending the illumination of divine light to the levels of the universe below them. Finally, the lowest rank of the celestial hierarchy was formed by the principalities, archangels, and angels, who presided over the human world. In their spiritual purity, the angelic beings of this lowest rank protected human beings, but also directed them to rise above the dark and defiling world in which they were alienated from God. According to Dionysius the Areopagite, therefore, the sacred order of the heavens was a celestial hierarchy that proceeded out from the supreme Godhead through the three ranks of angelic beings that represented perfection, illumination, and purity. On earth, the human soul could embark on a journey back to God, a spiritual or mystical trajectory that moved through three stages—purification, illumination, and perfection—and ultimately promised to end in union with God.[1]

A different Christian image of hierarchy on earth, however, emerged at the same time as a system of worldly order based on three social classes. For example, as the end of the first Christian millennium approached during the 990s, the Anglo-Saxon monk Aelfric used familiar terms to identify the basic structure of a Christian social hierarchy of three earthly ranks. Maintaining that human society depended upon a division of labor, Aelfric identified the three social orders as workers, fighters, and ritual experts who specialized in speaking, praying, and mediating between human beings and God. Arguably, this division of social classes preserved the class system of Indo-European paganism, the tripartite social order of priests, warriors, and householders that was widely distributed in the ancient world. In that Indo-European system, these three social classes represented functions—ritual authority, physical force, and material well-being—that were supported by different orders of divine beings. For the monk who invoked this image of social order, however, these three social classes were necessary for maintaining a specifically Christian world.

First, as Aelfric explained, the *laboratores,* the economically productive class of workers, farmers, and traders, "are those who by their labor provide our means of subsistence." Engaged in material production and economic exchange, this broad class of people who operated within the world of work supported the other two social classes. Through tribute, taxes, and rents, the workers sustained a ruling class or nobility of warriors, the *bellatores,* as Aelfric identified them, "who protect our cities and defend our soil against invading armies." And through regular tithes, donations, and gifts, both the workers and the warriors supported a priestly class, the *oratores,* literally meaning those who pray, as Aelfric explained, in order to "intercede for us with God." In Aelfric's view, therefore, these three Christian social classes, the social orders of working, fighting, and praying, made Christianity more than merely a church in the sense of a gathering of believers. By encompassing every aspect of human activity, Christianity was a total social world.[2]

PRAYING

The social class of *oratores,* those who prayed for a living, can be broadly divided into the monks and nuns who lived in religious communities and the priests who administered the formal liturgy of the church. Although these *oratores* operated in different contexts, they shared two basic assumptions about the nature of Christian prayer. First, prayer was essentially a collective act. For monks and nuns, praying alone was certainly possible, but according to the influential *Rule of St. Benedict,* private prayers should be kept very brief unless they were unavoidably prolonged by the direct inspiration of God. Under normal circumstances, prayer was collective, a group activity regulated by the hours of the day, coordinated around the hymns from the book of Psalms that were prescribed for each hour, and sung together in community. Likewise, the prayers spoken or sung by priests in the formal ritual of the liturgy were public acts. Although some prayers, such as the words that consecrated the bread and wine of the Eucharist, were uttered by the priest before the audience of the church, other prayers required the collective participation of the entire church in a carefully scripted performance. In these respects, therefore, prayer was not a private, but a shared, collective, and even public activity that built a sense of community, whether in the monastery or the church, through group participation in ritual speech.

Second, prayer was used as an instrument for the sanctification of time. Although the *oratores* were concerned about the ultimate salvation of Christians in eternity, they were also interested in developing Christian techniques for sanctifying the hours, days, weeks, and years, the ordinary temporal cycles of the world. In the monastery, for example, monks and nuns observed a liturgy of the hours, a ritual pattern that came to be known as the Offices, which effectively sanctified each ordinary day by making it into a regular, predictable, and repeatable cycle of prayer. The

Sunday liturgy in the church sanctified the week, and the entire year was regulated by a sacred calendar, revolving around the complicated and often disputed calculation of the date for Easter, that defined the repeating cycle of the Christian liturgical year. Accordingly, although Christians prayed for salvation, they also prayed collectively to sanctify the recurring cycles of ordinary time.

As the monastic ideal developed in the Egyptian desert spread with the expansion of Christianity into Europe, it was formalized during the sixth century in the *Rule of St. Benedict.* At his monastery of Monte Cassino in Italy, Benedict of Nursia (ca. 480–547) established the framework for a life of prayer that merged the Eastern asceticism of Pachomius with the Western piety of Augustine. Although recent scholarship has questioned Benedict's authorship of the rule bearing his name, this manual extensively influenced the development of monasticism in the West, not only among the Benedictines, but also among other religious orders. According to the *Rule of St. Benedict,* different types of monks could be observed— solitary hermits, wandering holy men, and dubious pretenders—but the best form of monastic life was led in community under the discipline of a rule and the authority of an abbot. The monastic life of prayer, therefore, was based on obedience. "The first degree of humility is obedience, without delay," instructed the *Rule of St. Benedict,* citing as its ultimate authority the biblical text "At the hearing of the ear he hath obeyed me" (Ps. 17:45). As the antidote to the sin of pride, which could be regarded as the root of all sin, the monastic rule and abbot enforced a discipline of obedience that promised to cultivate humility.

The religious life of prayer in a monastery, however, also promised to create a kind of heaven on earth. Anticipating the timeless eternity of heaven, each day in the monastery was a sacred day. According to the *Rule of St. Benedict,* in winter, the monks would rise at 2:00 A.M. for the first prayers, the Nocturns, which later came to be known as Matins, from 2:10 to 3:30 A.M. Following these prayers, after two and a half hours of reading, the next daily prayers, Lauds, were observed from 5:00 to 5:45. These prayers led into another period of reading for two and a half hours that was interrupted by the twenty-minute observance of Prime. From 8:15 to 2:30 the monks engaged in work, stopping at three points to observe the prayers of Terce, Sext, and None, each of which lasted ten minutes. From 2:30 to 3:15 in the afternoon they enjoyed their daily meal, which for all their ascetic discipline was quite ample, since it comprised an estimated 6,000 calories, nearly three times the caloric intake considered normal in the twentieth century, and included a ration of as much as a quart and a half of wine or beer. This meal was followed by another hour of reading. As the day drew to a close, the final prayers, Vespers, with collation, or reading, followed directly by Compline, were observed between 4:15 and 4:45. Half an hour later the monks were in bed, to sleep until they awoke at 2:00 A.M. to begin the cycle again.

During the longer days of summer, monks awoke earlier, before 1:00 A.M., and went to bed later, after 8:00 P.M., with the daily routine of prayer, reading, and work broken by a siesta from 12:30 to 2:00 P.M. and two meals. Nevertheless, the timetable of monastic life in both winter and summer was a daily cycle of ritual prayer structured according to the hours of the Office; this cycle was the *opus Dei*, the "work of God," and was regarded as the primary responsibility of both monks and nuns. As *oratores* who were employed in this daily work of God, therefore, monks and nuns lived a life of liturgy in sacred time.[3]

In addition to being a vehicle for acting out heaven on earth on a daily basis, monasticism was crucial to the expansion and development of Christianity in Europe. First, the establishment of Christian communities in many regions resulted not from the efforts of bishops, deacons, priests, or other agents of the church, but from the missions established by monks. In Ireland during the eighth century, for example, Christianity flourished in monastic estates and towns, with monasteries often serving as residences for royalty. Second, as new monastic orders multiplied throughout Europe, by the twelfth century monks exercised a powerful and extensive influence over the church. In particular, the French monastic centers of Cluny, under the leadership of Peter the Venerable, and Cîteaux, under the leadership of Bernard of Clairvaux, vied for religious authority over Christendom. Third, the influence of the monastic ideal increasingly extended to ordinary people in the world, the laity. During the twelfth and thirteenth centuries, many ordinary Christians in Europe experienced what has been called an "evangelical awakening," in which they were inspired to engage in popularized forms of monastic ritual practices—at least one Communion a year at Easter, at least one confession of sins a year to a priest, and at least one prayer, the Lord's Prayer, that could be recited from memory.

Finally, the mendicant orders originating in the thirteenth century—the Dominicans and the Franciscans—directly worked for this popularization of religious activity. The Spanish Castilian monk Dominic of Guzmán (1170–1221) founded the Dominicans, in the year before his death, as a monastic order dedicated to teaching Christianity and fighting heresy among the people. The Italian visionary Francis of Assisi (1181–1226) founded the Franciscans as an order devoted to a life of prayer circumscribed by vows of poverty, chastity, and obedience. In the evocative prayers composed by Francis, however, these vows pointed to commitments binding not only upon monks, but upon all Christians. For example, within the context of an emerging market economy in Europe, where pride had been replaced by greed, avarice, and desire for material gain as the root of all evil, Francis prayed for a "holy poverty" that trusted only in God. Francis prayed:

> Holy Obedience
> confounds all self-will and all sensual will,
> And keeps its body
> Obedient to the spirit
> And obedient to its neighbor
> And makes men subject
> To all the men of this world,
> And not only to the men
> But also to all animals and wild beasts,
> So that they can do with him
> Whatever they wish,
> As far as God above allows them.[4]

In this prayer of St. Francis, therefore, the monastic ideal of obedience was extended to the entire world, indicating a way of life in which everything was based on cultivating humility under God. For a visionary such as St. Francis, the monastery was the world.

Within the formal liturgy of the church, prayer was also a direct intervention in the world. Whether performed in the East or the West, the liturgy dramatically transformed the ritual elements of ordinary bread and wine into the extraordinary presence of God. In the West, that transformation was achieved through the priestly words of consecration, "This is my body, this is my blood." In the East, those words of institution had to be completed by the *epiklepsis,* the invocation of the Holy Spirit. As the central prayers of the Christian church, these words could only be uttered by an ordained male priest in the context of a ritual drama that came to be increasingly formalized and elaborated. In the historical development of the liturgy, priestly *oratores* played a mediating role in a ritual of exchange between God and the church.

In the East, the basic format of the liturgy had been developed by the ninth century. As people gathered in the church, in another room the priests prepared the elements for the Eucharist, reciting prayers over the bread and wine. The bread was pierced with a liturgical spear. Wine and water were mixed in a chalice. A piece of sanctified bread from a previous Mass was put in the chalice to link the present ritual with all previous performances. Following these ritual preparations, the Liturgy of the Word began with the procession of priests into the sanctuary. Accompanied by the singing of hymns, the light of candles, and the fragrance of incense, this procession, known as the Little Entrance, marked the beginning of the part of the service for both the baptized faithful and the unbaptized catechumens. All chanted the prayer known as the Trisagion, "Holy God, Holy Mighty, Holy Immortal, have mercy on us." Scripture readings from the Letters and gospels of the New Testament were alternated with the chanting of psalms. A sermon marked the close of the Liturgy of the Word. As the catechumens were formally dismissed, the doors of the church were closed.

Reserved for baptized Christians in good standing in the church, the Liturgy of the Faithful began with the Great Entrance, the procession in which the bread and wine for the Eucharist were brought to the altar with the chanting of prayers. After greeting each other with the Kiss of Peace, the people recited the Nicene Creed. Silently or in a quiet voice, priests prayed, culminating in the words of institution that were spoken loudly and clearly: "Take, eat, this is my body. . . . Drink of it, all of you, this is my blood." As the bread and wine were raised in offering to God, the priest quietly recited the memorial prayer, recalling that this central act of the liturgy commemorated "the cross, the tomb, the resurrection on the third day, the ascension into heaven, the enthronement at the right hand of the Father, and the second, glorious coming." Then, in a loud voice, the priest addressed the congregation with the words "We offer to You these gifts from Your own gifts in all and for all." The transformation of the bread and wine was not complete, however, until the priests had quietly recited the prayer of invocation for the Holy Spirit:

Send down Your Holy Spirit upon us and upon these gifts here
    presented:
And make this bread the precious Body of Your Christ,
And that which is in this cup, the precious Blood of Your Christ,
Changing them by Your Holy Spirit. Amen, Amen, Amen.

Following their recitation of the Lord's Prayer, the people were invited
to come to the altar and share the communal meal. Accompanied by
chanting, Communion was offered by means of a spoon. At its conclusion, the priest recited a blessing, "O Lord, save Your people and bless
Your heritage," which was followed by the singing of a prayer of gratitude. Although the people were dismissed from the church at that point,
the service ended only when the priests had recited silent prayers of
thanksgiving and gathered behind the altar to intone the secret prayers
that would close the liturgy. Therefore, although the congregation actively
participated in the ritual drama of the liturgy, the priests played a special
mediating role in the exchange between God and human beings that was
particularly evident in the quiet, silent, or secret prayers recited at crucial
points of the service.

Likewise, the liturgy in the Latin West developed as a ritual of
exchange in which priestly specialists in prayer played a crucial role in
mediating between heaven and earth. According to Gregory the Great,
in the sacrificial ritual of the Mass, the heavens were opened "at the
words of the Priest." With the words of consecration spoken over the bread
and wine, Christians saw "that high things are accomplished with low,
and earthly joined to heavenly, and that one thing is made of visible and
invisible." As in the East, the Western ritual was divided into two basic
sections—the Liturgy of the Catechumens and the Liturgy of the
Faithful—which reserved participation in the communal meal of bread
and wine for baptized Christians. Opening the first section of the liturgy,
the ceremonial entrance of the bishop, presbyters, deacons, subdeacons,
acolytes, and chorus was accompanied by antiphonal singing. The hymns
that marked the entrance—the Introit, the Kyrie Eleison, the Gloria in
Excelsis—evoked moods of expectation, sorrow, and celebration. The
deacons and finally the bishop kissed the altar. As the bishop stood before
the congregation, he recited the first prayer, the Collect, that formally
"collected" and offered the individual prayers of all the people in one
voice. After the seating of the bishop on an elevated throne, which was

sometimes accompanied by shouts of triumph from the congregation, the people also sat for readings, alternated with hymns, from the texts of the Old Testament and the New Testament Letters that had been assigned for that day. At the announcement of the opening and reading from the gospels, the congregation stood, faced the east, and made the sign of the cross. Following the reading from the gospels, two candles, representing the Law and the Prophets, were extinguished and the catechumens were dismissed.

As the Liturgy of the Faithful began, the members of the congregation brought forward their offerings of candles, bread, and wine. In exchange, they participated in the central act of the Mass, the sacrifice on the altar, which was conducted by a priest who led the congregation through prayers for the universal church, both the living and the dead, that was unified as the mystical body of Christ. Step by step, in word and gesture, the ritual proceeded to recall the crucifixion, suffering, and death of Jesus. With the words of consecration, the sacred bread, known as the Host, from the Latin *hostia,* meaning "victim," referring to Christ as the sacrificial victim, was believed to be transformed into the body of Christ on the altar. The Host was raised so that it could be seen by the entire congregation. In this elevation of the Host, which eventually became the most important moment of the Mass in the medieval West, people saw the merger of the invisible and the visible. By viewing the Host, they saw the invisible realities of the sacrificed body of Christ in heaven and the social body of the church on earth. After Communion, the liturgy concluded with the blessing of the people as they left the church.[5]

Although the congregation could share in the communal meal of the Eucharist, many Christians in the West apparently felt that eating and drinking were unnecessary because it was sufficient to be in the presence of God by seeing the elevated Host. As we will see in the next chapter, the Host became increasingly important in the West as the crucial object that linked the material and spiritual worlds. Like the icon in the East, the Host came to be regarded in the West as the visible presence of an invisible reality. The link between heaven and earth that was forged in the Host, however, was effected by the sanctifying speech of ritual experts in prayer, the *oratores,* who mediated the exchanges between human beings and God.

FIGHTING

Identified by the monk Aelfric as those "who protect our cities and defend our soil against invading armies," the social class of *bellatores* comprised a ruling class of nobility and knights within the feudal system that had been established by the tenth century in Europe. As a type of government based on the division of political power among many lords, who each regarded that power as their private possession, feudalism was supported by vassals (from the Celtic word for "servants") or knights (from the Anglo-Saxon word for "servants") who served the interests of their lords by means of military force. While mobilizing their armies and exploiting the peasantry, the feudal nobility of *bellatores* occasionally came into conflict with the *oratores* of the church.

For those who adopted the perspective of the fourth-century monk St. Martin of Tours, any kind of military service was inconsistent with service to Christ. "I am Christ's soldier," Martin had observed. "I am not allowed to fight." As Christianity was adopted by a dominant warrior class in Europe, however, elements of a Germanic religion that valued military courage, strength, and force were transposed into Christian terms. In ancient Germanic religion, the warrior deity Wodan had been praised as "the father of slaughter, God of desolation and fire; the active and roaring deity, he who gives victory, and revives courage in the conflict, who names those who are slain." A century after the death of St. Martin of Tours, the Frankish king Clovis recognized the archangel Michael as a Christian Wodan. He regarded the apostle Peter as a supporter in warfare. According to an eighth-century Frankish history, Clovis constructed a church dedicated "in honor of the most blessed Peter, prince of the apostles, in order that he may be a helper in battle." For the warrior nobility that succeeded Clovis in Europe, therefore, Christianity provided spiritual weaponry to be deployed on the battlefield.[6]

While this warrior class in Europe appropriated Christianity for its military interests, the clergy struggled to establish terms that would contain the nobility within the church. At the end of the tenth century in southern France, clergy and monks initiated a peace movement—the Peace of God—that attempted to assert church control over the unrestrained violence of the feudal nobility. Proponents of the Peace of God accused the nobility of attacking clergy, expropriating church property, stealing from merchants, taking livestock from farmers, and holding peasants for ransom. At a series of peace councils, the church required all knights to take an oath to support the peace and threatened anyone who committed acts of violence with excommunication. For example, at the monastery of Limoges in November 1033, ten bishops gathered to denounce all knights who had refused to keep the peace and promote justice. Holding lighted candles, the bishops declared, "Let them and their henchmen be cursed; let their weapons and horses be cursed. Let them be thrown alive into hell with the fratricide Cain and the traitor Judas." As they threw their candles on the ground and snuffed them out, the bishops concluded, "And just as these lights are extinguished, let their happiness be extinguished in sight of all the saints and angels, unless they come to the court of their bishop before they die to make amends and pay the penalty that is due." If they refused to repent before their deaths, these cursed perpetrators of violence would be denied burial in sacred ground.[7]

In addition to the Peace of God, the clergy could invoke the principles of justice in warfare developed in the fourth century by Augustine of Hippo to address the question "When is a Christian justified in participating in war?" As an attempt to restrain military violence, this theory of the just war identified legitimate terms for declaring and conducting war. The principles of justice in beginning a war—*ius ad bellum*—were only fulfilled if war was declared by a duly constituted civil authority, for a good cause, and with the intention of restoring peace. In terms of just-war theory, resort to military violence could only be justified in the interests of defending the ethical imperative of Christian love by protecting the innocent or redressing wrongs. Once war had been declared, however, justice in the conduct of warfare—*ius in bello*—was measured by the principles of discrimination and proportionality. The principle of discrimination distinguished between combatants who were exposed to military violence and noncombatants who were supposed to be protected, and the principle of proportionality held that the conduct of warfare could only be regarded as just if a greater proportion of good than evil resulted from the violence. In this theory of the just war, therefore, the church developed a set of ethical standards that might be invoked against the unlimited exercise of military violence.

Peace and justice, however, were redefined by the incorporation of the *bellatores* into the church. By the middle of the eleventh century, the church in France had gained control over the ritual initiation of warriors into knighthood. In a formal ceremony of ordination, the church effectively sanctified knights as servants of Christ. Usually performed on Easter or Whitsunday, this sacrament of knighthood required the candidate to prepare the day before by confessing his sins, taking a purifying bath, dressing in white linen, and meditating throughout the night in an armed vigil in church with his sword on the altar. In the morning, the presiding priest prayed over the candidate:

> Hearken, we beseech Thee, O Lord, to our prayers, and deign to bless with the right hand of Thy majesty this sword with which Thy servant desires to be girded, that it may be the defense of churches, widows and all Thy servants against the scourge of the pagans, that it may be a terror and dread of other evil doers, and that it may be just both in attack and defense.[8]

After a short sermon on the virtues of knighthood, a special Mass was celebrated in which each part of the initiate's armor and weaponry was blessed, anointed with oil, and put on. In a final ritual gesture, the priest struck the initiate to signify the last blow that the knight would ever receive and not return. With the final prayers of blessing and thanksgiving, the initiate emerged from this ordination as a Christian knight. In the development of this ritual, therefore, the initiation of a knight became a kind of Christian sacrament for the warrior nobility.

The "pilgrims' wars" that came to be known as the Crusades tested all of these principles of peace, justice, and Christian knighthood. As noted in the previous chapter, Pope Urban II declared a "Truce of God" that drew inspiration from the peace movement to insist that all internal conflicts among Christians in Europe had to end. Furthermore, the pope invoked the theory of the just war to argue that a military campaign against Muslims in Jerusalem was justified because it was declared by legitimate papal authority, in support of a good cause, and for the purpose of redressing an injury. However, since he regarded the occupation of Jerusalem by Muslims as an injury against Christ, and therefore as an injury of infinite proportion, the pope called for an extraordinary war, a holy war, that transcended these ethical concerns about peace or justice by promising salvation. At Clermont in 1095, Pope Urban II offered a plenary indulgence, a full remission of sins, for Christian knights who embarked upon the armed pilgrimage to Jerusalem. Celebrated by clergy and monks, these military campaigns opened a new path to salvation through holy war. "In our own time," the monastic author Guibert of Nogent declared, "God has instituted a holy manner of warfare, so that knights and common people who, after the ancient manner of paganism, were aforetime immersed in internecine slaughter, have found a new way of winning salvation."⁹ By taking up arms and "taking up the cross" (Matt. 10:38), Christian knights embarked on the way of winning salvation through slaughtering the enemies of God.

Although the First Crusade, conducted between 1096 and 1099, succeeded in capturing Jerusalem and establishing a Latin kingdom in Palestine, which finally fell in 1291, every subsequent crusade over the next two centuries was a complete failure. Besides failing to conquer Jerusalem, the "pilgrims' wars" contributed to the division between Western and Eastern Christendom, especially when the Fourth Crusade culminated in 1204 with the siege, capture, and looting of Constantinople. Nevertheless, the ideal of holy war persisted as a religious commitment in the Christian West. One of the strongest advocates of holy war was the mystic, theologian, and monastic leader Bernard of Clairvaux (1090–1153). As abbot of the Cistercian monastery of Clairvaux in France, Bernard was a leading figure in the monastic reforms of the twelfth century. Emphasizing simplicity, humility, and poverty, he accused other monastic orders, especially the French Benedictines centered at Cluny, of being seduced by wealth in their social organization and ostentation in their liturgy. While developing a mystical theology of Christian love, Bernard vigorously campaigned for support, funds, and recruits to wage holy war.

As an effective administrator, Bernard went further than merely lending his support to the Crusades. He organized Christian knights into a military order of armed monks. The Knights of the Temple of Solomon, known as the Knights Templar, had originally been formed in 1119 as a police force to protect Christian pilgrims in Jerusalem. Under Bernard's direction, however, the Knights Templar were transformed into a monastic order, with their own monastic rule, in the armed service of Christ. In the rule that Bernard composed for this monastic order of warriors, Christian knights were bound to vows of obedience, simplicity, and chastity. Like other monks, these Christian warriors prayed and read, but their prayers consisted of a series of Pater Nosters recited several times daily, and their readings were taken from the more militant passages of the books of Joshua, Judges, and Maccabees. The essential *opus Dei*, "work of God," of these military monks was not prayer and reading, however, but fighting against evil in the world. In celebrating the *novae militae,* this new monastic order of armed "ministers of God," Bernard argued that their acts of killing should not be understood as homicide. They should be regarded as *malecide,* the killing of evil. "The soldiers of Christ can fight the Lord's battles in all safety," Bernard declared, "for whether they kill the enemy or die themselves, they need fear nothing. To die for Christ and to kill his enemies, there is no crime in that, only glory." Whether killing or dying for Christ, the Knights Templar and other armed monastic orders of Christian knights represented a significant merger between the *oratores* and the *bellatores* in Western Christendom.[10]

WORKING

From the creation story in Genesis, Christians could derive an image of a working God, a God who labored for six days and rested on the seventh. With regard to human labor, however, the message of Genesis was ambiguous. Was human labor a service to God? According to Genesis, the first human beings were placed in the Garden of Eden "to dress it and keep it" as God's gardeners (Gen. 2:15). From this evidence, labor seems to have been part of the divine plan for humanity. Or was labor a punishment from God? Having been expelled from the Garden, Adam was condemned to work for food by the sweat of his brow and "to till the ground from whence he was taken" (Gen. 3:23). This evidence suggests that labor was a divine punishment resulting from the human fall from grace. Turning to the texts of the New Testament, Christians could also derive a mixed message about labor. Although Jesus exhorted people to be like the lilies of the field or the birds of the sky in trusting divine providence to provide for their needs (Matt. 6:25–34; Luke 12:27), Paul defended the inherent value of labor by insisting, "If any would not work, neither should he eat" (2 Thess. 3:10). Accordingly, Christians could argue with equal scriptural justification for the virtues of the contemplative life or the active life.

In the ongoing conflicts between clergy and nobility over which class was dominant in the social hierarchy, it was always clear that workers, the *laboratores,* were on the bottom. Within a social world that depended upon agricultural production for its survival, however, the labor of farmers had to be valued. Around the year 1100, for example, a monk of Autun by the name of Honorius composed a dialogue between a teacher and a student, the *Elucidarium,* that reviewed the prospects for salvation of people engaged in different occupations. According to the teacher, those employed as priests, monks, or nuns could expect to achieve salvation if they had lived a righteous life. Showing his preference for the *oratores,* the teacher insisted that nobility, knights, and soldiers would certainly be condemned to hell because they lived by robbery. Since their wealth was derived from expropriating the land and exploiting the labor of others, the teacher concluded, the *bellatores* had earned God's wrath and forfeited any hope of salvation.

Having clarified the prospects of those engaged in praying and fighting, the student turned the teacher's attention to the workers. "Do merchants have a hope of salvation?" the student asked. "A slim one," answered the teacher, "since they acquire almost all that they own by fraud, perfidy, and other dishonest methods. They make pilgrimages to holy places so that the Lord will increase their riches and preserve their property—and hell awaits them." "If merchants are destined for damnation," the student wondered, "what is the fate of various artisans?" With respect to those workers who produced manufactured goods out of stone, wood, iron, leather, and other materials, the teacher insisted, "Almost all of them will perish." Most of the artisans involved in building, bricklaying, woodworking, and other trades were destined for hell because, as the teacher explained, "Everything that they manufacture is based on fraud." Turning to the entertainment industry, the student wondered about the fate of minstrels, acrobats, mimes, jugglers, and dramatists. "Do jongleurs have any hope?" the student inquired. "None," the teacher replied, "for they are servants of Satan."

At last, the student asked, "And farmers?" In response to this question, the teacher held out the only hope through which a laborer might achieve salvation. "The greater part shall be saved," the teacher said about farmers, "for they live without guile and feed God's people by the sweat of their brow, as it is said, 'Thou shalt eat the labors of thy hands: blessed art thou, and it shall be well with thee'" (Ps. 127:2). In reviewing the prospects of the broad class of *laboratores,* therefore, in which merchants, artisans, and entertainers were destined for hell, the teacher in the *Elucidarium* of Honorius of Autun concluded that only those workers engaged in agricultural production had any hope of salvation.[11]

The expansion of Christianity from the Mediterranean into Europe was largely controlled by a landed aristocracy, whether feudal nobles or ecclesiastical landlords, who owned arable land and exploited the agricultural labor of peasants or serfs who were bound to the land. Beginning as early as the sixth century but culminating in the eleventh century, northern Europe underwent a gradual agricultural revolution largely driven by the introduction of the horse into farming. Replacing the slow-moving oxen, which remained in use in the Mediterranean world, farmers in northern Europe harnessed teams of horses to more efficient plows to increase dramatically their agricultural yield. Not only more productive, the faster horse allowed peasants in northern Europe to live at a distance from the fields, forming small hamlets, villages, or towns. The introduction of the horse, therefore, not only increased agricultural production, but also led to new patterns of human settlement in Europe.[12]

For the history of Christianity in Europe, this agricultural revolution was crucial to the development of the parish system, which extended the scope of the religion from the city to the countryside. By the beginning of the twelfth century, the parish represented the basic unit of Christianity for the European peasantry. Although linked to an urban "mother church," the parish had a degree of local autonomy. Parishioners assumed local responsibility for a range of religious activities, including building and maintaining churches, electing and supporting clergy, and forming chapters of religious associations such as the Peace of God movement. Through the parish system, therefore, European Christianity underwent a ruralization that integrated Christian beliefs and practices more directly into the lives of ordinary people, the rural peasantry that comprised up to 90 percent of the population of Europe.

At the center of the religious life of the parish system, the rituals of the penitential system were designed to integrate Christian values even further into the most personal and intimate regions of human thought, feeling, conduct, and relationships. Originally a public ritual that required the confession of wrongdoing before the entire Christian community, penance had been transformed in Europe by the seventh century into a private ritual. In Eastern Orthodox practice, laypersons, clergy, and monks turned to spiritual advisers, or "soul friends," to confess sins, receive advice, and perhaps gain absolution in private consultation. Performed in secret before a priest-confessor, who acted as both doctor and judge, private penance in the West was a ritual initially developed for the monastic life. Especially as the penitential system was developed in the monastic outposts of Ireland, the threefold process of feeling contrition, confessing sins, and undertaking acts of penance became an important part of the regulated life. For monks dedicated to a life of celibacy, the regulation of human sexuality was central to the penitential system. As the system was carried out of the Irish monasteries into the world, the concern with managing sexuality remained central. Although the *Penitentials,* which served as guidebooks for confessors, addressed sins of killing, theft, or perjury, they paid particular attention to the details of sexual conduct. In its attention to sexuality, penance developed in the West as a ritual in which a celibate male clergy exercised control over a married laity.[13]

The penitential system prescribed acts of penance, such as fasting, prayers, or fines, for a range of nonreproductive sexual activity. Even within the context of marriage, however, sex was subject to certain restraints. Urging married Christians to refrain from sex during the three forty-day periods of fasting—before Christmas, before Easter, and after Pentecost—and during all religious feasts and festivals, penitential manuals specified other days for abstaining from sex. According to one manual, married Christians should not engage in sexual relations on Thursdays (in memory of the arrest of Jesus), on Fridays (to honor his death), on Saturdays (out of respect for the Virgin Mary), on Sundays (in celebration of the resurrection of Jesus), and on Mondays (in commemoration of the dead). More than merely a ritual format for confessing sins and gaining absolution, therefore, the penitential system was a broader program for regulating the intimate life of ordinary Christians.[14]

During the twelfth century, new Christian evaluations of work appeared in the monasteries and expanding cities of Europe. The monastic understanding of work had been informed by the *Rule of St. Benedict,* which prescribed manual labor and holy reading as antidotes for idleness, the "enemy of the soul." As the French Benedictine monastery of Cluny grew in power, wealth, and property, however, its monks spent less time in manual labor and more time in the "work of God" by developing an elaborate, complex liturgy. As the Cluniacs acquired vast tracts of land by donation or purchase, the farm labor was performed by serfs who were tied to the land or by peasants who paid rents as tenants. Under the leadership of Bernard of Clairvaux, the rival French monastic order based in Cîteaux—the Cistercians—renounced these agricultural rents and services. Calling for a return to the purity, simplicity, and poverty of Benedict's rule, the Cistercians insisted that the manual labor required to work their fields should be performed by monks. As the agricultural estates of the Cistercians expanded throughout Europe, the manual labor of monks was increasingly supplemented by lay brothers who were incorporated into the broader monastic community. Within the Cistercian movement, manual labor was celebrated not merely as a cure for idleness, a penance for sin, or a necessity for survival, but as a positive religious program for developing the fundamental Christian virtue of humility. In this respect, Cistercian monks could regard work as a kind of prayer.[15]

Although they redefined the Christian meaning of manual labor for the monastic life, it was alleged that the Cistercians destroyed villages and removed peasants from the land in order to clear a space for their monastic estates. As the twelfth-century English author Walter Map observed, the Cistercians "raze villages and churches, and drive poor people from the land." Therefore, although they valued manual labor, the Cistercians did not necessarily respect the rights of the laboring peasantry with which they competed in agricultural production.[16]

In the expanding cities of twelfth-century Europe, however, the labor of merchants, artisans, and even entertainers came in for a dramatic Christian reevaluation. With the growth of trade, the emergence of markets, and the increasing use of money as a medium of exchange, the role of merchants was reassessed. According to tradition, Christian merchants could engage in buying and selling, but they were not allowed to make profits through interest gained on lending money. Defined as the serious sin of usury, lending money at interest was forbidden to Christians. Since they had no religious constraints on this kind of economic activity, Jews with the necessary means were able to provide financial services in feudal Europe. By the twelfth century, however, the emerging market economy in Europe drew wealthy Christians into banking and lending money at interest. As the socioeconomic status of Christian bankers, financiers, and merchants rose, usury became a less serious sin in the eyes of the church. At the same time the preaching of religious reformers within the church suggested the effect of these economic changes, as they shifted from attacking the sin of pride, which had traditionally been identified as the most basic sin, to identifying avarice, greed, or the acquisition of wealth as the root of all sin.

Along with the role of merchants, the Christian status of workers also changed during the twelfth century. Representing the interests of the increasingly specialized trades, occupations, and professions, labor guilds emerged as a new feature of European cities. They also assumed certain religious functions. Guilds organized Christian charity for the living and

Christian burial, prayers, Masses, and other rituals for the dead. Although conflicts occasionally arose in a city between churches and guilds over the control of these Christian rituals, the social organization of workers into guilds forced clergy to reassess the value of manual labor. In response to the specialization and organization of the social class of workers, dominant voices within the Roman Catholic Church abandoned the notion that there were three classes, *oratores, bellatores,* and *laboratores.* Lumping together all nobles, knights, merchants, artisans, and peasants in a single class, the *ordo laicalis,* church leaders insisted that a Christian society has only two social classes—the clergy and the laity. While the laity worked within the ordinary, everyday world of goods and services, the clergy operated on an entirely different level by performing the spiritual services and dealing in the sacred goods of the Christian tradition.

13

Objects

Although they failed to reach the holy city of Jerusalem, the armed pilgrims of the Fourth Crusade (1201–4) did succeed in returning to Europe with sacred objects from Constantinople. While crusaders were sacking and looting the imperial city of the East, the French bishop Nevelon removed sacred relics from its churches and brought them back to France.[1] According to one inventory, the bishop acquired objects that were sacred because they had been directly associated with Jesus and his mother. Bishop Nevelon brought back a thorn from the crown of thorns that had been placed on Jesus' head during the crucifixion, a part of the reed with which Jesus had been beaten, a small crucifix made from the wood of the True Cross, and fragments of a robe and a belt worn by the Virgin Mary. In addition to these objects, which had been in contact with the bodies of Jesus and Mary, the bishop also acquired body parts from first-century saints and apostles, including the finger of the apostle Thomas that had touched the resurrected body of Jesus, the forearm of John the Baptist, and the heads of John the Baptist, the apostle Thomas, the first martyr, Stephen, and Dionysius the Areopagite. These relics were received in France with great celebration and credited with extraordinary spiritual power. The weak, the infirm, and the sick were cured. A blind man recovered his sight. By seeing these sacred objects transferred from the East to the West, French Christians beheld with their own eyes the spiritual power of ancient Christianity in the present.

As Dionysius the Areopagite had observed, sensory images make invisible things visible.[2] In both the East and the West, Christian spirituality involved relations with sacred objects that could be seen and touched or smelled and tasted. Certainly, this appreciation of the spirituality of material objects reflected a Christian understanding of the incarnation in which spiritual and material worlds had been fused by God becoming flesh. However, Byzantine and medieval Christians did not operate within a strict conceptual dualism separating spiritual and material realms. Rather, materiality itself—the bread and wine of the Eucharist, the holy images of the church, and the sacred relics of the saints—contained and conveyed Christian spirituality. Ultimately, of course, Christians hoped for a salvation that was not purely spiritual, but was an embodied, fleshly, and material resurrection of the dead. In the meantime, however, they could anticipate that salvation in relation to certain material objects invested with extraordinary spiritual power.

Like the relics of saints, the holy images depicting Jesus, Mary, and the saints could be regarded as material points of intersection with the spiritual world. As the veneration of icons developed in Eastern Orthodoxy, the holy image was valued not merely as a representation, but as a presentation—both likeness and presence—of the spiritual power of holy persons. In the ritualized veneration of icons, Orthodox Christians used these images as windows through which the invisible could be seen. As an opening into the heavenly realm, according to St. Stephen the Younger, "the icon may be termed a door."[3] From the perspective of church leaders in the West, however, holy paintings had a purely pedagogical value, serving, as Gregory the Great put it, as an educational text for the illiterate, as the Bible of the *idiotae*. Continuing this particular reading of images in the West, the theologians at the court of Charles the Great at the end of the eighth century recognized the existence of certain sacred objects, the *res sacrata*, which included the Eucharist, the liturgical vessels, the cross, the scriptures, and the relics of saints, but argued that pictures could never be regarded as sacred objects worthy of worship. "God is to be sought not in visible or manufactured things," they insisted, "but in the heart; he is to be beheld not with the eyes of the flesh but only with the eye of the mind."[4] On a similar basis, opponents of the worship of images in the East, who were called iconoclasts, or "icon smashers," objected to what they perceived as a confusion of the visible and the invisible, the human and the divine, in the practice of venerating icons. For nearly two centuries, this controversy of the image divided Eastern Orthodoxy. Out of the iconoclastic controversy, however, the icon emerged as one of the central features of Orthodox spirituality.

As relics of the saints continued to provide a material focus for spiritual power, protection, and healing in the West, they also defined new European centers for pilgrimage. While the bones of Peter and Paul attracted pilgrims to Rome, new pilgrimage sites developed around the bones of St. James at Compostela in Spain and the corpse of St. Thomas Becket at Canterbury in England. Even greater numbers of pilgrims journeyed to many other sites dedicated to local saints. Enduring the expenses, hardships, and dangers of travel, pilgrims visited those sites to behold the fragments that remained on earth of the bodies of the saints in heaven. In this ritual attention to the physical remains of holy persons, however, the absent bodies of Jesus and Mary presented a problem. According to tradition, both had physically ascended to heaven, leaving behind no bones that could be venerated as relics. Certain traces had been found—drops of blood from Jesus that had been mixed with the dirt of Golgotha, drops of milk from the breasts of Mary—but the absence of physical remains resulted in the relative neglect of Jesus and Mary in early medieval European devotion and pilgrimage. During the thirteenth century, however, attention increasingly shifted to the more universal spiritual power represented by Jesus and Mary. Even that universal power, however, was localized, most evidently in the Host, the eucharistic wafer, which, after all, was regarded as the physical body of Jesus Christ. Through such media as relics, icons, and the eucharistic Host, therefore, Christians developed a spirituality that thoroughly embraced materiality.

RELICS

As we recall, the veneration of the physical remains of martyrs and saints, "the special dead," was an ancient Christian practice. Although the practice of sharing meals at cemeteries was discontinued, the ongoing connections between the living and the dead were sustained through prayers, services, and regular Masses performed for the dead. In European Christianity, as the church and churchyard became the preferred sites for Christian burial, the church itself assumed the ancient role of the cemetery as the meeting place of the living and the dead. As the rituals of the living were performed in the presence of the bones of the dead, both the living and the dead could look forward to a general resurrection of the flesh in which every particle of the human body, even those particles consumed by fire, dispersed by the winds, or eaten by animals, would be restored to form a fully human person to stand before the Last Judgment. In this hope of resurrection, therefore, soul and body together defined the person who was destined for damnation or salvation. The eternal fate of the soul depended on both spiritual status and material body.

In constructing a church as the meeting place between the living and the dead, the physical remains of the saints were crucial. Since they acted as patrons, protectors, and intercessors between material and spiritual worlds, the saints had to be present in a church. In fact, their bones had to be located within the most sacred center of the church, the altar, in order for the building itself to be sanctified. According to a ninth-century formula for consecrating a church in Europe, the bishop of its diocese sprinkled the building with water before performing the first Mass. After completing the Mass, the bishop took the consecrated bread of the Eucharist and other relics and placed them in the altar. In this formula, the Host was regarded as a powerful relic to be joined with other relics, the physical remains of the saints, in the construction of an altar. Although this ninth-century formula suggested that if the bishop was unable to find other relics for the church the Host would be sufficient, since it was effectively the relic of the body and blood of Jesus Christ, churches increasingly required relics of the saints. In the early ninth century, a church council in Carthage ruled that altars lacking relics had to be destroyed and reconsecrated with the physical remains of saints. As this ruling was followed throughout Europe, churches and monasteries embarked on a quest for relics, struggling to secure these material signs of the presence of powerful spiritual patrons.

By the ninth century in Europe, relics had become a crucial focus for religious attention. Not only necessary for sanctifying an altar, relics were also used for swearing oaths, for rituals of healing, and for religious devotions that brought pilgrims from great distances to be in the presence of a holy patron. In response to the increasing demand for relics, new methods were developed for acquiring the physical remains of saints. Certainly, relics might be simply discovered, as the empress Helena had found relics in fourth-century Jerusalem, but this method became extremely rare in medieval Europe. In some cases, a saint could be found in the midst of a religious community. In the case of Thomas Becket, the archbishop of Canterbury who was murdered in his cathedral on December 29, 1170, a local martyr was found. During the fifteen years following his death, over seven hundred miracles were credited to the intervention of this new saint. Becoming a popular pilgrimage site, the shrine of St. Thomas at Canterbury drew pilgrims from all over Europe, vying in importance with Rome and Compostela as a destination for medieval pilgrims.

For the most part, however, the bones of martyrs could not simply be found. Especially in France, martyrs were in short supply. In order to sanctify their altars, bishops and abbots sought to acquire the bones of martyrs from elsewhere, preferably from Rome, but also from the Spanish martyrs of Córdoba. As the European demand for relics increased, a class of professional relic merchants emerged to serve the expanding international trade in the bodies of saints. Relic salesmen acted as middlemen in sacred exchanges between Rome and the rest of Europe. Crossing the Alps, they secured a supply of relics by digging them up from the catacombs, buying them from clerics, or stealing them from unguarded churches. The most prominent ninth-century relic merchant, Deusdona, who served as deacon of a Roman church, became the head of a large and highly organized business. Through the services of Deusdona and other relic merchants, the bodies of many early Christian saints were transferred from the catacombs of Rome to the altars of France.

Although relic merchants assured their customers that the bones they were purchasing were genuine, the question of authenticity was ultimately settled in practical terms. If the bones worked miracles, inspired the faithful, attracted pilgrims, secured funds from donors, and added prestige to the community, then they had to be regarded as authentic relics. The proof of a relic, therefore, was in its effects. Bishops and abbots who purchased relics could be assured the bones they bought were genuine if they worked like relics.

Better than buying relics, however, was stealing them. By stealing the body of a saint, a community could be assured not only of the authenticity of the relic, but also of the blessing of the saint, since saints would certainly not allow their bodies to be moved without their spiritual approval. The bones of St. Benedict, for example, were stolen from his monastery of Monte Cassino in Italy and taken to the monastery of Fleury on the Loire River in France. To certify their claim on the spiritual power of St. Benedict, the monks of Fleury told elaborate stories about stealing the bones, with the implicit permission of the saint, and transferring them to France, where they subsequently conveyed their miraculous power. The successful theft of the body, however, was itself a miracle, which was celebrated in the annual feast of the "translation" of St. Benedict from Monte Cassino to Fleury. Back at Monte Cassino, the Italian monks argued that they still benefited from the spiritual power of their founder, since the saint's body had decomposed into the ground of the monastery, but they recognized that the physical relics of St. Benedict had been taken from them. By an act of sacred theft, therefore, the French monks of Fleury had succeeded in acquiring the spiritual power of an Italian saint.[5]

Throughout Europe similar accounts of stealing relics, known as *translationes,* certified local claims on the bodies of saints and martyrs. In many instances, regional competition among monasteries inspired monks to acquire relics through theft. Vying for pilgrims, status, and wealth with the French monastery of Figéac during the 860s, the French monks of Conques wanted to secure the body of a saint. Hearing of the fame of St. Foy, a twelve-year-old child-martyr killed in the Diocletian persecution of 303, whose body was maintained at the monastery of Agen in France, the monastery of Conques entrusted a monk by the name of Arinisdus with the task of acquiring her remains "for the health of the area and for the redemption of its inhabitants." Posing as a priest, Arinisdus served for ten years as a kind of religious undercover agent, gaining the confidence of the Agen community, until he was appointed guardian of the church. Left alone in the church one night, he broke open the tomb and encountered the sweet fragrance of sanctity from the body of St. Foy. Returning to Conques, Arinisdus and St. Foy were received with great joy. Within twenty years of this theft, the shrine of St. Foy at Conques had become an important pilgrimage site supported by the donations of lay patrons. As a countermaneuver, the monks of Figéac stole the remains of a French bishop, St. Bibanus, from the church of Saintes. St. Bibanus, however, was never able to achieve the prominence of St. Foy as an object of religious devotion.[6]

By assuming the spiritual complicity of the saint in the theft of his or her remains, stories about stealing relics played an important role in validating their authenticity. Ironically, therefore, the theft of a relic was regarded as the best guarantee of its legitimacy. In the case of the relics of Mary Magdalene preserved at the monastery of Vézelay in southern France, monks produced stories about the theft of her relics even though they had not actually been stolen. As a composite saint in medieval Europe, Mary Magdalene combined several biblical characters—the penitent sinner who anointed Christ's feet (Luke 8:36–50); Mary, the sister of Martha (Luke 10:38–42); and Mary, the sister of Lazarus (John 11:1–45). Devotion to Mary Magdalene began at Vézelay in the middle of the eleventh century. As Mary Magdalene emerged as the patron saint of the monastery, her remains had to be present. In 1050 the monastery announced that a monk had brought the body of Mary Magdalene back from a pilgrimage to Jerusalem. A century later, however, a different story was published about the acquisition of Mary Magdalene. In this new account, after the crucifixion of Jesus, Mary Magdalene had fled Jewish persecution in Palestine and along with her brother Lazarus and sister Martha had settled in southern France. Living the rest of her life in penance in the wilderness, Mary Magdalene died and was buried in the town of Aix-en-Provence. When southern France was threatened during the ninth century by foreign invaders—whether by Muslims or Normans, depending upon the version of the story—the body of Mary Magdalene was stolen from Aix-en-Provence by the monks of Vézelay and brought back to the safety of their monastery. Far from regarding the theft of relics as a crime, therefore, the monks of Vézelay celebrated stealing the relics of Mary Magdalene as the founding moment in the spiritual life of their monastery.[7]

Like monasteries, urban churches engaged in the theft of relics. Perhaps the most popular saint in the Christian world, St. Nicholas, was translated in 1087 from the monastery of Myra in Syria to the trading city of Bari in Italy. Competing for lucrative Byzantine markets with the city of Venice, the merchants of Bari sought to acquire the body of a powerful patron saint. According to one account, when the merchants of Bari learned that merchants from Venice planned to steal the body of St. Nicholas, they decided to get there first. Arriving at the shrine of St. Nicholas in Myra, the Bari merchants gained entrance from the monks who guarded the tomb. Assuming that the merchants had come to worship, the monks showed them the sacred oil that flowed in the shrine. Recently, one of the guardians revealed, St. Nicholas had appeared in a vision to announce that he wanted to move to another place, but moving his body was impossible. Even emperors had tried and failed. When the merchants of Bari opened the tomb, however, they had no difficulty in removing the relics of St. Nicholas. The beautiful fragrance from the tomb, which emanated for miles around, was understood by the merchants as further evidence that the saint wanted to be stolen. Although the people of Myra tried to prevent them, the merchants escaped and returned to Bari, where a magnificent basilica was built for the relics of St. Nicholas. Rapidly emerging as a popular pilgrimage site, the port city of Bari could attribute its prosperity to the presence and power of St. Nicholas, the patron saint of merchants.[8]

Although they became focal points for religious devotion, spiritual healing, and supernatural miracles, relics also performed important social functions. Relics represented a kind of "symbolic capital" that enhanced the local, regional, or international status of a church or a monastery. In

most instances, the presence of a saint contributed directly to the accumulation of wealth by attracting gifts from pilgrims and lay patrons. But
relics performed at least three other social functions as media for myth,
ritual, and competition over the spiritual resources of Christianity.

First, the relics of saints operated as the main characters in the compelling stories about the spiritual foundation of a monastery, church, or
other religious community. For the development of European Christianity,
stories about the translation of saints from the East were important
because they assumed a transfer of sacred power to Europe. Each story
about relics operated as a social myth of origin, providing a sacred charter
to a local community. Whether they were bought from Rome, stolen from
Spain, or produced locally, as in the case of Thomas Becket in Canterbury,
martyrs represented the original "seed of the church," as Tertullian had
proposed, that grew into religious communities.

Second, relics were used in regular rituals for the regeneration of society.
Every altar was expected to contain the relics of saints, and each Christian
community, from the urban cathedrals to the parish churches, celebrated
the feast days of those saints who resided in its altar. Through annual rituals for patron saints, a local community reaffirmed its identity as a community. As the relics of the saints were removed from the altar on those
occasions for public display, procession, and celebration, the local
Christian community that comprised both the living and the dead could be
revitalized.

Finally, relics became important symbolic markers of social competition among Christian communities. Relics not only attracted pilgrims and
donors, but also generated spiritual prestige that operated as a form of
symbolic capital in a competitive religious market. The competition over
the acquisition of relics was waged as fiercely between the French monasteries of Conques and Figéac as it was between the Italian trading ports of
Bari and Venice. In these social competitions over power, status, and prestige, which were simultaneously spiritual and material, Christian communities deployed the relics of the saints to assert their distinctive local
character. At the same time they participated in a broader Christian communion of the living and the dead that was most clearly and powerfully
embodied in the physical remains of holy persons that had been left in the
world. In the end, therefore, despite the often intense social competition,
the presence of those physical remains in the world anticipated the resurrection of the flesh that was the ultimate hope of all Christians.

ICONS

How were Christians supposed to recognize Jesus Christ at the resurrection of the dead? They could study, revere, and honor the holy images of Christ in order to prepare for the Second Coming. In Orthodox practice, the media of salvation included not only the words of the gospels, but also the images of Christ, Mary, and the saints as they were depicted in paintings. By venerating his image that appeared on the materials of wood, cloth, metal, or glass, Christians would be able to recognize Jesus Christ when he returned.

As the icon developed into a focal point for religious devotion, the holy image was regarded as a likeness, similar to a modern photograph, that accurately portrayed its subject. Although depictions of saints and martyrs often relied on oral or written traditions about their appearance, a visual vocabulary developed in which holy persons could be recognized by certain features—St. Peter's short hair, St. Paul's baldness—that gave each a distinctive pictorial identity. In the case of Jesus and Mary, however, certain holy images were held to be accurate representations because they were thought to be portraits either painted from life or miraculously produced. According to tradition, St. Luke the Evangelist, as a medical doctor, was allowed access to the mother and child, who sat for him while he painted their portrait, which depicted the Virgin Mary holding the infant Jesus on her knee. Regarded as an authentic likeness, the portrait attributed to St. Luke set the standard for visual representations of the holy mother and child.

Images of the mature Jesus that had been miraculously produced, however, were even more important than this portrait from life. The most authentic images of Jesus were those imprinted on cloth. In the East, an image on cloth known as the Mandylon, which had reportedly been sent by Jesus himself to Abgar, King of Edessa (d. 50), protected the city of Constantinople. In the West, the most important cloth image was the Veronica. According to tradition, this image had been miraculously produced when a woman by the name of Veronica—meaning "true image"—had wiped the face of Jesus with a cloth while he was carrying the cross to his crucifixion. Since these "unpainted" images had not been made by human hands, they were regarded as not only the most lifelike, but also the most sacred images of Jesus.

By the sixth century, icons had assumed an important role in the religious practices of Eastern Orthodoxy. In general terms, holy images were used for education, veneration, and protection. Although icons were often characterized as if they were a visual scripture, the Bible of the illiterate, their pedagogical role was superseded by their status as sacred objects effectively conveying the spiritual power of holy persons. Although great value was placed on the accuracy of a representation, an icon was more than a mere likeness; it was a presence. Through ritual acts of veneration—bowing, kneeling, and kissing the image—devotees could gain access to the spiritual power of the holy person represented by the icon. By such acts of veneration, Christians entered into ritual exchanges with Jesus, Mary, and the saints, who were the heavenly "prototypes" of the material images. As John of Damascus explained, "The honor given to the image is transferred to its prototype." In exchange for this transfer of honor, the heavenly prototypes of Jesus, Mary, and the saints extended spiritual healing, strength, and protection to Christians. As they came to be widely used in personal devotion, church liturgy, public processions, and even in defending a city against invaders, icons emerged as crucial intercessors between heaven and earth. "We offer the proper honor to them," as the patriarch of Constantinople Nikephoros explained, "and entreat their sacred intercessions."[9]

During the eighth century, however, the Orthodox Church entered a period of crisis for the image. Known as the iconoclastic controversy, this crisis called into question the legitimacy of venerating icons within the Christian tradition. To a certain extent, the controversy was waged in the broader context of an interreligious argument about images among Jews, Muslims, and Christians. Generally, Jews and Muslims rejected the use of visual images in their own religious worship. However, they also developed criticisms of the Christian veneration of icons. As the Islamic tradition developed, all visual representations of human beings were held to be blasphemous attempts to imitate God's creativity. The act of venerating such visual representations represented an even greater sacrilege. Indicating that Christians were concerned about these Muslim criticisms, Theodore abu Qurra (ca. 750–ca. 825) wrote a defense of icons in Arabic to assure them that they should not allow Muslims or Jews to make them feel ashamed for kneeling and bowing in front of icons.[10]

Although these interreligious criticisms were taken seriously, the iconoclastic controversy was primarily an internal argument among Christians who, unlike Jews and Muslims, regarded Jesus Christ as divine.

According to the defenders of icons, the merger of spiritual and material in these holy images corresponded directly to the merger of divinity and humanity in the incarnation of Christ. "I do not draw an image of the immortal Godhead," John of Damascus observed, "but I paint the image of God who became visible in the flesh." Therefore, according to the "icon lovers," who became known as *iconophiles* or *iconodules,* the icon presented the central mystery of Christianity. However, the opponents of images, who became known as iconoclasts, were convinced that icons had drawn Christians into violating the Second Commandment. Not only idolatrous, the veneration of icons was useless. According to the iconoclasts, Christians should not rely on "inanimate and speechless images, made of material colors, which bring no benefit." In place of the holy images, iconoclasts directed Christian attention to the text of the Bible, the bread and wine of the Eucharist, and the "victory-bringing" sign of the True Cross. Only these objects, they argued, could be regarded as bearing the spiritual power of Christ.[11]

The iconoclastic controversy, therefore, was an argument about the material location of the sacred. As the reference to the victory-bringing Cross should suggest, however, the controversy over holy images occurred in the midst of military conflict. Between 700 and the early 840s, Constantinople was attacked almost every year by the military forces of an Islamic empire that was ten times larger and fifteen times richer than the Byzantine Empire. Although outnumbered on the battlefield by as much as five to one, the Byzantine Greeks managed to maintain the independence of Constantinople. Following a military victory against Arabs and a volcanic eruption in the Agean in 726, Leo III (717–41) was the first Byzantine emperor to act against icons. Removing the icon of Christ at the entrance to his palace, Emperor Leo III replaced it with a cross. In a directive to the bishops of the Orthodox Church, he encouraged the destruction of holy images as if they were pagan idols. His son and successor, Constantine V (741–75), vigorously pursued this war against images. Convening a church council at Nicaea in 754, Emperor Constantine V made sure that icons were condemned. Lovers of icons, according to this iconoclastic council, were guilty of "two blasphemies"—they limited God by confining divinity within material forms, and they confused the human and divine by assuming that products of human art could hold and convey divinity. The only true image of Christ, the council concluded, was found in the consecrated bread and wine of the Eucharist.[12] Over the next three decades, prominent monks who defended icons were attacked, humiliated, and in some cases killed. Holy images were destroyed or removed and replaced with simple, unadorned crosses. In the great church of Hagia Sophia, crosses replaced mosaics of Jesus, Mary, and the saints. Throughout the empire, the holy icons of the Orthodox Church were under siege.

In 787, however, the first phase of the iconoclastic war against images ended abruptly with another church council that restored the veneration of icons. Defending the orthodoxy of images, the council of 787 reaffirmed the incarnational character of icons. But iconoclasm was revived again in 815 in response to a new military crisis, the threat of the Bulgars from the Balkans. Associating iconoclasm with military strength, Emperor Leo V concluded that the idolatry of image worship had made Greek Christians vulnerable to defeat by pagan nations. Following the military defense of Constantinople against Arab forces in 843, however, the second phase of iconoclasm ended. Celebrated as the "triumph of Orthodoxy," the restoration of icons reestablished the importance of ritual attention to holy images that has continued to characterize the beliefs and practices of the Orthodox Church.

With the restoration of the icons in the 840s, the question of the location of the sacred was resolved for the Orthodox Church. Although iconoclasts had insisted that Christian spiritual power could only be found in the consecrated Eucharist, the text of the Bible, and the sign of the True Cross, leaders of the Orthodoxy who emerged from this controversy reaffirmed the inherent spirituality of the material world. The merger of the spiritual and material was most evident in the icon, but it could be discerned everywhere. As Leontius of Neapolis (fl. ca. 610–40) had maintained before the controversy broke out over icons, God was to be worshiped through both creation and created objects not only in "heaven and earth and sea," as Leontius clarified, but also through "wood and stone, through relics and church-building."[13] From this perspective, the entire world could be regarded as iconic, as a world of windows and doors into the spiritual realm. According to the iconoclasts, this iconic vision of the world had to be controlled by the textual authority of the Bible. Otherwise, any prophet, seer, or dreamer could claim Christian authority for his or her religious visions. Accordingly, iconoclasts such as John the Grammarian defended writing against painting, words against images, and hearing the texts of scripture against seeing any kind of image.

In the restoration of the icons of the 840s, however, Orthodox church leaders emerged to reaffirm the visual vocabulary of Jesus, Mary, and the saints appearing in holy images. Against the iconoclasts, they asserted the primacy of sight over hearing. For example, Nikephoros observed that "we all know that sight is the most honored and necessary of the senses and it may allow apprehension of what falls under perception more distinctly and sharply (than hearing)." Speech can be distorted by altering texts, he argued, but visual representations remain clear and distinct. Therefore, visual images, Nikephoros concluded, are more trustworthy than documents. Similarly, the patriarch of Constantinople, Photius, asserted the primacy of sight, but he extended the argument by maintaining that images were not only more trustworthy, but also more powerful in their effects. Affirming the superior power of sight over hearing in the formation of memory and knowledge, Photius maintained that seeing a holy image "sends the essence of the thing seen on to the mind, letting it be conveyed from there to the memory for the concentration of unfailing knowledge. Has the mind seen? Has it grasped? Has it visualized? Then it has effortlessly transmitted the forms to the memory." Delivering a sermon in 867 in the Hagia Sophia under the holy images of Jesus and Mary, Photius reminded his audience that "before our eyes stands motionless the Virgin carrying the creator in her arms as an infant, depicted in painting as she is in writings and visions, an intercessor for our salvation." As they were represented in sacred writings, but also as they were immediately present in visions, dreams, and holy icons, Jesus, Mary, and the saints interceded on behalf of Christians for their protection and salvation.[14]

When European crusaders looted the imperial city of Constantinople for its gold, silver, and relics in 1204, they also stole icons. Under the profound impact of these powerful images from the East, devotional images also developed in the West. A century after the sack of Constantinople, an Italian commentator such as Giordana da Rivalto revered the pictures from Greece in which the saints "are depicted exactly as they appeared in real life." Referring to a picture of Jesus on the cross painted by Nicodemus, who had been present at the crucifixion, and the portrait of the Virgin Mary painted by Luke the Evangelist, Giordana da Rivalto concluded that "the old images imported from Greece long ago possess the greatest possible authority and as proof are just as compelling as

Scripture." In both the East and the West, therefore, the authority of Christianity was reinforced by both holy scriptures and holy pictures. In supervising the architecture, sculptures, stained-glass windows, and other magnificent artworks of the Gothic cathedral dedicated to St. Dionysius in Paris, Abbot Suger had inscribed on the door, "The dull mind rises to truth through that which is material."[15]

HOST

As the body of Christ that appeared in the church, the eucharistic bread could be regarded as both the supreme relic and the supreme icon of Christianity. However, the Host was also food. Celebrated as heavenly flesh, the consecrated bread was eaten for spiritual nourishment. In both East and West, mainstream theologians insisted that the body of Christ was actually present in the Eucharist, but theologians in medieval Europe particularly insisted on the physical, carnal, or fleshly character of that presence. The ninth-century theologian Paschasius Radbertus, for example, held that the bread and wine of the Eucharist changed at the priestly words of consecration into exactly the same body that Christ had received from the Virgin Mary. By eating the consecrated bread of the Eucharist, he insisted, Christians were actually consuming the very same flesh of Jesus that had been born in first-century Bethlehem. This fleshly, physical, or material understanding of the consecrated bread and wine continued to inform the spirituality of the Eucharist.

During the eleventh century, however, the theologian Berengar of Tours (d. 1088) proposed a less materialist understanding of the Eucharist. "A portion of the flesh of Christ cannot be present on the altar," he argued, "unless the body of Christ in heaven is cut up and a particle that has been cut off from it is sent down to the altar." In the face of this physical impossibility, Berengar proposed that Jesus Christ could only be said to be spiritually present. However, this symbolic interpretation of the Eucharist exposed Berengar to accusations of heresy. Forced to renounce his position, Berengar finally agreed to support an explicitly carnal understanding of the Eucharist. As he was required to confess, "The bread and wine which are placed on the altar are after consecration not only a sacrament, but also the real body and blood of our Lord Jesus Christ." Bread and wine, therefore, became body and blood in the Eucharist not merely as a sign or symbol of Christ, but as a reality. Emphasizing the physical character of that reality, Berengar was required to conclude that in the Eucharist the actual body of Jesus Christ was "taken and broken by the hands of the priest and crushed by the teeth of the faithful." By breaking, crushing, grinding, and chewing the flesh of Jesus Christ with their teeth, therefore, Christians ate God.[16]

At the Fourth Lateran Council, in 1215, the Roman Catholic Church affirmed the physical presence of Christ in the Eucharist. Observing that no salvation was possible outside of the universal church in which Jesus Christ was both priest and sacrifice, the council stated that "his body and blood are really contained in the sacrament of the altar under the species of bread and wine." In affirming the reality of the body and blood on the altar, the council used a term, "transubstantiation," that would be developed by medieval scholars, following the lead of Thomas Aquinas, into a theory of the Eucharist. According to this theory, the external appearance of bread and wine remained unchanged, but their substance, essence, or underlying reality was transformed into the body and blood of Christ. Therefore, although the bread and wine might still look, smell, or taste the same, their substance had been changed. Although this theory of transubstantiation, with its scholarly precision and logical distinctions, became the official doctrine of the Eucharist within the Roman Catholic Church, other European theologians insisted that the mystery of the Eucharist was simply beyond rational understanding. As Hugh of St. Victor had insisted:

> Here is a marvel indeed. The flesh that is eaten below remains whole in the heavens. Why do you start up with your logic, dialectician? What do you think of this, sophist? Why are you seeking arguments? That would be to sprinkle dust on the stars. Your logic does not reach so high.

Whether this mystery could be rationally comprehended or not, the denial that Christ's body really became holy food on the altar was regarded as the defining feature of heresy. According to Hildegard of Bingen, heretics "deny the most holy humanity of the Son of God and the sanctity of the body and blood which are in the offering of bread and wine."[17]

Beyond the direct control of church councils, scholars, or heretic hunters, the eucharistic Host functioned in popular religious beliefs and practices as holy food, relic, and icon. Miraculous stories related how on rare occasions the Host had actually turned into bleeding flesh. According to one story, a certain priest doubted the presence of Christ in the Eucharist. While he was performing the Mass, however, "the Lord showed him raw flesh in the Host." In other stories, priests beheld a sacrificial lamb, the crucified Christ, or the infant Jesus miraculously appearing in the Host. According to his biographer, Bishop Hugh of Lincoln (ca. 1140–1200) often saw the appearance of a beautiful child in the eucharistic bread he held between his hands when he performed the Mass. Although an avid collector of relics, Hugh of Lincoln maintained that the holy relics diminished in significance before the miracle of the Mass. Although relics might contain minute fragments of divinity, Hugh argued, the consecrated Host held the entire divinity of Jesus Christ.

Hugh's attitude toward relics was dramatically demonstrated on a visit to the monastery of Fécamp in northern France, which had preserved an arm of Mary Magdalene. Wanting to take a piece of the arm, but finding it difficult to cut with a knife, Hugh chewed off some of the bone with his teeth. When the monks of Fécamp angrily objected, Hugh explained, "If a little while ago I handled the most sacred body of the Lord of all the saints with my fingers, in spite of my unworthiness, and when I partook of it, touched it with my lips and teeth, why should I not venture to treat in the same way the bones of saints?" Accustomed to eating the body of God, therefore, Hugh of Lincoln saw no problem in chewing on the bones of saints.[18]

These visions of physical flesh and blood in the Eucharist supported the development of what might be called the spirituality of eating God. For the thirteenth-century poet Mechthild of Magdeburg (ca. 1207–ca. 1294), for example, the ritual of the Eucharist and the spiritual experience of ecstasy could both be described as "eating God." "Yet I, least of all souls," Mechthild wrote, "take Him in my hand, eat Him and drink Him, and do with Him what I will!" Similarly, writing between 1220 and 1240, the Flemish poet Hadewijch proposed that the closest union with God was achieved by eating and being eaten. "Love's most intimate union is through eating, tasting, and seeing interiorly," Hadewijch proposed. "He eats us; we think we eat him, and we do eat him, of this we can be certain." In this spirituality of eating God, the Eucharist provided a model for a style of religious experience that was both intensely personal and universal. Directed toward the universal sanctity of Jesus Christ or the Virgin Mary, rather than to a local saint, relic, or icon, this new style of spirituality corresponded to changing medieval attitudes toward the Host.[19]

During the thirteenth century, the eucharistic Host clearly emerged as the supreme relic. In declaring that every particle of the Host contained the entire body of Christ, the Fourth Lateran Council (1215) prohibited the practice of taking pieces of the consecrated bread out of the church. Apparently, the council wanted to prevent people from treating the Host as if it were like any other relic, a sacred object of power that could be used for healing, protection, or personal devotion. Nevertheless, popular accounts of miracles performed by the Host suggest that it was used as a relic. At the same time, however, with the increasing importance of the elevation of the Host in the Mass, the Host became the supreme icon. By seeing the Host held up by the priest, Christians beheld God. This visual theophany, or manifestation of God, became the most important moment in the ritual of the Mass. Reportedly, in some towns on Sunday, people ran from church to church, from Mass to Mass, to see as many elevations of the Host as possible. In these popular attitudes toward the Host, therefore, it was not necessary to eat the body of Christ to be in the presence of God.

The increasing importance of the Host as relic and icon resulted in a new annual festival, the Feast of Corpus Christi. Originally a local French development in 1246, this festival devoted to the "body of Christ" was formally established in the Christian sacred calendar by Pope Urban VI in 1389 as a holy period with the same status as Christmas, Easter, Pentecost, and the Assumption. In practice, the festival was distinguished by the public procession of the Host. Placed under a special canopy, the Host was paraded with the cross, relics, holy water, candles, banners, and other sacred regalia. In this procession, the Host was taken from church to church. But it was also carried around the perimeter of the village, town, or city. As the Host blessed the boundaries that enclosed a community, it also reinforced them against any dangers that might come from outside. By celebrating the Host, therefore, the annual procession of the Feast of Corpus Christi marked out a community—a social body—under the protection of the body of Christ. In the midst of increasing social, economic, and occupational differentiation in medieval society, the Feast of Corpus Christi enacted a ritual drama of social unity.

From the Christian social unity defined by the body of Christ, however, Jews in Europe were clearly excluded. According to the twelfth-century abbot of Cluny, Peter the Venerable, Jews might even be excluded from the definition of humanity. "I really do not know whether a Jew is a man," Peter wrote, "given that he does not yield to human reason, nor does he assent to the divine authorities which are his own."[20] Although Jews were outsiders in the Christian community, they nevertheless featured prominently in the central myths and rituals of the Christian tradition. Every time the Mass was performed, Christians were reminded not only that their salvation depended upon the death of Jesus, but that the death of Jesus had been caused by Jews. By the twelfth century, the notion had developed among Christians in Europe that Jews had intentionally killed Jesus Christ. Ignoring the New Testament passage in which Jesus had said of his persecutors, "Forgive them for they know not what they do," Christians began to accuse Jews of premeditated murder. As the consecrated bread of the Eucharist grew in importance as the body of Christ, however, strange stories developed about Jews desecrating the Host to make Christ suffer again. According to widely believed rumors, Jews stole the Host and then proceeded to torture the consecrated bread by stabbing it, pounding it, or throwing it into a fiery oven. After desecrating the body of Christ, they supposedly cast the Host into a river only to find that the water ran red with the blood of Jesus. By the fourteenth century, such impossible stories about Jews ritually torturing and murdering the Host came to be widely believed among European Christians.

Between 1336 and 1339, Christian armies of *Judenschläger,* "Jew killers," exterminated hundreds of Jewish communities in the southern German region of Bavaria. Where Jews had been massacred, Christian clergy and nobles established shrines to the Bleeding Host. As popular pilgrimage sites, especially for knights on horseback, Christian shrines of the Bleeding Host were created throughout Germany on the ruins of Jewish synagogues, urban ghettos, or rural communities. At those shrines, the same kinds of miracles were reported, especially healing cures, that had been attributed to the relics of saints. More powerful than any saint's relic, however, the Bleeding Host conveyed the saving blood of Jesus, which, as Pope Clement VI had declared in 1343, was so potent that one drop was sufficient "to redeem the entire human race." Adding to the infinite saving power of the blood of Jesus Christ, the virtues of Mary and the saints created a Christian "treasury of merit" without limit.[21]

No longer the "Vicar of Peter," but now the "Vicar of Christ," the pope in Rome carried the responsibility of administering the infinite spiritual treasury of the body of Christ, Mary, and the saints. Following the fall of the Latin outpost of Acre in Palestine in 1291, Pope Boniface VIII had proclaimed a Jubilee Year in 1300 that called all Christians to embark not on a crusade to the Holy Land, but on a pilgrimage to Rome that would earn them full or plenary indulgences releasing them from punishment for sins. During 1300, as many as 2 million Christians journeyed to Rome to participate in this sacred exchange of spiritual merit.[22] In the process, Christian redemption was both centralized in the power of the pope in Rome to grant indulgences and universalized in the power of any consecrated Host in any Christian church to convey the saving body and blood of Christ. As the most material of the spiritual resources of Christianity, the sacrificial blood, flesh, and body of Christ might have been controlled by the priesthood of the church, but it also represented the promise that anyone could "taste and see" (Ps. 34:8).

14

Scholars

In Christian ritual, the Bible functioned as a sacred object. The text of the gospels was placed on the altar, kissed by priests, carried in public processions, and used for swearing legal oaths. Like relics, icons, and the eucharistic Host, the Bible was an object of religious power. However, the Bible was also an object that could be read and interpreted. Since most Christians did not have access to the specialized techniques of literacy, the words of the Christian scriptures were not read, but only heard as oral performances within the liturgy. Clergy, monks, and nuns were distinguished by their ability to read the ecclesiastical languages of Greek or Latin, but the Christian laity was generally nonliterate. For the majority of Christians, therefore, scripture was the oral, or spoken, word encountered in ritual. Certainly, being literate was not a prerequisite for being a Christian. According to the New Testament, Jesus and his disciples had not relied upon literacy. In the book of Acts, for example, the disciples Peter and John spoke eloquently before large crowds, even though they were illiterate and *idiotae* (Acts 4). Without benefit of formal education in reading and writing, these "ignorant" disciples of Jesus nevertheless taught Christian wisdom in public. By the twelfth century in the West, however, literacy defined the standard for religious authority. In contrast to a literate clergy, the term *idiotae* was used for lay Christians who knew only how to speak and understand their native tongue, but could not read or write in Latin. Even the illiterate, however, increasingly lived in a culture that was oriented toward the written word, literary texts, official documents, and the authority of the literati, scribes, and scholars.

As noted, reading was an important feature of monastic life. The devotional reading of religious texts—the *lectio divina*—integrated the Bible and patristic writings into the daily rhythm of the monastery. In this ritual context, reading was like prayer. The words of the text were murmured quietly or uttered out loud. Sound, tone, pace, and rhythm were important aspects of devotional reading. By being read aloud, texts were also carefully assimilated. In monastic practice, reading was something to be digested. The words were to be ruminated over like a cow chewing its cud. While vocalizing the words, monastic readers absorbed religious texts into memory. In the process, the practice of devotional reading internalized both the sound and the sense of religious texts in the formation of a personal identity that was shared with others who lived within the same textual community.[1]

In the specialized work of scholars, however, reading was a matter of silent reflection. Replacing oral recitation with the visual contemplation of texts, scholarly reading was private, individual, and solitary. Instead of emphasizing memory and community, the silent reading practiced by scholars stressed critical reason and individual powers of textual interpretation, intellectual argumentation, and convincing persuasion. For guidance in these silent arts of literacy, Christian scholars turned to the ancient sciences of grammar, logic, and rhetoric. As the classical *trivium,* these three disciplines represented the foundation of ancient Greek and Roman education. In simple terms, grammar was the science of reading and writing correctly, logic was the science of rational proof and demonstration, and rhetoric was the science of verbal eloquence and persuasion. For Christian scholars, the ancient sciences of grammar, logic, and rhetoric could be adapted to the requirements of a literacy that was necessary for reading and writing about the Word of God.

As the apostle Paul had observed in the first century, reading and interpreting biblical scripture required distinguishing between the letter and the spirit of the text. In the historical development of Christian biblical scholarship, this distinction between literal and spiritual levels of meaning became standardized in reading the Bible. Gregory the Great, for example, distinguished the literal or historical meaning of biblical texts from their spiritual significance for the Christian church or for the individual Christian soul. According to Gregory, reading biblical texts spiritually meant discerning the allegorical references to the church and the tropological references to moral guidance for the soul. Although the literal sense of a biblical text might refer to historical events in ancient Israel, a scholar could nevertheless uncover spiritual messages hidden in the Bible for Christians in the present.

By the eleventh century, this method of reading the Bible had become formalized as the fourfold method of biblical interpretation. According to Guibert of Nogent:

> The first is history, which speaks of actual events as they occurred; the second is allegory, in which one thing stands for something else; the third is tropology, or moral instruction, which treats of the ordering and arranging of one's life; and the last is ascetics, or spiritual enlightenment, through which we who are about to treat of lofty and heavenly topics are led to a higher way of life.

In illustrating these four levels of scripture, Guibert cited the standard example of the word "Jerusalem." On the literal or historical level, "Jerusalem" referred to a specific city in Palestine. Spiritually, however, the same word could be read as referring to the church, the soul, and the mystical or anagogic destiny of Christians in the heavenly kingdom of God. Although the biblical term "Jerusalem" literally referred to a historical city, as Guibert explained, "in allegory it represents the holy Church; tropologically or morally, it is the soul of every faithful man who longs for the vision of eternal peace; and anagogically it refers to the life of the heavenly citizens, who already see the God of Gods, revealed in all his glory in Zion." In this fourfold method of biblical interpretation, the literal meaning of any passage of the Bible could be related to the church, the soul, or the ultimate destiny of Christians. The literal words of the Bible operated as points of departure for elaborating spiritual commentaries, extensions, and applications deemed to be relevant for Christians.[2]

At the same time, however, Christian scholars were interested in establishing reliable terms for adjudicating the literal, factual, or essential truth of Christianity. Following Paul's distinction between the spirit and the letter, the sixth-century author of the texts ascribed to Dionysius the Areopagite asserted that biblical tradition had both its mystical and its literal dimensions. According to Dionysius, the "tradition has a dual aspect, the ineffable and mysterious on the one hand, the open and more evident on the other. The one resorts to symbolism and involves initiation. The other is philosophic and employs the method of demonstration."[3] Although the fourfold method of biblical interpretation might have effectively entered the mysteries of Christian symbolism, a different method was necessary for the open, evident, and philosophical demonstration of

Christian truth. As masters of literacy, Christian scholars used the ancient sciences of grammar, logic, and rhetoric as methods for assessing the truth of Christianity. Although they generally accepted the spiritual truth of Christian revelation, Christian scholars sought to work out the terms and conditions of establishing the literal truth of Christian claims on reality.

SETTING CHRIST ASIDE

Anselm of Canterbury (1033–1109) was a Benedictine monk who served as prior and abbot of the Norman monastery of Bec in England. Elevated as archbishop of Canterbury in 1093, Anselm played an active role in church politics. Coming into conflict with English kings over the ownership of church property, the investiture of bishops, and other issues of church and state, Anselm spent much of his tenure as archbishop in exile. Gaining the favor of the pope, however, he spent many years of that exile in Rome. As part of the Roman delegation, Anselm was a leading participant at the Council of Bari, which negotiated Western church policy toward the Byzantines in the wake of the schism in 1054 between the Greek and Roman churches. In the midst of all these responsibilities, however, he was a prolific author on matters of Christian faith. In keeping with the Augustinian tradition, he wrote in the service of *fides quaerens intellectum,* "faith seeking understanding," in his efforts to provide rational grounds for Christian beliefs. Explaining the nature of his enterprise, Anselm described himself as "one who strives to lift his mind to the contemplation of God, and seeks to understand what he believes." Rational understanding, however, required a method of inquiry that in principle set aside biblical revelation. Anselm claimed to have developed a method of reasoning that proceeded "as if nothing were known about Christ." Although ostensibly setting aside the faith of biblical authority, this method nevertheless concentrated on providing rational arguments for basic doctrines of Christian faith.

In the text of his *Monologion,* prepared around 1077, Anselm provided an extended meditation on the rationale for holding basic tenets of the Christian faith. Beginning with four chapters on the existence of God, he proposed three rational arguments designed to prove that God exists. First, observing relative degrees of goodness in a world in which some things are better than others, he concluded that there must be some absolute good that sets the supreme standard for goodness. Second, noting that everything in the world was caused by something to come into existence, he concluded that there must be a supreme cause that was originally responsible for causing everything to exist. Third, maintaining that finite beings in the world are more or less perfect, he concluded that there must be an infinitely perfect being that is superior to all beings in perfection. At the end of each argument, Anselm wanted Christians to understand that this is what they meant when they used the word "God." For a Christian with faith seeking understanding, these rational arguments were designed to clarify that the term "God" meant the highest good, the original cause, and the infinite perfection. Beginning with such definitions, Anselm developed a kind of grammar of faith for reasoning about the existence, nature, and activity of God in the world.

Two years later, Anselm produced a sequel to the *Monologion* that presented a new argument for the existence of God. In the first four chapters of that text, the *Proslogion,* he introduced a rational proof that did not depend upon drawing conclusions from things, like goodness, causation, or degrees of perfection, that could be observed in the natural world. Instead, his new argument was based solely on analyzing the meaning of words. Anyone who uses the word "God," Anselm proposed, must understand that term to mean "that than which nothing greater can be conceived." By definition, the term "God" refers to the greatest that can be thought, conceptualized, or imagined. Even the fool who says, "There is no God" (Ps. 14:1) can understand that the phrase "that than which nothing greater can be conceived" refers to God. As a result, that phrase exists in his understanding. However, Anselm argued, if it only existed in the understanding, it would then not be "that than which nothing greater can be conceived" because a greater could be imagined that exists both in the understanding and in reality. In order to avoid this contradiction, "that than which nothing greater can be conceived" must exist not only in the understanding, but also in reality. Therefore, Anselm concluded, God must exist in reality.

Anselm's proof for the existence of God, which later came to be known as the ontological argument, was attacked by other Christian scholars. The French monk Gaunilo even rose to the defense of the fool by insisting that Anselm could not make such a leap from the existence of something in the understanding to its existence in reality. For example, Gaunilo observed that when we imagine a perfect island, it might be said to exist in our understanding. Even if we admit that it would be better for that perfect island to exist both in our understanding and in reality, we have no reason to conclude that it therefore must exist in reality. In response, Anselm insisted that he was not talking about perfect things like a perfect island, but about perfection itself. Accordingly, his argument only applied to this one case—"that than which nothing greater can be conceived"— which Christians understood as God. Everything else, he acknowledged, could be imagined not to exist. Only the existence of God, when properly understood as "that than which nothing greater can be conceived," was impossible to think of as not existing.[4]

Subsequent Christian thinkers were divided over the validity of Anselm's argument. During the thirteenth-century expansion of academic theology in Europe, the Franciscan Bonaventure adopted it, while the Dominican Thomas Aquinas rejected it. More influential than his argument for the existence of God, however, was Anselm's rethinking of why God became a human being in the person of Jesus Christ. In his book on why God became man, *Cur Deus Homo,* Anselm again tried to proceed on the basis of rational arguments "as if nothing were known about Christ." On the basis of his definition of God as the highest good, the original cause, and infinite perfection, Anselm felt that he could logically establish the necessity of God becoming human. His argument revised conventional Christian understandings of the role of the life, suffering, and death of Christ in the economy of salvation. By many accounts, the death of Jesus Christ was a payment made to the devil to ransom human beings from the damnation they deserved as a result of original sin. Taking the devil out of the equation, however, Anselm proposed that the death of Jesus Christ was actually a payment to God. In his *Cur Deus Homo,* Anselm worked out new terms for understanding the logical necessity of such a payment.

In turning against God through their disobedience, Anselm proposed, the original human beings had incurred an enormous debt to God. In fact, because the divine honor they had offended by their disobedience was infinite, their indebtedness was infinite. As finite, limited, and temporal beings, however, they were actually incapable of making the necessary restitution. Even by living a perfect life of obedience, human beings were only able to give God what they owed for their own personal lives and therefore could not begin to make payments on the infinite debt incurred by their original ancestors. According to Anselm, therefore, human beings were bound to pay a debt to God that they could never pay. Only a divine being who was

infinite would ever be able to make that payment. Therefore, Anselm concluded, the logic, economy, and history of salvation required a God-Man.
As a being who was simultaneously human and divine, the God-Man
would pay the debt on behalf of his humanity because he was actually
capable of paying the debt on account of his divinity.

Like other human beings, however, the God-Man would find that his
virtuous, sinless, and even perfect life was not sufficient to pay the debt.
To pay the infinite debt of humanity, the God-Man could not merely balance his own personal account. He had to give something beyond the
scope of the ordinary goods and services that any human being owed to
God. For the God-Man, that payment was death. Assuming that he lived
a sinless life, the God-Man would not have had to undergo death, "the
wages of sin." By giving himself to death, however, the God-Man paid
back the original debt through a surplus that was not required of him personally, but that benefited all humanity. In Anselm's account, therefore,
the Christian faith that God had become human was invested with a kind
of logical necessity. Since humans had to pay an infinite debt that only an
infinite God was capable of paying, a God-Man was logically required to
pay something—his death—that was human but was also of infinite value
because it was beyond what was owed by any human being who had ever
lived. By setting Christ aside, therefore, Anselm arrived at the logical
necessity of Christ.[5]

Anselm's account of why God became man profoundly affected the
development of Christian theology in the Latin West. Although he imagined that the power of his rational arguments was derived from setting
Christ aside, by pretending as if "nothing were known about Christ," the
impact of his arguments in *Cur Deus Homo* seemed most attractive to
other Christian scholars because they set the devil aside. By implicitly
denying any claim the devil might have on humanity, Anselm presented a
self-contained Christian economy of salvation based solely on relations
among God, human beings, and the divine-human being who was incarnated as Jesus Christ. Certainly, the Christian economy of salvation that
Anselm outlined was consistent with the feudal relations of honor and
shame, service and obedience, lifelong debt and perpetual payment that
had been established in the economy of Europe. Nevertheless, Anselm
remained interested in clarifying a grammar of faith. He wanted to work
out a rationale in which the basic terms of Christian faith—God, man,
and God-Man—could be meaningful for both faith and reason.

As a result of Anselm's abiding concern with the grammar of faith, he sought to define Christian terms not only for understanding the God-Man, but also for understanding the God-Woman. In his *Monologion*, Anselm wondered "whether it is more fitting to call them father and son than to call them mother and daughter." Setting aside the authority of the Bible, which referred to God and Christ as masculine, how could Christians rationally respond to this question? Why should God and Christ not be female?

In wrestling with this question of divine gender, Anselm revealed the basic workings of his theological method by first referring to principles of grammar. In Latin grammar, he observed, both God and Christ are *Spiritus,* which is a masculine noun. Certainly, Anselm's observation about Latin grammar raised other profound theological questions, not least of which was the notion that the Holy Spirit proceeded from both the Father and the Son. In the West, that assumption was embodied in the alteration of the creed—the notorious *filioque* clause, which affirmed that the Spirit issued from Father and Son—but it was adamantly rejected in the East. Although the issue of the Holy Spirit proceeding from both the Father and the Son had divided Christendom, Anselm casually alluded to the controversy by treating it as a simple matter of Latin grammar in which the masculine noun, *Spiritus,* necessarily linked the third Person of the Trinity with the first and second in a common masculinity. In this unity of grammatical gender, Anselm proposed, God and Christ had to be understood as masculine.

By relying on grammar alone, however, Anselm had to face the problem that sometimes God and Christ could be referred to by such Latin terms as truth *(veritas)* or wisdom *(sapientia),* which grammatically were feminine nouns. Perhaps, he reflected, Christians should adopt the terms "Goddess" and "Daughter" in the place of "Father" and "Son" when speaking about the persons of the Trinity. Resisting this conclusion, however, Anselm shifted from the science of grammar to other sources of scientific knowledge that might support rational reflection on the truths of Christian faith. Looking to biological sciences for inspiration, Anselm observed the "natural fact" that in most instances the male was superior, larger, and stronger than the female in the animal kingdom. Even in the natural sciences, however, he found contradictory evidence, because in some species "the contrary is true, as among certain kinds of birds, among which the female is always larger and stronger, while the male is smaller

and weaker." Like the science of grammar, therefore, the scientific investigation of the natural world did not provide Anselm with a solid foundation for resolving the question about the gender of the Christian divinity.

In the end, Anselm asserted that the masculinity of the Trinity was a
fundamental Christian truth on the basis of his understanding of human
biological reproduction. Assuming that the male seed was the cause of
human reproduction, he asserted that it was appropriate to call the cause
of everything "Father." As Anselm explained, "It is more consistent to call
the supreme Spirit father than mother, for this reason, that the first and
principal cause of offspring is always the father." On the basis of another
assumption about human biological reproduction, he asserted that sons
rather than daughters always bear a greater likeness to their fathers. "If
the son is always more like the father than is the daughter," Anselm proposed, "nothing is more like the supreme Father than his offspring."
Therefore, he concluded, "It is most true that this offspring is not a
daughter but a Son." Out of these rational, grammatical, and scientific
deliberations, therefore, Anselm felt that he had reinforced the Christian
practice of referring to God as male.[6]

Although this question of the gender of God was not Anselm's major
concern, it did reveal his basic theological method. Setting aside the biblical authority that had clearly revealed God and Christ as masculine, he
was willing to consider other reasons. As his preferred method of reasoning, the science of grammar provided an intellectual discipline for defining
terms, using terms, and clarifying the implication of terms. When grammar failed to settle an argument, however, he turned to the natural sciences. Although his observations about the natural world and biological
reproduction were certainly limited, they nevertheless represented new
grounds for questioning the truth of basic assertions of Christian faith.

YES AND NO

While Anselm of Canterbury sought to clarify the grammar of faith, the
most controversial scholar of twelfth-century Europe, Peter Abélard
(1079–1142), employed the tools of philosophical analysis to investigate
the logic of faith. Born in Brittany in a noble family, Abélard renounced
the status of knighthood for the life of a scholar. Having studied with the
most eminent philosophers and theologians of his day, he rejected all of
their methods and conclusions and established himself as an independent

master in Paris. As he admitted years later, Abélard came to regard himself as "the only philosopher remaining in the world."[7] Attracting students from all over Europe, Abélard also became entangled in a personal scandal through a love affair with a young student, Héloïse. Although they secretly married and had a child, Héloïse's family felt that it had been dishonored by this relationship. Her relatives avenged that dishonor one night by leading a crowd to attack and castrate Abélard. After his mutilation, Abélard retreated to the abbey of St.-Denis in Paris, and Héloïse entered a convent, eventually assuming the leadership of a community of women dedicated to the Holy Spirit. Maintaining a regular correspondence for the rest of their lives, Abélard and Héloïse consulted each other on the spiritual, educational, and disciplinary life of this religious community, the community of the Paraclete.

Recovering from his wounds at St.-Denis, Abélard embarked upon philosophical investigations that led to new scandals. Clearly, he had not lost his intellectual combativeness, because he was soon arguing with his hosts at the abbey that their St. Denis of Paris could not possibly have been the same historical person as St. Dionysius the Areopagite. However, it was in the field of theological combat that Abélard created controversy. Applying the discipline of logic to Christian faith, he set out to analyze the received authority of patristic writings. The first product of this research was a book entitled *Sic et Non—Yes and No*—in which Abélard collected statements from ancient Christian authorities that apparently contradicted each other on questions of doctrine. Identifying 158 doctrinal questions, Abélard simply juxtaposed direct quotations from ancient authorities who had answered affirmatively with those who had answered negatively. By focusing on these contradictions, Abélard challenged the assumption that there was an underlying consensus among the early fathers of the church. Although he proposed methods for determining if the contradictions he had uncovered were real, such as establishing whether two authors used different words to convey the same sense, Abélard left the abiding impression that the ancient authorities of Christianity did not agree with each other on basic questions of faith.

By his own account, Abélard hoped to use the research gathered in *Sic et Non* to develop new methods of biblical interpretation and logical analysis for reconciling the contradictions that appeared in the ancient authorities of the church. As he worked out those methods in numerous books, however, he produced results that some of his contemporaries saw as dangerous innovations. For example, in denying the transmission of original sin from Adam to all humanity, Abélard proposed that Jesus Christ did not die to ransom human beings from the devil or to make a payment to God. Rather, Jesus Christ lived as the embodiment of perfect love in order to set a moral example for humanity to follow. Although he argued that this conclusion was derived from the authority of the Bible and the logic of faith, Abélard was nevertheless attacked and condemned as a heretic. Leading the campaign against the "new theologian," the church leader, crusader, and mystic Bernard of Clairvaux declared that Abélard had to be condemned because he "corrupts the integrity of the faith and the chastity of the church. He oversteps the landmarks placed by our Fathers in discussing and writing about the faith, the sacraments, and the Holy Trinity." According to Bernard, "He is a man who does not know his own limitations, making void the virtue of the cross by the cleverness of his words."[8] In 1141 Bernard arranged for a synod of bishops to issue a formal condemnation of Abélard and his teachings. Given refuge in the Cluniac monastery of Peter the Venerable, Abélard wrote one final book, a confession of faith, and died the following year.

Although he was rejected by the church, Peter Abélard introduced methods of theological inquiry that had a lasting effect on Christian scholarship in the Latin West, especially in a new institution, the university. Anticipated in Italy in the 1150s, universities were established throughout Europe during the thirteenth century. They emerged as vibrant centers of learning in Paris, Rome, Bologna, Oxford, Cambridge, and elsewhere. Universities generally supported the kind of intellectual inquiry that Abélard had pioneered. Certain developments, however, he would not necessarily have anticipated.

University education in theology called for textbooks that summarized and synthesized basic Christian doctrine. Adapting material from Abélard, the most popular textbook, the *Four Books of Sentences,* was compiled around 1150 by Peter Lombard (d. 1160), who briefly served as bishop of Paris. In Peter Lombard's *Sentences,* basic Christian teachings were collected about God, Christ, the Holy Spirit, creation, angels, humanity, sin, redemption, sacraments, and eschatology. For nearly four hundred years, the *Sentences* was used as the basic introductory text for theological studies. Although this textbook provided a summary of Christian doctrines, it also raised questions for logical investigation, philosophical argumentation, and theological disputation. In other words, like Abélard, the scholars within the new universities found that the "sentences" could also be challenged. In the new intellectual environment of the universities, these challenges were formulated in terms of academic procedures that came to be known as Scholasticism.

As a broad intellectual trend, Scholasticism represented a range of critical methods in the science of logic devoted to the analysis and demonstration of the truth of propositions. Commonly referred to as *dialectics,* these logical methods, which were derived from ancient Greek philosophy, investigated the validity of truth claims. For example, the logical syllogism—"If Socrates is human and all humans are mortal, then Socrates is mortal"—was a simple but basic method for establishing truth. In the dialectical method employed by Abélard, the search for truth was guided by principles of logic particularly associated with the work of the Greek philosopher Aristotle. During the thirteenth century, however, scholars in the Latin West were increasingly exposed to a broader range of ancient texts by Aristotle, not only on the science of logic, but also on the science of nature (physics), the science of reality (metaphysics), and the science of knowledge (epistemology). In the process of discovering these ancient intellectual resources for the first time, scholars in the universities of the Latin West came to refer to Aristotle simply as "the philosopher."

This discovery of Aristotle by Christian scholars in Europe was facilitated by an extraordinary interreligious exchange. Although European Christians had generally lost track of these ancient Greek texts, they had been preserved by Muslim scholars in Arabic translations. Stimulating significant developments within Islamic philosophy and science, the texts of Aristotle were translated, commented upon, and adapted by Muslim scholars. Before the rise of universities in Europe, the Muslim university in Baghdad had emerged as an important center of learning. Prior to the emergence of a university-based class of Christian philosophers, experts in Muslim philosophy—*falsafah*—were in conversation with ancient Greek philosophy. Not merely translating or transmitting the texts of Aristotle, these Muslim philosophers became international experts in Aristotelian thought. Although they wrote in Arabic, Muslim theologians, especially Ibn Sina (980–1037) and Ibn Rushd (1126–98), known in the Latin West as Avicenna and Averroës, were regarded in Christian Europe as philosophical authorities. At the same time, Jewish philosophy, most prominently developed in the work of Mosheh ben Maimon (ca. 1135–1204), known as Maimonides, sought to adapt Aristotle to the demands of faith.

During the thirteenth century, therefore, if Christian theology was to be reconciled with philosophy, it had to come to terms with the Aristotelian philosophy that was being developed by Muslim and Jewish philosophers.

In their theological method, Scholastics posed their inquiries, like Abélard, in terms of "yes" and "no." They tended to resolve contradictions, however, not only by trying to reconcile biblical or patristic authorities, but also by invoking the philosophical authority of Aristotle. The influential Dominican theologian Albert (ca. 1200–1280), for example, who was so renowned for his mastery of Aristotelian logic, ethics, politics, physics, and metaphysics that he was commonly referred to as Albert the Great, used the Scholastic method of weighing the relative merits of "yes" against "no."

For instance, in considering the question of the gender of Christ, which had been raised by Anselm, Albert the Great asked whether Christ ought to have assumed humanity in the female sex. On the positive side, he cited three reasons why Christ ought to have been a woman: first, since death had entered the world through a woman, Eve, eternal life should have come into the world through a woman, Christ. Second, since the second Person of the Trinity is wisdom—*sapientia*—this feminine noun suggests that Christ should have been a woman. Third, because Christ performs the maternal role of "giving birth" to human beings in their new life of salvation, Christ should have been a woman.

On the negative side, however, Albert countered these propositions with three arguments. First, although Christ certainly performs the maternal role of giving new life, Christ is also the head of the church, which according to biblical authority is not a role fit for women, since women are instructed by Paul to remain silent in church. Therefore, Christ had to be male. Second, although "wisdom" is a feminine noun, this grammatical consideration must give way before the science of Aristotle. According to Aristotle, a woman is a defective man. Since Christ ought to represent spiritual perfection rather than natural imperfection, Christ had to be male. Third, although recalling that death had entered the world through a woman, Albert noted that God had produced Eve as a woman through a man without a woman. In overcoming death, God had to reverse that process by producing Christ as a man through a woman without a man. Therefore, instead of being born as a female like Eve, Christ had to be a male born of a virgin who had never known a man.[9]

In this demonstration of Scholastic method, Albert the Great showed how thirteenth-century Christian scholars could reason about questions of faith by drawing on a combination of biblical authority, Aristotelian science, and their own speculations about what was logically fitting. Although the works of the philosopher could be invoked to establish scientific "facts," such as the mysogynistic definition of women as defective males, Aristotle also provided an entire philosophical system that formed the basis for Scholastic thought. While trying to establish philosophical clarity, however, Scholastics could not entirely avoid the ambiguities of a biblical tradition that spoke in at least four voices—literal, allegorical, moral, and anagogical. Furthermore, while working out a logic of faith, Scholastics often made assertions based less on logic than on rhetoric, poetics, or aesthetics. For example, when Albert the Great decided that it was more "fitting" that the birth of Christ should reverse rather than correspond to the birth of Eve, his decision had less to do with logic than with an aesthetic judgment about what should "fit" within the drama of Christianity. Christian scholars, therefore, were faced with the challenge of making sense out of both the philosophy and the poetry of their religious tradition.

PHILOSOPHY AND POETRY

Emerging as the supreme master of Scholasticism, Thomas Aquinas (1225–74) elaborated an Aristotelian science of theology. Born in southern Italy, Thomas rejected the career in law his parents had planned for him in order to join the Dominicans. Although his relatives kidnapped him and held him captive to get him to change his mind, the young man insisted on pursuing the religious life. Developing as a master teacher, eventually at the University of Paris, Aquinas was a prolific author of books of patristic commentary, philosophical reflection, and systematic theology. The most influential of his many works was the monumental survey of Christian theology, the *Summa Theologiae,* which developed the Scholastic method. Guided by the Bible, the church fathers, especially Augustine and Dionysius, and a thorough grounding in the philosophy of Aristotle, the *Summa Theologiae* became the standard compendium of Christian Scholasticism.

Like Anselm, Thomas Aquinas tried to establish rational proofs for the existence of God. Asking, "Is there a God?" he proceeded to consider arguments for answering that question with "no." First, if God is supposed to be limitless good, then the presence of evil in the world entails that God does not exist. Second, if everything in the world can be explained by natural causes, then there is no reason to suppose that God exists. However, Aquinas cited biblical authority to recall that the Christian scriptures presented a God that exists, a God who declares, "I am who I am" (Exod. 3:14). In turning from "no" to "yes" in answer to the question "Is there a God?" Aquinas proposed that there were five ways of proving the existence of God. As he laid out these five proofs, Aquinas illustrated how much his method of reasoning depended upon integrating the philosophy of Aristotle into Christian theology.

First, we can observe that everything in the world is changing. In Aristotle's terms, change is the transition from potentiality to actuality. For example, water has the potential to become hot, but it actualizes that potential when it is heated by something else that is actually hot. All change, according to Aristotle, involves such a transition from the potential to the actual. However, there must be some original mover at the start of this whole process of change. There must be some pure actuality that has brought the potentiality of everything into existence. As Aquinas concluded, that unmoved mover, or pure actuality, is precisely what Christians understand by "God."

Second, we can observe that everything in the world is caused by something else. According to Aristotle, everything is an effect of some cause. In the natural series of causes and effects, however, there must be a first cause that itself was not caused by anything else. Otherwise, the causal series would regress to infinity. Concluding that there must have been an efficient cause at the beginning of the entire series of causation, Aquinas maintained that the original cause of everything is known by Christians as "God."

Third, we can observe that everything in the world is dependent for its existence on something else. As a result, things in the world are contingent on the existence of other things. However, there must be something that is not contingent but necessary, that is dependent on nothing else but itself for its existence. That original necessary being, Aquinas held, is what Christians call "God."

Fourth, we can observe that everything in the world is more or less perfect. Since we know that some things are more perfect, true, or noble than others, we have to assume that there is an absolute standard of perfection, truth, and nobility. Anselm was content to identify that standard of per-

fection as God, but Aquinas brought Aristotle into the discussion to identify perfection not merely as a standard, but also as a cause. According to
Aristotle's philosophy, everything has four causes—an efficient cause that
puts it in motion, a material cause that gives it distinctive characteristics,
a formal cause that defines its ideal shape, and a final cause that directs it
toward a specific goal or end. Using Aristotle's terms, Aquinas could identify perfection as a formal cause. As Aristotle had observed, fire, the
hottest of all things, is a formal cause that causes all other things to be
more or less hot. Accordingly, Aquinas concluded, the absolute perfection
that Christians call "God" must exist as the formal, ideal, or essential
cause that makes things in the world to be more or less perfect, good, true,
or noble.

Fifth, we can observe that everything in the world tends toward some
goal or end. Like an arrow launched by an archer, everything is on a trajectory toward a destination. In Aristotle's terms, the final cause of any
process of change is its goal, end, or *telos*. By developing this principle
into a teleological argument, Aquinas proposed that God was the
supreme cause not only at the beginning, but also at the end of the world.
Since the order, design, or goal-oriented behavior of the universe could
not have happened by accident, there must be some intelligence guiding
things toward their ends. As Aquinas concluded, that guiding intelligence
is what Christians understand by "God."

In all of these five proofs for the existence of God, Thomas Aquinas
began with things that could be observed in the natural world. His observations, however, were clearly guided by the philosophy of Aristotle.
Noticing relations of cause and effect in the world, for example, he analyzed those relations according to the four types of causes that had been
identified by Aristotle. In the end, however, Aquinas was only able to
answer his first argument that God does not exist—because of the existence of evil—by bringing in the authority of Augustine to support
Aristotle. "Since God is supremely good," Augustine had proposed, "he
would not permit any evil at all in his works, unless he were sufficiently
almighty and good to bring good even from evil." By this logic of faith,
therefore, the limitless goodness of God was actually confirmed by the
fact that God allowed evil in the world in order to draw out the good. In
working out a thirteenth-century synthesis of faith and reason, therefore,
Aquinas relied as much on Augustine as he did on Aristotle to establish
Christian doctrine.[10]

Although Thomas Aquinas frequently quoted the writings of Augustine, the Aristotelian theologian also consistently cited the works of the Neoplatonist Dionysius the Areopagite to clarify the logic of Christian teachings. On many occasions, Aquinas invoked the distinction that Dionysius had drawn between two aspects of Christian tradition, "the ineffable and mysterious on the one hand, the open and more evident on the other." Although primarily concerned with demonstrating the open and evident truth of Christian doctrine, Aquinas also recognized that the mysteries of faith were both revealed and disguised in poetic figures of speech. According to Aquinas, "holy Scripture delivers spiritual things to us beneath metaphors taken from bodily things." In metaphoric terms, the Bible depicted God the Father as embodied—as speaking, displaying anger, placing Christ at his right hand, and so on—when God was actually beyond such bodily characteristics. Theology uses metaphors, as Aquinas quoted Dionysius, because the "divine rays cannot enlighten us except wrapped up in many sacred veils." Although Christians could see through the metaphoric veils to behold the truth, the truth was at the same time protected by these metaphors from being penetrated by those who were unworthy. Therefore, although philosophy gave Christians tools to demonstrate sacred doctrine openly, poetry provided metaphoric figures of speech that both revealed and concealed the sacred mysteries of Christianity.[11]

A century after Thomas Aquinas, the Italian poet, storyteller, and literary commentator Giovanni Boccaccio (1313–75) explored these themes in an essay, "On Poetry and Theology." He noted that the Christian scriptures employed poetic fictions in describing Christ as a lamb or a lion, a serpent or a dragon, or the rock of the church. In the appearance of such figures of speech throughout the New Testament gospels, the holy language of theology was thoroughly infused with poetry. Through its use of poetic techniques of metaphor, allegory, and parable, Boccaccio asserted, "theology is nothing less than the poetry of God." At the same time, when addressing sacred subjects, poetry could operate as theology. As Aristotle had maintained, the ancient Greek poets who composed songs about the pagan gods had been the first theologians. The ancient poets provided a model for developing a Christian rhetoric of faith in which theology was poetry and poetry was theology.[12]

The supreme exemplar of Christian poetic theology in the West was the Italian scholar and poet Dante Alighieri (1265–1321). Born in northern

Italy to a family of minor nobility, Dante devoted his early life to studies in literature, poetry, and drawing. Married with four children, he became actively involved in the political life of Florence. After the city was captured by French forces allied with the pope in 1302, Dante spent the rest of his life as an author in exile with the support of patrons in various Italian cities. Although he wrote scholarly treatises on philosophy, language, civil society, and politics, Dante became renowned for his poetry. In the monumental three-volume poetic journey through hell, purgatory, and heaven called the *Divine Comedy*, however, Dante claimed to have produced not merely a work of poetry, but "a sacred song to which both Heaven and Earth have set their hand" (*Paradiso* 25.2–3). According to Dante, the intention of the *Divine Comedy* was "to remove those living in this life from a state of misery, and to bring them to a state of happiness." As poetic theology, therefore, the *Divine Comedy* promised not only aesthetic pleasure, but also a taste of Christian redemption.

As a youth, Dante had written poetry in a new style that merged romantic love with philosophy. In this "sweet new style," the poet exalted a specific woman as the inspiration for both romantic love and sacred devotion. For Dante, this poetic inspiration was derived from Beatrice, a young woman of Florence whose very name suggested to the poet "one who brings blessed joy and salvation." After her death in 1290, Beatrice continued to inspire Dante's poetry, eventually emerging in the *Divine Comedy* as his spiritual guide on a journey through the celestial realms of heaven. In this poetic theology, therefore, a woman such as Beatrice was not denigrated according to Aristotle's formula by being defined as a "defective male." Rather, she was idealized as a divine presence, as a poetic metaphor for divine grace, salvation, the church, and even Christ. As her character was developed in the *Divine Comedy*, Beatrice was both an actual woman and a spiritual allegory for the Christian community, the moral progress of the soul, and the ultimate vision of God in heaven. In this regard, the figure of Beatrice in the *Divine Comedy* demonstrated Dante's contention that the meaning of poetry could be interpreted on four levels—literal, allegorical, moral, and anagogical—just like the theology of the Bible.

According to Dante, Aristotle was the "master among those who know," the "leader of human reason," who had developed a philosophical system that by the fourteenth century could be regarded by Christians in the West as "almost Catholic opinion." In the *Divine Comedy*, however, it was not the Greek philosopher but the Latin poet Virgil who served as Dante's initial guide on his visionary journey into the world beyond death. As the author of the epic poem of ancient Rome, the *Aeneid*, Virgil was an appropriate guide to the underworld, since he had described an afterlife in which "souls are trained with punishment and pay with suffering for old felonies." In the first volume of the *Divine Comedy*, the *Inferno*, Virgil led Dante on an explicitly Christian tour of hell. After visiting Limbo, where virtuous pagans lingered without hope of salvation but also without being otherwise punished or tortured, they descended through nine levels of hell. On each level, they saw the damned being punished. They saw the lustful locked in embrace, the gluttonous wallowing in mire, the greedy rolling huge rocks, the wrathful submerged in a slimy swamp, the heretics confined in fiery tombs, the violent trapped in burning sands, the fraudulent scourged by demons, and the traitors buried in the deepest abyss of hell. At the bottom of hell, they found the supreme traitor—the angel Lucifer, the devil Satan—who had betrayed the original divine order. Ultimately, therefore, sin was revealed in the depths of hell to be a betrayal of God.

In the second volume of the *Divine Comedy*, the *Purgatorio*, Dante was led through an afterlife realm between heaven and hell. Still under the guidance of Virgil, he ascended the mountain of Purgatory, where sinners were both punished and purified. In Dante's visionary journey, the levels of Purgatory were organized according to the standard medieval catalogue of the seven deadly sins—pride, envy, anger, sloth, greed, gluttony, and lust. As Dante proposed, these sins were different forms of what he called "misdirected love," love directed toward the world instead of toward God. Pride, envy, and anger were "perverted love"; the boredom and laziness of sloth were "defective love"; and greed, gluttony, and lust were "excessive love." In Dante's geography of the Christian afterlife, the purpose of Purgatory was to correct these deviant forms of love and redirect human desire toward the love of God.

His final volume, the *Paradiso*, celebrated the divine love that pervaded the universe. Replacing Virgil as his guide, Dante's beloved Beatrice initiated him into the highest celestial spheres. As he looked into her eyes, Dante was enveloped in radiant light, "passing beyond humanity" so he could ascend through the levels of heaven (1.70). Rising above the seven planets, he entered the spheres of the zodiac, the unmoved mover, and the Empyrean, beyond time and space, where God appeared as divine light and love. At the culmination of his visionary journey, Dante realized that his heart had become perfectly synchronized with the divine source of all love. "My desire and will, like a wheel that spins with even motion," he declared, "were revolved by the Love that moves the sun and other stars" (33.143–45).[13]

During the fourteenth century, Dante's poetic accomplishment in the *Divine Comedy* was widely regarded by Italian scholars as an advance in Christian philosophy. "Dante, the theologian," one of his colleagues wrote, was "skilled in every branch of knowledge that philosophy may cherish in her illustrious bosom." In commenting on the *Divine Comedy*, his son observed that Dante was a "glorious theologian, philosopher, and poet."[14] By developing his philosophy through the medium of poetry, however, Dante opened up new possibilities for a Christian rhetoric that combined beauty with sacred truth. In its classical formulation, the science of rhetoric used language to teach, persuade, and please. When poetry turned to divine subjects, its rhetorical capacity for giving pleasure, persuading, and instructing could produce the kind of powerful poetic theology that appeared in the *Divine Comedy*. From this perspective, therefore, Christian truth was best explored not through the sciences of grammar or logic, but through the beautiful rhetoric of the poet.

15

Mystics

According to the Irish monk Columbanus (ca. 543–615), who directed sixth-century Roman Catholic missions into the continent of Europe, the course of a human life proceeds along a path that leads from earth to either heaven or hell. "Here is the way the human being's miserable life runs," he observed. A human life moves "from the earth, on the earth, in the earth, from the earth into the fire, from the fire to judgment, from judgment either to Gehenna or to life." As Columbanus explained, human beings are earthlings. They are made from the earth, walk briefly on the earth, and then are buried in the earth. At the resurrection of the dead, however, human beings will rise from the earth to be tested by fire and judged by God. Based on that Last Judgment, Columbanus promised, "either torture or the kingdom of heaven will be yours forever."[1] By contrast, the sixth-century Greek author who adopted the name of Dionysius the Areopagite developed a different account of the course of a human life. On a trajectory that moves through three ascending stages—purification, illumination, and perfection—a human being can proceed toward union with God. According to Dionysius, therefore, humans are not merely creatures of the earth. They are beings of the heavens.

The spirituality of Dionysius the Areopagite, which was thoroughly informed by the philosophy of Plotinus and other Neoplatonists, has often been identified as one of the major inspirations of Christian mysticism, that broad tradition of Christian beliefs and practices directed toward an immediate, personal, and often intense experience of God. In his *Mystical Theology*, Dionysius began with a prayer invoking some of the central themes that would be developed in the Christian mystical tradition. As Dionysius called upon the Trinity, he prayed:

> Lead us up beyond unknowing and light,
> up to the farthest, highest peak

of mystic scripture,
where the mysteries of God's Word
lie simple, absolute and unchangeable
in the brilliant darkness of a hidden silence.

As this prayer suggests, the journey to God is an ascent to a divine insight that is beyond ordinary ways of knowing. Characteristically, Dionysius described this insight as an entrance into silence or darkness, pointing to the resounding silence of the divine Word and the bright darkness of the divine light. Clearly, in a phrase such as "brilliant darkness," Dionysius tested the limits of language to evoke a divine reality beyond sense perception or mental concepts. Although affirming that God was the supreme cause of everything, Dionysius also followed a path of negation—a *via negativa*—that denied the capacity of words to represent God. Abandoning language, concepts, and perceptions, the ascent toward God was a plunge into the "truly mysterious darkness of unknowing." In his *Mystical Theology*, Dionysius advised, "Leave behind you everything perceived and understood, everything perceptible and understandable, all that is not and all that is, and, with your understanding laid aside, strive upwards as much as you can toward union with him who is beyond all being and knowledge." By renouncing everything, especially any sense of self, he promised, "you will be uplifted to the ray of the divine shadow which is above everything that is."[2]

Although the mystical theology of Dionysius was further developed in the Greek East, it was also influential in the emergence of mysticism in the Latin West. The ninth-century Irish theologian John Scotus Eriugena (fl. 847–77) made direct use of the texts of Dionysius, following the Areopagite along a *via negativa* that led beyond knowledge or language. Since divine ignorance, unknowing, and darkness pointed to the highest wisdom, he held that nothing could actually be said about God. Ignored by his contemporaries, the texts of John Scotus Eriugena were widely studied in Europe during the twelfth-century revival of interest in the soul's ascent to union with God. In that context, however, a new emphasis was placed on the unifying power of love and the affective powers of the soul—desire, emotional longing, and even erotic passion. This new mystical spirituality evoked an intimate experience of loving union with Jesus Christ.

Although no mention of the role of love in the soul's ascent to God appeared in Dionysius's *Mystical Theology*, love became the dominant preoccupation of the leading exponent of twelfth-century mystical theology in the West, Bernard of Clairvaux. In developing his spirituality of love, Bernard relied on a text that has often been identified as the second major source of Christian mysticism, the erotic poetry of the biblical Song of Songs. From the ancient theologian Origen, Christians had learned to interpret the text's passionate lyrics about the bride and bridegroom, the lover and the beloved, as an allegory for the relations between the church and Christ. As Bernard personalized the Song of Songs, however, the bride became the human soul in loving intercourse with Christ, the bridegroom. In the development of Christian mysticism, therefore, these two themes— the ascent of the soul to God, the intimacy of the soul with Christ— defined the broad parameters of discourse on spirituality in which mystics spoke extensively about what was beyond words.

LOVE

In his role as a Cistercian abbot, Bernard of Clairvaux (1090–1153) was responsible not only for the administration of the monastery, the reform of its liturgy, and the discipline of its monks, but also for the direction of its spiritual life. As a preacher, Bernard selected the biblical text of the Song of Songs, known in Latin as the Canticles, for a remarkable series of sermons on spirituality. Addressing an audience of celibate monks, he transposed the erotic wedding poetry of the Song of Songs into a spirituality based on stages of ascent that culminated in a loving union with God. In the first line of the biblical text, for example, Bernard found the passionate entreaty of the bride, "Let him kiss me with the kiss of the mouth." As he explained to his monastic audience, this kiss signified a direct encounter with the Divine Lover, Jesus Christ. Before it was ready for the kiss of the mouth, however, the soul had to go through two stages of preparation. First, the soul had to kiss the feet of Christ, indicating through that act of humility that it had embraced the contrition, confession, and repentance of the Christian penitential system. Second, the soul had to kiss the hands of Christ, indicating that it was devoted to a life of Christian virtue. Only after the soul had kissed Christ's feet and hands was it ready to experience the intimate enjoyment of Christ signified by the third and highest kiss, the kiss of the mouth. In that intimate encounter with Jesus Christ, Bernard concluded, whoever "is joined to him in a holy kiss becomes through his good pleasure, one spirit with him."

The first line of the Song of Songs, therefore, provided Bernard with a textual point of departure for elaborating three stages of the spiritual path to God—confession, devotion, and contemplation. As Bernard explained:

> The heartfelt desire to admit one's guilt brings a man down in lowliness before God, as it were to his feet; the heartfelt devotion finds in God renewal and refreshment, the touch, as it were of his hand; and the delights of contemplation lead on to that ecstatic repose that is the fruit of the kiss of his mouth.

This entire movement of the soul toward God, however, was driven by love. According to Bernard, spirituality was both the science and the passion of divine love. In a treatise on the science of loving God, *De diligendo Deo,* Bernard carefully calculated four different ways in which love might be organized—the love of the self for the sake of the self, the love of God for the sake of the self, the love of God for the sake of God, and the love of everything, even the self, only for the sake of God. In this last type of loving, according to Bernard, a person achieves an "ordered love" that is organized solely by the will of God. Any consideration of the self, therefore, is completely submerged in this final stage in the science of conforming love to the selfless love of God. "To become thus," Bernard concluded, "is to be deified."

At the same time, however, the passion of love, including sexual desire, provided Bernard's most powerful metaphors for the loving union between the soul and Christ. In his description of the selfless love of God, Bernard had recourse to the passionate language of being "inebriated by his love," of being caught up in "swift and sudden rapture." His sermons on the Song of Songs further elaborated this imagery of erotic passion. In the figure of the Bride, who lives solely for love of the Bridegroom, Bernard found his controlling image for the highest love: "The individual soul, if it loves God, dearly, wisely, and ardently, is the Bride." By loving the Divine Lover in purity and wisdom, he observed, "if she loves with her whole heart nothing is lacking, for she has given all. Such love, as I have said, is marriage." The spiritual marriage, however, also involves a love that is burning with passion, energy, and even violence in its consummation. "What could be more violent?" Bernard asks with respect to this divine passion. "Love triumphs over God. But what is nonetheless so nonviolent? It is love." The passion of the soul, therefore, is suggested by this contradiction of a violent victory over God and nonviolent surrender to God through love.

In the spirituality developed by Bernard, the science of love was ultimately subsumed under the passion of love. Asserting the priority of divine love over human reason, Bernard observed that this "headlong love does not wait for judgment, is not chastened by advice, not shackled by shame nor subdued by reason." The marital embrace of the Bride and Bridegroom, which is only hinted at in the biblical text of the Song of Songs (2:6–7), is highlighted in Bernard's sermons as the consummating spiritual experience of the supreme Godhead entering into marriage with the exiled soul. In the union of lover and beloved on the marriage bed of the Song of Songs, Bernard found a model for the most intimate and profound spiritual experience in which "the soul, overcome by the loveliness of the place, . . . sweetly sleeps in the arms of her bridegroom, in ecstasy of spirit." In these terms, Bernard developed a Christian spirituality thoroughly imbued with images of erotic passion, perhaps drawing upon contemporary literary traditions of courtly love, but certainly drawing out the mystical implications of the erotic poetry of the Song of Songs. By loving, desiring, and adhering to God in this passionate embrace, Bernard concluded, the soul achieved the vision of God. "This kind of ecstasy," he proposed, "is called contemplation."[3]

Combining the passion of love with the soul's ascent to the vision of God, this ecstatic contemplation celebrated by Bernard was also the primary theme in the mystical theology developed by Hugh of St. Victor. "Love surpasses knowledge and is greater than intelligence," Hugh taught. "One loves more than one understands, and love enters and approaches where knowledge stays outside." As the leading teacher of the abbey of St. Victor, which had been established for canon regulars outside Paris, Hugh was a prolific author of biblical commentaries and treatises on theology and other arts, sciences, and disciplines of medieval learning. Inspired by Hugh, the school of the Victorines became particularly noted for its theoretical developments in mystical theology. With scholarly precision, Hugh of St. Victor outlined the stages of the soul's ascent to God as three types of intellectual vision: thinking, meditation, and contemplation. In thinking (cogitatio), the rational soul begins to discover its situation in the world, forming concepts about the order of things around it. In meditation (meditatio), the rational soul proceeds from forming concepts about the world to critical reflection on those concepts, developing its inherent rational capacity for distinguishing between true and false ideas. When the rational soul ascends to contemplation *(contemplatio)*, however, it achieves direct and immediate insight into reality. "Contemplation," according to Hugh of St. Victor, "is the attentive and free gaze of the intellectual soul poured out everywhere over the things to be discerned." Contemplation can discern the nature of the created world, but the supreme object of contemplation was identified by Hugh of St. Victor as the vision of God.

At first glance, the three stages of ascent toward God outlined by Hugh of St. Victor appear to describe a purely intellectual exercise. Certainly, Hugh regarded intellectual accomplishment as crucial because he argued that the integrity of human nature had been disrupted not only by sin, but also by ignorance. "The integrity of the soul, which ignorance shatters," he observed, "thinking discovers, meditation collects." This apparently cold rationality of thinking and meditation, however, was transformed by the divine heat generated in contemplation. According to Hugh, "Contemplation pours by its melting action into the die of the divine likeness in order to be reformed through the fire of divine love." In this vivid imagery of melting and being recast in the likeness of God, Hugh represented a stage of contemplation in which the rational soul was transformed by love.[4]

This mystical theology of divine contemplation, love, and union with God was further developed during the twelfth century by other masters, especially by the Cistercian William of St. Thierry and the Victorine Richard of St. Victor. In very general terms, all of these masters of mystical theology were engaged in a common project. First, they outlined a mystical program based on identifying a series of stages in the ascent of the soul to God. Drawing on the inspiration of Dionysius the Areopagite, those stages became standardized as three—purification, illumination, and perfection. By the following century, the mystical theologian Bonaventure (ca. 1217–74), who succeeded St. Francis as the head of the mendicant order of Franciscans, could assume that these three stages outlined the soul's journey into God. Second, however, these theologians merged the three stages of the soul's ascent found in the mystical theology of Dionysius with the erotic poetry of the Song of Songs to identify the highest stage of union as divine love. According to Bonaventure, for

example, the preparatory stages of moral purification and intellectual illumination ultimately led to the soul's union with God in divine love. In the
threefold process of the soul's ascent to God, as Bonaventure formulated
it, purgation leads to peace, illumination to truth, and perfection to love.[5]

Third, drawing inspiration from Dionysius and the Song of Songs, all
of these mystical theologians ultimately grounded their spirituality in
texts from the Bible. In this respect, their mysticism was a science of interpreting the Bible to chart the soul's journey to God. Finally, although their
writings celebrated the unifying power of divine love in vivid, intense, and
even sexual imagery of erotic passion, burning desire, and the heat of
love's consummation, these mystical theologians were essentially theoreti-
cians. Only rarely, if at all, referring to their own personal experiences of
divine love, ecstatic contemplation, or intimate union with God, they
instead outlined theoretical terms for understanding the relation between
the soul and God. These mystical theologians, therefore, did not claim to
see extraordinary visions or hear supernatural voices. Rather, they tried
to work out a Christian mystical logic of divine love.

The twelfth-century mystical theologian Hildegard of Bingen
(1098–1179), however, did claim to have direct personal experiences of
spiritual voices and visions. Writing to Bernard of Clairvaux around
1147, Hildegard sought advice about her extraordinary spiritual experiences. As Hildegard recognized, Bernard was a leader of the church in the
world, "who with burning love for the Son of God and great fervor won-
derfully enlists men in the army of Christ under the banner of the holy
cross for the worthy struggle against the ferocity of the pagans."
However, she also regarded him as an authority on the spiritual life of
Christians that transcended the world. Accordingly, Hildegard revealed
that from childhood she had experienced spiritual visions that urged her
to teach and preach. As she wrote to Bernard:

> I am most troubled about this vision which appeared to me in the spirit of
> mystery, and which I never saw with the eyes of the flesh. I, wretched and
> more than wretched in that I bear the name woman, have seen great mir-
> acles, which my tongue could not describe had not the spirit of God
> taught me.

As a woman, Hildegard had limited options for writing, teaching, or
preaching about her spiritual visions. Although Bernard gave only a brief

response to her letter, he defended Hildegard before Pope Eugenius at the Synod of Trier in 1147 so that she was granted permission in the name of Christ and of St. Peter to publish all that she had learned from the Holy Spirit.

Establishing an independent convent for nuns at Bingen, Hildegard proceeded to dictate books on the lives of the saints, monastic discipline, natural history, and medicine. As a gifted poet and musician, she composed seventy-seven hymns in praise of God. Her greatest accomplishments, however, were in the field of mystical theology. In three volumes on her spiritual revelations, Hildegard invoked the authority of what she had personally seen and heard through the Spirit of God. Although her personal revelations only served to reinforce a fairly conventional account of the Christian story from creation to salvation, Hildegard nevertheless introduced a new emphasis on the immediacy of spiritual sight and hearing. Not only pointing to the divine light or the vision of God, she also cultivated the capacity of spiritual hearing. "Then I saw in the luminous sky," she reported, "in which I heard different kinds of music, marvelously embodying all the meanings I had heard before." The divine light, according to Hildegard, perhaps drawing upon her experience as a musician and composer, enters the spiritual ears as music, as heavenly singing, as a divine symphony, as a celestial harmony. In the mystical theology of Hildegard of Bingen, therefore, spiritual experience was ultimately a harmonious orchestration of divine light and sound.[6]

LIGHT

In the spirituality of the Eastern Orthodox Church, the influence of Dionysius the Areopagite was crucial. In addition, however, mystical theologians in the East could build on the legacy of the three foundational Greek theologians—Basil of Caesarea (ca. 329–79), Gregory of Nyssa (ca. 335–ca. 395), and Gregory of Nazianzus (ca. 329–ca. 391)—who had pioneered ways of thinking about the soul's journey to God. Although they affirmed the absolute transcendence of God, the Greek theologians also held out the possibility that human beings could directly, immediately experience the presence of God. By entering the radiance of divine light, even through extraordinary spiritual experiences in this life, the soul could anticipate its ultimate deification *(theosis)* in the kingdom of God. Building on this foundation, Symeon (949–1022), who was known as the

"New Theologian," emphasized the direct experience of God through divine light. At the age of twenty, after a series of spiritual visions, Symeon entered a monastery in Constantinople. While assuming the responsibilities of abbot, Symeon also developed a mystical theology based on the conviction that God could appear directly to human beings. As he related his own visionary experience of God, Symeon testified to having had a direct experience of the divine light. While he had been standing one day reciting the prayer "God be merciful to me a sinner" (Luke 18:13), as Symeon recalled, "a divine radiance suddenly appeared in abundance from above and filled the whole room." Losing awareness of his surroundings, he had been "wholly united to nonmaterial light and, so it seemed, he had himself been turned into light." In the spirituality of Symeon the New Theologian, therefore, a direct personal experience of the divine light established the baseline for developing a mystical theology.[7]

As a monk and abbot of a monastery, Symeon pointed to an extraordinary spiritual experience of the presence of God that could be most effectively cultivated within the context of monastic life. By the thirteenth century, Greek Orthodox monasteries, especially the flourishing monastic communities of Mount Athos, had developed specific techniques of prayer, breathing, and bodily posture for inducing such spiritual experience. This spiritual practice came to be known as *hesychasm,* from the Greek word for "silence," because it was based on a technique of sitting and intoning a silent prayer. The words of the prayer were simple: "Lord Jesus Christ, Son of God, have mercy on me." But the effects of repeating this silent prayer were profound. In the rituals of the Orthodox Church, prayers were generally public events, spoken aloud, and recited while standing. Within the spiritual discipline of hesychasm, however, the "Jesus Prayer" was recited privately, silently, and while seated. As a ritualized performance, therefore, hesychasm effectively reversed or inverted conventional Christian expectations about the power of prayer. However, as this spiritual technique was developed in monasteries throughout the Greek Orthodox world, hesychasm provided monks with a practical method for achieving a personal experience of divinity.

First, this method of prayer required a particular bodily posture. Sitting on the ground or on a low stool, those who wanted to enter into the silence of prayer had to lower their heads and place their chins upon their chests; shoulders were bowed and backs bent. Having adopted this physical position, however, they had to focus all of their physical and spiritual attention into the center of their bodies. As one manual instructed, the physical posture of prayer required "resting your beard on your chest and directing your bodily eye together with your entire intellect toward the middle of your belly, that is, toward your navel." In other manuals, the attention of the physical and spiritual eye was directed toward the heart. In either case, prayer depended upon assuming a specific physical posture that prepared both the body and the mind for an experience of God.

Second, this method required control over breathing. "Restrain the inhalation of the breath through the nose," as one manual advised, "so as not to breathe in and out at your ease." Rather than breathing normally, the practitioner had to consciously direct the process of inhaling and exhaling. By slowing down the physical activity of breathing, the hesychast demonstrated a measure of spiritual control over such a basic physiological process. As a physical exercise, this control of breathing brought a sense of calm, but also a concentration of mind that created the perfect context for reciting the words of the "Jesus Prayer." As this practice developed, however, the recitation of the words of the prayer was coordinated with the rhythm of breathing. By synchronizing breath and prayer, the practitioner inhaled with the words "Lord Jesus Christ, Son of God," while exhaling with "have mercy on me." In the harmony of breathing and praying, the technique of hesychasm generated a personal sense of the immediate presence of divinity.

Third, as breath merged with prayer, the practitioner was directed to enter into the heart. As the center of both the physical and spiritual body, the heart represented the internal realm of heaven, because, as the biblical words of Jesus were generally understood, "the kingdom of heaven is within us." By centering prayer in the deepest recesses of the human heart, that internal kingdom of heaven, human beings could enter into a spiritual realm in which they might behold themselves as "entirely luminous." This simple practice of prayer, therefore, with its disciplined attention to posture, breathing, and the heart, promised direct access to an experience of the divine light of heaven.[8]

As both a physical and a spiritual exercise, the practice of Christian prayer in hesychasm resembles techniques that have been developed in other religious traditions. Like hesychasm, the practices of Hindu yoga, Buddhist meditation, Taoist alchemy, and many other religious disciplines begin with adopting a specific bodily posture, regulating the flow of breathing, and focusing attention in a particular region of the body. These

religious "techniques of ecstasy" use the physical body as a spiritual vehicle for rising above the ordinary world. From the perspective of the
monks who performed this Christian meditation, silent prayer was a technique of spiritual transformation. Although the physical posture might
initially be painful, the work of focusing attention on the heart, rhythmic
breathing, and silent repetition transformed physical pain into spiritual
power. Beyond ordinary thinking or imagining, according to the hesychasts, this technique of concentration led to a direct contemplation of the
light of God. Like the transfiguration of Jesus on Mount Tabor, this contemplation of divine light transformed the practitioners of hesychasm into
light.

During the fourteenth century, the Orthodox Church was briefly
divided by a controversy over the practice of hesychasm. A Greek scholar
from southern Italy, Barlaam the Calabrian (ca. 1290–1350), launched a
campaign against this technique and the monks who practiced it.
Deriding the hesychast monks as *omphalopsychoi,* "those who locate the
soul in the navel," Barlaam argued that these "navel-gazers" were
involved in nothing more than superstition. Rather than engaging in gen-
uinely religious prayer, he insisted, the hesychasts deluded themselves
through superstitious, magical, and materialist means into imagining that
they could see the divine light. According to Barlaam, however, such a
direct vision of God was not possible for human beings in this life.
Invoking the ancient authority of Dionysius the Areopagite, he argued
that God could not be seen or known directly because the divine light was
hidden in the radically transcendent "darkness of unknowing." Beyond
the reach of human perception, concepts, language, or experience, God
transcended the world to such an extent that in this life divine reality
could only be known indirectly through the scriptures, sacraments, and
traditions of the Orthodox Church. From this perspective, therefore, the
hesychasts were not only superstitious "navel-gazers," but also heretics
who denied divine transcendence by claiming immediate personal access
to the light of God.

Responding to this challenge, a Greek monk from Mount Athos,
Gregory Palamas (1296–1359), undertook a sustained defense of the theory and practice of hesychasm. As Gregory Palamas recognized, the theory
of hesychasm had to be defended by addressing Barlaam's interpretation
of the mystical theology of Dionysius the Areopagite. According to

Palamas, Dionysius had taught both a path of negation, which denied any direct knowledge of God, and a path of affirmation, which promised direct human experience of God "in the brilliant darkness of a hidden silence." At the level of theory, Palamas argued, both negation and affirmation were true because they referred to two different aspects of divinity, the essence of God and the energy of God. Palamas agreed that the essence of God could not be known. The divine essence, he observed, "in a manner beyond all being transcends every being." Palamas nevertheless affirmed that the energy of God could be directly experienced by human beings. As God in action, divine energy appeared as spiritual light. When hesychasts saw this spiritual light, therefore, they experienced God directly, not the essence of God, but the energy, activity, and manifestation of God.

In his defense of hesychasm, Palamas argued that the light experienced in this discipline of prayer was not merely a metaphor for spiritual insight. Rather, the divine light was the "nonmaterial" and "uncreated" energy of God. Following Dionysius the Areopagite, who had observed that the "divine darkness is the unapproachable light in which God is said to dwell," Palamas used the imagery of "bright darkness" to describe the spiritual light of God. "Even though it is darkness," he noted, "yet it is surpassingly bright; and in that dazzling darkness, as the great Dionysius says, things divine are granted to the saints." While the direct experience of divine energy was granted to the hesychasts, the divine light effectively changed them into light. Identifying this spiritual light as the primary agent in the process of deification, or *theosis,* he found that "the light alone shines through them and it alone is what they see." By seeing and being the divine light through the practice of silent prayer, according to Palamas, the hesychasts achieved a deification in which "God is all in all."[9]

In a series of church councils between 1341 and 1351, the defense of hesychasm worked out by Gregory Palamas was adopted by the Greek Orthodox Church. By practicing the power of prayer, including the physical discipline of the body, hesychasts anticipated the ultimate redemption in which the "body is deified along with the soul." In the subsequent development of the Orthodox tradition, the spiritual discipline of hesychasm continued to be practiced as a technique for uniting body and soul with the energy of the divine light of God.

NOTHING

In the development of medieval Christian spirituality in the West, women played a prominent role. As in the case of Hildegard of Bingen, the monastic environment provided scope for women to emerge as leaders in the theory and practice of mysticism. During the second half of the twelfth century, however, the movement of religious women known as Beguines provided a distinctive form of women's spirituality outside of the convent. Relatively independent of male authority or control, the Beguines formed a decentralized urban movement. Renouncing property, sex, and marriage, they lived alone with parents or formed small groups in ordinary houses to dedicate themselves to a religious life of purity, devotion, and service in the midst of the secular world. Developing initially in Belgium and the Netherlands, the Beguine movement spread into northern France and the Rhineland. Although the Fourth Lateran Council (1215) had forbidden the formation of any new religious orders, the Beguines had expanded to such an extent that the movement was granted papal approval the following year. Although women were increasingly joining the new mendicant orders of Franciscans and Dominicans during the thirteenth century, the Beguines provided an alternative avenue for the development of women's spirituality.

The distinctive character of this thirteenth-century women's spirituality can be suggested by the writings of the Dutch Beguine Hadewijch of Antwerp. From a wealthy, upper-class, and educated background, Hadewijch joined the Beguines and eventually became a spiritual adviser within the movement. Her visions, poems, and letters recorded not only a mystical theology, but also several incidents of intense personal experience of God. Like earlier mystical theorists, Hadewijch used erotic imagery of passion and intimacy to represent the soul's ascent to God. In the spiritual visions of Hadewijch, however, that erotic imagery assumed a new intensity. For example, one Sunday during Pentecost, while attending church at dawn, she experienced severe physical distress that she described as a mixture of madness, fear, and desire. "My heart and my veins and all my limbs trembled and quivered with eager desire," she recounted. "On that day my mind was beset so fearfully and so painfully by desirous love that all my desperate limbs threatened to break." In this physical agony, Hadewijch experienced an intense desire for God that could not be satisfied merely through partaking in the Eucharist, but longed for an intimate union with Jesus Christ. As Hadewijch reported, Jesus Christ "came himself to me, took me entirely in his arms, and pressed me to him, and all my members felt his in full felicity, in accordance with the desire of my heart and my humanity. So I was outwardly satisfied and fully transported." In recounting this intimate union, which was simultaneously spiritual and physical, divine and human, Hadewijch redefined what it meant to be a "bride of Christ" in intensely personal terms. The passionate consummation of that union effectively dissolved any difference between lover and beloved, she concluded, "so that I wholly melted in him and nothing any longer remained to me of myself." The fulfillment of desire, therefore, resulted in a disappearance of the self in union with God.[10]

In the mystical theology of Bernard of Clairvaux, the erotic imagery of the Song of Songs served as an allegory for the love between the soul and God. Developing this literary tradition, the Beguines also celebrated divine love in similar terms. For example, the German poet and visionary Mechthild of Magdeburg (ca. 1207–ca.1294) presented her understanding of the love of God in the form of five ecstatic declarations:

> O God! So generous in the outpouring of Your gifts!
> So flowing in Your love!
> So burning in Your desire!
> So fervent in union!
> O God, who rests on my heart, without whom I could
> no longer live![11]

Like her sister Beguine Hadewijch, however, Mechthild shifted from literary allegory to a personal account of divine intimacy. Beyond the circle of Beguines, other women authors in late medieval Europe provided similar accounts of intimate spiritual union. In England, for example, Julian of Norwich recounted her visionary experiences of intimate relations with Christ. Likewise, Margery Kempe reported a vision in which Christ said to her, "I will that thou lovest Me, daughter, as a good wife ought to love her husband. Therefore thou mayest boldly take Me in the arms of thy soul and kiss My mouth, My head, and My feet, as sweetly as thou will."[12] By holding Jesus Christ in such a passionate physical embrace, these women mystics developed a spirituality of both body and soul that announced a new intimacy with God.

Certainly, there were male mystics who evoked a similar intimacy. In a spiritual vision described by Rupert of Deutz (ca. 1075–1129), for example,

Jesus Christ was embraced as a lover. "I embraced him, I kissed him for a long time," Rupert reported, and "in the midst of the kiss he opened his mouth so that I could kiss more deeply."[13] For women mystics, however, intimate encounters with Christ assumed a different character within the context of Christian spirituality. As we recall, the ancient Christian ideal of female holiness proclaimed by Paul and the church fathers required a woman's body to be closed. Within the sacred space of the church, a woman's mouth was shut, her head covered by long hair, and her sexuality contained. In medieval Europe, male authorities of the church continued to imagine the female body as a network of dangerous openings that had to be monitored, controlled, and closed. For women mystics, however, opening the body to passionate intercourse with Jesus Christ radically altered the terms of female spirituality. Effectively, these women opened what the church had tried to close. In gendered terms, therefore, intimate union with Christ assumed a distinctive significance for women. Beyond the enclosures established by the church, women could be open to a direct, immediate, and transcendent experience of God.

Like earlier mystical theorists in the West, the Beguines focused on the ascent of the soul to God. According to Hadewijch, the self-fulfillment that she experienced in satisfying her physical and spiritual desires for Jesus Christ resulted in her own disappearance. As she melted into Christ, nothing of herself remained. In developing her mystical theology of the soul's ascent to God, Hadewijch placed this annihilation of the self at the apex of that journey. Consistently, she developed a mystical logic of contradiction to describe the stages of that journey. For example, although the three Christian virtues of faith, hope, and love represented steps on the journey to God, they were most profoundly experienced according to Hadewijch by their opposites. Accordingly, instead of advocating the Christian virtue of faith, Hadewijch celebrated "unfaith." As she observed in one vision of souls approaching God, "Unfaith made them so deep that they wholly engulfed Love." In a letter to one of her students, she observed that "this noble unfaith greatly enlarges consciousness." Faith seems to represent a narrow path, but the "unfaith" of Hadewijch is so deep and wide that it can completely encompass the love and vision of God. Similarly, Hadewijch replaced the Christian virtue of hope with despair. Souls ascending to God "keep their hearts devoid of hope," she observed. "This way leads them very deep into God, for their great despair leads them above all the ramparts and through all the passageways, and into all places where the truth is." Finally, in her supreme contradiction, Hadewijch proclaimed that the summit of divine love was the deep abyss of hell. At the height of her own experience of divinity, she reported, "I sank into the fathomless depth" and fell into "the abyss of love." As the culmination of the ascent to God, according to Hadewijch, the soul was submerged into the depths of hell.

> Forever to be in unrest,
> Forever assault and new persecution;
> To be wholly engulfed and devoured
> In her unfathomable essence.

According to Hadewijch, therefore, mystical theology followed a logic of contradiction. By cultivating an expansive unfaith and a profound sense of despair, the human soul ascended upward to a divine love that absorbed it into a deep abyss.[14] In similar terms of self-renunciation, Mechthild of Magdeburg celebrated a divine "foresakenness" in which the highest achievement of the soul was to be abandoned by God and dissolved into nothing. "You must love nothingness," Mechthild advised. "Thus you live in the true desert."[15] For these mystics, therefore, salvation was not a return to the original garden, but an absorption into the divine desert, ocean, or abyss that was beyond all things.

Arguably, like physical intimacy, this mystical imagery of self-annihilation meant something different to women than it did to men. Within a religious context in which their social roles were formally restricted, women might have had a specific interest in denying the validity of the female "self" constructed by the church. Explicitly prohibited from gaining access to the priesthood and generally inhibited from exercising religious knowledge, authority, and power, women might have understood the disappearance of the self as a liberation from those social constraints. Furthermore, the mystical logic of contradiction in which faith is unfaith, hope is despair, love is hell, and up is down might have resonated with the social situation of women who sought to reverse the discrimination under which they were cast as inferior human beings. While male Christian scholars were insisting that Jesus Christ could not possibly have been born as a woman, women mystics were asserting that they had in effect been reborn as Jesus Christ in ecstatic spiritual experiences in which they disappeared as individuals so that only Jesus Christ remained.

In the case of the French Beguine Marguerite Porete (d. 1310), the development of these mystical themes of intimacy, union with Christ, and the annihilation of the self led to her condemnation by Rome. Marguerite's text, *The Mirror of Simple Souls,* was an imaginative literary dialogue between the soul, reason, and divine love, which in keeping with the general style of Beguine spirituality appeared as "Lady Love" *(Dame Amour).* Defying the standards of rationality established by the scholars and theologians of the church, Marguerite cautioned,

> Theologians and other clerks,
> You will not have the intellect for it,
> No matter how brilliant your abilities,
> If you do not proceed humbly.
> And may Love and Faith, together,
> Cause you to rise above Reason,
> Since they are the ladies of the house.

As the dialogue moved beyond reason, the soul was directed by Lady Love toward its own annihilation. Like a river that loses its separate identity by flowing into the sea, the soul immersed in love was completely absorbed in God. As Lady Love explained, annihilation was "perfection, when the soul dwells in pure nothingness and without thought." Like other Beguine poets, Marguerite described the highest perfection of the soul as a fall into the deepest abyss. "Now this Soul has fallen from love into nothingness," Lady Love observed. But the nothingness of this divine abyss was actually everything because "without such nothingness she cannot be All." Losing herself in the depths of divine love, "the Soul, thus pure and clarified sees neither God nor herself, but God sees Himself of Himself in her, for her, without her." In the annihilation of the soul, "God shows to her that there is nothing except Him."

By becoming nothing but God, the soul no longer required the reason, virtues, sacraments, or authority of the organized institution that Marguerite identified as the "Lesser Church." In contrast to that inferior church that operated in the world, she pointed to the "Greater Church" of divine lovers who had become nothing by uniting with God. According to Marguerite, only God knew those souls, those "daughters of the king, sisters of the king, and brides of the king." Asserting that the "Lesser

Church" failed to recognize them because it was incapable of entering into their souls, Marguerite concluded that "none would understand such souls except God who is within them." Although Marguerite Porete echoed many of spiritual themes developed by Hadewijch, Mechthild, and other Beguines, this direct challenge to the authority of the church resulted in her formal condemnation. During eighteen months of imprisonment in Paris, Marguerite refused to appear before the ecclesiastical court to defend herself by explaining her teachings before the theologians of the "Lesser Church." In writing about the annihilated soul united with God, Marguerite had suggested that such a soul was not answerable to anyone. "This Soul responds to no one if she does not wish to," she observed. "This is why whoever calls this Soul does not find her, and so her enemies have no reply from her." Declaring Marguerite Porete to be an unrepentant heretic and a "pseudo-woman," the ecclesiastical court turned her over to the secular authorities of Paris to be burned at the stake on June 1, 1310.[16]

The teachings of Marguerite Porete fueled the church's growing suspicion of the Beguines. Nevertheless, in spite of official condemnation, the Beguine movement continued to flourish in the Netherlands and Germany into the fifteenth century. Marguerite's radical spirituality of the soul's annihilation, however, was generally abandoned by these later Beguines in favor of an emotive devotion to the infant Jesus and the suffering Christ. But the Christian spirituality of nothing was further developed by the Rhineland mystics who followed the German Dominican Meister Eckhart (1260–1327). Influenced by the writings of the Beguines, Meister Eckhart, who also suffered official condemnation, but not execution, pointed to a similar annihilation of the self through divine union in which the soul "has a will and a longing for nothing." In his analysis of divinity, however, Eckhart drew a crucial distinction between God—the deity of conventional Christian faith, hope, and love—and the Godhead, the "God beyond God." As the supreme "origin of all things beyond God," the Godhead was the primal ground of being, a divine unity in which "God's ground and the soul's ground are one ground." In terms that recalled the spirituality of the Beguines, Meister Eckhart described the soul's union with the Godhead as a fall into the profound and fathomless abyss of nothingness. "When the soul reaches the essence of the Godhead itself," he observed, "it sinks even deeper into the abyss of the Godhead so that it never comes to the bottom." In the depths of the Godhead, as Eckhart maintained, "God and I are one." Although he acknowledged the importance of God having been born in Bethlehem, Eckhart suggested that it was more important that God should be born within the human soul. In the bright darkness of the Godhead, Meister Eckhart found that the soul was nothing but God.[17]

16

Heretics

As an official inquisitor of the Roman Catholic Church, the Dominican Stephen of Bourbon (ca. 1180–1262) traveled widely throughout France to preach, hear confessions, and search out traces of religious error, superstition, or heresy. The pope had conferred this responsibility upon the mendicant orders of Dominicans and Franciscans in the 1230s. Stephen of Bourbon had become an inquisitor sometime around 1235. Although based in the city of Lyons, Stephen directed his ministry toward rural areas, where he worked to expose the persistence of pagan practices in the countryside. According to Stephen, even those who regarded themselves as Christians in rural areas worshiped trees, offered sacrifices, practiced divination by casting lots, and performed healing rituals at sacred sites. In some cases, they also revered saints who were unknown to the church. For example, while he was preaching and hearing confessions in the rural region of the Dombes, about forty kilometers north of Lyons, Stephen heard accounts of popular local devotion to a new saint. Reportedly, many women in the region took their children to the shrine of this saint—St. Guinefort—to receive spiritual blessings and physical healings. Since he had never heard of St. Guinefort, Stephen was eager to learn more about this holy person. When he arrived at the saint's shrine, however, he was surprised to discover that the saint was not exactly a holy person. According to the saint's devotees, St. Guinefort was a dog.[1]

In the popular tradition, St. Guinefort was a greyhound in the household of the Lord of Villars. One day, when the lord and lady left their infant child unattended in its cradle, a vicious serpent entered and approached the baby. Seeing this danger, the greyhound attacked the serpent. After a bloody battle, the dog succeeded in killing the intruder beneath the infant's cradle. Although he was seriously injured, the greyhound remained on guard until the parents returned. When they came back and saw the blood all around the room, however, they assumed that the dog had eaten their child. Drawing his sword, the lord killed the greyhound. But the lord and lady soon discovered the corpse of the serpent and their child sleeping peacefully. Realizing what had happened, they were overwhelmed with regret. Placing the dog's body in a well, they covered it with a large pile of stones and planted trees in memory of the heroic greyhound, Guinefort.

Although the castle was soon destroyed and abandoned, the shrine continued to attract local peasants who regarded the dog as a martyr. With its burial mound of stones and sacred grove of trees, the shrine of St. Guinefort became a popular pilgrimage site. In particular, women brought their sick or weak children to the shrine to be healed in the presence of the holy greyhound. Under the direction of an elderly woman, these mothers were instructed in the rituals of St. Guinefort. They presented offerings of salt at the well, drove nails into the trees, hung their babies' clothing in the bushes, and passed their naked children nine times between two tree trunks. After performing these preliminary rituals, the mothers placed their sickly infants at the foot of a tree and left them there during the time it took for two inch-long candles to burn down. During that time of separation, the mothers prayed to the woodland spirits of the shrine, asking for their healthy children to be restored to them. Apparently, they assumed that their real children had been stolen and replaced by demonic spirits. By leaving those "changelings" at the foot of the sacred tree, the mothers hoped for spiritual intervention in getting their human children back. If the children were still alive when their mothers returned to the tree, they were taken to a nearby river and plunged nine times into the cold water. Children who survived this final ritual ordeal were expected to be strong and healthy. Most important, however, the children who survived were thought to have been restored to a fully human identity. Under the auspices of St. Guinefort the dog, therefore, children could recover both their health and their humanity.

Stephen of Bourbon, however, attacked the devotion to St. Guinefort and its attendant rituals as dangerous superstition. During the thirteenth century, superstition was thought to assume three basic forms. First, superstition appeared in pagan rituals that perpetuated what Stephen called the "illusions of the Devil." In keeping with the ancient tradition of Christian demonology, Stephen concluded that the devotees of St.

Guinefort were engaged in the pagan worship of the devil and his demons. Second, superstition registered as idolatry. Based on the ancient authority of Augustine, Stephen could recognize idolatry as a serious form of superstition that transferred worship from the creator to the created world. As the definition of this type of superstition was formulated by Thomas Aquinas, idolatry consisted "in improperly according divine honor to a creature." In the devotions to St. Guinefort, Stephen found peasants who honored not merely a created object, such as a statue, but an actual creature—a dog—as a martyr, saint, and spiritual healer. Accordingly, he condemned these devotions as idolatry. Third, superstition appeared in its most subtle and devious form in what Thomas Aquinas would identify as "the superstition of the improper worship of the true God." In this form, superstition might look like genuine religion only to deceive. In the case of St. Guinefort, Stephen decided that the peasants "scorn the churches and holy relics" by imitating genuine Christian pilgrimages to sacred sites and authentic veneration of the relics of saints and martyrs who had been approved by the church.[2]

Finding that the devotion to St. Guinefort qualified as superstition on all three grounds—as demon worship, as idol worship, and as improper worship—Stephen of Bourbon had the shrine destroyed. Digging up the body of the dog, he ordered the sacred grove to be cut down and burned along with the remains of St. Guinefort. He secured the cooperation of the secular authorities to enforce his edict that any peasants who went to the shrine for any reason would have all their possessions confiscated and sold. Assuming that he had suppressed this evil superstition, Stephen of Bourbon could not have known that popular veneration of St. Guinefort the holy greyhound would persist in the region into the nineteenth century. As late as 1879, representatives of the Catholic Church in France continued to complain about religious devotions directed toward a saint who was a dog. The history of St. Guinefort, therefore, suggests the long-standing tension in European Christianity between two broad cultural formations, the folk culture of the people and the literate culture of the church. In consolidating its authority in Europe, the church struggled to establish control over both cultural spheres. While suppressing popular forms of religion as idolatry on the grounds that the superstitious were "improperly according divine honor to a creature," the inquisitors also fought what they saw as deviations in the literate religion of the church, those forms of superstition that appeared in what they regarded as "improper worship of the true God." In attacking religious deviations on both elite and popular fronts, the church deployed these definitions of superstition in its ongoing campaign against heresy.

PREACHERS

As the principal medium of religious communication, preaching was carefully guarded by the church. According to Roman Catholic tradition, the right to preach had been given to the pope and the bishops, as successors to Peter and the disciples, and to priests as heirs to the seventy who were sent to preach to all nations. The religious activity of preaching, therefore, was exclusively reserved for ordained clergy. Since the right to preach was conferred solely by the institutional authority of the church, other sources of authority, whether personal charisma, spiritual inspiration, or biblical interpretation, were excluded. Preaching, therefore, was not merely a form of religious communication; it was authorized religious communication.

Dreaming, for example, was regarded as a particularly unreliable source of religious authority. As the eleventh-century Cluniac monk Ralph Glaber (Ralph the Bald) recorded, heretical preachers were often inspired by strange dreams. In the major Italian city of Ravenna, a scholar of grammar by the name of Vilgard dreamed one night that he was visited by the spirits of three ancient Latin poets—Virgil, Horace, and Juvenal—who promised him fame. Inspired by this dream, Vilgard the scholar "began to preach many things contrary to the faith." Reportedly, he proclaimed that "the words of the poets ought to be believed in all cases." Although he was perhaps trying to reconcile the Christian gospel with classical learning, wisdom, and beauty, Vilgard was condemned as a heretic and forbidden to preach. In the French diocese of Châlons-sur-Marne, a peasant by the name of Leutard fell asleep in the fields after a hard day's work and dreamed that his body was invaded by a swarm of bees. Entering through his genitals, the bees moved through his body stinging him and buzzing loudly as they flew out of his mouth. He felt that the bees were "bidding him to do things impossible to men." When he awoke exhausted from this extraordinary dream, Leutard went to the parish church, where he broke the cross and destroyed an image of Jesus. Explaining to the local peasants that he was acting under divine revelation, he gained a following for his preaching. Apparently, Leutard com-

bined the authority of his personal experience with the authority of the
Bible, since he left his wife "as though he effected the separation by command of the Gospel." When the bishop intervened to condemn him as a
heretic, Leutard lost his following and drowned himself in a well.[3]

In citing these two examples, one a literate scholar, the other an illiterate peasant, Ralph Glaber warned that such false preachers would
increasingly appear as the world moved toward the end of the millennium. These heretics were agents of Satan and the Antichrist. Even within
the institutional church, however, millennial expectations of the end of the
world raised concerns about heretics. During the papacy of Gregory VII
(1073–85), for example, a program of reform was initiated to reinforce
the religious authority of the church. Among the many evils that beset the
world as it drew to its close, Gregory declared, were "certain ministers of
Satan and precursors of the Antichrist," ordained clergy who were nevertheless "trying to overthrow the Christian faith and calling the wrath of
God upon them." Seeking to reform the church from within, Gregory
attacked clergy who bought their positions in the church with money or
engaged in sexual relations. According to Gregory, these two sins—
simony and fornication—threatened the integrity of the church by revealing the corrupt dealings in money and sex among its ordained clergy.[4]

From the fourth-century Donatist controversy in North Africa, the
church had concluded that the effectiveness of its sacraments did not
depend upon the personal integrity or moral purity of its priests. Rather,
the sacraments worked—*ex opere operato,* "working by working"—
because of the apostolic authority invested in the institution of the church.
Nevertheless, the Gregorian reforms directly addressed the issue of the
moral status of clergy. While enforcing clerical celibacy as a standard of
purity, Gregory also tried to remove priestly offices from the cash nexus
of the emerging market economy in Europe. Religious authority could not
be bought or sold for money. Some reformers within the church, however,
went further in arguing that religious authority had to be entirely free
from the ordinary world of economic exchange. As the world drew to its
end, Peter Damian (ca. 1007–72) maintained, Christians were called to
return to their beginning, to restore the original pattern of life established
by the apostles of Jesus Christ. Holding all things in common, the apostles
had no personal possessions, private property, or wealth. According to
Peter Damian, only those who followed the model of the first Christian
community in Jerusalem by owning nothing of their own were fit to

assume the religious authority of preaching (Acts 4:32).[5] In the expanding economy of Europe, this link between poverty and preaching inspired the emergence of new Christian movements.

By the thirteenth century, itinerant preachers had become common throughout Europe. Taking their guidance from the biblical instruction of Jesus in Matthew 10:7–13, these homeless preachers traveled without shoes, money, or possessions. Embracing the poverty of the apostles, they also assumed the apostolic authority to preach the gospel. As Stephen of Bourbon complained, the world was plagued by "stupid and uneducated" preachers who "wandered through the villages, entered homes, preached in the squares and even in the churches." In defiance of a wealthy church and a wealthy bourgeoisie developing during an era of rapid economic growth, wandering preachers renounced worldly goods.

Around 1170, Valdes (Peter Waldo), a rich businessman of the French city of Lyons, saw a jongleur put on a play about St. Alexis. As the entertainer dramatized the story, Alexis underwent a conversion in which he renounced the wealth of his father, rejected his bride, and left home for a life of poverty. Returning to his home many years later as a beggar, Alexis was not recognized by his family and died destitute in his father's house. Moved by this play, Valdes decided to renounce his wealth. He even dramatized his own conversion by throwing money in the street and giving away his possessions. Providing for his wife and daughters, Valdes embraced what he understood as a Christian life of poverty. Rather than entering a monastery, however, he embarked upon a life of homelessness, preaching, and service to others. The guiding text of the Bible for Valdes was the injunction of Jesus: "If you wish to be perfect, go, sell your possessions, and give to the poor, and you will have treasure in heaven; then come, follow me" (Matt. 19:21). As he proclaimed this message of spiritual perfection and material poverty, Valdes insisted on the biblical basis for his preaching. According to Stephen of Bourbon, he "was not well-educated, but on hearing the gospels was anxious to learn more precisely what was in them." To facilitate access to the Christian scriptures, Valdes commissioned translations of the Bible from Latin into the vernacular French. Preaching in public on the basis of those translations, Valdes and his disciples rapidly acquired a large following in and around the city of Lyons.[6]

Rejected by the archbishop of Lyons, however, Valdes was forbidden to preach. With a group of followers, he took his case in 1179 to Pope Alexander III in Rome. Approving the ideal of voluntary poverty, the pope nevertheless denied Valdes and his followers the right to preach unless they were specifically invited to speak in a church by a local priest. Since the established clergy was unlikely to allow such local competition, this condition was effectively a papal ban on their preaching. When they refused to stop preaching, Valdes and his followers were formally excommunicated. By 1184, under the designation Waldensians, they were included in an official list of heretical sects threatening the church. As a result of being driven out of Lyons, however, the Waldensian movement actually grew. Despite official persecution, the Waldensians survived, with their primary centers emerging by the fourteenth century in Germany and central Europe.

Clearly, the Waldensians challenged the church's monopoly on the right to preach. Rejecting the apostolic authority of the Roman Catholic Church, they proposed that anyone who was pure in spirit and moral in lifestyle could act as a priest. They not only denied the special status of priestly ordination in the established church, but also ignored the church's exclusion of women from the priesthood and allowed women to preach. As the movement developed, the training of men and women as preachers became formalized. Preparation lasted one to two years in Lombardy and as long as six years in the north. At the end of their training, the preachers were presented with special sandals that conveyed the right to preach. Known simply as brothers, sisters, or the poor in spirit, these preachers maintained a life of poverty and preaching. They were financially supported by householders, known as "friends," who remained in the world but were devoted to the study of the Bible. By memorizing an impressive number of biblical texts in the vernacular, the preachers were able to present the Bible through the medium of preaching even to listeners who were unable to read.

Like unauthorized preaching, however, the vernacular translation of Christian scriptures worried the official church. In response to the increasing number of popular translations, Pope Innocent III maintained in the 1190s that the "desire for understanding the Holy Scriptures and a zeal for preaching what is in the Scriptures is something not to be reprimanded but rather to be encouraged." Nevertheless, the pope warned, "the secret mysteries of the faith ought not to be explained to all men in all places. For such is the depth of divine scripture, that not only the simple and illiterate but even the prudent and learned are not fully sufficient to try to understand it."[7] In trying to maintain control over the written and oral channels of religious communication, the Roman Catholic Church condemned the biblical translations and preaching of the Waldensians. Although the content of their message, including the ideal of voluntary poverty, might have been acceptable, they had no recognized authority to convey that message. In the struggle against the Waldensians, therefore, the church found a heresy that challenged its regulation of the popular media of religious communication.

Around 1205, Francesco Bernardone (1181–1226), the son of a wealthy merchant in the Italian town of Assisi, publicly renounced his father to adopt a life of poverty. Entering into a spiritual marriage with Lady Poverty, he dedicated himself to demonstrating humility, service to others, and obedience to the church. Gathering a small group of followers, Francis of Assisi drew up a rule for his Friars Minor, the "lesser brothers." In 1210 he went to Rome to appeal for the approval of Pope Innocent III. Initially reluctant, Innocent III nevertheless granted papal permission for Francis and his followers to form a religious order devoted to poverty and preaching. In their preaching, however, they were only permitted to call for penance, leaving the teaching of Christian doctrine to ordained clergy. After receiving this conditional approval, the religious movement grew rapidly, expanding to five thousand Franciscans by 1220. In addition to the order of Friars Minor, a second order was formed in 1212 under the leadership of Clare, a young noblewoman of Assisi. Like the "lesser brothers," the sisters of the Poor Clares took vows of poverty, chastity, and obedience. For laity, a third order, the Order of Penance, allowed men and women to identify with Franciscan spirituality while remaining in the world. Incorporated within the Roman Catholic Church, the Franciscans developed into a major religious force.

Since they were both dedicated to poverty and preaching, why was Francis of Assisi granted official approval when Valdes and his followers were rejected by the church? Certainly, Francis was a charismatic figure, renowned in his lifetime for his personal sanctity. He was described as an inspiring preacher. "He would suggest in a few words what was beyond expression," one of his brothers recalled, "and using fervent gestures and nods, he would transport his hearers wholly to heavenly things." Teaching less by words than by example, Francis had a theatrical flair for dramatizing his Christian commitment to holy poverty and absolute humility. One Easter, when the friars had prepared a table for dinner with linen and glassware, Francis came to the door disguised as a beggar, accepted a plate of food, and sat on the ground, saying, "Now I am sitting as a Friar Minor should sit." When he was invited to dine with nobility or church leaders, Francis would beg for food along the way and arrive to eat the scraps that he had collected. During an illness, he was given a piece of meat to eat, an indulgence that he punished by ordering his friars to lead him by a rope naked around the town, announcing, "Behold the glutton who has grown fat on the meat of chickens which he ate without your knowing it." In these and many other instances, Francis of Assisi drama- tized for his followers what he regarded as Christian poverty, humility, and obedience. He enacted an imitation of Christ that according to tradi- tion culminated in his receiving the wounds that Jesus had suffered on the cross—the stigmata—two years before his death.

The personal charisma of their founder, however, cannot account for the official acceptance of the Franciscans. From the beginning, they found powerful patronage within the church hierarchy. When Francis and his followers appeared in Rome to seek papal approval, they were sponsored by the church leader Cardinal Ugolino. Not only promoting the Franciscans, Ugolino—now as Pope Gregory IX—canonized Francis as a saint in 1233. Official patronage from the church leadership, however, was matched by Francis's absolute obedience to the authority of the church. Like humility, obedience was also dramatized. When he was once denied permission by a bishop to preach in his diocese, Francis left, paused briefly, and then returned to humbly resubmit his request. Impressed by this humble submission to authority, the bishop allowed Francis to preach. According to Stephen of Bourbon, Francis displayed an exemplary respect for the sacramental office of the priesthood. While Waldensians were attacking the legitimacy of the Roman Catholic clergy, the Franciscans followed the model of obedience established by Francis of Assisi.[8]

Nevertheless, the link between poverty and preaching remained poten- tially subversive. As the movement grew under papal guidance, the origi- nal Franciscan requirement of absolute poverty was relaxed. Growing in wealth and power, the Franciscans also entered the universities, playing an influential role not only in teaching, but also in reformulating Christian doctrine. At the end of the thirteenth century, however, factions within the movement objected that the Franciscans had become too wealthy and worldly to remain true to the ideal of holy poverty taught by Francis. Known as the Spirituals, these dissident Franciscans were condemned as

heretics and actively persecuted by the church. In response to the persistence of the Spiritual Franciscans, Pope John XXII in 1323 declared that
it was a heresy to hold the belief that Christ and his apostles had lived in
absolute poverty. Like the Waldensians, therefore, Spiritual Franciscans
were condemned by the church for insisting that holy poverty was a prerequisite for authentic Christian preaching.

DUALISTS

In 1206 Bishop Diego of Osma reflected on the failure of his Cistercian
monks to convert heretics in southern France. Sent on this mission by the
pope, the Spanish bishop only met with frustration. He found that no
matter how sincere or capable his monks might be, they failed to convince
people of their spirituality because they inevitably displayed traces of the
material wealth of the church. As a strategy for engaging heretics, Bishop
Diego proposed that the Cistercian monks under his direction should
dress simply, travel on foot, carry no possessions, and show no signs of
wealth. Although the monks refused, Bishop Diego's assistant, Dominic
of Guzmán (1170–1221), took this advice seriously as the basis for a new
religious order, the Order of Preachers, which came to be known as the
Dominicans. According to tradition, Dominic instructed his followers,
"Have charity, keep humility, and possess voluntary poverty."[9] Like the
Franciscans, the Dominicans developed into a powerful mendicant movement, with orders for men, women, and laity, that was incorporated into
the institutional structure of the Roman Catholic Church. At their inception, however, the Dominicans adopted poverty as a strategy for engaging
heretics, especially for confronting the Cathars, the Christian dualists who
had formed a church that during the thirteenth century rivaled the
Catholics in Europe. Flourishing in Italy and southern France between
about 1150 and 1250, the Cathars were regarded by the Roman Catholic
Church as the most dangerous heretical sect in Christendom.

Deriving their name from the Greek term *katharoi,* meaning "pure,"
the Cathars regarded themselves as authentic Christians, adherents of the
pure church of Jesus Christ. Accepting the New Testament as divine revelation, Cathars saw themselves at the center of a cosmic struggle between
the forces of good and the forces of evil. As the creation of an evil deity or
Satan, the world was understood by Cathars as a realm of darkness and
defilement. Cathar dualism recalled the ancient teachings of Mani (d. 276)

and the Manicheans, with their dualism of good and evil gods, but there does not seem to have been a direct historical connection. Although leaders of the Roman Catholic Church insisted on referring to them as "Manicheans," relying on the fourth-century accounts by Augustine, the Cathars appear to have had a more direct interaction with a church that developed in Bulgaria and spread throughout the Byzantine Empire, the Bogomil Church. Founded in the middle of the tenth century by the monk Bogomil, meaning "loved of God," the Bogomil Church developed a moderate dualism based on belief in one God who was the father of both Satan and Christ. Betraying the supreme God, Satan created the world and held human souls captive in its materiality. According to the Bogomils, Christ was born to liberate souls from an evil world. Following Christ, therefore, required as much spiritual detachment as possible from any physical involvement in that world. Adopting an extremely austere lifestyle, initiates who had received the spiritual baptism within the Bogomil Church renounced marriage, family, sex, and any food associated with sexual coition, including meat, milk, cheese, and eggs. Their supporters, remaining in the world of work and family, served the initiates and gained benefit from their spirituality.

With its dualism of good and evil, spiritual initiation, and ascetic lifestyle, the Bogomil Church grew not only in its Bulgarian homeland, but also in other parts of the Byzantine Empire. By the middle of the twelfth century, a Bogomil Church was firmly established in Constantinople. Bogomil dualism inspired intense theological controversies. From an Orthodox perspective, the suggestion that Satan had created the world contradicted both the unity of God as the supreme creator and the goodness of the world as God's creation. In its extreme spirituality, the Bogomil Church denied the efficacy of many features of Orthodox belief and practice that depended upon finding spiritual power in the material or physical world, such as the sacraments, saints, icons, the incarnation, and the cross. Reportedly, the Bogomils dismissed the Eucharist as nothing but a meal of ordinary bread and wine; they accused the Virgin Mary of complicity with Satan for trying to confine Christ in a body; and they identified the cross as an "instrument for the murder of Christ" that was not the salvation of Christians, but an "enemy of God." Deviating in these respects from Orthodox Christianity, the Bogomil Church nevertheless established a presence in Constantinople that survived until the city was conquered in 1453 by the Turks.

Although historians have debated the extent of Bogomil influence in Europe, by the twelfth century the Cathars of France and Italy had established relations with the Bogomil Church. Around 1172, Nicetas, the bishop of the Bogomil Church of Constantinople, came to the West to preside over a major council of the Cathar Church held near Toulouse in southern France. Attended by Cathars from Italy and France, the council reconsecrated Cathar bishops and reorganized Cathar dioceses. Under the influence of Nicetas, however, many Cathars were encouraged to adopt a more radical or absolute dualism that had become established in the Bogomil Church in Constantinople. Asserting that there were actually two gods, one good, the other evil, this absolute dualism gained some support among Cathars, although many persisted in the moderate dualism that saw the evil god, Satan, as originally and ultimately subordinate to the supreme God, the Father.

Whether absolute or moderate dualists, however, Bogomils and Cathars held much in common. They observed the same ascetic lifestyle, vegetarian diet, and renunciation of the world. Like the Bogomils, the Cathars organized their church on the basis of a division between initiates and supporters. As the leaders of the church, the Cathar initiates, who were known as the "perfect," or simply as the "good Christians," dedicated themselves to living the ascetic ideal. Their supporters, the "believers," provided a material base for the church. When meeting a Cathar perfect on the street, at home, or in church, the believer bowed three times and recited, "Pray God for me, a sinner, that he may make me a good Christian and lead me to a good end." In reply, the perfect said, "May God be prayed that he make you a good Christian." As the living model of a good Christian, therefore, the perfect represented the goal of ordinary Cathar believers.

Besides their ascetic lifestyle, the perfect were distinguished from the ordinary believers by having undergone the principal Cathar sacrament, the *consolamentum,* which was a ritual of spiritual baptism performed by the laying on of hands. Understood as the only sacrament to have been introduced by Jesus Christ, this ritual was received once in a lifetime. After receiving this initiation, the perfect were required to maintain a sinless life, making a public confession once a month of any minor transgressions, while awaiting the final spiritual liberation from the world that was anticipated to come at death. Transcending the mythic dualism of good and evil, therefore, the Cathar ritual of the *consolamentum* promised to restore the soul that had originally come from God, the Father, in expectation of the ultimate triumph of good.

During the thirteenth century, the Roman Catholic Church declared war on the Cathars. The church deployed two strategies—crusade and inquisition—to destroy Cathars in Europe. In the Languedoc region of southern France, where the Cathars were known as Albigensians, after the French town of Albi, the Cathar Church had become well established among nobility, peasantry, and artisans. Roman Catholic attempts at conversion had resulted in failure. In response to this religious resistance, Pope Innocent III in 1208 called for a new crusade, not to recapture the Holy Land in Palestine, but to subdue the heretics of southern France. Initially targeted at Toulouse, the Albigensian Crusade caused massive death and destruction throughout southern France. Inspired to take up the cross, Christian knights were also interested in pillaging the wealth of the region, in many instances failing to discriminate between orthodoxy and heresy. Nevertheless, the Albigensian Crusade devastated the Cathar movement. Their last outpost in southern France, a mountain castle near Foix, where the Cathar bishop of Toulouse had fled in 1232, was finally captured by the crusaders after a ten-month siege in 1244. Over two hundred perfect were executed by being burned alive. Cathar bishops who survived the crusade in southern France fled to Lombardy, where they continued to lead their church in secret.

Although this military crusade gained some success in suppressing heresy, the legal procedures of inquisition had a more enduring effect. Introduced in 1233 by Pope Gregory IX to address Cathars and Waldensians in southern France, the inquisition developed into the principal Roman Catholic institution for identifying and dealing with heretics. Regarded as an extension of the penitential system, the ecclesiastical inquisition was established to induce confessions and repentance for the sin of heresy. Accused heretics who confessed were able to perform acts of penance that would reincorporate them in the Catholic community. Those who refused to confess or who lapsed after their penance, however, could be given over to a local secular authority for punishment. Confirmed heretics might be executed by burning, but they could also have their property confiscated and their descendants deprived of any civil rights for two generations. Although inquisitions had these legal, social, and economic implications, they were essentially ritual institutions for the production of truth. In 1252 Pope Innocent IV approved the introduction of physical torture into that ritual, with the provision that torture should not result in shedding of blood, mutilation, or death. As further indication of the ritual character of these proceedings, even dead heretics could be punished as a result of the findings of an inquisition by having their corpses disinterred and burned. Although there was no single inquisition, with a centralized administration in the Roman Catholic Church, the institution nevertheless assumed an important ritual function in the production and reinforcement of a particular domain of religious truth.

More effective than crusading, the inquisitions established in northern Italy and southern France succeeded in destroying the Cathars, thus eliminating the Roman Catholic Church's principal rival. At stake were crucial issues of Christian doctrine, ritual, and society. Through military crusade and legal inquisition, the church found forceful ways of settling those issues. Nevertheless, those engagements with heresy involved church leaders in the complex and difficult task of trying to read outward signs of secret beliefs. During the Albigensian Crusade, for example, Catholic forces sought to establish signs of secret heresy in heretical habits of diet or heretical dispositions toward killing and eating animals. "I have heard that Catholic soldiers in France examined the heretics in the Albigensian territory in the following way," Stephen of Bourbon reported. "They gave the suspects chickens or other animals to kill, and if they did not wish to do so, they determined them to be heretics, or followers of them." Heretics, as the inquisitor Bernard Gui explained, "never eat, nor even touch meat, cheese or eggs." Although heretics inevitably abstained from certain foods, the inquisitors found, Christians would eat anything.[10] Combating heresy, therefore, involved more than merely searching out errors in Christian doctrine and practice. It required a close reading of everyday behavior to identify and expose those who deviated from what was regarded as normal. With the suppression of Christians such as the Waldensians and Cathars who were defined as heretics because of their "improper worship" and alternative lifestyles, a new threat emerged in fourteenth-century Europe in the form of the deviance of witchcraft.

WITCHES

In destroying the shrine of St. Guinefort, Stephen of Bourbon had determined that the women who participated were engaged in demon worship. Suffering under the "illusions of the Devil," they performed the "tricks of demons." As he worked to expose Waldensians and Cathars, Stephen also heard stories suggesting that demon worship was widespread, especially devotion to pagan deities, the gods and goddesses of ancient Europe, who conveyed extraordinary powers on men and women. Reportedly, there were women who gathered at night to worship the pagan goddesses Diana and Herodias. Calling themselves the *bonae res,* the "good ones," these women believed that they could fly through the night sky, pass through walls, and see the future. As Stephen related, an old woman told her priest that she had saved him from death at the hands of the goddesses. Out riding one night with the *bonae res,* she had entered his house to find him sleeping naked. The old woman had covered him, she said, because if Diana and Herodias had seen his nakedness, they would have whipped him to death. Instead of being grateful for receiving this spiritual protection, however, the priest called the woman a *sortilega*—a diviner, sorcerer, or witch—and subjected her to a beating.

Although Stephen found that women were most commonly involved in this type of demon worship, men also participated in pagan rites. In one rural area, he recounted, a group of men dressed as women visited the home of a wealthy farmer and promised to grant the farmer even greater prosperity. Demanding gifts from the farmer in return for their spiritual gift of prosperity, they danced around the house, singing, "We take one and give back a hundred." When the farmer refused to give them anything, they simply took all the goods from the house. "You shall be rich," they said, "because we are the *bonae res,* and your goods will be multiplied."

In these accounts, Stephen documented the persistence of pagan practices for achieving spiritual protection, prosperity, fertility, and well-being. But he identified the practitioners as witches. According to the traditional image of witchcraft in Europe, witches used a range of secret techniques for causing harm or bestowing protection. When they used occult means to harm persons or property, witches registered as dangerous, violent, and antisocial agents who had to be excluded from society. By arguing that witches actually worshiped demons, however, Stephen pointed to a new development—diabolical witchcraft—that came to dominate the Christian imagination. More dangerous than the deluded *bonae res,* he reported, were the witches who met secretly at night to participate in ritual services for the devil, suggesting that diabolical witchcraft was an organized anti-Christian movement devoted to the devil.

As the notion of diabolical witchcraft developed, certain stereotypes about witches—atheism, sexual promiscuity, and cannibalism—recalled Greco-Roman accusations against early Christian communities. Denying God, witches allegedly entered into a solemn pact with the devil that was reinforced through regular meetings in their demonic "sabbats" or "synagogues." At those nocturnal meetings, the devil appeared in the form of a cat, a toad, a duck, a goose, a man with goat's legs, or a black man to receive the devotion of witches who took turns kissing him on the buttocks. After a ceremonial meal of disgusting food, the witches engaged in an orgy of heterosexual and homosexual intercourse. Any children that might be born from this sexual activity were supposedly eaten eight days after birth. Their pact with the devil, however, enabled witches to fly through the air, change shape, acquire material wealth, and cause harm to others by secret means. The stereotype of diabolical witchcraft, therefore, combined certain features of the traditional image of the witch with the notion that witches were the supreme heretics, adherents of a secret, underground organization, the church of Satan.[11]

During the fourteenth century, this stereotype of diabolical witchcraft was employed in a series of political trials, most notably in the destruction and dispossession of the Knights Templar. At the instigation of the French monarch Philip IV, known as "Philip the Fair," who seized the property of the wealthy and powerful order of military monks, the Templars were accused in 1307 of worshiping the devil. Before a papal inquisition, they were charged with demonic practices drawn from the repertoire of diabolical witchcraft. Allegedly, all Templars formally denied God, Christ, and the Virgin Mary. They trampled, spat, and urinated on the cross. They kissed the buttocks of their prior, engaged in sodomy, and worshiped idols in the form of a golden calf, a bearded man, or the demon Baphomet, a term derived from the name of the prophet of Islam. Under interrogation and torture, members of the Knights Templar not only confessed to these anti-Christian practices, but added further testimony about demon worship, extraordinary sexual activity, and ceremonial cannibalism that filled in the details of the stereotype of diabolical witchcraft. Later, leaders and members of the order tried to retract their confessions, but in 1314 the Knights Templar was dissolved and its leaders were burned in public. Despite the transparent political motivation of the French king and the Catholic pope in destroying the order and appropriating its wealth, the trial of the Knights Templar was a significant public occasion for reinforcing the stereotype of diabolical witchcraft.

Sustained witch-hunts, however, were not conducted by ecclesiastical inquisitions until the fifteenth century. Between 1427 and 1486, witch-hunting flourished in northern Italy and southern Germany, as local inquisitions were established to identify witches and turn them over to secular authorities for execution. During the following three centuries, as local witch-hunts developed throughout Europe, an estimated hundred thousand people—80 percent women—were killed as witches. The primary guide for witch-hunting was a manual, the *Malleus Maleficarum (Hammer of Witches)*, which was originally published in 1486 by two Dominican inquisitors, Jacob Sprenger and Heinrich Kramer. As veterans of the inquisition in southern Germany instituted by Pope Innocent VIII in 1484, Sprenger and Kramer had been charged with the responsibility of seeking out, prosecuting, and executing witches. Within two years, they had supervised the execution of fifty accused witches, all but two of whom were women, in and around the city of Cologne. According to these inquisitors, witchcraft was the most serious heresy faced by the church, a heresy of disbelief, apostasy, and opposition to the Christian faith. "Since infidelity is a chief cause of man's separation from God," they wrote, "the infidelity of witches stands out as the greatest of sins. And this is given the name heresy, which is apostasy from the faith; and in this witches sin throughout their whole lives."

Sprenger and Kramer knew that skeptics might doubt the existence of witches. Accordingly, they began their manual by insisting that beliefs in the devil, demons, and witches were necessary features of Christianity. They asserted that "the belief that there are such beings as witches is so essential a part of the Catholic faith that obstinacy to maintain the opposite opinion manifestly savors of heresy." Not only witches, therefore, but also Christians who denied the existence of witches were classified by the inquisitors as heretics. Among medieval scholars, demonic influence was generally recognized. As Thomas Aquinas argued, however, the devil was the "indirect cause of all our sins, in so far as he induced the first man to sin, by reason of whose sin human nature is so infected, that we are all prone to sin." Although acknowledging the indirect influence of the devil through original sin, Aquinas maintained that "He is not, however, the direct cause of all the sins of men, as though each were the result of his suggestion."

By contrast, Sprenger and Kramer insisted that the devil and his demons directly entered into pacts with witches to promote sin, suffering, and misfortune. By acting through their human agents, the witches, these demonic forces were the direct cause of a host of evils. They stirred up wicked desires; inspired hatred, anger, and jealousy; interfered with sexual relations and childbirth; and brought diseases, madness, and death. In acting directly through witches to cause such enormous evil, the devil and his demons waged an incessant campaign against God. In order to avoid the dualistic conclusions of the heretical Cathars, however, the Dominican inquisitors had to maintain that all this evil was somehow part of God's plan. As they argued, God allowed evil to flourish because he planned to draw from it a greater good. Ironically, therefore, Sprenger and Kramer repeatedly observed that the evil of witchcraft that they so vigorously opposed in the name of God only existed in the world with the permission of God.

While elaborating all the features of the stereotype of diabolical witchcraft, Sprenger and Kramer also reinforced the assumption that most witches were women. In keeping with Scholastic prejudice against women, the inquisitors proposed that women were more susceptible to demon possession and the seductions of the devil "since they are feebler both in mind and body." Although witch-hunting was regarded as a crusade against evil, the numerous misogynistic passages of the *Malleus Maleficarum* suggest that witch-hunters were also waging a war against women. Certainly, the authors celebrated the divine female in the form of the Virgin Mary, proclaiming the "whole sin of Eve taken away by the benediction of Mary." An ordinary woman, however, could always be suspected of witchcraft, "since she is ever weaker to hold and preserve the faith." Throughout their manual, Sprenger and Kramer referred to the witch in the feminine gender, suggesting that their inquisition was specifically targeting women.

Against the evil of witchcraft, Christians could turn to certain ritual techniques for protection. As Sprenger and Kramer advised, Christians could defend themselves by devout prayer, the sacrament of confession, pilgrimages to holy shrines, and "the plentiful use of the sign of the Cross." Under the supervision of a priest, they could be protected from witchcraft and demon possession by rituals of exorcism. For judges who presided at the trials of accused witches, they recommended wearing a kind of spiritual armor of fabric in which was woven "consecrated salt and other matters, with the Seven Words which Christ uttered on the Cross written in a schedule, and all bound together." As a ritual means for "putting on Christ," this technique was recommended by Sprenger and Kramer because "it is shown by experience that witches are greatly troubled by these things." In fighting witches, therefore, the inquisitors encouraged certain practices that resembled the magic or sorcery for which witches stood accused.

Witches were most seriously troubled by the proceedings of an inquisition, however, which according to Sprenger and Kramer ultimately provided the best protection against witchcraft. In starting the proceedings, an accuser might come forward, but the accuser risked facing the same penalties applied to witchcraft if the case could not be proved. It was safer, therefore, to appear as an informer rather than as an accuser, since an informer was not liable to suffer any punishment if the case failed. Usually, however, a case was opened as a result of "a general report that there are witches in some town or place." In principle, a conviction required a confession from the witch. In order to obtain a confession, the inquisitors advocated the use of deception and force. Using false promises, for example, the inquisitor could assure the accused of mercy, but "with a mental reservation that he means he will be merciful to himself or the state; for whatever is done for the safety of the state is merciful." If such deception failed to produce a confession, Sprenger and Kramer advised that the accused should be imprisoned "in case perhaps, being depressed after a year of the squalor of prison, she may confess her crimes." When an accused witch persisted in refusing to confess, the inquisitors could resort to torture, "but not joyfully," Sprenger and Kramer noted. As a technique for inducing a confession, they recognized, torture might be unreliable, since the weak would confess anything and the strong would withstand the pain in silence. Nevertheless, in the search for truth, they regarded torture as a legitimate means for gaining a witch's personal confession, the only basis for a legal conviction. Once convicted, the witch was to be turned over to the local secular authorities for execution. On biblical authority, the inquisitors were instructed, "Thou shalt not suffer a witch to live" (Exod. 22:18). By sending witches to their death, inquisitors could be assured that they were defending the "Faith of the Holy Church of God."[12]

Identified by the Dominican inquisitors as the worst of all heretics, witches continued to be hunted in Europe; the most vigorous, extensive, and violent witch-hunts were conducted during the sixteenth and seventeenth centuries. These witch-hunting campaigns continued to be informed by the stereotype of diabolical witchcraft established by Sprenger and Kramer in their *Malleus Maleficarum*. However, that text was produced in the context not only of witch-hunting, but also of intense debates over the status of Mary, especially the proposition that she had been born without sin. In Germany, these debates became so intense that in the 1480s the pope threatened excommunication for anyone who argued about the topic. The Dominican inquisitors, however, were strong advocates of the veneration of Mary, having participated in the 1470s in their order's introduction of a new ritual technique, the rosary, for reciting and counting the repetitions of two prayers, the Ave Maria (Hail Mary) and the Pater Noster (Our Father). Around 1475, Jacob Sprenger had founded a new religious organization, the Confraternity of the Rosary, to promote and popularize this ritual technique for devotion to Mary. Attracting the participation of lay men and women, the Confraternity of the Rosary was dedicated to the regular recitation of the rosary, Bible reading, and the cultivation of a devotional spirituality particularly directed toward the Virgin Mary. In their struggle to assert orthodoxy against heresy, therefore, the Dominican inquisitors deployed two strategies that significantly altered the character of Christianity in Europe in the early modern era, the suppression of witches and the elevation of Mary.[13]

17

Mary

When the founder of the Dominican order, Dominic of Guzmán (1170–1221), became despondent about his failure to convert Cathars in southern France, he withdrew in 1214 to an isolated cave in the woods near Toulouse. Alone, without food or water, Dominic prayed for divine assistance. Suddenly, the Virgin Mary appeared. She kissed him and then satisfied his hunger and thirst by giving him milk from her breast. Before sending him back out into the world, the Virgin Mary instructed Dominic to preach her prayer, the Ave Maria: "Hail Mary, full of grace, the Lord is with you. Blessed are you among women, and blessed is the fruit of your womb, Jesus." This prayer, which had been used in varying forms in both the East and the West for centuries, was based on the biblical salutations of Mary by the angel Gabriel and her sister, Elizabeth, as recorded in the Gospel of Luke (1:28; 1:42). Exhorting Dominic to promote this prayer, the Virgin Mary left him with a string of beads to be used when reciting the Ave Maria. In this miraculous appearance by the Virgin Mary, therefore, the use of the rosary was introduced into Christian devotions.

This legendary account of the origin of the rosary, however, was first told in 1470 by the Dominican Alanus de Rupe (d. 1475). In a manual for praying to Mary, Alanus praised the power of the rosary to invoke the Virgin's mercy and protection. Apparently, the Dominican priest felt it was appropriate that the rosary should have been originally introduced by the founder of his order. In relating the story of the miraculous visitation of the Virgin to Dominic, he adapted the theme of receiving the holy mother's milk, which had featured in earlier devotional traditions. For example, Bernard of Clairvaux reportedly experienced a mystical vision of the Virgin Mary in which he received three drops of milk from the breast of the Mother of God. By the end of the fifteenth century, however, the Dominican Order of Preachers had assumed a special responsibility for promoting and organizing devotion to the Virgin Mary. Twenty years after the founding of the first Confraternity of the Rosary by the Dominican Jacob Sprenger, Pope Alexander VI gave formal approval for its use in 1495. Supported by lay organizations that developed in cities and towns throughout Europe, the recitation of prayers to Mary on the rosary became thoroughly integrated into Catholic religious practice.

Like the Jesus Prayer used by the hesychasts in the East, the Ave Maria gained its power through repetition. In many religions, prayer beads provide a ritual aid for repeating sacred tones, words, or prayers. As some historians have speculated, the Hindu use of the *japamala* prayer beads in chanting sacred sounds or reciting prayers might have influenced the development of similar practices among Muslims and Christians. In early medieval Europe, however, Christian monks were using a string of 150 beads as a device for monitoring their recitation from memory of the 150 Psalms. This counting device became so closely associated with the hymns of the book of Psalms—in Latin, the *Psalter*—that the string of beads was also referred to as the psalter. By the eleventh century, prayer beads were used to count the number of prayers offered for the dead. Since the most common prayer recited in these chantries was the Lord's Prayer, the "Our Father" (in Latin, the *Pater Noster*), the beads themselves came to be known as a paternoster. Adapting these ritual practices of reciting, repeating, and counting prayers, the Dominicans celebrated the rosary as "Our Lady's Psalter," the garland of roses that evoked the divine mercy and spiritual protection of Mary. In the prayers of the rosary, Mary was invoked as the "rose without thorns" (Ecclus. 24:14), the "rose of Sharon" (Song of Songs 2:1), the rose at the center of an enclosed garden (Song of Songs 4:12), the beautiful rose that gave birth to Christ on earth (Dante *Paradiso* 23.73), the blood-red rose of suffering and sorrow, and the mystical rose that unfolded its radiant petals in heaven.

Although principally focused on Mary, the prayers of the rosary provided a comprehensive tour through Christian faith. Beginning with the creed, which was recited holding the cross or medallion appended to the beads, the cycle of prayer on the rosary alternated one Pater Noster on a larger bead with repetitions of the Ave Maria on each of ten smaller beads. Arriving after these ten invocations of the Virgin Mary at another larger bead, the round of prayer was concluded with the Gloria: "Glory be to the Father, and to the Son, and to the Holy Ghost, as it was in the beginning, is now, and ever shall be." With the completion of that round, another round was begun, repeating the three prayers in a continuous cycle. Although a complete tour of the rosary required 150 rounds, it became common to recite a shorter version of 50. The rosary, as it was popularized by the Dominicans during the fifteenth century, with the Ave Maria framed by the prayers to the Father and the Trinity, effectively placed Mary, as the Mother of God, at the center of Christian devotion. Initially the Ave Maria consisted of the biblical praises to the Virgin, but during the sixteenth century it was expanded by adding the petition, "Pray for us sinners, now and at the hour of our death." Although this version of the prayer was only officially recognized by Pope Pius V in 1578, it reflected an understanding of Mary—as mediator, intercessor, and protector of Christian devotees in this life and the next—that had a much longer history.

While reciting each round of prayer on the rosary, the devotee was expected to visualize one of the fifteen mysteries of Mary, the joyful, the sorrowful, and the glorious. The Joyful Mysteries, which recalled the divine motherhood of Mary, were the Annunciation, the Visitation, the Nativity, the Presentation, and the Finding of Jesus in the Temple. As they were meditated upon during the tour of the rosary, the five Joyful Mysteries recalled important events in the relationship between the Virgin Mother and the Child God. By contrast, the Sorrowful Mysteries represented the betrayal, suffering, and death of Jesus from his mother's perspective. As subjects for meditation, the five Sorrowful Mysteries recalled Mary's profound emotional pain at her son's Agony in the Garden, his Scourging at the Pillar, his Crowning with Thorns, his Carrying of the Cross, and his Crucifixion and Death. Finally, the Glorious Mysteries—the Resurrection of Jesus, the Ascension of Jesus, the Descent of the Holy Spirit upon the early Christian community, the Assumption of the Virgin Mary into heaven, and her Coronation as the Queen of Heaven—celebrated the triumph of Christianity. Transcending suffering, death, and loss, these five mysteries recalled the ultimate glorification of Jesus and Mary as the divine king and the divine queen of the universe. With the final meditation that ended a complete cycle of the rosary, the verbal praise of the Virgin Mother of God expressed in the Ave Maria merged with a vision of Mary as the supreme Queen of Heaven. In all these mysteries, however, Mary remained a complex religious figure. As the joyful mother of the son of God and the sorrowful mother of a son who was cruelly tortured and executed, Mary was ultimately regarded in the spirituality cultivated by the rosary as the divine queen who reigned over heaven and earth. Punctuated by prayers to the Father and the Trinity, the rosary grew around the Mother.[1]

IMMACULATE CONCEPTION

As the eternal virgin, Mary was a model of purity. Devotees of the Virgin Mary in medieval Europe such as Bernard of Clairvaux held that she had maintained her virginal status not only before and after, but also during the birth of Jesus. "The Virgin's name was Mary" (Luke 1:27), Bernard observed, which means "star of the sea." This name was particularly appropriate for the Virgin, he explained, because as the "star sends forth its ray without harm to itself, in the same way the Virgin brought forth her Son with no injury to herself."[2] Bernard insisted that Mary had gone through childbirth effortlessly, like a star radiating light, with her virginal purity intact. Born of this virgin, Jesus was exempt from inheriting the original sin that had been transmitted through the human generations from the first parents. But what about Mary? If she had been born into sin like all other human beings, how had she achieved her sinless state of purity? The doctrine of the Immaculate Conception, which proposed that Mary had been born free of the taint of original sin, was one solution to this problem. An annual feast celebrating the miraculous conception of Mary, which had been observed within Eastern Orthodoxy since the eighth century, had been introduced into the Catholic calendar beginning around 1030 in England and thereafter increased in popularity through-out Europe.[3] The doctrine of the Immaculate Conception, therefore, emerged as a significant feature of the new devotion to the *Mater Matris*, the "Mother of the Mother."

Since Mary's mother did not appear in the gospels, Christians had to rely on textual sources not included in the New Testament canon. Written in the middle of the second century, the text known as the *Protevangelium of James* provided details about Mary's family. Allegedly written by James, who is referred to in the New Testament as the "brother of the Lord," this text stands in striking contrast to the relative neglect of Mary in the gospels and other early Christian writings. Identifying Mary's parents as Joachim and Anne, James's work described how the childless couple had miraculously conceived Mary and dedicated her to the temple in Jerusalem. When Mary reached puberty, her parents found her a husband, the elderly widower Joseph, who respected her virginity and stood by her when she became pregnant. According to the *Protevangelium of James,* Mary's virginity remained intact even during the birth of Jesus, a miracle witnessed by a woman named Salome who insisted on testing Mary's condition herself only to find that her hand caught on fire. As a virgin before, during, and after the birth of Jesus, therefore, Mary was affirmed by this popular and influential second-century text as the paragon of purity, a virgin mother who herself had been miraculously conceived by her own mother, Anne.[4]

Certain passages of the New Testament, however, called into question the perpetual virginity of Mary by referring to brothers of Jesus. On several occasions, his mother and brothers appeared together in stories about the ministry or miracles of Jesus. How could they be reconciled with the virginity of Mary before, during, and after the birth of Jesus? In the influential theological summary of the *Sentences,* Peter Lombard proposed that the brothers of Jesus ought to be understood either as sons of the elderly widower, Joseph, from a previous marriage or as cousins of Mary, interpreting the term "brothers" to refer to broader relations of kinship. Although the first option could be supported on the authority of the *Protevangelium of James,* the second solution became increasingly popular. During the fourteenth century, this dilemma of maintaining the virginity of Mary while accounting for the brothers of Jesus was resolved by the elaborate symbolism of the "holy kinship," the imagery of an extended divine family traced back to the mother of Mary, the matriarch Anne.

In the holy kinship, Anne was the source of a family tree in which she was the grandmother not only of Jesus, but also of several grandsons, such as James, the brother of the Lord, and John, the Evangelist, who were referred to in the New Testament as brothers of Jesus. However, Anne's own children, who became the mothers of these "brothers," were born out of three different marriages. In her first marriage to Joachim, Anne miraculously conceived a daughter, Mary. Then Joachim died. Following the levirate law of ancient Jewish tradition, in which a younger brother was expected to assume responsibility for an elder brother's widow, Anne married Joachim's younger brother, Cleophas. Anne and Cleophas had a daughter, also named Mary, who was called Mary Cleophas to distinguish her from the other Mary. Then Cleophas died. At the death of her second husband, Anne married her third husband, a man by the name of Salome. Anne gave birth to a third daughter, who was once again named Mary, but was distinguished from the other two Marys by being known as Mary Salome. According to this medieval reconstruction, therefore, over the course of three marriages, which were celebrated as the holy *trinubium,* Anne gave birth to three Marys.

Eventually, Anne's daughters became mothers in their own right of sons who featured prominently in the Christian story. The Virgin Mary inherited her mother's spiritual gift of immaculate conception by conceiving her son, Jesus, through the Holy Spirit; Mary Cleophas became the mother of James, the "brother of the Lord"; and Mary Salome became the mother of John, the Evangelist. Within the extended family of the holy kinship, therefore, Anne was the root of an extensive Christian family tree.[5]

As this symbolism of the holy kinship was developed in medieval Europe, the central role of Anne, as the Mother of the Mother of God, became increasingly important in Christian devotion. At the beginning of the thirteenth century, for example, the cathedral of Chartres in northern France, with its magnificent Gothic architecture dedicated to the Virgin Mary, received the head of the matriarch Anne from the knights who were returning from the Fourth Crusade. According to a contemporary commentator on this event, "The head of the mother was received with great joy in the church of the daughter."[6] Three hundred years later, the Dominicans of the German monastery at Mainz also kept a head of the matriarch Anne, until it was stolen and turned over to the Franciscans in Düren, near Aachen, which subsequently became a popular pilgrimage site. Between roughly 1200 and 1550, devotion to Anne as the matriarch of the holy kinship was anchored not only in such relics, but also in pictorial representations. In depicting the incarnation of God in human flesh, artists frequently represented Christ as a child who was accompanied not by his mother and father, but by his mother and grandmother. Although Joseph might appear at a distance, looking old, tired, and feeble, perhaps even separated from the child by a wall, the human father of Jesus was not central to the mystery of the holy kinship. In contrast to the genealogies of Jesus that appeared in the gospels of Matthew and Luke, which had derived the patriarchal lineage of Jesus from Jesse, the father of King David, this medieval symbolism of the holy kinship emphasized matriarchy. Accordingly, in the holy kinship the Tree of Jesse was replaced by the rose tree of Mary.

Objections were raised to the doctrine of the Immaculate Conception.

Anselm of Canterbury, for example, was devoted to Mary, but assumed that she had been born into original sin like every other human being. Thomas Aquinas offered a compromise by proposing that Mary had been conceived normally, but sanctified spiritually while in her mother's womb.[7] With the support of both the Dominicans and the Franciscans, however, the doctrine of the Immaculate Conception gained considerable force during the fifteenth century. Although it was declared a doctrine of faith at the church council held in Basel in 1438, the doctrine of the Immaculate Conception remained such a source of disagreement that its supporter, Pope Sixtus IV, in 1483 forbade any further argument about the topic on pain of excommunication. This papal silencing of debate about the Immaculate Conception, however, only seemed to increase Anne's popularity, although Christian scholars often challenged the entire notion of the holy kinship by pointing out its arbitrary construction from biblical materials. In reconstructing Anne's family tree, the advocates of the *trinubium* had given her third husband, Salome, a woman's name. As the name appeared in the New Testament (Mark 15:40; 16:1), Salome clearly referred to a woman and therefore could not be the name of the third husband of Anne. According to the anti-Salomites, the entire family tree that was traced back to the matriarch Anne fell apart because of such careless use of biblical evidence. Despite these objections, however, the *trinubium* became generally accepted, largely because it was incorporated in the popular text of the *Legenda Aurea,* the "Golden Legend," which was widely circulated throughout Europe.

In the midst of controversy over the Immaculate Conception, the *trinubium,* and the holy kinship, Anne continued to inspire religious devotion. The fourteenth-century visionary Bridget of Sweden (d. 1373), a widow, Franciscan tertiary, and founder of her own religious order, reported a miraculous vision in which she witnessed the birth of Christ. Surrounded by heavenly light and music, Bridget beheld the Virgin Mary painlessly give birth to Jesus and then kneel down to worship the child. Bridget also reported receiving a spiritual vision of Mary's mother, Anne, who introduced herself as the "lady of all wedded folk." In the exemplary marriage of Anne and Joachim, which was distinguished by "godly charity and honesty," Bridget observed that God had found the perfect parents for Mary. "Hence it pleased him that the body of his most glorious mother," Bridget explained, "should be begotten in this holy wedlock." In this vision, Anne appeared as the most appropriate patron saint for married Christians.[8]

Religious women who had taken vows of celibacy could also be devoted to St. Anne. In the case of Colette of Corbie (1381–1447), the Franciscan reformer of the Poor Clares, St. Anne was established as the focus for special devotions in the chapels of her convents. According to her biographer, as a child Colette had refused to pray to St. Anne because she was disgusted by the story of her three marriages. Praying only to saints who were famous for their virginity, Colette unexpectedly received a visit from St. Anne, who appeared before her "with glorious ornaments bringing with her all her glorious progeny, her three most glorious daughters, and her noble son." In this extraordinary vision, St. Anne reportedly revealed to Colette that "although she had several times copulated in marriage no one in the whole church militant and triumphant was so adorned for her progeny and honored with fame." Justifying her three marriages by their glorious fruits, therefore, St. Anne appeared to Colette as the root of the tree of holy kinship that had produced the Christian church. In her efforts as organizer of the Colettine convents of the Poor Clares, Colette regarded St. Anne as playing a special role in mobilizing the support of the saints in heaven for her religious work on earth.[9]

By the beginning of the sixteenth century, devotion to St. Anne was popular in Europe. Supported by accounts of popular devotion, with their visions, miracles, and spiritual interventions in the world, St. Anne became a powerful Christian symbol of female authority, reproductive fertility, and spiritual glory. Around 1550, however, a shift can be observed from this devotion to the holy kinship, which revolved around St. Anne, to an interest in the holy family of Joseph, Mary, and the Child. As this nuclear family was elevated in importance, the earlier imagery of Joseph as a tired old man was gradually replaced by one of a hardworking carpenter, provider, and protector of Mary and the infant Jesus. It was not until 1564 that the first Western church was dedicated to St. Joseph, built in Toledo, Spain, under the influence of Teresa of Ávila (d. 1582), who regarded Joseph as the best saint because he was the stepfather of Jesus and the supporter of Mary. Corresponding to new patterns of family life emerging among urban elites and middle classes in Europe, the holy family of father, mother, and child increasingly displaced the extended kinship system headed by the holy grandmother. Certainly, Catholic religious devotion continued to be directed toward St. Anne, a devotion certified in 1854 by the papal authorization of the dogma of the Immaculate

Conception. However, with the historical changes in the understanding and organization of the European family, Anne lost her preeminent place as the matriarchal head of the holy household of God.[10]

MOTHER OF SORROW

In Christian symbolism, the Virgin Mary has represented both glory and humility. As the *Theotokos* of Eastern Orthodoxy and the *Mater Dei* of Roman Catholicism, Mary was glorified as the Mother of God who gave human flesh to Jesus Christ. By her willingness to undertake that awesome responsibility, however, Mary also demonstrated a profound humility, describing herself as the "handmaid of the Lord" (Luke 1:38). Therefore, Mary was both the mother and the servant of God. While serving "Lady Poverty," Francis of Assisi was also interested in cultivating the devotion for the humility of Mary. With his flair for the theatrical, Francis prepared a new display for the midnight Mass at Christmas, a crib that would suggest the humble conditions suffered by mother and child at the birth of Christ. Francis introduced this nativity scene, he explained, "For I wish to do something that will recall to memory the little Child who was born in Bethlehem and set before our bodily eyes in some way the inconveniences of his infant needs, how he lay in a manger, how, with an ox and an ass standing by, he lay upon the hay where he had been placed."[11] In this theater of the nativity, therefore, a popular image of the lowly birth of the divine Jesus was cultivated and spread widely in European Christianity.

In keeping with this imagery of the humility of Christ's birth, between 1400 and 1600 in Europe a new emphasis on the physicality of Jesus emerged in Christian theology, literature, and art. Although the mainstream Christian understanding of Jesus as God incarnate had always emphasized the body, a new interest in meditating on the physical details of the body of Jesus Christ became prominent in European Christianity. When representing the nativity, for example, artists increasingly depicted the infant Christ as a realistic, recognizable, and fully human male child, using precise anatomical detail that frequently included the display of the holy genitals. In paintings of Anne, Mary, and the infant Jesus, for example, the grandmother of Christ is often shown holding or pointing to the child's penis. According to some historians, the growing concern with the physicality of Christ, reflected in this new artistic attention to the penis of the infant Jesus, reinforced the Christian doctrine of the incarnation by showing that God had been born in a real, physical, gendered, and even sexual human body.

By contrast, however, other historians have argued that these depictions of the genitals of Jesus did not represent the relatively abstract modern notions of embodiment, gender, or sexuality. Rather, they pointed to an important Christian holiday, the Feast of the Circumcision, which was celebrated on the first day of January to mark Jesus' first shedding of blood when he was circumcised according to Jewish practice eight days after birth. The holy circumcision featured prominently in late medieval spirituality. Catherine of Siena, for example, was said to have miraculously received the holy foreskin of the infant Jesus to wear as a wedding ring. Since the blood of Christ was regarded as the source of salvation, this first wound that Jesus suffered at his circumcision prefigured the last wounds he would suffer on the cross.[12]

In any event, the evidence from Christian art suggests a new interest in visualizing the physical details of Christ's body at birth and in death. Mother Mary, of course, was present at both events. As the Mother of Sorrow, the *Mater Dolorosa*, Mary had undergone the supreme agony of watching her only son betrayed, arrested, tortured, and cruelly executed by crucifixion. The burden of her sorrows, however, could be shared by all Christians. An influential thirteenth-century monastic text for meditating on the life of Christ urged Christians to adopt the perspective of the mother when contemplating Christ's death. By assuming the vantage point of the Virgin Mary, the mind's eye had to behold "the cross, the nails and hammer, the ladder and other instruments, some giving orders, others stripping him." In this flurry of activity, Jesus is taken from his mother, "torn furiously from her hands to the foot of the cross." Identifying with the agony of Mary, the meditator experienced the mother's terror, sadness, and shame at the humiliation of her son.

> Now for the first time the Mother beholds her Son thus taken and prepared for the anguish of death. She is saddened and shamed beyond measure when she sees him entirely nude; they did not leave him even his loincloth. Therefore she hurries and approaches the Son, embraces him, and girds him with the veil from her head. Oh, what bitterness her soul is in now!

By visualizing Jesus naked, exposed, and tortured, this meditation certainly emphasized the physical torment of the Son of God. In adopting the perspective of the Virgin Mary, however, the meditator embraced the pain, agony, and loss that only a mother could experience at the death of her only son.[13]

Another thirteenth-century text, the Latin verse of the Stabat Mater, which came to be recited and sung throughout Europe, evoked Mary's pain as she stood at the foot of the cross. Sharing the mother's grief, the song demanded, "Who would not weep to see the mother of Christ in such torment?" In a prayerful petition to Mary, the singer asks to bear not only her pain, but the pain of Christ. "Holy Mother, do this for me: fix the wounds of the crucified deeply in my heart." At the conclusion of the Stabat Mater, the singer prays to be united with the sorrow of the mother and marked by the wounds of the son in the hope of entering the heavenly paradise.[14] The mother's anguish was evoked in meditation, poetry, and song, but the visual arts also dwelt on her pain. European artists depicted the mother's suffering in the *pietà*, the representation of the mother grieving over the dead body of her son. They presented both the physical reality of the son's death and the spiritual anguish of the mother's loss. In this imagery of suffering, the Mother of Sorrow emerged as the exemplary model for a Christian theology and practice of pain.

In the sacrament of penance, the Christian tradition had developed a ritual that managed pain. Required for every Christian by the Fourth Lateran Council (1215), penance imposed a certain degree of suffering in this life to avoid punishments in the next. The three stages of the ritual—contrition, confession, and acts of penance—were premised on penitents experiencing the emotional pain of sorrow *(contritio)* that would move them to confess their sins to a priest. By the thirteenth century, the mental and emotional anguish of contrition had come to be emphasized as the most important aspect of the ritual of penance. In this respect, a person's guilt for sins became less an objective condition than an emotional state. Not merely representing a kind of legal status before the judgment of God, guilt gradually came to be seen as a painful feeling of remorse. Although the sacrament was understood to provide objective absolution from the effects of sins, that forgiveness increasingly came to depend upon cultivating the subjective emotional pain of sorrow.[15]

In the practice of penance, monks and nuns held themselves to a more severe discipline than the laity. Introduced in the eleventh century, the devotional discipline of flagellation had become a well-established feature of monastic penance by the thirteenth century. Inflicting pain by beating or scourging, the discipline of flagellation was adopted as a monastic technique not only for performing penance, but also for acquiring physical wounds on the body that imitated the saving wounds of Christ. Although beatings could be administered by another monk or nun, the practice of self-flagellation was often preferred. As a kind of physical meditation on the suffering of Christ, flagellation also produced intense emotional pain and spiritual anguish. Describing his own use of this technique, the Dominican mystic Henry Suso (1300–1366) recounted that one winter's night he locked himself in his room, stripped himself naked, and beat himself with a leather whip with sharp metal spikes on the end. While blood poured from his torn flesh, he beat himself so hard that the scourge broke and flew against the wall. When he stopped to reflect on himself, Henry Suso beheld an image of the suffering Christ:

> He stood there bleeding and gazed at himself. It was such a wretched sight that he was reminded in many ways of the appearance of the beloved Christ, when he was fearfully beaten. Out of pity for himself he began to weep bitterly. And he knelt down, naked and covered in blood, in the frosty air, and prayed to God to wipe out his sins from before his gentle eyes.[16]

This prominent Rhineland mystic adhered to the conviction of his teacher, Meister Eckhart, that it was possible for Christ to be born within the human soul. While celebrating a spirituality of joy, however, Henry Suso also demonstrated a spirituality that depended upon the physical production of emotional pain.

As a ritualized means for inducing pain, remorse, and sincere contrition, flagellation moved out of its monastic context during the thirteenth century and became the basis for popular religious movements. Started in 1260 by a hermit in Perugia, the earliest flagellant movement expanded rapidly throughout Italy, drawing widespread support in towns and cities that had recently suffered famine, an outbreak of plague, and warfare. Usually led by priests, groups of flagellants marched in procession to a church, beat themselves for hours, and implored the mercy of the Virgin Mary and Jesus Christ. Although the movement died out in Italy, it spread within a few years to southern Germany and the Rhineland. The German flagellants observed the same rituals of procession, self-torture, and devotion to the Virgin Mary, but they also had a copy of a heavenly letter warning that God had decided to punish human beings for their sins by killing every living creature on earth. Learning of this divine plan, as the letter explained, the Virgin Mary had fallen at God's feet to beg that human beings be given one last chance. As a result of the Virgin's intercession, God had agreed to spare human beings if they would renounce sin, change their ways, and undertake a flagellant procession for thirty-three and a half days in recollection of the number of years that Jesus Christ had spent on earth.

By claiming this special mission, the German flagellants came into conflict with the established church. Excommunicated, suppressed, and driven underground, the movement resurfaced, however, in 1348 with the outbreak of the plague. Known as the Black Death, this epidemic of bubonic fever spread rapidly throughout Europe, accounting for the sudden death of between one-third and one-half of the population. "On all sides is sorrow," as the poet and philosopher Petrarch (1304–74) described the effects of the Black Death. Reviving the processions and self-torture, the flagellants organized in bands of fifty to five hundred to devote themselves to suffering and sorrow. Significantly, this movement was not led by clergy and often came into conflict with the church. As martyrs in imitation of Christ, the flagellants also regarded themselves as new crusaders. Wearing uniforms of white robes marked by red crosses, the flagellants took up the cross not only by suffering the wounds of Christ, but also by declaring war on people they imagined as Christ's enemies. In the large-scale massacres of European Jews during the Black Death, the flagellants were active participants. Like the "Jew killers" of the previous decade who had accused Jews of torturing the eucharistic Host, the flagellants promoted anti-Jewish propaganda that blamed Jews for causing the plague by poisoning water supplies.

Although the bubonic plague did not discriminate between European Jews and Christians, the disease was used as a pretext to kill Jews. In expressing his church's opposition to the movement, Pope Clement VI complained that the flagellants, "beneath an appearance of piety, set their hands to cruel and impious works, shedding the blood of Jews, whom Christian piety accepts and sustains." Despite this official opposition, the flagellants continued to play a leading role during the years of the Black Death in the massacres of Jews that resulted in the extinction of entire Jewish communities in much of Germany and the Netherlands. Where churches or shrines were built on the ruins of a Jewish community, they were typically dedicated to the Queen of Heaven.[17]

QUEEN OF HEAVEN

From humble beginnings, according to Christian tradition, Jesus and Mary rose to become royalty. In the Gospel of Matthew, the designation of Jesus as "king of the Jews" was ascribed to the "wise men" *(magoi)* from the East who were guided by a star to come and worship the king. Finding the mother and child in Bethlehem, they presented precious gifts of gold, frankincense, and myrrh. Although these eastern visitors were variously identified during the first four centuries as astrologers, Zoroastrians, or devotees of Mithras, they gradually emerged as three kings, foreign royalty in their own right, who had made their procession bearing gifts in political supplication to the king of kings. According to a Byzantine tradition, the three kings even placed their own crowns under the feet of Mary and Jesus to acknowledge the eternal sovereignty of Christ. As this royal imagery was developed in the civic ceremonies of Eastern Orthodoxy, the Magi were drawn into supporting not only the royalty of Jesus, but also the royal power and authority of the Byzantine emperor. For example, in a tenth-century celebration of the divine status of the emperor, the priests recited: "Heaven sends the star to direct the magi to the birth. The earth prepares the cave to receive the author of all things! But may Jesus himself, having taken our earthly flesh from the virgin, guard in the royal purple your royal power, crowned by God!"[18] In this imperial tribute, the three foreign kings appeared in supplication before both Jesus and the Byzantine emperor. Until the fall of Constantinople during the conquest in 1453, this identification of the emperor with the royalty of Jesus Christ remained an important feature of Eastern Orthodoxy.

The divine royalty of Mary, however, also became important to the religious politics of Eastern Orthodoxy. In selecting the ancient Greek city of Byzantium as the site for his capital, the Christian emperor Constantine chose a city that had originally been dedicated to the goddess Rhea, the "mother of the gods." By the fourth century, Rhea was generally identified with other goddesses—Athena, Hecate, Cybele, and more recently Isis—who were divine mothers. Under the title of the Magna Mater, the Great Mother was the focus of religious devotion throughout the Roman Empire. In the founding myth of the city of Byzantium, the Great Mother had been present at the beginning as Rhea. When he rebuilt Byzantium as the imperial city of Constantinople, Constantine dedicated the city to another goddess, Tyche Anthousa. Although the Tyche of a city was understood as its goddess of fortune or luck, a divine patron of the welfare of the city, the designation Anthousa translated into Greek the Latin name Flora, the goddess of Rome. Suggesting that the power of the Tyche of the old Rome had been transferred to the Tyche of the new Rome, Constantine marked the consecration of his capital with a civic ceremony performed before two statues, one of himself and the other of Tyche Anthousa. As Constantine instructed, this ceremony was to be reenacted every year to ensure the power, protection, and prosperity of the city.

The Christian city of Constantinople, therefore, inherited a tradition of two goddesses, the mother of the gods and the protector of the city. On the one hand, the Magna Mater, under many names, was praised as the royal mother who provided both physical and spiritual nourishment. "Divine are your honors, O mother of the gods and nurturer of all," the *Orphic Hymns* declared. "For in the cosmos yours is the throne in the middle because the earth is yours and you give gentle nourishment to mortals."[19] Assuming different roles as mother, bride, and virgin, the goddess was the source of life, which was rendered in political symbolism by her throne, suggesting that the Magna Mater was not only mother, but also empress or queen of the gods. Under the reign of the divine mother, power was knowledge. Celebrated as guide, initiator, and savior, the mother goddess led human beings into saving knowledge. In the *Orphic Hymns,* Rhea was described as "redeemer" and "savior." On the other hand, the Tyche Anthousa was a goddess who ensured the well-being and safety of the city. Wearing a crown that was a duplicate in miniature of the city walls, she was the goddess of fortune who presided over the walls, bulwarks, towers, and military defenses that protected Constantinople. Like the goddesses of fortune in other cities in the Mediterranean world, the Tyche of Constantinople was responsible not only for political security, but also for agricultural fertility. As protector and provider, the Tyche was revered in temples, statues, mosaics, and the sacrifices performed by her organized priesthood. In dedicating Constantinople to Tyche Anthousa, Constantine indicated the royal status of the goddess of fortune who watched over the interests of the imperial city.

As the Virgin Mary of Byzantine Christianity rose in royal status, she assumed the basic roles of divine mother and urban defender that had been fulfilled by the goddesses Rhea and Tyche. In the sixth-century Greek Akathistos Hymn, these roles are clearly evident in the praises bestowed upon the holy virgin, bride, mother, and queen. As the oldest hymn to Mary continuously performed in the Eastern Orthodox Church, the Akathistos Hymn has played a significant role in translating the functions of the ancient goddesses into Christian terms. In its recurring refrain, the hymn declared, "Hail bride, unwedded." Around this paradoxical mystery, the Akathistos Hymn praised the Virgin Mary as a divine being who had absorbed all the basic functions of the ancient goddesses. In one verse, for example, Mary is praised as military champion of the city, healer of the body, and savior of the soul:

> Hail to you, through whom trophies of victory are assured,
> Hail to you, through whom enemies are vanquished,
> Hail to you, who are the healing of my body,
> Hail to you, who are the salvation of my soul.

Like Rhea, the mother of the gods, the Virgin Mary gave birth to divinity. Celebrated in Eastern Orthodoxy as the *Theotokos*, the mother of God, Mary provided the spiritual nourishment—the flesh and blood, which was present in the eucharistic bread and wine—that led to salvation. Accordingly, the Akathistos Hymn celebrated Mary as the initiator of Christians into the mysteries of God. "Hail to you," the hymn declared, "who enlighten the initiates of the Trinity." In this initiation, Mary was the divine source of the knowledge, wisdom, and enlightenment that led to the "salvation of the soul." By offering nourishment, enlightenment, and salvation, therefore, the Theotokos fulfilled the essential functions of the divine mother in ancient religion.

By emerging as the spiritual protector of the city, however, the Virgin Mary gradually displaced the Tyche of Constantinople in military defense, agricultural fertility, and urban welfare. Mary the *Theotokos*, the Akathistos Hymn declared, was the royal defender who brought home "trophies of victory" and ensured that "enemies are vanquished." As her icon was ceremoniously paraded around the city or strategically placed on the battlements, Mary became the imperial and spiritual defender of Constantinople. At the same time, the Virgin Mary was increasingly entrusted with the city's economic prosperity. For farmers, she was fertility; for artisans, she was weaving; and for sailors she was "a haven for all life's seafarers." Although the statue of the Tyche remained in Constantinople until the ninth century, Mary had clearly absorbed many of the functions of the goddess in representing, protecting, and providing for the city.[20]

In their efforts to maintain the unity of God, some theologians in the East objected to what they saw as the deification of Mary. Rejecting the entire notion of the *Theotokos* because it implied that Jesus Christ was "second to the blessed Mary," the patriarch Nestorius and his Church of the East were alienated from Constantinople. But an Orthodox theologian such as John of Damascus could also complain that Christians were worshiping Mary with the same rituals and praises employed by pagans in their devotion to the divine mother of the gods. Insisting that the Virgin Mary was not a goddess, John of Damascus warned that she should not be worshiped as a deity, but instead venerated as a saint. However, it was conceivable that people might regard Mary as a deity. Suggesting that the deification of Mary was possible, from fourth-century Arabia there were reports of a priesthood of women who worshiped Mary as a goddess. At their meetings, the devotees reportedly offered loaves of bread to Mary. Like certain women of ancient Judah, as one Orthodox commentator suggested, these worshipers of the goddess Mary presented "sacrifice to the queen of heaven."[21] Although Eastern Orthodoxy clearly rejected such worship, the veneration of Mary remained central to the religious and political life of Constantinople until its fifteenth-century conquest.

In the Latin West, the Virgin Mary also assumed a divine status in the political economy of the kingdom of heaven. The theologian Anselm of Canterbury, for example, glorified Mary by defining her as divine perfection that was only transcended by God. Having defined God as "that than which nothing greater can be conceived," Anselm described Mary as "so great that nothing greater under God can be imagined." In his treatise on why God became human, *Cur Deus Homo,* Anselm had emphasized the debt that human beings owed to God for both their own sins and original sin. Justice demanded payment. Turning to Mary in his prayers and meditations, however, Anselm found a source of divine mercy that contrasted with the strict justice of God. By praying for the intercession of the Queen of Heaven, he observed, "the accused flees from the just God to the good mother of the merciful God."[22]

As the divine royalty of the Virgin Mary rose in importance in the Latin West, the royal role of Jesus Christ gradually shifted from mercy to justice. Increasingly, Christ was represented as a severe judge, presiding over the justice of God and the final judgment of souls. An influential thirteenth-century monastic text suggested that Mary "chose the better part, because she was made Queen of Mercy, while her Son remained King of Justice." As this text concluded, "mercy is better than justice." In this formula, Mary was celebrated not as the good mother of the merciful God, but as the divine mediator, intercessor, and advocate who asked for mercy on behalf of human beings before the court of Jesus Christ, the King of Justice. As expressed in the popular hymn to the Queen of Mercy, the Salve Regina, Christians could hope for salvation through the merciful intervention of the Virgin Mary:

> Hail, Holy Queen, Mother of Mercy, our life, our sweetness, and our hope. To thee do we cry, poor banished children of Eve. To thee do we send up our sighs, mourning, and weeping in this valley of tears. Turn then, most gracious advocate, thine eyes of mercy toward us, and after this our exile show unto us the blessed fruit of thy womb, Jesus.

Like the *Theotokos* in the Byzantine empire, the Queen of Heaven played a role in the religious politics of the West. In 1491, for example, Emperor Frederick III and Duke George the Rich formed a political alliance marked by formally placing the Holy Roman Empire under the spiritual protection of the Immaculate Conception. At the same time, however, the Virgin Mary—as Mother of God, Mother of Sorrow, and Mother of Mercy—provided a multifaceted focus for personal devotion and spirituality. As suggested in the Salve Regina, Mary has represented the hope that Christians banished in the valley of tears might experience the mercy of coming home from exile.[23]

18

Renaissance

Born out of the frothing waves of the sea, she stands naked on a conch shell, her long golden hair blowing in the wind of the heavens as her body is about to be covered by the beautiful tapestry of the earth. Presiding over the rites of spring in a forest meadow, she stands clothed in a diaphanous gown, her right hand held up, perhaps blessing, perhaps orchestrating the dance that surrounds her of spirits, nature, fertility, wisdom, and love. In these two images, the Greco-Roman goddess Venus was vividly depicted by the Italian painter Sandro Botticelli (1444–1510). Among the most compelling works of European visual art, Botticelli's *Birth of Venus* and his *Primavera* reflect the broader interest among his contemporaries in adapting representational styles and mythological themes from pagan antiquity. Accordingly, Botticelli's paintings of Venus can be regarded as landmarks in the general revival of the creative arts at the end of the fifteenth century that later came to be known as the Renaissance, the era of cultural rebirth.

Botticelli's paintings of Venus, however, appear to have had a more specific religious intention. Under the patronage of the wealthy banker and de facto ruler of Florence Lorenzo de Medici (1449–92), artists, poets, musicians, and philosophers were reinterpreting the pagan deities of antiquity. In a letter that might have referred directly to these paintings, the priest, doctor, and scholar Marsilio Ficino (1433–99) advocated the spiritual value of meditating on the image of Venus. According to Ficino, the practice of meditating on such an image did not imply an anti-Christian revival of Greco-Roman paganism. Rather, if properly guided, the meditation would reveal layers of meaning in the image of Venus crucial for leading a Christian life. Just as the theologians had read different levels of meaning in sacred scripture, Ficino proposed that Christians could also recognize the allegorical, moral, and ultimately spiritual significance contained in the mythological imagery of pagan gods and goddesses. Interpreting the imagery of Venus, he maintained that the goddess represented all the virtues of *humanitas,* the moral qualities of love, dignity, liberality, modesty, and so on that defined the contours and content of a humane life. As the most beautiful goddess of the heavens and the earth, Venus stood for this moral humanism.

Understanding the humanism of Venus, however, required the skills acquired from two divine sciences, astrology and psychology. Growing out of her role as a goddess in Greco-Roman myth, Venus was identified with one of the planets among the seven in the ancient science of astrology. Each planet, according to Ficino, represented a specific quality. The moon stood for spiritual motion, interest, or attention; Mars was speed; Saturn was slowness; the sun was God; Jupiter was law; Mercury was reason; and Venus, the morning star, was *humanitas.* These heavenly bodies, therefore, comprised a cosmic allegory. In applying the specific terms of this allegory, Ficino advised that the moon, which signified the movements of the spirit, should be neither too fast like Mars nor too slow like Saturn. By achieving a balance or harmony in motion, spiritual attention could then be focused on God, symbolized by the sun, which would lead to the higher planetary spheres of law, reason, and *humanitas.* Culminating with Venus, this allegorical ascent celebrated the humane virtues in the figure of a beautiful female spirit. As Ficino explained:

> For Humanity herself is a nymph of excellent comeliness born of heaven and more than others beloved by God all highest. Her soul and mind are Love and Charity, her eyes Dignity and Magnanimity, the hands Liberality and Magnificence, the feet Comeliness and Modesty. The whole, then, is Temperance and Honesty, Charm and Splendor. Oh, what exquisite beauty!

Ficino called for the soul to unite in holy wedlock with this noble and beautiful nymph of *humanitas.* Moral exhortation through words alone, however, was regarded by Ficino as insufficient to awaken virtue. Through the immediacy of sight, he proposed, "virtue herself (if she can be placed before the eye) may serve much better as an exhortation than the words of men." If they recalled Ficino's astrological allegory, therefore, Botticelli's paintings of Venus might have placed before the eye the multifaceted virtue of *humanitas* in the visual form of a beautiful goddess.

The goddess Venus also featured in Ficino's psychology. Like his moral allegory of the planets, Ficino's psychological theory used imagery drawn from the science of astrology. Shifting from the heavens to the self, he developed a psychology based on recognizing the harmony and conflict of heavenly bodies that resided within human beings. "We must not look for these matters outside ourselves," he advised, "for all the heavens are within us and the fiery vigor in us testifies to our heavenly origin." As Ficino interpreted the myth of the birth of Venus, he found an account of a spiritual faculty within the human self. Located between the intellectual soul and the material world, this spiritual faculty was able to move both upward to the heavens and downward to the earth. The spiritual faculty "creates Beauty within itself," he explained, "by an upward movement of conversion toward supra-intelligible things; and by a downward movement it gives birth to the charm of sensible things in matter." As Ficino concluded, "This conversion into Beauty and its birth from the soul is called Venus." In this interpretation of the birth of Venus, Marsilio Ficino found a distinctively human spiritual capacity for interchange between heavenly and material realms. While the beauty of Venus was being memorably represented in Renaissance art, therefore, it was also being incorporated in the Renaissance spirituality of Christian humanism.[1]

HUMANISM

Although often regarded as a modernizing movement, the Christian humanism of the Italian Renaissance was based on the recovery, interpretation, and application of ancient texts. For the humanist scholar and poet Petrarch, Francesco Petrarca (1304–74), the relevant sources were found in the classical Latin texts of ancient Roman civilization. Petrarch developed his Christian humanism during an era of institutional turmoil for the Roman Catholic Church. Between 1309 and 1378, the pope was exiled from Rome to the southern French city of Avignon. The papacy came under the influence of the French monarch to such an extent that when the pope finally returned to Rome in 1378, the French cardinals elected their own pope, resulting in an ongoing conflict between two competing claimants to the papacy that lasted until 1417. During the exile of the central institution of the Roman Catholic Church in southern France, Petrarch led a revival of interest in the literary glory of ancient Rome.

Rejecting Christian Scholasticism for its dependence on Greek philosophy, Petrarch disdained the philosophy of Aristotle as barbaric. Adopting ancient Roman models, he embraced the poetry of Virgil, Ovid, and

Juvenal, the rhetoric of Quintillian, and the public philosophy of Cicero. In developing a distinctively Christian humanism, however, Petrarch felt that he was guided by the example of Augustine, whose *Confessions* in particular demonstrated an introspective self-examination before God that he emulated. Going back to the ancient sources for Petrarch, therefore, meant recovering both the Latin classics and the Latin church fathers from what he regarded as the alien and corrupting influences introduced into Christian theology from Greek and Arabic philosophy.

In his *Ascent of Mount Ventoux,* which was addressed in 1336 to the professor of theology who had first introduced him to Augustine, Petrarch illustrated this Augustinian self-examination by means of a literary allegory about climbing a mountain. In recounting this ascent, Petrarch described how his brother, Gherardo, who became a monk, took a shortcut to reach the summit, while Petrarch stumbled around lost in the valleys, unable to find a path that would lead to the top. Frustrated and tired, he sat down to reflect on his situation. As his thoughts shifted from his physical to his spiritual condition, he said to himself, "What you have so often experienced today while climbing this mountain happens to you, you must know, and to many others who are making their way toward the blessed life." Seeking to follow the "narrow path" that leads to the summit of salvation (Matt. 7:14), Petrarch reflected that he had wandered in sin through the valley of "darkness and the shadow of death" (Ps. 107:10; Job 34:22). By ascending "from virtue to virtue," however, he concluded that the heights of the blessed life could be achieved.

Refreshed by these thoughts, Petrarch resumed his climb, meditating along the way on the course of his life until he reached the peak. On the summit of the mountain, he took out his small volume of Augustine's *Confessions,* which he carried with him everywhere, and opened its pages at random. Reading the first passage that struck his eyes, Petrarch found: "And men go to admire the high mountains, the vast floods of the sea, the huge streams of the rivers, the circumference of the ocean, and the revolutions of the stars—and desert themselves." Regarding this passage as a divine oracle from Augustine, Petrarch concluded that nothing in the world could compare to the inestimable value of the human self. In support of Augustine, he cited the Roman philosopher Seneca, who had observed that "nothing is admirable besides the mind; compared to its greatness nothing is great." In the allegory of climbing Mount Ventoux, therefore, Petrarch displayed a Christian humanism that employed classical Latin texts of Christian and pagan antiquity in the service of an intro-spective exploration of the self.[2]

During the fifteenth century, a different style of Christian humanism was inspired in Europe by Greek scholars from the East. With the Byzantine Empire under increasing pressure from invading Turkish armies, representatives of the Orthodox Church sought to negotiate terms for unifying the estranged churches of the East and West in the hope that Christian unity would also result in military assistance against the Muslim Turks. At the council held in the northern Italian cities of Ferrara and Florence during 1438 and 1439, Orthodox and Catholic delegates dis-cussed the issues of doctrine, practice, and ecclesiastical authority that divided East and West. On all these matters, compromises were struck. The Orthodox Church agreed to accept the contentious doctrine of the *fil-ioque,* the teaching of the Latin church that the Holy Spirit proceeded from both the Father and the Son, but was not required to add that phrase to its creed. The Catholic Church acknowledged that distinctively Eastern styles of worship, liturgy, and priesthood, including the marriage of priests, should not stand as obstacles to union. In the interest of unity, the Orthodox patriarchs were allowed to retain their traditional rights, while agreeing in general terms to accept the spiritual primacy of the pope. Out of these negotiations, the unification of East and West was proclaimed.

Although the unification announced in 1439 never actually material-ized, the council nevertheless stimulated new intellectual exchanges between East and West. Leading Byzantine scholars, such as the Platonist Gemistus Pletho (ca. 1360–ca. 1452), his prominent student, the arch-bishop of Nicaea, Bessarion (ca. 1403–72), and their Aristotelian rival, George of Trebizond (1395–1484), created a new interest in Greek phi-losophy. In particular, the lectures given by Pletho in Florence generated enthusiasm for the teachings of Plato, which had previously been inacces-sible in the Latin West. With the assistance and instruction of Byzantine scholars, however, a new generation of humanists during the fifteenth cen-tury gained familiarity with the primary texts of Greek philosophy. In the process, they developed a Christian humanism that incorporated not only classical poetry, rhetoric, and virtues, but also the textual sources of what came to be regarded as ancient wisdom.

Emerging as the leading Christian Platonist of the Renaissance, Marsilio Ficino was commissioned by his wealthy and powerful patron, Cosimo de Medici, to translate the Greek texts of Plato into Latin.

Established in a villa outside of Florence in 1462, Ficino began translating the ancient writings not only of Plato, but also of Plotinus and other Greek Neoplatonists. As a circle of scholars, poets, and artists gathered around him, Ficino seemed to be the leader of a new Platonic academy. Cultivating a religious devotion for the wisdom of Plato and the central figure of his dialogues, Socrates, this group of scholars reportedly revered a statue of the philosopher and petitioned his mentor, "Holy Socrates, pray for us." Ficino was convinced, however, that Christianity and Platonism were in complete harmony because they led to the same end—the Good, the True, and the Beautiful. In developing a Christian Platonism in his *Theologia Platonica,* Ficino could cite both Augustine and Dionysius the Areopagite as Christian authorities who had recognized the wisdom of Plato. Consistent with the humanistic emphasis on exploring the self, however, Ficino maintained that the highest Platonic ideals could be found within the human soul. As the ultimate promise of his Christian Platonism, Ficino proposed that even the supreme God of Christian faith could be discovered within the soul.

In addition to the philosophy of Plato, other sources of ancient wisdom informed Ficino's distinctive Christian humanism. Before beginning his translations of Plato, he had been instructed by his patron to translate a collection of Greek manuscripts ascribed to the ancient Egyptian priest, philosopher, and visionary Hermes Trismegistus. In the writings of the "Thrice-Great" Hermes, the *Corpus Hermeticum,* Ficino found confirmation of the greatness of the human soul in which the supreme God resides. Although actually written during the second or third century of the common era, the Hermetic texts were thought to convey a wisdom from ancient Egypt that was contemporary with the revelations to Moses. Perhaps, as Ficino suggested, Hermes might even have predated Moses, since he was "the first author of theology," the first to reveal the primordial wisdom of God and the soul.

However, this same revealed wisdom, Ficino maintained, had appeared not only in ancient Egypt and Israel, but also in ancient Persia through the inspired prophet Zoroaster and in ancient Greece through the divine poet Orpheus. In the sacred scriptures of the *Chaldean Oracles* and the *Orphic Hymns,* which were also second- or third-century Hellenistic texts, Ficino found what he assumed was the ancient wisdom revealed to the Persian Zoroaster and the Greek Orpheus. Since all of these texts emerged out of the same historical milieu, it should not be surprising that they incorpo-

rated similar Neoplatonic and Gnostic themes. According to Ficino, however, these texts from different parts of the ancient world spoke with one
voice about the discovery of God within the human soul. Although Ficino
was convinced that they anticipated and supported Christianity, he maintained that these texts pointed to the "ancient theology" at the root of all
religions.[3]

During the 1480s, the cathedral of the Italian city of Siena was installed
with a new pavement of mosaics. At the cathedral's entrance, the mosaic
on the floor depicted a majestic image of Hermes Trismegistus with the
caption "Hermes Mercurius, Contemporary of Moses." While Hermes,
the "first author of theology," was being installed in the Siena cathedral,
one of the members of Ficino's circle, Giovanni Pico della Mirandola
(1463–94), was attempting to take the ancient theology from Florence to
the center of theological education in Europe at the University of Paris. In
December 1486, at the age of twenty-three, Pico published an extensive
list of theological propositions—a total of nine hundred theses—and
invited all interested theologians to come to Paris the following month for
a public debate. Most of the nine hundred theses drew conclusions from
the *Corpus Hermeticum,* the *Chaldean Oracles,* the *Orphic Hymns,* and
other primary sources of the ancient theology. Arguing for a harmony
between Plato and Aristotle in Christian theology, Pico ultimately
grounded his theological synthesis in the apparent consensus of ancient
wisdom about the unity of the soul with God.

Pico's distinctive contribution to the ancient theology, however, grew
out of his study of Hebrew under the guidance of Jewish teachers of the
mystical wisdom of Kabbalah. As developed in medieval Spain, the Kabbalah was understood as an orally transmitted mystical tradition, going
back to Moses, that supplemented the written tradition of the Torah.
According to Pico, his Jewish teachers had instructed him in two forms of
the Kabbalah. On the one hand, the Path of the Names revealed the secret
power of the letters of the Hebrew alphabet, which could be combined
and recombined in different ways to disclose divine truth. Understood as
the primordial language of God, the Hebrew alphabet was both meaningful and powerful. Present at the beginning when God first spoke, the
alphabet was a force that created and sustained the universe. In the methods developed by the Spanish Kabbalist Abraham Abulafia, the letters of
the Hebrew alphabet were combined in endless permutations as a focus
for meditation. On the other hand, the Path of the Sephiroth revealed the

ten levels of reality that proceeded from the material world through various spiritual powers to the supreme divinity—the En Soph—that was beyond being. As a path toward union with the En Soph, the Path of the Sephiroth led the soul toward its own unconditional identity in the nothingness of God.

According to Pico, both forms of the Kabbalah, the "ancient theology of the Hebrews," actually supported Christianity. In following the Path of the Names, for example, Pico felt that his kabbalistic experiments with the Hebrew alphabet had shown that the combination and recombination of the letters of the name Iesu "signified God, the Son of God, and the wisdom of the Father through the divinity of the Third Person." Likewise, in following the Path of the Sephiroth, Pico found confirmation of the Christian teachings of Dionysius the Areopagite, who had also outlined the ascending levels of angelic beings that led up to the supreme mystery of the Godhead. According to Pico, the Kabbalists agreed with Dionysius in pointing toward the darkness, emptiness, and nothingness of the ultimate, unknowable Godhead. By embracing the wisdom of Jewish mysticism, therefore, Pico was convinced that he was supporting Christianity, "confirming the Christian religion from the foundations of Hebrew wisdom."

Pico hoped to debate these matters at the University of Paris, but Pope Innocent VIII intervened, canceled the event, and set up a commission to investigate the nine hundred theses. Finding evidence of heresy, especially in the assertion that Jewish mysticism supported Christian truth, the commission condemned Pico and forced him into exile in France. Although he would return to Florence before his death in 1494 at the age of thirty-one, Pico spent the rest of his life in conflict with the church. His introductory speech for the great debate that never happened, however, was published after his death and widely circulated. Known as the *Oration on the Dignity of Man,* the speech that Pico had intended to deliver before a learned audience of theologians in Paris emerged as one of the most important documents of Christian humanism in Italy during the Renaissance. Outlining the evidence from ancient theology for the central importance of the human self, including references to the authority of Hermes, Zoroaster, and Orpheus, Pico's oration was remarkable for its inclusion of Muslim and Jewish wisdom. In the end, Pico found that the wonder of humanity was revealed in the human potential for unity with God. The ultimate dignity of a human being, according to Pico, was realized when "he withdraws into the center of his own unity, his spirit made one with God, in the solitary darkness of God, who is set above all things." Like Marsilio Ficino, therefore, Pico advocated a Christian humanism that drew on the interreligious resources of ancient wisdom. But he went further in recognizing the wisdom of Muslims and Jews, who had been declared enemies of Christ. In the process, however, Pico himself was condemned as a heretic by the Roman Catholic Church.[4]

PSYCHOLOGY

In his *Oration on the Dignity of Man,* Pico della Mirandola pointed toward the ultimate union of the soul with God. Nevertheless, he recognized that most human beings find themselves short of this goal, suspended between the material world and the heavenly realm. This middle ground that most people occupy, however, also revealed the wonder of humanity. Poised between the spiritual heavens and the physical earth, as Pico observed, the human being has the "power to degenerate into the lower forms of life, which are brutish," and the "power, out of the soul's judgment, to be reborn into the higher forms, which are divine." In this dual capacity, the human spirit is a dynamic movement that can be directed upward or downward. According to this account, therefore, a human being has no single, fixed identity. Rather, the human spirit is a nexus between the higher intellectual heavens and the lower material earth.

Clearly, this understanding of what it means to be human was based on a Platonic dualism that distinguished between a higher realm of ideal forms and a lower realm of material appearances. However, the Christian Platonists of the Renaissance also developed a psychology that relied heavily on assumptions drawn from medieval Aristotelianism. Although they did not employ the modern term "psychology," they were nevertheless concerned with working out a science of the *psuche,* or the soul, that would have both analytical and therapeutic benefits. By the time of the Renaissance, a general understanding of the basic structures and functions of human psychology had become common. On the authority of the Arabic Muslim interpreters of Aristotle, this psychology drew together ancient philosophical resources from Stoic, Platonic, and Aristotelian schools of thought. As formulated in the eleventh century by Ibn Sina (980–1037), who was known in the West as Avicenna, the basic structure of human psychology was determined by three souls—the vegetative soul, the sensitive soul, and the intellective soul. Every human being is comprised of all three of these souls. As the lowest structure in human psychology, the vegetative soul animates the physical body. It drives the basic physical functions of nutrition, growth, and reproduction. Without consciousness, the vegetative soul automatically performs these functions as long as there is life in the body. Because this vegetative soul also operates in animals, the presence of the other two souls makes human beings distinctively human.

As the highest psychological structure, the intellective soul is the location of consciousness, reason, and will. According to Ibn Sina and other Aristotelians, this intellective soul actually contains two intellects, one passive, the other active. The passive intellect receives information from the senses, and the active intellect transforms that sensory data into rational concepts. The active intellect, therefore, was crucial for the production of ideas, from the general principles of mathematics to the ideal forms of goodness, truth, and beauty. Since these ideas were regarded as eternal and universal, the active intellect of the highest soul must also be eternal. Within the Aristotelian tradition, however, considerable controversy was generated over the question of whether or not the active intellect was also universal. For Ibn Sina, the active intellect was not universal but personal, since each human person was endowed with this faculty of the intellective soul. Arguing that the active intellect was both eternal and personal, Ibn Sina concluded that it was this faculty that enabled human beings to exist after the death of the body with a personal identity.

By contrast, the Aristotelian commentator Ibn Rushd (1126–98), who was known in the West as Averroës, insisted that because the active intellect was in contact with eternal and universal ideas, it should not be understood as a personal faculty residing within an individual human being, but must be seen as a universal intellectual capacity that could in principle be accessed by all human beings. In adopting this position, however, Ibn Rushd had to conclude that Aristotelian psychology denied the existence of a personal intellectual soul that could survive death, stand before the judgment of God, and experience rewards or punishments in the afterlife. Accordingly, he came under attack from Muslim, Jewish, and Christian scholars who sought to preserve the notion of personal immortality, even when they accepted the basic framework of Aristotelian psychology. In late medieval Latin Christianity, the teachings of Ibn Rushd, identified by the label Averroism, were consistently condemned by ecclesiastical authorities on the grounds that they denied the immortality of the soul by positing a single active intellect. By insisting that the active intellect was both eternal and individual for each human being, however, Christian Aristotelians could affirm the personal immortality of every intellective soul.

As the psychological structure located between the vegetative and intellective souls, the middle region of the sensitive soul was certainly the most complex. Between the intellect and the body, the sensitive soul contains faculties that interact with both. At its base, the sensitive soul has faculties of movement that engage the body by governing the voluntary motion of the limbs and the involuntary motion of the circulatory system. But the basic faculties of movement also govern emotional desire. In the Aristotelian psychology, those basic desires were identified as sex and aggression. As the Latin Aristotelians put it, the lower part of the sensitive soul is driven by the concupiscent and irascible appetites. Long before Sigmund Freud identified the id as the region of the unconscious motivated by sex and aggression, this medieval psychology had located these basic drives in the sensitive soul.

Rising above the basic drives, however, the sensitive soul also includes faculties of perception. Although the five external senses perceive objects that are present to sight, hearing, smell, taste, and touch, the highest faculty of the sensitive soul consists of internal senses. Capable of generating perceptions when objects are absent, these internal senses are functions of the human imagination. Although defined differently by various authorities, the internal senses in Aristotelian psychology fulfill imaginative functions of memory, fantasy, and reflection. Situated between the animal body and the eternal soul, the internal senses provide the psychological media of communication between the two worlds of the body and the soul.[5]

Assuming the general validity of this outline of Aristotelian psychology, Ficino, Pico, and other Christian Platonists of the Renaissance simply referred to the imaginative capacities of the sensitive soul as spirit. "Without doubt three things are in us," Ficino asserted, "soul, spirit, and body. The soul and body are very different in nature; they are joined by means of the spirit." Thin, clear, airy, and vaporous, the spirit was understood as a dynamic medium of communication between body and soul. The spirit was moved not only by lower drives of sex and aggression, but also by the higher imagination. By working creatively with the spiritual imagery of memory, fantasy, and visualization, the Renaissance Platonists tried to move the spirit upward in the direction of the soul. Just as Renaissance artists became experts in the visual media of drawing, painting, and sculpting, the Platonists developed expertise in using the internal vision of the imagination. Through the inner media of spiritual images, as Ficino maintained, "the soul conceives in itself images similar to them, but much purer; and such conception is called imagination or fantasy." Spiritual imagination, therefore, was conceived as a kind of internal art of the soul.

In the ancient art of memory, the Platonists found a precedent for using vivid imagery to memorize concepts. As a branch of classical rhetoric, the art of memory provided imaginative techniques for memorizing the text of a speech. The Renaissance Platonists extended their inner vision to meditate on images that supposedly imprinted higher spiritual qualities on the sensitive soul. For Ficino, the most powerful spiritual images were derived from the science of astrology. By visualizing the signs and symbols of the planets and constellations, he assumed that their heavenly influences could be drawn into the human spirit. Accordingly, he recommended the use of astrological emblems or talismans to inspire the spirit. Through meditating on such visual imagery of the heavens, including artistic representations like Botticelli's *Primavera* and *Birth of Venus*, Ficino felt that the spirit could be shaped into a higher form and moved toward the celestial realm of the highest soul.

In addition to visual imagery, however, Ficino also advocated the use of music to inspire the spirit. According to Ficino, music itself should be understood as "a heavenly spirit, arranging everything with its movements and tones." Composing vocal pieces that he sang while accompanying himself on a lyre, Ficino experimented with the spiritual effects of song. Like his astrological imagery, Ficino's songs tried to imitate the spiritual influences he ascribed to the seven planets. In between the dull, heavy music of Saturn and the sharp, fast music of Mars, the songs of the moon proceeded at a moderate pace, neither too quick nor too slow. Ficino's spiritual music, however, was directed toward the four higher planets. The songs of the sun were simple, smooth, and graceful, yet carried a subtle intensity. Jupiter's music could be serious or happy, Mercury's relaxed or strenuous, and Venus's lascivious or voluptuous with softness. By attuning melody, rhythm, and lyrics to these planets, especially to the music of the sun, Jupiter, Mercury, and Venus, Ficino imagined that singers could spiritually absorb their heavenly influence. Playing and singing, therefore, provided a practical technique for tuning the spirit to the higher heavens.

In this practical psychology of the spirit, with its astrological imagery and heavenly music, Ficino was convinced that he had discovered methods for maintaining the health of the body and realizing the divinity of the soul. As a general designation for these spiritual methods, Ficino used the term "magic." Along with superstition, witchcraft, and heresy, the art of magic had been consistently condemned by church authorities, who regarded magic as secret and sinister relations with demons. According to Ficino, however, there was a crucial difference between the evil magic based on the worship of demons and "that natural kind of magic which seizes, from the heavenly bodies through natural things, benefits for helping one's health." This natural magic also drew the spirit toward the soul in ways that according to Ficino were essentially Christian. As an expert in natural magic, the magus should not be feared by Christians because he bore "a name pleasing to the Gospels, not something wicked and venomous, but signifying a wise man and a priest." Recalling the Gospel account of the three magi who followed an astrological sign to find the birthplace of Jesus, Ficino asked, "Was not such a Magus the first worshiper of Christ?"[6]

Despite his claim to be performing Christian magic, Ficino was investigated for heresy by a papal commission in 1490. When Pope Innocent VIII decided not to prosecute him for his magical astrology, however, Ficino showed his gratitude by casting Innocent's horoscope to determine the appropriate medicine to prepare as a gift for the pope. Marsilio Ficino, the Christian magus, provided the model for an esoteric subtradition of magic that developed in early modern Europe. Informed by the ancient theology, these magicians, most notably Henricus Cornelius Agrippa (1486–1535), John Dee (1527–1608), and Giordano Bruno (1548–1600), often came into conflict with the authority of the church. Although their magic has sometimes been regarded as a prelude to modern science, they were actually concerned with developing a spiritual psychology that linked body and soul. Like Ficino, early modern magicians in Christian Europe believed that they were operating through images, harmonies, and correspondences within the middle region of the spirit that moved between the heavens and the earth.

PROPHECY

During his exile from Florence, Pico della Mirandola became impressed by a preacher, the Dominican monk Girolamo Savonarola (1452–98), who was warning Christians in northern Italy to repent before the judgment of God. When he heard Savonarola preaching his fiery sermons in which he predicted an imminent destruction comparable to Noah's flood, Pico was reportedly so electrified that his hair stood on end. Perhaps on Pico's recommendation, in 1490 Lorenzo de Medici invited the preacher to Florence, where he was installed as prior of the Dominican monastery of San Marco. Working from that monastic base, Savonarola began his public campaign to reform the religious and moral life of Florence. His sermons on selected texts from the Bible drew large and enthusiastic audiences. In addition to calling upon his listeners to repent, Savonarola criticized the clergy for corrupting the church. He argued that they had betrayed the ancient office of the priesthood for power, wealth, and other vanities of the world. "There once were priests of gold and chalices of wood," he asserted, but "now it is the reverse of those ancient days and there are priests of wood and chalices of gold." According to Savonarola, the general corruption of church and society indicated that the end would come soon. Preaching this apocalyptic message, Savonarola emerged not only as a popular prophet, but also for a brief period as the political leader of the city of Florence.

In addition to interpreting the Bible, Savonarola preached on the authority of his own dramatic spiritual visions. During the Lenten season in 1492, for example, he declared that he had been granted a prophetic vision of the coming destruction that would soon befall the world. On the night of Holy Friday, Savonarola declared, he had beheld two crosses— the cross of divine anger and the cross of divine mercy—which signified the unfolding drama of the immediate future. The first cross was black. Centered in Rome, it reached up into the heavens, while its arms stretched out all over the world. Above this massive black cross, he saw the words *"crux irae Dei,"* which identified it as the cross of the anger of God. As soon as this first cross appeared, Savonarola reported, "the weather became disturbed; clouds came flying through the air bringing winds, and hurling lightning and arrows, and it rained hail, fire and swords, and killed a great number of people so that few remained on earth." The cross of the anger of God, therefore, foretold the coming destruction. He warned that God's penitential whip, the *flagellum Dei* of righteous anger, was already raised over the city of Florence. "Behold," he declared in his Lenten sermon of 1492, "the sword of the Lord will descend suddenly and quickly upon the earth."

Significantly, in his vision of the first cross, Savonarola saw the divine anger centered in the papal city of Rome, suggesting that the Roman Catholic Church would provide no sanctuary from the coming destruction. Instead of offering a safe haven, the church of Rome appeared to be the focus of the divine anger that would soon be unleashed over the entire world. After witnessing this widespread destruction, Savonarola beheld a time of peace and tranquillity. As the skies cleared, he saw a second cross, which was as large as the first, but it was a radiant, golden cross centered not in Rome, but in the holy city of Jerusalem. "It was so resplendent," Savonarola declared, "that it lit all the world, and above it was written: *crux misericordiae Dei*." Identifying this cross as the mercy of God, he reported that "all the generations of men and women from all parts of the world came and adored and embraced it." In this prophetic vision, therefore, Savonarola promised that the purifying punishment of the world would be followed by an era of peace. Centered in Jerusalem rather than Rome, the millennial reign of peace promised to unify humanity under the mercy of God. As he frequently repeated this vision of the two crosses in his popular sermons, Savonarola urged the city of Florence to prepare for the tribulations that would precede the appearance of the New Jerusalem.[7]

In this prophecy of destruction and renewal, Savonarola adapted basic themes of Christian millennialism, drawing particularly from the book of Revelation, which anticipated a period of trials and tribulations before the establishment of the reign of Christ on earth in the New Jerusalem. Since the twelfth century, millennial prophecy in Latin Christianity had been influenced by the work of the Italian monk Joachim of Fiore (ca. 1135–1202). Recognized as a prophet during his lifetime, Joachim claimed to have been granted a spiritual understanding that enabled him to unlock the mysteries of the Bible and interpret their significance for the course of human history. Joachim's prophetic vision was organized by his innovative understanding of the three ages of the world, the ages of the Father, the Son, and the Holy Spirit. According to Joachim, the age of the Father, which had upheld the law of ancient Israel, ended with the coming of grace through Jesus Christ that initiated the age of the Son. In the near future, however, Joachim expected that the age of the Son would end with the unfolding of the apocalyptic events outlined in the book of Revelation. Those events would usher in the final age of the Spirit. Characterized by divine love, spiritual contemplation, and political liberty, the age of the Spirit would continue until the second coming of Jesus Christ to establish his kingdom of heaven on earth. Under the influence of Joachim, therefore, Christian millennialists looked not merely for signs of the end of the world, but for contemporary historical incidents that might indicate the advent of the new age of the Spirit.[8]

At the end of the fifteenth century, Christian Platonists in Florence also spoke of the beginning of a new Golden Age centered in Florence. As Savonarola developed his prophecy, the beginning of the new age was also clearly located in the city of Florence. During the 1490s, the tribulations faced by the city could be identified as the military threat posed by the French monarch, Charles VIII (1483–98). While the French forces prepared to invade northern Italy, Savonarola preached about the impending danger of this new Cyrus, recalling the Persian king who had conquered ancient Jerusalem. When King Charles finally entered Florence in 1494, however, he banished the ruling Medici family, leaving a political vacuum in which Savonarola soon established a theocratic government. No longer seeing Charles as the punishing Cyrus, Savonarola agreed with many of his French supporters in seeing him as the second Charlemagne, the divine king of a new Christian political order. Identifying Florence as God's chosen city, however, Savonarola proclaimed, "God alone will be thy king, O Florence, as He was king of Israel under the Old Covenant." Although he denied any influence from Joachim of Fiore, Savonarola nevertheless declared that Florence had entered a new spiritual age that recalled the final age, the age of the Holy Spirit, promised by the twelfth-century prophet. In the process, Savonarola shifted in his preaching from threatening destruction to promising peace and prosperity under a new spiritual regime.

Savonarola's preaching of a new spiritual age in Florence was supported by his account of another vision. During 1495 he claimed that he had ascended into paradise. In this vision, he was met by several women who offered to accompany him. Refusing the offers of Lady Philosophy and Lady Rhetoric, he chose to go with the Ladies of Faith, Simplicity, Prayer, and Patience. At the throne of the Virgin Mary, he was given a crown and a precious stone. Holding the infant Jesus in her arms, the Virgin petitioned the Holy Trinity on behalf of Savonarola and the city of

Florence. Although the people of Florence would undergo sorrows, he learned that they would soon enter an era of prosperity. In another sermon delivered in 1495, Savonarola explained that the throne of the Virgin Mary was based on the model of the throne of Solomon described in the Old Testament. Every detail of the throne, he proposed, revealed important aspects of the sanctity of the Virgin Mary. Its ivory was her purity and its gold her charity; the rotunda above the throne signified her divinity, without beginning or end, which encircled the world. Leading up to the throne, the six steps represented the six ages of the world that led to the final age at the end of the world. Having ascended to the throne of the Virgin Mary, Savonarola was in a position to proclaim the advent of that final apocalyptic age in Florence.

While developing basic Christian millennial themes, Savonarola also showed that he was adept in the rhetorical use of powerful visual imagery. His preaching was based on mobilizing imagery. As Savonarola explained in the treatise *The Triumph of the Cross,* visual images were both necessary and useful for retaining religious truths in memory and for understanding their complexity. In thinking about the saving works of Christ, for example, he recommended the visual image of a triumphal chariot. As an image easily pictured in the mind, the chariot of Christ could be imagined as a whole and it could be divided into specific parts that recalled different aspects of the life and death of Christ. The human ability to create and use such meaningful imagery, Savonarola observed, was a divine gift.[9]

Like the Christian Platonists, therefore, the apocalyptic preacher relied on the power of striking visual imagery. In relation to the visual arts, however, he introduced a new moralism by insisting that artists devote their skills to depicting compelling Christian images. Attacking representations of nude men and women in obscene poses, Savonarola called upon artists to picture Christian truths of heaven and hell. Although he defended religious images as the Bible of children, the poor, and the illiterate, he adamantly rejected visual arts demonstrating what he regarded as the sin of vanity. In the service of an ethics and aesthetics of Christian simplicity, Savonarola organized the public burning of "vanities," those objects he identified as trifles of luxury, including what he regarded as obscene books and paintings. Since he encouraged the production of Christian imagery for religious instruction and devotion, Savonarola was clearly not an iconoclast. Nevertheless, he tried to exercise a measure of religious control over the production and reception of imagery.

In the shifting political fortunes of Florence, however, Savonarola's theocracy was short-lived. By proclaiming the French king as the divine champion of the city, he isolated Florence from the rest of Italy. The failure of French support to arrive further weakened his position. When he defied the command of Pope Alexander VI (1492–1503) to appear in Rome, which eventually resulted in his excommunication, Savonarola further alienated the city. Placed under the threat of a papal ban for harboring the prophet, the people of Florence started to turn against Savonarola. Franciscans in the city began to challenge the Dominican prophet, culminating in their proposal of a trial by fire to be held in the same public square in which the burning of the vanities had been staged. Although preparations were made for him to prove the divine inspiration of his prophecy by being set on fire, Savonarola managed to avoid going through this public test. Soon after, however, a mob broke into the monastery of San Marco and captured Savonarola and two other monks. Turned over to the civil authorities, they were interrogated and tortured. On May 23, 1498, Savonarola and his two associates were hanged and burned in the public square. Having killed the prophet, the city of Florence nevertheless continued as a Savonarolan republic until 1512, when the Medici family was restored to the rulership of the city by Spanish troops. Even after this restoration of oligarchy, the followers of Savonarola, who were known as the *piagone,* continued to dream of the theocracy promised by the visionary prophet.

During the fifty years after the death of Savonarola, prophecy flourished in Italy. The artist Sandro Botticelli, for example, painted a nativity surrounded by rejoicing angels that was completed in 1500, as he noted, during "the troubles of Italy in the half time according to the 12th chapter of St. John in the second woe of the Apocalypse in the loosing of the devil for three and a half years."[10] While an artist such as Botticelli was facing the apocalypse, prophetic texts were being widely distributed through the new medium of print. As the discernment of signs of the end became increasingly popular, the evidence provided by contemporary events for an impending apocalypse was publicized not only through books, but also through pamphlets, handbills, posters, and other printed forms. In this new communication media, the signs of the times—rumors of war, changes of weather, and unnatural occurrences—were broadcast as evidence of the impending end of the world.

An unnatural birth, for example, could be regarded as evidence that the end was near. On December 8, 1522, a deformed fetus was found in the uterus of a cow in the German region of Saxony. This unborn calf had a large fold of flesh on its neck that looked like a monk's hood. As an unnatural birth, this fetus was regarded as a monster. When the report of the monstrous birth reached Italy, it was widely publicized through the new media of printed pamphlets. In the northern Italian city of Modena, the journalist and chronicler Tommasino Lancellotti reported that in May 1523 a picture of the deformed cow fetus had been received in his city. "There was brought to Modena," he recounted, "a picture of a monster born of a cow in Saxony that has a quasi-human head, and it has a tonsure and scapular of skin like a friar's scapular, and arms in front and legs and feet like a pig's and the tail of a pig." More than merely an unnatural birth, however, this cow fetus was a sign of the disturbances, evil, and heresy that could be expected at the end of the world. Specifically, as Lancellotti explained, the deformed fetus was said to represent "a friar who is called Martin Utero, who is dead and who several years ago preached heresy in Germany." This deformed fetus of a cow, therefore, was popularly interpreted as a symbol of the anti-Christian heresy that was being unleashed upon the world during its last days. By identifying the monster in this case as the monk Martin Utero, referring, of course, to the reformer Martin Luther, who was not actually dead but instead was actively mobilizing a religious revolution in Germany, the Italian commentator used this vivid image to present Luther as a prophetic sign, like a war, earthquake, or lightning storm, indicating that human beings were entering the final days at the end of the world.[11]

19

Reformation

In the midst of a thunderstorm during the summer of 1505, a terrified university student, Martin Luther (1483–1546), invoked the spiritual protection of the grandmother of Christ. "St. Anne help me!" he cried. "I will become a monk!" When he survived the thunder and lightning, Luther made good his vow by abandoning his studies in law and entering an Augustinian monastery. Two years later, he was ordained as a Catholic priest. As Luther later recalled, performing the ritual of the Mass for the first time left him nearly paralyzed with awe before the presence of God on the altar. "Who am I," he wondered, "that I should lift up my eyes or raise my hands to the divine Majesty?" Comparing himself to a "little pygmy" standing before a great prince, Luther recalled that he had been struck by the vast difference between human sinners and God. "For I am dust and ashes and full of sin," he observed, "and I am speaking to the living, eternal, and the true God." Convinced of his unredeemable sinfulness in the eyes of a righteous God, Luther devoted himself to praying, fasting, and confessing what he regarded as his innumerable sins. Even a pilgrimage to the holy city of Rome, where he performed Mass and engaged in acts of penance at the most sacred sites, failed to bring him relief. Although he made every effort to obtain spiritual merit from these rituals, including the papal indulgences that bestowed forgiveness from the church's "treasury of merit," Martin Luther continued to feel unworthy of divine mercy.[1]

Tortured by his own sense of inadequacy in relation to an angry, righteous God, Martin Luther experienced a sudden breakthrough while wrestling with the meaning of the phrase "the righteousness of God" in Paul's Letter to the Romans. He realized that divine righteousness was not the "active" justice in which an angry God punished sinners, but the "passive" justification that sinners received from a merciful God through faith. As Luther later recalled:

Then I began to comprehend the "righteousness of God" through which the righteous are saved by God's grace, namely, through faith; that the "righteousness of God" which is revealed through the Gospel was to be understood in a passive sense in which God through mercy justifies man by faith, as it is written, "The just shall live by faith." Now I felt exactly as though I had been born again, and I believed that I had entered Paradise through widely opened doors.[2]

Even within Luther's lifetime, these dramatic stories of his encounters with the awesome power and mercy of God, his personal hell, and his evangelical rebirth became part of the foundational myth of the Protestant Reformation. Out of thunder and lightning, fear and trembling, and soul-searching anguish over the unbridgeable gap between a righteous God and his sinful self, Luther made an "evangelical discovery" that launched the Reformation. Relying solely on the authority of Christian scriptures, Luther found that salvation was an undeserved gift of divine grace received through faith. The principles *sola scriptura, sola gratia, sola fides*—only according to scripture, by grace, through faith—were regarded by Luther and his followers as marking the new divide between Protestants and Catholics in European Christianity.

The Protestant Reformation, however, emerged in the context of a changing Catholic environment in Europe. From his childhood schooling, Luther had been influenced by the Brothers and Sisters of the Common Life, a movement of clergy and laity committed to the "modern devotion"—*devotio moderna*—which cultivated a simple Christian piety. Founded by Gerhard Groote (1340–84), this devotional movement spread widely, especially in the Netherlands and the Rhineland. Like the Confraternity of the Rosary, the Brothers and Sisters of the Common Life required no vows from lay members, allowing them to remain in their ordinary vocations, while providing manuals, instructions, and other guidance for Christian spirituality. For *devotio moderna*, however, spiritual devotion was focused not on the Virgin Mary, but on the Eucharist. Instead of celebrating Mary as the Queen of Heaven, adherents of the modern devotion, such as Thomas à Kempis (ca. 1379–1471), author of the influential guide *The Imitation of Christ*, saw her as a humble servant of God. Although *devotio moderna* encouraged frequent Communion, it also diminished the importance of saints, relics, and rituals of pilgrimage. As Thomas à Kempis insisted, Christians did not need "to run to divers places" to behold the relics of saints or benefit from their miracles because the supreme God was "present on this altar here before me." Supported by regular reading of the Bible and mystical literature, particularly the collection known as the *Theologia Germanica,* which contained excerpts from Meister Eckhart and other Rhineland mystics, *devotio moderna* promoted a simple and humble Christian life devoted to the presence of God.

At European universities, academic theologians also developed what was widely regarded as new and modern ways of inquiring about God, the soul, and the world. Challenging the synthesis of Christian faith and Aristotelian reason worked out by Thomas Aquinas, late medieval scholars adopted new critical methods that separated faith and reason. Influenced by the work of William of Ockham (ca. 1280–1349), this *via moderna* found that theology had to be derived from biblical revelation rather than rational argumentation. Often identified as nominalists, because they insisted that ideas, concepts, or "universals" were merely names—*nomina*—with no independent or real existence, followers of Ockham criticized any attempt to establish the Christian religion on rational grounds. According to Ockham, reason had its legitimate place, which was limited to providing rational accounts of processes in the world. Ockham's famous "razor" called for cutting away all unnecessary philosophical assumptions—the fewer assumptions the better—when developing rational or scientific explanations. Philosophy, however, provided no access to the truths of Christian theology, which could only be gained through revelation. Faith rather than reason, therefore, had to guide Christian thinking about God.

Inspired by the humanist movement in Italy, Christian humanists in Germany and the Netherlands recovered classical Greek and Latin literary models. As the leading figure of this "northern Renaissance," the Dutch humanist Desiderius Erasmus of Rotterdam (ca. 1469–1535) developed a "philosophy of Christ" that set out a program for reforming Christian moral and religious life. Advocating reform through education, Erasmus recommended the ancient pagan poets and philosophers, but only if they were read allegorically so that "everything can be related to Christ." Drawing on classical models for the rhetorical style of his Christian philosophy, Erasmus adamantly rejected both the theological style and content of Scholasticism. According to Erasmus, all that the various schools of theology had accomplished was to create a labyrinth of "tortuous obscurities" that the original apostles of Jesus Christ would never have understood. The apostles would have needed a new holy spirit, he once remarked, to lead them through the intellectual maze created by Christian Scholasticism. Like Petrarch, therefore, Erasmus and other Christian humanists in northern Europe dismissed Scholasticism as nothing more than convoluted exercises in logic expressed in an awkward technical style.

In place of the complexities of Scholastic theology, Erasmus advocated the simplicity of a Christian faith based on the Bible. Supporting this biblical faith with his classical scholarship, Erasmus produced a new edition of the Greek New Testament, originally published in 1516, that provided European scholars with a more accurate version of the primary Christian scriptures. He hoped that his corrected Greek edition would provide the basis for new translations of the Christian scriptures into every vernacular language. In developing new historical and linguistic methods of biblical scholarship, Erasmus discovered that the author of the texts ascribed to Dionysius the Areopagite could not possibly have been the same historical person as the Dionysius of the New Testament. Following suggestions originally made by the Italian humanist Lorenzo Valla (1407–57), Erasmus argued that the Greek style, historical references, and elaborate ceremonies described in the Dionysian texts placed their author in the sixth rather than in the first century. As Erasmus publicized these research findings, the texts of Dionysius the Areopagite, which had assumed almost biblical authority, began to decline in importance as a basis for Christian thought in the West. Ultimately, however, the "philosophy of Christ" developed by Erasmus was a moral philosophy, a "design for Christian living" for both clergy and laity. "The end and aim of the faith of the Gospel," Erasmus asserted, "is conduct worthy of Christ." In his Christian humanism, therefore, Erasmus advocated an educational program in language, literature, and Christian scriptures in which faith was fulfilled in an ethical life.[3]

FREEDOM OF A CHRISTIAN

Shaped by these late medieval Catholic developments in spiritual devotion, academic theology, and Christian humanism, Martin Luther precipitated a break with the Roman Catholic Church over the question of the authority of the pope. As he developed his "theology of the cross," which promised forgiveness only through the divine grace received by faith,

Luther rejected most of the sacramental channels—confession, acts of penance, pilgrimage to holy shrines, miracles of the saints, and indulgences bestowed by popes—through which divine mercy was sought by Christians. Retaining only the sacraments of baptism and the Eucharist, Luther attacked the entire ritual system of the Roman Catholic Church. But he directed his initial attack at what he regarded as the system's weakest link, the practice of granting papal indulgences. Although forgiveness from afterlife punishment in purgatory could be acquired through penance or pilgrimage, indulgences could also be obtained in exchange for a donation to the church. As they were aggressively marketed in the early sixteenth century to support building projects in Rome, indulgences appeared to Luther merely as a way of selling grace. When he published ninety-five theses against indulgences for academic debate in 1517, Luther argued that "indulgences, which the merchants extol as the greatest of favors, are seen to be, in fact, a favorite means for money getting." Such exchanges of money for forgiveness, he insisted, "are not to be compared with the grace of God and the compassion shown in the Cross." At stake for Luther, therefore, was not merely the practice of granting papal indulgences, but the economy of grace in which forgiveness was a free gift of mercy that was received in faith, but was only offered once through the sacrificial death of Jesus Christ on the cross.[4]

When Luther published his ninety-five debating points, the new technology of printing rapidly took the debate out of the confines of the university. Although German publishing houses had been printing about forty titles a year since 1500, Luther's controversy stimulated the publication of over five hundred new books a year. Not only books, but also a multitude of pamphlets and tracts, journals and cartoons, flowed from the presses and were absorbed by an expanding reading public. Between 1517 and 1525, Luther and his followers effectively used this new communication medium to widely publicize their challenge to the church. Unable to ignore this challenge, church leaders, especially representatives of the Dominican order, mounted a counterattack. During 1518, the Dominican theologian Johann Tetzel (ca. 1465–1519) argued that Luther's attack on the pope's capacity to grant indulgences had disastrous implications. If papal authority was undermined, even in this one relatively minor respect, then Christians would neglect the sacraments, doubt the preachers, and read the Bible without the guidance of tradition. "Everyone will interpret Scripture as takes his fancy," Tetzel warned. "And all sacred Christendom must come into great spiritual danger when each individual believes what pleases him most." Taking action against Luther, a papal decree issued in June 1520 identified a list of his statements that were "heretical, offensive, erroneous, scandalous for pious ears, corrupting for simple minds, and contradictory to Catholic teaching." Given sixty days to recant, Luther instead burned the text of the papal decree in public, a defiance of papal authority that resulted in his excommunication in January 1521. Luther, his followers, and anyone who sheltered them were declared to be enemies of Christendom. In support of the church, Charles V, the emperor of the Holy Roman Empire, condemned Luther to death. Like many heretics before him, therefore, Luther was formally excluded from church and society in the interests of preserving Christian unity.[5]

However, under the political protection of the German prince of Saxony, Frederick the Wise, Luther was able to defy the authority of both the pope and the emperor. Between 1520 and 1525, he published a series of influential books on faith, the sacraments, and the church. Attacking papal authority and the sacramental system as symptoms of "the pagan captivity of the church," Luther developed the implications of his "evangelical discovery." In his *Freedom of a Christian,* Luther proposed the enigma that a Christian is "a perfectly free lord of all," but at the same time "a perfectly dutiful servant of all." Christian freedom, according to Luther, was the divine grace through faith that liberated Christians from the law, ritual, and works. Under divine law, all human beings stood condemned as sinners. No amount of merit gained through rituals or good conduct could alter this condition. By means of an unmerited gift of divine grace, however, God liberated faithful Christians from judgment under law. Remaining sinners, Christians were nevertheless justified, as Luther understood the significance of Paul's assertion in Romans that whoever "through faith is righteous shall live" (Rom. 1:17). Since Christ was the "end of the law," the grace of Christ meant that "everyone who has faith may be justified" (Rom. 10:4). Freedom through faith, however, did not imply that Christians could do anything they wanted. Although faith set them free, love bound them to serve the good of others. As Luther put it, the Christian "lives in Christ through faith, in his neighbor through love."[6]

Striking at the ritual and moral order of the church, Luther's declaration of Christian freedom also undermined any notion of human free will. Since good works could only flow from a good faith, a faith passively received from God, then human beings were not capable of willing to be good or do good. With his commitment to moral education, however, Erasmus argued against this passive construction of the human will. In a treatise published in 1525, *On the Freedom of the Will*, he asserted that the will was free to cooperate with divine grace to live a moral life based on "conduct worthy of Christ." According to the Christian humanist, human beings were free to make that moral choice. Having hoped that Erasmus would support his campaign for reform, Luther registered his disappointment in a response, *On the Bondage of the Will*, which insisted that human beings were absolutely dependent on the will of God. Following the lead of Augustine, who in his later work emphasized the pervasive corruption of the will, Luther insisted that the human will was not free to choose good. "The human will is like a beast of burden," he asserted. "If God rides it, it wills and goes as God wills; if Satan rides it, it wills and goes as Satan wills; nor can it choose to run to either of the two riders or to seek him out, but the riders themselves contend for the possession and control of it." According to Luther, therefore, the freedom of a Christian was only realized in being possessed by God.[7]

Outside of academic debates and theological disputations, however, Luther's declaration of Christian freedom seemed to take on a life of its own in both town and countryside. Certainly, his protector in Saxony, the elector Frederick the Wise, welcomed a religious rationale for declaring freedom from the Roman Catholic Church. Having already denounced papal taxes and refused to allow agents of the church to offer indulgences in his territory, Frederick was in the position of many German princes who were seeking political independence from the Roman Catholic Church and the Holy Roman Empire. For the German princes, therefore, the freedom of a Christian could signify independence from the political authority of Rome. At the local level, however, the Lutheran movement found a following in the imperial cities and towns of Germany that had emerged as centers of social and economic power. As an urban phenomenon, the Reformation spread—city by city, town by town—in a changing political environment. In some cases, religious change was inspired by town councils that attempted to assert control over civic life by replacing Roman Catholic clergy with Lutherans. Absorbing land, property, and other forms of wealth from the church, urban magistrates could expect Lutheran ministers to be better citizens, since they were accountable not to Rome, but to the local town council. In other cases, religious change resulted from local struggles over the control of an urban center between councils, a wealthy ruling class, and trade guilds. The Protestant movement developed as a "magisterial" Reformation to the extent that it relied upon local magistrates for the religious conversion of an urban center. From this magisterial perspective, therefore, the freedom of a Christian entailed establishing local political control over the material and human resources of the city.

During the 1520s, however, the vast majority of the people of Europe did not live in towns or cities. Out of an estimated population of 70 million, only 10 percent were urbanized. As Luther's evangelical message reached the countryside, peasants developed an alternative understanding of Christian freedom. For those inspired by a biblically based call for freedom, the gospel promised liberation from oppressive working and living conditions. In a document drawn up in March 1525 by the tanner Sebastian Lotzer and the pastor Christoph Schappeler, the *Twelve Articles of the Peasants,* long-standing grievances over rents, taxes, servitude, and forced labor were reformulated in evangelical terms. The authors called for certain reforms in the church. For example, they proposed that a congregation should be allowed to select its own minister and to see that the funds donated to the church were redistributed to the poor. They also quoted passages from the Bible to demonstrate the injustice of preventing an already impoverished peasantry from pursuing a livelihood. Peasants were generally forbidden access to rivers, forests, and woodlands and suffered under heavy taxes and rents from both wealthy landlords and the church. Coerced into working for the wealthy nobility, peasants were treated like property, "which is deplorable," the authors observed, "since Christ redeemed us all with the shedding of his precious blood—the shepherd as well as the most highly placed, without exception." On behalf of all peasants, Lotzer and Schappeler insisted that "the Scripture establishes that we are and will be free." As widely dispersed groups of peasants rose up in rebellion during 1524 and 1525, many understood the freedom of a Christian to signify a new peasantry—both egalitarian and evangelical— that was liberated from feudal oppression.

Although Luther recognized the legitimacy of their grievances, he quickly moved to denounce the rebellious peasants. In a response to the *Twelve Articles of the Peasants,* Luther counseled both peasants and princes to seek a peaceful resolution to the conflict. Calling the princes and nobility to account, he asserted, "as temporal rulers you do nothing but cheat and rob the people so that you may lead a life of luxury and extravagance. The poor common people cannot bear it any longer." Luther warned the rulers that their injustice would bring down the wrath of God. Suggesting that God might use peasant uprisings to punish the ruling class, Luther adamantly rejected the peasants' use of God and the evangelical gospel in their revolt. By invoking the Bible in support of worldly rather than spiritual goals, he argued, the peasants showed that they did not understand the meaning of Christian freedom. Rather than promising that peasants would be freed from their servitude, the Bible actually supported slavery. All the patriarchs and prophets of the Old Testament had slaves, and the apostle Paul of the New Testament called upon slaves to accept their condition. In offering similar advice to the German peasants, Luther further warned them not to commit the crime of "robbery" in which "every man takes his body away from his lord, even though his body is the lord's property."

More seriously for Luther, however, the peasants' demand for liberty violated a crucial distinction between the kingdom of God and the kingdom of the world. As a result of its inherently sinful nature, the world could never conform to the spiritual kingdom in which all Christians, both slave and free, were equal in Christ. By demanding their liberty, Luther insisted, the peasants "would make all men equal, and turn the spiritual kingdom of Christ into a worldly, external kingdom; and that is impossible." Unlike the equality of the spiritual kingdom, he argued, "a worldly kingdom cannot exist without an inequality of persons, some being free, some imprisoned, some lords, some subjects." In assessing the positions of both princes and peasants, Luther concluded that "there is nothing Christian on either side and nothing Christian is at issue between you; both lords and peasants are discussing questions of justice and injustice in heathen, or worldly, terms." According to Luther, therefore, the Christian freedom of the gospel was found in a spiritual kingdom beyond such worldly concerns. Nevertheless, Luther sought to distance his reform movements from the peasants, writing a few weeks later in a tract, *Against the Robbing and Murdering Hordes of Peasants,* that anyone who killed a rebellious peasant was performing a service to God. As the widespread revolts were forcefully suppressed by the German princes in 1525, over a hundred thousand peasants were killed. Taking the side of the rulers not only against the peasants, but also against a variety of radical reformers known as Anabaptists, or "rebaptizers," who were forming alternative Christian communities, whether militant or pacifist, Martin Luther clearly aligned his reform with the interests of the cities.[8]

WAR AGAINST IDOLS

By 1526 evangelical reformers were established in cities throughout central and southern Germany. To the evangelicals, this early expansion seemed like the work of God. While he was busy drinking good Wittenberg beer with his colleagues, Luther later recalled, the reform was advanced solely by the Word of God. According to Luther, an authentic Christian faith was received by hearing the Word of God through the words of preaching and the words of the Bible. In proclaiming this faith through hearing—*fides ex auditu*—Luther asserted that "a right faith goes right on with its eyes closed; it clings to God's Word; it follows that Word; it believes the Word." Hearing rather than seeing, therefore, defined Luther's gospel. "The kingdom of God is a kingdom of hearing," he maintained, "not of seeing." Under the influence of this new kingdom of hearing, Luther argued that Christian worship required no material support from things that could be seen. In 1522, for example, he insisted that proper worship needed no lights, candles, paintings, images, or altars. "For these are all human inventions and ornaments," he explained, "which God does not heed, and which obscure the correct worship, with their glitter." As the Protestant Reformation developed, genuine Christian religion came to be defined by the reformers as an ongoing war against idols.[9]

In a treatise published in 1522, *On the Abolition of Images,* the reformer Andreas Karlstadt (ca. 1480–1541) announced this new Protestant iconoclasm by insisting that the use of images in worship was forbidden by the Ten Commandments. According to Karlstadt, "God has forbidden images with no less diligence than killing, stealing, adultery and the like." Instead of following Gregory the Great in regarding Christian imagery as the Bible of the illiterate, Karlstadt argued that images were actually responsible for the anti-Christian materialism, moral corruption, and spiritual seduction that had drawn Christians into the sin of idolatry. To avoid being defiled by such a serious sin, Karlstadt urged Christians to take immediate action in removing images from churches. He called upon the "common people" to destroy the idols. Inspired by this radical iconoclasm, crowds in Wittenberg stormed into churches and monastic cloisters to attack statues, destroy paintings, and overturn altars. Luther reasserted his authority over the city by opposing this destruction. Against the iconoclasm of Karlstadt, he argued that since images were merely "outward things" that were neither evil nor good in themselves, then "we may have them or not, as we please." If they were to be permitted in church, however, then evangelicals only had "to preach that images are nothing."[10]

Parting ways with Martin Luther on this issue, most Protestant reformers during the sixteenth century did not regard images as neutral. Like Karlstadt, they called for their destruction. Under the leadership of Ulrich Zwingli (1484–1531), a parish priest who had been influenced by the Christian humanism of Erasmus, the Swiss city of Zurich was converted to the Protestant cause. From his arrival in Zurich in 1519, Zwingli had preached against the veneration of saints, arguing that "no one other than Christ alone can mediate between God and us." Gaining the support of the city council in 1522, Zwingli launched a campaign to remove all religious images from the churches of Zurich. After considerable public debate, which was punctuated by a few random acts of destruction, the city council finally agreed to supervise the orderly removal of images. Giving private citizens one week to recover images they had sponsored, the council followed Zwingli in ruling that only the crucifix could remain in churches "because it does not signify any deity but only the humanity and suffering of Christ, and because it is a sign to Christians." By official edict rather than mass action, therefore, Zwingli succeeded in removing images from the churches of Zurich.

As Zwingli developed his "theology of idolatry," the use of religious images in worship defined the essence of the "false religion" opposed to the "true religion" of Christ. In his *Commentary on the True and False Religion,* Zwingli argued that adherents of the true religion "will disregard those fallacious hopes which certain persons have told us to place in sacraments, ceremonies, and created things, and will see that all his hopes are placed in God." Since the true God was purely spiritual, any material image used in worship, whether a painting, statue, or relic, became the locus for what Zwingli called "strange gods." Proposing a psychological explanation, he argued that the human mind is so bound by materiality that "there is no one who, as soon as he hears God spoken of, or any other thing which he has not already seen, does not picture a form for himself." According to Zwingli, therefore, the mental production of "strange gods" in the imagination preceded the construction of the idols of wood and stone used in religious worship. By removing the external images from Christian churches, Zwingli hoped to erase the "strange gods" in the imagination that had turned people away from the true religion of the spiritual God.[11]

This strict separation of the spiritual and the material also extended to Zwingli's understanding of the Eucharist. Arguing against any presence of the physical body of Jesus Christ in the bread and wine, he interpreted the sacrament as a symbolic commemoration of the death of Jesus and a sign of the spirituality of Christ. Although Luther had rejected the Catholic doctrine of transubstantiation, partly on the grounds that it owed too much to the philosophy of that "pagan rascal" Aristotle, he still maintained the real presence of the body of Jesus Christ in the bread and wine. Their different understandings of the Eucharist had caused a rift not only between Luther and Zwingli, but also between the German and Swiss reformers. As Luther told the Swiss representatives at a conference at Marburg in 1529, "Our spirit has nothing in common with your spirit." Although Zwingli encouraged Luther to rise to a spiritual understanding of the Eucharist, citing in support the biblical passage "The flesh is of no avail" (John 6:63), the German reformer insisted, "I know God only as he became human, so I shall have him no other way."[12] From Zwingli's perspective, however, Luther's assumption that God was actually present in the material forms of the Eucharist was idolatry. On this issue, the Lutheran movement in Germany split from the Protestant initiatives emerging in Switzerland and France. Following the spiritual lead of Zwingli, this Reformed movement continued to declare war against idols, even engaging in the military battles between Swiss Catholics and Protestants in which Zwingli himself was killed in 1531. Like Ulrich Zwingli, the new Reformed leaders—his successor Heinrich Bullinger (1504–75) in Zurich, Martin Bucer (1491–1551) in Strassburg, and Guillaume Farel (1489–1565) in Bern—understood the Protestant Reformation as both theoretical and practical opposition to idolatry.

As they wrote and preached against idols, Reformed leaders frequently inspired people to take mass action against Catholic churches. By 1534, in the Swiss city of Geneva, for example, people were taking the Reformation into their own hands by overturning altars, breaking statues, and stealing consecrated Hosts to subject them to public ridicule. "Behold the god of bread," children sang in the streets. Giving force to the theological arguments of the reformers, these acts of desecration advanced the

Reformation in Geneva. For the "common people" who participated, destroying a statue was a revolutionary act that asserted the power of the people over ruling institutions. In the midst of public rioting, the council of Geneva tried to contain that popular revolt by ordering the removal of images from churches and prohibiting the Mass. By establishing the Reformation in Geneva, therefore, the council reasserted its control by containing the revolutionary impulses of popular iconoclasm.

When he arrived in the Protestant city of Geneva in 1536, the French lawyer, humanist, and reformer John Calvin (1509–64) found that the city was "reformed" only to the extent that the council had formally adopted a policy of iconoclasm. "They were good at seeking out idols and burning them," he observed, "but there was no Reformation. Everything was in turmoil." Invited to stay in Geneva to assist the process of reform, Calvin was driven out of the city in 1538 only to be invited back in 1541. From that point until his death in 1564, John Calvin devoted his efforts to transforming the urban "turmoil" of Geneva into Protestant order. As a result, Calvin's Geneva became the model city of the Reformed movement. The city was governed by the consistory, a body of clergy and laity, who monitored private and public morality and supervised the establishment of the Reformed faith. In support of these efforts, Calvin developed a Reformed theology of the majesty of God, which asserted that human destiny was entirely determined by the divine will that predestined a few, the "elect," for salvation and condemned the vast majority to eternal damnation. In the first edition of his *Institutes of the Christian Religion*, which had been published a few months before he arrived in Geneva, Calvin outlined and defended this Reformed theology of the supreme majesty and sovereignty of God. When he entered the war against idols in Geneva, however, Calvin further developed this Reformed theology as a critique of the "false religion" of idolatry.

According to Calvin, the world was created for human beings to know and glorify God. Insisting that God can only be known through biblical scripture, the Word of God, Calvin maintained that God was glorified in practice through obedience to the divine will and through spiritual acts of worship. A God who is entirely spiritual, he argued, can only be glorified through spiritual worship. "God wholly calls us back and withdraws us from petty carnal observances, which our stupid minds, crassly conceiving of God, are wont to devise," Calvin observed. "And he makes us conform to his lawful worship, that is, a spiritual worship established by himself." By bringing the spiritual into the material, the finite into the infinite, acts of worship that used material objects were indicted by Calvin as dishonoring rather than glorifying God. As Calvin insisted, "Nothing belonging to God's divinity is to be transferred to another." Relics, icons, and even the eucharistic Host received as the real presence of God were all identified by Calvin as acts of worship that transferred God's divinity to another. Like Zwingli, Calvin developed a psychology of worship in which he argued that the human imagination had been thoroughly corrupted by its tendency to attach divine significance to material objects. Assuming that all human beings had an inherent sense of divinity, or seed of religion, Calvin argued that the human capacity for spiritual worship had been almost universally destroyed by its entanglement with material objects. As a result, spiritual religion had been subsumed under superstition, magic, and idolatry.

Certainly, Calvin was familiar with arguments in defense of images advanced by John of Damascus in the eighth century. Rather than worshiping an object as if it were a deity, Christians who venerated a relic or icon were directing their devotion to the invisible reality that the material object represented. According to Calvin, however, all idolaters defended their material worship as if it were spiritual, but "they never stopped until, deluded by new tricks, they presently supposed that God manifested his power in images." Not merely false and illusory, these acts of material worship effectively dishonored God and thereby represented a serious act of sacrilege that would be met with divine punishment. Accordingly, Calvin urged Christians to disassociate themselves entirely from any worship involving images or objects. In the interest of maintaining their spiritual purity, Christians had to avoid any contact with images, whether "by look, access, or nearness," in order to remain free of the "guilt or stain" of impure worship and to honor the supreme power of God.[13]

PROTESTANTS AND CATHOLICS

As the Reformation expanded into France, Scotland, the Netherlands, and Poland, Calvinism emerged as the major Protestant alternative to the Roman Catholic Church. Affirming the sovereignty of God, the sole authority of the Bible, the centrality of spiritual faith, and the human dependence upon divine grace, this Reformed movement also defined itself in opposition to Roman Catholic tradition. When reflecting on the long historical development of the Christian church in Europe, the Protestants traced a counterhistory of forerunners, such as Valdes in France, John Wycliffe in England, and John Huss in Bohemia, who had promoted Bible-based preaching that seemed to anticipate the Protestant Reformation. Claiming these Catholic heretics as Protestant heroes, the Protestant reformers castigated the Roman Catholic Church, which had condemned them, as the church of the devil or the Antichrist. By the middle of the sixteenth century, the Protestant war against idols had developed into widespread and often violent conflict between two religions, Catholic and Protestant.

In the interest of internal reform, in the 1530s the Roman Catholic hierarchy decided to hold a major church council. Only partially inspired by the Protestant challenge, this council was designed to revitalize a church whose administrative center had in 1527 suffered a devastating invasion by the troops of Emperor Charles V. The sack of Rome was widely interpreted by Catholic leaders as a symptom of the spiritual decline of the church. According to the Catholic theologian Giles of Viterbo, for example, God had used the imperial troops to punish the pride of a city that had turned from authentic religion to worldly pursuits. As Giles explained, "You must understand just how wicked are these days and how angry is Heaven at the rabble now admitted everywhere to the exalted office of the priesthood (lazy, untrained, disorganized and immoral, mere youths, bankers, merchants and soldiers, not to mention usurers and pimps)." As Giles concluded, "The ungodly say 'If God cares for sacred things, why does he allow this?' I reply that it is because God cares that he not only allows this thing, but even carries it out himself." From the perspective of this Catholic reformer, therefore, the violent destruction of sacred objects could be interpreted as God's punishment of the pride, wealth, and power of a corrupt religion. Out of the ashes of that destruction, however, Catholic reformers anticipated a renewal of the church. In its report on the status of the church in 1537, a papal commission called for a church council because the "spirit of God decrees that Christ's church, almost collapsed, should be restored to its early glory."[14]

For centuries, popes had been reluctant to convene general church councils because they felt threatened by advocates of an alternative model of church governance, conciliarism, that would have made papal authority subject to the approval of bishops meeting at regular councils. However, when Charles V indicated that he would follow the precedent of the Christian emperor Constantine in convening a church council, Pope Paul III began preparations for a general council. The Council of Trent opened in 1545, beginning an eighteen-year process of reviewing crucial issues of Catholic doctrine, ritual, and organization. Although it was a general council for the entire church, the Council of Trent was dominated by Italian bishops, who accounted for about 75 percent of the representatives. Nevertheless, the council succeeded in introducing reforms that reorganized the priesthood, the parish system, and the monastic orders in Catholic territories.

At the same time, the Council of Trent responded to the Protestant challenges to Catholic faith and worship. The council maintained that the justification by faith proclaimed by Luther actually had a long history in Catholic tradition. Affirming justification through faith as Catholic teaching, the council condemned any notion that a human being "can be justified before God by his own works, whether done either by his own natural powers or through the teaching of the law, without divine grace through Jesus Christ." Faith alone, however, was not sufficient for salvation, since faith had to be manifested in good works and required participation through acts of worship in the community of the faithful. With respect to worship, therefore, the Council of Trent addressed the sacramental system of the Roman Catholic Church. At the final sessions during 1563, the council formulated a creed that placed the Mass at the center of religious worship. According to the council, "The true God is offered in the Mass, a proper, propitiatory sacrifice for the living and the dead, and in the Holy Eucharist there are truly and substantially the body and blood, together with the soul and the divinity of Our Lord Jesus Christ." Reaffirming the presence of God in the Eucharist, the creed of the Council of Trent also reasserted the value of prayers for the dead in purgatory, the veneration of saints and their relics, and the benefit of papal indulgences. Through the deliberations of the Council of Trent, therefore, the power of the sacraments for Christian faith was reaffirmed.[15]

By the end of the Council of Trent, one of the primary agencies for revitalizing the power of the church had emerged in the new religious order of the Society of Jesus—the Jesuits—founded by Ignatius of Loyola (1491–1556). As he recounted in his autobiography, Ignatius of Loyola had been a Spanish soldier fighting in France in 1521 when he was wounded. While confined to bed reading about the lives of Christ and the saints, Ignatius asked himself, "Suppose that I should do what St. Francis did, what St.

Dominic did?" The following year, while keeping a vigil at the shrine of the Virgin Mary at Montserrat in Spain, Ignatius had a spiritual experience that confirmed his belief in this special mission. After studying at the university, in 1534 Ignatius and six companions decided to go to Jerusalem to preach the Christian gospel to Muslims. Failing to establish that mission in Jerusalem, they decided to present themselves to the pope in Rome and ask the Vicar of Christ to make use of them for "God's glory and the good of souls." In 1539 Ignatius of Loyola announced the formation of the Jesuits, "a community founded principally for the advancement of souls in Christian life and doctrine," but also a religious order "for the propagation of the faith by the ministry of the word, by spiritual exercises, by works of charity, and expressly by the instruction in Christianity of children and the uneducated." As "soldiers of God," the Jesuits pledged obedience to the pope in engaging Protestants in Europe, Muslims in the Middle East, and pagans in the new territories being discovered by Europeans all over the world.

In addition to this militant mission to the world, Ignatius of Loyola also introduced a reformation of the imagination. In his *Spiritual Exercises,* Ignatius developed techniques for working with mental imagery, emotions, and the internal senses. Adapting techniques of visualization from *devotio moderna* and other mystical traditions, Ignatius advocated a regulated practice of meditation "to help the exercitant to conquer himself." To stimulate contrition for sin, for example, Ignatius recommended five meditations on hell that corresponded to the five senses so that the imagination could experience in succession the sight of burning bodies, the sound of the screams of the damned, the smell of abysmal stench, the taste of bitter tears, and the searing touch of flames. Meditating on hell, therefore, required an intense sensory experience of an interior place in the imagination. Likewise, when meditating on Christ or the Virgin, Ignatius insisted that it was essential to picture "with the mind's eye the physical place where the object that we wish to contemplate is present." By forming a detailed and vivid mental image of a specific place, whether a home, a mountain, or a temple, Ignatius found that the imagination was able to make Christ or the Virgin directly present to the powers of the soul. Through such interior spiritual exercises, therefore, it was not necessary to travel to distant shrines to be in the immediate presence of the sacred. In the internal space of the imagination, the sacred was present in vivid images that evoked religious thought and emotion.[16]

Like Ignatius of Loyola, other Spanish reformers fought heresy by cultivating a mystical spirituality. Teresa of Ávila (1515–82), for example, reformed the Carmelite order of nuns, establishing sixteen convents dedicated to countering heresy through contemplative prayer. From a family of *conversos*, Spanish Jews forcibly converted to Christianity, Teresa took the Carmelite vows of poverty, chastity, and obedience in 1535. In 1562 she opened the first convent of reformed Carmelites. As she pursued the administrative work of reorganizing the order, Teresa felt herself to "be addressed by interior voices and to see certain visions and experience revelations." Ironically, Teresa claimed to suffer from an undeveloped faculty of imagination. "So inert is this faculty in me," she observed, "that despite all my efforts I can never picture or represent to myself the Holy Humanity of our Lord." Nevertheless, her classic text on mystical spirituality, *The Interior Castle,* provided an imaginative account of the soul's journey toward union with God. Picturing the soul as a castle of many rooms but made from a single diamond or clear crystal, Teresa led the reader into the central room, the chamber of the spiritual marriage, "where the most secret things pass between God and the soul." Her Carmelite colleague, the Spanish poet John of the Cross (1542–91), developed the vivid imagery of the "dark night of the soul" to evoke an internal union with God. Picturing the rungs of an internal ladder rather than the rooms of an interior castle, John of the Cross nevertheless developed an imaginative spirituality independent of place. In fact, due to conflicts within the Carmelite order, John actually wrote many of his mystical texts while he was confined in prison. By developing imaginative techniques of visualization that transcended the ordinary limits of space, however, the Spanish mystics could find the sacred anywhere because they experienced it through internal senses in the interior places of the soul. As both mystics and reformers, Ignatius of Loyola, Teresa of Ávila, and John of the Cross had a profound impact on revitalizing a Catholic spirituality of images.[17]

The sixteenth-century controversy over images, however, continued to take place in public. In Lyons, for example, a growing community of French Protestants, who came to be known as Huguenots, struggled to establish their place in the city. As an international city, Lyons was home to people from all over Europe. Between 1550 and 1580, Lyons experienced religious conflicts between Catholics and Protestants that were also appearing in other urban centers of Europe. Although they represented a minority of perhaps one-third of the population, the Protestants in Lyons declared their own war against idols. Inspired by the iconoclastic preaching of their Reformed ministers, Protestant crowds broke into churches, threatened priests, destroyed statues, and mocked the consecrated Host. While Protestants attacked "idols," engaging in a kind of symbolic warfare against statues, paintings, and the Host, Catholics responded by attacking "heretics," directing their violence against the Protestants themselves in order to prevent or avenge their acts of desecration. In the midst of this religious conflict, Catholics and Protestants worked out different approaches to defining the sacred space of the city. Carved into nine traditional parishes, the Catholic space of Lyons allowed for each church in the city to develop a distinctive identity associated with its relics and saints. During the religious processions held to mark feast days and other holy days, Catholics engaged in public rituals that sanctified the city as a whole. Marching around its perimeters with banners, torches, pictures, relics, and the consecrated Host, they sanctified Lyons as a space of purity and protection. Nevertheless, those public rituals of urban unity allowed for considerable diversity among the nine parishes and the many religious guilds and confraternities of the city.

Rejecting this diversity in the sacred space of the city, the Protestants organized their congregations according to the more uniform division of the population into new urban wards. Furthermore, in keeping with the Protestant war against idols, they insisted that no object, altar, or place could actually contain the sacred. According to the Protestants, a place was sanctified not by the presence of relics or the veneration of saints, but only by the activity of preaching and praying. As a result, the Protestants introduced a new sense of homogeneity into urban sacred space. Since they assumed that any building could in principle be consecrated for worship, Protestants ignored the Catholic sensitivity to the subtle and complex differences among sacred sites, each with its own relics, saints, and traditions. As they sought to establish a new uniformity of sacred places in the city, with each church being the same in its preaching and praying, Protestants in Lyons also celebrated the opening of the city to new commerce, communication, and immigration. Significantly, most Protestants in Lyons were relatively recent arrivals in the city and could be expected to encourage regional and international exchanges. Rather than sanctifying the boundaries of the city to maintain its purity and protection, the Protestants opened Lyons to new economic relations of an expanding market. In the classic formulation of the sociologist Max Weber (1864–1920), the Protestants anticipated the uniformity, homogeneity, and rationalization of space that would be crucial for the rise of capitalism in western Europe.

Although they briefly established a Protestant regime in 1562, the Huguenots of Lyons experienced a fierce Catholic backlash that drove many from the city. As one observer reported in 1567, the violent anti-Protestant riots succeeded in unifying the Catholics of Lyons because "in an instant the Catholics were united and conforming, so that one could finally say that in such a town, composed of so many sorts of nations, there was only one heart, one will and one head." Beyond the city of Lyons, conflict between Catholics and Protestants, each of which experienced the internally unifying effect of violence against the other camp, became a constant feature of European politics. One attempt at international compromise was proposed in the formula *cuius regio, eius religio,* which meant that the ruler of a territory determined its religion and the people of a region were subject to the religion of their ruler. However, the wars of religion continued. During the Protestant and Catholic reformations of the sixteenth century, Christianity entered a new era of unprecedented violence. As religion was increasingly linked with the political interests of rising European nationalisms, the violence of intolerance, persecution, and warfare only escalated. In the early modern era, Christian Europe was a region of religious conflict conducted in the name and under the banner of Christianity.[18]

20

Europe

After the fall of Constantinople in 1453, Pope Pius II wrote a letter to the conquering Turkish sultan Muhammad II to warn the Muslim ruler about the "power of the Christian people." Surveying Christian Europe, Pius pointed to the strong Spanish, the bellicose French, the numerous Germans, the powerful British, the bold Poles, the vigorous Hungarians, and the rich Italians, who were especially spirited and skilled in warfare. In presenting this inventory of European nations as if it comprised the full extent of the "Christian people," Pope Pius indicated that he saw Christianity as the religion of Europe. In fact, the pope informed the sultan that these European Christians were the only genuine Christians in the world. Although Sultan Muhammad might imagine that he controlled Christians within his recently conquered domain, the Eastern churches of the Armenians, Syrians, Egyptians, and others, according to Pius, were "all tainted with error, despite their worship of Christ." Likewise, the pope declared that the Greek Orthodox Church should not be regarded as Christian. "The Greeks fell away from union with the Roman church when you invaded Constantinople," the pope told the sultan. "They had still refused to accept the settlement achieved at Florence and remained in error." According to Pope Pius II, therefore, the only true Christianity was found in the nations of Europe.

This assertion by Pope Pius II, of course, was highly prejudicial in denying the legitimacy of the ancient Christian churches of the East. Not only continuing the conflict between the Latin West and the Greek East, the pope dismissed the validity of all Eastern Orthodox churches. Tracing its origin to the missions of the disciples Thaddeus and Bartholomew, the Armenian Church understood itself to be the oldest Christian communion in the world. The so-called Nestorians and Jacobites, the East Syrian and West Syrian Orthodox churches, might have emerged out of ancient theological controversies, but they understood their religious beliefs and practices as authentic Christianity. In North Africa, where Christianity had flourished for centuries, the Coptic Church, which traced its origin to Mark the Evangelist, preserved an ancient orthodoxy in Egypt. Further south, in the ancient African kingdom of Abyssinia, the Ethiopian Church maintained a distinctive form of Christianity that featured certain practices—circumcision, dietary regulations, and observance of Saturday as Sabbath—that Ethiopian Christians, who also saw themselves as the oldest church in the world, regarded as signs of their authentic roots in ancient Israel. By rejecting the validity of these ancient forms of Christianity, Pope Pius II tried to confront the Muslim sultan with the image of a unified religion exclusively centered in the combined national force of Europe.

The pope left Sultan Muhammad with a threat and a promise. If the Turkish sultan pursued his wars of conquest into their territory, then all those Christian nations would overcome their differences to prevent his entry into "the interior of Christendom." However, if Muhammad accepted conversion to Christianity, then he would gain the admiration of the entire Christian world, "of all Greece, of all Italy, of all Europe." Either way, Pope Pius concluded, the Muslim ruler would have to contend with the military, political, and religious power of "the Europeans, or those who are called Christians."

As Pope Pius II indicated, by the 1450s the terms "European" and "Christian," from a European perspective, had become interchangeable. In contrast to earlier ideals of Christendom that had in principle affirmed the "global" or "universal" unity of Christianity, this emerging image of Christian Europe presented the basic unity of Christianity as exclusively European. Certainly, any broader notion of Christian unity had been frustrated by the ongoing disagreements between East and West over doctrine, ritual, and organization. Unresolved by the Conference of Florence, this basic ecclesiastical division gave Latin Christians their justification for dismissing the orthodoxy of the East from the world of authentic Christianity. With the advance of Turkish conquests, however, European Christians felt increasingly isolated as the last bastion of Christianity in the world. During the reigns of Otman (d. 1326) and his successor Orkhan (d. 1360), the Ottoman Turks had occupied nearly every Greek town south of the Bosphorus. Armenia, which had been invaded by Egyptian forces in 1373, was next occupied by the Ottoman Empire, as was Georgia, where Christians were divided over allegiance to

Constantinople or Rome. From the Nestorians and Jacobites in Asia to the Coptic Church in Egypt, Christians in the East came under Muslim control; only the Ethiopian Church maintained a measure of political independence in the Christian kingdom of Abyssinia.

In administering the religious diversity within their empire, the Ottoman Turks developed a system of "nations," or *millets,* to manage the affairs of Christians in their domain. With no control over any territory of its own, a nation was defined by a common language, religion, and ethnicity. For example, the patriarch of Constantinople was established as the head of the Orthodox Christian *millet,* which gradually expanded to other Eastern Christians under Turkish control. Exercising both religious and civil functions, the Greek patriarch supervised the collection of taxes and ensured the loyalty of Christians to the centralized Muslim government of the empire. Generally tolerated within the world of Islam, Christianity was redefined by the *millet* system as the minority religion of ethnic nations that had no independent control over any territory.

As indicated by the letter of Pius II to Sultan Muhammad, Latin Christians had their own way of defining nations. At the Council of Constance in 1415, different schemes were proposed to identify the nations of Europe that would be represented in the deliberations. For all their differences in language, ethnicity, and history, these nations supposedly shared a common Latin religious culture. Even political regime, wealth, and power were too changeable to provide a solid basis for classifying nations. In response to this dilemma, English church leaders argued that only a map of the world could provide the basis for a "natural" division of the nations of Europe. The entire world was divided into three parts—Asia, Africa, and Europe—and the region of Europe was divided according to the four directions:

> The Eastern region or Christian church owing obedience to the pope in Europe comprises Hungary, Bohemia, Poland and Germany. The Western part or church is France and Spain. The Northern part or church in Europe as a whole is England, Wales, Scotland and Ireland (with their islands), Denmark, Sweden and Norway. The Southern is Italy and those of the Greeks in our obedience—that is to say the Cypriots and the Cretans.

One of the effects of the Protestant Reformation, of course, was to shatter this map of Europe. Under the formula *cuius regio, eius religio,*

European nations were defined not merely by language, ethnicity, or history, but by religious control over a territory. Following the map prepared for the Council of Constance, the southern and western nations remained Catholic, while many of the eastern and northern nations developed new Protestant establishments. Certainly, regional variations appeared under this new religious mapping of the nations of Europe. Although the Huguenots struggled as a Protestant minority in Catholic France, significant Catholic churches in Ireland, Poland, and Germany managed to maintain their religious identity in regions dominated by Protestant nations. Nevertheless, the unity of Europe could no longer be defined in terms of a shared religion.[1]

OUT OF EUROPE

In the middle of the fourteenth century, an unknown author adopted the name Sir John Mandeville to produce a remarkable book about the world beyond Europe. Presented as if it were an authentic report of the adventures of an English knight, *Mandeville's Travels* described distant lands, unfamiliar people, and strange customs. For centuries, Mandeville was accepted as an authority on the non-European world. Mercantile interest in *Mandeville's Travels* was widespread, since the book presented a merchant's dream, with vivid descriptions of gold, silver, jewels, and "plenty of goods" that could be acquired through trade in distant lands. Mandeville opened these lands for the European imagination. In the early seventeenth century, he was still regarded by a prominent editor of travel literature as "the greatest Asian traveler that ever the world had." Although most of the details of his adventures were plagiarized from ancient and monastic sources, suggesting that the author never actually left home, Sir John Mandeville nevertheless profoundly influenced the European Christian picture of the world.[2]

Setting out on a pilgrimage to Jerusalem, Mandeville restated the Latin Christian assumption that the Holy Land, which Jesus had chosen "to environ with his blessed feet," was the rightful inheritance of Christians. "For we are called Christian men, after Christ our father," he asserted. "And if we be right children of Christ, we owe for to challenge the heritage that our father left us, and do it out of heathen men's hands." When he arrived in Jerusalem, however, Mandeville found that the religion of Muslims was not entirely strange. Instead, he realized that Islam contained "many good articles of our faith." Since they were already so similar to Christians in matters of religion, Muslims could be converted, he advised, not by mounting another military crusade, but through the "preaching and teaching of Christian men." Renouncing the crusading ideal of "armed pilgrimage," therefore, Mandeville advocated interreligious conversation between Christians and Muslims.[3]

Nevertheless, Mandeville still understood his travels in the Holy Land as a pilgrim's journey to the sacred Christian sites. He visited Bethlehem to see a stone stained by the milk from the breasts of the Virgin Mary. He walked up the Mount of Olives to see a stone that preserved the footprints of Jesus. At the Dome of the Rock, however, he beheld the stone—the foundation stone of the world—sacred to Jews, Christians, and Muslims. As Mandeville observed, the Muslim guardians of the Dome of the Rock normally prohibited Jews and Christians from entering, "for they say that so foul sinful men should not come into so holy a place." With the special permission of the sultan who ruled Jerusalem, however, he was allowed to enter that holy place and stand before the sacred stone at the center of the world. In his account of entering the Dome of the Rock, therefore, Mandeville pointed to the possibility that Muslims and Christians might stand together in the same sacred place.[4]

As he suggested new opportunities for interreligious communication and cooperation between Muslims and Christians in the Holy Land, Mandeville also looked back with a critical eye to Christian Europe. While in Jerusalem, he was granted a private audience with the sultan. Asked to explain how Christians governed their territories in Europe, Mandeville replied, "Right well, thanked be God." Contradicting the European traveler on this assessment, however, the sultan proceeded to describe the ignorance, greed, and hypocrisy of princes and priests in Christian Europe. Through the sins of pride and avarice, he observed, the rulers of Christian Europe had betrayed their own God. In response to this attack, Mandeville could only ask the sultan how he came to know so much about the current state of Christianity. As a critique of European Christianity, therefore, Mandeville's conversation with the sultan reflected back on the failings of the rulers of church and state in Christian Europe. According to Mandeville, the sultan concluded that it was the moral failure of Christian Europe and not the presence of Muslims that prevented Christians from recovering their inheritance in the Holy Land.[5]

Having related his pilgrimage to Jerusalem, Mandeville shifted abruptly to speak of the diverse lands and peoples beyond the Holy Land. Traveling through Chaldea, Persia, Armenia, Libya, and Ethiopia, he discovered unfamiliar forms of Christianity, including the Christianity of the legendary Christian king Prester John. Inspired by the twelfth-century forgery of a letter from this Christian king of the East to Manuel I, emperor of Byzantium, medieval Christians had imagined Prester John as a wealthy and powerful ruler, presiding over a vast territory extending from India to Ethiopia, who was waiting to assist Christendom against the Muslim world. "I am a zealous Christian and universally protect Christians of our empire," the letter from Prester John explained. "We have determined to visit the sepulcher of our Lord with a very large army, in accordance with the glory of our majesty to humble and chastise the enemies of the cross of Christ and to exalt his blessed name." Reinforcing the crusading ideal of capturing the holy sepulcher in Jerusalem, this letter from Prester John also pointed to mysteries of the East, such as a healing stone, a sea of sand, and abundant wealth in gold, silver, and jewels, that captured the European imagination. All of these wonders, according to the legend, were controlled by the powerful Christian king who was also a "prester," a priest who presided over a court attended every day by twelve archbishops and twenty bishops.

Claiming to have found Prester John, Mandeville related that the Christianity practiced in his kingdom had been preserved unchanged from that of the original apostles. According to Mandeville, "they say not but only that that the apostles said, as our Lord taught them, right as Saint Peter and Saint Thomas and the other apostles sung the Mass, saying the Pater Noster and the words of the sacrament." This foreign Christianity practiced in the kingdom of Prester John, therefore, had not been altered by any of the changes in worship introduced over the centuries in the Latin West. Unlike European Christians, who were characterized by Mandeville as driven by greed and divided by conflict, the Christians of the kingdom of Prester John were unified by a simpler and more primitive Christian faith.[6]

Continuing on his travels through Asia, Mandeville observed the many different religious beliefs and practices in India and China. Entering the land of India, he found considerable religious diversity. "The folk of that country have a diverse law," Mandeville reported, "for some of them worship the sun, some the moon, some the fire, some trees, some serpents, or the first thing that they meet at morrow." In organizing this religious diversity, Mandeville made a distinction between two types of religious imagery, simulacra and idols, used by the people of India in their worship of these different things. Simulacra were identified by Mandeville as images of things found in the natural world, but idols were bizarre products of the human imagination, such as a human form with four heads or a creature that was half human and half ox, distortions of nature. According to Mandeville, the simulacra were legitimate expressions of devotion to the God who had created the natural world. As Mandeville observed, "There be no folk, but they have simulacras," and even "we Christian men have images." The worship of monstrous idols, however, gave rise to abuses, such as child sacrifice or self-sacrifice, that seemed to Mandeville to go against nature. In drawing this distinction between simulacra and idols, therefore, Mandeville clearly preferred the religious images that operated as signs of a "natural religion" serving the supreme God of Nature.

On the Isle of Bragman, however, Mandeville found mystics who were distinguished by their natural spirituality. Known as the "Land of Faith," this island was inhabited by people who "believe well in God, that made all things, and him they worship." Drawing upon popular accounts of the mystics, Brahmins, or gymnosophists of India, Mandeville stood in a long European tradition of idealizing the spirituality of the East. In the legendary adventures of Alexander the Great that circulated widely in Europe, for example, the gymnosophists appeared as spiritual experts who criticized the worldly ambitions of the Greek conqueror. As one Brahmin explained to Alexander, the spiritual conquest of the body and its desires was greater than any accomplishment in the world. "We Brahmins, since we have won the inner battles," he explained, "do not fight in external war." In claiming to have visited the land of the Brahmins, Mandeville observed that the worship of these non-Christian mystics was certainly accepted by God. "And albeit that these folks have not the articles of our faith as we have," he maintained, "nevertheless, for their good faith natural, and for their good intent, I trust fully that God loves them and that God takes their service." Although he objected to the unnatural practices of idol worshipers, Mandeville displayed remarkable respect for the non-Christian religions of India.[7]

When he entered the Far Eastern land of Cathay, Mandeville found that a policy of religious toleration had been established by the Mongol ruler of China, the Great Khan. Although he "believeth not faithfully in

God," the Great Khan nevertheless would "gladly hear speak of God." According to Mandeville, the Great Khan was attended by Christian physicians and served by Christian knights. Allowing Christians to dwell freely in his pagan kingdom, the Great Khan also permitted his people to convert to Christianity if they wished. In fact, as Mandeville explained, the Great Khan had ruled that his subjects could subscribe to whatever religious law they liked. This account of a flourishing Chinese Christianity might have been influenced by the long presence of Nestorian Christians in China, although they were never more than a small religious minority. Mandeville's report about China, however, was remarkable not only for finding Chinese Christians, but also for celebrating the official toleration of religious diversity established by the pagan ruler of China.[8]

Returning to Europe, Mandeville advised European Christians to recognize and respect the religious diversity of the entire world. In conclusion, he observed that "of all the diverse folk, that I have spoken of before, and of diverse laws, and of diverse beliefs that they have, yet is there none of them all but that they have some reason within them and understanding." By recognizing human reason operating in the midst of this religious diversity, Mandeville also found an underlying similarity with Christianity. People all over the world, he maintained, "have certain articles of our faith and some good points of our belief, and they believe in God, that formed all things and made the world, and call him God of Nature." Having discovered common ground among the world's religions in both reason and faith, Mandeville insisted that Christians should never despise the different religious laws or sects in the world. In this remarkable spirit of toleration, therefore, Mandeville concluded the narrative of his travels by urging European Christians to accept the religious diversity of the world.[9]

Although certainly fictional, *Mandeville's Travels* nevertheless provided an opportunity for European audiences to imagine the bewildering variety of religious laws and sects that flourished in the world outside of the familiar orbit of Christianity. By advising respect for that religious diversity, Sir John Mandeville countered the conventional assumption within medieval Christianity that no salvation was possible outside of the church. Implicitly, he challenged the Christian church's exclusive control over the knowledge, means, and scope of salvation. However, Mandeville returned home to reinforce relations of authority, opposition, and exchange that were central to the formation of European Christianity.

First, Mandeville recounted that upon his return he presented his travel book to the pope for the formal blessing and approval of the church. While advancing a subtle critique of Christian Europe, therefore, he ironically linked the authority of his narrative to the authority of the Roman Catholic Church. According to Mandeville, the pope found that his travels only confirmed what was already known from a Latin text in the papal library that gave the map of the world—the *Mappa Mundi*—describing all the nations of the world. Accordingly, he reported that the pope had ratified and confirmed the truth of his book on all points. Of course, this papal certification of the book, like the book itself, was part of the fiction of *Mandeville's Travels*. Nevertheless, as a rhetorical device in the narrative, Mandeville's visit with the pope could be read to reinforce the centralized authority of European Christianity.

Second, the Jews of Europe occupied a blind spot in Mandeville's spirit of religious toleration. In reporting on his travels, Mandeville repeated familiar Christian libels against Jews. For example, he related that Jews were preparing poisons from plants grown in the remote islands of Borneo that would be used to kill all Christians. In the land of Gog and Magog beyond China, he reported, Jews were gathering to attack Christians in Europe, with the support of European Jews, when the Antichrist appeared at the end of the world. Within the context of fourteenth-century genocidal Christian campaigns against Jews on the pretext that they had desecrated the Host, poisoned the water wells, or caused the plague, Mandeville's reports about the larger world only reinforced those prejudices at home. At the very least, *Mandeville's Travels* suggested that Christian toleration of religious diversity was easier at a distance. Closer to home, the nearest "other," the proximate "other," was most violently opposed.

Finally, Mandeville ended his book with an appeal to all Christians to pray for his soul not only for his own benefit, but for the exchange of merit that they would gain from his pilgrimage. He asked that "all those that say for me a Pater Noster, with an Ave Maria, that God forgive me my sins, I make them partners, and grant them part of all the good pilgrimages and all the good deeds that I have done." Since his pilgrimage to the Holy Land was linked in the narrative to his travels in Africa, India, and China, pilgrimage and travel were fused in this exchange. Increasingly, European travelers, explorers, and discoverers would look for the benefits of pilgrimage not in the Holy Land, but in Africa and Asia.[10]

1 Jesus as the Good Shepherd:
Revered as a teacher of wisdom, a worker of wonders, and a preacher of the kingdom of God, Jesus was depicted in early Christian art as a youthful shepherd. During the first four centuries, Christian imagery did not focus on the sacrificial death of Jesus on the cross but on symbols of spiritual support, strength, peace, and prosperity that included anchors, doves, boats, olive branches, palm trees, bread, fish, vines, and grapes *(page 73)*.

2 Christ as the Sun:
As the cosmic Christ, Jesus was a transcendent deity, like the sun, rising above and going beyond the world. At the end of the world, Christians could anticipate meeting Christ "in the air" *(page 41)*. Adopting the Sun-Day in the Roman week for their religious gatherings, Christians by the fourth century had identified the annual festival of *Sol Invictus*—the invincible Sun —as the birthday of Jesus Christ *(pages 60–61, 92)*.

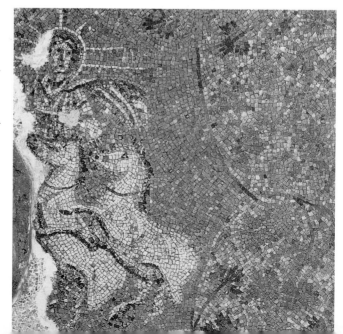

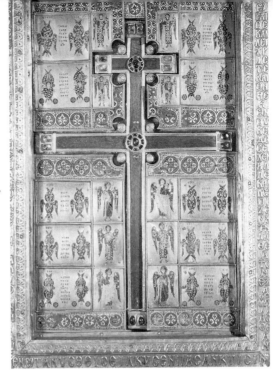

3 True Cross:

According to tradition, Helena, the mother of the Roman emperor Constantine (*ca.* 273–337), discovered the cross upon which Jesus had been executed and brought it to the new center of Christian empire, Constantinople. As a holy relic, the True Cross was valued for providing spiritual protection, especially during times of war *(page 105).* Surviving the sack of Constantinople by Latin crusaders in 1204, the reliquary of the True Cross depicts the celestial hierarchy of angels.

4 Christian Empire:

In consolidating the Byzantine empire in the East, Emperor Justinian (526–65) declared that its Christian unity was derived from God's two greatest gifts to humanity, "the priesthood and the imperial dignity" *(pages 162–63).* In Justinian's formula, these two spheres, church and state, were not separate, since they both were subject to the authority of the Christian emperor. While the emperor represented Christian unity in the Greek East, the bishop of Rome, as pope, emerged as the center of a unified religious and political order in the Latin West.

5 Paradise:
The Christian heaven has been identified both as a time in the future, anticipated at the general resurrection of the dead, and as a space above the world. In his *Divine Comedy*, the poet Dante Alighieri (1265–1321) saw souls ascending into heavenly realms. At the end of his imaginative journey through the Christian otherworldly geography of hell, purgatory, and heaven, Dante described a mystical union with God in which his "desire and will, like a wheel that spins with even motion, were revolved by the Love that moves the sun and other stars" *(pages 234–35)*.

6 King and Queen of Heaven:
As Holy Virgin, Mother of God, and Queen of Heaven, Mary has been celebrated as a merciful mediator who intercedes on behalf of human beings at the divine court of justice. According to an influential thirteenth-century monastic text, Jesus and Mary represented justice and mercy, but Mary "chose the better part, because she was made Queen of Mercy, while her son remained King of Justice" *(page 291)*.

7 Protestant Reformation:
As a leader of the Protestant Reformation, Martin Luther insisted that Christianity had to be based solely on the authority of the Bible. Declaring war on images, Protestant reformers developed their Christianity of the Word in opposition to what they regarded as the idolatry of the Roman Catholic Church *(pages 321–25)*. Although branded as a heretic, and even depicted as a "monster born of a cow in Saxony" *(page 311)*, Martin Luther proclaimed a Christian "justification by faith" that was also affirmed by the Catholic Counter-Reformation *(page 327)*.

8 Monstrous Races:
On the authority of the ancient Roman author Pliny, medieval theologians asked: Are they human? Do they have souls? Can they be converted to Christianity? *(pages 341–42)*. Moving out of the Mediterranean into the Atlantic and Pacific worlds, Christian explorers raised similar questions about indigenous people who were subject to European conquest and colonization in America, Africa, Asia, and the Pacific Islands.

9 Christian Virgin, Mexican Patron:

During the sixteenth century, Spanish conquerors invaded the Aztec empire under the sign of the cross and under the divine patronage of the Virgin Mary. Demonizing and destroying the indigenous religion of Mesoamerica, the Spanish colonizers also tried to prevent Indians from claiming Christian symbols in ways that were independent of the authority of the church. Although Indians who claimed visions of the Virgin Mary were generally suppressed by church authorities, especially those visionaries who inspired militant resistance to Spanish control by Indian "Soldiers of the Virgin" *(pages 366–69)*, the Virgin of Guadalupe became the divine patron of Mexico.

10 Christian God, Inca Deities:

In response to the Spanish conquest and colonization of Peru, the Andean nobleman Guamán Poma (1532–1614) published a book that wove together religious resources from Christianity and indigenous Andean tradition. Within the proper order of the world, as illustrated by Guamán Poma, the Christian God upheld the divine sun and moon of Andean religion. Under foreign domination, however, the indigenous people of Peru found that the world had been turned upside down. Only by restoring Inca sovereignty, Guamán Poma argued, would a new order of the world be revealed in which Christianity supported the people of the Andes and the Andean people supported Christianity *(pages 361–65)*.

11 Jesuits in China:

The first Jesuit missionary to China, Matteo Ricci (1552–1610), initially wore the priestly robes of Buddhist monks but eventually identified with the Confucian elite of scholars, philosophers, and scientists. Admiring the traces of "natural religion" that he found in the texts of Confucius, Ricci tried to use Confucian texts as a basis for presenting the "revealed religion" of Christianity. Ricci's Chinese critics, however, argued that this "Western man of letters" was neither a good Buddhist nor a good Confucian *(pages 435–38).*

12 St. Thomas in India:

Tracing their heritage back to the first-century mission of the apostle Thomas to India, Thomas Christians of the Malabar coast maintained links with Orthodox churches of Syria. During the sixteenth century, Portuguese Catholics captured control over their most sacred shrine, the site of the martyrdom of the apostle Thomas at Mylapore, which had been revered as a holy place by Hindus, Muslims, and Christians. The shrine became a pilgrimage center that featured the bones of St. Thomas and a miraculous bleeding cross *(pages 456–57).*

13 African Cross:
In the seventeenth-century BaKongo
Christian kingdom, African Christianity
depended upon intercultural translation.
While foreign missionaries condemned
indigenous African ritual objects, the *nkisi*
used by traditional diviners and healers, the
BaKongo king adopted the Christian cross as
his *nkisi* and the Bible, *mukanda nkisi*, as the
most powerful ritual object *(pages 413–14)*.
Throughout Africa, the expansion of
Christianity raised questions not only about
spirituality, but also about the meaning and
value of materiality.

14 Secret of the Cargo:
Under the banner of
"Christianity, Commerce and
Civilization," Christian missions all over the world linked
religion with the promise of
material prosperity. In the cargo
movements that arose during
the twentieth century in
Melanesia, Christianity
appeared as a religion for gaining access to the world of manufactured goods. Suspecting that
the white people hid the secret
of the cargo, these movements
anticipated an apocalyptic
return of Jesus, angels, and
ancestors who would bestow
the wealth of material goods
upon the indigenous people of
the islands *(pages 473–79)*.

15 Nazism and Christianity:
Adolf Hitler believed that
Christianity was incompatible
with the political religion of
German nationalism, observing
that "one is either a Christian or
a German. You can't be both."
Nevertheless, leaders of Protestant
and Catholic churches in Nazi
Germany, such as the Lutheran
bishop Ludwig Muller, shaking
hands with Hitler, accompanied
by the Benedictine abbot Alban
Schachleiter, gave Christian support to the German nationalism
of the Nazi party. While some
Christian leaders struggled to
keep their religion out of politics,
the German Christian movement
actively promoted a Nazi
Christianity *(pages 495–501)*.

16 Communism and Christianity:
After the Cuban revolution of
1958, Fidel Castro distinguished
between two types of Christianity,
one progressive and revolutionary, which he identified as the
original religion of Jesus, the
other oppressive and reactionary,
the religion of European colonialism. In the face of criticism from
the Roman Catholic Church,
Castro argued that "those who
condemn a revolution like this
are betraying Christ" *(pages
527–29)*. During his pastoral visit
to Cuba in January 1998, Pope
John Paul II met with Fidel
Castro. Delivering a sermon in
which he criticized both communism and global capitalism, the
pope offered Mass in Havana's
Revolution Square.

MAP OF THE WORLD

In medieval European maps of the world, Jerusalem stood at the center of the three continents, Europe, Asia, and Africa. As *Mandeville's Travels* indicated, Asia and Africa were strange and marvelous regions that contained not only strange kingdoms, people, plants, and animals, but also the earthly paradise and the mouth of hell. Past the easternmost reaches of Asia was located the earthly paradise. As the original birthplace of humanity, the earthly paradise was also the source of the four great rivers of the world. According to Mandeville, the earthly paradise was protected by high walls that prevented any living human being from gaining access. Besides the earthly paradise in the east, medieval maps also included heavenly islands in the west. Off the coast of Ireland, the islands of St. Brendan and Brasil—Hy-Brasail, "the land of the Blest"—were imagined to hold sacred power and significance. In the northwestern corner of Ireland, the island in Lough Derg emerged as the site of St. Patrick's Purgatory, a popular destination for pilgrimage that was suppressed by Pope Alexander VI in 1497 because he saw Ireland as the end of the world. Like the earthly paradise at the edge of the world to the east, therefore, the sacred islands of Ireland could be regarded as the outer limit of the world in the northern Atlantic Ocean. By stark contrast, Mandeville reported that in the domain of Prester John was found the Valley of Devils, which marked the entry to hell, where abundant gold and silver was found, but few came out alive. Within the medieval imagination, therefore, the map of the world was intersected by the hellish and heavenly regions of Christian myth.[11]

In locating the different people of the world, medieval maps often identified the three continents with the descendants of the three sons of the biblical Noah. Accordingly, they assigned Europe to Japheth, Asia to Shem, and Africa to Ham. The medieval view of the world, however, contained a greater diversity of races than could be easily traced back to a single ancestor. From ancient classical encyclopedias, European Christians had learned about the existence of strange peoples in Asia and Africa who might not actually qualify as human beings. Among the "monsters of the East," they imagined the dog-headed people, the one-eyed people, the long-eared people, the mouthless people, and the androgynous man-woman people. In some cases, these strange races were distinguished by their diet, such as those who ate raw meat, fish, or other people. However, the races were most often identified by distinctive physiological features, such as the opposite-footed people, who walked upside down, the no-headed people, who had their eyes, nose, and mouth in their chests, and the one-legged people, who ran very fast and used the large foot on their one leg to shade themselves from the hot sun. Looking east, therefore, European Christians saw a world populated with strange, monstrous races. Christian theologians asked, "Were these races human?" "Did they descend from the common biblical ancestor Noah?" "Did they have souls capable of salvation?"

In Christian art of both the East and the West, representatives of these strange races appeared in depictions of the original Pentecost in which the disciples of Jesus spoke the languages of all nations. Within the debates of medieval Scholasticism in Europe, however, the question of the humanity of these strange races was often contested. According to the Franciscan theologian Alexander of Hales (ca. 1185–1245), for example, the strange races were "propagated from the body of the first man," but were severely deformed as a result of their sin. Recognizing their humanity, therefore, Alexander argued that these deformed, sinful races were on earth to show by contrast the beauty and sanctity of Christianity. The Dominican theologian Albert the Great (ca. 1200–1280), however, argued that the strange races were not actually human. Focusing on the race of small people known as pygmies, Albert argued that although they appeared to be similar in some respects to human beings, they lacked the essential defining characteristic—reason—that made human beings human. Although they might be "the most perfect of animals," Albert the Great concluded that pygmies were not actually human.[12]

During the fifteenth century, as European travelers in Africa and Asia failed to find the legendary monstrous races, they transferred these questions about the humanity of strange people from the mysterious lands of the East to the unconquered islands of the West. As a prelude to European expansion across the Atlantic Ocean, in 1436 Pope Eugenius IV authorized the Christian kingdom of Portugal to subdue and convert all the unbelievers on the Canary Islands. According to King Duarte I of Portugal, the people of the islands might appear to be human, but they "are not united by a common religion, nor are they bound by the chains of law; they are lacking in normal social intercourse, living in the country like animals." Like the monstrous races or wild animals, therefore, the people of the Canary Islands could not be regarded as humans by European Christians. When the islands were finally conquered in 1496, the brutality was justified by this contrast between Christian humanity and the wild "bestiality" of the natives. As the monstrous races of the East receded from the European imagination, therefore, their place was taken in the map of the world by a new category, the "savages."[13]

Looking west, European Christians moved into an expanding Atlantic world. The interest in seafaring at this time was largely inspired by the closure of land routes to Asia by the Turkish conquest of the Byzantine Empire. However, European navigators entered the Atlantic as if the ocean itself represented the supreme test of Christian faith. For example, the Portuguese explorer Vasco da Gama (1469–1524), who set off in 1497 in search of a sea route to India around the tip of Africa, exhorted his sailors to maintain their Christian faith at sea. As their ship was threatened with destruction by torrential winds and rain, he invoked the protection of Christ and the Virgin Mary. But he also challenged his sailors to prove their Christian faith. "If you have faith in God, the storm will soon die down," Vasco da Gama exclaimed. "I want my men to prove that they have a true faith in the mercy of Our Lord Jesus Christ!" Upon their return to Portugal, the sailors simply yet triumphantly declared, "God has brought us hither." In these pious formulas, which were perhaps intended more for a Portuguese reading public than for Portuguese sailors, the sea was represented as the new proving ground for Christianity. Venturing out upon the Atlantic Ocean, therefore, seemed to mark the beginning of a new Christian mission and a new Christian crusade.[14]

During the travels of Vasco da Gama, the Portuguese entered regions of Africa and Asia that had already been penetrated by Christianity. When they landed on the southeast African coast of Mozambique, for example, the Portuguese Christians were surprised to be met by three African Christians from the land of Prester John in Ethiopia. As Christians of the Ethiopian Church, these Africans recognized a painting of the archangel Gabriel that the Portuguese had brought ashore. Falling on their knees before the image of the angel, the Africans recognized the Portuguese as fellow Christians. Finally arriving on the western coast of India, Vasco da Gama found a flourishing Christian community that traced its lineage back to the apostle Thomas and maintained relations with Syrian Christianity. By taking to the sea, therefore, these Portuguese Christians discovered that Christianity was more broadly established in the world than they had imagined.

For Vasco da Gama, however, the truth and power of Christianity had to be proven not only at sea, but also in trading relations. In the capital city of Calicut, the Hindu rajah who ruled over the southwestern coast of India was known as the "Lord of the Sea." Entering into trading relations with the Portuguese Christians, the rajah began to suspect that they did not know how to conduct business. When the Portuguese paid too much for trade goods, the rajah's adviser concluded, "If these Portuguese were real merchants they would not accept bad goods at double their proper value. These Christians are not traders at all. They are soldiers and they have come to destroy our kingdom." Arguing that the Portuguese should be killed and their ships burned, the royal adviser urged the rajah to ensure "that none of them can return to their own country and reveal the way they have discovered across the ocean!" Instead of following this advice, however, the rajah granted the Christians an audience in which he challenged them to prove their good faith in trading relations. "You say you come from a very powerful kingdom," the rajah said, "yet the gifts you have brought me from your ruler are of trifling value." Pointing to a golden statue that the Portuguese had brought with them, the rajah requested that image as a more valuable gift than what he had been given. Vasco da Gama refused. "It is the statue of the Virgin Mary," he explained, "and I shall never be separated from it, for Our Lady has guided me across the ocean and will lead me back to my own country." The rajah concluded from this exchange that the Portuguese Christians would never make good trading partners. They paid too much for worthless things, suggesting that they did not know how to value trade goods, and they refused to part with things of value for strange religious reasons. Sending the Portuguese on their way, the rajah never imagined that they would soon return to establish settlements, take over the spice trade, and try to convert the Indian Christians to the Christianity of the Roman Catholic Church.[15]

RELIGIOUS DIVERSITY

The adventures of Sir John Mandeville were widely read in England, giving English readers a profoundly unreliable, but nevertheless expanded, perspective on the complex diversity of customs, laws, and sects of the world. However, the English word "religions" was not used for that diversity. Following medieval Latin usage, in which the term *religio* referred to faithful attention to God, the word religion in English did not have a plural. Instead, it had an opposite suggested by the Latin term *superstitio*. As we have seen, medieval Christians developed many terms for superstition, such as heresy, witchcraft, or idolatry, but religion remained a singular term. In the 1590s, however, the English word "religions" was used for the first time by the Protestant theologian Richard Hooker, who proposed that there were two religions, Protestant and Catholic. The term "religions," therefore, emerged in England as a new mark of difference in the interreligious conflicts of the Protestant Reformation.[16]

The earliest Protestant reformers would probably have been surprised by the term "religions." According to Martin Luther, for example, there was only one religion—a biblical faith that led to salvation through divine grace—which was in opposition to all other forms of false belief and worship. As Luther often observed, Jews, Muslims, and Roman Catholics were essentially the same, because they were opposed to that true religion of Christian faith. "Jews, Turks, papists, radicals abound everywhere," Luther observed. "Even if they do not all pursue the same course, but one chooses this way, another that way, resulting in a variety of forms, they nonetheless all have the same intent and ultimate goal, namely, by means of their own deeds they want to manage to become God's people." Instead of faith, they relied on human reason, he argued, and therefore fell from grace because "reason never finds the true God, but it finds the devil or its own concept of God, ruled by the devil." Rather than regarding them as alternative religions, therefore, Luther saw Jews, Muslims, Catholics, and all others "sects" or "laws" as the opposite of religion. At best they were the result of human invention; at worst, or perhaps, inevitably, they were in the service of the devil.[17]

While Luther distinguished true religion from what he regarded as the "Judaizing" effects of human reason, works, and law, John Calvin contrasted Christian religion with pagan idolatry. As noted in the previous chapter, Calvin assumed that humanity had a religious sense, the *semen religionis,* or seed of religion, that prepared human beings for the call of divine election. However, that inherent potential for religion had been so thoroughly corrupted by ignorance, fear, and fraud that most human beings had succumbed to the seductions of idolatry. In this respect, Calvin argued, Roman Catholics were no different from Jews, Muslims, or pagans. Developing a critique of Roman Catholicism, Calvinists fused "papism" with paganism to form the stereotype of "paganopapism." Not genuine religion, according to Calvinists, this "paganopapism" of the

Roman Catholic Church was ignorant, dangerous, and even demonic superstition. Like Luther, therefore, Calvin defined Roman Catholicism not as a different religion, but as the absence of religion.[18]

During the sixteenth century, as reports of travel, exploration, and discovery in the Atlantic world arrived in Europe, Europeans learned that an absence of religion had supposedly been discovered in the New World. Although he "found no human monstrosities, as many expected," Christopher Columbus reported in 1492 that the inhabitants of the islands "do not hold any creed nor are they idolaters." Confirming this discovery in 1504, Amerigo Vespucci insisted that "they have no church, no religion and are not idolaters." Allegedly lacking the basic human characteristic of religion, the indigenous people of the New World were represented by terms—"wild men," "barbarians," and "savages"—that called into question their humanity.[19] Rarely were these stereotypes challenged, but, most notably, the French humanist Michel de Montaigne (1533–92) did turn the accusation of barbarism back on Europe. In response to travelers' reports about savages who lived in the recently discovered South American land named Brazil, Montaigne introduced a note of cultural relativism by observing that "each man calls barbarism whatever is not his own practice." Like Mandeville, however, Montaigne used the reports about strange people in distant places to advance an internal critique of European society. Comparing European civilization to the natural nobility of savages, he found that Europeans "surpass them in every kind of barbarity."[20] In these new calculations of savagery and civility, therefore, Montaigne proposed that the global comparison revealed the barbarism of Christian Europe.

During 1580 Montaigne undertook his own travels of discovery through Europe. Seeking relief from his physical ailments at healing baths in Switzerland and Italy, he recorded his observations about local languages, customs, and religions. In both regions, Montaigne found that people "were not in agreement over their religion." As a result of the religious controversies and conflicts of the Reformation, Montaigne found "some calling themselves Zwinglians, others Calvinists, others Martinists; and indeed he was informed that "many still fostered the Roman religion in their heart." Despite the notion of religious uniformity within the various regions of Europe, therefore, Montaigne discovered considerable religious diversity.

While in Rome, Montaigne paid particular attention to Christian relations and exchanges with Judaism and Islam. For example, he observed a Jewish congregation in the city that followed a "renegade rabbi who preaches to the Jews on Saturday after dinner in the Church of the Trinity." Recognizing that Italy was on the Mediterranean frontier with the Turkish empire, Montaigne recorded a "memorable incident" of religious conversion from Christianity to Islam. As related by a woman living across the street from Montaigne's residence, her son, a soldier by the name of Giuseppe, was captured by the Turks in a sea battle. To gain his freedom, Giuseppe converted to Islam and settled in Muslim territory. When he joined a Turkish raiding party in pillaging the Italian coast, however, he was captured by the Italians, but he "had the presence of mind to say that he had come to surrender deliberately, that he was a Christian." Set free, Giuseppe returned home to his mother and the church. In a special ceremony presided over by the bishop of Lucca, he publicly renounced Islam and received the sacrament of the Eucharist. "It was just humbug," however, as Montaigne recounted, because Giuseppe "was a Turk at heart." At the first opportunity, Giuseppe took off for Venice, where he could associate with Muslims and resume his travels. Captured again by the Genoese Christians, however, Giuseppe, the Italian Turk, was forced to remain in the employment of the Genoese navy.[21]

As Montaigne observed on his travels, therefore, Europe was a region of religious diversity. Noting the complex religious divisions among different "laws" or "sects" of Christianity, he recorded striking illustrations of local relations and exchanges in an Italian religious economy that included Christians, Jews, and Muslims. However, unlike Sir John Mandeville, who found universal traces of reason and faith in the religions of the world, Montaigne saw all this diversity as an opportunity for self-reflection. "I do not talk about others," he observed, "except to talk better of myself." Whether traveling through Europe or reading reports from America, Montaigne confronted religious differences as part of his struggles to understand himself. If we were to survey the diversity of the world from God's perspective, he suggested, we would find that there are no "monstrous races" out there. "Those which we call monsters," he observed, "are not so with God, who in the immensity of his work sees the infinite forms therein contained." The real monsters, Montaigne proposed, reside within the self. "I have seen no such monster or more express wonder in this world than myself," he declared. "With time and custom a man does acquaint and enure himself to all strangeness; but the more I frequent and know myself the more my deformity astonishes me, and the less I understand myself."

By exploring the inner monsters and strange miracles of the human self, therefore, Montaigne cultivated an introspective sensibility. As his motto he adopted the question "What do I know?" Skeptical of the competing claims to religious knowledge advanced by the different Christian factions in Europe, Montaigne concluded that nothing could actually be known about God. "We may use words like Power, Truth, Justice, but we cannot conceive the thing itself," he observed. "None of our qualities can be attributed to the Divine Being without tainting it with our imperfection." Doubting the validity of all religious claims to knowledge, Montaigne proposed that people should simply remain in the faith of their birth, since changing faiths would require knowing the relative merits of their truth claims, something that could not actually be known. Instead, Montaigne adopted a simple faith in God while pursuing a complex, detailed investigation of the imperfection and variability of the human self.[22]

Two years after Montaigne's visit to Italy, an Italian miller by the name of Domenico Scandella (1532–99), who was known as Menocchio, was put on trial for heresy. Married with seven children, Menocchio supported his family by working primarily as a miller, but he also engaged in carpentry, bricklaying, plastering, and other manual labor. In addition to these skills, Menocchio knew how to read, write, and add. He became a prominent figure in his village, serving for a time as mayor and administrator of the parish church. His neighbors reported Menocchio to the Holy Office of the inquisition, however, for speaking "heretical and most impious words." During a preliminary inquest, the inquisitors learned from the villagers that Menocchio expressed strong opinions about the priesthood. "Priests want us under their thumb, just to keep us quiet, while they have a good time," Menocchio said, according to one witness. Another observed that "he has evil ideas like those of the sect of Luther." Although many witnesses noted that he was well liked in the village, regarded as "everybody's friend," they provided the inquisitors with sufficient evidence of heretical opinions and statements to go to trial in 1584. After months of questioning, he was released, but fourteen years later he was again arrested and brought before the inquisition.

During the long course of his two trials, Menocchio revealed that he held unconventional religious opinions about God, creation, the virgin birth, the crucifixion of Christ, and the sacraments of the church.

Believing that the world had emerged naturally out of chaos, he denied that Mary was a virgin, proposed that Jesus had been a prophet like many others who had appeared in the world, and criticized the sacraments as artificial inventions of priests designed to enrich themselves and exploit the poor. As for the human soul, he held that it died with the body. Menocchio testified that he had been influenced in forming these ideas by reading a book about the travels of the English knight Sir John Mandeville, in which he had learned that "out of many different kinds of nations, some believe in one way and some in another." Although he was initially troubled by reading the strange tales of many nations, Menocchio indicated that he had accepted both the critique of European Christianity and the tolerance of religious diversity he found in *Mandeville's Travels*.

At his second trial in 1599, the inquisitor accused Menocchio of saying that he had been "born a Christian and so desired to live as a Christian, but if he had been born a Turk, he would have wanted to remain a Turk." Admitting that he had in fact spoken those words, Menocchio related the parable, which he had learned from Boccaccio's *Decameron*, about a great lord who had declared that his heir would be identified by a special ring but had three identical rings made for his sons so that each would think that he was the legitimate heir in possession of the true ring. "Likewise," he told the inquisitor, "God the Father has various children whom he loves, such as Christians, Turks, and Jews, and to each of them he has given the will to live by his own law, and we do not know which is the right one." The inquisitor challenged Menocchio on this point. Certainly, Christians knew which religious law was the right law. "Yes sir," Menocchio replied, "I do believe that every person considers his faith to be right, and we do not know which is the right one; but because my grandfather, my father, and my people have been Christians, I want to remain a Christian, and believe that it is the right one." Like the French humanist Montaigne, therefore, the Italian miller Menocchio asked himself, "What do I know?" Deciding that it was impossible to adjudicate among the many faiths of the world, both Montaigne and Menocchio concluded that it was most appropriate to remain within the religious community of one's birth. Consistently, Menocchio told the inquisitors that he only wanted to "do good and walk in the path of my ancestors and follow what Holy Mother Church commands."

According to Menocchio, however, the many religions represented different but equal paths to salvation. As Menocchio told the inquisitor,

"The majesty of God has given the Holy Spirit to all, to Christians, to heretics, to Turks, and to Jews; and he considers them all dear, and they are all saved in the same manner." Even those faiths identified by the church as heretical, he argued, had received the Holy Spirit and would be saved by God. Accused of being a heretic himself, however, Menocchio was eventually condemned by the inquisition. For denying the virginity of Mary, the divinity of Christ, and the providence of God, he was executed in November 1599. Like the distinguished scholar Montaigne, however, the humble peasant Menocchio suggested that an alternative trajectory was possible for European Christianity. It was possible to be a Christian, he held, by remaining in the religious faith of one's ancestors while recognizing that other religions presented valid ways to salvation.[23]

PART III
GLOBAL TRANSFORMATIONS

21

New World

For the Catholic monarchs of Spain, 1492 was a landmark year. Having joined forces through marriage, Ferdinand of Aragon and Isabella of Castile succeeded in January 1492 in defeating the last Muslims remaining in Granada, thus bringing Spain under Christian rule. During March of the same year, they issued an edict of expulsion that required all Jews to leave their territory. By driving Muslims and Jews out of Spain, the Catholic monarchs established a single, unified Christian domain. During the same year, however, that domain was opened to new worlds by the unexpected discoveries of the navigator Christopher Columbus (1451–1506).

"God made me the messenger of the new heaven and the new earth of which he spoke in the Apocalypse of St. John," Columbus wrote eight years later, "and he showed me the spot where to find it." Immersed in apocalyptic expectations, Columbus interpreted his voyages as crucial events in the unfolding of the last days. Even his own first name, which Columbus rendered in Latin as *Christoferens*—"Christbearer"—suggested his special status as servant and messenger of Christ. By bringing the message of Christ to new lands, as well as by gaining wealth from those lands which he hoped would finance a new crusade to wrest Jerusalem from Muslim control, Christopher Columbus was convinced that he had opened the door to the apocalypse.

Two religious commitments—conversion and crusade—animated Columbus's understanding of his mission. Ultimately, Columbus found his mandate for extending the Christian gospel in New Testament passages that linked the Christian proclamation with the end of the world. According to the Gospel of Matthew, for example, "This gospel of the kingdom will be preached throughout the whole world, as a testimony to all nations; and then the end will come" (Matt. 24:14). But Columbus read that biblical prophecy under the influence of medieval commentators, especially the Spiritual Franciscans, who believed that the world was in its last age, the "Age of the Holy Spirit," and the scholar Pierre d'Ailly (1350–1420), who provided calculations for the end that indicated to Columbus that only about 150 years remained before the return of Christ. In his *Book of Prophecies,* Columbus insisted on the urgency of the work of conversion. "Our Lord is hastening these things," he wrote; "the Gospel must now be proclaimed to so many lands in such a short time." Beginning with his first landing of October 12 on the island he called San Salvador, Columbus set about the work of Christian proclamation.

In his diaries, Columbus indicated the procedures he followed in bringing the Christian gospel to new lands. First, his proclamation of Christianity was enacted by the performance of ritual, especially by the ritualized planting of the Christian cross. On each island, Columbus and his crew set up a large cross to symbolize the Christian presence in the land and the Christian claim over the indigenous people. Eventually, Columbus involved local people in setting up crosses, noting that they eagerly offered prayers before this central Christian symbol. Second, Columbus identified the essential content of Christian teaching as ritual formulas designed for repetition. "They say quickly any prayer that we tell them to say," he observed, "and they make the sign of the cross." According to Columbus, by repeating the Pater Noster, the Ave Maria, and the sign of the cross, the local inhabitants of the islands indicated that they had internalized the Christian message. Third, since these outer signs could not conclusively be read as evidence of inner assent, the advance of Christianity depended upon translation. For this purpose, Columbus proposed kidnapping local people and transporting them to Spain so that "returning, they might be interpreters for the Christians, and so that they would take on our customs and faith." Out of twenty-four people taken to Spain after the first voyage, six survived to return with Columbus on his second voyage to act as translators in proclaiming the Christian gospel. Through such procedures, Columbus advised the Catholic monarchs, "Your Highnesses ought to resolve to make them Christians: for I believe that if you begin, in a short time you will end up having converted to our Holy Faith a multitude of peoples."

Although proclaiming the gospel to new lands extended Christianity to the farthest periphery of the world, a new crusade promised to capture its most sacred center. Columbus had declared this intention to provide financial backing for a new crusade against the Muslim rulers of

Jerusalem before his first voyage. As he reminded the Spanish monarchs, "I urged Your Highnesses to spend all the profits of this my enterprise on the conquest of Jerusalem, and Your Highnesses laughed and said that it would please them and that even without this profit they had that desire." In his *Will and Testament,* Columbus reaffirmed his ambition to provide revenue that the Spanish monarchs "should determine to spend in the conquest of Jerusalem." Acquiring gold from the New World, therefore, was understood by Columbus as a religious mission. He instructed the men under his command to secure gold "in such quantity that the Sovereigns, before three years are passed, will undertake and prepare to go conquer the Holy Sepulchre." Instead of launching a new crusade, however, the Spanish sovereigns used the proceeds from the voyages of Columbus to pay debts already incurred fighting Muslims in Spain. Having seen the first sign of the end of the world with the proclamation of Christianity to new nations, Columbus died in 1506 without witnessing the second sign, the conquest of Jerusalem, he thought would usher in the millennial reign of Christ on earth.[1]

SPANISH CONQUESTS

During the era of extensive Spanish conquests in the Americas between 1512 and 1573, the conquerors were instructed to act as messengers of Christianity. A formal speech devised by Catholic theologians designed to be read before a gathering of indigenous people, called the *Requirement,* set the terms and conditions for the entry of the Christian message into the New World. In the *Requirement,* however, that Christian message was introduced not as a gift, but as a ceremony of possession.

First, the conqueror established the Christian terms of his authority. Like Columbus, he announced himself as a messenger. However, instead of presenting himself as a messenger of the second coming of Christ, which would signal the end of the world, the conqueror declared himself as "servant, messenger" of the God who was responsible for the creation of heaven and earth in the beginning. Ultimately, as the *Requirement* proclaimed, the conqueror's authority was derived from God's original act of creation, but that authority depended upon a chain of references in which the conqueror acted on behalf of the Spanish monarch, who acted on behalf of the pope, who acted on behalf of St. Peter, who acted on behalf of the supreme God. As the text of the *Requirement* proclaimed, "God our Lord," who created heaven and earth, "gave charge [of all peoples] to one man named St. Peter, so that he was lord and superior of all the men of the world . . . and gave him all the world for his lordship and jurisdiction." Curiously, the *Requirement* did not mention Jesus Christ. Nevertheless, the conqueror proclaimed his authority as Christian.

Second, the *Requirement* issued an invitation to the natives to convert to Christianity. If the people converted and became subjects and vassals of the Christian monarch of Spain, the text proclaimed, all would be well. No harm would befall them. They could keep their women and children. "Almost all who have been notified have received His Majesty and obeyed and served him," the *Requirement* declared, "and turned Christian." This decision to convert, the text advised, must be freely made. The conqueror was instructed to inform the natives: "We will not compel you to turn Christians." With this promise of freedom and protection, the conqueror pleaded with those gathered before him to accept conversion to the Christian church.

Finally, the invitation to conversion was followed by a threat. As a warning to all those who refused to convert, the conqueror declared, "With the help of God, I will enter forcefully against you, and I will make war everywhere and however I can, and I will subject you to the yoke and obedience of the Church and His Majesty and I will take your wives and children, and I will make them slaves . . . and I will take your goods, and I will do to you all the evil and damages that a lord may do to vassals who do not obey or receive him." For any who resisted conversion, therefore, the *Requirement* promised destruction. However, the Christian conqueror was instructed to disavow any responsibility for the suffering and dispossession that would follow. "I solemnly declare," the text of the *Requirement* concluded with a final warning to the natives, "that the deaths and damages received from such will be your fault."[2]

With such a Christian justification, which transferred the blame for their military aggression to the victims, Spanish conquerors succeeded in destroying the Aztec, Inca, Maya, and other polities in the Americas and subjecting indigenous people to Spanish rule. As an exemplary conqueror, Hernán Cortés (1485–1547) in 1519 established a town on the Mexican coast, La Villa Rica de la Vera Cruz, the Rich City of the True Cross, in order to bypass the authority of the governor of Cuba and claim an imperial mission of conquest into the interior of Mesoamerica. Adopting for his banner the motto of Constantine—*"In hoc signo vincemus"* ("Under

this sign we conquer")—Cortés led a small band of Spanish soldiers, supported by a large force of Indian allies, against the center of the Aztec
empire, the city of Tenochtitlán.

According to Spanish accounts, the Aztec emperor, Moctezuma II (r.
1502–20), initially tried to interpret the arrival of Cortés in religious terms.
Reportedly, he wondered if Cortés's arrival represented the return of the
god Quetzalcoatl, the Feathered Serpent, the Warrior of the Dawn, the god
of the winds, the deity of solar light and power. Fourteen years earlier,
Moctezuma had constructed a special temple for Quetzalcoatl in the sacred
precincts of Tenochtitlán near the Great Temple with its two shrines, one
dedicated to Tlaloc, the god of rain and agriculture, the other to
Huitzilipochtli, the god of tribute and war. According to the cycles of the
Aztec calendar, 1519 was Quetzalcoatl's year, the year "One-Reed," which
marked the anniversary of his birth. Did it also mark the year of his return?

For their part, the Spanish Christians also struggled to translate the
intercultural contact into religious terms. Recalling their procession into
the political and religious capital of the Aztec empire, Bernal Díaz
reported, "Our Lord Jesus Christ was pleased to give us grace and
courage to dare to enter into such a city."[3] In addition to the cross of
Christ, the Spaniards relied upon the support of two divine patrons, the
Virgin Mary and St. James, known as Santiago, or Santiago Matamoros,
the "Killer of Moors," who was depicted as a warrior on horseback wav-
ing a sword over his head. From both Aztec and Spanish perspectives,
therefore, the confrontation of alien cultures involved the presence and
power of superhuman beings.

Entering the city of Tenochtitlán, the Spaniards were struck by the elaborate ceremonials of Aztec religion. Comparing these unfamiliar practices
to their own religious life, they found many recognizable elements—
temples, high altars, statues, offerings, and even "symbols like crosses."
Even the practice of human sacrifice, in which Aztec priests periodically
consecrated and killed captives in rituals that sanctified their body and
blood, seemed strangely similar to the Christian sacrificial offering and
consumption of Christ's body and blood in the Eucharist.

In drawing these comparisons, however, the Spanish Christians concluded that Aztec religious ritual was a perversion of Christian ritual.
Instead of serving God, they insisted, Aztec ritual served the devil. As
Cortés said to Moctezuma when the Aztec emperor allowed him to enter
the shrines at the summit of the Great Temple, "I do not understand how

such a great lord or wise man as you has not realized that these idols are not gods, but bad things, called devils. So I hope you will allow us to place our sign of the cross here as well as a picture of the Virgin Mary and you will see how afraid your gods will be." In reply, Moctezuma reportedly said, "Had I known that you would say such dishonorable things, I would not have shown you my gods. We hold these beings to be good; they bring us health, water and good crops, rain, and when we need them, victories, and so we sacrifice to them. I request that you not say other things like that to their dishonor." Before engaging each other on the battlefield, therefore, Spaniards and Aztecs entered a war of religions.

This interreligious conflict might have remained at an impasse. Moctezuma adopted a policy of accommodation, permitting the Catholics to build a chapel in a minor palace near the precincts of the Great Temple. Cortés, however, was not content with coexistence. In effect, he declared war on the Aztec gods. Cortés reinforced his interpretation of the Aztec deities by destroying and replacing them with Christian symbols. Ascending the Great Temple, he entered the shrine of Tlaloc and attacked the statues there. According to one account, with a "superhuman leap," Cortés destroyed the shrine, yelling, "Something must be done for the Lord!" His men removed the statues from both the Tlaloc and Huitzilipochtli sanctuaries, which were appropriated for Christian worship. They were washed, whitewashed, and then adorned with a crucifix and images of Mary, Christopher, and other saints. Cortés finalized his Christian appropriation of these Aztec shrines by organizing a ritual procession up the steps of the temple, to the singing of psalms, in order to perform the Mass at the summit of the Great Temple. Through such ritual maneuvers, the Spanish conqueror defeated the Aztec gods as a prelude to defeating the Aztec empire.[4]

These Christian strategies of interreligious engagement—demonization, destruction, and appropriation—were repeated throughout Central and South America during the era of Spanish conquests. Even before the arrival of the first Catholic priests, monks, and missionaries, Christian adventurers like Cortés initiated the "spiritual conquest" of the Americas. In the earliest contacts between Spaniards and Aztecs, the Catholic conquerors tried to impose specific Christian terms for translating religious difference. However, as Moctezuma's policy of accommodation suggested, Aztecs could translate Catholic symbols into the familiar terms of their own religious world. The warrior Santiago and the Virgin Mary, for example, could be recognized as divine beings analogous to the holy warrior and the earth mother of Aztec religion. From this perspective, the sacred symbols of the two religions could be regarded as basically interchangeable representations of martial power and agricultural fertility. By rejecting such an intercultural translation, however, Spanish Catholics denied any possibility of religious exchange. Instead, they insisted on the total removal of the local religion and its complete replacement.

When Catholic priests arrived, beginning with the twelve Franciscans who were received by Cortés in Tenochtitlán in 1524, they continued this policy of demonizing, destroying, and replacing local religion. Attacking Aztec and other Mexican religious sites throughout the region, they directed a campaign of "extirpation" against indigenous religion and conducted mass baptisms to Christianize the Indian population. Following the Franciscans, other religious orders—the Dominicans, the Augustinians, and, later, the Jesuits—arrived to work on this massive project of religious conversion. While the indigenous people were subjected to military conquest, dispossession of land, forced labor, and large-scale reduction in population through imported European diseases, a demographic disaster that reduced the native population of Mexico, for example, from 25 million to 1 million within a century, they were also drawn into the systematic project of Christianization.

In Europe the legitimacy of the Spanish conquests in the Americas was rarely questioned. In the debates held in the city of Valladolid in 1550, however, the Christian justification for the subjugation of the people of the Americas was challenged by Bartolomé de las Casas (1484–1566), who, having served as priest and administrator in New Spain, had firsthand experience of the cruel treatment of the Indians. Las Casas argued that the indigenous people of the Americas were human beings and therefore had to be dealt with in a humane fashion. Although he assumed that the humanity of the Indians could ultimately only be fulfilled by Christian conversion, Las Casas insisted that conversion must be a matter of persuasion rather than coercion.

By contrast, his opponent in the Valladolid debates, Juan Ginés de Sepúlveda (ca. 1490–1574), defended the justice of the Spanish conquests on the grounds that the indigenous people of the Americas were less than fully human. Rather, they were what the ancient Greek philosopher Aristotle had called "natural slaves," who must be forced to submit to the authority of superior human beings. According to Sepúlveda,

This war and conquest are just because these barbaric, uneducated, and inhuman [Indians] are by nature servants. Naturally, they refuse the governance which more prudent, powerful, and perfect human beings offer and which would result in their great benefit. By natural right and for the good of all, the material ought to obey the form, the body the soul, the appetite the reason, the brutes the human being, the woman her husband, the imperfect the perfect, and the worse the better.

Recalling Augustine's fourth-century arguments for the use of force against the Donatists, Sepúlveda asserted that it was proper to employ not only persuasion, but also coercion to compel the indigenous people of the Americas to submit to Christianity, because they were "barbarians, violators of nature, blasphemers, and idolaters." Drawing inspiration from Aristotle's theory of natural hierarchy and Augustine's battles with Christian heresy, therefore, Sepúlveda developed terms for defending the justice of the political and religious conquest of the Americas.[5]

Certainly, although some resisted Christian incursions by maintaining traditional forms of religious life, many indigenous communities in New Spain adopted the Christian religion by accepting baptism and participating in the new parish system of churches, which by 1540 had spread throughout Mesoamerica. However, since that parish system was constructed along the same lines as the traditional administrative system that had organized the Aztec empire, the *altepetl,* which had revolved around local gods, festivals, and celebrations, much of the earlier social allegiances and religious rhythms persisted. In general, the indigenous response to Christianity was neither outright rejection nor the total acceptance that might be suggested by the term conversion. Between rejection and acceptance, indigenous people negotiated distinctive forms of local Christianity. For example, according to legend, in 1531 an Indian by the name of Juan Diego was walking by the hill of Tepeyac, an ancient shrine and pilgrimage site of the mother goddess, Tonantzin, when a young Indian woman met him and told him to gather flowers to take to the Catholic bishop of Mexico. When Juan Diego unwrapped the flowers he had gathered in his cape before the bishop, the image of the Virgin Mary—the Indian Virgin Mary—was revealed on the cloth. In this merger of the ancient Mexican mother goddess and the new Christian mother of God, the shrine at Tepeyac was revitalized as a devotional site for the Virgin of Guadalupe, who would eventually emerge as the divine patron of Mexico. Similar local revelations of the Virgin Mary and other Christian saints occurred throughout the Americas. Beyond acceptance or rejection, therefore, Christianity in the Americas developed through local initiatives as an indigenous Christianity.[6]

THE TALKING BOOK

Like the Aztecs, the Incas who ruled the Andean region of Peru were conquered and colonized by Spain. Beginning in 1532 with the invasion led by Francisco Pizarro, who also fought under the banner of the Virgin and Santiago, the Inca empire collapsed and the Andean people were placed under Spanish colonial subjugation. From the earliest contacts, Spanish observers reported that the religion of the Inca empire was devoted to the devil and his demons. Under the authority of the Spanish vice-royalty of Peru, missionaries waged vigorous campaigns for the "extirpation of idolatries" that sought to expunge all traces of indigenous religious practices devoted to the sun, the holy places, the oracles of the gods, and the deceased rulers and other ancestors who were revered in the imperial and popular religion of the Andes. Throughout the sixteenth century, each campaign of extirpation revealed that these traditional practices persisted under Christian rule, requiring continued religious warfare against the ancient gods and ancestors of Peru.

Even among Indian converts to Christianity, however, ancient patterns of thought provided resources that could be drawn upon in trying to make sense out of the disaster that had befallen Andean people under colonization. For example, about fifty years after the fall of the Inca empire, a descendant of Andean nobility, Felipe Guamán Poma de Ayala (1532–1614), began work on an illustrated book that presented a monumental history of the Andean world. Writing in Spanish and his native Quechua, Guamán Poma supported his text with vivid pictures depicting the ancient history and current society of Peru. He called it the "Talking Book." Completed in 1613 under the title *Nueva corónica y buen gobierno (New History and Good Government),* the book was dedicated and addressed to King Philip III of Spain (r. 1598–1621). Weaving together Christian and indigenous traditions, the "Talking Book" of Guamán Poma presented a striking religious examination of colonial conditions in Peru.

Although he was born of Andean nobility, Guamán Poma acquired skills in the Spanish Christian religion, language, and literacy that placed him in the role of an intermediary between two cultures. As a translator and interpreter, he served the colonial authorities during 1594 in their program to reallocate Andean land to new Spanish owners. At the same time, however, he fought this dispossession of Indian lands by pursuing an unsuccessful court case to reclaim his family's hereditary estate and by teaching Indians to read and write so they could assert their own claims for restitution. In part, his "Talking Book" was an appeal to King Philip of Spain to restore that land to its rightful owners, the indigenous people of the Andes, on both indigenous and Christian grounds.

According to Guamán Poma, the conquest and colonization of Peru had produced a world that was upside down. The established order of preconquest Andean society had been reversed. Andean nobles were dispossessed and impoverished, while Andean commoners who paid tribute to colonial officials were treated like nobility. In one of his illustrations, Guamán Poma depicts "Don Juan Capcha, tribute paying Indian, great drunkard," who is dressed in Castilian finery, as an image of "Don Juan World-Upside-Down." All Andeans were subjected to the reversals of colonial rule in which Spanish foreigners assumed grand titles, Catholic priests lived in luxury, and the Indians, mulattos, and mestizos in their service conspired with them to rob the poor. "The world is upside down," Guamán Poma declared. "It is a sign that there is no God and no king." The reversal of the world, therefore, suggested to Guamán Poma that Peru had been abandoned by both the God of Christianity and the king of Spain. As a result, the Andean people suffered without divine support or good governance. God and king were absent from Peru, Guamán Poma concluded with some irony—"They are in Rome and Castile."

What caused this situation? How did the world come to be upside down? On the one hand, Guamán Poma proposed a Christian explanation: the world was upside down as a result of human sinfulness. He was well aware of the standard Catholic missionary texts that represented the conquest of Peru as an act of divine justice that had punished the natives for their sins of idolatry. By contrast, Guamán Poma took a broader view of human sinfulness by identifying the crucial sin in the colonial context as the sin of pride. Originally introduced into the world by Lucifer, the sin of pride, arrogance, or *soberbia* had severely corrupted human nature. By identifying pride as the "root of all sin," Guamán Poma stood in a long tradition of Christian reflection on the corrupting effect of self-interest, which alienated human beings from God. However, he also applied this analysis of the sin of pride to the history of the Inca empire. The empire fell, he argued, not because the Spanish conquerors acted on behalf of God to punish the Inca for their sin of idolatry, but because the empire had already been weakened as a result of a civil war between the legitimate ruler, Atahualpa, and his rival, Huascar, who displayed the sin of "Lucifer-like pride." Therefore, the Spanish did not conquer on behalf of God. After all, Guamán Poma reflected, they could not have represented God since they suffered from the sin of greed for gold and silver. Rather, the Inca empire fell, like Lucifer fell from grace, as a result of internal divisions caused by the sin of pride.

In this explanation, therefore, Guamán Poma affirmed a Christian conviction that sin is the cause of evil, suffering, and misfortune and that sin—in this case, the sin of pride—is punished by God. The problem with this formula of human sin and divine punishment, however, was that those in colonial Peru who most obviously displayed the sin of pride—the colonial officials, the priests, and the tribute-paying Indians—were not in fact punished for their sin in this world. While poor Indians suffered for God, losing their lands, laboring in the mines, and dying by the thousands from unknown diseases, Guamán Poma observed, the priests dined, drank, and played cards with the colonial officials of Spanish Peru. Therefore, he found that the good were punished unjustly, while the wicked were not punished at all, but prospered. Once again, Guamán Poma observed that the world was upside down. If the sin of pride went unpunished, he concluded, then God must be absent.

In the human relations of a colonial world that had been turned upside down, Guamán Poma found one exception, the Christian hermit. With no vested interest in either church or society, the hermit represented for Guamán Poma an image of proper religious and social order. In one illustration, he depicted an Andean of low social status kneeling behind a Christian hermit, saying, "Obedience, saint, I respect you, saint." In striking contrast to the pride and ambition displayed by "Don Juan World-Upside-Down," this Andean commoner demonstrated the proper signs of respect for someone of his social station. Another illustration depicted the hermit kneeling before an Andean nobleman who says, "Here is alms, Father." The hermit replies, "For God." Not the church, therefore, but the Christian hermit, who stood outside of society, symbolized for Guamán Poma the possibility that the proper order of the social world could be restored. However, the humility of the hermit, which was respected by both the commoner and the nobleman, only magnified by contrast the sin of pride that Guamán Poma saw permeating the colonial world.[7]

On the other hand, Guamán Poma proposed an indigenous explanation for the colonial situation. According to Andean tradition, history was a series of epochs each of which ended with a dramatic event of destruction. That disaster, however, was followed immediately by the renewal of the world. In each cycle, or *pachacuti,* an old order ended only to be replaced by a new order, a new god, and a new king. Each *pachacuti,* therefore, effectively began the world again. As Guamán Poma reported, Andeans knew of a great flood, the "*pachacuti* by water," that had destroyed the world in ancient times so it could be renewed. In this instance, the world had simply decided to reverse itself without any concern for human beings. More recently, however, the historical epochs of destruction and renewal were marked by transitions in human society, especially by the death of a ruler and his succession. The last historical era before the coming of the Spanish, for example, was the epoch of the Inca, the era in which each new Inca emperor began the world again. The Inca Yupanqui, who consolidated the Inca state as an empire in the fifteenth century, was known as Pachacuti, "he who turns [or turns around or transforms] the world." The Inca Atahualpa, who was deposed and executed by the Spanish conquerors, was known as "Original Ruler," the emperor who had restored the world by guiding it through the destruction of a *pachacuti* into a new origin. This indigenous understanding of history, therefore, led Guamán Poma to view the Spanish conquest as another *pachacuti* in which the old world was replaced by a new order, a new god, and a new ruler.

In this new historical epoch under Spanish domination, however, Guamán Poma found that the world had not been renewed, but had been turned upside down. According to the Spanish conquerors, the God of heaven and earth was represented by the pope, who was represented by the king of Spain, who was represented by the Spanish colonial agents in Peru who had deposed the Inca emperor, imposed Christian conversion, and forced Indians to labor in the silver mines. A genuine renewal, Guamán Poma proposed, depended upon restoring the Inca emperor, a renewal of indigenous sovereignty that would reveal the order of a new world in which the mineral wealth of Peru supported Spain, which supported the church, which supported the Christian faith in the supreme God of heaven and earth. In his caption to an illustration of the mining capital of Peru, Guamán Poma observed, "Thanks to this mine exists Castile, Rome is Rome, the pope is pope and the king is monarch of the world, and holy mother church is defended and our holy faith is preserved by the four kings of the Indies and by the Inca emperor." Therefore, Peru was not subject to Spain, the Roman Catholic Church, and the Christian God; instead, the very existence of Castile, Rome, and the "holy faith" depended upon Peru. The return of Inca political sovereignty, Guamán Poma suggested, was crucial not only for the renewal of the Andean world, but also for the preservation of the Christian faith. In the meantime, however, reciting an ancient Andean prayer, Guamán Poma asked, "Where is God?"[8]

SOLDIERS OF THE VIRGIN

The Maya of Yucatán, Chiapas, and Guatemala also came under Spanish control during the sixteenth century. Although the classic era of Mayan civilization had long passed, the Maya maintained an indigenous religious life that was dramatically disrupted by the Spanish conquests. Like Guamán Poma in Peru, Mayan priests and prophets struggled to make sense out of the catastrophic changes brought about by colonization. Prophetic books, such as the *Book of Chilam Balam of Chumayel,* presented a Mayan perspective on the coming of the Spanish: "Here they arrived, with the true God, the true Lord, the cause of our misery." In this Mayan account, the Spanish brought not only the true God, but also a world of pain and suffering. The arrival of the Spanish Christians marked the origin of colonial tribute and church dues, rape and robbery, debt and poverty, torture and inquisition, and forced service to the Spaniards and their priests. Furthermore, colonization fomented internal divisions in Mayan communities that surfaced in witchcraft accusations and "hair-pulling quarrels." Divided and conquered, the Maya suffered under the rule of "human leeches, the suckers of poor commoners."

Nevertheless, with a cyclical view of history, the Mayan prophets anticipated a future reversal of the present colonial order. As the *Book of Chilam Balam of Chumayel* promised, "Well, it shall come to pass on the day that tears come to the eyes of our Lord, God, there will descend the justice of our Lord, God, everywhere in the world." Although the "true God" that arrived with the Spaniards was identified as the origin of misery, the God of the Maya would one day restore justice. Ironically, however, that

Mayan God was explicitly identified with the Christian God. The Mayan prophets proclaimed, "He is coming here, among us, our savior, that Jesus Christ, the guardian of our souls. Just as here on earth, so he is going to receive our souls in Holy Heaven also, O ye sons. The true God. Amen."[9]

While awaiting that global restoration of justice, however, the Maya under Spanish colonization developed local religious initiatives in claiming direct access to the power and protection of the Virgin Mary and Christian saints. In the highlands of Chiapas, for example, a series of village-based movements between 1708 and 1713 asserted local Indian claims on the ownership of Christian sacred symbols. As the authorities of the Spanish church acted to suppress these movements, Chiapas became a religious battlefield. Although indigenous resistance to the Spanish imposition of the new religion continued, the movements in Chiapas displayed widespread Indian interest in appropriating the meaning and power of Christianity.

In 1708 a hermit gained a large following by proclaiming that the Virgin had descended from heaven to offer assistance to Indians. Preaching from the hollow trunk of an oak tree, he displayed an image of the Virgin that gave off rays of light. Indians came from local villages to offer food and incense at the hermit's shrine. When the Catholic bishop learned of the hermit and his miracle, he sent Father Joseph Monrroy, a parish priest, to investigate. Father Monrroy found a small painting, which had been placed in a hole in the tree, and a notebook calling for repentance and the love of God. Ordering the tree to be cut down and chopped up, Father Monrroy imprisoned the hermit. Released two years later, the hermit resumed preaching. Indians built him a chapel with an altar to display an image of the Virgin and to receive offerings. When church officials again came to investigate, they burned the chapel and captured the hermit, taking him to Ciudad Real, the administrative capital of the region, where he was interrogated and found to be possessed by the devil. Exiled to Mexico, the hermit died on the way.

During 1711, an Indian woman, Dominica López, reported that the Virgin had appeared to her in a cornfield. Four days later, when her husband also witnessed this miracle, the Virgin asked them to build a house for her because she would rather live in town than "die among sticks and stones in the woods." With the support of the traditional leadership of the town, a chapel was built that housed two images of the Virgin and images of the patron saints of three local villages. Speaking only to Dominica López, the Virgin gave divine encouragement to the Indians, promising prosperity in this world and salvation in the next. Pilgrims were drawn to the chapel from all over the region to offer chickens, flowers, incense, candles, firewood, and silver money before the altar of the Virgin. Father Joseph Monrroy was again sent to investigate. He convinced the Indians to take the image of the Virgin on a procession to Ciudad Real, where, he proposed, the Indian Virgin would receive greater honor. However, after arriving at the administrative capital with an entourage of two thousand Indians, the image was confiscated and Dominica López and other religious leaders were imprisoned and put on trial. Although the inquisitors accused her of being a Mayan shaman in Christian disguise, Dominica López insisted that the worship of the Virgin had been conducted according to orthodox Catholic rites observed for patron saints. Nevertheless, the inquisition found that the worship of the Indian Virgin was a revival of the beliefs and practices of Mayan religion. Regarding that ancient religion as demonic, the Spanish Catholic authorities sentenced Dominica López and other leaders to death.

In response to these Indian initiatives, therefore, the authorities of the Catholic Church acted swiftly to close any alternative avenues of access to Christian sacred power. Since church and state were coordinated in maintaining colonial rule, any Indian independence in matters of religion, even if that independence was only the attempt to develop authentically Indian forms of Christian worship, appeared as a threat to the authority of Spanish rule over Indian populations. One movement, however, advanced an explicit challenge to the religious and political basis of Spanish rule. The Virgin movement of Cancuc, which began in 1712 during the trial of Dominica López and her associates, mobilized widespread enthusiasm for military opposition to Spanish colonial domination. Its followers became "soldiers of the Virgin."

The Cancuc movement also began with a miraculous appearance of the Virgin, in this case to a young Indian woman, Maria de la Candelaria, who was instructed to place a cross at the spot. When the parish priest of Cancuc learned that Indians were lighting candles and burning incense before the cross, he confiscated it and had Maria de la Candelaria whipped, insisting that her vision had been an invention of the devil. Refusing to accept the priest's interpretation, Indians built a chapel where the cross had stood. Kneeling in the chapel, making the sign of the cross, and counting the rosary, many participants understood their worship of the Virgin as orthodox Catholic practice. They even sent a delegation to Ciudad Real to obtain official recognition from the bishop, asking for permission to perform the Mass in the chapel. Refusing to recognize the legitimacy of their worship, the bishop sentenced the members of the delegation to prison and ordered the chapel to be destroyed.

Unlike the earlier Virgin movements, however, the movement of Cancuc resisted the official denial and destruction of indigenous worship. Under the leadership of Sebastián Gómez, who claimed to have risen to heaven to speak with God, the Virgin, Jesus Christ, and St. Peter, the Indians of Cancuc turned that rejection back on the authorities of the church by renouncing Spanish priests and establishing an indigenous priesthood. The movement also tried to reverse the power relations in the region by renaming their small town "Ciudad Real," thus identifying Cancuc as the true Royal City of the Virgin. The Spanish administrative capital was renamed "Jerusalem," suggesting that the city was being held captive by infidels, the Spanish, and therefore must be reconquered through a new Christian crusade led by Indian "soldiers of the Virgin."

During 1712, the leaders of the movement called upon all the Indians of Chiapas to enlist in this crusade. In the name of the Virgin, they issued a call to the Indian leaders of surrounding towns:

> I, the Virgin, who has descended to this sinful world call you in the name of Our Lady of the Rosary and order you to come to this town of Cancuc and to bring with you all the silver of your churches, and the ornaments and bells . . . because there is no longer God, nor King; and thus come at once because otherwise you will be punished if you do not respond to my summons and God's Ciudad Real of Cancuc.

As the Indian towns of Chiapas responded to the call, Sebastián Gómez ordained a bishop, priests, and assistants to take over the religious functions of celebrating the Mass, administering the sacraments, and preaching sermons in a church now headed not by the Spanish God and king, but by the Indian Virgin Mary. Like the Spanish church, the Church of the Virgin of Cancuc was intolerant of alternative claims to sacred power. The Indian leaders of a competing Virgin movement in another town were taken to Cancuc and hanged; an Indian who claimed to be Jesus Christ was also brought to Cancuc and executed. In these instances, the leaders of the Virgin movement asserted supreme power over life and death while assembling an army for battle against the Spanish.

After some successes on the battlefield, the "soldiers of the Virgin" were defeated when Spanish troops broke through the defenses of Cancuc in November 1712. Since the Spanish also saw themselves as "soldiers of the Virgin," their victory over Cancuc was celebrated in Ciudad Real with a public procession in honor of the Virgin of Charity. Although Indian resistance continued during the following year, the Spanish succeeded in subduing the other towns, destroying Indian chapels to the Virgin, and capturing Sebastián Gómez and other leaders of the movement except for Maria de la Candelaria, who was never found. Clearly, the Virgin movement did not reject Catholicism, because it faithfully adopted the symbols, rituals, and organization of the Catholic Church. However, the movement did reject Spanish control over Catholic Christianity. Denied official recognition by the authorities of the Spanish church, the Virgin movement of Cancuc returned that denial by creating an alternative religious, political, and military order centered in a new "Ciudad Real," the true royal city of the Virgin. Although that new order was destroyed with the restoration of Spanish colonial rule, the alternatives represented by Indian Virgins and saints continued to be developed in working out the meaning and power of Christianity in the New World.[10]

Five hundred years after the first voyages of Columbus, every Mayan town in southern Mexico and Guatemala featured a Catholic church housing the images of a saint who served as the spiritual guardian of the crops, health, and well-being of the community. For example, in the town of Santiago Chimaltenango, which the Mayan residents called Chimbal, the local church housed two statues of the town's patron saint, Santiago Matamoros, "St. James the Moorkiller." The saint was the focal point for private devotions and public religious life. Accompanied by his wife, St. Anne, Santiago participated in the local feasts and festivals, enjoying the prayers, music, fireworks, and offerings of incense, flowers, candles, and rum, as the statues, which were dressed in the distinctively local styles of clothing, were paraded through the town.

Although Santiago Matamoros had been invoked by the sixteenth-century Spanish conquerors, the Maya of Chimbal did not associate their patron saint with that ancient history of conquest and colonization. Instead, they regarded Santiago as a saint who had been discovered and domesticated by their Mayan ancestors. According to one account, their ancestors had found Santiago living in the mountains. Building a church for him, they convinced the saint to come to town. The next morning, however, the saint was gone. Returning to the mountains, the ancestors found the saint and brought him back to the church. Once again, however, the saint was gone by morning. When they finally found him again in the mountains, Santiago resisted being carried back to town, miraculously making himself so heavy that he could not be lifted. In their frustration, the ancestors were forced to beat him to get him into the church. The marks left by their whips can still be seen today on a statue of the saint. From that day, however, the patron saint had resided in the church and protected the town.[11]

According to this account, therefore, Santiago had not been inherited from the Spanish conquerors, but had been discovered and even conquered by the ancestors of the town. As the ancient Mayan ancestors were thereby recalled as the founders of Christianity in Chimbal, the Christian St. Santiago absorbed many of the functions, such as healing, agricultural fertility, and protection from disaster, that had been the responsibility of the "earth lords" or "owners of the earth" in ancient Mayan religion. By drawing together Christian and indigenous religious resources, the Mayan Catholics of southern Mexico and Guatemala redefined Christianity as a religion both universal in scope and local in its meaning and power. In similar ways, throughout the Americas and other colonized regions of the world, Christianity became a local production.

22

Holy Russia

The year 1492 was highly significant in the world of Eastern Orthodoxy. According to the Byzantine calendar, which calculated human history from the creation, exactly seven thousand years would have elapsed in 1492. The end of the seventh millennium would mark the end of the world. Accordingly, the liturgical texts of the Orthodox Paschal Canon, including the calculation of the annual celebration of Easter, only went as far as 1492. During the fifteenth century, as Orthodox commentators anticipated the end, the fall of the sacred city of Constantinople to the Turks in 1453 seemed to signal the last days. Forced to submit to the Muslim authority of the Turkish empire, the Greek Orthodox Church was divorced from its political foundation. For Orthodox Christians, the destruction of the Byzantine Empire was more than a political disaster. Commentators concluded it was a divine punishment for the religious betrayal of orthodoxy at the Council of Florence during 1438–39 when delegates of the Eastern Church accepted union with Rome in exchange for Western military assistance against the Turks. Having betrayed the true faith by aligning with the Roman Church, Constantinople fell under Muslim rule. But the prospect of the imminent end of the world promised the appearance of a liberating emperor who would reconquer the sacred city in preparation for the return of Christ. Where would that liberating emperor appear? According to a Russian account of the fall of Constantinople, that emperor would emerge from Russia. In fulfillment of prophecy, "the Russian tribes will battle against the Ishmaelites," this account promised, and in defeating the Turkish Muslims, the Russians "will conquer the city of the seven hills [Constantinople], and will reign there." In these prophetic terms, Russia claimed a special role in the divine drama that would unfold at the end of the world with the reconquest of the sacred city, the confrontation with the Antichrist, and establishment of Christ's reign on earth.

Although this prophecy linked Russia and Constantinople in the future, that connection had already been established during the late tenth century when Russians began converting on a large scale from Slavonic paganism to the Christianity of the Greek Orthodox Church. As a result, many of the familiar religious institutions of the East—the Greek liturgy, monasticism, hesychast spirituality, scholarship, and artistic traditions— were transplanted into Russia. Between 1240 and 1380, while Russia was subject to the foreign rule of the Tatars, Russian Orthodoxy survived in the monasteries established on Greek models imported from Byzantium, Mount Athos, and the Balkans. The center of Russian Orthodox life, which had been located in Kiev prior to 1240, shifted to Moscow, where a close relationship developed between church and state. Supported by the religious, cultural, and educational work of the St. Sergius Trinity Monastery, which expanded under the leadership of the ascetic, mystic, and abbot Sergii of Radonezh (d. 1392), Moscow became both the political and the religious center of the Russian world.

Following the Council of Florence in 1438–39, many Russians began to identify Moscow as the center of the Orthodox world. When the metropolitan bishop of Moscow, Isidore, who was Greek by birth, returned from Florence to announce the union, he was deposed by the Russian monarch, Vasili II, for advocating a merger with heretics. Having learned from the Greek Orthodox Church that Roman Catholics upheld a heretical faith, Vasili could only conclude that Isidore and other Greeks had betrayed the Greek faith. Although a new metropolitan bishop— Jonas, a Russian—was installed in 1448, Vasili was proclaimed not only as the "supporter of the Orthodox faith and of all Russia," but also as the "upholder of the Greek faith." As noted, after the fall of Constantinople the conviction that Moscow was the supreme guardian of the Greek Orthodox faith was reinforced by that catastrophe. It was further reinforced in 1472 when Ivan III, who adopted the title Tsar, which was adapted from the Roman imperial title Caesar, married an heiress of Greek royalty, an event widely understood to symbolize the transfer of the "Byzantine inheritance" from the East to Russia. As the year 1492 approached, therefore, Russia had established its position as heir, guardian, and liberator of Byzantium.

The world, however, did not come to an end. In drawing up a new Paschal Canon in 1492 for the beginning of the eighth millennium, the metropolitan bishop of Moscow, Zosimius, cautioned that Christians could not predict the precise timing of the last days. "We are awaiting the advent of the Lord," he affirmed, "even although, according to the Holy Writ, the day and the hour of His coming cannot be established." Instead of looking to the fulfillment of prophecy in the future, Russian Christians should remember the crucial events of their sacred history. They should recall the founding of Constantinople, the New Rome, by the Emperor Constantine; the baptism of Russia by St. Vladimir; and the imperial expansion of Russia under Tsar Ivan III, who was proclaimed "the new Emperor Constantine of the new Constantinople—Moscow." In this account, Zosimius did not identify Ivan as the liberating emperor who would go to Constantinople. Instead, he proposed that Constantinople had already come to Moscow. Its religious authority, political power, and historical significance had already been symbolically transferred to the imperial capital of Russia. Accordingly, there was no imperative to recover the "Second Rome" from its Turkish captivity, because it had been effectively replaced by Moscow, the "Third Rome."[1]

OLD BELIEVERS

As the Constantine of the Third Rome, the tsar assumed divine status as a mediator between heaven and earth, even being praised for being "like the Highest God." Around 1511 a Russian monk, the Elder Philotheus, reinterpreting apocalyptic literature in the wake of the failure of the apocalypse of 1492, declared, "the Holy Catholic and Apostolic Church of the East shines more brightly than the sun in the universe, and only the great Orthodox Tsar of Russia, like Noah saved from the flood in the ark, directs the Church."[2] Although the Greek Orthodox Church did not officially recognize that the metropolitan of Moscow held independent status equal to those of ancient Rome, Constantinople, Antioch, Alexandria, and Jerusalem until 1589, the Russian Church had already claimed a unique independent status in the Orthodox Christian world by proclaiming the tsar as the supreme defender of the faith. Taking that responsibility seriously, the tsars periodically sponsored projects to reform the liturgical texts and practices of the Russian Church. Under the authority of Tsar Alexis in the 1650s, for example, scholars, linguists, and priests undertook a review of ritual, morality, and spirituality within the Russian Orthodox Church. As patriarch between 1652 and 1658, Archbishop Nikon briefly assumed a prominent role in that project of reform. Nikon's reforms, however, deeply divided the Russian Church and resulted in religious schism and conflict that persisted for the next two hundred years. In trying to go back to the earliest and most authentic Greek sources of Orthodox Christianity, Nikon's reforms inspired a movement of resistance—known as the "Old Ritualists" *(Staroobriadtsy)*, the "Schism" *(Raskol)*, or the "Old Believers"—that opposed the Russian Orthodox Church on the grounds that it had actually betrayed the faith of Russian orthodoxy.

According to Archbishop Nikon (1605–81), the standard for religious belief and practice was set by the Greek Orthodox Church. "I am Russian," he declared, "but my faith and religion are Greek." In reviewing Russian religious practice, Nikon noticed certain minor points of divergence from the Greek model. Russian Orthodox Christians made the sign of the cross with two fingers instead of with three; they recited the hallelujah of the liturgy two times instead of three; and they also differed in the number of prostrations performed before the altar. Through a series of church councils, Nikon had succeeded by 1656 in imposing the Greek standard for making the sign of the cross, reciting the hallelujah glorification, and performing ritual prostrations. Only a few priests, led by the archpriest Avvakum (1621–82), opposed these changes as an unwarranted deviation from both Russian tradition and the most ancient texts of the Christian church. Why should the Russian Church adapt to current Greek practice, they argued, when the Greeks themselves had deviated from their most ancient sources? Avvakum adhered to traditional Russian practice. "I hold to this even unto death, as I have received it," he declared. "It has been laid down before us: let it lie thus unto ages of ages." However, at a church council in 1667, which was presided over by the patriarchs of Antioch and Alexandria, Avvakum and his supporters were condemned as heretics. Avvakum was exiled to the north and imprisoned, along with three of his fellow priests, who had their tongues cut out. In 1682, Avvakum and his colleagues were burned at the stake. Even in the face of death, however, they remained faithful to what they regarded as the authentic beliefs and practices of the old Russian religion.[3]

By the 1680s, however, the religious and secular authorities were not able to suppress resistance by killing four priests. Spreading throughout Russia, especially in regions farthest from Moscow's imperial control, the *Raskol* movement of Old Believers emerged to challenge the changes introduced by the patriarch and tsar of Moscow. In response to mass protests, a law in 1684 made adherence to the Old Believers a crime punishable by death. Nevertheless, Old Believers persisted in their opposition to the religious and political authority of Moscow. At stake was the special status of the Third Rome as the guardian of Orthodox religion. By introducing even minor changes to that religion, Nikon and Tsar Alexis threatened Moscow's continuity with the past. Reviving the apocalyptic expectations of 1492, Old Believers generally accepted that the precise "day and hour" of the second coming of Christ could not be foretold. However, the Antichrist was a different matter. Whether in spiritual or physical form, the Antichrist could be recognized in the exercise of arbitrary power, the betrayal of tradition, and the captivity of the church. Applying these tests to current events, the Old Believers concluded that the Russian tsar was not "like the Highest God," but was actually the Antichrist.

Trying to escape the Antichrist, communities of Old Believers retreated to the forests or remote monasteries. However, they were pursued by forces of the tsar, not only by church officials in search of heretics, but also by soldiers, census takers, and tax collectors who were actively extending the scope of Moscow's rule throughout Russia. Refusing to submit to these agents of the Antichrist, many Old Believers chose death as a means of salvation. Beginning in the 1660s, whole communities committed mass suicide by locking themselves in a church, monastery, or farmhouse and setting the building on fire. As one leader explained before dying with his community in a burning chapel, "Because of the many present burdens on the people, no man in the world can save himself by any means, but if they burn themselves, then they can obtain salvation." Death by fire, therefore, appeared to many Old Believers as a way of escaping from the world of the Antichrist, maintaining Christian purity, and achieving martyrdom, even if self-inflicted, which guaranteed salvation.

During the reign of Peter the Great between 1682 and 1725, the official persecution and mass suicides of Old Believers reached their peak. Ironically, in 1702 Peter had issued a proclamation of religious toleration, but Old Believers were treated as a special case: they were free to practice their faith, although they were forbidden from preaching and had to be registered as Old Believers and pay double the amount of taxes to Moscow. The issue of taxation, in particular, convinced Old Believers that Peter was the Antichrist. A personal tax, known as the "soul tax," was required of all subjects of Russia. In taxing souls, they concluded, the tsar had made himself a god, but he was the god of this earth, the Antichrist, an evil force in opposition to the supreme God of heaven and earth. By refusing to pay the "soul tax," Old Believers rejected the ultimate authority of the Antichrist over human life in the world. In response to this opposition, Peter issued another law that equated the religion of the Old Believers with treason to the state. Although proclaiming religious toleration, officials of church and state pursued a policy of persecution by interrogating, torturing, and executing adherents of the faith of the Old Believers. Those not executed were sentenced to serve long terms of hard labor. In this context of official persecution, Old Believers increasingly turned to mass suicide as their only hope of salvation.[4]

Both sides in this religious struggle were working out the implications of the doctrine of Moscow, the Third Rome. Since there would not be a Fourth Rome, the role of Moscow as the last guardian of the Christian faith assumed ultimate proportions in the world. During the reign of Peter the Great, the Russian Church celebrated the tsar as a divine ruler like Constantine, proclaiming him as *zemnoi bog,* the god on earth, who presided over an expanding Christian empire. However, for the Old Believers and others who resisted this imperial ideology the symbol of Rome recalled not the New Rome of Constantine, but the old Rome of persecution and martyrdom, the Roman imperial power identified in the book of Revelation as the Antichrist. Nevertheless, Old Believers also argued that Moscow had a special role in defending the faith, but that some of the changes introduced by Peter further confirmed his role as the Antichrist precisely because they betrayed the ideal of Moscow, the Third Rome. As "god on earth," Peter reorganized sacred space and time in Russia. Moving his capital from Moscow to St. Petersburg, Peter abolished the Moscow patriarchate, presenting the sacred headdress, the "white klobuk," worn only by the patriarch of the "Third Rome," to all the metropolitan bishops in Russia. Intervening in sacred time, Peter introduced a reform of the Russian calendar so that time would be calculated not from creation, which had been so important in anticipating the events of the last days, but forward and backward from the birth of Christ. Accordingly, Old Believers saw his "reforms" as serious disruptions of the sacred space and sacred time of Russian religion.

According to the Old Believers, Peter had reversed the proper relationship between church and state. They insisted that the political order of the state ought to serve the religious salvation gained through the church, but

Peter had introduced a series of imperial laws in the 1720s that placed the church in the service of maintaining the law and order of the state. Fines were imposed on anyone who did not attend Communion or make confession at least once a year. Church attendance was mandated by law on certain religious and imperial holidays. Parish priests were enjoined to file reports on all those who did not attend church or confess yearly and to report any secrets divulged during the confession that might suggest that a person held criminal intentions or had performed criminal acts. In addition to prosecuting those who revealed any criminal thoughts or deeds during confession, secular courts were given jurisdiction over all offenders who neglected to perform their "Christian duties" of annual confession and church attendance. Peter thus introduced new techniques of surveillance and discipline that required the coordination of church and state in monitoring and controlling the Russian population. In this religiously and politically regulated Russian society, therefore, the religion of the Old Believers registered not only as a heretical schism within the Russian Orthodox Church, but also as a crime against the Russian state.

COERCION AND EDUCATION

If Christian heresy was regarded as a crime against the state, then the presence of non-Christian religions within the borders of the Russian empire represented an even more serious threat to the religious unity of the Christian state. Following the Russian conquests of the 1550s, which brought large populations of Muslims but also smaller yet significant numbers of Jews, Buddhists, and Slavic pagans under Moscow's domain, a new missionary spirit was introduced. Embracing this missionary project as part of the divine destiny of the Third Rome, the Russian tsar Ivan IV (1530–84) embarked upon a campaign of religious conversion. In the region of Kazan, for example, where Muslim Tatars had formed a ruling elite, Ivan's missionary policy involved a blend of coercion, persuasion, and education. In an effort to undermine Muslim authority in Kazan, the tsar prohibited the construction of any new mosques and ordered all existing mosques destroyed and replaced by Christian churches. Turning to the pagans of Kazan, however, Ivan advocated the persuasive force of education. In his instructions to the new archbishop of Kazan, Ivan advised that the Russian Church "should teach these 'children' not only to read and write, but to make them understand truly what they read, and then they will be able to teach others, including the Muslims." Converts should freely turn to Christian faith, hope, and love, but the process of conversion could be facilitated, the tsar proposed, by condemning all criminals to death, even those guilty of minor crimes, and then forgiving them, thus demonstrating a Christian love that would turn them to Christ.[5]

Despite these measures, however, conversions in Kazan and other conquered regions were rare. Although some prominent non-Christian nobles converted and formed alliances with Moscow, and in the process gained the title of Russian nobility, grants of land, and annual compensation in cash, ordinary non-Christians resisted conversion. During the seventeenth century, Russian legislation turned from converting to constraining the adherents of other religions. In the comprehensive legal code of 1649, any Muslim convicted of trying to convert a Christian to Islam was to be burned at the stake. Jews found guilty of trying to convert Christians were later subject to the same law. Although these laws sought to restrict the expansion of other religions, non-Christians were also vulnerable to the government policy of confiscating their land and reallocating it to Russians and converts. Coercion, therefore, remained a feature of the state's missionary policy.

Deployed primarily against Muslims, the use of force demonstrated Russia's continuing religious warfare against Islam. Fearing an Islamic military alliance, the tsars persisted with a policy of suppressing Islam within the orbit of the Russian empire. Certainly, a military threat had occasionally arisen when the Ottomans and Crimeans attempted to organize Muslims in the conquered territories against the political authority of Russia. But the Buddhist Kalmyks were also drawn into these anti-Russian campaigns. Nevertheless, the tsars continued to see Islam, which Peter the Great referred to as the "disgusting faith of Muhammad," as the principal spiritual enemy of church and state. Even attempts to convert pagans to Christianity, therefore, were understood as maneuvers against Islam because they were targeted not merely at gaining souls for Christ, but more specifically at preventing pagans from becoming Muslims.

By the reign of Peter the Great, the general failure of the Christian missionary project had become evident. The philosopher Ivan Pososhkov, for example, observed in 1719 that the Russian government had failed to extend Christianity to its own subjects while the Roman Catholic Church had succeeded in converting people of foreign lands all over the world.

Although the pagans who lived close to home within the Russian empire had been Russian subjects for two hundred years, Pososhkov complained, "they did not become Christians and their souls have perished because of our negligence." It was not enough, however, merely to make them Christians; they had to be made good Christians through missionary preaching and teaching for the sake of the salvation of their souls.[6]

During the 1720s, a renewed emphasis on Christian education was instilled into missionary campaigns. Established by Peter the Great in 1721, the Holy and Governing Synod assumed collective responsibility for the administration of the Russian Orthodox Church and its missions. At Peter's insistence, the synod decreed that no convert should be baptized without first being carefully instructed in the principles and practices of the Christian faith. Peter ordered the synod to arrange for Russian missionaries to live in remote villages among non-Christians, learn their various local languages, and translate the Bible so they could more effectively provide religious instruction. At the same time, they were told to set up schools in local monasteries to teach the Russian language and Christian laws. In some cases, students would be brought to St. Petersburg for further education. All of these educational initiatives indicated that the government and church had recognized by the 1720s that a policy of coercion had failed. Genuine conversion to Christianity required converts to internalize the norms of Russian language and law that supported both church and state. Conversion required education.

However, the educational campaign initiated by Peter the Great also failed to produce Christian converts in any substantial number. Russian missionaries complained of the difficulties of learning local languages, the stubborn resistance of non-Christians, the lack of sufficient financial support to create schools, and the corruption of priests and government officials who accepted bribes from Muslims and pagans so they could continue practicing their religions. In the wake of the failure of the educational mission to produce results, the Russian government reverted to coercion. In 1740 it established the Agency of Convert Affairs to coordinate a sustained assault against non-Christian religions in the Russian empire. Under the direction of Father Dmitrii Sechenov, the agency initially focused its efforts on the Muslims of Kazan. Revitalizing the earlier government policy of destroying mosques, the agency ordered the destruction of 418 out of the 536 mosques in Kazan, only sparing the remainder, which had been built before the Russian conquest, due to fear of a popular uprising against a government that would cause the desecration of such ancient sacred sites.[7]

In some cases, the destruction of mosques, cemeteries, and other places of Muslim worship did inspire revolt, causing the senate of the government and the synod of the church in St. Petersburg to caution restraint in forcing conversions because they feared further uprisings. Nevertheless, under the auspices of the Agency of Convert Affairs, coercion continued. In addition to eliminating mosques in Kazan, by 1756 the government had destroyed 98 out of 133 mosques in Siberia and 29 out of 40 mosques in Astrakhan. As a result of such interventions, the agency could claim by 1763 that it had converted about one-third of the Muslim population of Kazan to the Christian faith. With the adherents of indigenous religions in other provinces, the agency claimed even greater success for its policy of combining force with financial rewards by reporting that 95 percent of the pagans had converted to Christianity. Once again, however, officials of church and state could not be certain that such conversions were sincere. In fact, local missionaries complained that people were converting several times in order to receive financial benefits. The government recognized that although the coercive policy of the Agency of Convert Affairs had increased the number of Christian converts, it had not produced the religious or spiritual unity required by the Russian state. Over the span of one hundred years, the official Russian missionary policy had alternated between coercion and education. Neither had succeeded.

Closing the Agency of Convert Affairs in 1764, Empress Catherine II (1729–96) issued a decree of religious toleration. Regarding herself as an enlightened monarch in conversation with the leading philosophers of Europe, Catherine renounced the religious persecution of her subjects. In letters to some of the most eminent French philosophers of the European Enlightenment, Catherine described her impressions of a tour of Kazan. The religious diversity in that province, she realized, suggested that the Russian empire stood at the intersection of the cultural and spiritual traditions of Europe and Asia. Although the Russian state had perceived that intersection as a great danger, Catherine proposed that the meeting of Europe and Asia also held great potential for the world.

Reflecting on this long history of efforts by the Russian church and state to convert non-Christian subjects of the empire, Prince Mikhail Scherbatov observed in 1776 that the exercise of coercion violated not only the religious freedom of non-Christians, but also the religious integrity of Christianity. As a result, any conversions that might occur were suspect. Relying upon military force, tax exemptions, and financial rewards, the Christian missionaries of the Russian church and state, as Mikhail Scherbatov observed, "neither attempted to teach converts first, nor sent preachers who knew their language, and instead brought them to baptism in the same way they would have been brought to a bath, and gave them a cross, which, in their ignorance, they consider some kind of a talisman, and an image of Christ, which they regard as an idol, and forbade them from eating meat on fasting days, which they do not follow, and the priests take bribes from them for overlooking this." The recently appointed archbishop of the province of Kazan, Amvrosii Podobedov, agreed with Scherbatov's assessment. "I find that the ignorant non-Christian peoples," he wrote, "have not only insufficient, but not even the slightest notion about the precepts of faith into which they were converted by holy baptism." Such conversions could not count as Christian conversions.[8]

By 1776, therefore, Russian Christians had experienced over two hundred years of frustration in the missionary enterprise of unifying the empire under a single religious domain. Coercion had produced converts who were not Christian, while education had produced programs of Christian instruction but no converts. Certainly, this missionary dilemma was not unique to the Russian Orthodox Church. Roman Catholic and Protestant missions experienced a similar dilemma all over the world. However, by adopting the spiritual and political mantle of the Third Rome, the Russian Church assumed a special role in destroying heretics, defeating Muslims, and redeeming pagans. Unable to achieve those goals within the Russian empire, some leaders within the Russian Orthodox Church began to look outside of the territorial boundaries of Russia for a field to pursue religious missions. Some even looked to America.

RUSSIAN AMERICA

The establishment of Russian America in what is now Alaska began as an imperial project of Peter the Great. On his deathbed in 1725, the tsar instructed a Danish captain in the Russian service, Vitus Bering, to organize the discovery and exploration of America. Unlike the Spanish conquests, the initial Russian engagements with America were not conceived in religious terms as a Christian campaign for land and converts. Rather, entry into America was motivated by the scientific interests of the academy of sciences organized by Tsar Peter and by economic interest in the lucrative fur trade with China. Although the ships in Bering's small fleet bore the Christian names *St. Gabriel, St. Peter,* and *St. Paul,* the earliest Russian explorations of America between 1728 and Bering's death in 1741 received no explicitly Christian justification. With the increase of Russian incursions into the Aleutian Islands, indigenous inhabitants were occasionally taken to Siberia, baptized in the Russian Orthodox Church, and taught the Russian language so they could serve as interpreters, but no large-scale effort was directed toward Christian conversion. Yet religion was also put to sea with the eighteenth-century Russian navigators, adventurers, and traders. For example, when one Russia ship, the *Sts. Zosima and Savatii,* was blown off course in the Pacific Ocean, the crew deposed the ship's captain. As one passenger explained, "Their ikons were carried on deck as was that of the Mother of God, and we promised with tears that from whatsoever direction God would now send the wind we would follow it." When the ship unexpectedly found land, passengers and crew regarded their deliverance as a divine act of mercy. Under the auspices of Russian Orthodox divinity and saints, therefore, Christianity was carried along networks of navigation, exploration, and trade into the Pacific Ocean.[9]

Like these ships, the earliest Russian settlements in America were dedicated to Orthodox saints. On Kodiak Island, for example, the first Russian settlement in 1784 was named Three Saints Bay, drawing together the divine protection of Sts. Basil the Great, Gregory the Divine, and John "the Golden-Mouthed" Chrysostom. Off the Alaskan mainland, the earliest settlement in Sitka was named New Archangel. However, beyond the naming of ships and settlements, the Russian church and state showed little interest in advancing Christian missions in America. Russian trade in America was controlled by the Russian-American Company, a privately controlled and stockholder-owned corporation. Although the company charter invoked "God Almighty," the Russian-American Company did little to sponsor Christian missions to the indigenous people of Alaska. Beginning in 1823, however, a large-scale missionary effort was led by Ioann Veniaminov (1797–1879). He served as the first priest of Unalaska Island, as the first bishop of Alaska, and eventually as the metropolitan patriarch of Moscow. In 1977, as St. Innocent, Veniaminov was canonized by the Russian Orthodox Church.

Born in a rural village in Irkutsk as Ivan Popov, he took the name Ioann Veniaminov in honor of a local bishop when he entered the local theological seminary at the age of nine. In addition to academic subjects, Veniaminov studied science, carpentry, mechanics, and watchmaking. Leaving the seminary at the age of twenty, married to the daughter of a priest, he assumed the responsibilities of a deacon in the diocese of Irkutsk. As a member of the married clergy, known as the White clergy, Veniaminov was prevented from rising to a position of power and authority within the Russian Orthodox Church. Bishops were drawn only from the celibate Black clergy, who lived under monastic rule. When he was elevated to the priesthood in 1821 at the age of twenty-four, Veniaminov had reached the highest level he could expect to achieve within the church hierarchy. Two years later, however, he unexpectedly volunteered for America. With his wife, son, mother, and brother, Veniaminov established a mission in 1826 on Unalaska, an island in the Aleutian chain. There he built a church, the Church of the Holy Ascension, established a school, and set up an orphanage for an indigenous population on Unalaska Island of about five hundred people and another thousand people living on other Aleutian islands. Ten years later, Veniaminov reported, all had become Christians.

Apparently, Veniaminov found a receptive audience among the Aleuts for his Christian mission. According to the testimony of one Aleut, "When he preached the Word of God all the people listened, and listened without moving, until he stopped. Nobody thought of fishing and hunting while he spoke; nobody felt hungry or thirsty as long as he was speaking, not even little children." His ability to communicate his religious message depended upon mastering the Aleut language. Becoming fluent in the local Fox-Aleut dialect, Veniaminov also composed an alphabet, a dictionary, and a grammar to transform Aleut from a spoken into a written language. He translated prayers, the Catechism, and the Gospel of Matthew. In 1833 he published a small book in Aleut, *Indication of the Way into the Kingdom of Heaven,* that outlined basic Christian doctrines. "It is the binding duty of every Christian," Veniaminov held, "to know his faith thoroughly; because anyone who does not have a solid knowledge of his faith is cold and indifferent to it and frequently falls either into superstition or unbelief." Veniaminov claimed that his Aleutian converts had been rescued from both superstition and unbelief by developing a Christian interiority based on educated faith. "I do not mean that they know only how to make the sign of the cross, bow, and mutter some prayer," he exclaimed. "No! Some can pray from their souls, not only in church, but also in solitude." The ultimate goal of Veniaminov's work on the Aleut language, therefore, was to cultivate this interior language of silent, solitary prayer.[10]

The persistence of indigenous Aleut religion could be found in the work of traditional shamans. As specialists in ritual techniques of trance, healing, and spiritual power, shamans continued to play a significant role in Aleut religious life even in a new Christian context. As Veniaminov found in one village in 1828, an elderly man by the name of Ivan Smirennikov, who had been baptized into the Russian Orthodox Church, was regarded by the local people as a shaman because of his familiarity with spirits. In a letter to his bishop, Veniaminov recounted some of the miracles ascribed to his extraordinary power. First, Smirennikov had gained a reputation for his spiritual ability to heal. When a woman was caught in a fox trap and so seriously injured that her family expected her to die, they secretly contacted the shaman to cure her. "After thinking the matter over," Veniaminov recalled, "he said that the patient will be well in the morning. And, indeed, the woman rose in the morning from her deathbed, and is even now entirely well, not suffering any pain." Second, Smirennikov had become known for saving a village from starvation. During the winter of 1825, when the people of a local village suffered from lack of food, they approached the shaman to pray for a whale to be washed ashore. In response to their request, Smirennikov specified the precise location where the people would find a fresh whale carcass. Third, Smirennikov had displayed powers of clairvoyance, knowing in advance, for example, when the Russian priest would be visiting his village. As healer, protector, and clairvoyant, therefore, the old man demonstrated to Veniaminov's satisfaction that he was a "shaman, not an ordinary person, at least."

When the priest finally met the shaman, he learned that shortly after his baptism in 1795 Smirennikov had been visited by two spirits who related that they had been sent by God to instruct him in Christian teachings. Almost daily, over the next thirty years, the spirits appeared to him. Although they provided Christian instruction, the spirits told him not to listen to the Russians or to confess his sins to their priests. Without access to priests, teachers, or the Bible, Veniaminov found, the old man had learned in detail the Christian stories of creation, the fall of the angels, the tree of knowledge of good and evil, Cain and Abel, Noah, Abraham, John the Baptist, and the annunciation of the birth of Christ. To Veniaminov's surprise, therefore, he found that Smirennikov had also become an informed Christian through the mysterious intervention of the two spirits.

As in other situations of intercultural contact, Veniaminov's meeting with the Aleut shaman raised the problem of alternative claims on sacred knowledge and power. Certainly, the Christian character of Smirennikov's religious knowledge assured the Russian priest that the shaman was not drawing his spiritual knowledge and extraordinary power from demons. Although Veniaminov raised this possibility of demonic influence, he became convinced that the Aleut shaman's spirits provided confirmation rather than competition for his Christian gospel. "When I preached," Veniaminov recalled, "he was the first to confirm the truth of my words in the tone of a person conversant with the Holy Writ." The two spirits, according to Smirennikov, were even prepared to reveal themselves to the Russian priest, although they chastised him for his curiosity: "What does he want? Does he consider us demons? If he insists, he can come and converse with us." Realizing that his meeting with the spirits would be motivated by idle curiosity, Veniaminov declined this invitation. "Why should I want to see them personally," he concluded, "when their teaching is Christian teaching."

Accordingly, the Russian priest was prepared to recognize the essentially Christian character of the Aleut shaman. However, Veniaminov still insisted on asserting the ultimate authority of the Russian Orthodox Church over religious knowledge and action. As he informed his bishop, Veniaminov issued the following ruling to Smirennikov:

> I see that the spirits which appear to thee are not demons and therefore I instruct thee to listen to their teachings and instructions, as long as these do not contradict the teachings I deliver in assembly; just tell those who ask your advice about the future and request your help to address themselves directly to God, as He is common Father to all. I do not forbid thee to cure the sick, but ask thee to tell those thou curest that thou doest so not by thy own powers, but by the power of God and to instruct them to pray diligently and thank the Sole God. I do not forbid thee to teach either, but only instruct thee to confine this teaching to the minors.

In this formulation, therefore, the Aleut shaman was allowed to maintain his conversation with the spirits and to continue advising, healing, and teaching the people. However, Veniaminov concluded, "I told the other Aleuts who were present not to call him a Shaman, not to ask him for favors, but to ask God." Apparently, Smirennikov agreed with this resolution, since he had never wanted to be a shaman and the spirits had always taught him to pray with a pure heart to God alone. The bishop, however, was skeptical. His response a year later ordered Veniaminov to return to the shaman's village to meet with the spirits. When he arrived in the village, however, Veniaminov learned that Smirennikov had died. Nevertheless, however briefly, the Russian priest had found in the Aleut shaman a collaborator in the work of advancing Christianity in Alaska.[11]

Although the success of his mission depended upon interventions in local language, Veniaminov expressed some ambivalence about his attempts to standardize a written Aleut. "I considered the writing of the Fox-Aleut grammar an almost useless task," he observed. "The Aleuts do not need it. They can communicate with each other without the grammar." Although it was unnecessary for effective verbal communication, the real problem with the grammar was that it was rapidly becoming obsolete under the impact of Russian colonization. Linked with Russian culture, colonization, and trade, Veniaminov's mission was entangled with forces that were eroding the indigenous language he was working to preserve through his Christian texts and scholarly research. The Aleuts did not need a grammar for their dying language, he observed; and "Foreigners do not need it either." In the end, he imagined that only European scholars would find the grammar useful "for speculations about origins of that language and for historical conjectures." Ironically, therefore, Veniaminov's efforts to translate, standardize, and preserve an indigenous language turned it into a historical artifact.[12]

After ten years on Unalaska Island, Veniaminov relocated in 1834 to New Archangel on the island of Sitka, off the Alaskan mainland, where he served as priest, teacher, and missionary to the indigenous people, the Tlingit, who had adamantly resisted Christian conversion. Again, he began his work by mastering the Tlingit language, but he achieved little success in gaining converts. Two years later Veniaminov traveled by ship to California to stay at the Russian settlement at Fort Ross, founded in 1811, which had never been visited by a priest. While in California, he also visited the Spanish Franciscan missions of San Rafael, San José, Santa Clara, and San Francisco de Assisi. The Russian had never seen a Roman Catholic; the Roman Catholics were equally intrigued in encountering a priest of the Orthodox Church. Impressed by the prosperity of the missions, with their fields, orchards, and workshops, Veniaminov was particularly interested in observing Roman Catholic ritual. "I saw the burial ceremony and the christening of children," he recalled, "and was four times at Mass and saw all the sacred vessels and vestments." In spite of liturgical differences, however, Veniaminov found common ground with Roman Catholic monks, whom he described as "most learned and virtuous." When he finally returned to the island of Sitka, Veniaminov went into his own workshop and made several barrel organs for the mission of San Francisco de Assisi. Given the long history of Russian animosity toward the Roman Catholic Church, Veniaminov's encounter with the Spanish Franciscan monks of California was a remarkable instance of mutual recognition.[13]

Perhaps his observations about the relative prosperity of the Roman Catholic missions in California inspired Veniaminov to journey in 1838 to St. Petersburg to appeal for financial support. While the case was before the Holy Synod, his wife died. Taking monastic vows and entering the Black clergy, Veniaminov was elected by the Holy Synod as the first bishop of a new diocese. As the bishop of Kamchatka, the Kurile, and the Aleutian Islands, Veniaminov returned to Sitka in 1841, now with the monastic name of Innocent. Continuing his commitment to education, Bishop Innocent still sought to cultivate a Christian interiority of the heart. As he wrote to one of his priests,

> In order to influence the heart one must speak from the heart, because our lips speak from the plenitude of the heart. Therefore, only he who is filled and overflowing with faith and love can have eloquence and wisdom which are not going to be resisted by the hearts of the listeners.

When Bishop Innocent left in 1851 to serve as archbishop of a new see in the Yakutsk region of eastern Siberia, he reported that nearly half of the indigenous population of Russian America had converted to Christianity. Under the leadership of Bishop Innocent, the Russian Orthodox Church had become firmly established in North America.

In 1867, Bishop Innocent was chosen as the metropolitan of Moscow, the highest office in the Russian Orthodox Church. During that year Alaska was sold to the United States. Rather than mourning the loss of the Russian colony in America, Bishop Innocent embraced the sale of Alaska as a new opportunity for the missionary expansion of Russian Orthodoxy. Characteristically, Bishop Innocent regarded this new opportunity for the Russian Orthodox mission as a matter of mastering the local language of the indigenous population. However, as the United States expanded across the continent, the relevant indigenous language became English. Recommending that the residence of the bishop should be moved from Sitka to San Francisco, Bishop Innocent specified that a new bishop should be appointed, with new clergy and staff, and that only those speaking English should be selected. The liturgy and other divine services, he advised, should all be conducted in English with the relevant sacred texts translated into English. "The courses in the newly established schools for training of missionaries and priests in San Francisco and elsewhere," he proposed, "should be taught in the English language and not in the Russian language, which sooner or later will be replaced by the English language." Ironically, therefore, Bishop Innocent saw the Russian language, like the Aleut language, as destined to disappear in North America. The end of Russian America, however, did not signal the end of the Russian Orthodox Church in America. The Russian Orthodox Church would survive and even flourish, Bishop Innocent anticipated, but only if it successfully adapted to the dominant English-speaking culture of the United States.[14]

23

American Zion

In 1578 Queen Elizabeth of England instructed her navigators "to discover and take possession of such remote, heathen, and barbarous lands, as were not actually possessed by any Christian prince or people." For this Protestant queen, therefore, Christianity represented an entitlement to land, a right not recognized as being held by heathens or barbarians. Unlike the Spanish Catholic conquerors, however, who claimed land under the authority of the pope, English Protestants relied upon two sources of authority—the Bible and natural law. In a sermon to a group of Puritans departing for America in 1630, the Reverend John Cotton (1585–1652) combined both the Bible and natural law in celebrating "God's Promise to His Plantations." "It is a principle of nature," Cotton declared, "that in vacant soil, he that takes possession of it, and bestows culture and husbandry upon it, his right it is." By this reading of natural law, therefore, land could be considered vacant not only if it was uninhabited, but also if the inhabitants did not plant and cultivate the land through settled agriculture. According to English commentators, Native Americans did not cultivate the land. As the explorer Thomas Harriot observed in 1585, "The ground they never fatten with muck dung or any other thing, neither plough nor dig it as we in England." Since Native Americans reportedly lived by hunting, fishing, and gathering food, rather than by settled agriculture, their land was defined as vacant in terms of this understanding of natural law.[1]

This principle of nature, however, was ultimately based on the Bible. As John Cotton reminded the Puritans, "The ground of this is from the Grand Charter given to Adam and his posterity, Genesis 1:28, 'Multiply, and replenish the earth, and subdue it.'" Most European Protestants of the era understood this biblical passage—"Be fruitful and multiply"—to refer to human sexual activity and procreation. In Germany, for example, the Protestant reformers Martin Luther and Philip Melanchthon had used

Genesis 1:28 to argue that the Roman Catholic promotion of celibacy violated divine law. Only in England, where Genesis 1:28 had traditionally been chanted as a prayer over fields, was the passage associated with agricultural rather than sexual fertility. In colonizing North America, English Protestants consistently invoked Genesis 1:28 as a warrant to "fill the earth and subdue it" by means of settled agriculture. In staking their Christian claim to what they insisted was vacant land, these Protestant colonizers did not set up a cross, enact a ceremony, or recite a ritual formula, as in the *Requirement,* in the presence of the indigenous people in the New World. Instead, they simply built houses and planted gardens. However, since those acts of establishing settled agriculture were done in accordance with the laws of God and nature, they should also be understood as rituals of possession that asserted a Christian entitlement to land.[2]

In his 1630 sermon, Reverend John Cotton advised the Puritans to deal kindly with Native Americans. "Offend not the poor natives," he exhorted, "but as you partake in their land, so make them partakers of your precious faith." Seventeenth-century English settlements in North America generally proclaimed a religious mission. In addition to planting gardens, the settlers also declared an intention to plant Christianity. However, little was actually done to extend the Christian faith to Native Americans. In the Puritan Massachusetts Bay Colony, the Reverend John Eliot (1604–90), who established "praying towns" for Indians, was an exception. Beginning his work with official sponsorship from the General Court, Eliot was not merely interested in conveying the message of Christian faith. "Religion would not consist of a mere receiving of the word," Eliot declared. "Practical religion will throw down their heathenish idols and the sachem's tyrannical monarchy." In other words, Eliot proclaimed a mission that promised to free Native Americans from the "superstition" of their traditional religion and the "tyranny" of their traditional chiefs. That religious and political freedom, Eliot argued, could only be achieved by putting on the "yoke of Christ."[3]

Within the "praying towns," Native Americans were introduced to this new freedom of serving Christ not only by praying, listening to the Bible, and cultivating faith, but also by learning the Protestant disciplines of building permanent houses, cultivating the land, and wearing English clothing. As John Eliot insisted, "We labor and work in building, planting, clothing ourselves, etc., and they doe not." In order for Native Americans to be converted to "Christian civility," therefore, they had to adopt certain styles of English clothing, which included short hair, cobbled shoes, and a working-class suit; they had to submit to the demands of agricultural labor; and they had to live within the confines of a Protestant "praying town." These were the outer signs of an inner religious conversion. By 1676, however, most of the "praying towns" had been dismantled in the wake of a disastrous war, known as King Philip's War, in which Christian Native Americans allied themselves with other Native American forces against the Puritan colonists. Subsequently, New England Puritans showed little interest in missions to the Indians.

Puritans of the Massachusetts Bay Colony were more directly concerned with preserving the religious freedom they had found in America. Objecting to the centralized authority of the Church of England, which had been formalized in the Act of Supremacy in 1534 under King Henry VIII, Puritanism had begun as a reform movement. At the end of the sixteenth century, Puritans were seeking to purify the Church of England of heretical clergy, unwarranted ceremony, and the ecclesiastical hierarchy of bishops. Adopting a congregational model of church polity, in which membership was comprised of individuals who declared their personal experience of grace, and leadership was elected from among those members, the Puritans came into conflict with the established Church of England. Under the Stuarts (1603–49), several congregational groups separated from the Church of England and departed for the Netherlands or the New World. Although the Puritans of New England had left England with a royal charter, they nevertheless saw their migration as an exodus from captivity in Pharaoh's Egypt, as a liberation "from Egypt land through seas with watery walls." As the Puritan historian Edward Johnson declared in 1654, these Puritans had escaped captivity in the Old World "to rebuild the most glorious Edifice of Mount Zion in a Wilderness, knowing this is the place where the Lord will create a new Heaven and a new Earth in new Churches and a new Commonwealth." Liberated from bondage to the Old World, the New England Puritans, like many other European settlers in North America, rejoiced in the religious, political, and economic freedom of the New.[4]

CITY UPON A HILL

Puritan leaders of the Massachusetts Bay Colony imagined that their new Zion in the American wilderness was a covenant community, a "chosen people," like the ancient Israelites, in a special bond, agreement, or relationship with God. In a sermon delivered on the ship carrying them to America, their first governor, John Winthrop (1588–1649), declared, "We shall find that the God of Israel is among us." The covenant between the God of Israel and this new chosen people in America, however, entailed both a divine promise and a divine threat. If they ordered their lives, churches, and government according to divine law, they could expect to be rewarded with God's favor and blessings. However, if they violated the terms and conditions of their covenant with God, they could only expect to be punished. In the Puritan imagination, God's "chosen people" stood directly under divine judgment. The hardships they experienced in building a settlement in America were signs of God's involvement with this covenant community. Long after the Massachusetts Bay Colony had been established, this link between divine grace and divine punishment continued to define the Puritans' understanding of their covenant with God. As the Puritan theologian Increase Mather wrote in 1675, "God has covenanted with his people that sanctified afflictions shall be their portion." Divine providence and divine judgment merged in the Puritan understanding of their Christian covenant with God. "Christ by a wonderful Providence caused as it were New Jerusalem to come down from Heaven," Increase Mather concluded. "He dwells in this place; therefore we may conclude that he will scourge us." In this confidence of divine grace and anxiety before divine wrath, Puritans in New England defined their covenant with God.[5]

Puritan leaders hoped that their covenant community in New England would stand as an exemplary model for other settlements, but they also feared that failure would bring their religious and political faith into disrepute in the eyes of the world. Accordingly, John Winthrop exhorted Puritan settlers to remember that their holy experiment in the New World was being closely watched by the Old. "We must Consider that we shall be as a City upon a Hill," he proposed, "the eyes of all people are upon us." Twenty years after the first migration, the Puritan theologian Peter Bulkeley echoed this concern:

> We are as a city set upon a hill, in open view of all the earth, the eyes of the world are upon us, because we profess ourselves to be a people in covenant with God, and therefore not only the Lord our God, with whom we have made covenant, but heaven and earth, angels and men, that are witness to

our profession, will cry shame upon us if we walk contrary to the covenant which we have professed and promised to walk in.[6]

In these terms, therefore, Puritans of Massachusetts saw themselves at the center of a divine drama displaying the covenant community before the world. Ironically, however, the Puritan community was largely ignored back in England. Nevertheless, the conviction that the Puritan settlers were a community in covenant with God and exposed to the critical scrutiny of the world became a standard theme in New England theology.

In general, Puritans looked for two signs indicating that a person was a member of the covenant community. First, the personal experience of conversion, an inner experience of the transforming power of divine grace, marked an individual's entrance into the covenant. Subscribing to the Calvinist position worked out at the Synod of Dort in 1617, Puritans assumed that this conversion experience resulted from an unmerited gift of grace. Rejecting any reliance on human will, individual decision, or personal merit, they reaffirmed the Calvinist doctrine of predestination. Due to the original sin that pervaded and corrupted human nature, all humanity deserved eternal damnation; but God demonstrated divine mercy by selecting a few to receive the undeserved gift of grace. Accordingly, Puritans searched their hearts, minds, and actions for evidence of that gift. No evidence, however, could ultimately confirm that a person was among the elect. In fact, if a person did find proof of divine election, that sense of certainty could just as easily be interpreted as evidence that he or she suffered from the sin of pride and was therefore destined for damnation. In this Puritan dilemma, a false sense of assurance was avoided by constant scrutiny of the conscience. As the Puritan theologian Arthur Hildersam proposed, "It were better for a man to be vexed with continuall doubts and feares, than to be lulled asleepe with such an assurance."

Although no evidence could produce final certainty, Puritans persisted in agonized soul-searching for signs of grace. In rare cases, this uncertainty was unbearable. John Winthrop, for instance, wrote about a woman in the Boston congregation who was experiencing intense distress about her spiritual state. He recounted that "one day she took her little infant and threw it into a well, and then came into the house and said now she was sure she would be damned." To some extent, the Puritans of New England resolved this dilemma by making personal conversion a public event. To become a member of the church, an individual had to stand before the congregation and give an account of his or her personal experience of God's grace. If the church members acknowledged this testimony as legitimate, then the individual was admitted into the covenant community with full rights to participate in its sacrament of Communion. By granting public authentication to personal accounts of conversion, therefore, Puritan congregations eased some of the tension surrounding the question of salvation.

A second sign of election was found in the public commitment to a calling, or vocation, that took the form of disciplined and productive work. Like Catholic monastic communities in the European Middle Ages, the Puritans of New England held that "to work is to pray." Rather than retreating from the world, however, Puritans were called to live a pure, disciplined, and productive life by working in human society. Work became a test of faith. Instead of avoiding the worldly temptations of pride, greed, or lust, Puritans were called to confront and conquer them in their vocations. As John Winthrop put it, "For such trials as fall within the compass of our callings, it is better to arm and withstand them than to avoid and shun them." A calling, therefore, was an opportunity to demonstrate ascetic self-denial and spiritual discipline in the midst of the world. It was also a commitment to serving the community. True faith found its expression in a calling that was of service to others. According to Cotton, God approved of those who "live by faith in vocations, in that faith, in serving God, serves men, and in serving men, serves God." However, Cotton warned, "if thou has no calling, tending to the public good, thou art an unclean beast." Along with the personal experience of conversion, therefore, the public commitment to a useful vocation was a sign of inclusion within the Puritan covenant community.

In the interest of the public good, God had mandated a hierarchy of vocations. "God Almighty in his most holy and wise providence," John Winthrop declared, "has so disposed the Condition of mankind, as in all times some must be rich, some poor, some high and eminent in power and dignity, others mean and in subjection." While the rich found themselves in vocations through which they could develop the virtues of temperance, mercy, and charity, the poor labored in vocations that required learning the virtues of faith, patience, and obedience. When all these moral virtues were activated, Winthrop concluded, the social order was a harmony of mutual dependency in which "every man may have need of each other."

Clearly, this vision of social harmony lent a sacred aura to inequalities of wealth and power in the Puritan communities of New England. However, the hierarchical model of social harmony governed by a spiritual aristocracy, who were endowed with divine "gifts and experience," was the Puritan ideal of God's government. "Theocracy," as John Cotton and other Puritan leaders held, was "the best form of government in the commonwealth, as well as in the church." In this theocratic system, the role of the church was to prepare "fit instruments both to rule and to choose rulers." Only full members of the covenant community were fit for political participation. By contrast, Puritans found democracy to be lacking in biblical precedent and contrary to Paul's injunction in Romans that "civil authorities were appointed by God" (Rom. 13:1). "A democracy," according to John Winthrop, was "the meanest and worst of all forms of government." Although certain democratic impulses were evident in the practice of voting for ministers of congregational churches and voting for magistrates of New England towns, the vote was reserved for church members who had certified their inclusion within the covenant community.[7]

Although the Puritan covenant community was defined by these principles of inclusion—conversion and calling, communion and franchise—it was also reinforced by principles of exclusion. Rituals of exclusion, such as public humiliation, confinement, banishment, and execution, maintained the spiritual purity of the community. In particular, spiritual purity required the expulsion of the defiling influence of heretics. In trying to establish a theocratic society, Puritans were committed to a policy of religious intolerance. "I dare to take upon me to be the herald of New England," the Puritan Nathaniel Ward declared, "as far as to proclaim to the world in the name of our colony, that all Familists, Antinomians, Anabaptists, and other enthusiasts shall have the liberty to keep away from us; and such as will come, to be gone as fast as they can, the sooner the better."[8] In the first decade of the Massachusetts Bay Colony, Governor John Winthrop resorted to banishment as a ritual of exclusion in the cases of Roger Williams and Anne Hutchinson. In both instances, Winthrop banished Puritans who had argued that the Puritan establishment in the Massachusetts Bay Colony was not sufficiently pure.

According to Roger Williams (ca. 1603–83), the Puritan theocracy had tried "to pull God and Christ and Spirit out of Heaven, and subject them unto natural, sinful, inconstant men." Since they referred to purely spiritual states, Williams argued, the new Israel, the new Jerusalem, or the new Zion could not be established by human beings in America. Banished to Rhode Island, where he introduced a separation of church and state, Williams wrote to John Winthrop, "Abstract yourself with a holy violence from the Dung Heap of this Earth." In response, Winthrop described Rhode Island as the "cess pool of the world." Like Roger Williams, Anne Hutchinson (1591–1643) accused the Puritan establishment of spiritual impurity. Giving weekly Sunday lectures at her home, Hutchinson taught a radical spirituality based on the conviction that "the person of the Holy Ghost dwells in a justified person." When she examined the Puritan clergy from this spiritual perspective, she found only two who were part of the covenant of grace that led to salvation. All the rest, she argued, were damned because they relied upon the merit of good works rather than the Holy Spirit. During her trial for heresy in 1637, Anne Hutchinson attacked the colony's religious establishment. "God will ruin you," she warned, "and your posterity and this whole state." On behalf of the court, John Winthrop asked, "How do you know that it was God that did reveal these things to you, and not Satan?" Claiming an immediate revelation from God, Anne Hutchinson insisted that she knew these things by "the voice of his own spirit in my soul." Finding this claim to receiving direct revelations from God too much to tolerate, the court found Anne Hutchinson guilty of heresy, excommunicated her from the church, and banished her and her followers to Rhode Island. In working out a Christian theocracy in America, therefore, the Puritan establishment was entangled in controversies over spiritual purity and power, which it tried to resolve through rituals of exclusion.[9]

Although the banishment of Roger Williams and Anne Hutchinson attempted to resolve internal Puritan disputes, the policy of religious intolerance directed against missionaries of the Society of Friends, known as Quakers, represented an effort to exclude outsiders. The founder of the Society of Friends, George Fox (1624–91), was born in Leicestershire, England, and apprenticed as a shoemaker. Although Fox was of a serious religious disposition, he despaired of finding God in any of the existing churches. Unexpectedly, he began to have religious experiences that convinced him that any person could have direct access to God through the Holy Spirit. In rejecting the churches, Fox felt that he had found the Christ within. "When all my hopes in them and in all men were gone," Fox declared, "I heard a voice which said, 'There is one, even Christ Jesus,

that can speak to thy condition.'" Traveling around England preaching a
religious message based on this direct experience of God, George Fox was
ridiculed by crowds, beaten, and imprisoned. In 1652, he formed the
Society of Friends as a religious association dedicated to a mysticism of
the inner light. Fox promised that anyone who discovered this inner light
would find the indwelling power of Christ. "Now I was sent to turn people
from darkness to the light," he asserted, "that they might receive Christ
Jesus, for to as many as should receive him in his light, I saw that he would
give power to become the sons of God." In these terms, the early Quakers
cultivated a religious enthusiasm, a sense of spiritual power within themselves derived from the inner light of Christ.[10]

From the perspective of the Puritan establishment, the religious enthusiasm of the Quakers was a serious heresy, similar to the spiritual claims
made by Anne Hutchinson, that threatened the Christian foundation of
the Massachusetts Bay theocracy. Arriving in Massachusetts in 1656,
Quaker missionaries entered New England during a time of transition following the deaths of the first generation of Puritan leaders. As new
Puritan leaders emerged to reinforce the boundaries of the covenant community, they directed punitive measures against Quakers. The first two
Quaker missionaries, Mary Fisher and Ann Austin, were arrested in
Boston, stripped, searched for marks of witchcraft, and deported. When
other Quaker missionaries followed, New England magistrates drafted a
series of anti-Quaker laws. In this legislation, membership in the Society
of Friends was rendered a crime because Quakers met in small groups for
religious meetings and refused to take off their hats before magistrates. In
other words, Quakers allegedly defied the public authority of both church
and state. Those who entered the Massachusetts Bay Colony risked having their ears cut off or holes bored through their tongues with a hot iron
before being either banished or executed. Quakers tested these laws. One
Quaker leader declared, "All these as one come together in the moving
and power of the Lord to look your bloody laws in the face." Although he
was reluctant to resort to capital punishment, Governor Endicott nevertheless determined that it was necessary to maintain the integrity of the
theocracy. Other Puritans, however, were more enthusiastic about the
execution of Quakers. John Wilson, for example, was reported as
exclaiming, "Burn all the Quakers in the world."[11] This anti-Quaker campaign was halted, however, by the intervention of King Charles II, who
prohibited any form of corporal punishment of Quakers in the English

colonies. As the intensity of their legal persecution diminished, Quakers seemed to lose interest in Massachusetts. They found a more congenial home in Rhode Island and by 1681 in Pennsylvania, where the Quaker William Penn established a colony in which the Society of Friends could flourish in America.

The Puritan covenant community in America, therefore, depended upon both rituals of inclusion and rituals of exclusion. Constant vigilance was necessary to maintain the purity of the community. By monitoring the center and guarding the peripheries, leaders of the Puritan community imagined that they could create a pure domain of Christian faith, conduct, and social order in the world. By the 1650s, however, the covenant community was faced with a growing population of second-generation Puritans who had been baptized, but had not had the inner experience of conversion necessary for full membership in the church. At a general church council in 1662, a compromise was worked out that came to be known as the Half-Way Covenant. Under the terms of this compromise, the children of church members would be eligible for partial membership in Puritan churches even if they could not provide an acceptable testimony of conversion. Supported by covenant-renewal ceremonies in which the whole community was encouraged to participate, the Half-Way Covenant sought to broaden the base of the Puritan covenant community. However, by blurring the distinction between the converted and the unconverted, this compromise arguably led to the dissolution of the Puritan project in America.

SLAVE AND FREE

By stark contrast to the Puritan theocracy in New England, the forms of Christianity that emerged out of the American Revolution of 1776 were innovations in democracy. A new emphasis on individualism, anti-authoritarianism, freedom of association, and democratic participation infused the most popular Christian movements during the era of the early republic. The primary theorists of revolution, independence, and the new constitutional order of the United States were religious rationalists. Influenced by the philosophy of the European Enlightenment and the theology of deism, revolutionary leaders such as Benjamin Franklin (1706–90), Thomas Jefferson (1743–1826), James Madison (1751–1836), John Adams (1735–1826), and Thomas Paine (1737–1809) were committed to a rational Christianity. Imagining God as the designer and legislator of the universe, these revolutionary rationalists explored both the potential and limits of reason in matters of religion. Assuming that the existence of a divine architect of the universe could be inferred on rational grounds, they nevertheless held that God was beyond human comprehension. According to John Adams, for example, God was "an Essence that we know nothing of, in which Originally and necessarily reside all energy, all Power, all Capacity, all Activity, all Wisdom, all Goodness." The God of the rationalists, therefore, was not a personal deity, but an abstract essence. As divine architect and legislator, however, this unknowable God had organized the universe according to natural laws that could be discerned through reason.[12]

According to the rationalists, human beings had the rational ability and moral responsibility to organize civil society according to the pattern of natural law. Emphasizing the importance of moral reason in both religion and politics, they were skeptical of any claims to divine revelation. For the rationalists, the revealed doctrines of Christianity had to be subjected to the tests of reason. Thomas Jefferson, for example, produced an edited version of the Christian New Testament in which he carefully extracted only the words of Jesus to which he could give rational assent. As Jefferson explained, he was able to extract the philosophy of Jesus "by cutting verse by verse out of the printed book and arranging the matter which is evidently his and which is easily distinguished as diamonds in a dunghill." Out of the "dunghill" of revelation, therefore, Thomas Jefferson thought he could recover a rational moral philosophy that he described as "the most sublime and benevolent code of morals which has ever been offered to man."[13] In a more extreme version of this rationalist critique of revelation, Thomas Paine attacked any revealed religion on the grounds that it tended to suppress the free exercise of reason under the weight of orthodoxy and tradition. According to Thomas Paine, "every national church or religion has established itself by pretending some special mission from God, communicated to certain individuals—as if the way to God were not open to every man alike."[14] Such churches were nothing more than "human inventions, set up to terrify and enslave mankind and monopolize power and profit." In the interest of freedom, therefore, religious rationalists declared independence from slavery to religious dogmas, institutions, and traditions based on revelation.

American rationalists also saw a more positive role for religion in maintaining public order, inspired by Enlightenment political philosophers such as Charles Louis Montesquieu (1689–1755), who held that "religion and the civil laws should principally contribute to making men good citizens." Like civil legislation, religion restrained social deviance. According to Benjamin Franklin, a great part of humanity "consists of weak and ignorant men and women . . . who have need of the motives of religion to restrain them from vice." Agreeing that religion had a positive function as an instrument of social control, Thomas Jefferson observed that there were religions "of various kinds, indeed, but all good enough; all sufficient to preserve peace and order." As they imagined the role of religion in a democratic polity, therefore, the rationalists sought to establish a freedom from religion—by guaranteeing the free exercise of reason, opinion, and conscience—and a freedom for religion to flourish beyond government control in the hope that religion would contribute to making peaceful, disciplined, and productive citizens.[15]

Within this new political order, Thomas Jefferson expected that some form of rational Christianity would become dominant in the United States. He speculated that perhaps Unitarianism, which stressed personal responsibility, the humanity of Jesus, and the unity of God against the doctrine of the Trinity, might be that rational religion. Instead, an intensely emotional and dramatically experiential type of Christianity flourished. Although the older Anglican (or Episcopalian), Presbyterian, and Congregationalist denominations continued to have a place in the Protestant landscape, American Christianity increasingly came to be dominated by the more recent Methodist and Baptist churches, which vigorously promoted that experiential religion. Anticipated by the transatlantic revivals of the 1740s, known as the "Great Awakening" in America, the religious revivals of the early republic also made Christianity a personal matter of religious conversion. In starting his reform movement within the Church of England, John Wesley (1703–91), the founder of Methodism, had located Christianity in the personal experience of "the heart strangely warmed." By contrast to this intimately personal experience, questions of Christian doctrine, ritual, and organization were relatively insignificant. As Wesley observed:

> Methodists do not impose in order to their admission any opinions whatever. Let them hold particular or general redemption, absolute or conditional decrees; let them be churchmen or dissenters, Presbyterians or Independents [i.e., Congregationalists], it is no obstacle. Let them choose

one mode of baptism or another, it is no bar to their admission. The Presbyterian may be Presbyterian still; the Independent and Anabaptist use his own worship still. So may the Quaker; and none will contend with him about it. They think and let think. One condition, and only one is required—a real desire to save the soul. Where this is, it is enough; they desire no more; they lay stress upon nothing else; they only ask, "Is thy heart herein as my heart? If it be, give me thy hand."[16]

In colonial America of the 1740s, prominent evangelists—George Whitefield (1714–70), Jonathan Edwards (1703–58), Gilbert Tennant (1703–64), and others—exhorted their congregations to experience that personal conversion of the heart. After the American Revolution, this distinctive Christianity of the heart, rather than Jefferson's rational Christianity, swept through the new democracy.

Between 1780 and 1830, the United States underwent dramatic social changes, marked by exponential increases in population, agricultural development, industrial growth, and territorial expansion, that were accompanied by changes in religion. Adapting opportunities provided by new frontier settlements, more efficient transportation, and an expanding print media, itinerant preachers created a Christian communication network that was most evident in the camp meeting revivals that inspired widespread enthusiasm throughout the United States. With their emphasis on intense personal experience, which was often demonstrated through emotional displays of religious fervor, such as fainting, falling, shaking, jerking, shouting, crying, laughing, and even barking, these camp meetings became occasions for individuals to participate directly in the Christian drama of salvation. The prominent Methodist preacher Peter Cartwright (1785–1872) described his own experience of conversion at a camp meeting:

On the Saturday evening of said meeting, I went, with weeping multitudes and bowed before the stand, and earnestly prayed for mercy. In the midst of a solemn struggle of soul, an impression was made on my mind, as though a voice said to me, "Thy sins are all forgiven thee." Divine light flashed all round me, unspeakable joy sprung up in my soul. I rose to my feet, opened my eyes, and it really seemed as if I was in heaven; the trees, the leaves on them, and everything seemed, and I really thought were, praising God. My mother raised the shout, my Christian friends crowded around me and joined me in praising God; and though I have been since then, in many instances, unfaithful, yet I have never, for one moment, doubted that the Lord did, then and there, forgive my sins and give me religion.[17]

In cultivating this intense personal experience of forgiveness, the revivals marked a shift in Christian doctrine. Rejecting the Calvinist doctrine of predestination, Methodist and Baptist preachers promoted an understanding of Christian salvation based on personal decision, emotional engagement, and immediate access to spiritual power. In both style and substance, therefore, Christianity was recast during the early republic as a democratic religion.

In the democracy of the United States, however, the enslavement of African Americans remained a serious anomaly. Proclaiming their own liberty from tyranny and oppression, the framers of the U.S. Constitution had supported the institution of slavery. Reflecting the racial prejudice of his era, Thomas Jefferson held that African Americans were "inferior to the whites in the endowments of body and mind."[18] Like children and women, African Americans were excluded from voting rights under the original Constitution on the grounds that they supposedly lacked sufficient rationality and independence of will. Although excluded from democratic participation, African Americans were nevertheless drawn in increasingly large numbers to Methodist and Baptist churches, where many found a kind of spiritual freedom even in the midst of slavery.

Although the ambivalent relationship between Christianity and slavery can be traced back to the New Testament, it was particularly evident in America. The orthodox Calvinist position on slavery was clearly stated by the Dutch Reformed Church at the seventeenth-century Synod of Dort: slaves who converted to Christianity "ought to enjoy equal right of liberty with other Christians." In colonial America, however, Protestant slaveowners resisted the proposition that baptized slaves ought to be freed. As the Anglican Thomas Secker insisted in 1740, "The Scripture, far from making any Alteration in Civil Rights, expressly directs, that every Man abide in the condition wherein he is called, with great Indifference of mind concerning outward circumstances." This implicit distinction between religious rights and civil rights was established in a series of colonial laws specifying that conversion and baptism granted slaves the religious right to participate in a Christian church, but no civil right to freedom from slavery. Although it was clear that American religious and political leaders had no intention of freeing Christian slaves, colonial enactments banning African American Christians from preaching, assembling for prayer, building a house of worship, or conducting public funerals raised questions about the scope of religious rights gained by conversion and baptism.[19]

Even in the 1830s, there were white clergy who thought that making African Americans better Christians was a way to make them better slaves. For example, the Presbyterian Charles Colcock Jones (1804–63), a leader of interdenominational missions to slaves in the South, tried to use the Christian gospel as an instrument of social control. In his *Catechism for Colored Persons,* published in 1834, Jones exhorted slaves "to count their Masters 'worthy of all honor,' as those whom God has placed over them in this world." He warned slaves to "serve their masters as faithfully behind their backs as before their faces" because "God is present to see, if their masters are not." In these terms, therefore, Christianity represented an invisible system of behavioral controls. But as Charles Colcock Jones found, however, slaves were not generally responsive to this Christian gospel of slavery. For example, while delivering a sermon to a group of slaves on the New Testament theme "Servants, obey your masters," he was met with disbelief. As Jones recalled:

> I was preaching to a large congregation on the Epistle to Philemon; and when I insisted on fidelity and obedience as Christian virtues in servants, and upon the authority of Paul, condemned the practice of running away, one-half of my audience deliberately rose up and walked off with themselves; and those who remained looked anything but satisfied with the preacher or his doctrine. After dismission, there was no small stir among them; some solemnly declared that there was no such Epistle in the Bible; others, that I preached to please the masters; others, that they did not care if they never heard me preach again.[20]

On rare occasions, African Americans drew on Christian resources to inspire and mobilize revolts against slavery. For example, in 1800 Gabriel Prosser (ca. 1775–1800) was inspired by his reading of the Bible to assume the role of the "Black Samson." Claiming a divine mandate to establish a black kingdom in Virginia, Gabriel led an army of a thousand slaves in an unsuccessful attack on Richmond. In 1822 Denmark Vessey (ca. 1767–1822), an African American Methodist, was inspired by the biblical model of Joshua and the battle of Jericho to lead a slave revolt. Proclaiming that he was guided by the Lord in the form of an angel with a sword, Vessey organized an attack on Charleston, but his plans were exposed and he and his followers were executed. In 1831 the Baptist preacher Nat Turner (1800–1831) declared a Christian holy war against slavery in Southampton, Virginia, that resulted in hundreds of deaths and executions. As he was led to the gallows to be hanged, Nat Turner reportedly observed, "Was not Christ crucified?" These three revolts, therefore, suggested that African American leaders—a black Samson, a black Joshua, a black Messiah—could translate Christian resources into political action against the conditions of slavery. Rather than a system of social control, therefore, Christianity appeared in these slave revolts as an impetus for liberation.

Although actual slave insurrections were rare, the biblical myth of liberation from slavery in Egypt informed the sermons, hymns, and devotions of an emerging African American Christianity. Popular religious songs— "When Moses Smote the Water," "Did Not Old Pharaoh Get Lost," "Oh Mary, Don't You Weep (Pharaoh's Army Got Drownded)," and "Go Down, Moses"—developed this theme of liberation from captivity.

> Go down, Moses
> Way down in Egyptland
> Tell old Pharaoh
> To let my people go.

Jesus Christ appeared in African American songs and sermons as a righteous man who suffered with silent courage under injustice. "They crucified my Lord," as one hymn recalled, "and he never said a mumbling word." But Jesus was also "King Jesus," the eschatological deliverer, whose imminent return from his throne in heaven was anticipated as the ultimate liberation from slavery. As promised in the book of Revelation, King Jesus would appear on a white horse, with a rainbow around his shoulders, to redeem his people. "Ride on King Jesus!" one hymn exclaimed; "No man can hinder him!" In the rhythms and words of this sacred music, an entire Christian story—the exodus from Egypt, the crucifixion of Jesus, and the apocalypse of freedom from this world—could be compressed into a single hymn: "Jesus Christ, He died for me, / Way down in Egyptland. / Jesus Christ, He set me free, / Way down in

Egyptland." As captain of the "Old Ship Zion," King Jesus—crucified, yet triumphant—was coming soon to liberate all those who were enslaved in Pharaoh's Egypt and "carry us all home."[21]

Although forced relocation, the dispersal of communities, and the oppression of slavery radically disrupted African religious heritage, African American Christianity nevertheless displayed some continuity with Africa. As the historian of slave religion Albert J. Raboteau observed, "The African heritage of singing, dancing, spirit possession, and magic continued to influence Afro-American spirituals, ring shouts, and folk beliefs."[22] In dramatic ritual performances and ecstatic spiritual experiences, African American Christianity developed a distinctive character. Likewise, in other slave societies of the New World—in Brazil, Haiti, Jamaica, and elsewhere—new forms of Christianity emerged that drew upon both African and Christian religious resources. Under the bondage of slavery, Christianity provided a religious vocabulary for liberation in the formation of supportive communities and social networks. In response to the dehumanizing conditions of slavery, Christian churches represented a recovery of humanity.

As black churches developed and black clergy emerged in leadership roles, African American Christianity became an avenue for religious independence. Growing out of the work of black Methodists under the leadership of Richard Allen (1760–1831) in Philadelphia, the African Methodist Episcopal Church was formed in 1816 as the first independent black denomination in the United States. In 1824 a second denomination, the African Methodist Episcopal Zion Church, was formed in New York. Although these independent churches grew rapidly in the North, they also sent missions to the American South, competing there with Methodist and Baptist churches for the religious affiliation of slaves and freed blacks. Increasingly, these evangelical churches lent their support to the movement for the abolition of slavery in the United States. The Anti-Slavery Society, organized by William Lloyd Garrison (1805–79), for example, drew considerable support from Methodists and Baptists. Nevertheless, Christianity continued to maintain an ambivalent relationship with the institution of slavery. As noted, Christianity both provided legitimation for slavery and promised liberation from slavery. Poised between accommodation and protest, however, African American Christianity created a distinctive religious space of freedom in the midst of oppression.

LATTER-DAY SAINTS

The evangelical revivals of the early nineteenth century generated more than merely a new Christian enthusiasm. They also gave impetus to Christian experiments in social reform. In addition to the Anti-Slavery Society, evangelical crusades for temperance, women's rights, public schools, prison reform, and other causes attracted Methodists and Baptists. More dramatic social reforms, however, appeared in utopian communities. For example, the United Society of Believers in Christ's Second Appearing, who came to be known as the Shakers, established a network of communes in the United States. Founded by Mother Anne Lee (1736–84), who was held to embody the feminine aspect of God, the Shakers were dedicated to simplicity, celibacy, and the communal ownership of property. In keeping with broader Christian concerns of the period, the Shakers looked back to an original Christianity and forward to the imminent return of Christ.

As they sought to recover the simple Christian life of the earliest disciples of Jesus, the Shakers were engaged in a project similar to other attempts at restoration. Rejecting the ecclesiastical organization of all Christian denominations, a series of American reformers insisted on restoring what they understood as "primitive" Christianity. Between 1790 and 1815, they adopted the title "Christians" or "Disciples of Christ" to signal this restoration of the original Christianity, which had allegedly been distorted by church doctrines, rituals, and leadership structures. According to a popular song of the Christian restoration movement, the existing churches had produced a "World Turned Upside Down." To restore the proper order of the world, as one leader declared, all the churches had to be rejected in favor of "Bible government, Christian equality, and the Christian name." Under the leadership of Barton Stone (1772–1844) and Alexander Campbell (1788–1866), this movement for Christian restoration developed into a distinctive denomination, the Disciples of Christ, which gained a large following, becoming the fifth largest Protestant denomination in the United States. More generally, however, the restorationist quest to reestablish an original Christianity characterized many American Christian initiatives in the early nineteenth century.[23]

At the same time, in defining themselves as "Believers in Christ's Second Appearing," the Shakers joined other Christians during the era who were looking for signs of the return of Christ in the immediate future.

The most popular millennial movement was inspired by the predictions of the Baptist William Miller (1782–1849). Having converted to the piety of the evangelical revivals in 1815, Miller devoted himself to farming and Bible study. He was particularly absorbed with the problem of calculating Christ's second coming on the basis of the symbolism of the biblical prophets. Based on a passage in the book of Daniel, which he subjected to elaborate mathematical calculations, Miller determined in the 1820s that the return of Christ would occur around 1843. Ordained as a Baptist minister, Miller lectured at churches and conducted revivals. While giving a series of lectures in Massachusetts, Miller met the Baptist preacher Joshua V. Himes, who assumed the management of publicity, publications, and camp meetings for the millennial campaign. Under the direction of Joshua Himes, the millennial prediction of William Miller became the basis for the mass movement known as the Millerites.

As 1843 approached, Miller gained an enormous following throughout the United States for his message that the end of the world was at hand. He urged his listeners to recognize that they lived in the last days: "At this dread moment, look! The clouds have burst asunder; the heavens appear; the great white throne is in sight! Amazement fills the Universe with awe! He comes! He comes! Behold the Savior comes!"[24] With the passing of 1843, however, the leaders of the movement recalculated the prophecy for the Second Coming and decided on October 22, 1844, for the end of the world. In preparation, many quit their occupations, left their homes, and wore white ascension robes to prepare for the "rapture of the saints" that would carry believing Christians into the air with the second coming of Christ. When the prophecy failed, the Millerite movement dispersed. However, although temporarily discredited by the "Great Disappointment," millennial anticipation of the return of Christ continued to be a significant feature of American Christianity. Expelled from the Baptist church, William Miller formed a small Adventist church to keep alive his millennial vision until his death in 1849. By the end of the nineteenth century, new churches had emerged—Seventh-Day Adventists, Jehovah's Witnesses—to revive the Millerite expectation of the end of the world and the millennial reign of Christ.

The most successful new Christian movement to be forged out of this context of revival and reform was the Church of Jesus Christ of Latter-day Saints, which came to be known as the Mormons. This new church embodied both the impulse to restore an original Christianity and the assumption that the world was in its latter days prior to the return of Christ. Restoration and millennium, however, were both clearly centered in America. The founder of the church, Joseph Smith, Jr. (1805–44), represented himself as an American Christian prophet who was aided by extraordinary revelations. In 1820, as Smith later recalled, he had been praying alone when he was seized by a strange power, surrounded by a brilliant light, and confronted by God the Father and the Savior, who warned him that the teachings of all existing churches were false. During the following decade, by Joseph Smith's account, he was able to recover the truth of Christianity through the miraculous discovery and translation of ancient texts, inscribed on golden plates, that came to be known as the *Book of Mormon*.

Published in 1830, the *Book of Mormon* supplemented the biblical history of the world, the people of Israel, and the early Christian church by providing a new account of the sacred history of America. According to that account, around 600 B.C.E. a group of ancient Israelites were directed by God to emigrate to America. As God told the family of Lehi, "Inasmuch as ye shall keep my commandments, ye shall prosper, and shall be led to a land of promise; yea, even a land which I have prepared for you; yea, a land which is choice above all other lands" (1 Nephi 2:20). Led to the "promised land" of America, the family of Lehi divided into two factions, the Lamanites, who were cursed for their rebellion with darkened skin, and the Nephites, who were eventually exterminated around 400 C.E. by the Lamanites. Although the Nephites left no trace in America, the descendants of the ancient Lamanites, with their roots in the holy land of Israel, supposedly survived as the American Indians. Therefore, the sacred history of ancient Israel was revealed by the *Book of Mormon* to be continuous with the sacred history of America. More significantly, however, the sacred history of America was an explicitly Christian story. Consistently, the pre-Christian Nephite prophets recorded in the *Book of Mormon* speak of salvation through Christ. For example, although living around 80 B.C.E., the prophet Alma exhorted a gathering of Nephites in the tones of a revivalist preacher:

> Have ye walked, keeping yourselves blameless before God? Could ye say, if ye were called to die at this time, within yourselves, that ye have been sufficiently humble? That your garments have been cleansed and made white through the blood of Christ, who will come to redeem his people from their sins?
>
> (Alma 5:26–27)

Anticipated by pre-Christian American prophets, Jesus Christ actually appeared in America, according to the *Book of Mormon*, shortly after his resurrection in Judea. Preaching to the Nephites, Jesus established a church, which lasted for about two hundred years, and promised to return at the end of the world to establish the millennial kingdom in America.

Therefore, the *Book of Mormon* presented a distinctively American revelation. With the second coming of Christ to America, the New Jerusalem, the City of Zion, would be built on the American continent as the center of the kingdom of God on earth. By 1831 Joseph Smith had identified the precise location of the American Zion. According to another revelation, God had disclosed to his prophet that "the land of Missouri is the land which I have appointed and consecrated for the gathering of the saints. Wherefore this is the land of promise, and the place for the city of Zion" (*Doctrine and Covenants* 57:1–2). However, his growing following, which was supplemented after 1837 by successful missions to England, had difficulty in finding a home. Besieged by external persecution and internal dissension, the church moved through New York, Ohio, Missouri, and Illinois during the decade of the 1830s. As the church grew, Joseph Smith consolidated its authority structure under his presidency, a body of twelve apostles, and the priesthood of all male believers. Attributing this structure to revelations received from the apostles Peter, James, and John, Joseph Smith claimed to have achieved the only authentic restoration of the original church of Christ.

During the early 1840s, as the church established its temple in Nauvoo, Illinois, Joseph Smith claimed further revelations introducing new doctrines and practices that distinguished Mormon Christianity from other forms of Protestant Christianity in America. In developing a Mormon doctrine of God, for example, the prophet revealed that God had once been a human being. If God had once been human, then humans could aspire to becoming Gods. "You have got to be Gods yourselves," Smith exhorted, "and to be kings and priests to God, the same as all Gods have done before you." This Mormon doctrine echoed the biblical promise that "ye shall be as gods," a prospect of deification that has appeared in other forms of Christianity, such as Augustine's doctrine that the grace of God "makes his worshipers into gods," the Eastern Orthodox promise of *theosis,* or the experience of union between the soul and God in medieval mysticism. However, Joseph Smith's teachings on this point seemed to imply a plurality of Gods. Under the authority of the "head God," who "has a body of flesh and bones as tangible as man's," other human beings had achieved "Godhood." With the restoration of the true church of Christ, Mormons could work toward achieving that divine perfection.[25]

Mormons also could extend salvation to those who had died before the restoration of the church. Baptism for the dead, in which the living are baptized by proxy in the temple on behalf of deceased ancestors, became an important Mormon ritual. By receiving this baptism, deceased relatives and ancestors could enter into the Mormon community in the afterlife. While promising personal deification, therefore, the church also reinforced the collective relations of kinship, affirming that connections with ancestors are necessary, as Joseph Smith explained, "For we without them cannot be made perfect" (*Doctrine and Covenants* 128:5, 18). This collective character of perfection was further reinforced through Mormon rituals of marriage, which under Joseph Smith's leadership allowed for plural marriages in which one man could have several wives who were all sealed to their husband for eternity. Although the Mormon practice of polygyny was eventually discontinued in the 1890s, it caused considerable controversy both within and outside of the community. According to Joseph Smith, however, plural marriage was justified not only by the example of biblical patriarchs and kings, but also by the need to provide bodies for the preexistent souls waiting to be born into the community of salvation.

Perhaps motivated by his millennial expectations for America, in 1844 Joseph Smith ran for the office of president of the United States. In the midst of his campaign, however, anti-Mormon sentiment in Illinois led to his arrest by the state militia and murder by an angry mob. The community in Nauvoo was attacked by the state militia, and the Mormons were forced to leave Illinois. In the process, the community underwent a degree of fragmentation, with as many as six different churches claiming to be the authentic heirs to the original church created by the martyred prophet, Joseph Smith. Moving to Iowa, a minority formed the Reorganized Church of Jesus Christ of Latter-day Saints, which by 1860 was led by a son of the prophet and centered in Missouri, the anticipated site of the "American Zion." A larger contingent, under the leadership of Brigham Young (1802–77), ventured into the western territory of Utah, which became the sacred center of a new Mormon theocracy. Reportedly, when Brigham Young first saw Utah he exclaimed that he beheld "the future glory of Zion." In what became Salt Lake City, Utah, the Mormons set out to establish an American Zion that by the end of the twentieth century could claim the religious adherence of over 10 million Americans and millions of others all over the world. In keeping the millennial vision of Zion alive, the twelfth president of the Mormon Church, Spencer W. Kimball (1895–1985), declared that the prospect of Christ's return "causes me to rejoice over the many opportunities for service and sacrifice afforded me and my family as we seek to do our part in establishing Zion." Like the seventeenth-century Puritans of New England, Mormons have seen Zion in America, the holy city of God that will be the center of a new heaven and a new earth.[26]

24

African Prophets

During their fifteenth-century explorations of the West African coast, Portuguese navigators planted crosses or erected limestone pillars with crosses on top to indicate the southernmost point they had reached on each voyage. Serving as navigational markers, the pillars—or *padraos*—also asserted a Portuguese claim to land. Standing six to eight feet in height, each pillar featured a square stone on which the date, the name of the explorer, and the name of the Portuguese king were carved in Latin and Portuguese. By the time the Portuguese navigator Bartholomew Dias had planted a *padrao* at the eastern Cape of southern Africa in 1488, these Portuguese monuments appeared all along the west coast of Africa. Often accompanied by a performance of the Catholic Mass, the act of setting up a *padrao* was another European "ceremony of possession" with religious, political, and economic significance.

Although it conveyed the message of a prior Portuguese claim to any European navigators who might follow, the *padrao* must also have posed a problem of interpretation for Africans. Allegedly, Africans regarded these stone monuments as objects of worship. According to a nineteenth-century British account, a limestone *padrao* the Portuguese had dedicated to St. George at the mouth of the Congo River was worshiped by Africans. They reportedly regarded it as a fetish, an object of spiritual power. Their religious regard for the fetish of St. George supposedly continued until 1859 when some British seamen, trying to remove it, accidentally dropped it overboard. By that point, however, Christian missions, both Catholic and Protestant, which had been carried by commerce, conquest, and colonization all over sub-Saharan Africa, had raised new problems of interpretation for both Africans and Europeans.[1]

From the earliest reports, European Christians insisted that Africans lacked any indigenous religion. As the west coast of Africa developed into a mercantile trading zone, European travelers and traders reported that instead of religion Africans engaged in the superstitious worship of fetish objects. Drawn from the Portuguese word *feitiço*, which referred to an object used in magic or witchcraft, "fetish" became a term employed by European Christians to designate the absence of an indigenous African religion. Insisting that Africans lacked any religion to organize relations between the spiritual and material realms, Europeans reported that Africans were unable to evaluate objects. From the European perspective, Africans overvalued trifling objects—a bird's feather, a pebble, a piece of cloth, a bundle of sticks—by regarding them as fetishes, but they under-valued trade goods. Emerging out of intercultural trading relations in west Africa, therefore, the term "fetish" raised the problem of the meaning and value of material objects.

For the Portuguese navigators who erected stone pillars on the African coast, there was a link between spiritual power, which had been exercised by the pope in granting rights over trade in recently discovered lands, and the economic exchange of material objects. Certainly, the Portuguese monopoly was disputed in Europe, especially by English and Dutch com-petitors; Queen Elizabeth declared in 1562 that Portugal had no domin-ion over lands discovered and the Dutch legal theorist Hugo Grotius in 1605 ruled that Portugal had not discovered new lands, but had only "pointed them out."[2] As long as the *padrao* stood, however, it asserted a spiritual claim. For Africans, as well as for Europeans, it raised profound spiritual questions.

From an African perspective the *padrao* focused new questions about the spiritual relations between sea and land. Among the BaKongo, for example, the universe was divided into two realms, the living and the dead, which were separated by water. In ritual practices, the transition between the world of the living and the world of the dead—the ancestors whose spiritual presence was the source of knowledge, power, and heal-ing—could be marked by crossing any body of water. In 1483 a Portuguese expedition captured BaKongo hostages and transported them to Portugal. When they were returned two years later, the BaKongo king and his court reportedly received them "as though they had seen them resuscitated from under the earth." More likely, however, the BaKongo realized that they had undergone an extraordinary initiation by crossing the water. As they embraced Christianity, the BaKongo consistently trans-lated the new religion into a local African idiom. For example, a priest was a *nganga*, the term for an African ritual specialist, and the crucifix was a *nkisi,* the term for a ritual object. The Bible—*mukanda nkisi*—was a particularly potent ritual object. In the BaKongo kingdom, therefore, Africans who supposedly had no religion succeeded in making Christianity an indigenous African religion.[3]

As historian Richard Gray has observed, "The growth, expansion and development of Christianity south of the Sahara has depended on, and been distinctively molded by, African initiatives."[4] In contrast to earlier missionary literature that celebrated the foreign "planting" of the gospel in Africa, recent research on Christian missions has shown how Africans have developed local forms of African Christianity. Most evident in the work of African prophets, independent churches, and revitalization movements, African leadership also shaped the character of religious life in churches that maintained connections with foreign churches in Europe or North America. In both independent and mission churches, African religious innovators, ritual specialists, and spiritual workers struggled to solve local problems of translation and application that would make Christianity not an alien import, but an indigenous African religion.

MISSIONS

Among English-speaking Protestants in Britain and North America, the enthusiasm for missions to Africa was stimulated by the transatlantic evangelical revivals. As a broad religious trend that produced Methodist and Baptist churches, but also influenced Anglican, Congregational, and Presbyterian churches, evangelical Christianity represented a revitalization movement to convert individuals in societies that were already nominally Christian. Taking seriously the biblical mandate to evangelize all the nations, Protestant missionary agencies—the London Missionary Society (1795), the Church Missionary Society (1799), the Wesleyan Methodist Missionary Society (1813), and the American Board of Commissioners for Foreign Missions (1810)—began working actively in Africa at the beginning of the nineteenth century. The central doctrines of evangelicalism—what William Wilberforce in Britain called "the peculiar doctrines of Christianity"—were specified as original sin, which resulted in human depravity, the atonement provided by the sacrificial death of Christ, and the sanctifying power of the Holy Spirit. In evangelical preaching, these doctrines formed the basis for a gospel that aimed to humble sinners, exalt the Savior, and promote a life of holiness. In practice, therefore, evangelicalism was a campaign to activate what the secretary of the Church Missionary Society, the Anglican pastor Henry Venn, called "the vital operation of Christian Doctrines upon the heart and conduct."[5]

Although pursued under different colonial conditions, nineteenth-century European missions raised similar problems for Christianity throughout sub-Saharan Africa. First, as noted among the BaKongo in the fifteenth century, Christianity was initially engaged by Africans as a question of the relationship between sea and land. For example, in response to the British incursions and depredations in southern Africa during the early nineteenth century, the Xhosa chief Ngqika observed that since the Europeans were people of the sea they should have stayed in the sea. The Xhosa religious visionary and war leader Nxele developed this observation about sea and land into an indigenous theology that identified two gods, Thixo, the god of the white people, who had punished white people for killing his son by casting them into the sea, and Mdalidiphu, the god of the deeps, who dwelled under the ground but had ultimate dominion over the sea. Similarly, during the first half of the nineteenth century, a Zulu emergence myth was reconfigured in terms of this colonial opposition between land and sea. In the beginning, according to an account recorded in the 1850s, uNkulunkulu created human beings, male and female, but also black and white. Black human beings, according to this myth, were created to be naked, carry spears, and live on the land, and white human beings were created to wear clothing, carry guns, and live in the sea. In southern Africa, as elsewhere in sub-Saharan Africa during the nineteenth century, most Africans rejected the Christian mission, but recognized that a new opposition had been established between sea and land.[6]

Second, whatever their spiritual intentions, European and North American missionaries in Africa were inevitably involved with material concerns. In West Africa, for example, the missionary gospel required converts to declare their allegiance to a foreign church and to reject their indigenous tradition. African converts had to observe Sunday, but they also had to destroy fetishes and refuse to participate in traditional sacrifices for ancestors. At the same time, however, Christian conversion was defined by specifically European material practices in which the convert "wore western clothes, built a western-style house, married only one wife, and cultivated gardens of flowers." Similarly, in southern Africa, according to the LMS missionary Robert Moffat (1795–1883), the Christian mission brought two sacred symbols that promised to transform Africa, the Bible and the plow. There also Christianity registered as an intervention in "the heart and conduct" not only because it set a new religion in opposition to indigenous forms of religious life, but also because it sought to bring labor, gender, and sexual relations into conformity with a particular European pattern.[7]

Third, the Christian mission was immediately and consistently translated into local African idioms. In their work of translation, European missionaries appropriated terms from indigenous African vocabularies. Among the Tswana in the northern Cape of southern Africa, for example, the term for God, *Modimo*—perhaps a collective noun for the power of ancestral spirits, *badimo,* but also a word apparently used in the northern Cape for mysterious, creative, and effective power—was appropriated and deployed by the Christian mission. Although the Tswana generally seem to have located that mysterious power underground, the European missionaries placed Modimo in the heavens, while at the same time trying to demote the *badimo* to the status of demons. Understandably, this curious intervention in an indigenous vocabulary produced moments of incomprehension, bafflement, and even amusement. For example, after recounting his gospel of God and demons, heavenly light and eternal damnation, the missionary Robert Moffat reported that a Tswana chief asked his people, "Did you ever hear *litlamane* [fables] like these?" The chief's question "was followed by a burst of deafening laughter," Moffat recalled, "and on its partially subsiding, the chief man begged me to say no more on such trifles, lest the people should think me mad!" Therefore, many Tswana apparently saw the missionary's curious appropriation of their religious vocabulary as a kind of madness.

However, Africans found other ways to translate the Christian mission into local terms. Although they generally rejected the claims of Christianity throughout the nineteenth century, Africans nevertheless recognized familiar features of religious practice in the Christian mission. As they observed the Sunday services of the mission, for example, Khoisan people of the northern Cape reportedly concluded that Christian rituals were techniques that white people used to keep their encampment pure and safe. The Tswana reportedly found that Sunday services were actually rainmaking rituals, while the Bible, like the divining bones of the *ngaka,* or ritual specialist, was a ritual instrument for discerning the will of God and the ancestors. Not merely sin and salvation, therefore, but purity and protection, fertility and divination, God and ancestors, and many other African religious concerns were at stake in the production of distinctively African forms of Christianity.[8]

Foreign missionaries in Africa were incapable of resolving the problems of interreligious relations and intercultural translations posed for Africans by the Christian mission. African clergy, deacons, teachers, nurses, and lay workers addressed those problems within the mission churches. At the same time, African prophets appeared all over the continent during the twentieth century to propose novel ways of redefining Christianity as an African religion independent of white missionary control.

In West Africa, for example, the prophet William Wade Harris (ca. 1865–1928) led a mass movement of Christian conversion that not only inspired independent churches, but also swelled the membership of mission-based Protestant and Catholic churches. Born in Liberia, which had been settled since 1821 by African American immigrants, Harris was exposed from an early age to Christianity. Following his education at a Methodist mission school, he became a seaman, a schoolteacher, a government interpreter, and a lay preacher. Involved in a rebellion against the colonial government of Liberia in 1909, Harris was imprisoned for treason because he had raised a British flag. While in prison, reading the Bible and praying, Harris had a vision of the angel Gabriel, who revealed to him that he was God's last prophet with a destiny to bring Christian conversion to Africa.

When he was released from prison in 1913, Harris adopted what he regarded as the dress of a biblical prophet—a long white robe, a round white hat, and black sandals—and embarked on his prophetic campaign in the French colony of the Ivory Coast. During the preceding two decades, the government-sponsored Catholic mission there had achieved very little success, gaining only four hundred converts. Within a year, however, Harris had baptized over a hundred thousand new converts to Christianity before he was deported by the French colonial authorities. Calling on his converts to reject the practices of their indigenous religious heritage, the prophet directed them to the "teachers of the Bible." As a result, the Catholic missions were overwhelmed with new members; the Methodist missionaries who arrived in the Ivory Coast in 1924 found that they already had a large membership of tens of thousands of Harrist Christians. In addition, independent churches proliferated—the Harrist Church, the Church of the Twelve Disciples, the Deima Church, and many others—that all owed their origin to the mission of William Wade Harris.

As an African prophet, Harris advanced his religious campaign on two fronts. On the one hand, he attacked the beliefs and practices of African traditional religion. He insisted that people destroy the altars, masks, and other ritual objects of their indigenous religious heritage. Echoing the missionary opposition to African traditional religion, Harris instructed:

> All the fetiches, Koubos, and the ju-jus must be destroyed. Burn them all in the fire. Evil befall him who secretly keeps them in his house! May the fire from heaven devour him! All must adore the only true God in Jesus Christ and Him alone must you serve.

According to legend, when Harris entered some villages, the buildings in which traditional religious objects were kept burst into flames and the traditional deities told their priests that they had to flee before the coming of a stronger God. Harris demonstrated the superior power of his God by performing miraculous healings that confounded the traditional African priests. In all these respects, therefore, Harris's prophetic mission demanded the removal of African indigenous religion and its replacement with the Christian gospel in ways that were entirely consistent with the aims and objectives of foreign missionaries.

On the other hand, however, Harris challenged the authority of foreign Christian missionaries. For example, when they realized that Harris was performing baptisms, the Catholic missionaries in the Ivory Coast insisted that the African prophet lacked the proper authority to perform that ritual. Furthermore, they were shocked to discover that Harris was baptizing converts who had not received any instruction in the Christian faith. However, the prophet explained his practice in specifically African terms as a ritual of purity and protection. Typically, when Harris and his followers entered a village, they attracted a crowd by singing and shaking gourd rattles. After preaching his message of a new, more powerful God, the prophet invited his listeners to be baptized with water from a gourd bowl while the Bible was placed over their heads. As a ritual of purity, baptism washed away past sins; but it also washed away the traditional religious allegiances that many Africans felt had failed to protect them in the colonial era from foreign military conquest, political oppression, and economic exploitation. As a new ritual of protection, Christian baptism promised to strengthen converts by forging an alliance with a stronger God. By rejecting the foreign missionaries' insistence on instruction before baptism, therefore, Harris denied the authority of European Christians to define the character of Christian beliefs and practices in the African context.[9]

The African Christianity that William Wade Harris negotiated by rejecting both African traditions and foreign missions was worked out in similar ways by other African prophets. Also in West Africa, for example, Yoruba prophets in Nigeria during the 1920s—Moses Orimolade, Abiodun Akinsowon, Joseph Babalola, and others—engaged in a Christian mission of preaching, healing, and destroying the "fetishes" of African traditional religion. In the process, however, they inspired the formation of a distinctive Yoruba Christianity, known as Aladura, the "owners of the prayer," that transposed many features of African traditional religion, such as proverbial wisdom, a sense of the soul's destiny, respect for ancestors, divination, healing, and protection from the evil forces of witchcraft, into a vibrant Christian context that affirmed the power of both African ritual speech and Christian prayer.[10]

In Central Africa, Simon Kimbangu (1889–1951), from a Baptist background, failed his examination to enter the Baptist ministry, but during a typhoid epidemic in 1918–19 he heard a prophetic call in which Jesus appeared to him saying, "I am Christ. My servants are unfaithful. I have chosen you to bear witness before your brethren and convert them. Tend my flock." Like Harris, Simon Kimbangu rejected both African traditional religion and the foreign Christian mission. Arrested in 1921 by Belgian colonial officials in the Congo, Simon Kimbangu spent the rest of his life in prison. Under the leadership of his son, however, the church that Simon Kimbangu founded, with its focus on prayer, faith healing, and egalitarianism, had grown to 4 million members by 1990.[11]

In southern Africa during the 1930s, John Maranke (1912–63), who had been baptized as a Methodist, received a prophetic calling to start a new church, the New Revelation of the Apostles. According to John Maranke, a bright light and heavenly voice had instructed him, "You are John the Baptist, an Apostle. Now go and do my work. Go to every country and preach and convert people." With a ministry based on baptism and spiritual healing, John Maranke developed a prophetic reputation as "he who speaks with God." In South Africa, the Zulu prophet Isaiah Shembe (ca. 1870–1935) developed a Christian faith-healing ministry opposed to both traditional and Western medicine. Under conditions of colonial oppression, dispossession of land, and exclusion from economic opportunity, Isaiah Shembe created a religious order of divine power, purity, and protection at the holy village of Ekuphakameni, the "exalted place," and the holy mountain of Inhlangakazi, a site for annual pilgrimage. Like other African prophets, Shembe was opposed by a colonial government that sought, at the urging of Christian missionaries, to "deal with this mischievous growth swiftly and destroy the trouble in its inception." In spite of that opposition, however, the Christianity of Isaiah Shembe, like the Christianity of other African prophets, survived and continued to find a devoted following in Africa.[12]

These and many other African prophets, therefore, developed indigenous Christian missions in Africa. Although they were accused by European and North American missionaries of syncretism—the heresy of mixing Christianity with indigenous religion—these African prophets were adamantly opposed to African traditional religion. However, they were also opposed to any foreign monopoly on Christianity. By rejecting both African tradition and foreign missions, they engaged in the struggle—the term that the Aladura Christians of Nigeria have used for prayer, ritual, or spiritual work—to fashion authentic forms of African Christianity. During the twentieth-century expansion of Christianity in Africa, most African Christians affiliated with churches that had roots in Europe. Nevertheless, even in the Protestant and Catholic mission churches, Africans struggled with the same challenge faced by Harris and other African prophets of making Christianity an African religion.

WATCHTOWER

In the early twentieth century, colonial missions in Africa experienced new competition from recently formed millennial and charismatic churches from America. Founded in the United States during the 1870s by Charles Taze Russell (1852–1916), the Watchtower Bible and Tract Society, which came to be known in the 1930s as Jehovah's Witnesses, had a profound impact on the emergence of millennial expectations in central and southern Africa. Russell had been inspired to start the Watchtower society by William Miller's prophecy in the 1840s of the second coming of Christ. Publishing biblical commentaries, pamphlets, and the *Watchtower* magazine, which was originally titled *Zion's Watch Tower and Herald of*

Christ's Presence, Russell created the basis for a new Christian church dedicated to the worship of Jehovah and preparation for the return of Christ. Arguing that a Christian life must be based solely on the Bible, Russell rejected the rituals and traditions of conventional churches as deviant accretions. Since all members were preachers, no formal clergy was established. Although Sunday was observed for meetings in homes or "kingdom halls," the Christian holidays of Christmas and Easter were not celebrated. The ritual of Communion was replaced with an annual Lord's Meal. The ritual of adult baptism by immersion was retained, but all previous baptisms were ruled invalid. The study of the Bible, which was regarded as literally true in every respect, was the only authentic form of worship. The Bible was also understood as a prophetic guide to historical events.

Based on his reading of the Bible, Russell calculated that the end of the world would happen in 1914 with the cataclysmic warfare of Armageddon, the return of Christ, and the establishment of God's kingdom. The failure of this prophecy in 1914 led to schisms, but the leadership of the society, which was assumed in 1916 by Joseph Franklin Rutherford (1869–1942), held the Watchtower society together by insisting that the battles marking the last days had in fact already begun and that events from 1914 were gradually unfolding in fulfillment of the prophecy of the end. While waiting for that culmination, followers of Watchtower teachings were enjoined to avoid participation in conventional politics, including voting, swearing oaths of allegiance, or serving in the military, on the grounds that all existing institutions in society were ruled by Satan. This political stance brought the Watchtower into conflict with earthly governments and popular patriotic sentiments. During World War I, for example, members in the United States were attacked by angry mobs, and Rutherford and other leaders were imprisoned under the Espionage Act for giving aid and comfort to the enemy. Anticipating the theocratic rule of Christ on earth, however, the followers of the Watchtower society prepared for the end by remaining as aloof as possible from their prevailing social environment.

In central and southern Africa, Watchtower teachings were enthusiastically received as an alternative to both the mission churches and colonial rule. In the British colony of Malawi, for example, the relationship between mission church and colonial state was challenged by the eccentric reformer Joseph Booth (1851–1932). A British businessman who had converted to evangelical Christianity in Australia, Booth became a Christian activist in Africa, settling first in Malawi in 1892, where he established churches, schools, and Christian organizations. Booth traveled to the United States in 1897 with John Chilembwe (ca. 1860/71–1915), who returned three years later as an ordained Baptist minister to establish an industrial mission for the agricultural training and economic uplift of Africans. Supporting Baptist, Seventh-Day Adventist, and other Christian alternatives, however, Joseph Booth came into conflict with both the mission church and the colonial administration in Malawi.

Relocating to Cape Town, South Africa, in 1902, Booth became interested in the millennial teachings of the Watchtower society. He convinced Charles Taze Russell that his church should start an African mission. Booth began teaching and disseminating Watchtower literature from Cape Town. While working as a migrant laborer in South Africa, Elliot Kenan Kamwana studied the Watchtower teachings for eight months with Joseph Booth. In 1908 Kamwana returned to Malawi to preach the millennial promise of the Watchtower society. By the time he was deported for sedition just over a year later, Kamwana had baptized as many as twelve thousand people into the Watchtower community of the kingdom of God. Certainly, he preached against the established mission church and colonial administration, accusing the mission of propagating a "false Christianity" and the government of upholding the rule of Satan. These accusations were entirely consistent with the Watchtower understanding of Christian corruption and Satanic government in the world, as the cosmic battle between the spiritual forces of good and evil was being waged during the last days before the end. However, they also addressed specific African problems with the mission church and colonial state in Malawi.[13]

The African Watchtower movement broke the mission's monopoly on the ritual of baptism. Since the mission required converts to be instructed, examined, and certified before baptism, Africans often had to wait as long as four years before being baptized. During that period of waiting, candidates for baptism were investigated to assess their moral character, which also meant ensuring that they had rejected aspects of African culture the mission church found unacceptable—engaging in polygamous marriage, performing ancestral rituals, or seeking ritual protection against witchcraft. Even applicants found worthy, however, might still be denied baptism on the grounds that they had failed to contribute money to the church. As a result of these controls, during any given year the mission church might admit about half of the eligible candidates who had applied for Christian baptism. Under the leadership of Elliot Kamwana, however, the Watchtower movement baptized anyone who was willing to receive the millennial message of the return of Christ.

In liberating the ritual of baptism from missionary control in Malawi, Kamwana also gave it a distinctively African content not only by linking it with purity and protection, but also by making it the sign of entry into a theocratic community free from colonial domination. Accordingly, baptism into the Watchtower movement registered as a political act of defiance against a colonial government that oppressed Africans by taking their land, imposing heavy taxes, and coercing them into wage labor to gain cash in order to pay those taxes. When the colonial government proposed doubling taxes in 1902 to encourage Africans to work in the South African mines, even the missionaries at the Livingstonia Mission of the Free Church of Scotland realized that the proposal meant "scarcely veiled slavery." In place of the coercion of tax slavery, the missionaries countered with a "gospel of work," which promised to instill a new sense of discipline giving Africans an "indigenous stimulus" to work for the white-controlled mines, farms, and industries. According to the head of the Livingstonia Mission, the Reverend Robert Laws, the mission church cultivated an "internal motive" in African converts by showing them a new spiritual life. "Combine this with education," Reverend Laws concluded, "and new needs will be felt, requiring more work, and eventually steady industry to supply them."[14] However, a different analysis provided by the Watchtower movement revealed that the taxation imposed on Africans by the colonial government was not merely a policy of coercion; it was effectively a declaration of war on Africans by a Satanic regime.

As in many millennial movements, including, perhaps, the movement started by Jesus in first-century Galilee, the exaction of taxes, especially when imposed by an alien, colonizing government, posed a profound spiritual problem for Africans who were drawn to the Watchtower movement in Malawi. For Elliot Kamwana, the Watchtower promised freedom from the evil realm of oppression most clearly exemplified by colonial taxation. Calling on people to be baptized rather than to take up arms, however, Kamwana invoked the Watchtower's policy of "passive resistance" to earthly governments. People did not have to do anything but be baptized and wait for the end. However, while the Watchtower looked forward to participating in the spiritual war of a colonial Armageddon, others in Malawi took matters into their own hands. In 1915, for example, John

Chilembwe, who had dedicated his life to education, agriculture, and industry, led an armed revolt against the colonial government. For the followers of the Watchtower prophecy, the violent suppression of that revolt only confirmed that a transcendent spiritual power would be necessary to overthrow colonial domination.[15]

In Zambia the Watchtower also inspired mass religious movements. When World War I broke out in 1914, the British colonial government shifted from increasing taxes to direct coercion to force Africans to labor for the war effort. During 1917 the teachings of the Watchtower provided a vehicle for African resistance to colonial oppression. The most prominent leader of the movement in Zambia, Hanoc Sidano, had been introduced to Watchtower teachings as a migrant laborer and had gone to Cape Town for further study. When he returned to Zambia in 1917, Sidano and his colleagues proclaimed the imminent end of the world. Those who had been baptized by Watchtower preachers would enter "a new chieftainship under God," while the unbaptized would die and all whites would be driven from the country or enslaved. Clearly, this millennial message addressed widespread African resentment against forced labor by promising the future reversal of the colonial social order. Pointing at the colonial officials, Hanoc Sidano declared, "There they are, they who overburden us with loads, and beat us like slaves, but a day will come when they will be the slaves." But this promise of liberation from colonial oppression was ultimately framed in religious terms; as Hanoc Sidano insisted, "God only is to be respected and obeyed."[16]

As the baptizing movement grew, this exclusive allegiance to God, which effectively denied the authority of the colonial missions, government officials, and traditional chiefs, was celebrated in nightly prayer meetings featuring loud drumming, singing, shouting, and speaking in strange tongues. Although baptism marked an individual's entry into the community, these prayer meetings devoted to speaking in tongues, which Zambian Watchtower enthusiasts called *chongo,* reinforced the community's collective spiritual power. In the United States, the leaders of the Watchtower society generally rejected the practice of speaking in tongues. They were suspicious of the charismatic revival that began in 1901 at Bethel Bible College in Topeka, Kansas, under the leadership of Charles Fox Parham (1873–1929) and was carried in 1906 to the Azusa Street Baptist Church in Los Angeles by the Reverend William J. Seymour

(1870–1922). An African American preacher converted by Parham, Seymour led thousands of enthusiastic Christians into a second baptism, the "baptism in the Holy Spirit," which was evidenced by speaking in tongues. This revival seemed to reenact the original Christian Pentecost, described in the book of Acts, in which the early Christians "were filled with the Holy Spirit and began to speak in other tongues, as the Spirit gave them utterance" (Acts 2:1–4). Out of the Azusa Street revivals, new Pentecostal churches emerged—the Apostolic Faith Mission, the Church of God in Christ, the Assemblies of God, and others—dedicated to cultivating what they regarded as the special gifts, or *charismata,* of the Holy Spirit, which included not only speaking in tongues, but also faith healing and casting out demons.

Speaking in tongues, or glossolalia, represented an extraordinary language event. As a worldwide phenomenon in the history of religions, glossolalia occurs in many different ritual contexts as an extraordinary type of speech. Ordinary speech is limited by grammar and syntax, sense and reference, but glossolalia presents the possibility of speech as pure performance. As anthropologist Felicitas Goodman has argued, the performance of glossolalia flows out of a psychological dynamic, the experience of trance, that alters speech patterns. But the performance of glossolalia is also social; it is learned and shared among people in a community. For those outside the community, glossolalia seems to be nothing but meaningless noise. In response to the Azusa Street revival in 1906, for example, the *Los Angeles Times* ran the headline, "Weird Babel of Tongues; New Sect of Fanatics Is Breaking Loose." In Zambia during 1917, colonial officials likewise found the performance of glossolalia within the Watchtower movement incoherent. According to colonial administrator Charles Draper, it was nothing more than "gibbering, shivering, and generally mad fits." Participants in the performance, however, found meaning in the "meaningless" utterances of glossolalia, understanding the "gibbering" as evidence of positive spirit possession. By contrast with the negative possession associated with evil spirits, sorcery, and witchcraft, positive possession by an ancestral spirit was valued in African indigenous religion. However, in opposing both the "heathen" religion of traditional chiefs and the "false Christianity" of the colonial mission, the glossolalia of the Watchtower movement in Zambia represented a new kind of spirit possession, through the power of the Holy Spirit, that announced a new world.[17]

To the extent that they regarded the power to exorcise demons as one of the gifts of the Holy Spirit, Pentecostals generally located the performance of glossolalia in a broader spiritual economy of good and evil spirits. The good power of the Holy Spirit was deployed against the evil spiritual power of demons. In Zambia during 1925 another Watchtower revival suggested how the ability to distinguish between good and evil spirits could be mobilized in the context of an indigenous African understanding of evil. Basically, the cause of any illness, suffering, and misfortune could be traced back to the displeasure of ancestral spirits, the violation of an ethical or ritual prohibition, or the evil actions of an antisocial agent. Termed a "witch" in English, such an antisocial agent was thought to use spiritual or medicinal techniques to cause harm to other persons. Under the leadership of Tomo Nyirenda, who had been educated by teachers from the Free Church of Scotland, but had been baptized by Watchtower preachers in 1925, the Watchtower movement waged war against those agents of evil.

Preaching against the colonial officials and their taxes, Tomo Nyirenda urged people to be baptized in order to prepare for the imminent coming of the Son of God—Mwana Lesa—who would arrive soon with the Americans to drive all aliens from the country. He enjoined his followers to love each other, share food with the needy, and care for the sick. Pointing to witchcraft as the opposite of that social solidarity, he warned them "that if people did not throw away their witchcraft medicine he would know them for witches and would kill them."[18] As his following grew, however, Tomo Nyirenda broadened the definition of witches to include all who had not received the Watchtower baptism. In his work as a witch-finder, Tomo Nyirenda was supported by chiefs and headmen of local villages, who often invited him to come and identify the witches among them. Adopting the sacred name Mwana Lesa, Son of God, Tomo Nyirenda traveled around Zambia with an entourage of deacons, elders, pastors, teachers, and singers, each of whom played a different role in the spiritual work of baptizing converts and killing witches. Before he was arrested and executed by the colonial government in 1926, Tomo Nyirenda had created a mass movement by transforming baptism into a ritual technique not only for incorporating converts into the community of salvation, but also for exposing and eliminating witches, those evil, disruptive, and antisocial agents that threatened the community.

AFRICAN ZION

While the Watchtower movements in Malawi and Zambia found different ways to anticipate the sacred time of the millennium in Christian eschatology, other movements produced a new Christian sense of sacred space in Africa. In South Africa during the twentieth century, for example, the two most powerful spatial symbols for African Christianity have been Ethiopia and Zion. For the independent African churches that emerged in the 1890s in the new urban centers of Pretoria and Johannesburg, the symbol of Ethiopia signified not only freedom from white ecclesiastical control, but also a new pan-African identity. Founded in 1892 by Mangena M. Mokone, a former minister in the Methodist mission church, the Ethiopian Church embraced the symbol of "Ethiopia" as a multilayered Christian symbol. First, it appeared in the biblical psalm that declared, "Ethiopia shall stretch forth her hands unto God" (Ps. 68:31). Although European missionaries had occasionally used this passage to refer to Christian conversion in Africa, the Ethiopian Church reappropriated the psalm as a biblical promise of independence. Second, to some extent, it referred to the nation of Ethiopia, the Christian kingdom of Abyssinia, which had remained independent from the European colonization of Africa. After the Abyssinian victory over European troops at the battle of Adowa in 1896, Ethiopia rose in prominence as a spatial symbol of African independence. Finally, "Ethiopia" was employed as a symbol of pan-African unity shared by African Americans. As a common motif in African American preaching, "Ethiopia" represented the promise of black redemption and liberation. Under the leadership of Bishop Henry M. Turner (1834–1915), the African Methodist Episcopal Church aspired to create a "highway across the Atlantic" that would link Africans and African Americans in a pan-African Christian unity. Responding to that call, the Ethiopian Church of Mangena Mokone decided in 1896 to affiliate with the African Methodist Episcopal Church, thereby initiating an ongoing "Ethiopian" connection between South Africa and African America.

At the same time, new churches in South Africa emerged out of a "Zionist" connection with America. Although it might refer to the holy mountain of God or the New Jerusalem, the term "Zion" in South Africa gained its specific reference to a spiritual life of moral discipline, faith healing, and ecstatic prayer on the model of an American religious community near Chicago—Zion City, Illinois—established in 1893 by John

Alexander Dowie (1847–1907). Announcing himself as "Elijah the Restorer," the biblical prophet destined to appear in the end times, Dowie advertised Zion City, Illinois, as the perfect Christian city without "breweries or saloons, gambling halls, houses of ill-fame, drug or tobacco shops, hospitals or doctors' offices, theaters or dance halls and secret lodges or apostate churches." In keeping with the biblical avoidance of pork, Dowie ensured that Zion City would permit no "hog raising, selling or handling." At its peak Zion City held about six thousand residents.

The absence of hospitals or doctors' offices in Zion City followed from Dowie's commitment to faith healing. Dowie was convinced that modern medicine, like alcohol, gambling, prostitution, tobacco, and heresy, led the faithful away from God. "God has but one way of healing," Dowie declared. "The Devil has a hundred so-called ways. Zion cannot go to medicine for healing. There is no fellowship between the blood of Christ and medicine."[19] At the turn of the century, many Americans were looking for alternatives to modern medicine. Christian Science, for example, founded in 1875 by Mary Baker Eddy (1821–1910), relied upon the power of "Divine Mind" for health and healing. Through the power of positive thinking and spiritual affirmations, "New Thought" churches— the Unity School of Practical Christianity, Religious Science, Science of Mind, and others—made healing a central part of their religious work. In developing his healing ministry, however, Dowie relied not upon positive thinking, but upon faith, prayer, and a life of rigorous moral discipline. In addition to his Christian utopia of Zion City, Illinois, Dowie established a church, the Christian Catholic Apostolic Church in Zion, and the widely distributed magazine *Leaves of Healing,* which extended the influence of his faith-healing ministry all over the United States.

In South Africa, however, the Zionist mission had already firmly taken root. After a visit to America in 1897, a South African Congregationalist minister, J. U. Buchler, had been placed by Dowie in charge of "African work." In 1904 one of Dowie's associates in Zion City, Daniel Bryant, had arrived in Johannesburg and baptized nearly thirty people, mostly black South Africans, into the faith of Zion. Out of these initial exchanges with America, however, Christian Zionism in South Africa developed in a distinctively African direction. When he was refused ordination by Daniel Bryant in 1907, the African Zionist convert Lucas Zungu founded his own church. From Zungu's example, a remarkable proliferation of new African Zionist churches followed—the Christian Apostolic Church in

Zion, the Christian Catholic Apostolic Holy Spirit Church in Zion, the Holy Catholic Apostolic Church in Zion, and a multitude of others—so that by 1990 there were as many as five thousand different Zionist denominations, which together accounted for the religious affiliation of about 30 percent of the African population of South Africa. Clearly, the Zionist exchange between America and South Africa produced unexpected results that have been crucial to the formation of an African Christianity.

The Zion Christian Church (ZCC), founded in 1910 by Ignatius Lekganyane, emerged as the largest of the Zionist denominations in South Africa. Avoiding the schisms that divided other Zionist churches, the ZCC maintained a centralized, hierarchical organization that held together a network of hundreds of local congregations. Like the Christian Zionism of John Alexander Dowie, the ZCC stressed moral discipline, including the avoidance of alcohol, tobacco, and pork, along with faith healing, the power of prayer, and dramatic spiritual experience. In the South African context, however, the ZCC carved out alternative enclaves of Christian sacred space that transcended the conditions of political oppression, land dispossession, racial segregation, and economic exploitation under which Africans suffered. The ZCC produced Christian sacred space along two dimensions, a central sacred space, at Moria, which became the holy site for annual pilgrimage, and a local sacred space, within each congregation, that could be produced every Sunday through the ritual practices of Zionist worship. In the process of historical exchange, therefore, Christian Zionism might have been initiated in Zion City, Illinois, but its African character as a distinctive form of Christianity was worked out through the production of sacred space in South Africa.

Unlike most Zionist churches, which attracted the poor, disenfranchised, and disempowered in South Africa, especially among the urban working class, the ZCC maintained access to sacred land. Twenty-five miles from Pietersburg in the northern Transvaal, the sacred center of Moria stood apart from the political center of Pretoria and the economic center of Johannesburg in the symbolic landscape of a modernizing South Africa. Adopting a biblical name for Jerusalem, which itself had been taken from the ancient religious site at Mt. Moriah in the northern kingdom of Israel, the ZCC established Moria as a sacred city (2 Chron. 3:1; Gen. 12:6; 22:2). In the broader context of African poverty, Moria displayed its sacred power in part through its concentration of symbols of

wealth, through the opulence of its buildings, the expanse of its farm-
lands, the Rolls Royce driven by Ignatius Lekganyane, the fleet of forty-
five automobiles maintained by his successor, Edward Lekganyane, and
the business empire overseen by his successor, Barnabas Lekganyane. In a
capitalist world, the ZCC thereby demonstrated its spiritual power in the
idiom of material symbols. However, the ZCC also demonstrated its
power by drawing pilgrims three times a year, but especially at its annual
Easter festival, when hundreds of thousands of ZCC members journeyed
to Moria for sermons, prayer, healing, and celebration.

As a powerful sacred center in South Africa, Moria revolved around
the person of the ZCC bishop. In trying to understand the leadership provided by the Lekganyanes, scholars have drawn analogies with the traditional African chief or diviner. Rather than reproducing the authority of a
traditional chief, however, the bishop stands at the top of a church hierarchy that is organized along the bureaucratic lines of the colonial government. From the sacred center of Moria, the bishop exercises ultimate
administrative authority over prophets, ministers, secretaries, and trea-
surers at local congregations. In the spiritual work of the church, the focus
on healing diverges from the practices of the traditional diviner, who has
relied upon the power of ancestral spirits and knowledge of medicines, to
incorporate basic Pentecostal techniques of prayer, invocation of the Holy
Spirit, and laying on of hands. Sometimes supplemented by water, ash,
and other blessed objects, these Christian ritual techniques are understood
within the ZCC to be in opposition to the practices of traditional diviners.
Instead of perpetuating the traditional roles of chief and diviner, therefore,
the Zionist bishop represents an innovation in leadership within African
Christianity.

Although Moria stood as the sacred center of the Zion Christian
Church, each Sunday Zionists living in townships all over South Africa
also created enclaves of sacred space through ritual. Often meeting in a
private home, the Zionist congregation participated in rituals that sanctified that space as a center of spiritual power, purity, and protection. The
pattern of Zionist ritual followed three basic movements. As the service
began, the gatekeeper shut the doors and windows to block out the township and create a self-contained space in which worshipers could work to
build up a reservoir of spiritual power. That power was referred to as
umoya, a term associated with air, breath, or spirit, but specifically referring to the Holy Spirit in the Zionist context. During this first part of the

service, spiritual power was generated through prayer, both formal prayers such as the Lord's Prayer as well as spontaneous prayer that might include speaking in tongues. The middle stage of the service was devoted to preaching. As the Zionist minister opened the Bible, the doors and windows of the meeting room were thrown open so that the outside world of the township could hear the message of the sermon. During the final stage of the service, the energy of *umoya* was redirected into the most important ritual work of the Zionist congregation, spiritual healing. As the doors and windows were again shut, the service shifted from building up the power of the community to addressing the illness, suffering, or misfortune of individuals. While the Zionist prophet brushed off evil or impure influences from the afflicted person's body, the congregation participated in the healing ritual through ecstatic praying, singing, and dancing. As the culmination of the weekly service, healing ritual directed the spiritual energy generated within the meeting room toward the physical body.[20]

Although they emerged from the global Pentecostal movement of the twentieth century, Christian Zionist churches in Africa have often been represented in theological literature as if they were distinctively African. In South Africa, for example, theologians representing non-Pentecostal mission churches have depicted Zionist churches as a syncretism of Christianity and African traditional religion, an illicit mixture of "pure" Christianity with indigenous religion. Theologians have criticized Zionist churches as "bridges back to heathenism" or as "post-Christian" sects. However, the notion of a "pure" Christianity, which has usually been associated with European Protestant Christianity, certainly cannot be sustained. As this chapter has shown, the origin and development of Christianity in Africa cannot be represented as the transmission or transplanting of a "pure" religion outside of history. In the African context, part of that history necessarily involved African initiatives in finding new ways to relate to the spiritual resources of indigenous tradition. In the case of some Zionist Christian churches, for example, relations with ancestors have been incorporated into a basic Christian framework, while other Zionist churches have dismissed any Christian role for ancestors, even regarding the ancestral spirits as demonic. As these different Christian approaches to ancestors suggest, African Christianity has emerged out of complex local negotiations with indigenous religion.[21]

In reflecting on the emergence of Christianity in Africa, African theology has sought to recover and reappropriate an indigenous heritage for the Christian church. According to the most influential African theologian, John Mbiti, Africa knew the God of Christianity long before the arrival of any European Christian missionaries. Referring to the presence of a supreme being in African traditional religion, Mbiti insisted that "God, the Father of our Lord Jesus Christ, is the same God who has been known and worshiped in various ways within the religious life of African peoples." The missionary proclamation of the name of Jesus Christ only completed what was already inherent in African tradition. As an affirmation of both Christianity and African tradition, therefore, African theology has been celebrated by its proponents as the recovery of an authentic Christianity for Africa. In the process, African theology has supported a new sense of self-respect, as the Anglican archbishop of Cape Town, Desmond Tutu, observed, by countering the lie "that religion and history in Africa date from the advent in that continent of the white man." As Archbishop Tutu continued:

> It is reassuring to know that we have had a genuine knowledge of God and that we have had our own ways of communicating with deity, ways which meant that we were able to speak authentically as ourselves and not as pale imitators of others. It means that we have a great store from which we can fashion new ways of speaking to and about God, and new styles of worship consistent with our new faith.

This recovery of African tradition, however, has not only been the work of academic theologians and church leaders. For many African Christians, drawing upon both Christian and indigenous religious resources, including ritual sacrifices for ancestors, initiation into adulthood, and techniques of healing, has been a way of life. In his autobiography, for example, South African president Nelson Mandela recalled that the people of his community in the rural eastern Cape saw no conflict between attending the mission church and maintaining the traditional ritual of circumcision that marked a boy's passage into manhood. Accordingly, Nelson Mandela underwent both the rite of baptism in the local Methodist church and the rite of circumcision required by African tradition. Arguably, Nelson Mandela's dual initiation into Christianity and indigenous religion did not represent a "recovery" of African tradition, because his community had no idea that the tradition had been lost. Instead, Christians in the eastern Cape, like Christians all over Africa, drew upon the living spiritual resources in their midst. Beyond missionary control, Africans found new ways of negotiating relations between Christian innovation and indigenous tradition. As a result, many African Christians came to regard Christianity as the indigenous religion of Africa.[22]

25

Asian Heavens

When the first Jesuit missionaries, led by the Italian Matteo Ricci (1552–1610), entered China in 1583, they hoped that if they converted the emperor, then the conversion of his subjects would follow. Initially, they wore the priestly robes of Buddhist monks in pursuing their Christian mission, but when they learned that monks and priests were not held in high regard at the Chinese court, they adopted the style of dress of the Confucian literate elite of scholars, philosophers, and scientists. By 1595, Matteo Ricci was presenting himself not as a man of religion, but as a "Western man of letters." In order to advance Christianity in China, Ricci decided to "open neither church nor temple, but simply a preaching house, as do their most famous preachers."[1] What Ricci called a "preaching house" was a philosophical school, or a private academy, where distinguished teachers expounded on moral questions and interpreted the wisdom of the four Confucian classics. Like the teachers in these Confucian schools, Ricci mastered the Chinese language and literature while memorizing the classics. In addition, he taught mathematics, mechanics, and astronomy, and became widely known for displaying strange artifacts that inspired curiosity—clocks, telescopes, hydraulic pumps, maps, bound books, and religious paintings. "He is an altogether remarkable man," the Confucian philosopher Li Zhi (1527–1602) observed. But the philosopher wondered why Ricci had come so far to live in China. "I still do not know what he is here for. I think it would be much too stupid for him to want to substitute his own teaching for that of Confucius. So that is surely not the reason."[2]

Of course, replacing the Confucian, Taoist, and Buddhist traditions of China with Christianity was precisely what Matteo Ricci intended. His exclusive understanding of religion, in which Christianity was the sole means of salvation to the exclusion of all others, was at odds with the more flexible Chinese understanding of religious traditions as philosophical and practical resources to be drawn upon in making sense out of and living a fully human life. It was possible to enter a temple, for example, and find statues of Confucius, the Buddha, and the founder of Taoism, Lao Tsu, on the same altar. Although he wanted to replace all these Chinese religious resources with Christianity, Ricci found much in the ancient Confucian classics that was admirable, even locating some passages reminiscent of Christianity, such as the moral exhortation, "Do not do unto others what you would not have them do unto you." Although the Chinese lacked the revealed religion of the Bible, Ricci proposed that they showed traces of a "natural religion" that had been preserved in the Confucian texts. "Of all the pagan nations that are known to our Europe," he observed, "I know of none which has made fewer errors contrary to the things of Religion than the nation of China in its early Antiquity." Although praising the Confucian tradition, Matteo Ricci vigorously attacked the teachings of Taoists and Buddhists, arguing that they were based on a philosophy of nothingness that had become mixed up with idol worship. Those religions eventually had to be destroyed, but Confucianism used a philosophical vocabulary that could be appropriated, reworked, and replaced by Christian religious terms. In the style of a Confucian philosopher, therefore, Matteo Ricci composed his major text, *The True Meaning of the Doctrine of the Master of Heaven,* as an important step in his campaign to replace the "natural religion" of Confucianism with the revealed religion of Christianity.[3]

TRUE DOCTRINE

As Matteo Ricci explained, his book set out the three basic doctrines of Christian faith: "God, the creator of heaven and earth, the immortal soul, recompense for the good and punishment for the wicked—all things that are unknown to them and have not, until now, been believed." In identifying the Christian God, Ricci selected the Chinese term *Tianzhu,* "Master of Heaven." In the Confucian classics, references could be found to *Shangdi,* the "Sovereign on High," who was to be served and respected by human beings. "Having leafed through a great number of ancient books," Ricci asserted, "it is quite clear to me that the Sovereign on High and the Master of Heaven are different only in name." Presenting himself as an interpreter of Confucian texts, therefore, Ricci proposed that he understood the tradition better than previous commentators, because he had discerned the true nature of the Sovereign on High. Although Chinese scholars generally understood that heavenly sovereign as an impersonal power representing the order and vitality of the universe, Matteo Ricci insisted that the Sovereign on High mentioned in the ancient texts was the Master of Heaven, a personal, unique, and all-powerful creator God.[4]

Although this interpretation seemed strange to Confucian scholars, it could nevertheless be discussed and debated along with other questions of morality, mathematics, and science that formed the "heavenly studies" in the school of Matteo Ricci. A few scholars even embraced these teachings about the Master of Heaven as Christian converts. However, when they learned that Ricci and other missionaries were convinced that the Master of Heaven had been born as a human being, most Confucian scholars expressed shock and disbelief. For example, one Chinese scholar was surprised to discover that the missionaries "held Yesu, a man of the period of the emperor Ai, or the Han dynasty, to be the Sovereign on High to whom the Chinese do homage." How could this man, Yesu, who was born during the ancient Han dynasty, but lived far away in the West, where he was executed as a criminal, possibly be the Sovereign on High of Chinese tradition? Matteo Ricci, as another Chinese scholar noted, was careful not to call attention to the role of the man Yesu, especially his "lawful execution," when expounding his teachings about the Master of Heaven. "Thus all the literate elite have been deceived and duped," the scholar concluded. "That is what makes Ricci a great criminal."[5]

In the *Doctrine of the Master of Heaven*, however, Ricci had tried to explain the incarnation of Christ in terms that could be translated into familiar Chinese religious concepts. He recalled a time in human history when "those who followed their own desires had become daily more numerous while those who obeyed the principle of universal order had become increasingly rare." Any Confucian would understand that following personal desires, or acting out of self-interest, disrupted the harmony of universal order—*li*—that was maintained by observing ritual performances, moral propriety, and civic responsibility. During a time of such disruption, Ricci continued, "The Master of Heaven emitted a great thought of compassion and came in person to save the world so as to awaken beings everywhere." In these terms, the compassion of the Master of Heaven recalled the compassion of the Buddha, the Enlightened One, who came in person to enlighten others, awakening them to the futility of desire, the illusory character of the world, and the ultimate liberation from the cycle of birth, death, and rebirth. As he tried to present the Christian doctrine of the incarnation using a Chinese vocabulary, therefore, Matteo Ricci inadvertently transformed it into one that could be recognized as Confucian or Buddhist.[6]

Chinese critics of the Christian mission, however, argued that Jesus was neither a good Confucian nor a good Buddhist. According to a Confucian polemicist, Yang Guangxian (1597–1669), if Jesus had been the Confucian Sovereign on High, then Jesus would have taught Confucian propriety *(li)* in ritual and aesthetics, which in turn would have cultivated the principal Confucian ethical virtues of humanity *(jen)* and righteousness *(yi),* which ultimately would have resulted in peace, harmony, and prosperity in human society. "Instead of that," Yang Guangxian continued, "he only performed minor beneficent acts, such as healing the sick, raising the dead, walking on water and producing foods by magic means," acts the Confucian critic dismissed as insignificant. Christian claims about the miracles of Jesus had caused some resentment among Chinese intellectuals, however, because the Christian missionaries seemed to hide these reports of miracles from the philosophers while relating them to ordinary people to prey on their credulity. According to Yang Guangxian, however, the notion of miracles, which, in any case, were only "minor beneficent acts," was not the most serious problem with the Christian account of the life of the Master of Heaven on earth. Instead of showing a healthy Confucian interest in the well-being of human beings in society, the Master of Heaven, as represented in the teachings of Matteo Ricci, "only concerned himself with matters of paradise and hell." By only showing an interest in other worlds, Yang Guangxian concluded, the Christian Master of Heaven betrayed a contempt for life in this world.[7]

Matteo Ricci's doctrine of heaven and hell, an idea that many Chinese scholars accused him of stealing from the Buddhists, came in for special criticism. Since the human soul was immortal, Ricci taught, it would survive death to be rewarded or punished for its conduct. As Ricci knew, the Confucian, Buddhist, and Taoist traditions of China all insisted that conduct could only be regarded as moral if it was performed not out of self-interest—fearing punishment, desiring reward—but because it was right. In cultivating moral behavior, therefore, afterlife places of punishment and reward were at best irrelevant, at worst counterproductive, because believing in such places tended to cause people to act out of self-interest rather than a sense of ethical duty. Referring to the ancient Confucian classics, Ricci recalled that a sage of olden times said: "What need is there to believe in the existence of paradise and hell? If paradises exist worthy people certainly ascend there. And if hells exist, the wicked surely go there. All we have to do is act as worthy people." But Ricci countered this conclusion. "If one does not believe in paradise and hell," he insisted, "one is certainly not a worthy man."[8]

However, this insistence on believing in afterlife rewards in heaven and punishments in hell inspired human beings to act on the basis of what one Confucian scholar called "ignoble calculations founded upon self-interest." Even worse, entry into paradise was determined not on the basis of good conduct, but on the whim of the Master of Heaven. According to Xu Dashou, "The books of the Barbarians say: if you have done good throughout your life but have not made yourself agreeable to the Master of Heaven, all your goodness will have been in vain. If you have done evil all your life but for one single instant did make yourself agreeable to the Master of Heaven, all the evil you have done will immediately be absolved." In all this, the critic Yang Guangxian complained, the Christians were not being good Buddhists. "Hells and paradises," he observed, "were thought up by the Buddhists as a means to encourage stupid people to be good." However, as every Buddhist philosopher knew, such places of punishment and reward were ultimately not real:

> It is not as if there are really any hells or paradises: the blessings that result from good actions and the misfortunes that come in the wake of bad ones— these are the only true paradises and hells of the present world. . . . But these people teach, absurdly, that paradises and hells truly do exist above and below us and they say that those who honor their doctrine of the Master of Heaven go up to paradise while the rest go down to hell. Their Master of Heaven is just a rogue then, inciting people to flatter him.

In the end, therefore, Christian afterlife rewards and punishments had nothing to do with morality. All those who lived good lives, even the ancient sages who were moral exemplars for China, were condemned to hell if they had failed to flatter the Master of Heaven. The worst criminal, however, could enter heaven by gaining the favor and forgiveness of Yesu, his mother, and the Master of Heaven. "In all conscience," Yang Guangxian exclaimed, "their paradise must be a proper den of thieves!"[9]

After 1620, under the weight of such criticisms, Chinese scholars generally lost interest in the teachings of the Master of Heaven. Increasingly, they perceived the Christian teachings about God, immortality, and the afterlife as a distortion or perversion of Chinese religion. However, they also had fundamental problems with the Aristotelian logic employed by the Jesuit missionaries in expounding their Christian doctrines. Following a long Greco-Roman philosophical tradition, the missionaries distinguished between substance and accidents, cause and effect, the physical and the spiritual, and other binary oppositions, in ways alien to Chinese patterns of thought. On purely philosophical grounds, therefore, Chinese intellectuals questioned the logical distinctions imposed by Christian doctrine, even as they also recognized its potentially disruptive influence on moral conduct, ritual propriety, and social relations in China.

At the same time, religious thinkers in Japan also raised critical questions about both the logic and the desirability of the new Christian religion. Having been influenced by the religious traditions of Confucianism and Buddhism from China, as well as maintaining indigenous traditions that came to be known as Shinto, Japan also had a difficult relationship with Christian missions. In 1620, for example, Fabian Fucan (ca. 1583–1607), a Japanese convert who had renounced Christianity, identified the danger of the new religion. "The first commandment says: 'Love your God above all else,'" he noted. "You must therefore place him above both sovereign and parents and disobey the orders of your sovereign and your parents if they are not in agreement with the will of God." By asserting this transcendent claim on loyalty, therefore, the Christian religion threatened to undermine the practices of filial piety and reverence for rulers cultivated in Japanese religion. "Is this not proof," Fabian Fucan demanded, "that they desire to destroy the religions and state of Japan?"

Written at a time during which the Japanese *shogun* was consolidating his political power over all of Japan, Fabian Fucan's critique of Christianity recalled the history of Christian conquests elsewhere in the world. "They have sent troops and usurped power in countries such as Luzon [the Philippines] and New Spain," he wrote. "Hence their ambition to spread their doctrine throughout our land and thus take over our country even if it should take them a thousand years to do so."[10] Since Christianity represented the prospect of both internal subversion and foreign conquest, rulers in China, Japan, and elsewhere in Asia took measures to block the progress of Christian missions within their territories. Therefore, although the initial overtures of Matteo Ricci and his colleagues had initiated an Asian conversation about the doctrines of the Master of Heaven, the result was political opposition to Christian missions.

HEAVENLY KINGDOM

At the beginning of the nineteenth century, Christianity was a prohibited religion within the Chinese empire, although the Roman Catholic Church had persisted, counting perhaps 250,000 Chinese converts by 1800. Protestantism, however, had no discernible presence in China. Identified as the "English religion," Protestant Christianity was specifically forbidden by the emperor of China. Nevertheless, the London Missionary Society sent the first Protestant missionary to China, Robert Morrison (1782–1834), who arrived in the European trading enclave of Canton in 1807. Since his personal contacts with the Chinese living outside of Canton were restricted by law, Morrison devoted his time to learning the Chinese language, acting as interpreter for the East India Company, and translating the Bible, the *Book of Common Prayer* of the Church of England, and the shorter catechism of the Church of Scotland. Although converts were few, these publications occasionally got through the cultural embargo around the European settlement of Canton and circulated among a literate Chinese public.[11]

A prominent Chinese convert to the Protestant mission, Liang Afa (1789–1855), who had been originally hired by the London Missionary Society as a printer, produced his own book, which was published in 1832 as *Good Words for Exhorting the Age*. In nine chapters, Liang Afa related biblical stories of the creation of the world by the Heavenly God, the evil serpent, the expulsion of Adam and Eve from the garden, the flood and Noah's Ark, the destruction of Sodom and Gomorrah, the warnings of the prophets, the promises of Jesus in the Sermon on the Mount, and the end of the world foretold in the book of Revelation. Traveling throughout the countryside around Canton, Liang Afa distributed thousands of copies of his book and other Christian tracts, especially targeting students preparing for the official Confucian examinations. *Good Words for Exhorting the Age* had a dramatic and unexpected impact on one Confucian student, Hong Xiuquan (1813–64), who used the text as an entry into a religious world that inspired him to renounce Confucianism, embrace Christianity, and discover his own divine destiny as the second son of God, the younger brother of Jesus Christ.

Although he received a copy in 1836, Hong apparently did not read the book carefully at that time. Preparing to take the provincial Confucian examinations in Canton, which he had failed twice before, Hong was concentrating on demonstrating mastery of Confucian principles of ritual, ethics, and governance. However, when he failed the exams again, Hong became seriously ill. During his illness, convinced that he was dying, Hong dreamed that he was carried to the heavens, where he was met by attendants dressed in dragon robes who cut him open, replaced his internal organs, and resealed his body. They gave him texts to read. Then a woman appeared, calling him "son," and said, "Your body is soiled from your descent into the world. Let your mother cleanse you in the river, after which you can go to see your father." Appearing as a tall man with a golden beard, his father welcomed Hong by saying, "So you have come back up?" His father proceeded to explain to Hong that the world had been led astray by evil demons. People had even been deceived into presenting offerings before the images of these demons. Hong begged his father to allow him to go into battle against the forces of evil. Armed with spiritual weapons and assisted by his elder brother, Hong fought the demons through thirty-three levels of heaven. When he rested from battle with his wife, First Chief Moon, Hong received moral instruction from his father in the company of his elder brother and his elder brother's wife. Finally, bestowing upon him the title "Heavenly King," Hong's father sent him back to earth to continue his fight against demons and establish his authority as the "Son of Heaven in the Period of Great Peace *(Taiping)*."

When Hong related the details of this vision to his family and neighbors, they concluded that he was insane. Gradually he returned to his Confucian studies. But when he again failed the examinations in 1843, Hong returned to Liang Afa's *Good Words for Exhorting the Age* and found the key for interpreting his dreams. "These books are certainly sent by heaven to me," he observed, "to confirm the truth of my former experiences." In the process of carefully rereading Liang Afa's text, Hong realized that the "Highest God of Heaven," the supreme Ye-huo-hua, was the heavenly father he had met in his visions; the "Son of God," who had descended to earth to save people from Confucian, Taoist, and Buddhist idolatry, was his elder brother, whose birth had been proclaimed by angels singing, "Glory to God in the Highest, and on earth Great Peace and good will toward men." Having already battled demons on behalf of his father in heaven, Hong embarked upon a religious campaign against demons in this world. Forming the God Worshipers Society, Hong had succeeded by 1848 in attracting a following of about ten thousand adherents to his religious message of the One True God and the two Sons of God.

Although he had spent about two months with the Baptist missionary Isaachar Roberts, where he learned something about praying, singing hymns, and preaching sermons, Hong for the most part adapted his Christian beliefs and practices from the biblical texts and religious pamphlets distributed by the Protestant missionary society. However, he composed a *Book of Heavenly Precepts* to clarify the Christian gospel in the light of his own revelations. The ritual of baptism that marked initiation into the community of God Worshipers indicated a commitment to live by the heavenly precepts. Initiates were brought before an altar on which three cups of tea were placed. They read a confession of faith, recorded their names on paper, and then burned the documents to send their message of conversion up to the Heavenly Father. Renouncing the worship of images and evil conduct, the initiates drank the three cups of tea, sprinkled water over their foreheads and hearts, and then were immersed by attendants in water. Led by a lay preacher on the Sabbath every Saturday, the congregation recited Hong's prayers, sang Christian hymns, and listened to a sermon on such topics as God's mercy, Jesus' merits, and the importance of cultivating "sincerity of heart." The service concluded with a song composed by Hong on the virtues of the Trinity. The God Worshipers Society also supported ethical ideals of egalitarian participation in society, gender equality in the allocation of land, and mutual support through the pooling of all financial resources in a common "Sacred Treasury." During a time of drought, famine, and warfare in southern China, the God Worshipers Society provided a haven of peace in the world.

After 1848, two changes occurred in the religion of the God Worshipers. First, the heavenly precepts that Hong had derived from biblical texts and his own revelations were supplemented by new sources of religious knowledge and power that came directly from heaven. Two prominent disciples of Hong began to deliver divine oracles similar to those spoken by the shamans of Chinese popular religion, but they spoke on behalf of the Christian divine beings. Xiao Chaogui (d. 1852) conveyed messages from Jesus, the Elder Brother. For example, in support of Hong, the King of Great Peace, Jesus was recorded as saying, "You should acknowledge him. In Heaven you should trust Heavenly Father and me; on earth you should follow his instruction." Later, Yang Xiuqing (d. 1856) transmitted messages directly from God, the Father. Although only Hong had ascended to heaven to see the Heavenly Father and Elder Brother, the Christian divine beings regularly descended to earth to speak through the mouths of Yang and Xiao. Furthermore, Yang introduced techniques of spiritual healing, again drawing on practices associated with Chinese shamans, that gained him the titles of "Redeemer from Disease," "Comforter," and "Wind of the Holy Spirit." Therefore, the entire Christian Trinity—Heavenly Father, Elder Brother, and Wind of the Holy Spirit—were felt to be present among the community of God Worshipers.

Second, the God Worshipers' struggle against demon worshipers took on a new militant character. Hong formulated that conflict as a strict opposition between good and evil, God and demons, heaven and hell. As he taught,

> Those who truly believe in God are indeed the sons and daughters of God; whatever locality they come from, they have come from Heaven, and no matter where they are going they will ascend to Heaven. Those who worship the demon devils are truly the pawns and slaves of the demon devils; from the moment of birth they are deluded by devils, and at the day of their death the devils will drag them away.

In 1850, as the Manchu government sent troops to suppress the movement, the God Worshipers explicitly identified the emperor, officials, and army as demons. Shifting from spiritual to earthly warfare, the God Worshipers were organized into an army to overthrow the Manchu demons and establish the Taiping Heavenly Kingdom. After a series of military successes, the Taiping army in 1853 captured the city of Nanking. Declaring the city to be the Heavenly Capital, or the "New Jerusalem," of the kingdom, Hong established himself in imperial splendor. The Taiping Heavenly Kingdom, under the authority of God's second son, was established on earth for over a decade.

In transforming Nanking into the capital of a Christian theocracy, the Taiping leaders had to confront the religious diversity of the city. Since they had consistently demonized adherents of other Chinese religions as devil worshipers, the new officials of the Heavenly Kingdom immediately set about burning Confucian, Taoist, and Buddhist temples, smashing statues, and killing priests. Survivors were forced to adopt the Taiping religion. The Temple of the God of Literature, a shrine for Confucian scholars, was taken over for printing the Bible and other religious texts. Catholic converts, however, who numbered about two hundred, posed a special problem because their religious beliefs seemed so close to the Christianity of the God Worshipers. Nevertheless, on Good Friday in 1853, Taiping soldiers stopped the Catholic service by bursting into the church, destroying the cross, and overturning the altar. Catholics who refused to recite their prayers according to the Taiping liturgy were threatened with death, military conscription, or forced labor.

As religious alternatives were closed, the Taiping leadership organized the population of the city along both military and religious lines in which all families formed one "family of the Lord their God on High." Private surpluses were pooled in public treasuries for redistribution in keeping with the economic principle of the Heavenly Kingdom, which held that "when people of this earth keep nothing for their private use but give all things to God for all to use in common, then in the whole land every place shall have equal shares, and every one be clothed and fed." Under this regimental system, therefore, the military, political, and economic life of the city was coordinated around the worship of the One True God who had sent Hong, "the Taiping Heavenly Lord to come down and save the world."[12]

Although the Taiping theocracy drew on the Bible, the Ten Commandments, and the Lord's Prayer, these Christian resources were specifically interpreted in the light of Hong's visions. Accordingly, Taiping teachings were often disputed by Protestant missionaries who came into contact with them. For example, the Baptist missionary Isaachar Roberts, who had met Hong in 1847, was invited in 1861 to the Heavenly Capital of the Taiping Kingdom. During his fifteen-month stay, Roberts decided that Hong's religious teachings were "abominable in the sight of God." Furthermore, Roberts concluded, "I believe he is crazy, especially in religious matters." Although Roberts himself had been described as "partially deranged" by a fellow missionary, Roberts and other missionaries objected to Taiping teachings on the nature of God and the person of Jesus.[13]

The missionaries insisted that God was invisible. As one Chinese missionary text explained, "God is without form, sound, scent or taste; we can neither observe His form, nor hear His voice, nor feel nor perceive Him by any bodily organs." On the contrary, Hong referred to the authority of his own visionary experiences to maintain that God "can be seen only by those who ascend to Heaven." Having made that heavenly ascent, Hong could describe in detail the physical features of God, his height, breadth, and weight, the length and color of his beard, and the character of his cap and clothing. As for Jesus, who was explained by the missionaries as being one with God, Hong argued that the Father and the Son could not be the same. Missionaries accused the Taiping movement of adopting the Arian heresy by denying the coequal divinity of the Son of God. However, Hong again referred to his own visions. "If Christ were God, and ascended to Heaven where he and God became as one," Hong demanded, "then how could it be that when I myself ascended to Heaven I saw that in Heaven there was God the Father, there was the Heavenly Mother, and there was also the Elder Brother Christ and the Heavenly Elder Sister-in-law?" Although the foreign Christian missionaries came from nations that had long worshiped God and Jesus, their religious beliefs were based only upon what they had heard. However, Hong advised, "it is always the same: hearing with one's ears is not as good as seeing with one's own eyes."

Basing his religious teachings on the evidential authority of what he had seen, Hong also found confirmation for his understanding of God and Jesus in the Bible. In the Chinese translation of the book of Exodus, for example, he found that God had written the Ten Commandments "with his own hand" and had spoken to Moses "with his own mouth." Such biblical texts, therefore, supported Hong's vision of the materiality of God. In the martyrdom of Stephen described in the book of Acts, when Stephen says, "Behold, I see the heavens opened, and the Son of Man standing at the right hand of God," Hong found confirmation for his understanding of the separate identities of Father and Son. As Hong argued, this text "clearly proves that one is Father and one is Son." However, the Bible was not always reliable because it had allegedly been distorted during the long process of its transmission. In correcting the biblical texts, Hong removed references to sexual improprieties, drunkenness, and other immoral behavior that might lead the people astray. He clarified the nature of God, inserted Jesus, the Elder Brother, into Old Testament stories, and, in one of his most significant corrections, deleted the word "only" from the New Testament identification of Jesus as God's "only begotten son." Through careful editing, therefore, the Bible could be restored as a sacred text consistent with the teachings of the Heavenly

Father, the Elder Brother, and the Younger Brother, the Heavenly Lord of the Taiping Kingdom.

In developing his distinctive Taiping Christianity, Hong rejected the ancient Confucian texts and traditions of China. In his spiritual visions, he saw a confrontation between God and Confucius that clearly subordinated the Chinese sage to heavenly authority. As he was bound and whipped in heaven, Confucius begged before the Heavenly Father and the Elder Brother to be spared. Taking mercy on Confucius, they allowed him to remain in heaven, but prevented him from ever descending again into the world. Although his books contained references to heaven and morality, the Confucian texts would eventually be burned during the era of Great Peace. However, the very notion of Great Peace, Taiping, had been developed by Confucian scholars during the ancient Han dynasty as an ideal of social harmony based on moral conduct, filial piety, and loyalty to the emperor. Although Hong established himself as a new Christian emperor of a heavenly kingdom on earth, Taiping ideals of morality, family, and loyalty recast important aspects of the Confucian tradition.

In the end, however, this innovation in Chinese Christianity could not be sustained. Worn down by internal dissension, military defeats, and a long siege by imperial troops, the capital of the Heavenly Kingdom finally fell in 1864 to the forces of the Manchu rulers. Dying of illness six weeks before the destruction of his capital, Hong did not witness the mass executions of his family and followers. However, death had been a familiar feature of the Taiping Kingdom. During the process of creating a new heaven on earth between 1851 and 1864, the Taiping rebellion had resulted in the death of as many as 40 million people through warfare, starvation, and executions in southern and central China. "I have received the sacred command of God, the sacred command of the Heavenly Brother Jesus," Hong reasserted just before his death, "to come down into the world to become the only true Sovereign of the myriad countries under Heaven." Although his religious mission ended in destruction, Hong had fashioned a blend of Christianity, Confucianism, and socialism that briefly promised to establish heaven on earth.[14]

NO CHURCH

In Japan, where Christianity had been banned since 1638, the Meiji government, which came to power in 1868, reinforced the prohibition of the "heretical religion Christianity." When the ambassadors from European nations objected to this denigration of Christianity as a heretical religion, the Meiji government rewrote the proclamation as two paragraphs, one prohibiting heretical religions, the other prohibiting Christianity. However, despite the official prohibition of Christianity and persecution of Christian converts, Roman Catholic and Protestant missions increased their activities in Japan. The French priest B. T. Petitjean (1829–84) discovered a group of peasants in Urakami who had secretly preserved the Catholic faith that they traced back to the Portuguese Catholic missions of the sixteenth century. Protestants from North America, Britain, and the Netherlands conducted secret missions. Influenced by missionaries of the American Presbyterian Church and the Dutch Reformed Church, a group of students in Yokohama in 1872 formed the Church of Christ in Japan, *Nihon Kirisuto Kōkai,* as the first independent Japanese Protestant church. Acceding to the demands of European and North American diplomats, but also recognizing this proliferation of Christian activity, the Meiji government withdrew its prohibition of Christianity in 1873. Although never more than a small minority, Japanese Christians could freely participate in churches, schools, and religious associations.[15]

The Japanese government's commitment to religious freedom was restated in the Meiji constitution of 1889, which guaranteed freedom of religious belief to all Japanese subjects as long their religion was "not antagonistic to their duties as subjects." A year later, the emperor issued the Rescript on Education, which specified that all subjects were bound to "guard and maintain the prosperity of Our Imperial Throne coeval with heaven and earth." As the master of heaven and earth, therefore, the Meiji emperor was to be revered by all Japanese subjects. In the schools, where Western science and Christian culture were beginning to exert an influence, the Rescript on Education assumed a special role. As every school displayed a copy of the document, along with pictures of the emperor and empress, new rituals were developed for reciting and respecting what became a sacred text of an official religion, the civil religion of state Shinto. By bowing before the emperor's signature on the text, students and teachers in Japanese schools were required to display their loyalty to the imperial throne.[16]

In 1891 Uchimura Kanzō (1861–1930), a lecturer in the First Junior College, refused to bow before the imperial Rescript on Education and was dismissed from his teaching position. As a Christian, Uchimura

Kanzō felt that he could not perform such an act of religious devotion to the emperor. In response to his refusal to respect the imperial edict, anti-Christian sentiment was renewed in Japan. The leading anti-Christian spokesman, Inouye Tetsujirō, professor of philosophy at the Tokyo Imperial University, published *A Conflict Between Religion and Education,* in which he argued that the Christian teachings about universal love were inconsistent with the Confucian respect for parents and the Shinto reverence for the emperor enshrined in the Rescript on Education. Christianity, therefore, was found to be subversive of the domestic, social, and political order of Japan.[17]

Uchimura Kanzō was well aware that Christianity was widely perceived in Japan as a strange foreign import. Recalling his first exposure to Christianity, he related that a school friend had encouraged him to attend a church for its entertainment value. Uchimura Kanzō began attending church every Sunday, not for truth seeking, he recalled, but for sightseeing. "Christianity was an enjoyable thing to me so long as I was not asked to accept it," he remembered. "Its music, its stories, the kindness shown me by its followers, pleased me immensely." After five years of regular attendance, Uchimura Kanzō was formally requested to convert. He refused to convert to Christianity, however, not only because it would require submitting to Christian laws and church discipline, but also because it seemed to him to represent a serious betrayal of Japan. As Uchimura Kanzō explained,

> I early learned to honor my nation above all others, and to worship my nation's gods and no others. I thought I could not be forced even by death itself to vow my allegiance to any other gods than my country's. I should be a traitor to my country, and an apostate from my national faith by accepting a faith which is exotic in its origin.

When he enrolled in the Protestant agricultural college at Sapporo, Uchimura Kanzō found that all the senior students had already converted to Christianity. As students of the incoming class also converted, he found himself alone in the school as an adherent of the ancestral religion of Japan. However, he found himself tormented, as he later put it, "with the most unwelcome persuasion to accept the new faith." Shortly afterward, Uchimura Kanzō made a commitment to the "strange god," a commitment that was strengthened a few years later during a period of working and studying in the United States, where he "meditated upon Christ, the Bible, the Trinity, the Resurrection, and other kindred subjects." In the crucifixion of the Son of God, he found, all debts were paid, purity restored, and salvation promised in the kingdom of heaven.

Returning to Japan, however, Uchimura Kanzō found that his religious commitment was in tension with Japanese society. After he was dismissed as a teacher for his refusal to bow to the signature of the emperor in 1891, Uchimura Kanzō worked as a journalist, eventually becoming the editor of Japan's largest daily newspaper. But his outspoken Christian pacifism cost him his job. He turned to publishing a monthly series of Bible commentaries—*Seisho no kenkyū* (Biblical Studies)—that became the basis for a new Japanese Christian movement. Known as *mukyōkai* or *mukyōkai shugi,* which meant "no church," "nonchurch," or "Christianity of the no-church principle," this movement was dedicated to establishing a relationship between human beings and God through the prayerful use of the Bible alone.

The true form of the Christian church, Uchimura Kanzō argued, was *mukyōkai,* "no church." He insisted that this principle of "no church" should not be understood as anarchism or nihilism; he did not call for the rejection or destruction of existing churches. Rather, he pointed to the eschatological church in the kingdom of heaven. "There is no organized church in heaven," he observed. "The Revelation of John says, 'I saw no temple (church) within the city (heaven).'" Looking toward that final kingdom, Uchimura Kanzō found that there would be no church sacraments of baptism or Communion; no church leadership of bishops, deacons, preachers, and teachers; and no church organization because the New Jerusalem, the city of God, would reign supreme in a new heaven and a new earth. The nonchurch movement, therefore, anticipated the fulfillment of that future promise in the present. "*Mukyōkai,*" he explained, "hopes to introduce this sort of church to the world."

Acknowledging that many people needed churches built of stone, brick, or wood, Uchimura Kanzō dedicated his nonchurch movement to "God's universe—nature," a natural universe, between the blue skies and green fields, of beauty, colors, and music, in which the only preacher was God. "This is our church," Uchimura Kanzō concluded. "No church, whether in Rome or in London, can approximate it. In this sense, *Mukyōkai* has a church. Only those who have no church as conceived in conventional terms have the true church."

Therefore, in the future promise of heaven and the present order of nature, Uchimura Kanzō discerned a universal true church that was "no church." The universal character of his nonchurch movement, however, raised again the national question of this religion's specific place in Japan. For most Japanese, Christianity was a foreign religion, but Uchimura Kanzō consistently maintained that the nonchurch movement supported a national loyalty to Japan. "I love two J's and no third," Uchimura Kanzō wrote. "One is Jesus, and the other is Japan. I do not know which I love more, Jesus or Japan." By merging what Christians regarded as a universal religious truth with a particular national identity, Uchimura Kanzō came into conflict with both Japanese traditionalists and foreign Christian missionaries. "I am blamed by missionaries for upholding Japanese Christianity," he observed. "They say that Christianity is a universal religion, and to uphold Japanese Christianity is to make a universal religion a national religion." However, no universal Christianity exists, Uchimura Kanzō argued, that is not infused with a specific local, cultural, or national character. Setting the model for the expansion of Christianity, the apostle Paul, a Hebrew to the Hebrews, had been a Hebrew Christian. In Europe, he argued, the six hundred different forms of Christianity all assumed distinctive national forms, English Episcopalians, Scottish Presbyterians, German Lutherans, and so on, each giving Christianity a specific location. By affirming both Jesus and Japan, therefore, Uchimura Kanzō imagined a Japanese Christianity that would make Japanese better Christians and Christians better Japanese.

Uchimura Kanzō continued to be in conflict with Japanese nationalists and foreign missionaries. Toward the end of his life, however, he experienced further distress when his followers tried to create a church based on his "Christianity of the no-church principle." How could a church be built on the doctrine that there should be no church? While they awaited the imminent second coming of Christ, Uchimura Kanzō advised, Christians of the nonchurch movement could find their true church only in the beauty of nature and the hope of heaven. In the context of the long interchange between Asia and Christianity, this movement represented a significant attempt to formulate an indigenous Asian Christianity. As we have seen, many previous attempts had been made to locate Christianity in Asia as an indigenous religion. Although Matteo Ricci had found the Master of Heaven in the Confucian classics, Hong Xiuquan had found himself, as the younger brother of Jesus, in the Christian Bible. Uchimura

Kanzō, however, developed his Japanese Christianity on the basis of the more general principle that all Christianity is indigenous Christianity. Although representing a universal truth that requires no church to defend, Christianity necessarily assumes local forms that anchor it in the real world. In composing the inscription for his tombstone, Uchimura Kanzō stated his vision of an indigenous Japanese Christianity that led from the particular to the universal: "I for Japan; Japan for the World; the World for Christ; and all for God."[18]

26

Hindu Christians

Arriving in southern India in 1606, the Italian Jesuit missionary Roberto Nobili (1577–1656) endeavored to learn the local vernacular languages of Tamil and Telegu, the sacred language of Sanskrit, and the religious traditions of the Brahmins, the priestly class of Hindu tradition. Like Matteo Ricci in China, he also sought to identify himself and his mission with the interests of local scholars. Asserting that the Brahmins were teachers rather than priests, Nobili adopted the dress, eating habits, local dialect, and rituals of purification of these Hindu authorities. Like the Brahmins, he anointed his body with sandalwood paste. In terms of the detailed ranking of social classes and occupations within the Hindu caste system, these signs of priestly status and ritual purity placed Roberto Nobili in an upper-class position. When he learned that the brahmanic scholars revered the ancient sacred texts of the Vedas, Nobili proposed that his Christian mission had brought a lost Veda, the Veda of salvation, that would rescue India from its pagan idolatry. Drawing a stark contrast between two religions—Christian salvation and Hindu paganism— Roberto Nobili imagined that his mission in India would inspire a mass conversion similar to the conversion from paganism of "the first Christians in Europe."

Nobili's mission, however, did not mark the earliest introduction of Christianity to India. A small group of Roman Catholic converts, the fishing community known as the Paravas, traced their allegiance to Christianity back to the mission in the 1540s of the Portuguese Jesuit Francis Xavier (1506–52). Considered lower class within the Hindu caste system, these Christian converts were prohibited from entering Hindu temples, shrines, or other sacred precincts. Furthermore, since most roadways were used for the frequent religious processions that celebrated Hindu deities or Hindu rulers, these lower-class Christians were banned from the streets of towns and villages throughout southern India. By the time Roberto Nobili arrived, the Christian community of Paravas was served by a Portuguese Jesuit, the former soldier Gonçalo Fernandes. Identifying with his lower-class community, Fernandes complained about Nobili's adoption of the upper-class dress and manners of the religious teachers and renunciates, as well as his wearing of the sacred thread associated with the priestly and ruling class. Fernandes also opposed Nobili's adoption of Hindu religious practices, especially his use of sandalwood paste. The sandalwood "is blessed by him on Sunday before Mass and then distributed," Fernandes complained. "Rubbing sandal on the forehead is the ceremony used by the pagans when they offer their *puja* [worship]." By assimilating and adopting these local signs of Hindu social status and ritual purity, Fernandes insisted, Roberto Nobili had betrayed the Christian mission in India.

Countering this accusation, Nobili argued that if he only wanted to save his own soul he could dress and act as he pleased; but if he wanted to teach, gather disciples, and save other souls "he had as far as he could to adapt himself to the manners, customs, and ideas of this country." Therefore, Nobili explicitly advocated an assimilationist approach to advancing the Christian mission in foreign lands. According to Fernandes, however, this capacity to assimilate other religious beliefs and practices was not Christian, but Hindu. "The Brahmins are obliged to defend their law," he observed, "but in such a manner that it may not discredit other laws, because they say that all other laws have something of their own law." Unlike the Hindu priests, who easily assimilated other religious teachings into their own flexible framework, Fernandes assumed that Christians had to defend their religious law as a unique revelation by taking a confrontational stance against heathen or pagan "superstition" in India.[1]

Clearly, this early seventeenth-century argument between two Jesuits was about both religion and social class, since Nobili and Fernandes disputed the place of Christianity within the Hindu caste system. However, long before either of their missions to India, a Christian community in southern India had worked out its own position in that traditional network of social classification based on kinship, occupation, social status, and ritual purity. Known as "Thomas" or "Syrian" Christians, that community had flourished for centuries as a Christian church at home in a larger Hindu environment.

THOMAS CHRISTIANS

According to their traditional account, Thomas Christians could be traced back to the first-century mission of the apostle Thomas, the "Doubting Thomas" of the New Testament, who arrived on the Malabar coast in 50 C.E. to evangelize and build churches throughout southern India. During his travels, Thomas reportedly founded at least seven of the ancient churches of the region before undergoing a violent martyrdom.[2] Accordingly, Thomas Christians claimed an apostolic lineage going back to one of the original disciples of Jesus. Historians have suggested that the community was originally formed by the descendants of West Asian traders involved in the international pepper market and their local converts, since connections were maintained with West Asian Christian centers in what is now Turkey and Iraq. Using Syriac as their language of worship, the Thomas Christians seem to have been in conversation with the doctrinal controversies and ecclesiastical divisions of Syrian Christianity. Having had ties with the "East Syrian" church, which adopted the Nestorian distinction between the divine and human persons of Christ, by the middle of the seventeenth century Thomas Christians were linked to the "West Syrian" or Jacobite church, through the patriarch of Antioch, which advocated the Monophysite understanding that the human and divine in Christ formed a single, indivisible Person. More important than these doctrinal issues, however, was the spiritual power and authority conveyed by the bishops of West Asia. Regarded as a source of extraordinary sacred energy, the West Asian patriarch transmitted that energy through rituals of consecration and ordination. For the hereditary priesthood of the Thomas Christians, an ongoing connection with West Asia, which was marked by the occasional visits of bishops, monks, and other holy men and by acquiring holy oil from the patriarch, renewed the sacred energy of the community in India. The holy men who possessed this spiritual power were revered not only during their lives, but also after their deaths. Their tombs became important sites of pilgrimage for devotional rituals that celebrated the saints and heroes who gave life to the community. Although located in southern India, these sacred sites anchored the sacred power drawn from the Syrian holy men of West Asia.

In addition to maintaining these Syrian connections, Thomas Christians formed local links with the Hindu priestly and ruling classes in southern India. The ruling nobility of Hindu warriors, known as Nayars, had developed a religious culture of instruction in the arts of warfare.

Under the guidance of master warriors, or *panikkars,* disciples learned both spiritual discipline and the use of weapons. Similarly, Shafi'i Muslims in the region had formed schools for religious and military training. In this context of military prestige and power, Christian *panikkars* created their own schools of martial instruction, building networks of Christian and Hindu disciples in the spiritual arts of warfare. As a result, Thomas Christians acquired an important place in southern Indian society as an elite warrior group known as the "bearers of the curved sword," which was regarded by Hindu rulers as a superior caste group of the same status as Nayar warriors. They so thoroughly integrated the customs of this Hindu upper-class status that, as an early European traveler observed, "there is no distinction either in their habits or in their hair, or in any thing else, betwixt the [Thomas] Christians of this diocese and the heathen Nayars."[3]

In matters of religion, interchange between Hindus and Christians was common. Although the rajas were patrons of Hindu temples, they also occasionally financed Christian churches, placed their sacred sites under royal protection, and participated in their festivals. In exchange, Thomas Christians donated financial support for Hindu shrines and festivals. When Hindu temples and Christian churches were built on adjoining sites, they shared the same ritual regalia—the torches, umbrellas, banners, and even elephants—that were familiar features of both Hindu and Christian processions. During the holiest days of their sacred calendar, the *cattam* festivals that commemorated the anniversaries of the deaths of their saints and holy men, the Thomas Christians led processions through the streets, offered sacrificial cocks at the shrine of the Nayar warrior goddess, and distributed sacred food in ways that resembled the familiar practices of Hindu festivals. Furthermore, in their domestic rituals, Thomas Christians observed rites of birth, initiation into adulthood, marriage, and death, including the *sraddha* rites for the deceased that removed the pollution associated with death, thus ensuring their status as a "clean" caste in the Hindu caste system. In all these respects, therefore, Thomas Christians developed a Christian way of life based not only on an apostolic succession of sacred power and authority that could be traced back to a disciple of Jesus, but also on local patterns of religious conduct in southern India.

Under the influence of the Portuguese, who established their first trading station on the coast of southern India in 1498, the Thomas Christians entered a new era of religious conflict as they were caught between the competing claims to sacred authority asserted by Rome and West Asia. Within the terms of the pope's *padroado real,* or "royal patronage," the Portuguese were granted rights over all churches in their overseas territories. As they established fortresses, settlements, and trading posts to take over the spice trade, the Portuguese also tried to assert control over Christianity in southern India. This assertion of religious authority, however, was in conflict with the traditional allegiance of Thomas Christians to the sacred power and authority of holy men from West Asia. Between 1503 and 1583, an increasing number of West Asian monks and bishops arrived in southern India to be enthusiastically received by the Thomas Christians as miracle-working holy men. From the Portuguese perspective, however, these were "vile Nestorian heretics."[4] In order to combat the influence of West Asian clergy, the Portuguese captured the sacred shrine at Mylapore, the site of the martyrdom of the apostle Thomas, and transformed it into a new pilgrimage center under Roman Catholic control.

Mylapore was an interreligious sacred site revered by southern Indian Hindus, Muslims, and Christians. It drew its name from the Tamil word *mayil,* or "peacock," which was the sacred bird of the local Hindu deity, Lord Murukan. The apostle Thomas was also associated with the peacock. In one popular account of his martyrdom, Thomas transformed himself into a peacock but was shot by a hunter, who found that only a human footprint remained where the bird had been killed. With its connection to both a Hindu deity and Christian resurrection, therefore, the peacock was an important interreligious symbol in Mylapore. Portuguese navigators entering Mylapore in 1517 were surprised to find the tomb of the apostle Thomas guarded by a Muslim, who pointed out the footprint of the apostle and claimed to have been cured of blindness by the spiritual power of the saint. Apparently, the shrine of Thomas was revered as a site of sacred energy and healing by both Christians and Muslims. The Portuguese Catholics, however, took over the site and dug up bones they certified as relics of the apostle Thomas. They built shrines and cathedrals for the apostle, the most prominent being located on two hills, St. Thomas's Mount, where the church featured a cross that was miraculously seen to bleed, and Little Mount, where the St. Thomas Cathedral housed the relics of the apostle. Organizing large-scale pilgrimages to these shrines of Thomas, the Portuguese also introduced the Roman Catholic veneration of the Virgin Mary. Through all these measures,

Portuguese Catholics hoped to reorient the Thomas Christians away from their adherence to West Asia to a new allegiance to Rome.[5]

Influenced by new demands for Catholic orthodoxy emerging out of the Council of Trent (1545–63), the Portuguese authorities succeeded in 1599 in convincing the Thomas Christians to reject their West Asian tradition and accept the religious authority of the Roman Catholic Church. In the 1650s a substantial minority of Thomas Christians, outraged by the alleged murder of a visiting West Asian bishop by Portuguese officials, broke with Rome and eventually established a formal link with the West Syrian or "Jacobite" church of Antioch. In the space of a century, they had moved through three different doctrinal positions. Originally subscribing to the Nestorian doctrine of the East Syrian Church, which separated the human and divine Persons of Christ, they had been converted to the Chalcedonian doctrine upheld by the Roman Catholic Church, which identified two natures in one Person, but had finally identified with the Monophysite doctrine of the West Syrian Church, which insisted on a single divinely human nature in the Person of Christ. Clearly, the differences between these doctrinal options were less important for the Thomas Christians than ensuring access to the sanctifying power associated with the holy men of West Asia and anchored in the tombs of the saints and martyrs in southern India.

Although Portuguese interventions had created a bitter and occasionally violent division of the community into Roman Catholics and Jacobite Syrians, from the perspective of Hindu rulers Thomas Christians generally maintained their higher caste status. To the horror of European Catholics, Thomas Christians continued to patronize Hindu temples, share in Hindu festivals, and present offerings to the Hindu warrior goddess. The integration of Thomas Christians into Hindu society, however, changed dramatically under the impact of the British East India Company. Beginning in 1758, the East India Company gradually established political control over various regions throughout the Indian subcontinent. By 1795, Hindu rajas on the western coast of southern India had entered into a tributary alliance with the British East India Company. As a result of paying tribute to the British, the Nayar warrior class lost power and prestige. Since they were linked with the Nayars, the Thomas Christian priests and *panikkars* also suffered a decline in status. Between 1810 and 1819, the British Resident, Colonel John Monro, embarked on a campaign for the Protestant reformation of the Thomas Christians. As an ardent evangelical, Monro abhorred "heathenism" and "popery" with the same passion. He saw no difference between the Roman Catholic and the Jacobite factions of the Thomas Christians; both displayed what he regarded as the "popish superstition" of worshiping the dead in their reverence for saints and worshiping objects in their ritual attention to relics, icons, and statues. Recruiting agents from the Church Missionary Society and the London Missionary Society, Colonel Monro began a mission to convert Thomas Christians to the Protestant religion of their new colonial patrons.

The Jacobite branch of the Thomas Christians was hardest hit by this Protestant missionary campaign. When the Jacobite patriarch died in 1816, Monro prohibited the installation of his hereditary successor. Instead, he appointed a priest who was sympathetic to the new policy of Protestant reform. However, when that priest died within three weeks of his appointment and Monro's next three appointments also died in quick succession, the crisis of leadership among the Jacobite Thomas Christians resulted in chaos. As the connection with the sacred power and authority of West Asia was disrupted, the regional links between Christians and Hindus were also destroyed by Monro's reforms. Directing state funds for the construction and repair of Thomas churches, Monro made Thomas Christians exempt from paying taxes and tributes to Hindu officials. Since these funds were also used to support Hindu temples, shrines, and festivals, Thomas Christians were thereby removed from the system of mutual exchange by which high-caste Hindus and Christians had cooperated in financing religion. Increasingly, the preferential treatment they received from the British East India Company caused Thomas Christians to be viewed as ritually impure by high-caste Hindus.

Their loss of ritual purity was sealed during the 1850s when the Church Missionary Society launched a massive publicity campaign to enhance the status of low-caste or untouchable Hindus who converted to Christianity by asserting that they were all Thomas Christians. Instead of raising the status of these converts, however, the campaign only succeeded in certifying the impurity of the Thomas Christians in the eyes of high-caste Hindus. Where formerly they had access to Hindu temple precincts, Thomas Christians were now regarded as a seriously polluting influence to be excluded. They became associated with Christian converts from the ranks of the untouchables, some of whom had adopted a confrontational strategy, according to a report in 1867, of "forcing themselves into the presence of Nayars and Brahmins and 'polluting' them . . . and getting beaten or put into prison and then reporting themselves persecuted for Christianity's sake." During the 1880s, riots frequently developed out of conflicts between Hindus and Thomas Christians. Annual religious festivals, which had been events of interreligious celebration, became occasions for interreligious provocation as Hindu and Thomas Christian participants marched past each other's shrines, "howling, screaming, and crying out obscene words." The Protestant reforms, therefore, succeeded in reifying the boundaries between two religions—Hindu and Christian—that had been part of the same network of social class, martial culture, and religious worship in southern India.[6]

HINDU RENAISSANCE

During the nineteenth century, different reformers, drawing on Hindu tradition, worked to renegotiate the division between Hinduism and Christianity established by British colonialism.[7] A crucial figure in this process was Ram Mohan Roy (1772–1833), founder of the Brahmo Samaj, who became known as "father of modern India." Born into an orthodox Hindu family of the Brahmin class from a small town in West Bengal, Ram Mohan Roy was educated at Patna, a center of Islamic learning, where he studied Persian and Arabic. Under the guidance of his Muslim teachers, he became familiar with Islamic monotheism, which opposed any use of images in religious worship. After traveling through northern India, he settled in Banaras to study Sanskrit and Hindu scriptures. He also studied English, which enabled him to gain a position as an administrator in the British East India Company in 1803. After 1815, he moved to Calcutta, the political and intellectual center of India, and began a career as a Hindu reformer. During the 1820s he attended services of the Unitarian Church, attracted to the church's teachings about the simple unity of God. For a while, Ram Mohan Roy referred to himself as a "Hindu Unitarian." His book on Christianity, *The Precepts of Jesus,* published in 1820, depicted the Christian religion as a moral code that did not depend upon the divinity, miracles, or redeeming death of Jesus. In 1828, however, Ram Mohan Roy founded a new movement, Brahmo Samaj, as a religious organization dedicated to reforming Hinduism as the monotheistic worship of *brahman,* the one true God, who is designated by many different names in Hindu scriptures. By reinterpreting Hindu sacred texts, especially the most ancient Vedas, in the light of monotheism, Ram Mohan Roy hoped to enable Hindus "to contemplate, with true devotion, the unity and omnipresence of nature's God." Sailing to England in 1830, Ram Mohan Roy died of illness in 1833 before he could return to India.

In his book *The Precepts of Jesus,* which he subtitled, "The Guide to Peace and Happiness," Ram Mohan Roy represented Christ as a teacher of morality and belief in one Supreme Being. Hoping to convey this message of monotheism and morality to a Hindu audience, Roy extracted passages from the New Testament, mainly drawn from the Synoptic Gospels, that conveyed the ethical teachings of Jesus. Omitting any passages that referred to the miracles, resurrection, or divine nature of Christ, Ram Mohan Roy produced what he regarded as a rational Christian guide to a good life. "I feel persuaded," he wrote, "that by separating from the other matters contained in the New Testament the moral principles found in that book, these will be more likely to produce the desirable effect of improving the hearts and minds of men of different persuasions and degrees of understanding." Here Ram Mohan Roy was influenced by the "natural theology" of deism, growing out of the eighteenth-century European Enlightenment, which found the basic truths of religion not in revelation, but in reason, morality, and social order. Under the same influence, the American revolutionary leader Thomas Jefferson had produced his own edited version of the New Testament by extracting passages that he thought conformed to reason and morality. From the perspective of "natural theology," therefore, Christian doctrines concerning Christ's divinity, resurrection, and sacrificial atonement for the sins of humanity were unnecessary additions to the pure moral teachings of Jesus that could be found in the New Testament.[8]

Opposing the "natural theology" of Ram Mohan Roy, the Baptist missionary Joshua Marshman (1768–1837), who was working to expand the Baptist Church in Bengal, stated the terms of an "evangelical theology" that required a different understanding of Christ. In response to Roy's depiction of Jesus as a teacher of morality, Marshman insisted on an understanding of Christ as a savior, not because he gave moral precepts to human beings, but "because he died in their stead, to atone for their sins and procure for them every blessing, even his Spirit to enable them to trust in his death and merits for salvation, and from a principle of love cordially obey his precepts to the end of life."[9] This understanding of Christ as savior, however, could not be attained by reason; it depended upon accepting the Bible as a revelation from God that disclosed the truth of Christ. The entire Bible, Marshman insisted, testified to the divinity and saving power of Christ. By only extracting the moral teachings of Jesus, he concluded, Ram Mohan Roy had erased the evangelical theology of divine grace at the heart of Christianity.

As Marshman and Roy engaged in this controversy through a series of popular publications, the Hindu reformer expanded on his understanding of Christ as a teacher of morality. In the process, he interpreted basic Christian doctrines of the Trinity, the incarnation, and the atonement in the context of his campaign to reform Hinduism as an ethical monotheism. First, since Roy wanted to return the Hindu tradition to what he regarded as its original understanding of a single Supreme Being, he opposed any suggestion that there might be a plurality of gods. Polytheism, he held, had developed in the Hindu tradition as its original monotheism degenerated into a belief in the existence of many gods. According to Roy, the doctrine of the Trinity represented a similar degeneration in the Christian tradition by dividing the simple unity of God into three divine Persons. Although he cited specific New Testament passages in support of this argument, Roy's denial of the divinity of Jesus Christ was consistent with his attempt to maintain the unity of God against any notion that there might be more than one deity.

Second, Roy also wanted to reform Hinduism by removing what he regarded as the superstitious devotion to personal gods—the *avatars,* or human manifestations of a deity—which played such an important role in popular Hindu worship. In his critique of Hinduism, Roy championed reason and morality against the ritual practices of religious devotion—or *bhakti*—that appeared in the worship of divine beings, such as Rama or Krishna, who had assumed human form in the world. Accordingly, Ram Mohan Roy was equally unsympathetic to Christian *bhakti,* the devotional worship of Jesus Christ as a divine being in human form. In Roy's view, Jesus was the Messiah not because he was an incarnation or an *avatar* of God, but because he was the supreme messenger of God who lived and taught divine moral precepts.

Third, according to Ram Mohan Roy, Christian salvation was achieved by following those moral precepts. For the Baptist Joshua Marshman and other exponents of evangelical theology, however, Roy's identification of salvation with morality sounded like a gospel of works, the heretical assertion that righteousness could be attained by human effort. According to Marshman, salvation was gained not by moral righteousness, but by means of "Jesus' *expiating sin by his death,* his giving life to those who believe in him, his interceding with God for sinners and his forming of the *only medium* through which man can approach God." In response, Roy argued that the evangelical doctrine of the saving death of Christ was inconsistent with both divine justice and mercy. "Would it be consistent with common notions of justice," he asked, "to afflict an innocent man with the death of the cross, for sins committed by others, even supposing the innocent man should voluntarily offer his life on behalf of those others?" Although some of the authors of the New Testament had expressed their understanding of Jesus in terms of the blood offerings for purification from sin that had featured in the religion of ancient Israel, modern readers of the New Testament, Roy argued, had to extract the teachings of Jesus Christ from this ancient sacrificial system in order to discern their morality, rationality, and relevance for contemporary life. Acknowledging that the apostle Paul spoke of the saving power of the cross, Roy insisted that he could find no "single passage pronounced by Jesus enjoining a refuge in such a doctrine of the cross, as all-sufficient and indispensable for salvation." Instead, Roy found that salvation was granted "from the merciful Father through repentance, which is declared the only means of procuring forgiveness for our failures."[10]

In the wake of this controversy between the evangelical missionary and the Hindu moralist, the Brahmo Samaj movement continued to advocate a religion based on reason alone. During the 1860s, however, a new leader of the Brahmo Samaj emerged, Keshab Chandra Sen (1838–84), who valued reason and morality, but also added a new emphasis on the importance of religious devotion and divine revelation. Born five years after Roy's death, Sen was educated at Hindu College, Calcutta. After graduation he joined the Brahmo Samaj, becoming one of the movement's most prominent organizers. As a social reformer, he campaigned for overcoming traditional Hindu caste divisions, eliminating the social category of the "untouchable," prohibiting child marriage, and enabling the education of women. He broadcast his social and religious views by publishing a wide range of popular journals, magazines, and newspapers. In outlining his program for modern social reforms, Sen echoed many of the complaints about Hindu society expressed by British Christian missionaries.

Asserting that Christ was the greatest religious teacher, Sen rendered the British conquest of India as part of God's plan to direct India toward moral, social, and political reformation. Embracing the British colonizing mission, Sen imagined that the intercultural relations between England and India would involve a mutually beneficial exchange. "Let modern England teach hard science and fact," he proposed; "let ancient India teach sweet poetry and sentiment." By 1881, Keshab Chandra Sen was preaching a merger of Hinduism and Christianity that he called the New Dispensation. He held that this New Dispensation stood in the line of previous revelations—Hindu, Jewish, Muslim, and Christian—as their modern fulfillment.

According to Keshab Chandra Sen, Jesus Christ was revealed at the center of the New Dispensation. Although he regarded Jesus as the "Prince of Prophets," who had been preceded by earlier prophets and was subsequently succeeded by others who formed the links in a chain of revelation, Sen also saw Jesus Christ as the ultimate revelation of what he called "Divine Humanity." In Jesus Christ, Sen held, humanity and divinity were perfectly united. Sen identified that oneness of the human and divine in Christ as a Christian pantheism, an understanding that God's presence fills the world, which was also essentially a Hindu doctrine. In the original Hindu pantheism, Sen explained, all things were identified with God, but later developments in the tradition distorted this ancient conception. In this degenerate pantheism, he alleged, Hindus cultivated a passive, unconscious, trancelike absorption in the divine. Christian pantheism, however, stressed an active, conscious unity of the human will with the divine will. "Christ's pantheism is a pantheism of a loftier and more perfect type," Sen declared. "It is the conscious union of the human with the Divine Spirit in truth, love and joy." The perfect pantheism of Divine Humanity revealed in Jesus Christ, however, was also found by Sen at the heart of the most ancient Hindu sacred texts. Addressing his fellow Hindus, he concluded that since "the basis of early Hinduism is pantheism, you, my countrymen, cannot help accepting Christ in the spirit of your natural Scriptures."

Unlike Ram Mohan Roy, Sen embraced the Christian doctrine of the Trinity as the key to salvation. Picturing the Trinity as a triangle, with the Supreme God—Jehovah of the Hebrew Bible, Brahma of the Hindu Vedas—at the apex, Sen imagined that God descended to humanity as the Son and carried humanity back up to heaven as the Holy Spirit. During the 1880s, believing that he was directly inspired by the Holy Spirit, Sen announced himself as "a servant of God, called to be an apostle of the Church of the New Dispensation." As Sen understood it, the Church of the New Dispensation was a Christian church. Based on "a belief in the supremacy of Christ as the God-man," this church promised to overcome sectarian divisions among Christians in India. However, the Church of the New Dispensation was also a Hindu church. By embracing the Divine Humanity of Christ, Sen urged, Hindus would realize "the spirit of a devout Yogi and loving Bhakta, the fulfillment of [Hindu] national prophets and scriptures." In these terms, Sen imagined an indigenous Hindu Church of Christ. "Christ is not Christianity," he held. "If you have the true Christ in you, all truth, whether Jew or Gentile, Hindu or Christian, will pour into you through him, and you will be able to assimilate the wisdom and righteousness of each sect and denomination." Although centered on Christ, whose Divine Humanity represented the supreme standard of truth, the Church of the New Dispensation proposed a universal religion based on the harmony of all religions.[11]

One Hindu who translated this assumption about the truth of all religions into a distinctive religious practice was the devotional mystic Ramakrishna (1836–86). Having renounced the world, Ramakrishna embarked on a series of spiritual paths for achieving God-realization. Not only learning Hindu spiritual disciplines, he experienced devotion for the Buddha, Allah, and Jesus Christ. In the case of Jesus Christ, Ramakrishna was exposed to Christianity not by a Christian, but by a Hindu who had chosen Jesus as his personal deity for devotional worship. Regarding Jesus as a legitimate focus for Hindu *bhakti,* therefore, Ramakrishna reportedly experienced an intense spiritual union with Christ. One day, while meditating on a painting of the Madonna and child, Ramakrishna "became gradually overwhelmed with divine emotion and breaking through the barriers of creed and religion, he entered a new realm of ecstasy. Christ possessed his soul." Beholding a vision of Christ, Ramakrishna reportedly exclaimed, "It is he, the Master Yogi, who is in eternal union with God. It is Jesus, Love Incarnate." According to his biographer, this intense spiritual experience of divine love enabled Ramakrishna to realize his identity with Christ. That mystical union with Christ, however, was similar to Ramakrishna's identification with other manifestations of God. He had entered into the same devotional experience of union with the Mother Goddess, Kali, with the *avatars* Rama and Krishna, and with Muhammad, the Prophet of Islam. According to Ramakrishna, gods and goddesses, *avatars* and prophets, Buddhas and Christs, all represented different ways to experience the same union between the human and the divine.

Unconcerned with religious creeds, Ramakrishna sought direct religious experience through the spiritual disciplines of meditation and devotion. "For the purposes of meditation," he advised, "some persons find it helpful to concentrate on a certain aspect of the Godhead in a particular 'form'; others prefer meditation on the formless Absolute." Behind Jesus and all other divine forms, however, Ramakrishna could discern traces of the "formless Absolute," the impersonal sacred power of *brahman* that pervades the entire universe. By interpreting his religious experiences in terms of the ancient Hindu philosophy of Vedanta, his disciples saw Ramakrishna as providing contemporary confirmation of the Vedantic insight that a human being's highest self, the *atman,* is ultimately one with *brahman.*[12]

Ramakrishna's disciple, Narendranath Datta (1863–1902), who became known as Vivekananda, taught that the "formless Absolute" was the ultimate truth of all religions. As founder of the Vedanta Society in the West and the Ramakrishna Mission in India, Vivekananda made a substantial contribution to the revitalization of Hinduism. Although he had studied to be a lawyer, Vivekananda's meeting with Ramakrishna convinced him to become a renunciate and pursue the spiritual discipline of meditation. In 1893, Vivekananda journeyed to the United States to represent Hinduism at the World's Parliament of Religions in Chicago. Proclaiming the Hindu tradition's universal truth of the union of self and God, Vivekananda maintained that Jesus Christ was a mystic who had developed a spiritual realization of an inner kingdom of heaven and an ultimate union with God. Rather than teaching a gospel of sin and salvation, Jesus taught a way to overcome ignorance and achieve the liberating knowledge, a kind of Hindu *gnosis,* that the highest self is one with God. In Christ the "formless Absolute" had assumed human form so that Christ, the *avatar,* could direct human beings to a realization of their own divinity. "God became Christ to show man his true nature," Vivekananda concluded, "that we too are God."[13]

Under the impact of British colonialism and Christian missions, the religious leaders of the nineteenth-century Hindu renaissance recast the ancient tradition of Hinduism as a modern religion. In developing what might be called a "Protestant Hinduism," they sought to purify the tradition by recovering and reinterpreting its primary sacred texts. In the process, they also included Christ in their work of reforming Hinduism. As we have seen, however, vastly different images of Christ—the moral teacher, the model of divine humanity, the object of devotion, the yogi, the mystic, the gnostic, and the *avatar* of God—were produced by Hindu reformers, from Ram Mohan Roy to Vivekananda, who sought to incorporate Christ among the religious resources of modern India. Over the objections of foreign missionaries like the Baptist Joshua Marshman, they found different ways to claim Christ as an integral part of the Hindu religion.

EXPERIMENTS WITH TRUTH

Mohandas Karamchand Gandhi (1869–1948), who became known as the Mahatma, the "Great Soul," drew on religious resources of the Hindu renaissance to mobilize his campaign for the liberation of India from British rule. Born into a Hindu household in Gujarat, western India, Gandhi reflected in his autobiography that he had learned from his father to respect the adherents of all religions, the Hindus, Buddhists, Jains, Parsees, Muslims, and others who came to his home, except for the Christian missionaries, who were "pouring abuse on Hindus and their gods."[14] Although he regarded himself as a Hindu, Gandhi joined other Hindu reformers in looking for a common ground among religions. While studying law in London, he met leaders of the Theosophical Society, Helena Petrovna Blavatsky and Annie Besant, who had developed a blend of Western spiritualism and Eastern mysticism directed toward the realization that the self was divine. Under the influence of Theosophy in London, Gandhi read the sacred Hindu text of the *Bhagavad Gita,* Edwin Arnold's biography of the Buddha, *Light of Asia,* and the Christian Bible, in which he was especially impressed by the Sermon on the Mount. Reflecting on the devotion of Krishna, the compassion of the Buddha, and the self-sacrificial love of Jesus, Gandhi found that the truth contained in these different religions represented complementary paths to God.

Eventually, Gandhi identified truth as God, insisting that ultimately "there is no other God than Truth."[15] In the course of his "experiments with truth," Gandhi translated his understanding of God into a strategy, which he called *satyagraha,* or "truth force," for nonviolent political action against injustice, oppression, and colonial domination. Developed during his twenty-three years as a lawyer in South Africa, where he campaigned for Indian rights, *satyagraha* was tested after Gandhi returned to India in 1914 during the long struggle for liberation from British rule. Based on a principled commitment to nonviolence, which drew upon the religious ideal of *ahimsa*, or harmlessness, that Gandhi found in the Jain tradition, *satyagraha* was understood by Gandhi as the practical realization of divine truth that was supported by all religions. In the case of Christianity, that truth was reflected in the teachings, example, and divinity of Jesus.

First, for all practical purposes, Gandhi found that the teachings of Jesus were contained in the Sermon on the Mount. "It is that Sermon," Gandhi reflected, "which has endeared Jesus to me." Under the influence of the Russian novelist Tolstoy, whose Christian commentary in *The Kingdom of God Is Within You* had interpreted the Sermon on the Mount as a program for "passive resistance" to evil, Gandhi came to see nonviolent opposition to injustice as a way of putting that universal love into action. As he later recalled, the "Law of Love" in the Sermon on the Mount had awakened him to "the rightness and value of passive resistance." This Christian teaching about love in action, rather than the person of Jesus Christ, therefore, was what Gandhi found to be important in Christianity. Even if Jesus had never existed and the gospels were only literary fictions, he observed, "the Sermon on the Mount would still be true to me."[16]

According to Gandhi, the truth of the Sermon on the Mount did not belong exclusively to organized Christianity. Imagining that Jesus would disown many of the things that have been done in the name of Christianity, Gandhi argued that "where there is boundless love and no idea of retaliation whatsoever it is Christianity that lives." Therefore, he was convinced that "God and Christianity can be found also in institutions that do not call themselves Christian." Many people who had never heard of Jesus Christ or had rejected organized Christianity, he insisted, could be regarded as Christians based on their adherence to the divine truth of unconditional love and nonviolent resistance that Jesus taught in the Sermon on the Mount.

If Indian Christians will simply cling to the Sermon on the Mount, which was delivered not merely to the peaceful disciples but a growing world, they would not go wrong, and they would find no religion false. Cooperation with forces of Good and noncooperation with forces of Evil are the two things we need for a good and pure life, whether it is called Hindu, Muslim, or Christian.[17]

Second, the example provided by the life of the historical Jesus, who demonstrated love in action, served for Gandhi as a significant model for humanity. "The gentle figure of Christ," he recalled, "so patient, so kind, so loving, so full of forgiveness that he taught his followers not to retaliate when abused or struck but to turn the other cheek—it was a beautiful example, I thought, of the perfect man." The attention shown by Jesus to the poor and oppressed, to the "least of these among us," was recalled by Gandhi during his campaign to elevate the status of the outcasts—the "untouchables"—who were generally despised in India because they fell outside of the Hindu caste system. The example of Jesus' suffering, however, provided Gandhi with a compelling model of self-sacrifice in the service of nonviolent love. "Though I cannot claim to be a Christian in the sectarian sense," Gandhi noted, "the example of Jesus' suffering is a factor in the composition of my underlying faith in nonviolence, which rules all my actions, worldly and temporal. Jesus lived and died in vain, if he did not teach us to regulate the whole of life by the eternal Law of Love." By exemplifying nonviolence in his life and death, therefore, Jesus served for Gandhi as a significant model of a human life devoted to the truth of sacrificial love.[18]

Third, Gandhi rejected conventional Christian claims about the unique divinity of Jesus Christ. "It was more than I could believe," he recalled, "that Jesus was the only incarnate Son of God and that only he who believed in him would have everlasting life. If God could have sons, all of us were his sons. If Jesus was like God, or God Himself, then all men were like God and could be God Himself." Nevertheless, by adapting the Hindu understanding of *avatars,* Gandhi included Jesus among those human beings who had incarnated divinity. Accordingly, he found that Jesus was "as divine as Krishna or Rama or Muhammad or Zoroaster." Within the limits of the flesh, Gandhi proposed, Jesus had achieved the highest degree of perfection possible to human beings. Only God or Truth, however, could ultimately be regarded as perfect. In keeping with what Gandhi saw as the truth of all religions, the teachings and example of Jesus could inspire people to realize the perfection of divine truth in action.[19]

Certainly, Mahatma Gandhi was not a Christian in any conventional sense. "It was impossible for me to regard Christianity as a perfect religion or the greatest of all religions," he recalled. Like the reformers of the nineteenth-century Hindu renaissance, however, Gandhi found ways to integrate Christian resources, especially the Sermon on the Mount, into a broadly Hindu religious understanding and way of life. Although some Christian leaders objected to his appropriation of Christianity, many Christians found inspiration in Gandhi's interpretation of the teachings of Christ as a gospel of unconditional love, sacrificial service to others, and nonviolent resistance to injustice. The Indian Christian theologian S. K. George, for example, reported that Mahatma Gandhi had made Jesus a reality for him by demonstrating that "*Satyagraha* is Christianity in action." The American evangelical missionary E. Stanley Jones found that Gandhi was "a Hindu by allegiance and a Christian by affinity." In such interpretations of the life and work of Gandhi, therefore, both Indian and foreign Christians claimed the Mahatma as a Hindu Christian.[20]

In trying to clarify what it might mean to be a Hindu Christian, the Roman Catholic theologian Raimundo Panikkar (b. 1918) has affirmed the integrity of the two religions while at the same time advocating a mutually enriching interreligious dialogue between Hindus and Christians. Born of a Hindu father and a Spanish Catholic mother, Panikkar had to come to terms with his own interreligious background. In the process, however, he developed a global theology that placed the religious resources of India and the West in a dynamic relationship ultimately based on the model of the Christian Trinity. Describing himself as a Christian-Hindu-Buddhist, Panikkar found that God was revealed at the intersection of those three religious traditions. According to Panikkar, the supreme Godhead—God, the Father—was an unknowable reality best captured by the Buddhist silence about God. The second Person of the Trinity, the incarnation of God, had been revealed to Christians in the person of Jesus Christ, even though other incarnations, or *avatars,* of God had been beheld in other religious traditions. In Hinduism, however, the third Person of the Trinity, the Holy Spirit, had been developed through attention to the dynamics of spiritual experience. In developing a theology based on interreligious relations, therefore, Raimundo Panikkar acknowledged the contributions of Hinduism, Buddhism, and other religions to the quest for understanding such a basic Christian doctrine as the Trinity.[21]

In the Hindu tradition, however, the Lord, or the *Ishta Devata*, can appear in many different forms. Although academic theologians might try to rationalize the appearances of the Lord, popular religious devotion and practices in India have been known to follow their own logic. For example, while investigating religion in a village in southern India during the 1990s, researchers found that only 1 percent of the population regarded themselves as Christians. However, the researchers were surprised by the results when they asked, "Who is your *Ishta Devata*?" Although almost no one in the village chose to be identified as Christian, 15 percent of the villagers identified their Lord, the divine focus of their religious devotions, as Jesus Christ. Regarding themselves as Hindus, those people who had chosen Jesus as their personal Lord nevertheless were devoted to a deity, an *Ishta Devata*, who also happened to be the *Ishta Devata* of Christians. Although they performed Hindu practices of devotion, they directed their meditation, prayers, and offerings to the Lord who was worshiped by Christians all over the world. In that sense, therefore, these villagers in southern India might be regarded as Hindu Christians, even though they did not accept being designated as "Christians" because their devotion to Jesus Christ was lived and practiced within the broad religious matrix of Hinduism. As the history of Christianity in India has shown, however, the rigid distinction between Christian and Hindu was a product of European colonization and missionary interventions in Indian religious life. But that history has also suggested that Hindu Christianity is not necessarily impossible, especially given the fact that it has been formulated and lived in India by Hindu Christians.

27

Christian Cargo

The islands of the South Pacific were brought to European attention by the voyages of Captain James Cook, who explored Australia, New Zealand, Tahiti, and other islands until he was killed by Hawaiians in 1797. The death of Captain Cook was occasioned by a dramatic encounter between Europeans and adherents of an indigenous Polynesian religion. As Cook's ships arrived during the twenty-three-day Mahahiki festival, the Hawaiian king, nobility, and priests apparently incorporated the English captain into the ritual process by identifying him with the festival's deity, Lono. With ritual offerings, the Hawaiians entered into relations of exchange with that divine being. They sent him off with generous gifts of food, firewood, and ritual objects. In return, they expected the deity to bestow blessings on the people of the island. However, when Cook's ships unexpectedly came back for repairs, the Hawaiians perceived that Captain Cook had violated the ritual relations of exchange. Cook had previously received sacrificial offerings as a manifestation of the divine Lono, but when he came ashore again he became a sacrificial offering to the king. After a group of warriors killed him, the priests performed rituals on his body that sanctified James Cook as an ancestral deity of the Hawaiian royal household. Although the interpretation of these events has been disputed, the initial encounter between Europeans and Hawaiians suggests conflicting understandings of material goods. In sacrificial offerings and economic exchange, the meaning and value of material goods, which on many islands would come to be identified as the "cargo," inspired distinctive developments within Christianity on the islands of the Pacific Ocean.

Reports of Cook's voyages stimulated missionary interest in the Pacific Islands. Although Spanish Catholic missionaries had ventured from their base in the Philippines into the Mariana Islands as early as 1668, the first Protestant missionary effort in the Pacific was mounted by the London

Missionary Society (LMS) in 1797. As he surveyed the world to find a suitable site for the society's first mission, LMS director Dr. Romaine Haweis ruled out any place that had an inhospitable climate, a tyrannical government, an established religion, or people who spoke difficult languages. By process of elimination, Dr. Haweis chose the island of Tahiti as the best place to begin Protestant missionary work.[1] After initial difficulties, the LMS forged an alliance in 1815 with Pomare II, the principal ruler of Tahiti, that led to the adoption of Christianity as the established religion of the island. Conversion followed a similar pattern of gaining official royal support for the new Christian religion throughout the Pacific Islands. Extending its sphere of influence from Tahiti, the LMS gained royal support in Samoa and the Cook Islands. Arriving in the Hawaiian Islands in 1820, the American Board of Commissioners for Foreign Missions introduced a Protestant Christianity that was adopted by Queen Kaahumanu as the official religion of her kingdom. Methodist missionaries from Britain succeeded in establishing island churches by converting the rulers of Tonga in 1831 and Fiji in 1854. Beginning in 1851, French Catholic missions gained official support in New Caledonia that made Catholicism the island's majority religion. In a remarkably short period of time, therefore, varieties of Christianity became established in the Pacific Islands.

Although adopting Christianity required an adjustment of religious beliefs and practices, there was already some common ground between indigenous and foreign religion. For example, both Pacific Islanders and Christian missionaries imagined that the universe was occupied by good and evil spirits. LMS agent William Ellis (1794–1872) complained that the Tahitians suffered under a superstitious fear of demons. "No people of the world," he reported, "appear to have been more superstitious than the South Sea Islanders, or to have been more entirely under the influence of dread from imaginary demons or supernatural beings." But Ellis held his own Christian belief in demons and supernatural beings. Explaining the pervasive hold of superstition over the islanders as the result of demonic possession, Ellis observed that it was "recognized in the declarations and miracles of our Lord and his apostles" that "satanic agency affects the bodies of men." In their understanding of moral defilement and ritual purity, the missionaries and islanders also had much in common. In their indigenous religion, Ellis observed, the islanders offered blood sacrifices "to cleanse the land from pollution." Demanding that these ritual sacrifices for purification must cease, the missionary offered in their place the sacrifice of Jesus through which the islanders would be "purified from their moral defilement in that blood which cleanseth from all sin." Therefore, the missionary gospel of supernatural beings and demons, of moral defilement and ritual purity, could be translated into the religious life of the Pacific Islands.[2]

Translation broke down, however, over the value of material goods. In the Pacific Islands, the value of material goods was realized in and through reciprocal exchange. Reciprocity in giving and receiving reinforced social relations. Through the exchange of material goods, relations of kinship, friendship, and patronage were sustained. However, when foreign missionaries arrived in the Pacific Islands with an abundance of material goods, especially with the manufactured weapons, tools, and clothing that people had never seen before, they violated the principle of reciprocity by not giving them away. On Tahiti, for example, a high priest castigated the missionaries for withholding the manufactured goods in their possession. "You give me much *paraow* [talk] and much prayers," he complained, "but very few axes, knives, scissors, or cloth."[3] But the nineteenth-century missionaries operated with a different understanding of value based on a capitalist system of market exchange. As Christianity and European colonization developed in the Pacific Islands, conflict over the meaning and value of material goods produced dramatic innovations in religion that came to be known as cargo movements.

CARGO MOVEMENTS

In the Melanesian Islands, Papua New Guinea has developed the most characteristic forms of cargo religion. European Christian missions were relatively late in arriving there. Beginning with the Congregationalists of the LMS in 1871, the work of other Christian missions—Anglican, French Catholic, Australian Methodist, and German Lutheran—led to a diversity of Christian denominations on the island. Although missionaries saw the people of Papua New Guinea as potential converts, a series of colonial administrations appropriated their land for plantations, enforced new taxes, and coerced them into serving as cheap labor. As documented by the anthropologist Peter Lawrence, the history of southern Madang Province, on the eastern coast of the island, suggests the complex links between Christianity and the changing political economy of Papua New Guinea in this colonial situation.[4]

In 1871 the Russian scientist Nikolai Mikloucho-Maclay (1846–88) arrived in Madang. By presenting gifts of manufactured goods and new food plants, Maclay was gradually able to build trust with the people. In exchange for his gifts of steel axes, nails, mirrors, cloth, paint, and seeds, they gave the Russian food and handmade wares. Reportedly, people were convinced that this strange being, who brought such remarkable possessions, went about unarmed, and knew about people and places across the seas, must be something more than a human being. Using their indigenous terminology, the people of Madang speculated about his status. Although some wondered whether he was the spirit of one of their deceased ancestors and others thought that he came from the moon, many identified Maclay as a manifestation of one of the island's deities. According to an indigenous myth, two deities, the brothers Manup and Kilobob, had originally created the material resources and cultural practices that supported island life. Many of the islanders apparently identified Maclay with Kilobob, concluding that the original deity had returned to the island to introduce an entirely new order of material resources through his gifts of manufactured goods. Although no special rituals were performed in honor of Maclay, the reciprocal exchange of gifts assumed a ritualized quality as people came from remote regions of Papua New Guinea to participate. By the time he finally left in 1877, therefore, Maclay had introduced new symbols of wealth, the cargo, that could be incorporated in local myths about divine beings and in local rituals of exchange.[5]

Beginning in 1884, German settlers, with their superior weaponry of firearms, entered the Madang District and confiscated land, established plantations, and forced people to work. Under these oppressive conditions, people revised their view of the cargo. In a new version of the myth of origin, the deity Kilobob had built a great ship that he stocked with the indigenous people, artifacts, and food plants of the islands. At the same time, however, he created white people and European cargo, took them on board the ship, and hid them below deck. When the ship arrived in Papua New Guinea, Kilobob put the native people ashore and gave them the choice between the two types of material culture. In their ignorance, the people of the island rejected the European cargo. For example, they dismissed the rifles, because they looked like useless pieces of wood, in preference for the bows and arrows that were easy to carry and use. Leaving the native people with their chosen goods, Kilobob traveled to a distant country where he put the white people ashore and gave them all the cargo. He taught them the rituals and other techniques for acquiring new supplies. In this myth, therefore, the island deity, Kilobob, was identified as the ultimate source of the cargo, but the cargo had been given to white people by mistake. On account of the ignorance of their ancestors, the people had been denied the material wealth of European manufactured goods and made vulnerable to the German rifles that had conquered and colonized them. However, in the future, they could hope for the return of Kilobob bearing vast supplies of cargo, including rifles to use in overthrowing the German colonizers, that would usher in a new era of peace and prosperity. By reworking an indigenous religious myth, therefore, the people of Madang developed a millenarian expectation of the imminent return of their deity with the cargo.

When the German administration was replaced by an Australian military government in 1914, the people of Madang showed a new interest in Christianity. Applying to the Lutheran mission for baptism, they formed a new Christian congregation. As they learned Christian myths and rituals, however, the people generally interpreted them in the light of the cargo. In the stories of the Bible, they found a new explanation for their current situation. In the beginning, according to their reading of the Bible, God created Adam and Eve and provided them with tinned meat, steel tools, bags of rice, tobacco, and matches, but no cotton clothing. While enjoying this cargo paradise, Adam and Eve offended God by engaging in sexual intercourse. They were driven from paradise and deprived of the cargo. Living without these material goods, their descendants sank into depravity to such an extent that God decided to destroy them all except for Noah and his family. Showing him how to build a magnificent steamship, God guided Noah through the Great Flood and rewarded him with the cargo. Because they respected God and their father, Noah's sons Shem and Japheth, who became the ancestors of the white people, continued to receive regular supplies of cargo. Noah's son Ham, however, did not show the proper respect. God punished Ham by taking away his cargo and sending him to Papua New Guinea, where he became the ancestor of the island people who had to settle for an inferior material culture. Like the earlier adaptation of an indigenous myth, this particular reading of Christian myth explained the islanders' lack of material goods.

Christianity, however, also represented hope for the future as the religion followed by the white people who possessed the cargo. Linking the Christian religion with the Australian colonial administration, the people of Madang looked to the Christian heaven, which was located in or above Sydney, Australia, where God, Jesus Christ, and all the ancestors made cargo. Enjoying the abundance of material goods in heaven, the ancestors lived in European houses with beds, tables, and chairs. Eating tinned meat, rice, and other delicacies cooked by angels, the ancestors drank from an unlimited supply of whisky and beer. In exchange for these luxuries in heaven, the ancestors had agreed to assist God in the great work of redemption. When sufficient supplies had been prepared in heaven, the ancestors would carry them to the Sydney docks and load them on to the ships that would transport the cargo to Papua New Guinea for their descendants. However, the ancestors would only be enlisted in that great work if the island people worshiped and obeyed God. Therefore, the arrival of the cargo depended upon their devotion to Christianity.

Into the 1930s this Christian cargo movement mobilized tremendous support in Madang. Since Christian baptism, worship, and obedience were necessary for God to send the cargo, people turned in large numbers to the Lutheran and Catholic missions. The missionaries generally insisted that people reject the practices of their indigenous religion. Accordingly, Christian converts sought to eradicate rituals of initiation, marriage, dancing, fertility, healing, and homage to ancestors associated with their traditional culture. All these rituals, they decided, were given by Satan and the "satans," the old deities of Papua New Guinea. Even in discarding these traditional rituals, however, Christian converts incorporated their old deities into the Christian cosmos. As one explained, "The local deities always try to trick us into performing the old rituals again in their honor. But what they gave us was only rubbish—taro, yam, and all that stuff. If we yielded to temptation, God would not send us the real cargo—steel tools, tinned meat, and rice."[6] Interpreted as obstacles to the Christian cargo, the traditional deities of the island were transformed into evil demons in the service of Satan. As they awaited the arrival of the cargo, some thought it would come unannounced on European ships, while others expected it to come at the end of the world with the dramatic return of Jesus, who would be accompanied by the ancestors bearing gifts for all their Christian descendants in Papua New Guinea.

When Christ and the cargo failed to arrive soon, however, many people began to suspect that the missionaries were hiding something important about Christianity. By the middle of the 1930s, converts were leaving the mission churches. But religious visionaries emerged to recast both

Christian and indigenous myth. In the wake of the Japanese invasion of Papua New Guinea in 1942, for example, the visionary Tagarab inspired a revival of religious attention to the deity Kilobob, who turned out to be the supreme God of Christianity. Tagarab preached that God-Kilobob had not only made the original cargo, but that he had also dictated the Ten Commandments, entrusted Jesus with the responsibility of caring for the spirits of the dead, and sent the Christian missionaries to Papua New Guinea to teach the truth. However, the missionaries had failed to tell the truth of the cargo. Soon, Tagarab promised, God-Kilobob would arrive in a ship full of manufactured goods and weapons, accompanied by the ancestors disguised as Japanese soldiers, to drive all white settlers, including the missionaries, off the island. In preparation for this apocalyptic event, Tagarab instructed people to participate in church services, but he also instructed them to present food offerings at the graves of their ancestors and to build large storehouses for all the cargo that would soon be arriving. In addition to advocating Christian ritual, therefore, Tagarab revived an old ancestral ritual and introduced a new cargo ritual—the construction of a storehouse—in anticipation of the imminent apocalypse.

When this prophecy of the cargo also failed to materialize, many people in Madang became entirely disillusioned with Christianity. After World War II, some pursued the cargo through a revival of indigenous religion. Rejecting any dependence on the foreign Christian religion, prophets of the traditional revival proclaimed that all the local gods of Papua New Guinea were actually cargo deities. Long ago, the Christian missionaries had hidden the island's gods in Australia, but the deity Manup, who was also Jesus Christ, had found them and taught them how to make cargo. Although they remained imprisoned in Australia, these cargo deities would soon return to establish their millennial reign of peace and plenty in Madang. In the meantime, the island people had to reject all Christian teachings and forms of worship and return to the traditional rituals of initiation, dancing, feasting, and offering food to gods and ancestors. By 1950, therefore, the dominant cargo movement in Madang regarded Christianity as an obstacle rather than the road to the cargo.

As the history of the cargo in Madang reveals, cargo movements developed different strategies in relation to the Christianity brought by explorers, colonizers, and missionaries. Independent of Christian myth and ritual, cargo movements emerged that reconfigured indigenous religious resources to make sense out of the new world of material goods. Christianity, however, was also directly engaged by cargo movements. As noted, people might embrace the Christian church as the road to the cargo. The Christian gospel of the cargo, however, turned out to be a great disappointment. Many Christian converts in Papua New Guinea were convinced that "white men hide the secret of the Cargo. They say, 'Work for it,' but you do not get it. They say, 'Pray for it,' but you still do not get it." With the failure of wage labor or religious ritual to deliver the cargo, the only remaining way to get it was to steal it. According to many cargo myths, the secret of the cargo was the truth of theft: long ago, whites had secured the cargo by mistake—in effect, by stealing it—from its original producers and rightful owners, the deities and ancestors of the island people. In the colonial situation, therefore, this secret of the cargo revealed that private property was theft. The cargo millennium, however, promised to redress this act of theft by restoring material goods to their rightful owners in Papua New Guinea.[7]

The role of Christianity in cargo movements, however, has been complex. In explaining the formation of the movement in northern Madang during the 1930s led by Mambu, the "Black King," European missionaries and indigenous participants gave different accounts. According to the German Catholic missionary Father Georg Höltker, Mambu had been a Catholic convert assisting in the worship services at his local church, but had left to form a strange, subversive, and dangerous cult that mixed indigenous and Christian practices. According to the missionary, therefore, Mambu's cargo movement was a deviant form of Christianity. In an alternative account, however, an indigenous informant related that Mambu had stowed away on a ship to Australia, survived attempts by the ship's captain to throw him overboard, and learned the secret of the cargo, which was that the whites had robbed the island people of their rightful inheritance. Returning to Papua New Guinea, Mambu proceeded to raise money, perform miracles, and mobilize people to "be strong and throw the white men out of New Guinea and into the sea." In this version of the movement's origin, therefore, the relevant fact in Mambu's life was not that he had been in the church, but that he had been on the boat.[8]

In the islands of the South Pacific, Christianity was inextricably linked with new economic relations based not on reciprocity, but on the market realities of money, commodities, and wage labor. As the indigenous people of the Pacific Islands were forced by European colonization into this new world of commerce, they were confronted with the tremendous disparity between wealth and poverty. Whether formulated in traditional or Christian terms, the cargo promised the redemption of a human identity based on reciprocity from the dehumanizing conditions of market relations. The islanders were not alone, however, in attributing religious significance to new economic markets and the advance of commercial activity. During the nineteenth century, British Protestant missionaries often linked Christianity and commerce. In a sermon delivered in 1860, for example, Anglican bishop Samuel Wilberforce (1805–73) declared that "commerce is intended to carry, even to all the world, the blessed message of salvation." British commercial activity was thereby celebrated as if it were a Christian mission, and the Christian missions were credited with advancing commerce. Christianity, according to Wilberforce, had "the effect of training the human race to a degree of excellence which it could never attain in non-Christian countries." As a result, Wilberforce promised, indigenous people all over the world who converted to Christianity would became "a wealth-producing people, an exporting people and so a commercial people." Like Christian cargo movements, therefore, Bishop Samuel Wilberforce found that Christianity provided not only "the blessed message of salvation," but also a path for gaining access to the world of material goods.[9]

THE WORLD OF GOODS

Many historians have linked Christianity, especially the Protestant Christianity of Lutherans, Calvinists, and Methodists, with the rise of capitalism. According to the classic formulation by the sociologist Max Weber, the rise of capitalism in northern Europe was facilitated by the religious climate of Protestantism. As a distinctive economic system, capitalism had certain features that came to dominate the world of goods in Europe, North America, and eventually the entire world—the private ownership of property; the rational calculation of costs and profits; the accumulation of capital in the form of money and material assets; the borrowing, lending, and investment of money at interest; and the employment of laborers for wages in a labor market. By associating capitalism with Protestant Christianity, Weber did not argue that Protestantism had caused the rise of capitalism. Rather, he tried to indicate how certain Christian commitments derived from Luther and Calvin predisposed

Protestants to regard disciplined enterprise in the world as a virtue and thereby to participate in the kinds of economic activity that emerged as capitalism.[10]

Martin Luther, for example, gave new meaning to the medieval monastic ideal "To work is to pray." However, instead of retreating from the world into a monastery and assuming its spiritual disciplines of poverty, chastity, and obedience, Christians were exhorted by Luther to follow a life of religious devotion and self-discipline in the midst of the ordinary world. But Luther's notion of a Christian calling in the world was not sufficient to stimulate the kinds of economic activity that gave rise to capitalism. John Calvin's contribution was crucial. By reviving the doctrine of predestination, which affirmed that an all-powerful God had predetermined the ultimate fate of individuals and the world, Calvinism might have led to economic paralysis. Why would anyone be concerned about economic activity when human destiny—the few saved, the many damned—had already been determined by God? In practice, however, Calvinists looked for signs in both conscience and conduct that might suggest that they were among the saved elite. As noted among New England Puritans, any signs that might be found, such as a clear conscience, moral conduct, or material blessings, could never produce absolute certainty of salvation. Nevertheless, these signs were all that Calvinists had to go by to determine whether or not they were being used as an instrument of God's will in the world.

According to Max Weber, this ongoing practice of soul-searching for signs of election supported two dispositions—self-discipline and self-denial—that were conducive to capitalist economic activity. Under the influence of Calvinism, Protestants were driven to demonstrate disciplined, conscientious, and productive effort in fulfilling their callings in the world. As a result of all this disciplined effort, they tended to accumulate financial capital, perhaps even viewing their accumulation of wealth as an indication that they were among God's chosen. However, the religious disposition toward self-denial discouraged Calvinists from spending that wealth for purposes of pleasure or display. Rather than spending their wealth on immediate gratification, Calvinists were inclined to invest it in ways that eventually accrued profits and then led to further investment. This capitalist cycle of accumulation and investment, therefore, had an affinity with the Protestant ethical commitments to self-discipline and self-denial as signs of election by God. By the nineteenth century, Weber concluded, the economic system of industrial capitalism had become self-sustaining and therefore independent of the Protestant ethic that had been an integral part of its origin.

The Protestant entrepreneurial spirit of capitalism, however, was certainly only part of the story. Max Weber's account does not explain the relationship between Christianity and capitalism for those who were incorporated in its economic system as wage laborers. For people all over the world, colonization marked their entry into both a Christian and a capitalist world system. From an economic core in Europe, the colonization of the periphery was a significant feature of the rise of capitalism. Although European capitalist interests—mercantile, agricultural, and eventually industrial—were advanced by military conquest, dispossession of land, restrictions on trade, and forced labor, the entire enterprise was often justified as a providential extension to the rest of the world of "Christian civilization." At the European center, as the 1860 sermon by Bishop Samuel Wilberforce suggested, colonization could be celebrated as a force that was advancing both Christianity and commerce. On the colonized periphery, however, European missionaries often drew a different connection between Christianity and economic activity by advocating a "gospel of work." In the eastern Cape of South Africa, for example, the Presbyterian missionary James Stewart was an ardent proponent of a Christian gospel of productive labor. "The gospel of work does not save souls, but it saves peoples," Stewart declared. "Lazy races die or decay. Races that work prosper on earth. The British race, in all its greatest branches, is noted for its restless activity. Its life motto is Work! Work! Work!"[11] Rather than supporting free commercial activity, however, the "gospel of work" preached on the colonized periphery was designed to instill the self-discipline and self-denial that would make people good wage laborers for European-controlled enterprises. It taught the disciplines of punctuality, cleanliness, moral purity, self-restraint, and industriousness that were required of a good worker and a good Christian.

This Christian "gospel of work" was also advanced at the European center. In nineteenth-century Britain, for example, many historians have noticed the connection between Methodism and the spiritual incorporation of workers into an expanding industrial capitalism. Like Calvinism in general, the Methodist movement, initiated by John Wesley and George Whitefield, emphasized the Christian virtues of self-discipline and self-denial. According to John Wesley, for example, "Every man born into the world now bears the image of the devil, in pride and self-will; the image of the beast, in sensual appetites and desires." Human nature according to John Wesley was "altogether corrupt in every power and faculty." That corrupt human nature required constant monitoring, discipline, and denial. As demonstrated by the enthusiastic religious revivals in Britain and North America, however, Methodism gave this analysis an intensely emotional character. In weekly religious services, that emotion spilled out into what the poet Robert Southey called "a thing of sensation and passion." As the heart was "strangely warmed," the weekly Methodist service provided the occasion for a certain kind of self-expression that was rigorously denied during the rest of the week. In this weekly rhythm, as some historians have argued, the expression of religious emotion on Sunday served as a safety valve for all the pent-up emotions, repressed appetites, and frustrated desires that might be experienced in the regimen of self-denial required by disciplined labor during the week.[12]

In the context of industrial capitalism, commerce, and wage labor, this division of time into Sunday worship and weekday work held another implication for Christianity. As the nineteenth-century sociologist Herbert Spencer (1820–1903) noted, the British actually observed two coexisting religions, "the religion of enmity and the religion of amity." In Sunday worship services, Spencer noted, the "nobility of self-sacrifice, set forth in Scripture-lessons and dwelt on in sermons, is made conspicuous every seventh day." This weekly affirmation of the "religion of amity" supported religious values of self-sacrifice and reciprocity. By contrast, the "religion of enmity," which was practiced during the rest of the week, was based on self-interest and competition. During the working week, Spencer proposed, religious conduct was "ruled by the opposite code, egoism, aggression, and vengefulness." In the "religion of enmity," what had previously been regarded as vices—pride, greed, envy, and so on—became transformed by capitalism into Christian virtues. By dividing the days of the week between the church and the marketplace or workplace, Christians were able to adapt to what Herbert Spencer called the "glaring incongruities" of living in a society effectively based on two contradictory religions.[13]

The Protestant spirit of capitalism, with its temporal rhythms of work, worship, and leisure, also depended upon a spatial separation of work from the home. As commerce, industry, and labor became established as male domains, women were increasingly relegated to the domestic sphere of the family and household. A structural opposition was established between "economic men" and "domestic women." Like commerce and wage labor, however, female housekeeping demanded Christian discipline and self-denial. It required women to internalize certain Christian ideals of female character and conduct deemed appropriate for wives, mothers, and daughters within a patriarchal household. Under the terms of an emerging "cult of domesticity," women were expected to demonstrate Christian virtues—obedience, service, and purity—within the sphere of the home. For women, as historian Amaury de Riencourt has observed, the home became the "parallel of monasticism for men." By excluding women in principle from the public world of male work, the cult of domesticity tried to contain women within the private space of the Christian home.[14]

The evangelical revivals inspired by Methodism reinforced this cult of domesticity. Referring to the Christian gender roles prescribed in the first century by the apostle Paul, George Whitefield reminded Methodists that "the husband is the head of the wife, even as Christ is the head of the church." In this formula, a woman's insubordination to her husband was equated with disobedience to Christ. Female insubordination, as Whitefield declared, was the "fountain of domestic evil." The Christian home, therefore, was idealized as a domain of power relations in which wives and daughters were expected to obey the authority of husbands and fathers.[15]

At the same time, the Christian home was constructed as a sphere of purity. As a euphemism for sexual restraint, "purity" was an important feature of the cult of domesticity. But purity also became a Christian ideal of order within the household that brought some measure of symbolic control over the world of goods that entered the home. As anthropologist Mary Douglas has argued, the symbolic significance of "dirt" in any culture lies in its perceived violation of order. Essentially, dirt is "matter out of place." In the Christian cult of domesticity, cleanliness, which emerged as a sense of order "next to godliness," involved the ritualized organization of every object in the home in its assigned place. With meticulous attention to the arrangement of furniture, the placement of decorative and devotional ornaments, the tidying of surfaces, and the use of soap and other cleansing agents, the rituals of housekeeping reinforced the purity of the Christian home.[16]

For all its diversity, therefore, nineteenth-century Protestantism in Britain operated within a series of basic oppositions. It incorporated the class distinction between capital and labor, the colonialist distinction between metropolitan center and colonized periphery, the temporal distinction between Sunday worship and weekday work, and the spatial distinction between the different spheres occupied by economic men and domestic women. Receiving Christian legitimation from the Bible, churches, and theologians, all of these oppositions were established in relation to the world of goods. As in Papua New Guinea, Christianity represented more than a gospel of sin and salvation; it represented the religious road to the cargo.

CARGO HEAVENS

During the nineteenth century in Europe and North America, popular images of heaven adapted to the patterns and rhythms of the capitalist world of goods. Just as the home emerged as a haven from the working world, heaven came to be imagined as an afterlife place of domestic bliss that idealized the middle-class values of home and family. As historian Ann Douglas has documented, Christian sermons, hymns, and novels of the period described in detail the "eating habits, occupations, lifestyles, methods of child care and courtship current in Heaven." For example, *Gates Ajar*, a popular novel published in 1868 by Elizabeth Stuart Phelps (1844–1911), contrasted two visions of heaven. Focusing on the grief of a young woman named Mary who had lost her brother in war, the novel juxtaposed descriptions of heaven provided by the local Calvinist minister, Dr. Bland, and Mary's elderly Aunt Winifred. Dr. Bland's heaven was a cold, abstract "eternal state" in which the saved "shall study the character of God." Aunt Winifred's heaven, however, was a scene of domestic delight in which loving relatives were reunited after death in heavenly homes. As the men relaxed in conversation and the women played pianos in their parlors, children enjoyed eating their favorite sweets in heaven. In this popular vision of heaven, therefore, a Christian afterlife promised the fulfillment of desires for love, family, and material goods. As the Congregationalist minister Austin Phelps put it, heaven was a place "not unlike this world."[17]

Of course, many social critics noticed that the world of capitalism was nothing like heaven for the working class. During the first half of the nineteenth century, under the broad banner of Christian socialism, social critics sought utopian, revolutionary, or reformist solutions to the conditions of poverty and exploitation created by capitalism. As a utopian socialist, Claude-Henry de Rouvroy, known as Comte de Saint-Simon (1760–1825), proposed a "new Christianity" based on the rational organization of society for the benefit of workers. Similarly, Charles Fourier (1772–1837) advocated socialist cooperative communities as "the expression of the true Christianity of Jesus." The German evangelical and founder of the League of the Just, Wilhelm Weitling (1808–71), proposed a more radical solution by advocating a class war of the poor against the rich. In his repudiation of earthly power and riches, Weitling argued, Jesus had been the first socialist. However, the socialism of Jesus had been betrayed by the Christian church ever since the empire of Constantine. By initiating a revolutionary struggle against capitalism, Weitling hoped to recover what he regarded as the original Christianity, the "socialism of love." The more moderate Christian socialism of F. D. Maurice (1805–72) in Britain drew attention to the plight of workers and sought to ameliorate the more brutal aspects of capitalist industrialization.

In providing the most rigorous and sustained critique of capitalism, Karl Marx (1818–83) and Friedrich Engels (1820–95) argued that these Christian socialists were neither sufficiently scientific in their analysis nor revolutionary enough in their proposals to effect substantial change. Structurally, however, their own analysis and proposals bore certain traces of Christianity. Defining humanity as the free, conscious activity of self-creation through labor, Marx and Engels insisted that human beings were alienated from their fundamental humanity whenever the fruits of their labor were expropriated by others who employed or used them. Like original sin in Christian thought, the capitalist appropriation of the products of human labor led to the "total depravity" of workers. Deprived of ownership of the means of production, workers as a social class were locked in a system of wage labor that was effectively a system of slavery. Under those dehumanizing conditions, the humanity of workers could only be recovered through a revolutionary struggle that would overturn the relations of economic production. Like the Christian kingdom of God, however, this ultimate redemption of workers in a communist society was an eschatological promise. Although they operated from purely material premises, Marx and Engels nevertheless developed a critical theory and revolutionary program that resembled in broad outline the Christian myth of human depravity and redemption. At the same time, Marxism bore a striking resemblance to Melanesian cargo movements by anticipating the advent of an era of peace and plenty through the recovery of the human meaning and significance of material goods.

Clearly, Marx and Engels saw nineteenth-century European Christianity as an obstacle rather than as the road to the cargo. For the wage laborers of the working class, religion reinforced their alienation and oppression under capitalism. In the classic formulation of Karl Marx, religion was "the sigh of the oppressed creature," both a response to and a compensation for the dehumanizing conditions of capitalist economic oppression. Religion was the symbolic "opium of the people" that eased their pain, but also produced fanciful dreams of substitute gratification in imaginary heavens. Under the weight of this critique, therefore, the Christian religion, like every religion, was a delusion that had to be abandoned. In his critique of religion, Marx adapted the work of the Christian philosopher Ludwig Feuerbach (1804–72), who argued in his *Essence of Christianity* (1841) that Christian concepts of God were essentially imaginary projections of human ideals on to the blank slate of the heavens. By redefining God as a projection of humanity, Feuerbach proposed that the Christian church could reconstitute itself as a celebration of the truth and love that could be shared by human beings. For Marx, however, the false consciousness of the Christian church was beyond redemption to the extent that it reinforced the alienation and oppression of workers.

Friedrich Engels, however, developed this Marxist critique of religion in more detail in a series of works focusing explicitly on the Christian tradition. In the process of developing a historical critique, Engels discovered two basic types of Christianity. Relying upon the research of the New Testament scholar Bruno Bauer, Engels found the first type of Christianity in the mass movement of first-century Judea that mobilized slaves, debt-laden peasants, and poor freedmen—the "laboring and the burdened"— in a revolt against the Roman Empire. According to Engels, "socialism did in fact, as far as it was possible at the time, exist and even become dominant—in Christianity." This original socialist Christianity, therefore, was a militant struggle against the forces of economic oppression, including the power of the dominant religion, that might be established in any particular social formation. As a revolutionary movement, this original Christianity defied the cultural particularity of any national religion to present a universal vehicle for the protest and revolt of all humanity against oppression.

A second type of Christianity, however, had submerged this original Christian impetus for revolutionary liberation from economic oppression. According to Engels, this type of Christianity, which eventually became the dominant Christianity, established the orthodox doctrine of the Trinity and the standardized performance of the sacraments in order to enforce social conformity and thereby repress any protest or revolt against the prevailing social order. Demanding obedience, this second type of Christianity established an other-worldly gospel of sin and salvation that required an inward-looking response from Christians. By forsaking socialism in the interests of individual redemption, Engels argued, this type of Christianity actually betrayed the original Christianity.[18]

The Marxist challenge to Christianity, therefore, was twofold: Marxism posed both an alternative myth of redemption and an alternative analysis of the Christian myth of redemption. Simultaneously, Marxism announced a militant revolution against the prevailing Christian order and a recovery of the original socialism of Christianity. Christian reactions to the dual challenge of Marxism have been extremely diverse. Representing one extreme, Pope Leo XIII condemned socialism on behalf of the Roman Catholic Church as "a deadly plague" that undermined religion, state, family, and private property. Although he eventually recognized that under the modern economic relations of industrial capitalism "a small number of very rich men have been able to lay upon the masses of the poor a yoke little better than slavery itself," Pope Leo XIII continued to reject socialism as a legitimate Christian response to the world of goods. At the other extreme, the Christian socialist Karl Kautsky (1854–1938), in his *Foundations of Christianity* (1908), celebrated Jesus as an early socialist and condemned the other-worldly Christianity that reinforced capitalist oppression.[19]

In between these extremes of rejection and acceptance, however, Marxism has informed the social analysis of leading Christian thinkers in the modern era. In the United States, for example, Walter Rauschenbusch (1861–1918) developed a Christian "social gospel" that used Marxist analysis to expose the moral evils and injustices of capitalism. In a series of books, including *Christianity and the Social Crisis* (1907), *Christianizing the Social Order* (1912), and *A Theology for the Social Gospel* (1917), Rauschenbusch attacked the spirit of competition, the selfish profit motive, the irresponsible abuse of power, and the exploitation of workers inherent in the capitalist economic system. Without necessarily embracing the ideal of a communist utopia, Rauschenbusch's social gospel nevertheless advocated the public ownership of the basic means of production, economic equality, and democracy in the workplace as essentially Christian strategies for ameliorating the dehumanizing forces of modern industrial capitalism in America. During the 1920s and 1930s, the Protestant theologian Reinhold Niebuhr (1892–1971) called himself a "Christian Marxist." Using a Marxist analysis of class conflict, Niebuhr argued that the "comfortable classes" in capitalist America "do not suffer enough from social injustice to recognize its peril to the life of society." Although he objected to the tendency of Marxism to operate as an alternative religion, Niebuhr continued to develop a Christian social critique of the "immoral society" of industrial capitalism. Niebuhr expressed social concerns shared by many Protestant clergy in America during the 1930s. According to a survey of twenty thousand clergy in 1934, for example, only 5 percent favored capitalism as an economic system; 28 percent favored some form of socialism; 75 percent supported the Socialist Party candidate, Norman Thomas, for president. From the social gospel to Christian Marxism, therefore, Protestant clergy in the United States were critical of the social and economic conditions created by the capitalist system.[20]

In Russia, however, Marxism inspired the most dramatic social transformations. Following the Bolshevik revolution of 1917 under the leadership of Vladimir Ilyich Lenin (1870–1924), a communist program promised to create a classless society in which everyone would have equal access to the world of goods. As a militant atheist, Lenin saw Christianity in Russia as a reactionary opposition to this communist heaven on earth. "Every defense or justification of the idea of God, even the most refined, the best intentioned, is a justification of reaction."[21] Certainly, as the established state church, the Russian Orthodox Church had an interest in maintaining the old imperial order. Prior to the edict of toleration in 1905, the Russian Orthodox Church had been the only legally recognized religious body in the empire. Although the edict created greater legal freedom, the Russian Orthodox Church maintained a dominant position in the state, the schools, and other areas of Russian public life.

The new religious policy announced for the Soviet Union in 1918 explicitly separated the church from the state. Promising freedom of conscience, the legislation of 1918 defined religion as a private matter that should not enter the public arena. For example, clergy were prevented by law from teaching religion in public schools. The most serious attacks on the public standing of the church, however, were the provisions of this legislation that denied the right of churches to own property. Declaring all religious possessions, buildings, and land to be public property, the Communist party seized the wealth of the Russian Orthodox Church, promising to transfer the enormous wealth accumulated by the church to the working people of Russia. As the patriarch Tikhon (1865–1925) issued a formal condemnation of the Bolsheviks for which he was imprisoned, the new Soviet state embarked upon a campaign of violent repression of the Russian Orthodox Church. For resisting the nationalization of church property, dozens of bishops and thousands of priests, monks, nuns, and believers were arrested or killed. As the campaign to confiscate church property continued during the 1920s, it was directed by the Marxist theorist Leon Trotsky (1879–1940), who saw the campaign as a strategy for undermining both the social and the ideological power of the church. By applying a "short, sharp shock," he hoped to discredit the spiritual claims of the church in the eyes of the masses and thereby persuade people to embrace atheism. The conflict over ownership of church property, therefore, was seen by both the Russian church and the state as a spiritual battlefield.

In support of a broadly antireligious agenda, the Central Committee of the Communist party established an "Antireligious Commission" in 1922 to coordinate policy in three areas. First, the state introduced further measures to control religious organizations. Strict regulations governed the registration of churches, the censorship of sermons and religious publications, and the involvement of children in religious instruction. Second, the Communist party sought to promote atheism through antireligious propaganda. Although the Communist party cautioned that insulting the feelings of believers would be counterproductive, the commission supported programs in mass education in scientific materialism. Founded in 1925, the League of Atheists, which was later renamed the League of Militant Atheists, pursued this public campaign against religious belief. Third, a strategy was developed to infiltrate and divide the Russian Orthodox Church. With communist support, a group of reformers, known as the "Renovationists," succeeded in taking over the leadership of the church. Embracing the political, social, and economic goals of communism, the Renovationists sought to purge the church of counterrevolutionary clergy. When Patriarch Tikhon renounced his anti-Soviet position and was released from prison in 1924, however, the Communist party began to lose interest in the Renovationist Church. On behalf of the Patriarchal Church, Tikhon's successor, Patriarch Sergii (1867–1944), in 1927 issued a "Declaration of Loyalty" identifying the Russian Orthodox Church with the Soviet Union. "We wish to be Orthodox believers," Patriarch Sergii declared, "and at the same time to acknowledge the Soviet Union as our civil motherland, whose joys and successes are our joys and successes, and whose setbacks are our setbacks."[22] Nevertheless, the Russian Orthodox Church continued to be perceived by the Communist leadership as an obstacle to the progressive transformation of Soviet society. Although it had been stripped of its property, the church nevertheless represented a kind of spiritual capital that blocked the road to the communist cargo.

28

Holocaust

In developing his critical philosophy, which revolutionized European thinking about knowledge, morality, and aesthetics, the German philosopher Immanuel Kant (1724–1804) also advanced a critique of religion. Drawing on the intellectual inheritance of the European Enlightenment, Kant sought to work out the terms and conditions of a rational religion in his *Religion Within the Limits of Reason Alone* (1793). Traditionally, he observed, religion has portrayed God as a powerful being, beyond human comprehension or control, whose favor can nevertheless be gained by performing certain rituals or devotions. According to Kant, the observance of this external religion—the *cultus externus*—requires prayers and ceremonies, prescriptions and prohibitions, that are all designed to please God or the gods. However, Kant reasoned that a God who was truly all-knowing, ultimately powerful, and completely perfect would have absolutely no need for such religious displays. In fact, he insisted, such external displays of religion are not religion at all, but forms of superstition that are inconsistent with a rational understanding of God. By using reason alone without the aid of supernatural revelation or recourse to superstitious ritual, Kant concluded, human beings could realize that religion is morality and morality is religion.

Dismissing all other religions as servile attempts to manipulate supernatural powers, Immanuel Kant declared that Christianity was the only moral religion. He cited Jesus' exhortation in the Sermon on the Mount— "Be perfect as your heavenly father is perfect"—as evidence that moral reason was central to Christianity. According to Kant, Jesus had transformed the old law of Moses that governed the external observances of ancient Judaism into the new law of Christianity in which the internal dispositions of the human will conformed to moral reason. Clearly, Kant's distinction between Judaism and Christianity, which drew the stark contrast between the external ritual law of the one and the internal moral law of the other, recast familiar Christian polemics against Jews into a new philosophical key. Kant realized that Christianity had its roots in the religion of ancient Israel. Philosophically, however, he insisted that Christianity and Judaism had nothing in common. According to Kant, "It is evident that the Jewish faith stands in no essential connection whatever, i.e., in no unity of concepts, with the [Christian] ecclesiastical faith whose history we wish to consider, though the Jewish immediately preceded this church and provided the physical occasion for its establishment." Ancient Judaism was not really a religion, he insisted, "but merely a union of a number of people who, since they belonged to a particular stock, formed themselves into a commonwealth under purely political laws, and not into a church." By "completely forsaking the Judaism from which it sprang," Kant declared, Christianity "arose suddenly," a new religion of pure morality with no conceptual connection to the tribal laws or ritual observances of ancient Judaism.

Likewise, according to Kant, contemporary Judaism had nothing to do with the genuine religion of moral reason that could only be found in Christianity. Still, Judaism survived and even flourished in spite of persecutions and pogroms in Europe. At the beginning of the nineteenth century, 90 percent of the Jews in the world lived in Europe, with about two hundred thousand living in Germany. A rich culture of religious practice, philosophy, ethics, and spirituality continued to be developed in European Judaism. As we have seen, the persistence of Judaism has periodically been experienced by Christians as a scandal. According to Christian accounts, Judaism had been supplanted by Christianity and should have ended in the first century. Nevertheless, Judaism survived. Reviewing Christian explanations for the survival of Judaism, Kant noted previous attempts to account for the continuing presence of the Jewish tradition as the ruins of a destroyed and dispersed nation, as a sign of God's special preservation of a previously chosen people, or as evidence of God's special punishment of Jews because they "stiff-neckedly sought to create a political and not a moral concept of the Messiah." In place of these historical and theological speculations, however, Kant proposed that the survival of Judaism could be rationally explained as the persistence of a superstition that was the defining opposite of true religion.

Having no authentic religious value, Jewish religious practice, according to Kant, was based on the superstitious premise that it is possible to please God "through actions which anyone can perform without even needing to be a good man." Since such actions "contain nothing moral" and morality is the essence of religion, Kant concluded that the living tradition of contemporary Judaism, like the heritage of ancient Judaism, could not be regarded as a religion. In his *Conflict of the Faculties* (1798), Kant presented his ultimate solution to the problem of the persistence of Judaism. The time had come, he proposed, for Jews to allow themselves to be led to their "final end." Calling for the death of Judaism, he declared that the "euthanasia of Judaism is pure moral religion, freed from all the ancient statutory teachings." Judaism "must disappear," Kant concluded, so that a purely moral religion could emerge with "only one shepherd and one flock."[1]

While Immanuel Kant developed Enlightenment ideals of reason and morality, the German theologian Friedrich Schleiermacher (1768–1834) displayed the distinctive commitments to emotion and imagination associated with European Romanticism. Educated in the Moravian piety of the United Brethren, Schleiermacher joined the circle of intellectuals, poets, and artists that revolved around Friedrich Schlegel (1772–1829). Under the influence of this Romantic movement, Schleiermacher redefined religion as a distinctive kind of emotional experience. In his major work, *On Religion: Speeches to Its Cultured Despisers* (1799), he argued that religion is not essentially a matter of either knowledge or morality, since both can be achieved outside of the ambit of religion. Instead of being a way of knowing or doing, he proposed, religion is a way of feeling. According to Schleiermacher, the essence of religion can be found in an intuitive sense of the infinite, an emotional engagement with the unity of the world, and a feeling of absolute dependence upon God. By redefining religion as the human capacity for achieving a profound depth and intensity of feeling, Schleiermacher defended religion as an important feature of any authentically human life.

In his celebration of the emotional vitality of religion, however, Friedrich Schleiermacher singled out Judaism as an exception. Assuming that Jews were incapable of the depth and intensity of feeling necessary for genuine religion, he declared that "Judaism is long since a dead religion." Of course, he was well aware of the contemporary presence of living Jews who continued to practice their religion. Nevertheless, he insisted that Judaism was religiously dead. Because of its alleged legalism, ritualism, and traditionalism, Judaism represented for Schleiermacher the denial of a genuine living religion based on profound feeling. According to

Schleiermacher, Judaism was an "undecaying mummy"; it displayed the "unpleasant appearance of a mechanical movement after the life and spirit had long since departed"; it persevered just like "a single fruit, after all the life force has vanished from the branch, often remains hanging until the bleakest season on a withered stem and dries up on it." In these vivid and horrifying metaphors, therefore, Schleiermacher denied Judaism's status as a living religion by insisting that it was already dead.

Schleiermacher left Jews with an impossible religious dilemma: on the one hand, Schleiermacher thought that Jews should abandon their tradition because anyone who identified with Judaism displayed what he called a "pathological state of mind." Although he supported the "emancipation" of Jews in modern Europe, his polemical attacks on Judaism implied that the price of that freedom from legal restrictions on residence, occupation, and movement would be the betrayal of the Jewish tradition. On the other hand, Schleiermacher opposed the conversion of Jews to Christianity because he feared it would lead to what he called an undesirable "Judaization" of the churches. Although supporting the inclusion of Jews in civil society, therefore, Schleiermacher recommended their exclusion from Christianity on the grounds that they represented a "pathological" influence.[2]

How did Kant and Schleiermacher—the founder of modern philosophy and the founder of modern theology—become involved in these polemical attacks on Jews and Judaism? Representing the highest intellectual achievements of the European Enlightenment and the Romantic movement, they nevertheless perpetuated the ignorance, misunderstanding, negative stereotypes, prejudice, and even hostility that had characterized the long tradition of Christian anti-Judaism. Certainly, they inherited this "Jewish problem" as a problem in Christian theology. In his early work, Martin Luther had tried to solve this "problem" by insisting that Judaism had died at the birth of Christianity. According to Luther, what persisted of Judaism as a contemporary religion was a corpse, because "Judaism is withered and decayed in all the world." Like Luther, therefore, Kant and Schleiermacher proclaimed the death of Judaism. Yet they were still faced with the "scandal" of the persistence of Judaism in spite of the death certificate issued by Christians.

By the middle of the 1540s, Luther had shifted to recommending a more militant policy toward Jews and Judaism. In a polemical tract, *On the Jews and Their Lies* (1543), he advocated banning all rabbinic teaching, confiscating Jewish prayer books, and burning Jewish homes, schools, and synagogues. If they still refused to convert to Christianity, Luther proposed, then the Jews should be expelled from Germany, even though he thought that Christians would be "at fault for not slaying them." When his recommendations were ignored by the German political authorities, Luther finally concluded that the resolution of the "Jewish problem" had to be postponed until the return of Christ at the end of the world. In that eschatological event outside of human history, the problem posed by Jews, as well as by Roman Catholics, Muslims, and all other heretics and infidels, would be solved in a final cosmic drama of divine destruction and redemption.[3]

In that eschatological hope, however, Kant and Schleiermacher parted ways with Luther. Whether they defined religion as moral reason or as profound feeling, both placed religion firmly in the context of human history. As modern Protestant theology developed during the nineteenth century in Germany, this Christian discovery of history was evident in the search for the historical Jesus, the development of historical methods of biblical criticism, and the emphasis on the ways in which God works in and through human history. In the process of discovering history, Protestant theologians increasingly posed the "Jewish problem" as a historical problem. In Nazi Germany, however, the "final solution" to this Christian historical problem revealed the terror of history in the mass killing of Jews—the Shoah or Destruction and Desolation—that came to be known as the Holocaust.

GERMAN CHRISTIANS

As the leader of the National Socialist German Workers' party, which came to power in Germany in 1933, Adolf Hitler (1889–1945) proclaimed a German nationalism based on race and territory—*Volk* and *Vaterland*—that from the beginning declared war against the Jews. In his political manifesto, *Mein Kampf* (1924), Hitler announced the heroic struggle of the Aryan people to maintain racial purity and establish territorial dominion. According to Hitler, these nationalist goals were blocked by obstacles outside Germany, especially by Poles, Russians, Ukrainians, and other Slavic peoples, and by corrupting influences inside Germany, by the mentally retarded, the physically handicapped, the homosexuals, or the criminals that Hitler labeled as "defective" or "anti-social" Germans.

However, Hitler identified the most serious enemy of his German nationalism as people who could be found both inside and outside Germany—the Jews.

The relation between Nazism and Christianity was complex. Hitler's political party endorsed "positive Christianity" and guaranteed "freedom for all religious denominations in the State so far as they are not a danger to it and do not militate against the customs and morality of the German race." Since Hitler declared Jews to be enemies of the German race, however, Judaism was not included in this guarantee of religious freedom. But Christian churches might also be condemned if they were found to oppose the Germanic "customs and morality" of Nazism. From a Roman Catholic background, Hitler had personally abandoned Christianity. In private he confessed that he saw no common ground between German nationalism and the Christian religion. "One is either a Christian or a German," he remarked. "You can't be both." Publicly, his close associate Martin Bormann (1900–1945) declared that "National Socialism and Christianity are irreconcilable." Nevertheless, Hitler imagined that there was some continuity between Nazism and the Christian tradition. For example, when a delegation of Catholic bishops asked him in 1933 what he was going to do about the Jews, Hitler assured them that he intended to do exactly what Christian churches had been advocating and practicing for almost two thousand years. On that basis, Hitler and the Nazi party sought the help of mainstream Catholic and Protestant churches in the campaign to revitalize German nationalism.[4]

In his personal religious thought, Hitler drew inspiration from the mixture of religion, racism, and romantic nationalism in the work of the composer Richard Wagner (1813–83), observing that "whoever wants to understand national socialist Germany must know Wagner." As a prospectus for his last opera, *Parsifal*, Wagner prepared an essay on "Heroism and Christianity" in 1881 that anticipated the racial nationalism of Hitler. Drawing on the quasi-scientific speculations about race by Count Gobineau, Wagner had asserted the superiority of a white Aryan race, which he found in its purest form in Germany. The Christian religion, according to Wagner, had strengthened that race. Asserting that Jesus had been born of Aryan rather than Jewish parentage, Wagner claimed that Christianity had inculcated heroic ideals of courage, self-sacrifice, willpower, and commanding intellect in the German people. However, Wagner asserted that this nobility of the Germans had been damaged by racial intermixtures. In prophetic tones, Wagner declared that the pure Aryan blood of Christ would cleanse Germany of all defilement, so that the nation could "rediscover itself as a race of divine heroes living in a sanctified world." Once purified, he promised, the "superior" German race would master and exploit all "lower" races. In Wagner's operatic vision, therefore, Hitler and other Nazis found the apocalyptic promise that Germans were destined to dominate the world.[5]

In theory and practice, however, Nazism emerged as a religious movement in its own right. As many historians have observed, Hitler "deified himself and made himself into the savior of the German people." Ultimately, the Nazi movement mobilized a religious politics of redemption. Through the new medium of film, Nazi propaganda used striking religious imagery. A 1933 film on the Hitler Youth, for example, depicts two religions—Nazism and Communism—vying for the allegiance of German youth. Sneaking away from a Communist Youth Camp, the young hero, Heini, has a conversion experience at the Nazi summer solstice celebration. By their bonfire, Heini hears the Nazi leader declare: "Germany lies in chains, but as these flames rise to the skies, so will we rise up to free her from her bonds." Identifying with this myth of the bondage and freedom of the German will, Heini converts to Nazism. He adopts the oaths, symbols, and discipline of this political religion. Having gone through this conversion, however, Heini passes quickly into martyrdom. Killed by the Communists, Heini lies dead in the last scene of the film as the Hitler Youth sing in the background: "We will march for Hitler through night and through danger with the flag of youth for freedom and bread. . . . Our flag is the new era and this flag will lead us into eternity. Yes, the flag is greater than death." In such vivid cinematic imagery, therefore, a Nazi political religion was advanced. Under the ultimate authority of a Germanic God and divine leader, that religion promised a transcendence of death in an eternal era of national redemption.[6]

Although it clearly adapted certain Christian themes and motifs, Nazism nevertheless emerged as a pagan political religion. For that reason, Hitler felt that the German nationalism of the Nazi movement and Christianity were two different religions. Among his plans for after the war, Hitler hoped to solve the "church problem," which divided German religious allegiance between Christianity and Nazism. A considerable number of Christians in Germany, however, were convinced that Christianity and Nazism were not two but actually one religion. Primarily comprised of Protestant clergy and laypeople, the German Christian movement *(Glaubensbewegung Deutsche Christen)* celebrated the rise of National Socialism as a revitalization of Christianity. During the 1930s and 1940s, the "German Christians" formed a mass movement of over half a million members with branches throughout Germany. Dominating theological faculties and seminaries, the German Christians had a broad influence on Protestant church leadership and congregations. As they merged Christianity with German nationalism, German Christians praised both Jesus and Hitler in church services, rallies, books, pamphlets, hymns, and popular songs. Although they met with some Christian opposition, the German Christians also annoyed the Nazi hierarchy by trying to make the pagan Germanic religion of National Socialism into an essentially Christian crusade.

The German Christian movement was dedicated to a Christianity that was adamantly racist. In its statement of principles in 1932, the movement declared that "race" and "nation" were "laws of life that God has bequeathed and entrusted to us. It is God's law that we concern ourselves with their preservation. Mixing of the races, therefore, is to be opposed." Not only the creator of heaven and earth, God was also the maker of separations who had divided the many races, peoples, and nations of the world. Reflecting on Christian missions overseas, they insisted that even after their conversion African and Asian Christians had to be kept apart from German Christians. As one Christian missionary in the movement declared, "What God has put asunder let no man join together." This commitment to racist notions of blood, people, and nation, therefore, denied any possibility of a nonracial Christian "brotherhood" in foreign mission fields.

Within German territory, however, the German Christian movement targeted the racist principle of separatism directly against Jews. In its statement of 1932, the movement opposed any domestic missions to Jews in Germany on explicitly racist grounds, asserting, "That mission is the entryway for foreign blood into the body of our *Volk*." From the racist perspective of the German Christians, Jews threatened the "purity" of the German people. Although these church leaders could not prevent Jews from associating with Christians, marrying Christians, being citizens, or living in Germany, they could advocate the exclusion of Jews from the churches under their influence or control. Even before the Nazis took power in 1933, therefore, the German Christian movement had formulated racist policies against Jews for the churches that would eventually be enacted under Hitler by the German state.

As the German Christian movement developed, it proclaimed a Nazi Christianity based not only on blood, but also on certain ideals of masculinity that were responsive to the increasing militarization of German society under the Nazi regime. According to German Christian leader Joachim Hossenfelder in 1933, the movement would mobilize the "storm troopers of the church." Opposed to alternative forms of Christianity they characterized as "effeminate, soft, or weak," the German Christians envisioned a "manly church" for "real men." As another leader put it in 1935, Germany needed "a church of men, not a church of women of both sexes." By adding patriotic marches, military drills, and the display of Nazi flags to the Christian liturgy, German Christians proclaimed an aggressive Christianity that was prepared for war. Ironically, more women than men became formal members of the "manly church." Celebrated as mothers of the nation and as wives of soldiers, women in the German Christian movement formed service groups, assumed leadership roles, and edited publications in support of the Nazi ideals of racial purity. Alongside racism, therefore, German Christians tried to inculcate separate gender roles for men and women within a "manly church" dedicated to a militant Christian nationalism.[7]

Although most Protestants and Catholics were not formal members of the German Christian movement, their churches were nevertheless influenced by similar attempts to reconcile Christianity with the Germanic nationalism, racism, and anti-Judaism of National Socialism. Appealing primarily to Protestants, this brand of national Christianity nevertheless was also embraced by some Catholics. Representing about one-third of the Christians in Germany, German Catholics attempted to accommodate Christianity to the Nazi program. Shortly after Hitler came to power in 1933, a group of Catholic intellectuals started a periodical, *Reich und Kirche,* dedicated to "the building of the Third Reich from the united forces of the National Socialist State and Catholic Christianity." In the popular pamphlet *The Catholic Entree to National Socialism,* the Catholic historian Joseph Lortz (1887–1975) urged German Catholics to support Hitler as the savior of Christian Europe from the threat of communism. According to Lortz, Nazism represented "the salvation of Germany and therefore the salvation of Europe from the chaos of Bolshevism and the destruction of Christian Europe." Nazism was identified by Joseph Lortz as a new way "to be a German Catholic or a Catholic German." In another essay, "The German *Volkstum* and Catholic Christianity," the Catholic theologian Karl Adam (1876–1966) explicitly embraced the racist ideology of Nazism by celebrating Hitler's recovery of the "primeval powers, which created and formed our nationalistic consciousness: blood and spirit, blood and religion, German blood and Christianity." For these Catholic intellectuals, therefore, the racist and nationalist features of Nazism were consistent with the religious interests of German Catholicism.[8]

The German Christian movement saw World War II as the fulfillment of its ideals of race, gender, and militant nationalism. Mobilizing Christian resources for the German war effort, leaders of the movement celebrated the ideals of motherhood and martial sacrifice as if they represented the highest achievements of the Christian faith. During 1944 the German Christian theologian Walter Grundmann (1906–76) published an open letter depicting the German Reich at war as a "parable for the Kingdom of God." According to Grundmann, that divine kingdom was supported by two Christian symbols, the Madonna and the cross. The Madonna with child represented holy motherhood as the source of life for the German nation; the cross represented the sacrificial death of the nation's soldiers on the battlefield. As Grundmann appropriated these Christian symbols on behalf of the Nazi regime, he declared that "the Madonna and the Cross are the symbols of faith in the Reich!" By placing these powerful symbols of life and death at the service of Nazism, Grundmann concluded that "faith in the Reich is the German form of Christianity in the twentieth century."[9]

Of course, not all Christians in Germany subscribed to the Nazi Christianity of the German Christian movement. One of the most vocal critics was the Lutheran pastor Dietrich Bonhoeffer (1906–45). With a doctorate in theology from the University of Berlin, Bonhoeffer developed a Christian theology that emphasized social ethics, a sense of community, and service to others. In Hitler's Germany, Bonhoeffer urged Christians to adopt new strategies of social activism against the Nazi state. The rise of Nazism, he argued, "brought an end to the church in Germany." Far from seeing Nazism as the "German form of Christianity in the twentieth century," therefore, Bonhoeffer recognized that the Nazis had declared war on Christianity. For authentic Christians, he insisted, the "cost of discipleship" was resistance to the Nazi regime. "If we claim to be Christians there is no room for expediency," Bonhoeffer declared. "Hitler is the Anti-Christ. Therefore we must go on with our work and eliminate him whether he is successful or not." Arrested in 1943 on the suspicion that he was involved in a plot to assassinate Hitler, Bonhoeffer was executed in April 1945 along with five thousand others who had been accused of participating in the resistance. As the life and martyrdom of Dietrich Bonhoeffer demonstrated, some Christians in Germany were prepared to struggle against Nazism in both church and state.[10]

CHURCH STRUGGLES

As the Nazi party rose to prominence, a group of church leaders in 1928 signed a declaration against its professed anti-Semitism: "We are persuaded that the anti-Semitic movement, which in the aftermath of the World War has had so mighty a boom, is irreconcilable with the Christian point of view and is incompatible with our debt of gratitude to the cradle of Christianity."[11] Among the signatories of this anti-Nazi statement was the Protestant theologian Karl Barth (1886–1968). Often identified as the most important theologian of the twentieth century, Karl Barth had moved to Germany from his native Switzerland to assume university chairs in theology at Göttingen in 1921, Münster in 1925, and Bonn in 1930. Although he was forced out of Germany in 1935 for his opposition to the Nazi state, Karl Barth continued to exercise a commanding influence over the development of Protestant theology in Germany.

In his first major work, *The Epistle to the Romans* (1922), Barth announced a theology of the Word of God. Against all forms of institutionalized Christianity, Barth posed the God that he found revealed in the Bible, a God whose radical difference from human beings exposed the vain pretensions of human morality and religion. As Barth described his own project, "If I have a system, it is limited to a recognition of what [the Danish philosopher Søren] Kierkegaard called the 'infinite qualitative distinction' between time and eternity and to my regarding this as possessing negative as well as positive significance: God is in heaven, and thou art on earth." According to Barth, this infinite distance between God and humans could only be bridged by God. The Word of God issued a resounding "no" to human autonomy—which for Barth was the very definition of sin, the pride, ambition, and pretension of human independence from God—while conveying a "yes" through the gift of grace to God's own creatures in the kingdom of God. In his multivolume *Church Dogmatics,* begun in 1927, Barth continued to amplify this "dialectical" theology of God's simultaneous negation and affirmation of humanity through the Word of God in Jesus Christ, the Bible, and the preaching of the church.[12]

When Hitler came to power in 1933, Barth saw the "German people beginning to worship a false God." Convinced that the Nazi party ultimately intended to destroy Christianity, Barth argued against this false worship of the state. Insisting that Jesus Christ was the sole leader of the church, Barth inspired an emerging movement—the Confessing Church—that resisted Nazi interference in church affairs. Its slogan was "Church must remain church." The Confessing Church grew out of the Pastors' Emergency League established in 1933 by a Berlin pastor, Martin Niemöller (1892–1984), who mobilized Christian opposition to a piece of Nazi legislation known as the "Aryan clause," which removed Jews from the civil service. Following the Nazi lead, the German Christian movement proposed an "Aryan clause" for churches that would expel Christian converts with Jewish ancestry from the clergy. Although he was a self-professed anti-Semite, Martin Niemöller nevertheless organized resistance to this proposal because it denied the effectiveness of the Christian ritual of baptism. Without necessarily opposing the racism, anti-Semitism, or anti-Judaism of the German Christians, therefore, the Confessing Church movement developed from this interest in maintaining the autonomy and integrity of the Christian church.

At a conference held the following year in the town of Barmen, Karl Barth drafted a declaration of principles, which he understood as a confession of faith, for the Confessing Church movement. In the Barmen Declaration, the movement declared its opposition to the nationalist ideology of the German Christians and the interventions by the Nazi state in church administration by affirming sole allegiance to Jesus Christ. The first article read:

> In view of the destructive errors of the German Christians and the present national church government, we pledge ourselves to the following evangelical truths:
>
> "I am the way and the truth and the life: no man comes to the Father but by me" (John 14:6).
>
> "Truly, truly, I say to you, he who does not enter by the door into the

sheepfold but climbs up some other way is a thief and a robber. . . . I am the door: by me if any man enter in, he shall be saved" (John 10:1, 9).

Jesus Christ, as he is testified to us in Holy Scripture, is the one word of God which we are to hear, which we are to trust and obey in life and in death.

We repudiate the false teaching that the Church can and must recognize yet other happenings and powers, personalities and truths, as divine revelation alongside this one Word of God, as a source of her preaching.[13]

For Barth, the Barmen Declaration struck an evangelical blow against any form of "natural theology" that derived Christian principles from human reason or human interests. Under Nazism, however, the "natural theology" of the German Christians had drawn its Christian principles from the supposedly "divine revelations" of race, nationalism, and Aryan supremacy. By the doctrinal standards outlined in the Barmen Declaration, such a mixture of the Word of God with the truth claims of Volk and Vaterland was a false teaching to be condemned as a Christian heresy. Like any other "natural theology," according to Barth, German nationalist Christianity was a human fabrication condemned by God.

As Barth later recognized, the Barmen Declaration had failed to address the persecution of Jews under the Nazi regime. He regretted that he had not made the "Jewish question" a major theme in the declaration, but observed that "in 1934 no text in which I had done that would have been acceptable even to the Confessing Church, given the atmosphere that there was then." Among its supporters, the Confessing Church movement included anti-Semites, such as Martin Niemöller, and others who might have objected to the racial policies of the Nazis but were still opposed to Jews and Judaism on theological grounds. Some within the Confessing Church even argued that Jews and Nazis were essentially the same because they were both völkisch, or national, movements that rejected the supreme authority of Jesus Christ. In such an anti-Semitic atmosphere, Barth concluded, the "Jewish question" could not be raised.

On other occasions, however, Karl Barth clearly stated his opposition to the Nazi persecution of Jews on Christian grounds. For example, in a 1934 sermon on the theme "Christ was born a Jew," Barth asserted that "anyone who believes in Christ, who was himself a Jew, and died for Gentiles and Jews, simply cannot be involved in the contempt for Jews and ill-treatment of them which is now the order of the day." Although

Barth was opposed to the anti-Semitic hostility toward Jews that increasingly pervaded German society, he was not very well acquainted with Jews in Germany or with Judaism as a living religion in Europe. As Barth later confessed, he had no time to study recent developments in European Judaism because he was too occupied with the Christian theological significance of "Israel." Rejecting liberal ideals of interreligious toleration as hypocrisy, Barth insisted on affirming the Christian doctrine that Jesus Christ was the fulfillment of the promise of ancient Israel and therefore the ultimate replacement of the religion of Judaism. Absorbed in this Christian framework, however, Judaism registered as a series of stubborn refusals of God—the betrayal of divine election, the denial of Jesus Christ, and the rejection of the promise of grace within the Christian church—that denied Jews any religious authenticity independent of the "salvation history" of Christianity.[14]

Obviously, this Christian "doctrine of Israel" made any religious dialogue between Jews and Christians difficult. Nevertheless, largely through Jewish initiatives, attempts were made to find some common ground for interreligious communication. In January 1933, two weeks before Hitler assumed power, a Jewish educational organization, the *Jüdisches Lehrhaus,* sponsored a public dialogue on the topic "Church, State, Nation, and Jewry" between the Protestant theologian Karl Ludwig Schmidt and the Jewish philosopher, historian, and educator Martin Buber. This public event revealed both the character and the impossibility of meaningful religious dialogue between Christians and Jews at the dawn of the Nazi era.

As an opponent of the German Christians and the Nazi influence over the churches, Karl Ludwig Schmidt (1891–1956) rejected the racial and political anti-Semitism that was sweeping Germany. Like Karl Barth, he was eventually forced to leave Germany in 1935 on account of his resistance to Nazi interventions in the churches. In his opening remarks at this public dialogue, Schmidt expressed to his Jewish hosts his desire "to live together with you as Jews—as we must, as we wish—for as you are our brothers in the whole world so also in our German fatherland." However, Schmidt insisted that the fundamental differences between the two religions had to be taken seriously. According to Schmidt, Christians could only avoid the hypocrisy of liberal toleration by proclaiming the gospel to Jews. In that gospel, the Christian church appeared as the "true Israel," the heir to divine election. Christian salvation history, Schmidt insisted, had revealed that "Jewry is necessarily on the road to the Church." Having rejected Jesus of Nazareth as their Messiah, however, Jews remained on that road, but they also remained lost, disoriented, and dispersed in the world. "God has willed all this," Schmidt concluded. "Jesus, the Messiah, rejected by his people, prophesied the destruction of Jerusalem. Jerusalem has been destroyed, so that it will never again come under Jewish rule. Until the present day the Jewish diaspora has no center." According to Schmidt, only the Christian church, as "the Israel after the spirit," could ultimately provide Jews with a spiritual center that would be their home.

For decades, Martin Buber (1878–1965) had been working to foster mutual understanding between Christians and Jews. As he recovered and reinterpreted the heritage of Jewish philosophy, ethics, and spirituality, Buber also tried to communicate an understanding of that heritage to a literate Christian audience. Karl Ludwig Schmidt, for example, had written favorable reviews of Buber's writings. Struck by Schmidt's dogmatic approach in this public dialogue, however, Buber sought to shift the terms of the discussion away from doctrinal differences. Since Christian and Jewish beliefs were both based on revelation, he observed, their differences could not be resolved by rational argument. Acknowledging essential differences between Jews and Christians, Buber pointed to a common spiritual experience, a presence of the spirit, that presented the possibility of a basic unity in the midst of religious differences. As Buber explained:

> We feel ourselves, in fact find ourselves, in a world where differences are unresolved and appear by their nature to be irresolvable. To be sure, however, we also feel something else. We feel that the "Spirit"—a term of belief which we have in common with Christians, although they call it *pneuma hagion* (holy spirit) and we *ruach ha-kodesh* (spirit of sanctification or holiness)—is itself not bound by this differentiation. We feel that the Spirit alone wafts over our irresolvable differences, that though it does not bridge them, it nevertheless gives assurance of unity, assurance in the experienced moment of unity for the communality of both Christians and Jews.

By affirming the mystery of this spiritual reality, Buber asserted that it would be presumptuous of human beings to prescribe to God the manner of his revelation by saying, "God cannot reveal himself in this way." Certainly, Christians and Jews experience that spiritual mystery differently.

"How is it possible for the mysteries to exist side by side?" Buber asked. "This is God's mystery."

Nevertheless, Buber found remaining differences that had to be confronted. Appealing to Christians, he proposed that a genuine encounter with religious differences could only begin when they stopped regarding Israel as only a theological concept and recognized Judaism as a living community of faith. In that recognition, Buber suggested, Christians would learn that Jews had a very different experience of the history of salvation. "We know that universal history has not been rent to its foundations, and that the world has not yet been redeemed," he observed. "The Church may or must understand precisely this sensation of ours as the consciousness of our unredeemedness. But we know it otherwise." As Buber concluded, in their specific encounter with the divine mystery, Jews sense, experience, and know that they have not been rejected by God. Buber, therefore, proposed a dialogue based on the mutual recognition of different religious experiences in Jewish and Christian communities of faith.

Rejecting Buber's invitation to enter into this mutual recognition, Schmidt insisted that the Christian understanding of Jesus Christ was not negotiable. Christians were bound by their scriptures to proclaim Jesus as the redemption of humanity and the culmination of history. According to Schmidt, that proclamation of Jesus Christ necessarily brought Christians into conflict with Jews. In fact, Christians were obligated to confront Jews with the demands of their gospel. As the defining moment of the Christian tradition, the opposition between Christians and Jews was reaffirmed by Schmidt as essential to Christianity. "From the very beginning of Christianity, this sharp conflict has existed," he concluded. "We Christians must never tire of keeping this one conflict alive." As Karl Ludwig Schmidt demonstrated, therefore, at the beginning of the Nazi era even a liberal Protestant theologian could maintain that anti-Judaism was an essential feature of Christian faith.[15]

AFTER AUSCHWITZ

During World War II, the Nazi death squads, concentration camps, and killing centers caused the deaths of 15 million people. Slavs, Poles, gypsies, communists, dissidents, gays, lesbians, and many others were caught up in the Nazi killing machinery. As their Final Solution (*Endlösung*) to

the "Jewish problem" in Europe, however, the Nazis systematically murdered as many as 6 million Jews precisely because they were Jews. The
Nazis killed approximately two out of every three Jews who were living in
Europe in 1939; they killed over 90 percent of the 3.3 million Jews in Poland.
In the killing center constructed near the Polish town of Oswiecim, which
the Germans called Auschwitz, the Nazis killed an estimated 1.5 million
men, women, and children, of which 90 percent were Jews. As the principal site, emblem, and memorial of the Holocaust, Auschwitz has come to
represent a radical disruption of human history. For Jews, according to
Elie Wiesel, Auschwitz was the place in which time stopped and became
"eternal night." Some Christians have also recognized that Auschwitz
marked a historical break, an eruption of evil into the world that changed
human history. Did the Holocaust also change Christianity? "Never
again," the Roman Catholic theologian Johann-Baptist Metz urged other
Christians, "do theology in such a way that its construction remains unaffected, or could remain unaffected, by Auschwitz." After the horror of
Auschwitz, Christians have been challenged to confront the entanglements of Christianity in anti-Semitism, racism, and nationalism.[16]

In the wake of the Holocaust, historians have debated the relation
between Christian anti-Judaism and the Nazi anti-Semitism that resulted
in the legalized persecution and state-sponsored genocide of approximately 6 million European Jews. According to the Protestant theologian
Franklin H. Littell, the basic Christian doctrine that the church had
replaced the synagogue, thereby rendering Jews and their religion obsolete, "has murderous implications which murderers will in time spell out."
In Nazi Germany, "the murder of six million Jews by baptized
Christians," Littell concluded, "raises the most insistent question about
the credibility of Christianity." Along similar lines, the Catholic theologian Gregory G. Baum challenged Christians to consider the connection
between Christian anti-Judaism and the Holocaust. "What Auschwitz has
revealed to the Christian community," Baum proposed, "is the deadly
power of its own symbolism." According to these Christian theologians,
therefore, Christianity was clearly implicated in the Holocaust.[17]

Certainly, the Nazi hierarchy did not plan and execute its program of
genocide on explicitly Christian principles. As already noted, Nazi leaders
were for the most part neopagans who despised Christianity as an extension of Judaism. Adolf Hitler, for example, derided the Christian notion of
"turning the other cheek" as a "Jewish doctrine." Rather than drawing

inspiration from a long tradition of Christian anti-Judaism, therefore, the Nazis relied primarily on nineteenth-century theories of race—the classification and ranking of people into quasi-scientific racial categories—to justify a romantic nationalism based on the power and purity of an Aryan race. However, as many historians have observed, the racist anti-Semitism of the Nazi project emerged in the heartland of European Christianity. As we have seen, the German Christian movement enthusiastically embraced racist anti-Semitism as consistent with its Christian faith. But many Christians had been prepared by representations of Jews as rejecting Christ and therefore as rejected by God to be relatively indifferent to their plight. Therefore, although Christian anti-Judaism might not have been the cause of the Holocaust, it arguably prepared the ground for racist anti-Semitism to gain the force that it assumed in Nazi Germany.

After the war, the French Catholic scholar Jules Isaac, author of a seven-volume history of the world, began research on the history of Christian anti-Judaism that culminated in his book *Jesus and Israel* (1948). By reviewing Catholic and Protestant commentaries on the Bible, Isaac demonstrated that Christian theology was permeated with "teachings of contempt" for Jews and Judaism, which had played a contributing role in the Holocaust. Looking to the future, however, Isaac made specific proposals for improving Christian relations with Jews. Affirming the Jewishness of Jesus, his family, and his disciples, Isaac encouraged Christians to renounce the accusations that Jews had practiced a degenerate religion at the time of Jesus, that they were the enemies of Christ, or that they were guilty of deicide, the murder of God. Although a modified version was adopted by a conference of Christians and Jews at Seelisberg, Switzerland, in 1947, Isaac's proposals were largely ignored by the Roman Catholic Church until Pope John XXIII convened the council of Vatican II between 1962 and 1965 to review church doctrine, practice, and organization. Building on the work of Jules Isaac, the subcommittee considering relations with Jews issued its declaration, *Nostra Aetate,* which repudiated the entire history of the church's "teachings of contempt" against Jews and Judaism. Formally absolving Jews in the past or present of any guilt for the death of Jesus, this declaration also stated that the church was open to new initiatives in religious dialogue between Catholics and Jews. Likewise, many Protestants looked for new opportunities to redress anti-Jewish stereotypes and engage in Christian-Jewish dialogues that would foster mutual respect and understanding. By the

1960s, therefore, a small but increasing number of Christians were renouncing the anti-Judaism of the past and searching for common ground between Christians and Jews.[18]

One common concern shared by Jews and Christians has been the attempt to understand a God who operates in history. Both Jews and Christians hold beliefs about God acting through historical events—the exodus from Egypt, the revelation of the Torah to Moses, the inspiration of the prophets, and so on—that presume God's active involvement in human affairs. But where was God during the Shoah? "The Holocaust poses the most radical counter-testimony to both Judaism and Christianity," Rabbi Irving Greenberg observed. "The cruelty and killing raise the question whether even those who believe after such an event dare to talk about a God who loves and cares without making a mockery of those who suffered."[19] With a particular intensity, the Holocaust has forced theologians to return to the problem of evil—the question of theodicy, the justice of God—in any theistic understanding of an all-good and all-powerful governor of the world. In simple and stark terms, the Holocaust challenged the notion that God could be both all-good and all-powerful. If God was all-good, then God could not be all-powerful because God did not intervene to stop the slaughter of innocent men, women, and children. If God was all-powerful, then God could not be all-good because God allowed or caused this evil to be perpetrated. Characteristically, theists have assumed that the all-good and all-powerful God used his power to create human beings with freedom and responsibility, which represented a greater good than creating them for mechanical obedience, but that human beings abused their freedom by turning from God and acting in irresponsible ways. During the Holocaust, however, God seemed to have turned away from innocent human beings. From a variety of perspectives, Jews and Christians have tried to answer the question posed by the Holocaust: "Where was God?"

Attempts have been made to interpret the Holocaust as God's direct intervention in human history. The Reform rabbi Ignaz Maybaum, for example, argued that God acted through the Holocaust to bring the entire world into the modern age. As God's chosen people, the Jews were consecrated by God as the sacrificial victims whose deaths would change the world. Surprisingly, Maybaum interpreted the murder of 6 million Jews in the Holocaust according to the model provided by a Christian understanding of the sacrificial death of Jesus on the cross at Golgotha.

According to Maybaum, "The Golgotha of modern mankind is Auschwitz. The cross, the Roman gallows, was replaced by the gas chamber." Of course, in most Christian understandings of the crucifixion, Jesus went to his execution on the cross willingly. The innocent victims of the Holocaust certainly did not. Nevertheless, Maybaum tried to retain the notion of a good and powerful God acting in history. In the process, however, Hitler was transformed into an agent of God. Declaring, "Hitler, My Servant," according to Maybaum, "God used this instrument to cleanse, to purify, to punish a sinful world." Although this interpretation made God responsible for the degradation, torture, prolonged suffering, and mass murder of innocent victims, it was an attempt to render the Holocaust consistent with a biblical view of God's redemptive activity in the world, even if redemption in this case was only the blessings of modernity.[20]

A similar attempt to explain the Holocaust as God's direct intervention in history was made by the German Protestant church leader Heinrich Grüber. During World War II, Grüber had been imprisoned for three years in a concentration camp for his opposition to the Nazi treatment of Jews. From his biblical faith in a God who acts in history, however, Grüber maintained that the death of 6 million Jews was part of a divine plan for God's chosen people. "At different times God uses different people as His whip against His own people, the Jews," he insisted. In this instance, Grüber imagined that Hitler was the divine whip that God used to chastise or punish his people. "For some reason," he concluded, "it was part of God's plan that the Jews died."[21]

For some Jews and Christians, therefore, retaining a notion of God acting in history turned Adolf Hitler into an unwitting agent of God's plan for achieving some higher good—redemptive sacrifice, divine punishment—through the evil of the Holocaust. As the Jewish theologian Richard Rubenstein argued in *After Auschwitz* (1966), this belief that God worked through Hitler was unacceptable:

How can Jews believe in an omnipotent, beneficent God after Auschwitz? Traditional Jewish theology maintains that God is the ultimate, omnipotent actor in the historical drama. It has interpreted every major catastrophe in Jewish history as God's punishment of a sinful Israel. I fail to see how this position can be maintained without regarding Hitler and the SS as instruments of God's will. The agony of European Jewry cannot be likened to the testing of Job. To see any purpose in the death camps, the traditional believer is forced to regard the most demonic, anti-human explosion of all history as a meaningful expression of God's purposes. The idea is simply too obscene for me to accept.

According to Rubenstein, the Holocaust revealed the absence of God from human history, indicating that human beings had entered the era of the death of God. "When I say we live in the time of the death of God," he explained, "I mean that the thread uniting God and man, heaven and earth, has been broken. We stand in a cold, silent, unfeeling cosmos, unaided by any purposeful power beyond our own resources." After Auschwitz, Rubenstein argued, only a void remained where God was once felt to be present. The terror of history, therefore, revealed God's absence.[22]

During the 1960s, a group of radical Christian theologians also proclaimed the "death of God." Drawing inspiration from the prison writings of Dietrich Bonhoeffer, the "death of God" theologians proposed a "religionless Christianity" for a world that had "come of age" in the absence of God. Like Rubenstein, therefore, some Christian theologians rejected traditional theism in the wake of the horrors of recent history. More recently, however, both Christian and Jewish theologians have tried to recover what the Jewish philosopher Emil Fackenheim has called "God's presence in history." According to Fackenheim, God did not act through the Holocaust to redeem or punish Jews. Rather, God was present as a "commanding Voice."

> We are, first, commanded to survive as Jews, lest the Jewish people perish. We are commanded, second, to remember in our very guts and bones the martyrs of the holocaust, lest their memory perish. We are forbidden, thirdly, to deny or despair of God, however much we may have to contend with Him or with belief in Him, lest Judaism perish. We are forbidden, finally, to despair of the world as the place which is to become the kingdom of God lest we help make it a meaningless place in which God is dead or irrelevant and everything is permitted. To abandon any of these imperatives, in response to Hitler's victory at Auschwitz, would be to hand him yet other posthumous victories.[23]

Recovering the presence of God in history after the Holocaust, however, has required theologians to make certain modifications in the traditional understanding of God. According to the Christian theologian Paul Van Buren, for example, God was revealed in the Holocaust to be a God that suffers with his people. Although he was counted among the "death of God" theologians in the 1960s, Van Buren was led by his reflections on the Holocaust to conclude that God was not absent or remote from the world. Instead, God was immanently present because God shared the agony of Jews. "Where was God at Auschwitz?" he asked. According to Van Buren, God was there in the midst of the dehumanization, destruction, and death, suffering "in solidarity with His people." Affirming God's presence in Jewish suffering, Van Buren suggested that God's solidarity with Jews also sent a message to Christians. "Perhaps He was trying, by simply suffering with His people, to awaken His church to a new understanding of love and respect for them." Although he proposed that love and respect could be cultivated by interreligious dialogue, Van Buren recognized that the death of 6 million Jews was an extremely high cost for God to have paid to send a message to the Christian churches. In deciding among possible explanations for God's purpose in the Holocaust, he admitted, "silence may be the wiser choice."[24] Whether interpreted as the voice or the silence of God, the Holocaust cast a shadow over both Judaism and Christianity during the second half of the twentieth century.

29

Cold War

During the 1970s, the Reverend Sun Myung Moon and the Reverend Jim Jones gained international attention as leaders of unconventional Christian movements. Born in what became North Korea, Sun Myung Moon (b. 1920) claimed that a meeting with Jesus on Easter Day, 1936, had inspired him to become a Christian evangelist. Coming into conflict with the North Korean government, Moon was imprisoned for over two years until he was released by U.N. forces during the Korean War. In 1954 he founded the *Tong Il* movement in Korea, which would emerge internationally as the Holy Spirit Association for the Unification of World Christianity, or the Unification Church. Moon's teachings were collected in a text, the *Divine Principle,* which was understood as both interpreting and completing the Bible. The *Divine Principle* presented human history as a battle between forces of good and evil, which had resulted during the modern era in the division of the world between God-centered democracy and Satan-centered communism. According to the *Divine Principle,* the United States and the Soviet Union were locked in a conflict of cosmic significance.

As the Unification Church expanded in the United States during the 1970s, Reverend Moon called upon America to embrace its divine destiny. At a rally celebrating the U.S. bicentennial in 1976, for example, Moon declared that "God anointed America with oil." According to Moon, God-centered America was the world's only defense against Satan-centered communism. "Destroying America is the communist's final and ultimate goal," he declared. "They know America is God's final bulwark on earth." In Moon's apocalyptic scenario, therefore, the geopolitical conflict of the Cold War, which was being waged between the two "superpowers" of the modern world, was actually the final battle between God and Satan.

For the United States to fulfill its divine destiny, however, Americans would have to accept the messiah of this new age. In its reworking of the basic Christian myth, the *Divine Principle* recounted that the first messiah, Jesus of Nazareth, had been sent by God to restore the perfect pattern of God-centered family life that had been broken by Adam and Eve. On that mission from God, Jesus was supposed to marry and raise a God-centered family, which would have inspired a God-centered nation, which would have eventually resulted in the emergence of a God-centered world. Unfortunately, according to the *Divine Principle,* Jesus was crucified before he could fulfill that divine mission. Therefore, a second messiah—the Lord of the Second Advent—was required to perform the task that Jesus had failed. Where should the world look for this messiah? As the *Divine Principle* proposed, the birthplace of the messiah "must be God's front line and Satan's front line." In the war between God and Satan, that front line was the 38th parallel dividing North from South Korea. "Naturally," the *Divine Principle* insisted, "this 38th parallel is the very front line for both democracy and communism, and, at the same time, the front line for both God and Satan." Without specifically mentioning Sun Myung Moon, the *Divine Principle* nevertheless made it clear that the new messiah would appear from Korea to restore the perfect pattern of a God-centered family. In the international arena, however, the messiah would represent God during the impending World War III. After Satan-centered communism had been destroyed in that war, the *Divine Principle* promised, the entire world would be unified under a single messianic ruler in a new "Kingdom of Heaven on Earth."[1]

While Sun Myung Moon was developing his unconventional Christianity in Korea during the 1950s, Jim Jones (1931–78) was in the Midwest heartland of America, the state of Indiana, building a Christian ministry based on Pentecostal faith healing, social service, and racial integration. After reporting a vision of nuclear war in 1967, Jones moved his ministry to northern California, where he gained formal affiliation with the Disciples of Christ and attracted a large, primarily African American following. In sermons during the early 1970s, Jones attacked what he regarded as false notions of God as a transcendent person, deriding such notions by ridiculing the deity of conventional Christianity as the Sky God, the Mythological God, the Spook, or the Buzzard. However, Jones proclaimed a genuine God, which he identified as love. What was love? Citing Karl Marx, Jim Jones declared that divine love was a social system in which each according to their ability gave to each according to their need. In other words, for Jim Jones, God was socialism—"God Almighty, Socialism." While his sermons celebrated the Soviet Union, China, and Cuba as utopias of Divine Socialism, Jones identified the United States as a domain of evil. "Any system that fights against [socialism] is against God," he declared. "So, who is fighting against socialism? You are sitting in the midst of the anti-God system: American capitalism." Depicting American capitalism as a racist, fascist, and oppressive system, Jones informed his congregation that "America's system is representative of the mark of the Beast and America is the Antichrist."

Like Sun Myung Moon, therefore, Jim Jones worked out his novel form of Christianity on the international battlefield on which capitalism confronted communism. Of course, his deification of communism as Divine Socialism represented a vastly different solution to the religious significance of the Cold War than did Moon's demonization of communism. Still, they were operating in the same symbolic arena. Proclaiming himself as Christ, as God in a body, Jones declared, like Moon, his own messianic status. In one sermon, for example, he exclaimed: "You can call me an egomaniac, megalomaniac, or whatever you wish, with a messianic complex. I don't have a complex, honey. I happen to know I'm the messiah." However, since God was socialism, Jones explained, to be an embodiment of God, to be Christ, or to be the messiah meant that a person was a perfect socialist. As his followers became better socialists, he promised, they too could eventually achieve deification as living embodiments of Divine Socialism. Anticipating the apocalypse, Jones assured his congregation that they would see the culmination of the messianic age in the nuclear destruction of the third world war. When the nuclear bombs fell, the capitalist Antichrist would be destroyed. In the certainty of that ultimate redemption, Jones declared, "Already socialism has won the victory over the world. Hallelujah, socialism!"[2]

In the end, the Reverend Jones led over nine hundred of his followers into mass suicide in 1978, while the Reverend Moon revised his understanding of a God-centered America in 1981 after being indicted and imprisoned in the United States for tax fraud. Confronted with the innovations in Christianity proposed by Moon and Jones, most Americans found them strange and bizarre, deviant and dangerous, and refused to recognize them as bearing any relation to the Christian tradition. Nevertheless, mainstream American Christians also struggled to make religious sense of the socioeconomic realities, geopolitical conflicts, and nuclear threats of the Cold War. During the decade of the 1970s, the best-selling book in the United States was a guide to the apocalypse, Hal Lindsey's *The Late Great Planet Earth*. Set firmly within the context of the Cold War, that popular book interpreted biblical prophecy to indicate that the great battle of Armageddon would be started by the evil forces of the Soviet Union.

Adapting earlier traditions of millennial expectation, Hal Lindsey found a new impetus for discerning the signs of the last days in the establishment of the modern state of Israel in 1948 and the Israeli capture of the city of Jerusalem during the Six-Day War in 1967. As Lindsey argued, the establishment of a Jewish state and the recovery of its ancient sacred center fulfilled a biblical prophecy that a third temple would be built in Jerusalem. Within the span of one generation, roughly forty years from 1948, he promised, the world would see all the events of the last days unfolding. The Antichrist would emerge as an international dictator centered in Rome, the Whore of Babylon would bring all the "false religions" of the world together in one international religion, and the Soviet Union, with its evil allies, would attack Israel.

Based on a questionable reading of Ezekiel 38:2, Lindsey identified the biblical "Gog, of the land of Magog" with the modern Russia and the Soviet Union. In the book of Ezekiel, the prophet had declared that the Lord would bring Gog "up from the uttermost parts of the north and lead you against the mountains of Israel" (Ezek. 39:2). While the biblical author might have been referring to the allies of the Babylonians who threatened Israel from the north when the book of Ezekiel was written during the sixth century B.C.E., Lindsey found that "You only need to take a globe to verify this exact geographical fix. There is only one nation to the 'uttermost north' of Israel—the USSR." Under the leadership of the Soviet Union from the north, other evil forces, which Lindsey used biblical terms to identify as Iranian, Arab, Asian, African, and Eastern European, would all descend on Israel to begin World War III. Predicting an all-out exchange of nuclear weapons, Lindsey promised, "As the battle of Armageddon reaches its awful climax and it appears that all life will be destroyed on earth—in this very moment Jesus Christ will return and save man from self-extinction." After cleansing the world of the radioactive fallout from the nuclear Armageddon, Jesus Christ will establish the kingdom of God on earth.

Like Moon and Jones, therefore, Hal Lindsey adapted Christianity to the conditions of the Cold War. In his millennial scenario, the communism of the Soviet Union, the nuclear arms race between the United States and the Soviet Union, and the modern state of Israel were all incorporated into an evangelical Christianity that was prepared for the end of the world. As Lindsey stated the moral of his apocalyptic story, "If you are not sure that you have personally accepted the gift of God's forgiveness which Jesus Christ purchased by bearing the judgment of a holy God that was due your sins, then you should do so right now wherever you are." In conclusion, therefore, Lindsey urged his readers to invite Jesus to come into their hearts as the best way to prepare for all the chaos and destruction of the impending apocalypse.[3]

But other conclusions might be drawn from Lindsey's version of biblical prophecy. It could easily provide reinforcement for a militant anti-communism. When he was governor of the state of California in 1971, for example, Ronald Reagan remarked to a state senator over dinner that all the signs of prophecy were being fulfilled. As Governor Reagan observed:

> Everything is falling in place. It can't be too long now. Ezekiel says that fire and brimstone will be rained upon the enemies of God's people. That must mean that they'll be destroyed by nuclear weapons. They exist now, and they never did in the past. Ezekiel tells us that Gog, the nation that will lead all of the other powers of darkness against Israel, will come out of the north. Biblical scholars have been saying for generations that Gog must be Russia. What other powerful nation is to the north of Israel? None. But it didn't seem to make sense before the Russian revolution, when Russia was a Christian country. Now it does, now that Russia has become communistic and atheistic, now that Russia has set itself against God. Now it fits the description of Gog perfectly.

As president of the United States during the 1980s, Ronald Reagan continued to rely upon this understanding of biblical prophecy to identify the Soviet Union as a nation that lacked "the joy of knowing God" and was therefore "the focus of evil in the modern world." From the periphery to the center of American public life, therefore, varieties of Christianity were shaped in relation to the global forces of the Cold War.[4]

CRUSADES

After World War II, a Protestant revival in the United States coincided with the new Cold War crusade against communism. As the U.S. Congress conducted investigations against alleged communists during the early 1950s, these official proceedings were represented as one battlefield in a larger religious war. According to the chairman of the House Un-American Activities Committee in 1953, for example, communists were "foreign to our nation and to our God. In the world of humanity they are aliens." The battle with these "aliens" was not only over military superiority and economic advantage; it was also a war for hearts and minds. A widely distributed pamphlet in support of the anticommunist crusade accused communists of "stealing words, such as freedom, security, and equality from the Bible, and other good covenants, to confuse issues and deceive the mind into ensnarement." Even a politician opposed to the government "witch-hunt" for communists, such as Senator Ralph Flanders, imagined in 1953 that the conflict between the United States and the USSR was the final battle of Armageddon between the forces of good and evil. Flanders warned, "Now is a crisis in the agelong warfare between God and the Devil for the souls of men."[5]

As noted in Chapter 27, the Communist leadership of the Soviet Union had in fact waged a concerted campaign against religion. Initially directed against the Russian Orthodox Church, antireligious measures were eventually extended to Jews, Muslims, Buddhists, and other Christians. All religious organizations suffered under government restrictions on religious activity and periodic bursts of official persecution. The Law of Religious Associations of 1929, which remained in effect until 1990, confined religion to the performance of services in registered buildings. All other religious activities, such as evangelizing, educating children, producing or disseminating publications, or raising money for charitable purposes, were forbidden by law. Under Joseph Stalin during the 1930s, antireligious campaigns, including the closing of churches and the arrest of clergy, were intensified so that by 1941 Russian Orthodox churches and clergy had been reduced to one-tenth of their number before the revolution.

After World War II, however, the Soviet policy on religion relaxed to a certain extent. For the first time since the revolution, the Russian Orthodox Church was allowed to establish seminaries for the training of new clergy. As churches and monasteries were reopened, Russian

Orthodoxy experienced a revival. Furthermore, the All-Union Council of
Evangelical Christians and Baptists was formed to coordinate Protestant
missions. Lutheran churches in Estonia and Latvia, Reformed churches in
the Ukraine, and Roman Catholic churches in Lithuania and eastern
Poland also received formal government recognition. As the Soviet sphere
of influence expanded into Eastern Europe, Communist governments in
Poland, Yugoslavia, Czechoslovakia, Hungary, and the German
Democratic Republic of East Germany followed the Soviet policy of
granting some freedom for religious profession, however closely it might
be regulated, while engaging in state-sponsored campaigns in antireligious
propaganda and public education in Marxism.

With the success of the Chinese revolution in 1949, the expansion of
communism into Asia initiated new campaigns against religion. Chinese
Communists identified religious belief as a social evil that eventually had
to be eliminated along with feudalism, kinship loyalty, the oppression of
women, and subordination to foreigners. Excluding all foreign missionaries, the Chinese Communist party called for the formation of "patriotic
associations" that would represent the major religions of China. In addition to the China Buddhist Association, two Christian organizations—the
China Catholic Patriotic Association and the Protestant Three Self
Patriotic Movement—played important roles in supporting religion in the
People's Republic of China. Although never representing more than a
small minority, these Catholic and Protestant patriotic associations
struggled to reconcile Christianity with the new revolutionary nationalism emerging in Communist China.

Like the Soviet Union and other Communist countries, China found in
Marxism the basis for a political religion that was given a distinctively
national character through new myths of heroic sacrifice, new rituals, festivals, and celebrations of revolution, and new traditions of a common
past, a collective present, and a shared future in the progressive advance
of socialism. In the apocalyptic expectation that religion would eventually
disappear, Communist regimes tried to transfer religious impulses to the
state. With its own tradition of civil religion, the United States responded
to the Cold War challenge of religious nationalism through the symbolic
gesture of adding the phrase "under God" to the ceremonial pledge of
allegiance to its flag. Another response, however, took the form of a revitalized Protestant evangelicalism. As Americans were reeling from the
"loss" of China, the first Soviet atomic test, the Korean War, and the

suspicion of "Reds" in government, media, and education, Billy Graham (b. 1918) gained a wide popular following in the 1950s for his evangelical crusades. Beginning with his first rallies held in Los Angeles in 1949, Billy Graham emerged as the leading figure in a new Protestant campaign to win souls for Christ. During the early 1950s, Graham enthusiastically entered the Cold War against communism by declaring that "either communism must die or Christianity must die because it is actually a battle between Christ and Anti-Christ."[6]

From his religious background, education, and training, Graham had been influenced by the twentieth-century tradition of American Protestant fundamentalism. Owing its title to a series of pamphlets, *The Fundamentals: A Testimony of Truth,* published in 1909 by the Moody Bible Institute, fundamentalism emerged in America as an attempt to define the basic Christian doctrines that had to be protected against modernity. *The Fundamentals* identified five nonnegotiable Christian doctrines: the literal inerrancy of the Bible; the virgin birth of Christ; the saving sacrificial death of Christ; the resurrection of Christ; and the imminent return of Christ and the end of the world. Although fundamentalists asserted the factual authority of the Bible in reaction to the threat posed by modern science, they affirmed the premillennial dispensationalism that promised an imminent reversal of the social order in response to the increasing power of modern secular society. In its early twentieth-century origin, therefore, Protestant fundamentalism was a modern religious movement with an explicitly antimodern agenda.

Although he came out of this fundamentalist background, Billy Graham developed an approach to Christianity that was experiential, pragmatic, and ecumenical. Abandoning the fundamentalist concerns for doctrinal purity, he emphasized the evangelical experience of being "born again" as the heart of what it meant to be a Christian. The primary biblical text of this new evangelism was John 3: "Have you been born again?" Graham's nondenominational organization, the Billy Graham Evangelistic Association, developed new techniques for mass evangelism that were adopted by other ministries. Graham's crusades made extensive use of mass media, publicity, and advertising. Supported by a weekly radio show, the *Hour of Decision,* his crusades attracted widespread public attention and mobilized clergy from local Protestant churches across denominational divisions. Since Graham encouraged converts to join a local church of their choice, his crusades were generally embraced by mainstream Protestant denominations as a way of revitalizing their churches with increased membership. At the end of each rally, Graham invited his listeners to come up to the stage to accept Jesus as their savior. Reportedly, any given rally resulted in about 5 percent of the audience coming forward to pray with a member of Graham's large staff of counselors, who helped them make their "decision" for Christ.

Billy Graham was not alone in campaigning to win souls for Christ. For example, Campus Crusade, founded in Los Angeles in 1951 by Bill Bright, set out to win the world for Christ by beginning with students at American colleges and universities. As an ardent anticommunist, Bright warned that the only way to avoid the "universal tyranny" of a communist conquest of the world was through evangelical Christian conversion. In a simple and direct fashion, religious workers for Campus Crusade presented potential converts with "Four Spiritual Laws":

1. God loves you and has a wonderful plan for your life.
2. Man is sinful and separated from God; thus he cannot know God's love and plan for his life.
3. Jesus Christ is God's only provision for man's sin. Through him you can know and experience God's love and plan for your life.
4. We must individually receive Jesus Christ as Savior and Lord; then we can know and experience God's love and plan for our lives.

Like Billy Graham's crusades, Bill Bright's Campus Crusade urged people to make a decision for Christ. But that personal religious decision for Christ was also against international communism. Billy James Hargis, the leader of another 1950s evangelical campaign, the Christian Crusade, made that opposition between Christ and communism the heart of his ministry. Describing his converts, Hargis observed: "They loved Jesus, but they also had a great fear. When I told them that this fear was Communism, it was like a revelation." Eventually, these American crusades became international as Graham, Bright, Hargis, and many other evangelists traveled the world to call people to make their decision for Christ and be saved from both sin and communism.[7]

As celebrated in the magazine *Christianity Today,* which Billy Graham helped to found, the message of this new evangelism was explicitly addressed to the "man in the street." For example, *Christianity Today* quoted a "New York cabbie" as saying that his experience of Billy

Graham's crusade was "the first time I ever knew what a preacher was talking about." This pragmatic approach to conversion was opposed by many fundamentalists, who objected to Graham's casual approach to details of Christian doctrine and his open association with nonfundamentalists. His crusades also came under criticism from Christian liberals and social activists. The liberal Protestant magazine *Christian Century*, for example, in 1956 published criticisms of the new mass evangelism by the distinguished theologian Reinhold Niebuhr (1892–1971). Although Graham's simple and direct biblical preaching might appeal to the "man on the street," Niebuhr objected, it offered nothing for "modern cultured man." Niebuhr worried that the call to make a spontaneous decision for Christ resulted in a very superficial kind of Christian commitment.[8]

Given Niebuhr's understanding of human weakness in the face of "immoral society," the evangelical aim of bringing individual souls into a personal relationship with Christ did nothing to fulfill the Christian mandate to take concerted action against the social injustices of poverty, exploitation, and racism that plagued modern industrial society. By the 1950s, however, Niebuhr had been disillusioned by Soviet communism, which he described as "a demonic religio-political creed," and no longer described himself as a "Christian Marxist." Advocating what he called "Christian realism," Niebuhr called upon Americans to abandon their "illusions of innocence" and accept moral responsibility for the serious social and economic problems of the world. "The free world must cover itself with guilt," Niebuhr urged, "in order to ward off the peril of communism."[9] In contrast to what he saw as the easy innocence promised by the anticommunist evangelicals, therefore, Niebuhr tried to work out a Christian moral agenda that engaged the difficult challenges of the modern world.

In addition to Graham's Christian evangelism and Niebuhr's Christian realism, other Christian options came into prominence in the United States during the 1950s that were less directly engaged in the Cold War conflict between capitalism and communism. Among Christian intellectuals, the philosophy of existentialism, which posited a radical human freedom in the face of an absurd universe, found a significant following. As developed by the Russian philosopher Nicolas Berdyaev, Christian existentialism promised a spiritual independence not only from the world, but also from the state. Against the followers of Friedrich Schleiermacher, Berdyaev argued that religion was not a "sense of dependence," but a sense of independence. According to Berdyaev, "If God does not exist, man is a being wholly dependent on nature or society, on the world or the state. If God exists, man is a spiritually independent being; and his relation to God is to be defined as freedom."[10] In these terms, Christian existentialism advocated a personal freedom in relation to a God that was defined as the ultimate basis of freedom.

The most influential Christian existentialist was the German theologian Paul Tillich (1886–1965). Although during the 1930s he had been a religious socialist, an opponent of the German Christian movement, and a signatory of the Barmen Declaration, Tillich spent his exile in the United States as an academic theologian working out a Christian existentialism that was responsive to the crisis of meaning faced by people in the modern world. Religious questions, Tillich argued, were not resolved by the Word of the transcendent God of Christian theism. Rather, the questions themselves revealed what Tillich called an "ultimate concern," which by analogy hinted at an ultimate reality, a "Ground of Being," that was the power sustaining human existence and giving human beings the courage to be. In his existentialist reworking of Christianity, Tillich defined faith as "the state of being grasped by the power of being itself."[11] Although he challenged the faith in the personal God found in classical Christian theism, especially as it was formulated in the neoorthodoxy of Karl Barth and his followers, Tillich directed Christian theological reflection toward a recovery of its medieval traditions of mysticism and spirituality. This renewed interest in mysticism, which was stimulated by the work of the Catholic monk Thomas Merton (1915–68), whose best-selling autobiography, *The Seven Storey Mountain* (1948), described his spiritual journey to the monasticism of the silent order of Trappists, presented a Christian counterpoint to the religious, political, and social conflicts of the Cold War era.

As clergy of mainline Christian churches became involved during the 1960s in the social activism of the civil rights movement in America, the criticism of the social irrelevance of "born again" evangelism was increasingly heard. Ironically, Billy Graham himself had lent support to the racial integration of public schools in Little Rock, Arkansas, by recording a sermon to be broadcast by local radio stations in which he observed that "the violence, the hatred, the intolerance come from man's rebellion against the moral laws of God. We must love our fellow man . . . we must love him without even thinking about his race or the color of his skin."[12] But Graham's defenders insisted that positive social change only began with the spiritual regeneration of the individual who accepted Christ, reinforcing a focus on personal salvation that discouraged many evangelicals from getting involved in the civil rights movement. Under the leadership of Martin Luther King, Jr. (1929–68), however, the Southern Christian Leadership Conference was formed in 1957 to mobilize Christians against racial discrimination and segregation in America. In the civil rights movement, many American Christians became involved in a different kind of crusade.

LIBERATION

Advancing an activist program for African American rights in the United States, Martin Luther King argued for the connection between Christian faith and social action. According to King, the campaign of protest marches, economic boycotts, and civil disobedience in defiance of unjust laws was an extension of devotion to Jesus Christ. For inspiration, King drew upon the Christian identification with the poor, weak, and oppressed declared by Jesus in the Sermon on the Mount. But he followed the strategy and tactics that Mahatma Gandhi had identified as *satyagraha,* the "truth force" or "soul power" of nonviolent resistance to social injustice. As King recalled, "When the protest began, my mind, consciously or unconsciously, was driven back to the Sermon on the Mount, with its sublime teaching on love, and to the Gandhian method of nonviolent resistance."

By adapting Gandhian techniques, King advocated nonviolent civil disobedience as a way of producing confrontational situations in which public opinion could be mobilized to change unjust laws. By marching thousands of unarmed men, women, and children into a hostile community to defy a racist law, King's strategy was designed to create a dramatic tension between the marchers and the local authorities. When the authorities responded with violence, dogs, fire hoses, arrests, or beatings, the marchers would refuse to retaliate or defend themselves. As this official violence against innocent people was increasingly exposed through the media, King hoped an enraged public would demand basic social changes that would result in the extension of civil rights to African Americans.

Based on the example of Jesus, King saw nonviolent resistance to injustice as a source of spiritual strength. "Nonviolence is not a symbol of weakness or cowardice," he insisted, "but as Jesus demonstrated, nonviolent resistance transforms weakness into strength and breeds courage in the face of danger." For African Americans who had been deprived of voting rights, segregated by racist laws, and discriminated against in jobs, housing, and public services, King saw nonviolent resistance as an expression of Christian love that would transform the world. In that ideal of love, King refused the temptation to dehumanize the enemy. "Love your enemies," he exhorted. "Let no man pull you so low as to make you hate him." As King concluded:

> If you will protest courageously, and yet with dignity and Christian love, when the history books are written in future generations, the historians will have to pause to say, "There lived a great people—a black people—who injected new meaning and dignity into the veins of civilization." That is our challenge and our overwhelming responsibility.

Through the social activism of the civil rights movement, King saw the potential for creating what he called a "beloved community" based on Christian love. That sense of community, he argued, promised to fulfill the dream of equality enshrined in the American Declaration of Independence, but denied to African Americans. "I have a dream," King announced in 1963, "that one day this nation will rise up and live out the true meaning of its creed: 'We hold these truths to be self-evident, that all men are created equal.'" But King also developed a broader international vision of human community. In 1960, for example, King observed that he had "taken a particular interest in the problems in South Africa because of the similarities between the situation there and our own situation in the United States." Whether in the United States or in South Africa, racist oppression was a denial of humanity that prevented the emergence of King's "beloved community." Toward the end of his life, King increasingly saw the United States, which he identified as "the greatest purveyor of violence in the world today," as an obstacle to building any sense of community based on Christian love at home or abroad. Nevertheless, in his last speech before being assassinated by a sniper's bullet in 1968, King reaffirmed the promise of redemption for African Americans in the United States. "It really doesn't matter with me now, because I've been to the mountaintop," he said. "I may not get to the promised land with you, but I want you to know tonight that we as a people will."[13]

King's optimism, however, was not shared by all African American leaders. Although some entirely rejected what the Black Muslim leader Malcolm X called the "white slavemasters' Christian religion," a growing number of African American clergy embraced more militant forms of black theology in opposition to racist oppression. Adopting the slogan "Black Power," the National Committee of Negro Churchmen declared that God had "chosen black humanity as a vanguard to resist the demonic powers of racism, capitalism and imperialism, and to so reform the structures of this world that they will more perfectly minister to the peace and power of all people as children of God and brothers of one another." Taking a global perspective, this declaration affirmed a special covenant between God and black humanity to work for the liberation of all human beings from oppressive social structures. In working out a black theology of liberation, James Cone, professor of theology at Union Theological Seminary in New York, maintained that any theology that was not committed to the liberation of the oppressed was not a legitimate Christian theology. The God of a black theology of liberation had to be black, Cone insisted, because "either God is identified with the oppressed to the point that their experience becomes His or He is a God of racism." According to Cone, God was identified with the struggles of oppressed people, present with them in their bondage, and working with them for their liberation. Although directed primarily to black people who suffered under racist oppression, black theology also held the potential to liberate whites from the sinful complicity in the oppressive power structures from which they benefited. For whites to receive this revelation of God's identification with blacks, Cone suggested, "is to become black with him by joining him in his work of liberation."[14]

As a more militant strategy for achieving freedom from oppression, black theology in the United States was also in conversation with international efforts, especially within Latin American Catholicism, to work out a political theology of liberation that addressed the specific conditions of social and economic oppression under capitalism. Insisting that Christianity held a "preferential option for the poor," liberation theologians used Marxist class analysis to redefine the Christian gospel of sin and salvation in terms of social structures. According to the Catholic theologian Gustavo Gutiérrez, for example, "Sin occurs in the negation of man as brother, in the oppressive structures created for the benefit of the few and for the exploitation of peoples, races, and social classes." As a betrayal of the Christian mandate to love others as oneself, this violation of humanity within oppressive social structures revealed the essential character of sin. But it also defined the structural, systemic, or institution-alized violence under which the vast majority of Latin American people suffered under political regimes controlled by dictators, oligarchies, and corporations supported by the United States. If sin was the violation of humanity under such economic, social, and political systems of institu-tionalized violence, then salvation was a recovery of that humanity by the grace of God working through history for the liberation of the poor and oppressed. An essentially political definition of sin, however, demanded a political liberation. "Sin requires a radical liberation," as Gutiérrez observed, "but this necessarily includes liberation of a political nature." In the context of the global political conflicts of the Cold War, this Latin American political theology of liberation formulated in solidarity with the poor quickly found itself in conflict with the United States.[15]

"The United States shouldn't worry about the Soviets in Latin America, because they aren't revolutionaries any more," Cuban president Fidel Castro (b. 1927) observed. "But they should worry about the Catholic revolutionaries, who are." As leader of the revolution in Cuba that over-threw the dictator Fulgencio Batista in 1959, Fidel Castro had succeeded in mobilizing popular Catholic support. Although divided on the issue, the church hierarchy in Cuba lent tacit support by permitting Father Guillermo Sardinas to leave his parish and serve as chaplain for Castro's rebel army. By quickly introducing dramatic economic, agrarian, health, and educational reforms, however, Castro's new government met opposi-tion from elite and middle-class interests. While the United States formu-lated its foreign policy in opposition to Castro, the Catholic Church in Cuba tried to polarize religious and political debate into two foreign-policy options, "Rome or Moscow." As most Cubans suspected, the Roman option proposed by the Catholic Church entailed submitting to foreign control by the United States. That suspicion was confirmed by the Catholic involvement in the U.S. invasion of Cuba in April 1960 at the Bay of Pigs, which failed to inspire a popular uprising against Castro. Recalling the text of the *Requirement* designed to be read before gather-ings of natives in the era of Spanish conquests, Father Ismael de Lugo composed a text to be read to Cubans by the CIA-sponsored invaders.

> The liberating forces have disembarked on Cuba's beaches. We have come
> in the name of God, justice and democracy, with the goal of reestablishing

the rights which have been restricted, the freedom which has been trampled on, and the religion which has been taken over and maligned. . . . The assault brigade is made up of thousands of Cubans who are all Christians and Catholics. Our struggle is that of those who believe in God against the atheists, the struggle of democracy against communism. . . . Catholics of Cuba: our military power is overwhelming and invincible, and greater still is our moral strength and our faith in God, in his protection and his help. . . . Long live Christ the King!

As might be expected, this Catholic support for the CIA assault brigade at the Bay of Pigs, which comprised not thousands but under thirteen hundred Cuban soldiers, most of whom were immediately captured, seriously damaged relations between state and church in Cuba. Perceiving the church of Rome actually to be the church of Washington, D.C., the Cuban government arrested and deported many Catholic clergy. The government cut off the main source of income for the Catholic Church in Cuba by nationalizing all schools and universities. From the beginning of the 1960s, therefore, many Catholic Christians found themselves in conflict with Fidel Castro and the Cuban state.

Like Friedrich Engels during the nineteenth century in Europe, Castro saw two Christian faiths operating in Cuba, the one genuine, revolutionary, and progressive, the other false, reactionary, and oppressive. Declaring that a "true Christian is one who loves his neighbor, who makes sacrifices for others, who obeys the doctrines of Christ and gives what he has in order to go and serve his fellow human beings," Castro urged Cubans "to go out to the fields to help the sick, plant trees, build houses, assist the Agrarian Reform, sew smocks for the children who have no clothes. That's what being a Christian means!" Rather than supporting these social and economic initiatives, however, the leadership of the Church opposed the Cuban revolution. According to Castro, the Catholic Church hierarchy represented a false Christianity. When the Catholic Church published a pastoral letter in 1960 that warned against the danger of communism in Cuba, Castro responded, "I would like to see a pastoral letter condemning the crimes of imperialism, the horrors of imperialism. And then we would see that those who condemn a Revolution which is with the poor and the humble, which preaches love for one's neighbor and fraternity among men, which preaches equality, which practices love, generosity, and the common good; those who condemn a Revolution like this, are betraying Christ, and at the same time they'd be capable of crucifying him again." Over the next four decades, Fidel Castro continued to criticize the "unchristian conduct" of Christian churches that had betrayed what he saw as the original Christian gospel proclaimed by Jesus on behalf of the poor, the suffering, and the oppressed.[16]

At a major conference of bishops convened in 1968 at Medellín, Columbia, the changes in the Catholic Church initiated at Vatican II (1962–65) were translated into a new social gospel that sought to address the impoverished condition of the majority of people in Latin America. Reinforced by a subsequent conference at Puebla, Mexico, in 1979, this social gospel redirected the Latin American Church toward the "preferential option for the poor" of liberation theology. As this social definition of sin and salvation became integrated into Catholic discourse, a new emphasis on social practice, or *praxis,* emerged as the defining character of the Christian gospel. According to liberation theologians, Christians were called not only to act on behalf of the poor, but to act with the poor in social solidarity with those who directly suffered injustice, exploitation, and oppression. Opposing larger structures of oppression as institutionalized violence, Christians inspired by liberation theology supported local communities, which came to be known as Christian base communities, that involved ordinary people in the theory and practice of recovering humanity from its structural violation. Growing out of these experiments in local theory and practice, the work of Latin American liberation theologians—Leonardo Boff, José Miguez Bonino, Gustavo Gutiérrez, Juan Luis Segundo, Jon Sobrino, and others—had a tremendous global impact on redirecting Christian attention toward conditions of poverty, exploitation, injustice, and oppression.

KAIROS

In the United States, objections to any Christian involvement in social activism, liberation struggles, or the civil rights movement were often raised by white Protestant evangelicals and fundamentalists. In 1965, for example, a fundamentalist preacher delivered a sermon entitled "Ministers and Marchers" that chastised Christian clergy for their involvement in the civil rights movement. "Believing the Bible as I do," the preacher declared, "I would find it impossible to stop preaching the pure saving gospel of Jesus Christ, and begin doing anything else—including fighting communism, or participating in civil rights reforms. . . . Preachers are not called to be politicians, but to be soul winners." By the beginning of the 1980s, however, that fundamentalist preacher, the Reverend Jerry Falwell, had become one of the most prominent Christian politicians in the United States. Through his popular television ministry, the "Old-Time Gospel Hour," and the support of conservative political action commit- tees, Jerry Falwell mounted a Christian crusade against the moral, social, and political evils threatening American society. In a formal "Declaration of War," Falwell announced:

> Be it known to all that the Old-Time Gospel Hour hereby declares war against the evils threatening America during the 1980s.
> Furthermore, this shall be a Holy War, not a war with guns and bullets, but a war fought with the Bible, prayer, and Christian involvement.
> The Old-Time Gospel Hour hereby dedicates itself to spearhead the battle and lead an army of Christian soldiers into the war against evil.

This "Declaration of War" identified the evils threatening America as abortion, pornography, homosexuality, socialism, and the deterioration of the home and family. The church, as a "disciplined, charging army," was ready to confront all people with the truth of Protestant fundamen- talism, to "bring them under submission to the Gospel of Christ, move them into the household of God, put up the flag and call it secured."

As an extension of this Christian campaign, Jerry Falwell founded a national organization, the Moral Majority, dedicated to achieving conser- vative political goals in four areas: pro-life, pro-family, pro-moral, and pro-American. With the support of right-wing political organizers, the Moral Majority achieved prominence during the 1980s for its promotion of "family values" that opposed abortion, women's rights, and gay rights and its advocacy of a Christian nationalism based on prayer in schools, free-market capitalism, and increased military spending. In his appeal to America, Falwell's broadly conservative agenda was linked with a return to the fundamentals of the Bible. Falwell posed an absolute choice between national conversion or destruction. "Will it be revival or ruin?" he demanded. "There can be no other way." Ignoring the New Testament suggestion that the earliest Christians "held all things in common" (Acts 4:34–35), thereby practicing a kind of socialism, Falwell insisted that cap- italism had been ordained by God:

The free-enterprise system is clearly outlined in the Book of Proverbs in the
Bible. Jesus Christ made it clear that the work ethic was part of His plan for
man. Ownership of property is biblical. Competition in business is biblical.
Ambitious and successful business management is clearly outlined as a part
of God's plan for His people.

Since capitalism was part of God's plan, communism had to be
opposed by any means necessary. While arguing for cuts in social welfare
spending at home, therefore, Falwell advocated increases in the U.S.
"defense budget to whatever it takes to put us solidly back to No. 1 for
good." Increased U.S. military capacity, however, was necessary not only
to resist international communism, but also to follow the example of Jesus
Christ. According to Falwell, "Jesus was not a pacifist. He was not a
sissy." A strong U.S. military presence in the world, therefore, was
demanded by the capitalist plan of God and the militant model of Christ.[17]

Jerry Falwell's conservative Christian crusade defined the basic outlines
of political policy advocated by the "New Religious Right" or the "New
Christian Right" in the United States. That political policy was also a conservative Christian foreign policy that urged U.S. support for the modern
states of Israel, Taiwan, and South Africa. In South Africa, for example, the
ideological support provided by right-wing Christians from the United
States was welcomed by the National Party regime, which was attempting
to maintain the apartheid system of racist oppression that exploited the
black majority as labor while excluding them from any civil rights. As a frequent visitor during the 1980s, Jerry Falwell praised South Africa as a
"Christian country" in which human rights were upheld, that is, the rights
of the unborn, because abortion was illegal. Defending the apartheid
regime, Falwell castigated the anti-apartheid Anglican archbishop and
Nobel Peace Prize laureate Desmond Tutu, as a "phoney." According to
one conservative Christian publication in the United States, the *Family
Protection Scoreboard,* "in the area of traditional family values, South
Africa puts America to shame" because in South Africa there was no abortion, pornography, debates about women's rights, constitutional separation of church and state, or secular humanism, all of which had allegedly
eroded Christian "family values" in the United States. Conservative evangelist Jimmy Swaggert also praised South Africa as a "godly country" on
the front lines of the battle between the communist Antichrist and the
"Christian civilization" represented by the minority white regime.[18]

In 1986 a group of "concerned evangelicals" in Soweto objected to the fact that their "evangelical family has a track record of supporting and legitimating oppressive regimes here and elsewhere."[19] The National Party regime in South Africa, however, welcomed the support from U.S. evangelists and fundamentalists because the Dutch Reformed Church, which had been known as the "National Party at prayer," was no longer providing unconditional Christian justifications for the system of apartheid. During the 1930s and 1940s, the Dutch Reformed Church and the National Party had formed a close working relationship in the racist design of apartheid. Many of the leaders in both church and party had been educated in Germany, where they had been impressed by the ideology of *Volk* and *Vaterland* in Nazism and the German Christian movement. In South Africa, they proclaimed this racist ideology as if it were the divine plan for the world, asserting that the "preservation of the pure race of the *Boerevolk* must be protected at all costs in all possible ways as a holy pledge entrusted to us by our ancestors as part of God's plan with our People." Providing Christian legitimation for the National Party's policy of racist domination and separation, the Dutch Reformed Church worked out a theology of apartheid based on a reading of the Bible. As the Reverend J. G. Strijdom complained in 1938 in "Apartheid, a Matter of Faith": "There are people who falsely maintain on biblical grounds that apartheid is wrong. We, however, believe on the basis of God's Word that He had willed nations to be apart."[20]

As the National Party came to power in 1948, theologians of the Dutch Reformed Church read the Bible as an "apartheid Bible," finding that God was the "Maker of Separations." In the beginning, God had separated the light from the dark, the waters above from the waters below, the land from the sea, and so on, to indicate that separation—*apartheid*—was the divine plan for creation. When God instructed humans to "be fruitful and multiply," God meant that they should be fruitful and divide into separate groups, tribes, or nations. According to an official report by the Dutch Reformed Church published in 1948, the divine plan of apartheid operated in three spheres. First, spiritual apartheid was promised in the ultimate separation of the saved from the damned, the sheep from the goats, the wheat from the tares, and the light from the dark in the Last Judgment (Matt. 15:25). Second, social apartheid was justified by the biblical instruction that the ancient people of Israel should not have fellowship with any neighboring peoples (Deut. 7). Finally, political apartheid was mandated by God in the creation of separate nations, which had to be kept separate in order to follow the divine will (Gen. 11; Acts 2).

Within the Dutch Reformed Church in South Africa, a few notable theologians, such as Beyers Naudé, tried to counter apartheid by insisting on the "one-ness" of humanity in both church and society. Removed from his ministry, Naudé led the Christian Institute during the 1970s, which drew inspiration for opposing apartheid from the church struggles of the Confessing Church movement in Nazi Germany. Internationally, various church bodies recognized that "apartheid theology" in South Africa represented a crisis for the Christian tradition. In 1982, for example, the World Alliance of Reformed Churches found that apartheid was a "sin" for three reasons: it was based on an anti-Christian premise that human beings were irreconcilable; it was applied through racist structures that provided exclusive privileges to whites at the expense of blacks; and it created injustice, oppression, deportations, and suffering for millions of people in South Africa. Declaring any support for the sin of apartheid to be a Christian heresy, the World Alliance of Reformed Churches suspended the membership of the South African Dutch Reformed Church. At its general synod in 1986, the church responded by retracting its biblical support for apartheid, stating that "a forced separation and division of peoples cannot be considered a biblical imperative. The attempt to justify such an injunction as derived from the Bible must be recognized as an error and rejected."[21]

With this withdrawal of the church's biblical support for apartheid, however, the National Party turned for religious legitimation to the brand of Christian anticommunism proclaimed by right-wing Christians in the United States. Furthermore, as its constitution proclaimed South Africa to be a Christian country, the National Party invested the institutions of the state with a sacred aura as the schools instilled Christian nationalism, the military provided the nation with its "spiritual armament," and the police "maintained Christian norms and civilized standards." By claiming its own Christian legitimacy, therefore, this religious nationalism of the South African regime during the 1980s did not depend upon the support of any Christian church.[22]

In resistance to apartheid, forms of black theology and liberation theology were developed in South Africa. Under the leadership of Steve Biko (1946–77) until his death at the hands of the security police in 1977, the Black Consciousness Movement developed a Christian theological analysis of the class oppression and struggle for liberation in the midst of apartheid. Redefining the term "black" as a class location rather than as a racial classification, black theologians struggled for a psychological liberation from the "slave mentality" inculcated by apartheid. As Steve Biko declared at a conference on black theology in 1971, "The most potent weapon in the hands of the oppressor is the mind of the oppressed." However, black theology did not stop at this psychological liberation from the mental shackles of oppression. The recovery of black humanity required a militant solidarity of the oppressed in opposition to white racism and capitalist exploitation. As Biko insisted, the God of black theology was not a passive but a fighting God. By fighting to change the conditions of social exclusion and economic exploitation under which blacks had been dehumanized in South Africa, Biko concluded, black theology would fulfill its mission in "once more uniting the black man with his God." In the process, the "quest for a true humanity" undertaken by black theology promised also to liberate white oppressors from their bondage to a dehumanizing system and thereby "bestow upon South Africa the greatest gift possible—a more human face." After he was killed in police custody in 1977, Steve Biko was commemorated by the Christian Institute as a martyr for the cause of the "fullness of humanity and liberation which Christ proclaimed," thus strengthening Christian commitment to ensuring that apartheid's "ungodly and revolting society will be destroyed."[23]

As opposition to apartheid became increasingly militant with the intensification of the "armed struggle" of liberation movements in the 1980s, black consciousness and black theology continued to resonate with many Christians in South Africa. Increasingly, however, anti-apartheid theologians drew on the resources of Latin American liberation theology for a critique of the institutionalized violence of oppression. In the midst of the popular uprising and state repression of 1985, a group of theologians produced the *Kairos Document* as a critical reflection on the relations between Christianity and violence in the South African situation. Identifying the political struggle as a sacred time, the document declared "the present crisis, or *kairos,* as indeed a divine visitation." As the Kairos theologians tried to locate God in this struggle, they distinguished between three types of theology: state, church, and prophetic. A state theology had been developed to sanctify the current regime, and a church theology tacitly supported the regime by professing personal piety, neutrality, and nonviolence. The *kairos* of South Africa, however, required a prophetic theology that directly challenged the unjust rule of the state. Adopting this prophetic stance, the Kairos theologians argued that the heresy, sinfulness, and moral illegitimacy of the apartheid state required Christians "to confront and to disobey the State in order to obey God."

Although committed to nonviolent civil disobedience in the traditions of Mahatma Gandhi and Martin Luther King, Jr., the Kairos theologians opened the possibility that armed resistance to the apartheid state might be justified on Christian grounds. "Is it legitimate, especially in our circumstances," the *Kairos Document* asked, "to use the same word 'violence' in a blanket condemnation to cover the ruthless and repressive activities of the State and the desperate attempts of people to defend themselves?" The Kairos theologians therefore invoked what they regarded as a biblical distinction between the illegitimate violence of oppressors and the legitimate force necessary for self-defense against aggression or injustice. Under the extreme conditions of the struggle for liberation from apartheid, they concluded, the use of armed force by liberation movements was not only understandable, but even justifiable in terms of the Christian ethics governing a just war.[24]

As the Cold War ended with the "miracle" of 1989—the fall of the Berlin Wall, the collapse of Communist governments in central and eastern Europe, and the breakup of the Soviet Union—the war in South Africa also ended, not in military victory, but in the long process of negotiating a political settlement. In February 1990, African National Congress leader Nelson Mandela was finally released after twenty-seven years of imprisonment. "I stand here before you not as a prophet," Mandela told a crowd of a hundred thousand supporters in Cape Town, "but as a humble servant of you, the people. Your tireless and heroic sacrifices have made it possible for me to be here today. I therefore place the remaining years of my life in your hands."[25] Since the white South African regime was no longer of international strategic value as a bulwark against communism in the region, its leaders gradually and begrudgingly negotiated with the African National Congress for a democratic solution that resulted in the first elections of 1994.

As elsewhere in the world during the era of the Cold War, Christianity in South Africa had been profoundly ambivalent—justifying oppression, mobilizing liberation—in its political significance. Operating as an open set of sacred resources, Christianity was drawn into the political projects of capitalists and communists, U.S. racists and civil rights workers, Latin American dictators and base communities, apartheid ideologues and anti-apartheid activists, and many others who appropriated Christian symbols to maneuver within the violent contradictions of the global Cold War. Although Christians continued to link their religion with extremely diverse political programs, some decided from their experience during the Cold War that Christianity could not be contained with any single economic, social, or political system. For example, although he had been a long-standing crusader for Christian Americanism, Billy Graham responded to the rise of American right-wing political Christianity by warning that it was an "error to identify the Gospel within any one particular system or culture. This has been my own danger. When I go to preach the Gospel, I go as an ambassador for the Kingdom of God—not America."[26] In the end, therefore, the evangelist found that the struggles of the Cold War did not lead to an apocalyptic heaven on earth, but only confirmed Jesus' saying, "My kingdom is not of this world."

30

New World Order

In 1492 less than 20 percent of the world's population was Christian. Out of that Christian population, the vast majority, over 90 percent, lived in what eventually became Europe. For all its regional, confessional, and ecclesiastical differences, Christianity bore the imprint of a broadly European cultural identity. Only a small fraction of the non-Christian population of the world, estimated at 2 percent, had come into contact with Christianity. As the history of Christianity since 1492 has shown, however, European travel and exploration, conquest and capitalism, colonialism and imperialism dramatically altered the demography of Christianity in the world. Five centuries after Columbus, with roughly one-third of the world's population subscribing to Christianity, the largest concentration of Christians was found in Latin America and the fastest-growing Christian continent in the world was Africa. Recognizing that the center of gravity in world Christianity had shifted, some commentators identified Europe as the new "mission field" for Christian conversion.[1] As we have seen, U.S. Protestant missionaries representing recent developments in evangelical, fundamentalist, or Pentecostal Christianity actively promoted their gospel all over the world. Arguably, however, global conquests, colonization, and incorporation of people into international economic relations were more effective than any Christian mission in exposing the world to Christianity. By 1992, although only 33 percent of the world was Christian, an estimated 77 percent of the world's population had come into direct contact with some form of Christianity. Even non-Christians, therefore, lived in a world that featured Christianity.

At the beginning of the 1990s, as the Cold War abruptly, unexpectedly ended, one commentator proclaimed the end of history. According to the former U.S. State Department official Francis Fukuyama, the failure of Communism in the Soviet Union and Eastern Europe marked a victory for capitalism that had effectively ended all historical struggles. As the culmination of a long historical process, only the pattern of individualism, democracy, and market economy developed in the West remained to define the contours of a new world.[2] That "new world order" had been invoked in August 1990 by U.S. president George Bush as he mobilized international military action against Iraq in response to its invasion of Kuwait. In the midst of the war in the Persian Gulf, this "new world order" promised a new dispensation of global peace and prosperity under the political and economic leadership of the United States of America.

By the beginning of the 1990s, therefore, Christianity faced new challenges of globalization. According to many analysts, globalization marked significant shifts in the organization of the world economy in which industry was replaced by information; production gave way to consumption; and national economies were transcended by multinational or transnational corporations. To the extent that it was in the world, Christianity was inevitably entangled in these global transitions.

First, globalization involved new technologies for the transmission of information. Over its long history, Christianity had passed through several information revolutions that altered both the form and the content of Christian communication—from the spoken to the written word, from verbal metaphors to visible icons, from handwriting to movable type, from the monastic codex to the mass-distributed book. During the twentieth century, however, the explosion of electronic communications media ushered in a global revolution in information that changed everything, including Christianity. With the advent of radio and television, and subsequently with the appearance of computers and the Internet, Christians actively engaged in the new electronic forms of communication. Certainly, Christians continued to operate within the kingdom of print, even when print media developed new genres such as the comic book. For example, according to his unofficial Web site on the Internet, "the most widely read Christian communicator in history" may very well be the Christian cartoonist Jack T. Chick. With distribution centers all over the world, copies of Chick Christian Comix have been placed in public conveniences, bus stations, and phone booths to communicate a distinctive hellfire and brimstone evangelism. In Christian communication, however, the Internet seems to have provided the equivalent of public toilets, bus stations, and phone booths for leaving messages about the gospel. In a new world order given coherence by the flow of information, the Internet in particular held new potential for shaping the form and content of Christian communication at the end of the twentieth century.

Second, if globalization involved a shift from production to consumption in the organization of the world economy, then a new spirit of consumerism had entered Christianity. For many Christians, particularly, but not exclusively, in so-called economically developed countries, Christianity provided goods and services that could be consumed much like other consumer products available on the market. Although many Christians all over the world continued to maintain an essentially communal relationship with their religion, finding value in the immediate face-to-face relations with other Christians, the spirit of consumerism established a client relationship between people and their faith. In response to competition from other religions, spiritual movements, ethical orientations, or optional lifestyles, Christian entrepreneurs developed creative marketing strategies for "selling God."[3] As a consequence, however, the spirit of consumerism resulted in what might be called the commodification of the sacred. Bought and sold on the open religious market, Christian goods and services, whether musical recordings and clothing or the conviction of sin and the hope of salvation, were adapted to the demands of a global consumer culture. In a global economy that distinguished between work and leisure in principle, but depended upon both for its survival in practice, Christianity increasingly appeared to be a leisure-time activity, what Christians did for fun or fulfillment during their time off from the daily round of work.

Third, by definition, globalization entailed new international, multinational, or transnational relations. Some Christians were extremely unhappy with the transnational character of this new world order. In the United States, for example, Grace Baptist Church, a fundamentalist, independent Baptist church in Massachusetts, conducted its "Cutting Edge Ministries" over the radio to warn people about the "Satanic New World Order." According to the Cutting Edge broadcasts, "Satan has been manipulating world events to achieve his One-World Government, Economy, and Religion through Secret Societies, Communism, Nazism, the New Age, and UFOs." The new world order, therefore, was a conspiracy of evil forces, identified as the Illuminati and Masons, the atheistic communists and evil fascists, and the New Age paganism that allegedly appeared in the "nature worship" of environmentalism, the "goddess worship" of feminism, and the "antichrist worship" that was preparing in secret for the coming of Maitreya, the Christ, who would rule over a global government, economy, and religion. Even unidentified flying objects were exposed as Satan's demons circling the world to prepare for that new world order. At the very least, the Cutting Edge broadcasts suggested that not all Christians welcomed globalization.

However, significant Christian initiatives in the field of interreligious, interfaith, and intercultural relations responded creatively to the challenges of a new world order. Like any religion, Christianity contained foundational sacred myths, distinctive doctrines, and specific sacramental rituals that could not be shared by adherents of other religions. However, also like any religion, Christianity supported religious ethics, personal experiences, and social concerns that could in fact be shared by people of other faiths. Promoting a new sense of global unity during the 1990s, interfaith organizations sought to establish consensus about pressing social problems, trying to mobilize interreligious support for peace, human rights, gender equality, defense of the environment, social justice, economic empowerment, or the political liberation of the oppressed. Calling for unity, these interfaith organizations were well aware of the prejudice, divisiveness, and conflict that continued to be fueled by religious differences in the new world order. For Christian participants in these interfaith organizations, however, religious differences could no longer be resolved by dogmatically relegating those who were different to eternal damnation. Although they hoped for unity, the Christians involved in these interreligious initiatives also affirmed the intrinsic value of diversity in the new world order.

INFORMATION

The twentieth-century revolutions in electronic media have dramatically changed the character of Christian communication. Since Jesus had called upon Christians to preach the good news of the kingdom of God to all the nations of the world (Mark 16:15), Christians from the beginning have been in the information business. Jesus had instructed his disciples to leave home, wander from village to village, and convey the message "Peace be to this house" and "God's kingdom has come near to you" (Mark 6:8–11; Luke 9:3–5; 10:1–11; Matt 10:7–14; *Gos. Thom.* 14:2). With the new information technology, however, Christians did not have to leave home to fulfill the Great Commission; they could send a telegram, set up a radio station, gain access to television air time, develop satellite telecommunications networks, or establish a "home page" in cyberspace. During the twentieth century, Christianity had been an integral part of the development of new technologies for the dissemination of information.

When Samuel F. B. Morse installed the original telegraph line in 1844, his first transmission conveyed a sense of holy awe before the new communication technology by asking, "What hath God wrought?" The first successful voice broadcast over wireless radio, which was transmitted from the East Coast of the United States to ships at sea on December 24, 1906, consisted of a religious program of music and readings from the Gospel of Luke. Guglielmo Marconi, who has been credited with the discovery of wireless communication as early as 1896, assisted in the construction of the first global radio network, Vatican Network, which was completed in February 1931 to enable simultaneous communication with Roman Catholics all over the world. In December of the same year, the first international Protestant radio station, "Heralding Christ Jesus' Blessing," was established in Quito, Ecuador, to broadcast evangelical programs in Spanish from the Andes mountains to most of South America. After World War II, evangelical radio broadcasting expanded. The Far East Broadcasting Corporation, which was founded in the Philippine capital of Manila in 1948, was soon evangelizing over the radio in thirty-six languages and dialects to China and Southeast Asia. Trans World Radio, which started its radio ministry in 1954 with a Nazi propaganda transmitter captured in Tangier, Morocco, was quickly broadcasting in twenty languages to forty nations in North Africa, the Middle East, the Soviet Union, and Europe. For these Christian broadcasting networks, therefore, what God had wrought in the new information technology of radio was an opportunity to fulfill the Great Commission of evangelizing the entire world before the world's end.

While radio continued to provide global scope for Christian evangelizing, the emergence of television ministries mobilized even larger audiences. In the United States during the 1950s, the Roman Catholic bishop Fulton Sheen became the first religious celebrity on television by presenting a simple, inspirational, and entertaining religious message. During the 1970s, however, religious broadcasting on television was dominated by Protestant fundamentalist, evangelical, or Pentecostal programming. The new stars of the "electronic church"—Jerry Falwell, Jimmy Swaggert, Pat Robertson, Jim and Tammy Faye Bakker, and many others—might have emerged from "antimodern" Protestant backgrounds, but their sophisticated use of the television medium, with professional production values, cable distribution, and satellite technology, created modern broadcasting empires that eventually extended all over the world. Fitting the short attention span induced by the medium, these television evangelists delivered direct, simple messages, such as "Something good is going to happen to you," "You are loved," or "Jesus loves you," that established an emotional connection between the audience and the Christian gospel. Although some of the original celebrities of the electronic church were caught in financial or sexual scandals, Christian broadcasting continued to expand as an international medium.[4]

During the 1990s, the new technology of computers, electronic communication, the Internet, and the World Wide Web further altered the global character of information. On behalf of the Roman Catholic Church, Pope John Paul II delivered an address in 1990, "The Church Must Learn to Cope with Computer Culture." "With the advent of computer telecommunications and what are known as computer participation systems," the pope advised, "the Church is offered further means for fulfilling her mission."[5] Accordingly, the Roman Catholic Church set up its official home page on the World Wide Web. Likewise, the Russian Orthodox Church, which was experiencing a resurgence in Russia after the breakup of the Soviet Union, established its position in the new global village of the Internet with the official site of the Moscow patriarchate available in both Russian- and English-language versions.

Although Catholic and Orthodox sites emerged, Protestant Christians seemed to be most actively involved in the Internet. In addition to church-based home pages, Protestant fundamentalist and evangelical sites proliferated on the Internet, sites such as Worldnet Grace Ministries, JesusChristNet, Dial-a-Truth Ministries, the Biblical Discernment Ministries, and the Biblical Christianity for Regular People Home Page. These Internet sites transmitted Christian information on an unprecedented global scale. For example, the Global Christian Network, with its shopping service and its fun center for testing biblical knowledge through games and quizzes, proudly announced that it had conveyed 8 million pieces of information to over 130,000 people in eighty-two countries within the previous thirty days. In addition to the sheer volume of information made available on the Internet, however, the new information technology raised certain questions about the character of an emerging Christianity in cyberspace.

First, the Internet challenged conventional assumptions about geographical location. In early Christianity, the church, as *ekklesia,* had originally referred to a face-to-face gathering of people. Eventually, the church became a building, a specific site sanctified through ritual and thereby a localized community of the faithful. In cyberspace, however, the Christian *ekklesia* necessarily assumed a utopian character. The Vatican Web site, for example, was housed in the Apostolic Palace, three floors below the pope's personal quarters. It was supported by three machines named after the archangels Raphael, Michael, and Gabriel. However, the Web site could be accessed anywhere in the world. As Sister Judith Zoebelein explained in an interview on the religion site operated by *Time* magazine, God.com, the Internet was like the Holy Spirit, silent and invisible. Through this utopian character of the Internet, the Vatican Web site seemed to transcend the ordinary limits of spatial location in the world. Therefore, although its computer machinery was housed at the papal residence, the Vatican Web site itself was everywhere and nowhere, available in any place in the world and tied to no particular location.

Although this utopian character of cyberspace reinforced the universal orientation of the Church, it also provided scope for alternative maneuvers in spiritual geography. In January 1995, for example, the liberal Roman Catholic bishop Jacques Gaillot, who had come into conflict with the Church hierarchy, was transferred from his see in France to the inactive diocese of Partenia in the Sahara Desert. Without a local congregation, Bishop Gaillot created the "Virtual Diocese of Partenia" on the Internet. Relocated from the Sahara Desert to cyberspace, this "diocese without borders" could be visited almost instantly by anyone in the world who had access to the necessary information technology. In the case of the "Virtual Diocese," therefore, Christian information also appeared to transcend any specific location through the utopian character of the Internet. But the diocese without borders also seemed to provide an alternative site to the official Web site of the Roman Catholic Church. Although he was exiled to the Sahara Desert, Bishop Gaillot used the resources of the Internet to turn the desert into an alternative cybergarden.

Second, the Internet challenged conventional assumptions about Christian social formations. For decades, analysts in Europe and North America had been documenting the Christian trend of "believing without belonging." In Britain, for example, although less than 15 percent of the population belonged to a church, the overwhelming majority held beliefs in God, heaven, and prayer that were broadly Christian. The Internet seemed designed for precisely this kind of "believing without belonging."[6] In the anonymity of cyberspace, Internet users could sample a variety of beliefs and assertions of faith without ever joining a church, community, or religious organization. At the same time, they could visit the site of the Universal Life Church, which radically redefined religious belonging by including all human beings on the planet as church members. "We believe everyone is already a member of the church and is just not aware of it as yet." Committed to two tenets—freedom of religion and doing what is right—the Church of Universal Life represented an expanded sense of "belonging without believing." Whether in support of believing without belonging or belonging without believing, the Internet seemed to make the institutional dimension of Christianity increasingly irrelevant for leading a Christian life.

However, new Christian social formations developed on the Internet. For example, the First Church of Cyberspace provided a sense of community by holding online meetings every Sunday night. Anyone equipped with Netscape Navigator, Internet Relay Chat software, and a Real Audio Player was welcome to join. Like other sites on the Internet, this church transcended any particular geographical location. In addition to holding weekly church services, the First Church of Cyberspace offered an online sanctuary with sermons, music, and prayers, an art gallery, and a "faith forum" for feedback and discussion. The church also provided movie reviews, book reviews, and community services through links to other Internet sites. At the First Church of Cyberspace, therefore, "virtual parishioners" were invited to join and participate in a different kind of community.

As another example of a new Christian social formation on the Internet, Christian cell groups fit well with the global character of cyberspace. Founded in March 1996, the Christian Prayer Cell Network was organized on the principle that "Christians from all over the world do not have to be in the same room." By applying to the Christian Prayer Cell Network, Christians could be linked together, according to their similar concerns or interests, with up to six other Christians into a cell group that would then determine its own direction. Although the members of a cell group might never meet face to face, they could share a sense of participating in a small-scale community over the Internet.

Although most Protestant sites seemed to follow a conservative social agenda, emphasizing Christian prayer, personal morality, and "family values," the Cyber Center for Liberated Christians provided resources, support, and fellowship for sexually active Christians. Arguing that sexual monogamy was not based on the Bible, the Cyber Center for Liberated Christians proposed that responsible nonmonogamy, or "polyamory," was consistent with Christianity. Sharing sexual pleasure, according to Liberated Christians, was in keeping with the teaching of Jesus that the greatest commandment is love. With a worldwide ministry providing information, counseling, and even mechanical devices, the center encouraged the formation of local fellowship groups for the practice of Christian polyamory.

Third, like other electronic media, the Internet affected the ritual practices of Christianity. Obviously, certain Christian rituals, such as baptism and Communion, involved tangible elements of physical contact, such as immersion in water and taking bread and wine, that were impossible to transmit over the Internet. Other rituals, such as the ordination of ministers, were difficult, but not impossible. Nevertheless, even in the interactive space of the Internet, the Christian rituals transmitted through the electronic Web were almost exclusively verbal—sermons and hymns, testimonials and confessions, praise and prayer. Interactive prayer groups emerged as a significant feature of Christian life in cyberspace. At the BibleUSA.com Prayer Center, for example, participants were welcomed to "your Christian prayer and praise link to the World." Through the medium of electronic mail, Christians were invited to register their requests for prayer and their testimonials about what God had done in their lives. In such Internet Christian prayer circles, therefore, the ritual of prayer promised to generate a new sense of the global unity of Christianity.

Finally, the Internet gave rise to Christian concerns about the damaging effects of the new electronic medium. According to Christian evangelical author Douglas Groothuis, for example, Christians risked "losing our souls in cyberspace."[7] The disembodied character of communication over the Internet, Groothuis argued, lacked the personal presence necessary for genuine Christian discipleship, fellowship, and worship. As a result, the Internet denied the incarnational focus of Christianity, the embodiment of the word made flesh. In the anonymity of cyberspace, Internet users were "connected" to people and places all over the world, but in the process they tended to neglect spouses, families, neighbors, and local churches.

With his own Christian Web site on the Internet, Douglas Groothuis did not advocate destroying the technology, but he did recognize that the new information technology was not a neutral medium. By shaping the character of information, the Internet was altering the location, social formation, and ritual context of Christian communication in new and unpredictable ways.

CONSUMERISM

By the end of the twentieth century, most of the world had been incorporated into a global economy driven by consumerism. Although the Protestant ethic of hard work, discipline, and this-worldly asceticism had held an "elective affinity" with the productive economy of industrial capitalism, a different ethos appeared in the postindustrial capitalist economy. According to one commentator on the global economic transition from production to consumption, the Protestant ethic had been replaced by the "Romantic ethic and the spirit of modern consumerism."[8] In this Romantic ethic, commodities had more than merely use value. By stimulating the imagination and promising the immediate gratification of desires, the commodities that circulated in the modern economy of consumerism gave content to new personal and social identities.

In the spirit of modern consumerism, commodities could also promise a quasi-religious redemption. For example, Coca-Cola, a fizzy, caramel-colored concoction of water, sugar, and a secret formula of flavoring ingredients, became an emblem of this postindustrial economy of consumerism. But Coca-Cola also assumed a kind of religious character for its producers, advertisers, and consumers. From the beginning, the beverage was enveloped in a sacred aura, as its inventor, John Pemberton, referred to one of Coca-Cola's original ingredients, cocaine (which remained in the mix from 1886 until 1902) as "the greatest blessing to the human family, Nature's (God's) best gift in medicine." Asa Candler, the Atlanta entrepreneur who started the Coca-Cola empire, was described by his son as regarding the drink with "an almost mystical faith." Robert Woodruff, who became president of the company in 1923, "demonstrated a devotion to Coca-Cola which approached idolatry." Harrison Jones, the leading bottler of the 1920s, often referred to the beverage as "holy water." Even the bottle itself was a sacred object that could not be changed. At a 1936 bottlers' convention Harrison Jones declared,

"The Four Horsemen of the Apocalypse may charge over the earth and back again—and Coca-Cola will remain!" Archie Lee, who assumed direction of Coca-Cola advertising in the 1920s, complained that the "doctrines of our churches are meaningless words," but he speculated that "some great thinker may arise with a new religion." Apparently, Archie Lee, along with many other "Coca-Cola men," found that new religion in Coca-Cola.

As pioneers in new techniques of advertising for the era of consumerism, the Coca-Cola company succeeded in creating worldwide demand for a product that no one actually needed. Advertising was pursued with a missionary fervor. At the first international convention at Atlantic City in 1948 an executive prayed, "May Providence give us the faith . . . to serve those two billion customers who are only waiting for us to bring our product to them." As advertising director in the early 1950s Delony Sledge proclaimed, "Our work is a religion rather than a business." For the consumer, however, Coca-Cola has also assumed religious significance. It has "entered the lives of more people," as one executive put it, "than any other product or ideology, including the Christian religion." It gave the world a new image of Santa Claus in 1931 by presenting a fat, bearded, jolly old character dressed up in Coca-Cola red; it became the most important icon of the "American way of life" during World War II; it represented an extraordinary sacred time—the "pause that refreshes"—that was redeemed from the ordinary postwar routines of work and consumption; and from the 1960s it promised to build a better world in perfect harmony. As one indication of the popular religious devotion to the drink, public outcry at the changed formula of "New Coke" in 1985 caused one executive to exclaim, "They talk as if Coca-Cola had just killed God." In all these respects, therefore, the "religion of Coca-Cola" emerged as a competitor with Christianity for market share of the sacred.[9]

In the global economy shaped by this "coca-colonization" of the world, many Christian groups adopted new techniques of advertising, marketing, and business management. Christians found new ways for "selling God" in the cultural marketplace. For example, they could wear baseball caps in Coca-Cola red that appropriated the Coca-Cola advertising slogan "It's the real thing" by announcing, in Coca-Cola script, "Jesus Christ, He's the real thing."[10] Increasingly, Christianity was marketed as a leisure-time pursuit in competition with other leisure activities, such as sports, movies, and music. For many Christians, attending a church assumed some of the characteristics of these forms of popular entertainment.

At the same time, the sacred character traditionally associated with the church seemed to become diffused through popular culture. In the United States, for example, a popular television documentary on the history of baseball celebrated the religious character of the sport. Reflecting the "faith of fifty million people," the "church of baseball" functioned like a Christian church. According to journalist Thomas Boswell, his mother was devoted to baseball because "it made her feel like she was in church." Like her Christian church, Boswell explained, baseball provided his mother with "a place where she could—by sharing a fabric of beliefs, symbols, and mutual agreements with those around her—feel calm and whole." Boswell drew out a series of analogies between baseball and his mother's church: both featured organs; both encouraged hand clapping to their hymns; both had distinctive robes and vestments; and in both everyone was equal before God. Although his analogy between the basepaths of a baseball diamond and the Christian cross seems a bit strained, Boswell provided sufficient justification for asserting that his mother regarded her attendance of baseball games as roughly equivalent to belonging to a church. Like the "church of baseball" in the United States, other spectator sports all over the world have generated the sense of belonging, devotion, and enthusiasm traditionally located in a religious community.[11]

The Romantic ethic of consumerism was fueled by imagery and desires drawn not only from advertising, but also from motion pictures, television, and popular music. In the field of popular music, Christianity developed a particularly ambivalent relationship with rock 'n' roll. According to one academic theorist, rock music had revived the pagan pantheism associated with some of the poets and artists of European Romanticism. In broad agreement, other commentators found the music's performers to be divinely inspired shamans and its performances as occasions for an audience to participate in the "ecstasy ritual" of a new electronic paganism. When trying to interpret rock 'n' roll in Christian terms, the rock critic Dave Marsh observed that the total abandon evoked by the archetypal rock song "Louie, Louie" recalled the passage in the Gnostic *Gospel of Thomas* when "Jesus said, 'If you bring forth what is within you, what you bring forth will save you. If you do not bring forth what is within you, what you do not bring forth will destroy you.'" Whether defining rock music as paganism or heresy, these accounts of the religious character of rock 'n' roll placed the music in conflict with conventional forms of Christianity. Perceiving rock 'n' roll as a competing religious option in popular culture, many Christian commentators castigated this popular music not merely as an offensive art form—as "a cult of obscenity, brutality, and sonic abuse"—but also as a blasphemous, sacrilegious, and anti-Christian force in society. According to some conservative Christians, rock 'n' roll could be identified quite simply as the "Devil's music."[12]

At the height of the international popularity of the Beatles during the mid-1960s, John Lennon had inadvertently fueled this Christian opposition to rock 'n' roll by observing that the music had assumed the proportions of a global religion. "Christianity will go," Lennon remarked. "It will vanish and shrink. I needn't argue about that. I'm right and I will be proved right. We're more popular than Jesus now."[13] During the next decade, however, one of the most popular musical productions in the world was the rock opera *Jesus Christ, Superstar*. As a play, a motion picture, and a series of hit records, this production merged rock music with an account of the passion of Christ. Following the popularity of *Jesus Christ, Superstar,* an industry in Christian rock music developed that used the popular musical styles, rhythms, and amplification of rock 'n' roll for proclaiming an evangelical Christian gospel.

The Romantic ethic of imagination, desire, and personal fulfillment in the new global economy of consumerism was also evident in the growth of international tourism. Tourists represented a new leisure class that consumed not only commodities, but also experiences in distant places. Drawing on a religious analogy, many analysts have found that tourism enacted a new kind of ritual of pilgrimage. In medieval Europe, the pilgrim's journey to Christian sacred sites—Compostela, Rome, Canterbury, and so on—had marked a personal religious transformation in which pilgrims left their familiar social roles, adopted an alternative social reality of pure potential, and then returned home with new sacred power. Beyond this personal encounter with the sacred, however, pilgrimage routes created a network of sacred places that comprised the map of a unified European Christendom. At the end of the twentieth century, the pilgrimage routes of global tourism also created a symbolic map of the unity of the world. Although not exclusively Christian, the new world order mapped out by global tourism incorporated the cathedrals, shrines, and sanctuaries of an earlier Christian geography into the leisure industry of global tourism.

Traditionally, Christian pilgrims formed a communal relationship with each other and with the caretakers of the sacred sites through the ritual of pilgrimage. That communal relationship, which was forged through the hazards of the journey, the sharing of resources, and the entry into an alternative reality, defined the social character of the pilgrimage. In the modern tourism industry, however, the pilgrim's social role was defined as that of the client who paid for travel arrangements, airfare, tourist guides, comfortable accommodation, and prepackaged experiences of the sacred. According to John Benson, author of *Transformative Getaways: For Spiritual Growth, Self-Discovery, and Holistic Healing,* going on pilgrimage through a group package tour freed the traveler from the worries of travel arrangements. However, the package tour might also insulate the tourist from spontaneous experiences at the pilgrimage site or from interacting with other pilgrims outside the tour group. In any event, Benson advised pilgrims to be wary of being taken in by charlatans at pilgrimage sites who performed miracles for money. In tourist pilgrimage, therefore, the client relationship supposedly did not extend to the healing, spiritual enrichment, or religious experience that might be obtained at the sacred site. It only applied to the services provided by the tourism industry.

Nevertheless, Christian places of pilgrimage flourished at the end of the twentieth century as sacred sites of exchange. Like medieval European pilgrimage destinations, the modern sites of pilgrimage—Lourdes, in France, where the Virgin Mary was beheld by Bernadette Soubirous in 1858; Medugorje, in the former Yugoslavia, where the Virgin Mary appeared to six children in 1981; or many other Christian sites—places of pilgrimage were necessarily places of giving and receiving. Like traditional pilgrimage, the journey to these places involved an investment of a person's self, money, and time in exchange for the sacred. Christians continued to enter into those personal, economic, and social exchanges through pilgrimage. However, those exchanges were mediated by international agencies, such as the Center for Peace in the case of Medugorje, with offices on the East and West Coasts of the United States, that catered to consumers of both recreation and the sacred. As a privilege of the leisure class in the new consumer culture, the ritual of pilgrimage increasingly assumed the character of international tourism.

According to John Benson, consumers of modern pilgrimage were drawn to places where miracles occurred, whether those extraordinary events were attributed to the appearance of the Virgin Mary, the powers of a Hindu saint like Sai Baba, or the "psychic surgery" performed by shamanistic faith healers in the Philippines. From the perspective of the global tourism industry, all of these manifestations of the sacred were essentially the same because they attracted pilgrims in search of the sacred. With respect to Christian rituals of pilgrimage, therefore, the culture of consumerism opened the possibility for sacred journeys that were both international and interreligious. In the new world order, the tourist industry supported a transnational Christianity that was also in conversation with other religions.[14]

TRANSNATIONALISM

Whatever globalization might have meant at the end of the twentieth century, it impelled many Christians to forge new avenues of communication with adherents of other religions. Certainly, local religious conflicts persisted. During the 1990s, Catholics and Protestants continued to fight over the national identity and political future of Northern Ireland. In the former Yugoslavia, Serbian Orthodox Christians launched a crusade of "ethnic cleansing" against European Muslims that resulted in thousands of deaths. At Auschwitz, the most sacred and painful site of Jewish Holocaust memory, the Polish Catholic Church set off an international controversy by defending the conspicuous presence of a Catholic convent that displayed the Christian cross where Nazis had supervised the execution of 1.5 million Jews in a Christian country. Conscious of these conflicts and controversies, many Christians tried to work out new terms for interreligious understanding in a changing world.

During the twentieth century, Christian theological reflection on interreligious relations tended to follow one of three options—exclusivism, inclusivism, or pluralism. Taking the option of exclusivism, Christians could claim salvation for themselves, through the will of God and the grace of Jesus Christ, while relegating the adherents of every other religion in the world to eternal damnation. A classic statement of this exclusivist position appeared in the work of the Dutch missionary theologian Hendrik Kraemer (1888–1965), beginning in 1938 with his *Christian Message to a Non-Christian World*. According to Kraemer, a Christian approach to adherents of other faiths had to be guided by the conviction that "God has revealed *the* Way and *the* Life and *the* Truth in Jesus Christ, and wills this to be known through all the world." Influenced by the theology of Karl Barth, Kraemer held that all religions, including the religion known as Christianity, were human inventions that stood under the judgment of the Word of God. "I propose to set the religions, including Christianity," Kraemer asserted, "in the light of the person of Jesus Christ, who is the Revelation of God and alone has the authority to criticize—I mean, to judge discriminately and with complete understanding—every religion and everything that is in man or proceeds from him." Kraemer nevertheless appreciated religious traditions as significant human accomplishments and encouraged the comparative study of religions, interreligious dialogue, and interfaith cooperation on matters of common social concern. Ultimately, however, Christian relations with other religions were determined by the missionary imperative to proclaim the gospel.

The implication of the exclusivist position was that all those who had not heard, received, or accepted the Christian gospel were destined for eternal damnation. Some exclusivists have stated this position starkly, following the official statement of the Chicago Congress on World Missions in 1960 by concluding that in the non-Christian world billions of souls "went to the torment of hellfire without even hearing of Jesus Christ, who He was, or why He died on the cross of Calvary." Although he stood in a Calvinist or Reformed tradition that assumed that damnation was the final destination for the vast majority of humanity, Hendrik Kraemer tried to temper this Christian triumphalism by maintaining that the eternal fate of non-Christians was a divine mystery. Similarly, Leslie Newbigin maintained that Christians could not know anything about the fate of non-Christians except that they ultimately depended upon the justice and mercy of God. Other exclusivists, however, proposed that human beings might hear and receive the saving gospel of Jesus Christ in the afterlife. The Catholic doctrine of purgatory could be adapted for this postmortem missionary possibility, but even a Calvinist, such as the theologian George Lindbeck, could propose that non-Christians had the hope of salvation because they would encounter Christ after death.[15]

Under the auspices of a Christian inclusivism, however, Christians could speculate that people who belonged to other faiths might still receive salvation if they acted like Christians and mysteriously received the grace of God even though they were not members of a Christian church. A classic version of Christian inclusivism was proposed by the

German Jesuit theologian Karl Rahner (1904–84). In an essay "Christianity and Non-Christian Religions," Rahner tried to reconcile two Christian doctrines—the necessity of Christian faith for salvation and the divine will that salvation be extended to all human beings. As both a faith and a church, he observed, "Christianity understands itself as the absolute religion, intended for all men, which cannot recognize any other religion besides itself as of equal right." However, Rahner recognized that the fact that not all human beings had heard of Christianity seemed to limit Christian claims about the universal scope of God's saving will. In the church's "doctrine of Israel," however, he found a precedent for regarding a pre-Christian religion not only as "lawful," but even as a vehicle for divine grace through Christ. Turning to contemporary non-Christian religions, Rahner suggested that any religion might bear traces of divine grace. In their quest for truth, experience of the presence of God, or acts of selfless love, people of other faiths might turn out to be what Rahner called "anonymous Christians." Although they were not members of any Christian church, the "anonymous Christians" in other religions might still receive divine grace through Christ.

This inclusivist approach to religious diversity, therefore, affirmed the universal saving power of the Christian God by proposing, as Rahner put it, that "the Christian hope is present as a hidden reality even outside the visible Church." However, inclusivists also restated the exclusivist assumption that salvation was only possible through Christ. Furthermore, this position reaffirmed the historical importance of the Christian church. Those who found themselves in the body of the church, according to Rahner, "still had a greater chance of salvation than someone who is merely an anonymous Christian." As critics of this approach have observed, being classified as anonymous Christians can be offensive to Jews, Muslims, Hindus, Buddhists, and adherents of other religions who regard their religious way of life as inherently sanctifying or saving. As the theologian John Hick observed, the designation "anonymous Christian" is "an honorary status granted unilaterally to people who have not expressed any desire for it." Devout Christians might feel similarly offended if they were told that they were actually anonymous Jews, Muslims, Hindus, or Buddhists. By imposing Christian terms and conditions on interreligious relations, the inclusivist position blocked the mutual understanding that could be achieved through dialogue between people of different faiths. In that respect, inclusivism seemed to be a modified version of Christian exclusivism, triumphalism, and paternalism. However, advocates of the inclusivist position insisted that their reflections on religious diversity were directed not to people of other faiths but to Christians, who were encouraged to recognize that God had been revealed definitively but not exclusively in the Jesus Christ of the Christian church.[16]

The option of pluralism presented the more radical prospect that all religious paths might lead to salvation. Religious pluralism raised the possibility that salvation might be attained outside of the confines of the Christian church, the sanctifying power of its sacraments, or any specific religious beliefs in the saving power of Jesus Christ. As formulated by the British philosopher of religion John Hick, pluralism is a creative Christian response to the new problems posed by religious diversity. How should Christians regard the adherents of other faiths living in the same city, the same country, the same world? In the past, Christian emphasis on church membership and belief in Jesus Christ—the ecclesiocentric and Christocentric conditions for salvation—had erected barriers that separated Christians from the faithful of other religions. Furthermore, these church-centered and Christ-centered conditions supported what Hick regarded as the unchristian conclusion that God had "ordained that men must be saved in such a way that only a small minority can in fact receive this salvation." In the context of a new multifaith and multicultural global order, however, Hick called for a theocentric revolution that focused on an all-loving God as the ultimate source of salvation. Beyond the myths and doctrines, the ritual practices and social institutions, of the many religions of the world, Hick proposed that God, the "Eternal One," extended salvation to all human beings.[17]

For Christians, this theocentric understanding of religious diversity implied that a central Christian doctrine, the incarnation of Christ as the "God-man," was a particular myth that pointed beyond itself to the supreme God of all faiths. By relinquishing any claims to a monopoly on salvation, Christian pluralists were called to engage people of other faiths not through apologetics, polemics, or missions, but through dialogue. Through the process of interreligious conversation and mutual recognition, Christians would learn that their God actually has many names. While Hick tried to work out theological grounds for the unity of all faiths, other pluralists adopted approaches based on identifying common experiences or shared ethical concerns in different religions. For advocates of the "perennial philosophy," mysticism represented the common experiential core in all religions, even though that core only appeared in the secret or esoteric schools of religious mystics. By contrast, other Christian pluralists found that adherents of different religions shared ethical interests in addressing human suffering, demonstrating compassion, or even in mobilizing people toward political liberation from oppression.

Moving from theory to practice, Christians participated during the 1990s in the formation of interfaith organizations. A precedent for such interreligious cooperation had been set a century earlier by the World's Parliament of Religions at the Chicago World's Fair in 1893. Although the parliament was coordinated by a liberal Christian agenda that stressed the modern and progressive aspects of religion, it nevertheless drew together delegates from all over the world to affirm religious unity. In Britain, the World Congress of Faiths was founded in 1936 by Sir Francis Younghusband to support interfaith dialogue and cooperation in humanitarian projects. By the 1990s, such interreligious initiatives had expanded dramatically. A second parliament, now renamed the Parliament for the World's Religions, brought over eight thousand delegates to Chicago in 1993, concluding with a resolution to hold an interfaith parliament every five years. The World Congress of Faiths in Britain had been joined by other interfaith organizations—the World Conference on Religion and Peace, the World Interfaith Education Association, the International Association for Religious Freedom, the Global Dialogue Institute, and many others—in sponsoring publications, international conferences, educational programs, religious retreats, visits to religious communities, and group travel to religious sites. According to the World Congress of Faiths, interreligious communication was necessary for both personal growth and good community relations.

On a global scale, however, interfaith organizations proposed that the spiritual resources of all religions had to be drawn upon to address poverty, social injustice, and conflict in the world. For example, an organization based in Tübingen, Germany, Foundation Global Ethic, which was inspired by the work of the Catholic theologian Hans Küng (b. 1928), promoted the "Declaration Toward a Global Ethic," which had been endorsed by the Parliament for the World's Religions in 1993. This global ethic was based on the premise that there could be no peace among the nations without peace, dialogue, and mutual understanding among adherents of the different religions of the world. Toward that end, the declaration formulated four ethical commitments that could be supported by members of any faith:

Commitment to a culture of nonviolence and respect for life.
Commitment to a culture of solidarity and a just economic order.
Commitment to a culture of tolerance and a life of truthfulness.
Commitment to a culture of equal rights and partnership between men and women.

Although adherents of different religions might disagree about matters of myth, doctrine, and ritual, the sponsors of the "Global Ethic" believed that they could still find common ground in these ethical commitments to treating human beings humanely. The sponsors explicitly directed this interreligious ethic to the conditions of a new world order. "No global order," they declared, "without a new global ethic!"[18]

These initiatives in interreligious understanding in the 1990s, therefore, responded to challenges of globalization that had altered the social terrain in which Christianity and all other religions operated. For Christian participants, interreligious cooperation in social projects for peace, human rights, economic justice, gender equality, and environmental protection could be conceived as a transnational imperative. The unity of religions proclaimed by interfaith organizations was itself a confession of faith in the face of the disconfirming evidence provided by conflicts and warfare all over the world in which religion featured as a divisive force. Belfast, Sarejevo, and Beirut were only the most prominent locations in which Christians were engaged in armed interreligious conflict. Arguably, however, the entire "new world order" was emerging not as a unipolar world revolving around the global political power of the United States, but as a polarized world divided by new oppositions. With respect to interreligious relations, global relations between Christians and Muslims had become particularly polarized. Following the demise of the USSR as a global enemy, Islam seemed to replace international communism in the political rhetoric, popular media, and public prejudices of Christians in the United States. Denigrated under prejudicial stereotypes as fanatics and fundamentalists, as terrorist bombers and suicidal maniacs, Muslims suffered profound interreligious misunderstanding. As Christian-Muslim relations indicated, therefore, the new world order had not necessarily produced widespread interreligious understanding, respect, or unity.

According to many analysts, however, globalization was producing not unity, but hybridity, a mixing or grafting of cultural forms drawn from different parts of the world. Although this process of hybridity was born out of new global relations, it always displayed distinctively local features. For example, in 1993 when the Roman Catholic pope John Paul II—Juan Pablo Segundo—came to the Mexican state of Yucatán, he delivered a sermon in the small town of Izamal, where centuries before a Franciscan monastery had been built on a Mayan temple. As we recall, popular Mayan Catholicism had drawn together Catholic and indigenous resources, fashioning a religious life that merged the church and its saints with indigenous tradition and its ancestors. Clearly, if hybridity means mixing different cultural forms, then Christian hybridity has had a long history. But the pope's visit added new global features to the local mix in which the unity of the Church that was embodied by the pope was supported by advanced publicity and marketing and local entrepreneurs, who did a brisk business in selling specially designed baseball caps that featured a picture of the pope's face. Reportedly, only Mickey Mouse caps provided any competition for the sale of pope hats. As thousands of people of the Mayan region of the Yucatán flocked to this small-town audience with the pope, therefore, the event occurred at the intersection of local religious interests with the global forces of air travel, public relations, tourism, entertainment, and the commodification of the sacred.[19]

As Christianity approached the end of its second millennium, global changes in the flow of information, the attractions and seductions of consumerism, and the expanding scope of transnational relations raised profound questions about the location of Christianity in the new world order. On the one hand, Christianity itself seemed to be a global force. As a religion that was utopian because it was limited to no particular place and universal because it could potentially be in every place, Christianity was everywhere and nowhere. Accordingly, Christianity seemed particularly suited to the dislocations of an era characterized by many commentators as postmodern. On the other hand, every Christian was at home somewhere. Building a Christian home required attention to location. It depended upon the microscopic management of local religious resources. In the Mayan Catholic case, for example, a home was not built merely out of bricks and mortar. It was built out of human relations between males and females, elders and juniors, insiders and outsiders, and so on. Most significantly for the local character of Christianity, however, it was also constructed out of relations with saints and ancestors. Those ongoing religious relations produced the Christian home as a distinctive kind of sacred space. Even in the new world order, therefore, Christians were still faced with the challenge of using local materials to build a home that was in the world but not of it.

References

Abbreviations

AEW   J. H. S. Burleigh, trans. *Augustine: Earlier Writings*. London, 1953.

ALW   J. Burnaby, trans. *Augustine: Later Works*. London, 1954.

ANF   A. Roberts and J. Donaldson, eds. *Ante-Nicene Fathers*, 10 vols. Edinburgh, 1867–72; reprint: Peabody, Mass., 1996.

APW   P. Holmes, trans. *The Anti-Pelagian Writings*. Edinburgh, 1908.

ECF   C. C. Richardson, ed. and trans. *Early Christian Fathers*. New York, 1970.

JA   Josephus. *Antiquitates*, "Jewish Antiquities." In *Works*. Translated by H. St. J. Thackeray et al. London, 1927–43.

JW   Josephus. *Bellum Judaicum*, "The Jewish War." In *Works*. Translated by H. St. J. Thackeray et al. London, 1927–43.

LW   J. Pelikan et al., eds. *Luther's Works*. St. Louis and Philadelphia, 1955–86.

NPNF1   P. Schaff, ed. *Nicene and Post-Nicene Fathers: First Series*. 14 vols. Oxford and New York, 1886–90; reprint: Peabody, Mass., 1996.

NPNF2   P. Schaff and H. Wace, eds. *Nicene and Post-Nicene Fathers: Second Series*. 14 vols. Oxford and New York, 1890–1900; reprint: Peabody, Mass., 1996.

PL   J. P. Migne, ed. *Patrologia Latina Cursus Completus*. 221 vols. Paris, 1844–55.

1: Beginnings

1. *JW* 1.653.

2. Plutarch, *Moralia* 1102A, *Moralia*, trans. B. Einarson et al. (London, 1927); R. MacMullen, *Paganism in the Roman Empire* (New Haven, 1981): 40.

3. Plutarch, *On the E at Delphi* 393B; R. M. Grant, *Gods and the One God* (Philadelphia, 1986): 79.

4. G. Vermes, *The Dead Sea Scrolls: Qumran in Perspective,* 3d ed. (London, 1994).

5. D. A. Fiensy, *The Social History of Palestine in the Herodian Period: The Land Is Mine* (Lewiston, N.Y., 1991): 105.

6. *JW* 2.259–63; *JA* 18.85–87; 20.97, 188. On Judas, son of Hezekiah, see *JW* 2.56, 68; *JA* 17.271–72, 289.

7. *JW* 7.26–36, 116–57.

2: Jesus

1. J. P. Meier, *A Marginal Jew: Rethinking the Historical Jesus,* 2 vols. (New York, 1991, 1994): 1:407.

2. *JA* 18.63–64.

3. Tacitus, *Annals* 15.44, *Annals of Tacitus,* trans. A. J. Church and W. J. Brodribb (London, 1876): 304–5.

4. *JA* 13.296–98.

5. Philo, *De opificio mundi* 148, *Works,* trans. F. H. Colson and G. H. Whitaker (London, 1929): 117.

6. G. W. E. Nickelsburg, *Jewish Literature Between the Bible and the Mishna: A Historical and Literary Introduction* (Philadelphia, 1981): 184; J. J. Collins, *Between Athens and Jerusalem: Jewish Identity in the Hellenistic Diaspora* (New York, 1983): 182.

7. B. Mack, The *Lost Gospel: The Book of Q and Christian Origins* (San Francisco, 1993): 116; G. Theissen, *The Sociology of Early Palestinian Christianity* (Philadelphia, 1978): 8–16.

8. H. D. Betz, ed., *The Greek Magical Papyri in Translation* (Chicago, 1986): xli–liii; H. C. Kee, *Miracle in the Early Christian World* (New Haven, 1983): 3.

9. M. Smith, *Jesus the Magician* (New York, 1978): 54.

10. R. A. Horsley, *Jesus and the Spiral of Violence: Popular Jewish Resistance in Roman Palestine* (Minneapolis, 1987): 192.

11. Justin Martyr, *1 Apology* 17, ANF 1:168.

12. *JA* 18.116.

3: Christ

1. B. Mack, *A Myth of Innocence: Mark and Christian Origins* (Philadelphia, 1988); *The Lost Gospel: The Book of Q and Christian Origins* (San Francisco, 1993).

2. D. Boyarin, *A Radical Jew: Paul and the Politics of Identity* (Berkeley, 1994).

3. J. J. Collins, "A Symbol of Otherness: Circumcision and Salvation in the First Century," in J. Neusner and E. S. Frerichs, eds., *"To See Ourselves as Others See Us": Christians, Jews, and "Others" in Late Antiquity* (Chico, Calif., 1985): 163–86.

4. J. S. Siker, *Disinheriting the Jews: Abraham in Early Christian Controversy* (Louisville, Ky., 1991).

5. D. B. Martin, *The Corinthian Body* (New Haven, 1995).

6. E. Pagels, *The Origin of Satan* (New York, 1995).

7. A. Y. Collins, *Crisis and Catharsis: The Power of the Apocalypse* (Philadelphia, 1984); J. J. Collins, *The Apocalyptic Imagination* (New York, 1984).

4: Christians

1. Pliny, *Epistolae* 10.96, *Letters*, 2 vols., trans. W. Melmoth (London, 1915): 2:403–5.

2. R. Lane Fox, *Pagans and Christians* (New York, 1987): 268–73; R. MacMullen, *Christianizing the Roman Empire, A.D. 100–400* (New Haven, 1984): 109–10, 135 n. 26.

3. Tertullian, *Apologeticum* 7–9, ANF 3:23–26; Eusebius, *Historia Ecclesiastica* 5.1.7–10, NPNF2 1:212–13.

4. Justin Martyr, *1 Apology* 26, 58, ANF 1:171–72, 182; Tertullian, *Adversus Marcionem* 5.19, *Tertullian Adversus Marcionem*, 2 vols., trans. E. Evans (Oxford, 1972): 2:631.

5. S. G. Wilson, "Marcion and the Jews," in Wilson, ed., *Anti-Judaism in Early Christianity*, 2 vols. (Waterloo, Ontario, 1986): 2:45–57.

6. B. Layton, *The Gnostic Scriptures* (Garden City, N.Y., 1987): 265–75.

7. Irenaeus, *Adversus haereses* 1.21.4, ANF 1:346.

8. Irenaeus, *Adversus haereses* 1.2.6, ANF 1:318; *Gospel of Truth* 21.25, *Gospel of Truth: A Valentinian Meditation on the Gospel*, trans. K. Grobel (New York, 1960).

9. Justin, *2 Apology* 5, ANF 1:190.

10. Justin, *2 Apology* 13, ANF 1:193.

11. Justin, *1 Apology* 59–60, ANF 1:182–83.

12. Justin, *1 Apology* 5, 54, ANF 1:164, 181.

13. Justin, *Dialogus cum Tryphone* 16, ANF 1:202.

14. Justin, *1 Apology* 36, ANF 1:175.

15. Justin, *1 Apology* 60, ANF 1:183.

5: Churches

1. Justin Martyr, *Acta Justini* 3, H. Musurillo, ed. and trans., *The Acts of the Christian Martyrs* (Oxford, 1972): 49; G. Dix, *The Shape of the Liturgy* (London, 1945): 20.

2. Justin Martyr, *1 Apology* 67, ANF 1:185–86; Barnabas, *Epistle* 15.6, ANF 1:146–7.

3. *Didascalia apostolorum* 21, *The Didascalia Apostolorum in Syriac*, trans. A. Vööbus (Louvain, 1979): 199; Tertullian, *De baptismo* 19, *Tertullian's Homily on Baptism*, ed. and trans. E. Evans (London, 1964): 41.

4. Hippolytus, *Traditio apostolica* 20, *Apostolic Tradition of Hippolytus*, trans. B. S. Easton (Cambridge, 1934): 44.

5. *Didache* 7, ECF 174; E. Schürer, *The History of the Jewish People in the Age of Jesus Christ (175 B.C.–A.D. 135)*, 3 vols., rev. ed, M. Black, F. Millar, and G. Vermes (Edinburgh, 1986): 3:174; Tertullian, *De baptismo* 4, *Tertullian's Homily on Baptism*, 11.

6. Hippolytus, *Traditio apostolica* 21, *Apostolic Tradition*, 45.

7. R. H. Connolly, *Didascalia Apostolorum* (Oxford, 1929): 146–47.

8. Hippolytus, *Traditio apostolica* 21, *Apostolic Tradition*, 45–47.

9. Tertullian, *De Corona* 3, *Tertullian: Disciplinary, Moral, and Ascetical Works*, trans. E. A. Quain (Washington, D.C., 1959): 236–37.

10. Hippolytus, *Traditio apostolica* 16, *Apostolic Tradition*, 42–43.

11. Hippolytus, *Traditio apostolica* 4, *Apostolic Tradition*, 35–36; P. G. Cobb, "The *Apostolic Tradition* of Hippolytus," in C. Jones et al., eds., *The Study of Liturgy*, rev. ed. (London, 1992): 213–14.

12. *Didache* 9.2–3; 10.2–6, ECF 175–76.

13. Justin Martyr, *Dialogus cum Tryphone* 117, ANF 1:257.

14. Justin Martyr, *Dialogus cum Tryphone* 117; Tertullian, *De oratione liber* 18, *Tertullian: Disciplinary, Moral, and Ascetical Works*, 174; Ignatius of Antioch, *Ephesians* 5.2, ECF 89.

15. H. Hubert and M. Mauss, *Sacrifice: Its Nature and Function*, trans. W. D. Halls (London, 1964): 97.

16. Irenaeus, *Adversus haereses* 4.5.4, ANF 1:467.

17. Irenaeus, *Adversus haereses* 4.18.1, ANF 1:484.

18. Cyril of Jerusalem, *Mystagogical Catecheses* 5.10, *St. Cyril of Jerusalem's Lectures on the Christian Sacraments: The Procatechesis and the Five Mystagogical Catecheses*, ed. F. L. Cross, trans. R. W. Church (London, 1951): 75.

19. Tertullian, *Adversus Marcionem* 1.14, *Tertullian Adversus Marcionem*, 2 vols., ed. and trans. E. Evans (Oxford, 1972): 1:37; Ignatius of Antioch, *Ephesians* 20.1, ECF 93; Irenaeus, *Adversus haereses* 4.18.5, ANF 1:486; *Constitutiones Apostolorum* 8.13.16; D. A. Fiensy, *Prayers Alleged to Be Jewish: An Examination of the Constitutiones Apostolorum* (Chico, Calif., 1985).

20. G. F. Snyder, *Ante Pacem: Archaeological Evidence of Church Life Before Constantine* (Macon, Ga., 1985): 61.

21. Tertullian, *Apologeticum* 50, ANF 3:55.

6: Martyrs

1. Tertullian, *Apologeticum* 40, ANF 3:47.

2. Lucian, *Death of Peregrinus* 13.

3. Ignatius of Antioch, *Romans* 4–6, ECF 104–5.

4. *Martyrdom of Polycarp*, ECF 149–58.

5. Clement of Alexandria, *Paidagogos* 1.6, 3.12, ANF 4:136–48.

6. Origen, *Exhortation to Martyrdom* 30, *Origen*, trans. R. A. Greer (London, 1979): 62.

7. Tertullian, *Apologeticum* 49, ANF 3:54.

8. Tertullian, *Scorpiace* 8, ANF 3:641.

9. B. D. Shaw, "The Passion of Perpetua," *Past and Present* 139 (1993): 3–45.

10. Tertullian, *De anima* 9, ANF 3:188; Epiphanius, *Panarion* 49.1, *The Panarion of Epiphanius of Salamis: Books II and III*, trans. F. Williams (Leiden, 1994): 21–23; Tertullian, *Scorpiace* 6, ANF 3:639.

11. Eusebius, *Historia Ecclesiastica* 4.7.7, NPNF2 1:179; Clement, *Stromata* 4.9, ANF 12:171.

12. Clement, *Stromata* 4.4; 4.10; 4.7, ANF 12:147, 173, 159.

13. Eusebius, *Historia Ecclesiastica* 6.2.1–5; NPNF2 1:249–50; Origen, *Exhortation to Martyrdom* 47, 3, 13, 12, 22, 28, 30, *Origen*, trans. Greer, 76, 42, 50, 49, 56, 59, 61; Origen, *Dialogue with Heraclides* 24.10–15, *Treatise on the Passover and Dialogue of Origen with Heraclides*, trans. R. J. Daly (New York, 1992): 75.

14. *Martyrdom of Pionius* 20, H. Musurillo, ed. and trans., *The Acts of the Christian Martyrs* (Oxford, 1972): 163.

15. J. R. Knipfing, "Libelli of the Decian Persecution," *Harvard Theological Review* 16 (1923): 363.

16. Eusebius, *The Martyrs of Palestine* 1–2, NPNF2 1:343–44.

17. *Acts of Euplus*, 1–2, Musurillo, *Acts of the Christian Martyrs*, 311–13; Eusebius, *Historia Ecclesiastica* 8.6.6, NPNF2 1:328.

18. *Martyrdom of Polycarp* 17, ECF 155.

19. P. Brown, *The Cult of the Saints: Its Rise and Function in Latin Christianity* (Chicago, 1981).

20. P. Ariès, *Western Attitudes Toward Death: From the Middle Ages to the Present*, trans. P. M. Ranum (Baltimore, 1974): 16; Eunapius of Sardis, *Lives of the Sophists*, ed. and trans. W. C. Wright (London, 1961): 425.

7: Christian Empire

1. Lactantius, *De mortibus persecutorum* 48.2–12, ed. and trans. J. L. Creed (Oxford, 1984): 71–75; *Codex Theodosianus* 16.10.7, C. Pharr, ed. and trans., *The Theodosian Code and Novels and the Sirmondian Constitutions* (Princeton, 1952): 440.

2. *Panegyrici Latini* 6(7).21.3–6, J. Stevenson, ed., *The New Eusebius: Documents Illustrative of the History of the Church to A.D. 337* (London, 1960): 297–98.

3. Eusebius, *Vita Constantini* 1.26–9, NPNF2 1:489–91; A. Kee, *Constantine Versus Christ: The Triumph of Ideology* (London, 1982): 13–14.

4. Eusebius, *Vita Constantini* 4.20, NPNF2 1:545.

5. Eusebius, *Historia Ecclesiastica* 10.7, NPNF2 1:383.

6. Eusebius, *Oration* 2–3, NPNF2 1:583–85.

7. Eusebius, *Vita Constantini* 3.48, NPNF2 1:532.

8. Epiphanius, *Panarion* 69.6, *The Panarion of Epiphanius of Salamis: Books II and III*, trans. F. Williams (Leiden, 1994): 328–29.

9. J. N. D. Kelly, *Early Christian Creeds* (London, 1950): 215–16.

10. Hippolytus, *Philosophumena* 9.11–12, *Philosophumena or The Refutation of All Heresies*, 2 vols., trans. F. Legge (London, 1921): 2:124–32; Epiphanius, *Panarion* 62; *Panarion of Epiphanius of Salamis*, 121–28.

11. Athanasius, *De synodis* 45, NPNF2 4:473–74.

12. *Codex Theodosianus* 16.5.1, Pharr, *Theodosian Code*, 450.

13. Eusebius, *Vita Constantini* 3.26, 54–58, NPNF2 1:527, 534–36; Jerome, *Epistolae* 58.3, NPNF2 6:120; Socrates, *Historia Ecclesiastica* 1.17, NPNF2 2:21.

14. E. D. Hunt, *Holy Land Pilgrimage in the Later Roman Empire* (Oxford, 1982): 28–49; Cyril of Jerusalem, *Catecheses* 4.10, NPNF2 7:21.

15. Eusebius, *Demonstratio evangelica* 5.9, *The Proof of the Gospel*, 2 vols., trans. W. J. Ferrar (London, 1920): 1:252–54; JW 4.533; Eusebius, *Vita Constantini* 3.53, NPNF2 1:533; Sozomon, *Historia Ecclesiastica* 2.4, NPNF2 2:261.

16. Jerome, *Epistolae* 58.3, *NPNF2* 6:120; Eusebius, *Vita Constantini* 3.43, *NPNF2* 1:531.

17. *Acts of John* 97, E. Hennecke and W. Schneemelcher, eds., *New Testament Apocrypha*, 2 vols. (Philadelphia, 1963): 2:232; Eusebius, *Demonstratio evangelica* 6.18, *Proof of the Gospel*, 2:26–36; *Vita Constantini* 3.43, *NPNF2* 1:531.

18. *Itinerarium Egeriae* 47.5, *Egeria's Travels*, trans. J. Wilkinson (London, 1971): 146; J. Z. Smith, *To Take Place: Toward Theory in Ritual* (Chicago, 1987): 74–95.

8: Holiness

1. *Didascalia apostolorum* 1, *The Didascalia Apostolorum in Syriac*, trans. A. Vööbus (Louvain, 1979): 13; Jerome, *Epistolae* 22.28, *NPNF2* 6:34.

2. Tertullian, *De cultu feminarum* 1.1.2, *Tertullian: Disciplinary, Moral, and Ascetical Works*, trans. E. A. Quain (Washington, D.C., 1959): 118.

3. Athenagoras, *Legatio pro Christianus* 33, *Athenagoras: Legatio and De Resurrectione*, trans. W. R. Schoedel (Oxford, 1972): 81.

4. Justin, *1 Apology* 29, *ANF* 1:172; Tertullian, *De anima* 27.5, *ANF* 3:208; Tertullian, *De exhortatione castitatis* 10.1–2, *ANF* 4:56.

5. Clement, *Stromata* 3.57, *Stromateis, Books One to Three*, trans. J. Ferguson (Washington, D.C., 1991): 291; P. Brown, *The Body and Society: Men, Women, and Sexual Renunciation in Early Christianity* (New York, 1988).

6. Council of Elvira, Canon 33, E. J. Jonkers, ed., *Acta et symbola conciliorum quae saeculo quarto habita sunt* (Leiden, 1974): 12–13; Eusebius, *Demonstratio Evangelica* 1.8, *Eusebius: The Proof of the Gospel*, 2 vols., trans. W. J. Ferrar (London, 1920): 1:48.

7. Tertullian, *De carnis resurrectione* 61, *ANF* 3:593; Cyprian, *Habitu virginum* 20, *ANF* 8:347.

8. Jerome, *Epistolae* 48.21, *NPNF2* 6:79; Justin, *1 Apology* 29, *ANF* 1:172; Eusebius, *Historia Ecclesiastica* 6.8.2, *NPNF2* 1:254.

9. *Didascalia apostolorum* 14–15, *Didascalia Apostolorum in Syriac* 141–55; *Acts of Paul and Thecla* 4, W. Schneemelcher, "Acts of Paul," in E. Hennecke and Schneemelcher, eds., *New Testament Apocrypha*, 2 vols. (Philadelphia, 1963): 2:354.

10. *Codex Theodosianus* 9.25.1, C. Pharr, ed. and trans., *The Theodosian Code and Novels and the Sirmondian Constitutions* (Princeton, 1952): 246; Athanasius, *Apologia ad Constantium* 33.49, *Historical Tracts of Saint Athanasius*, trans. M. Atkinson (Oxford, 1843): 185.

11. Basil of Caesarea, *Epistolae* 199.18, NPNF2 8:237.

12. Ambrose, *De virginitate* 1.5.21, NPNF2 10:366.

13. Jerome, *Epistolae* 45.2; *Dialogus adversus Pelagianos* 2.24; *Adversus Jovinianum* 1.3; *Epistolae* 48.2; NPNF2 6:59, 470, 348, 66.

14. F. Lent, trans., "Life of Symeon Stylites," *Journal of the American Oriental Society* 35 (1915): 103–98; Athanasius, *Vita Antonii* 51, *Athanasius: The Life of Antony and the Letter to Marcellinus*, trans. R. Gregg (New York, 1980): 70.

15. Athanasius, *Vita Antonii* 14, *Athanasius: The Life of Antony*, 42–43.

16. *Poemen* 125, *The Sayings of the Desert Fathers*, trans. B. Ward (Kalamazoo, Mich., 1975): 156; *Olympios* 2, *Sayings of the Desert Fathers*, 135.

17. Palladius, *Historia Lausiaca* 22.9, *Palladius: The Lausiac History*, trans. R. T. Meyer (Westminster, Md., 1965): 79; *Isidore the Priest* 2; *Poemen* 67; *Sayings of the Desert Fathers*, 82, 148.

18. *Anthony* 30; *Macarius* 32; *Sayings of the Desert Fathers*, 6, 113.

19. V. Macdermot, *The Cult of the Seer in the Ancient Near East* (Berkeley, 1971): 766; *Pachomii vita prima* 112, *The Life of Pachomius*, trans. A. N. Athanassakis (Missoula, Mont., 1975): 155.

20. Vööbus, *A History of Asceticism in the Syrian Orient*, 1:141–44, 151; Sulpicius Severus, *Vita S. Martini Episcopi* 10, T. F. X. Noble and T. Head, eds., *Soldiers of Christ: Saints and Saints' Lives from Late Antiquity to the Middle Ages* (University Park, Penn., 1995): 13–14.

21. Plato, *Republic* 398c–403c; 614b–621d; W. Burkert, *Lore and Science in Ancient Pythagoreanism*, trans. E. L. Minar (Cambridge, Mass., 1972): 351, 357; Plotinus, *Enneads* 6.7.12, trans. S. MacKenna (London, 1956): 2:570–71.

22. Pseudo-Clement, *De virginitate* 2.6, ANF 8:63; Basil, *Epistolae* 207.2, NPNF2 8:247; Augustine, *De opere monachorum* 17.20, *Seventeen Short Treatises* (Oxford, 1847): 493.

23. Augustine, *Confessiones* 9.6.14, *The Confessions of St. Augustine*, trans. R. Warner (New York, 1963): 193–94; Ambrose, *Contra Auxentium* 34, NPNF2 10:436.

24. Photius, *Epitome* 2.2, *The Ecclesiastic History of Philostorgius as Epitomized by Photius*, ed. and trans. E. Walford (London, 1855): 434; Athanasius, *Ad Marcellinum* 16, *The Life of Anthony and the Letter to Marcellinus*, 115.

25. Synesius, *Epistolae* 148.105–14; J. Bregman, *Synesius of Cyrene: Philosopher-Bishop* (Berkeley, 1982): 75; Jerome, *Epistolae* 56.

26. John Chrysostom, *In Psalmum* 41.1–2; J. C. B. Petropoulos, "The Church Father as Social Informant: St. John Chrysostom on Folk-Songs," *Studia Patristica* 22 (1989): 159–64.

27. Augustine, *Enarrationes in Psalmum* 18.2; *Expositions on the Book of Psalms,* 6 vols. (Oxford, 1847–57); A. B. Wylie, "They've Gone Country: Popular Music and Christian Piety in Late Antiquity," unpublished paper, 1995.

9: Faith and Reason

1. R. Walzer, *Galen on Jews and Christians* (Oxford, 1949): 48.

2. Augustine, *Contra academicos* 3.20.43, *Saint Augustine Against the Academics,* trans. J. J. O'Meara (Westminster, Md., 1950): 150.

3. Augustine, *Confessiones* 1.9, 1.12, *The Confessions of St. Augustine,* trans. R. Warner (New York, 1963): 26, 30; Gregory Nazianzus, *Oration* 43.11, NPNF2 7:398.

4. Hippolytus, *Philosophumena* 9.13–17, *Philosophumena or The Refutation of All Heresies,* 2 vols., trans. F. Legge (London, 1921): 2:132–38; Eusebius, *Historia Ecclesiastica* 7.31, NPNF2 1:316–17.

5. Augustine, *Contra epistolam quam vocant fundamenti* 5, *On the Manichean Heresy,* trans. R. Stothert (Edinburgh, 1872): 100; *Confessiones* 4.16, *Confessions,* 87–88; C. R. C. Allberry, *A Manichean Psalmbook, Part 2* (Stuttgart, 1938): 215.

6. Augustine, *Confessiones* 5.3, 9.4, *Confessions,* 92, 191; D. Chidester, *Word and Light: Seeing, Hearing, and Religious Discourse* (Urbana, Ill., 1992).

7. Augustine, *Contra academicos* 3.18.41, *Saint Augustine Against the Academics,* 147–48; *Confessiones* 7.9, *Confessions,* 147.

8. Augustine, *Soliloquia* 1.2.7; 1.1.3, AEW 26, 24; *De civitate Dei* 12.2, *The City of God,* trans. M. Dods (New York, 1950): 382.

9. Augustine, *Soliloquia* 1.6.13, AEW 31.

10. Augustine, *De libero arbitrio* 2.6.14, AEW 144; *De vera religione* 31.57, AEW 254.

11. Augustine, *De magistro,* AEW 69–101; *Retractationes* 1.12; *Tractatus in epistolam Joannis ad Parthos* 3.13, NPNF1 7:481; ALW 285.

12. Augustine, *De consensu evangelistarum* 4.10.20, *The Harmony of the Evangelists* (Edinburgh, 1873): 502.

13. W. H. C. Frend, *The Donatist Church: A Movement of Protest in Roman North Africa* (Oxford, 1952): 171–75.

14. G. Bonner, *St. Augustine of Hippo: Life and Controversies* (London, 1963): 253–58; P. Brown, "St. Augustine's Attitude to Religious Coercion," *Journal of Roman Studies* 54 (1964): 107–16.

15. Jerome, *Epistolae* 123.17, NPNF2 6:237; Augustine, *Sermones* 296.6.

16. Augustine, *Enarrationes in Psalmum* 64.2; *De civitate Dei* 22.30, *City of God,* 867.

17. Augustine, *De civitate Dei* 10.1, *City of God,* 305.

18. Augustine, *De gratia Christi et de peccato originali* 2.14, 6, *APW* 2:58, 52.

19. Augustine, *De spiritu et littera* 53, *APW* 1:213.

20. Augustine, *De civitate Dei* 13.14; 14.15, *City of God,* 422–23, 462–63, *De gratia Christi et de peccato originali* 2.14, *APW* 2:58; *Sermones* 181.1–3.

21. Augustine, *De praedestinatione sanctorum* 5.10, *APW* 3:133; *Enchiridion* 26.100, *Enchiridion,* trans. A. C. Outler (London, 1955): 399.

10: Power

1. Hippolytus, *In Danielem* 4.5, *Commentaire sur Daniel,* ed. G. Bardy, trans. M. Lefèvre (Paris, 1947): 169–70; Barnabas, *Epistle* 15.4–5, *ANF* 1:146; D. Potter, *Prophets and Emperors: Human and Divine Authority from Augustus to Theodosius* (Cambridge, Mass., 1994): 106–9.

2. Athanasius, *Apologia ad Constantium* 33, *NPNF2* 4:252; Augustine, *De civitate Dei* 10.1, *City of God,* 305.

3. Council of Constantinople, Canon 3, J. Stevenson, ed., *Creeds, Councils, and Controversies: Documents Illustrative of the History of the Church A.D. 337–461* (London, 1966): 148.

4. Theodore, *On the Incarnation* 8; K. McNamara, "Theodore of Mopsuestia and the Nestorian Heresy," *Irish Theological Quarterly* 19 (1952): 254–78; 20 (1953): 172–91.

5. Cyril of Alexandria, *Epistolae* 4; 17.2, *Letters,* 2 vols., trans. J. I. McEnerney (Washington, D.C., 1987): 1:41, 90–92.

6. E. H. Blakeney, *The Tome of Pope Leo the Great* (London, 1923).

7. *Codex Theodosius* 16.1.2, *The Theodosian Code and Novels and the Sirmondian Constitutions,* trans. C. Pharr (Princeton, 1952): 448.

8. Tertullian, *Adversus Marcionem* 4.34, *Tertullian Adversus Marcionem,* 2 vols., ed. and trans. E. Evans (Oxford, 1972): 456–57; *De anima* 33; *Apologeticum* 49.

9. Origen, *Origen on First Principles,* trans. G. W. Butterworth (London, 1936); *Contra Celsum,* trans. H. Chadwick (Cambridge, 1953); H. Crouzel, *Origen,* trans. A. S. Worrall (San Francisco, 1989): 235–66.

10. M. Himmelfarb, *Tours of Hell: An Apocalyptic Form in Jewish and Christian Literature* (Philadelphia, 1983): 106–26, 68–105.

11. Tertullian, *De corona* 3–4, *Tertullian: Disciplinary, Moral, and Ascetical Works,* trans. E. A. Quain (Washington, D.C., 1959): 236–38.

12. Cyprian, *Epistolae* 51.20, *ANF* 8:144–45.

13. Lactantius, *Institutiones* 7.21, *The Divine Institutes,* trans. M. F. McDonald (Washington, D.C., 1964): 525; Ambrose, *In Psalmum* 118, sermo 20.

14. Augustine, *Enarrationes in Psalmum* 38.2–3, *NPNF1* 8:103.

15. Justin, *Dialogus cum Tryphone* 80, *ANF* 1:239; Hippolytus, *In Danielem* 4.5.

16. Irenaeus, *Adversus haereses* 5.35.1–2, *ANF* 1:565–66.

17. Augustine, *Confessiones* 10.40, *The Confessions of St. Augustine,* trans. R. Warner (New York, 1963): 252–53.

18. Aristotle, *Politics* 1253a9–12; *The Politics,* trans. H. Rackham (London, 1932).

19. Irenaeus, *Adversus haereses* 4.20.6, *ANF* 1:489; Augustine, *De civitate Dei* 22.30, *The City of God,* trans. M. Dods (New York, 1950): 867.

20. Cyprian, *On Mortality* 26, *ANF* 8:468.

21. Augustine, *De civitate Dei* 10.1, *City of God,* 305; Irenaeus, *Adversus haereses* 5.0, *ANF* 1:526; Athanasius, *De incarnatione Verbi Dei* 54.3, *NPNF2* 4:65.

11: Christendom

1. Sebeos, *History* 30, Sebeos, *Sebeos' History,* trans. R. Bedrosian (New York, 1985).

2. P. Brown, *The Rise of Western Christendom: Triumph and Diversity A.D. 200–1000* (Oxford, 1996): 216–32.

3. J. Meyendorff, *The Byzantine Legacy in the Orthodox Church* (Crestwood, N.Y., 1982): 48.

4. Gregory I, *Homilies on Ezechiel* 2.2.7–8, *The Homilies of Saint Gregory the Great on the Book of the Prophet Ezekiel,* ed. P. J. Cownie, trans. T. Gray (Etna, Calif., 1990): 174; *Cura pastoralis* 1.1, *Pastoral Care,* trans. H. Davis (Westminster, Md., 1950): 21.

5. Bede, *Historia Ecclesiastica* 1.32, Bede, *A History of the English Church and People,* trans. L. Sherley-Price, rev. ed. R. E. Latham (Harmondsworth, 1968): 90; Gregory I, *Epistolae* 11.66, *NPNF2* 13:82.

6. A. Gurevich, *Medieval Popular Culture: Problems of Belief and Perception* (Cambridge, 1988): 71–73.

7. Bede, *Historia Ecclesiastica* 1.32, 30, Bede, *History of the English Church,* 89, 86–87.

8. Boniface, *Epistolae* 16 [24], *The Letters of Saint Boniface,* trans. E. Emerton (Cambridge, 1940): 51; Willibald, *Life of Boniface* 7, T. F. X. Noble and T. Head, eds., *Soldiers of Christ: Saints and Saints' Lives from Late Antiquity to the Middle Ages* (University Park, Penn., 1995): 126–27; C. H. Talbot, *Anglo-Saxon Missionaries in Germany* (London, 1954): 45–46.

9. Boniface, *Epistolae* 47 [59], *Letters,* 101–4.

10. Boniface, *Epistolae* 40 [50], *Letters,* 82.

11. J. T. McNeill and H. A. Gamer, eds. and trans., *Medieval Handbooks of Penance* (New York, 1990): 419–21.

12. H. R. Loyn and J. Percival, *The Reign of Charlemagne: Documents on Carolingian Government and Administration* (New York, 1975): 52.

13. *The Message of the Qur'an,* trans. M. Asad (Gibraltar, 1980): 420, 246, 256, 169, 137, 134.

14. John of Damascus, *De Haeresibus* 100; D. J. Sahas, trans., *John of Damascus on Islam* (Leiden, 1972): 133.

15. J. Gil, ed., *Corpus scriptorum muzarabicorum,* 2 vols. (Madrid, 1973): 2:486–87; K. B. Wolf, "The Earliest Spanish Christian Views of Islam," *Church History* 55 (1986): 289–93.

16. A. C. Krey, ed., *The First Crusade: The Accounts of Eye-Witnesses and Participants* (Princeton, 1921): 30–32.

12: Hierarchy

1. Dionysius, *Pseudo-Dionysius: The Complete Works,* trans. C. Luibheid and P. Rorem (New York, 1987): 143–91; P. Rorem, *Pseudo-Dionysius: A Commentary on the Texts and an Introduction to Their Influence* (Oxford, 1993): 47–90.

2. G. Duby, *The Three Orders: Feudal Society Imagined* (Chicago, 1980): 102–5.

3. Benedict, *The Rule of St. Benedict,* trans. A. C. Meisel and M. L. del Mastro (New York, 1975): 54–55; D. Knowles, *Christian Monasticism* (New York, 1969): 212–13; C. Butler, *Benedictine Monachism,* 2d ed. (Cambridge, 1961): 275–88; M. Rouche, "The Early Middle Ages in the West," in P. Veyne, ed., *A History of Private Life: From Pagan Rome to Byzantium,* trans. A. Goldhammer (Cambridge, Mass., 1987): 445–46.

4. R. Brown, *Our Lady and Saint Francis* (Chicago, 1954): 24.

5. G. Dix, *The Shape of the Liturgy* (London, 1945); O. B. Hardison, *Christian Rite and Christian Drama in the Middle Ages* (Baltimore, 1965); H. Wegman, *Christian Worship in East and West: A Study Guide to Liturgical History* (New York, 1985).

6. Sulpicius Severus, *Vita S. Martini Episcopi* 4, T. F. X. Noble and T. Head, eds., *Soldiers of Christ: Saints and Saints' Lives from Late Antiquity to the Middle Ages* (University Park, Penn., 1995): 8; J. A. Aho, *Religious Mythology and the Art of War: Comparative Religious Symbolisms of Military Violence* (London, 1981): 81; R. Gerberding, *The Rise of the Carolingians and the "Liber Historiae Francorum"* (Oxford, 1987): 160–61; Gregory of Tours, *Historia* 2.37, *History*, trans. L. Thorpe (Harmondsworth, 1974): 152.

7. G. D. Mansi, ed., *Sacrorum concilorum nova et amplissima collectio*, 53 vols. (Florence, Venice, and Paris, 1759–1927): 19:530; S. D. Sargent, "Religious Responses to Social Violence in Eleventh-Century Aquitaine," *Historical Reflections* 12, 2 (1985): 224.

8. R. Barber, *The Knight and Chivalry* (New York, 1970): 26.

9. H. E. J. Cowdrey, "The Genesis of the Crusades: The Springs of Western Ideas of Holy War," in T. P. Murphy, ed., *The Holy War* (Columbus, Ohio, 1976): 23.

10. Bernard of Clairvaux, *In laude novae militiae* 3.1, "In Praise of the New Knighthood," trans. C. Greenia, *The Works of Bernard of Clairvaux*, vol. 7 (Kalamazoo, Mich., 1977), 134; R. Laffont, *The Ancient Art of Warfare*, 2 vols. (Paris, 1974): 1:356.

11. A. Gurevich, *Medieval Popular Culture: Problems of Belief and Perception* (Cambridge, 1988): 154–55.

12. L. White, Jr., "The Life of the Silent Majority," in R. S. Hoyt, ed., *Life and Thought in the Early Middle Ages* (Minneapolis, 1967): 85–100.

13. T. N. Tentler, *Sin and Confession on the Eve of the Reformation* (Princeton, 1977): xix.

14. D. S. Bailey, *Sexual Relations in Christian Thought* (New York, 1959): 133–34.

15. J. Le Goff, *Time, Work, and Culture in the Middle Ages*, trans. A. Goldhammer (Chicago, 1980): 114–15.

16. C. H. Lawrence, *Medieval Monasticism* (London, 1984): 162; Walter Map, *Master Walter Map's Book, De nugis curialium (Courtiers' Trifles)*, trans. F. Tupper and M. B. Ogle (London, 1924): 56–60.

13: Objects

1. A. J. Andrea and P. I. Rachlin, "Holy War, Holy Relics, Holy Theft: The Anonymous of Soisson's *De terra Iherosolimitana*: An Analysis, Edition, and Translation," *Historical Reflections* 18, 1 (1992): 147–75.

2. Dionysius the Areopagite, *Letter* 10, Dionysius, *Pseudo-Dionysius: The Complete Works*, trans. C. Luibheid and P. Rorem (New York, 1987): 289.

3. Bishop Kallistos of Diokleia, "The Meaning of the Divine Liturgy for the Byzantine Worshipper," in R. Morris, ed., *Church and People in Byzantium* (Birmingham, 1990): 8–11.

4. C. Chazelle, "Matter, Spirit, and Image in the *Libri Carolini*," *Recherches Augustiniennes* 21 (1986): 176.

5. B. Ward, *Miracles and the Medieval Mind: Record and Event, 1000–1215* (Philadelphia, 1982): 44.

6. P. J. Geary, *Furta Sacra: Thefts of Relics in the Central Middle Ages* (Princeton, 1978): 71; P. Sheingorn, ed. and trans., *The Book of Sainte Foy* (Philadelphia, 1995).

7. S. Haskins, *Mary Magdalen: Myth and Metaphor* (New York, 1993): 113–33.

8. Geary, *Furta Sacra*, 115–27; M. Ebon, *Saint Nicholas: Life and Legend* (New York, 1975); C. W. Jones, *Saint Nicolas of Myra, Bari, and Manhattan: Biography of a Legend* (Chicago, 1978).

9. John of Damascus, *Against Those Who Attack the Divine Images* 1.21, *On the Divine Images*, trans. D. Anderson (Crestwood, N.Y., 1980): 29; Nikephoros, *Antirrheticus* 2.353, J. Travis, *In Defense of the Faith: The Theology of Patriarch Nikephoros of Constantinople* (Brookline, Mass., 1984): 32.

10. S. H. Griffith, "Theodore abu Qurrah's Arabic Text on the Christian Practice of Venerating Images," *Journal of the American Oriental Society* 105 (1985): 53–73.

11. John of Damascus, *Against Those Who Attack the Divine Images* 1.8, *On the Divine Images*, 18; D. J. Sahas, *Icon and Logos: Sources in Eighth-Century Iconoclasm* (Toronto, 1986): 161.

12. C. Mango, *The Art of the Byzantine Empire* (Englewood Cliffs, N.J., 1972): 166.

13. N. H. Baynes, "The Icons Before Iconoclasm," *Harvard Theological Review* 44 (1951): 93–106; N. Gendle, "Leontius of Neapolis: A Seventh-Century Defender of Holy Images," *Studia Patristica* 18 (1985): 135–39.

14. Nikephoros, *Antirrheticus* 3.381–84, Travis, *In Defense of the Faith*, 48; Photius, *Homilies* 17.5–6, *The Homilies of Photius Patriarch of Constantinople*, trans. C. Mango (Cambridge, Mass., 1958): 294–95.

15. R. Davidsohn, *Geschichte von Florenz* (Berlin, 1927): IV.3:214; H. Belting, *The Image and the Public in the Middle Ages: Form and Function of Early Paintings of the Passion*, trans. M. Bartusis and R. Meyer (New Rochelle, N.Y., 1981): 22; E. Panofsky, ed. and trans., *Abbot Suger on the Abbey Church of St.-Denis and Its Art Treasures*, 2d ed. (Princeton, 1979): 49.

16. Lanfranc, *De corpore et sanguine Domine* 2, J. Pelikan, *A History of Christian Doctrine, Vol. 3: The Growth of Medieval Theology, 600–1300* (Chicago, 1978): 198.

17. Hugh of St. Victor, *Speculum de mysteriis ecclesiae, PL* 177:362; Hildegard of Bingen, *Epistolae 47, PL* 197:232; Ward, *Miracles and the Medieval Mind,* 14.

18. Caesarius of Heisterbach, *Dialogus miraculorum* 9.5, *The Dialogue on Miracles,* 2 vols., trans. E. Scott and C. C. S. Bland (London, 1929): 2:170; Adam of Eynsham, *Magna Vita S. Hugonis,* 2 vols., ed. and trans. D. L. Douie and H. Farmer (London, 1961–62): 2:92–94; 2:169–70.

19. C. W. Bynum, *Holy Feast and Holy Fast: The Religious Significance of Food to Medieval Women* (Berkeley, 1987): 133; Mechthild of Magdeburg, *The Revelations of Mechthild of Magdeburg (1210–1297) or the Flowing Light of the Godhead,* trans. L. Menzies (London, 1953): 48; Hadewijch of Antwerp, *Hadewijch: The Complete Works,* trans. C. Hart (New York, 1980): 353.

20. Peter the Venerable, *Adversus Iudeorum* 3.2.564–70, *Peter Venerabilis adversus Iudeorum inveteratam duritiem,* ed. Y. Friedman (Turnhout, 1958): 57–58.

21. J. Cohen, "The Jews as the Killers of Christ in the Latin Tradition, from Augustine to the Friars," *Traditio* 39 (1983): 1–27; G. I. Langmuir, *Toward a Definition of Anti-Semitism* (Berkeley, 1990): 300–301; L. Rothkrug, "Holy Shrines, Religious Dissonance, and Satan in the Origins of the German Reformation," *Historical Reflections* 14, 2 (1987): 161; D. J. Hall, *English Medieval Pilgrimage* (London, 1966): 13.

22. J. Sumption, *Pilgrimage: An Image of Medieval Religion* (Totowa, N.J., 1976): 235.

14: Scholars

1. M. Carruthers, *The Book of Memory: A Study of Memory in Medieval Culture* (Cambridge, 1990): 164; J. Leclercq, *The Love of Learning and the Desire for God,* trans. C. Misrahi (New York, 1961): 73.

2. Guibert of Nogent, *Liber quo ordine sermo fieri debeat,* trans. J. M. Miller, in J. M. Miller, H. Prosser, and T. W. Benson, eds., *Readings in Medieval Rhetoric* (Bloomington, 1973): 170–71.

3. Dionysius the Areopagite, *Letter 9.1, Pseudo-Dionysius: The Complete Works,* trans. C. Luibheid and P. Rorem (New York, 1987): 283.

4. Anselm, *Proslogion,* Preface; *Monologion* 1–4; *Proslogion* 2–5; *St. Anselm: Basic Writings,* trans. S. N. Deane (La Salle, Ill., 1962): 2, 35–45, 7–11.

5. Anselm, *Cur Deus Homo, Basic Writings,* 171–288.

6. Anselm, *Monologion 42, Basic Writings,* 104–6.

7. Peter Abélard, *The Story of My Misfortunes,* trans. H. A. Bellows (London, 1922): 5.

8. Bernard of Clairvaux, *Epistolae* 241, *The Letters of St. Bernard of Clairvaux*, trans. B. S. James (London, 1953): 321.

9. Albert, *Libros sententiarum* 3.d.12, a.10; Aristotle, *De generatione animalium* 737a25–30, *Aristotle's De Partibus Animalium I and De Generatione Animalium I*, trans. D. M. Balme (Oxford, 1972): 64–65; J. Gibson, "Could Christ Have Been Born a Woman? A Medieval Debate," *Journal of Feminist Studies in Religion* 8, 1 (1992): 71–72.

10. Thomas Aquinas, *Summa Theologiae* 1A.2.3; Aristotle, *Metaphysics* 2.1.993b30; Augustine, *Enchiridion* 11; *Summa Theologiae: Existence and Nature of God (1a.2–11)*, trans. T. McDermott (London, 1964): 13–17.

11. Thomas Aquinas, *Summa Theologiae* 1A.1.9; Dionysius, *Letter* 9.1; *Celestial Hierarchy* 1.2; *Summa Theologiae: Christian Theology (1a.1)*, trans. T. Gilby (London, 1964): 33.

12. Giovanni Boccaccio, *The Life of Dante (Trattatello in Laude di Dante)*, trans. V. Z. Bollettino (New York, 1990): 41.

13. Dante Alighieri, *The Divine Comedy*, 3 vols., trans. C. S. Singleton (Princeton, 1970–75); *Convivio* 4.2, trans. P. H. Wicksteed (London, 1924): 236; Virgil, *The Aeneid*, trans. P. Dickinson (New York, 1961): 141.

14. P. H. Wicksteed and E. G. Gardner, *Dante and Giovanni del Virgilio* (London, 1902): 175; Pietro Alighieri, *Super Dantis ipsius genitoris Comoediam commentarium*, ed. V. Nannucci and G. J. Bar. Vernon (Florence, 1845): 3; J. P. Bowden, *An Analysis of Pietro Alighieri's Commentary on The Divine Comedy* (New York, 1951).

15: Mystics

1. Columbanus, *Instructiones* 9, J. Le Goff, *The Birth of Purgatory*, trans. A. Goldhammer (Chicago, 1981): 100.

2. Dionysius the Areopagite, *Mystical Theology* 1.1, *Pseudo-Dionysius: The Complete Works*, trans. C. Luibheid and P. Rorem (New York, 1987): 135.

3. Bernard of Clairvaux, *Sermo super cantica canticorum* 3.5; 4.4; 73.10; 83.6; 64.10; 9.2; 52.2–6, Bernard of Clairvaux, *On the Song of Songs*, 4 vols., trans. K. J. Walsh and I. M. Edmonds (Kalamazoo, Mich., 1971–80): 1:20, 1:23, 4:82, 4:186, 3:177, 1:54, 3:50–54; *De diligendo Dei* 10, Bernard of Clairvaux, *On Loving God*, ed. H. Martin, trans. W. H. van Allen (London, 1959): 48; R. C. Petry, ed., *Late Medieval Mysticism* (Philadelphia, 1957): 64.

4. Hugh of St. Victor, *Commentariorum in Hierarchiam coelestem S. Dionysii Areopagitae*, PL 175; *In Salomonis Ecclesiasten* 1; *De arca Noe mystica* 9;

Miscellanea 173; P. Rorem, *Pseudo-Dionysius: A Commentary on the Texts and an Introduction to Their Influence* (Oxford, 1993): 217; B. McGinn, *The Presence of God: A History of Western Christian Mysticism*, 4 vols. (New York, 1994): 2:375, 383, 392.

5. Bonaventure, *The Works of Bonaventure*, 5 vols., trans. J. de Vinck (Paterson, N.J., 1960–70).

6. Hildegard of Bingen, *Epistolae* 1, *Secrets of God: Writings of Hildegard of Bingen*, ed. and trans. S. Flanagan (Boston, 1996): 154; *Scivias*, trans. C. Hart and J. Bishop (New York, 1990): 525; Z. Brunn and G. Epiney-Burgard, *Women Mystics in Medieval Europe*, trans. S. Hughes (New York, 1989): 19, 35.

7. Symeon the New Theologian, *Hymn* 27.128–29; *Catechesis* 22; K. Ware, "The Eastern Tradition from the Tenth to the Twentieth Century," in C. Jones, G. Wainwright, and E. Yarnold, eds., *The Study of Spirituality* (Oxford, 1986): 238–40; *Symeon the New Theologian: The Discourses*, ed. G. Maloney, trans. C. J. de Catanzaro (London, 1980): 245–46.

8. K. Ware, "The Hesychasts: Gregory of Sinai, Gregory Palamas, Nicolas Cabasilas," in Jones et al., eds., *The Study of Spirituality*, 244–45; E. Kadloubovsky and G. E. H. Palmer, *Writings from the Philokalia on the Prayer of the Heart* (London, 1951).

9. Gregory Palamas, *Triads* 1.3.8; 3.1.33; 1.3.18; 2.3.31; 1.2.10; 1.2.37; *Triads in Defense of the Holy Hesychasts*, ed. J. Meyendorff, trans. N. Gendle (New York, 1983).

10. Hadewijch of Antwerp, *Vision 7, The Complete Works*, trans. C. Hart (New York, 1980): 280–82.

11. Mechthild of Magdeburg, *Das Fliessende Licht der Gottheit* 17, *The Revelations of Mechthild of Magdeburg or the Flowing Light of the Godhead*, trans. L. Menzies (London, 1953): 11.

12. C. W. Bynum, *Holy Feast and Holy Fast: The Religious Significance of Food to Medieval Women* (Berkeley, 1987): 247.

13. Rupert von Deutz, *De gloria et honore filii hominis super Mattheum*, ed. H. Haacke (Turnhout, 1979): 383; J. G. Milhaven, "A Medieval Lesson on Bodily Knowing: Women's Experience and Men's Thought," *Journal of the American Academy of Religion* 57 (1989): 344.

14. Hadewijch of Antwerp, *Vision* 13.179; *Letter* 8.27; *Letter* 22.169; *Poems in Couplets* 16.158–61; *Complete Works*, 300, 65, 98, 356.

15. Brunn and Epiney-Burgard, *Women Mystics*, 60; Mechthild of Magdeburg, *The Revelations*, 17–18.

16. Marguerite Porete, *The Mirror of Simple Souls*, trans. E. L. Babinsky (New York, 1993): 79, 193, 102, 160.

17. Meister Eckhart, *The Essential Sermons, Commentaries, Treatises, and Defense,* trans. E. College and B. McGinn (New York, 1981): 200, 192, 203.

16: Heretics

1. J.-C. Schmitt, *The Holy Greyhound: Guinefort, Healer of Children Since the Thirteenth Century,* trans. M. Thom (Cambridge, 1983).

2. Thomas Aquinas, *Summa Theologiae* 2a–2ae.92–99; *Summa Theologiae: Superstition and Irreverence (2a2ae),* trans. T. F. O'Meara and M. J. Duffy (London, 1968): 3–127.

3. Ralph Glaber, *Raoul Glaber: Les cinq livres de ses histoires,* ed. M. Prou (Paris, 1866): 49–50; M. Lambert, *Medieval Heresy: Popular Movements from the Gregorian Reform to the Reformation,* 2d ed. (Oxford, 1992): 29; R. I. Moore, *The Origins of European Dissent* (London, 1977): 23–24, 35–36; W. L. Wakefield and A. P. Evans, eds., *Heresies of the High Middle Ages: Selected Sources Translated and Annotated* (New York, 1969): 72–73.

4. H. E. J. Cowdrey, ed. and trans., *Epistolae vagantes of Gregory VII* (Oxford, 1972): 14; Moore, *Origins of European Dissent,* 55.

5. Peter Damian, *Contra clericos regulares proprietarios* 6; B. H. Rosenwein and L. K. Little, "Social Meaning in the Monastic and Mendicant Spiritualities," *Past and Present* 63 (1974): 18.

6. A. L. de la Marche, ed., *Anecdotes historiques, légendes et apologues tirées du recueil inédit d'Etienne de Bourbon, dominicain du XIIIe siècle* (Paris, 1887): 290–92; Wakefield and Evans, *Heresies of the High Middle Ages,* 209.

7. O. Hageneder, W. Maleczek, and A. A. Strnad, eds., *Die Register Innocenz' III 2: Pontifikatsjahr, 1199/1200* (Rome, 1979): 272, 271–76, 432–34; M. Deanesly, *The Lollard Bible* (Cambridge, 1920): 31–33; Lambert, *Medieval Heresy,* 73.

8. *Celano* 2.107; 2.61; 1.52; Thomas of Celano, *Saint Francis of Assisi,* trans. P. Hermann (Chicago, 1968): 225, 189, 49; L. Lemmens, *Testimonia Minora s.xiii de S. Francisco Assisi* (Quaracchi, 1926): 93–94.

9. *Legenda sancti Dominici* 1, Peter Ferrand, *Legenda sancti Dominici,* ed. M.-H. Laurant (Rome, 1935): 248.

10. Marche, *Anecdotes historiques,* 301–2; Bernard Gui, *Practica inquisitionis heretice pravitatis,* ed. C. Douais (Paris, 1886): 5.1.1; D. M. Bazell, "Strife Among the Table-Fellows: Conflicting Attitudes of Early and Medieval Christians Toward the Eating of Meat," *Journal of the American Academy of Religion* 65 (1997): 73–99.

11. Marche, *Anecdotes historiques,* 319–25; H. C. Lea, *Materials Toward a History of Witchcraft,* 3 vols., ed. A. Howland (Philadelphia, 1939; reprint: New York, 1957): 1:174; J. B. Russell, *Witchcraft in the Middle Ages* (Ithaca, N.Y., 1972): 156–57.

12. Henrich Kramer and Jacob Sprenger, *Malleus Maleficarum,* trans. M. Summers (New York, 1971): 75, 1, 41–47, 170, 231, 205, 222–23, 231, 214, 275; Thomas Aquinas, *Summa Theologiae* 1a2ae.80.4, *Summa Theologiae: Sin (1a2ae. 71–80),* trans. J. Fearon (London, 1969): 229–31.

13. H. C. E. Midelfort, "Witchcraft, Magic, and the Occult," in S. Ozment, ed., *Reformation Europe: A Guide to Research* (St. Louis, 1982): 191; L. Rothkrug, "Holy Shrines, Religious Dissonance, and Satan in the Origins of the German Reformation," *Historical Reflections* 14, 2 (1987): 249.

17: Mary

1. B. R. Gaventa, *Mary: Glimpses of the Mother of Jesus* (Columbia, S.C., 1995); M. Warner, *Alone of All Her Sex: The Myth and Cult of the Virgin Mary* (London, 1976); E. Wilkins, *The Rose-Garden Game: The Symbolic Background to the European Prayer-Beads* (London, 1969); A. Winston-Allen, *Stories of the Rose: The Making of the Rosary in the Middle Ages* (Philadelphia, 1997).

2. Bernard of Clairvaux and Amadeus of Lausanne, *De laudibus beatae Mariae* 2, *Magnificat: Homilies in Praise of the Blessed Virgin Mary,* trans. M.-B. Saïd and G. Perigo (Kalamazoo, Mich., 1979): 30–31.

3. M. Clayton, "Feasts of the Virgin in the Liturgy of the Anglo-Saxon Church," *Anglo-Saxon England* 13 (1984): 226.

4. O. Cullman, "The Protevangelium of James," in E. Hennecke and W. Schneemelcher, eds., *New Testament Apocrypha,* 2 vols., trans. R. M. Wilson (Philadelphia, 1963); 1:370–88.

5. K. Ashley and P. Sheingorn, "Introduction," in Ashley and Sheingorn, eds., *Interpreting Cultural Symbols: Saint Anne in Late Medieval Society* (Athens, Ga., 1990): 1–68.

6. E. Mâle, *Religious Art in France: The Thirteenth Century,* ed. H. Bober, trans. M. Matthews (Princeton, 1984): 317; T. Brandenbarg, "St. Anne and Her Family: The Veneration of St. Anne in Connection with Concepts of Marriage and the Family in the Early Modern Period," in L. Dresen-Coenders, ed., *Saints and She-Devils: Images of Women in the Fifteenth and Sixteenth Centuries* (London, 1987): 102–3.

7. Anselm, *Cur Deus Homo* 2.16, *St. Anselm: Basic Writings,* trans. S. N. Deane (La Salle, Ill., 1962): 265; M. Levi D'Ancona, *The Iconography of the Immaculate Conception in the Middle Ages and Early Renaissance* (New York, 1957): 9.

8. Bridget of Sweden, *The Revelations of Saint Birgitta,* ed. and trans. W. P. Cumming (London, 1929); *"Liber celestis" of St. Bridget of Sweden,* ed. R. Ellis (Oxford, 1987): 467; *Revelations and Prayers of St. Bridget of Sweden,* trans. E. Graf (London, 1928): 30–31; H. Cornell, *The Iconography of the Nativity of Christ* (Uppsala, 1924): 12–13.

9. K. Ashley, "Image and Ideology: Saint Anne in Late Medieval Drama and Narrative," in Ashley and Sheingorn, eds., *Interpreting Cultural Symbols,* 119; Ashley and Sheingorn, "Introduction," 35.

10. Brandenbarg, "St. Anne and Her Family," 124; J. Bossy, *Christianity in the West, 1400–1700* (Oxford, 1985): 10–11; C. Hahn, "'Joseph Will Perfect, Mary Enlighten, and Jesus Save Thee': The Holy Family as Marriage Model in the Mérode Triptych," *Art Bulletin* 68 (1986): 54–66; P. Sheingorn, "Appropriating the Holy Kinship: Gender and Family History," in Ashley and Sheingorn, *Interpreting Cultural Symbols,* 193.

11. *Celano* 1.84, Thomas of Celano, *Saint Francis of Assisi,* trans. P. Hermann (Chicago, 1968): 75–76.

12. Leo Steinberg, *The Sexuality of Christ in Renaissance Art and Modern Oblivion,* 2d ed. (Chicago, 1996); C. W. Bynum, *Holy Feast and Holy Fast: The Religious Significance of Food to Medieval Women* (Berkeley, 1987): 246; *Fragmentation and Redemption: Essays on Gender and the Human Body in Medieval Religion* (New York, 1992): 79–117.

13. *Meditationes vitae Christi* 78, I. Ragusa and R. B. Green, eds., *Meditations on the Life of Our Lord,* trans. I. Ragusa (Princeton, 1961).

14. F. Brittain, ed., *The Penguin Book of Latin Verse* (London, 1962): 246–49.

15. B. Poschmann, *Penance and the Anointing of the Sick* (Harmondsworth, Middlesex, 1964): 157–58; T. N. Tentler, *Sin and Confession on the Eve of the Reformation* (Princeton, 1977): 16.

16. Heinrich Suso, *Deutsche Schriften,* ed. K. Bihlmeyer (Stuttgart, 1907): 43; N. Cohn, *The Pursuit of the Millennium: Revolutionary Messianism in Medieval and Reformation Europe and Its Bearing on Modern Totalitarian Movements* (New York, 1961): 124.

17. G. Deaux, *The Black Death 1347* (New York, 1969): 92–94; C. Baronius and O. Raynaldus, *Annales ecclesiastici una cum critica historico-chronologica* (Lucca, 1738–59): 25:471; Cohn, *Pursuit of the Millennium,* 139; L. Rothkrug,

"Holy Shrines, Religious Dissonance, and Satan in the Origins of the German Reformation," *Historical Reflections* 14, 2 (1987): 161.

18. R. C. Trexler, *The Journey of the Magi: Meanings in History of a Christian Story* (Princeton, 1997): 46.

19. A. Athanassakis, ed. and trans., *The Orphic Hymns* (Missoula, Mont., 1977): 27.

20. V. Limberis, *Divine Heiress: The Virgin Mary and the Creation of Christian Constantinople* (London, 1994): 158, 129–30.

21. Epiphanius, *Panarion* 78:13–17, Epiphanius, *The Panarion of St. Epiphanius, Selected Passages*, trans. P. R. Amidon (Oxford, 1990): 350–54.

22. Anselm, *De conceptu virginali* 18, *Why God Became Man, and the Virgin Conception and Original Sin*, trans. J. M. Colleran (Albany, N.Y., 1969): 194; *Prayers and Meditations of Saint Anselm*, trans. B. Ward (New York, 1973): 112.

23. H. C. Graef, *Mary: A History of Doctrine and Devotion*, 2 vols. (New York, 1963–65): 1:281–90; E. A. Johnson, "Marian Devotion in the Western Church," in J. Raitt, ed., *Christian Spirituality: High Middle Ages and Reformation* (New York and London, 1988): 402–3, 404.

18: Renaissance

1. Marsilio Ficino, *Opera Omnia* (Basel, 1576; reprint: Turin, 1962): 805, 807, 1217; E. H. Gombrich, "Botticelli's Mythologies: A Study in the Neo-Platonic Symbolism of His Circle," *Symbolic Images: Studies in the Art of the Renaissance II* (London, 1972): 41–42, 45, 73.

2. Francesco Petrarca, "The Ascent of Mount Ventoux," in E. Cassirer, P. O. Kristeller, and J. H. Randall, Jr., eds., *The Renaissance Philosophy of Man* (Chicago, 1948): 39, 44; Augustine, *Confessiones* 10.8.15; Seneca, *Epistles* 8.5, *Seneca: Ad Lucilium Epistulae Morales*, vol. 1, trans. R. M. Grummere (London, 1917): 37–40.

3. A. Athanassakis, ed. and trans., *The Orphic Hymns* (Missoula, Mont., 1977); B. P. Copenhauer, ed., *Hermetica: The Greek Corpus Hermeticum and the Latin Asclepius in a New English Translation* (Cambridge, 1996); R. Majercik, ed. and trans., *The Chaldean Oracles: Text, Translation, and Commentary* (Leiden, 1989); I. Merkel and A. G. Debus, eds., *Hermeticism and the Renaissance: Intellectual History and the Occult in Early Modern Europe* (Washington, D.C., 1988); D. P. Walker, *The Ancient Theology: Studies in Christian Platonism from the Fifteenth to the Eighteenth Century* (London, 1972); F. A. Yates, *Giordano Bruno and the Hermetic Tradition* (Chicago, 1964).

4. Giovanni Pico della Mirandola, *Opera Omnia* (Basel, 1572): 107–8; "Oration on the Dignity of Man," in Cassirer et al., eds., *The Renaissance Philosophy of Man*, 223, 225; *Conclusiones sive theses DCCCC*, ed. B. Kieszkowski (Geneva, 1973).

5. E. R. Harvey, *The Inward Wits: Psychological Theory in the Middle Ages and Renaissance* (London, 1975): 39–46; E. Kessler, "The Intellective Soul," in C. B. Schmitt, Q. Skinner, E. Kessler, and J. Kraye, eds., *The Cambridge History of Renaissance Philosophy* (Cambridge, 1988): 485–534.

6. Marsilio Ficino, *Commentary on the Symposium 6.6, Commentary on Plato's Symposium on Love*, trans. S. Jayne, 2d ed. (Dallas, 1985): 114–15; *De vita triplici* 3.21, *Apologia, The Book of Life*, trans. C. Boer (Irving, Tex., 1980): 162–63, 186.

7. Girolamo Savonarola, *Prediche sopra Giobbe*, 2 vols., ed. R. Ridolfi (Rome, 1957): 2:135, 1:203; R. M. Steinberg, *Fra Girolamo Savonarola, Florentine Art, and Renaissance Historiography* (Athens, Ohio, 1977): 75–76.

8. B. McGinn, *The Calabrian Abbot: Joachim of Fiore in the History of Western Thought* (New York, 1985); M. Reeves, *The Influence of Prophecy in the Later Middle Ages: A Study in Joachimism* (Oxford, 1969).

9. Savonarola, *Prediche sopra Giobbe*, 1:405–26; Girolamo Savonarola, *Triumphus Crucis. Testo latino e volgare*, ed. M. Ferrara (Rome, 1961): 293–96, 355ff.; Steinberg, *Fra Girolamo Savonarola*, 47–48, 67.

10. H. Ulmann, *Sandro Botticelli* (Munich, 1893): 148–49.

11. Tommasino Lancellotti, *Cronaca modenese*, 12 vols., ed. C. Borghi (Parma, 1863): 1:440; O. Niccoli, *Prophecy and People in Renaissance Italy*, trans. L. G. Cochrane (Princeton, 1990): 127.

19: Reformation

1. R. H. Bainton, *Here I Stand: A Life of Martin Luther* (Nashville, Tenn., 1950): 30.

2. E. G. Schwiebert, *Luther and His Times: The Reformation from a New Perspective* (St. Louis, 1950): 285–86.

3. Desiderius Erasmus, *The "Enchiridion" of Erasmus*, trans. and ed. R. Himelick (Bloomington, 1963): 51; "*The Praise of Folly" and "Letter to Martin Dorp, 1515,"* trans. B. Radice (New York, 1971): 156–57; *Christian Humanism and the Reformation: Selected Writings of Erasmus*, ed. J. C. Olin (New York, 1965): 59–60; M. M. Phillips, *The "Adages" of Erasmus: A Study with Translations* (Cambridge, 1964): 346; J. H. Bentley, *Humanists and Holy Writ: New Testament Scholarship in the Renaissance* (Princeton, 1983): 65, 186–87.

4. Martin Luther, *Martin Luther: Selections from His Writings*, ed. J. Dillenberger (New York, 1961): 497; *The Reformation Writings of Martin Luther, Volume 1:*

The Basis of the Protestant Reformation, trans. and ed. B. L. Woolf (London, 1953): 32–42.

5. D. V. N. Bagchi, *Luther's Earliest Opponents: Catholic Controversialists 1518–1525* (Minneapolis, 1991): 33–34.

6. Luther, *Selections from His Writings,* 53, 80; *LW* 31:333–77.

7. *LW* 33:67, 65–66.

8. Sebastian Lotzer and Christoph Schappeler, "Twelve Articles of the Peasants," in M. G. Baylor, ed. and trans., *The Radical Reformation* (Cambridge, 1991): 234; Martin Luther, "Friendly Admonition to Peace Concerning the Twelve Articles of the Swabian Peasants," *LW* 46:19, 35, 39, 40; "Against the Robbing and Murdering Hordes of Peasants, May 1525," in E. G. Rupp and B. Drewery, eds., *Martin Luther* (New York, 1970): 125–26.

9. *LW* 19:8; 51:11.

10. *LW* 51:86, 83.

11. Huldrych Zwingli, *Huldreich Zwinglis Sämliche Werke,* 13 vols., ed. E. Rivoire and V. Van Berchem (Geneva, 1900–1940): 2:217, 115–16; trans. Charles Garside, Jr., *Zwingli and the Arts* (New Haven, 1966): 94, 156–57; Huldrych Zwingli, *Commentary on True and False Religion,* ed. S. M. Jackson and C. N. Heller (Durham, N.C., 1981): 320, 330–37.

12. *LW* 38:3–90.

13. John Calvin, *Corpus Reformatorum: Joannis Calvini Opera quae supersunt omnia,* ed. W. Baum, E. Cunitz, and E. Reuss (Brunswick, 1863–80): 9:891; *Institutes,* 2.8.17; 1.12.1; 1.11.9, John Calvin, *Institutes of the Christian Religion,* vol. 1, ed. J. T. McNeill, trans. F. L. Battles (London, 1961): 383, 117, 110; *De fugiendis,* in *Corpus Reformatorum,* 5:250.

14. J. W. O'Malley, *Giles of Viterbo on Church and Reform: A Study in Renaissance Thought* (Leiden, 1968): 113; B. J. Kidd, ed., *Documents Illustrative of the Continental Reformation* (Oxford, 1911): 307.

15. H. J. Schroeder, *The Canons and Decrees of the Council of Trent* (Rockford, Ill., 1978): 34–35; Kidd, ed., *Documents,* 357–58.

16. Ignatius of Loyola, *St. Ignatius' Own Story,* ed. W. J. Young (Chicago, 1956): 9, 58; J. C. Olin, *Catholic Reform from Cardinal Ximenes to the Council of Trent, 1495–1563* (New York, 1990): 83–84, 86; Ignatius of Loyola, *The Spiritual Exercises of St. Ignatius,* trans. A. Mottola (New York, 1964): 47, 53–56.

17. Teresa of Ávila, "Interior Castle," in E. A. Peers, trans., *The Complete Work of St. Teresa of Jesus* (New York, 1946); John of the Cross, *Dark Night of the Soul,* trans. E. A. Peers (New York, 1959).

18. N. Z. Davis, "The Sacred and the Body Social in Sixteenth-Century Lyon," *Past and Present* 90 (1981): 59, 63.

20: Europe

1. Pius II, *Epistola ad Mahomatem II,* ed. and trans. A. R. Baca (New York, 1990); D. Hay, *Europe: The Emergence of an Idea* (Edinburgh, 1957): 84, 87, 79; L. R. Loomis, "Nationality at the Council of Constance," in S. Thrupp, ed., *Change in Medieval Society: Europe North of the Alps, 1050–1500* (London, 1965): 279–96.

2. J. Krasa, ed., *The Travels of Sir John Mandeville,* trans. P. Kussi (New York, 1983): 13; J. W. Bennett, *The Rediscovery of Sir John Mandeville* (New York, 1954): 250.

3. John Mandeville, *The Travels of Sir John Mandeville: The Version of the Cotton Manuscript in Modern Spelling,* ed. A. W. Pollard (London, 1900): 4–5, 92.

4. Mandeville, *Travels,* 54.

5. Mandeville, *Travels,* 92–93.

6. E. D. Ross, "Prester John and the Empire of Ethiopia," in A. P. Newton, ed., *Travellers of the Middle Ages* (London, 1926): 175; Mandeville, *Travels,* 197–98, 179.

7. Mandeville, *Travels,* 114, 206, 195; G. Boas, *Essays on Primitivism and Related Ideas in the Middle Ages* (New York, 1966): 142; Pseudo Ambrose, *The Brahman Episode,* trans. S. V. Yankowski (Ansbach, 1962): 21.

8. Mandeville, *Travels,* 161; John of Plano Carpini, "History of the Mongols," in C. Dawson, ed., *The Mongol Mission* (London, 1955): 22.

9. Mandeville, *Travels,* 206.

10. Mandeville, *Travels,* 207–8, 126, 175–76, 208.

11. J. K. Wright, *The Geographical Lore of the Time of the Crusades* (New York, 1925): 71–72, 261–65.

12. Alexander of Hales, *Summa theologica,* ed. B. Marrani (Florence, 1928): 574; Albert the Great, *De Animalibus,* ed. H. Stadler (Münster, 1920): 1328; J. B. Friedman, *The Monstrous Races in Medieval Art and Thought* (Cambridge, Mass., 1981): 186–87, 192.

13. J. Muldoon, ed., *The Expansion of Europe: The First Phase* (Philadelphia, 1977): 54; *Popes, Lawyers, and Infidels: The Church and the Non-Christian World, 1250–1550* (Liverpool, 1979): 120–21.

14. G. Renault, *The Caravels of Christ,* trans. R. Hill (London, 1959): 167, 169; E. G. Ravenstein, ed. and trans., *A Journal of the Voyage of Vasco da Gama 1497–1499* (London, 1898).

15. Renault, *Caravels of Christ,* 211, 216; M. Pearson, *The Portuguese in India* (Cambridge, 1987).

16. Richard Hooker, *Lawes of Ecclesiastical Politie* (London, 1593): 4.11; P. Harrison, *"Religion" and the Religions in the English Enlightenment* (Cambridge, 1990): 39.

17. *LW* 47:175; 19:55.

18. John Calvin, *Institutes of the Christian Religion,* 2 vols., trans. H. Beveridge (London, 1962): 1:62, 293.

19. S. E. Morison, *Journal and Other Documents on the Life and Voyages of Christopher Columbus* (New York, 1963): 65; Columbus, *The Journal of Christopher Columbus,* ed. and trans. J. Cecil, rev. L-A. Vigneras (London, 1960): 194–200; R. F. Berkhofer, Jr., *The White Man's Indian: Images of the American Indian from Columbus to the Present* (New York, 1978): 6–8; D. Chidester, *Savage Systems: Colonialism and Comparative Religion in Southern Africa* (Charlottesville, 1996): 11–16.

20. Michel de Montaigne, *Complete Works of Montaigne,* trans. D. M. Frame (Stanford, 1958); 152–53.

21. Michel de Montaigne, *Travel Journal,* trans. D. Frame (San Francisco, 1983): 14, 39, 80, 92, 124.

22. Michel de Montaigne, *Essais,* 1.31; 2.30; 3.11; 2.12, *The Essays of Michael Lord of Montaigne,* trans. J. Florio (London, 1891): 99–100, 362, 357, 252–53.

23. C. Ginzburg, *The Cheese and the Worms: The Cosmos of a Sixteenth-Century Miller,* trans. J. Tedeschi and A. Tedeschi (London, 1982): 2–3, 47, 49–50, 5, 51.

21: New World

1. P. M. Watts, "Prophecy and Discovery: On the Spiritual Origins of Christopher Columbus's 'Enterprise of the Indies,'" *American Historical Review* 70 (1985): 73; D. C. West and A. King, trans. and eds., *The Libro de las profecias of Christopher Columbus* (Gainesville, Fla., 1991): 109; O. Dunn and J. E. Kelley, Jr., *The Diario of Christopher Columbus's First Voyage to America 1492–1493* (Norman, Okla., 1989): 143–45, 291; J. B. Thacher, *Christopher Columbus: His Life, His Work* (New York, 1903): 3:652–53.

2. P. Seed, *Ceremonies of Possession in Europe's Conquest of the New World 1492–1640* (Cambridge, 1995): 69.

3. Bernal Diaz del Castillo, *The True History of the Conquest of New Spain,* 5 vols., ed. G. Garcia, trans. A. Maudslay (London, 1908): 2:42–43.

4. R. C. Padden, *The Hummingbird and the Hawk: Conquest and Sovereignty in the Valley of Mexico, 1503–1541* (New York, 1967): 170–73, 186; H. Thomas, *Conquest: Montezuma, Cortés, and the Fall of Old Mexico* (New York, 1993): 301, 328.

5. Juan Ginés de Sepúlveda, *De las justas causas de la guerra contra los indios* (Mexico, 1987): 153, 145.

6. M. P. Carroll, *The Cult of the Virgin Mary: Psychological Origins* (Princeton, 1986): 182–94; J. Lafaye, *Quetzalcóatl and Guadalupe: The Formation of Mexican National Consciousness 1531–1813*, trans. B. Keen (Chicago, 1976): 211–311.

7. R. Adorno, "The Rhetoric of Resistance: The 'Talking' Book of Felipe Guaman Poma," *History of European Ideas* 6 (1985): 452, 458; *Guaman Poma: Writing and Resistance in Colonial Peru* (Austin, Tex., 1986); Huamán Poma, *Letter to a King: A Picture-History of the Inca Civilisation*, ed. and trans. C. Dilke (London, 1978).

8. S. MacCormack, "*Pachacuti*: Miracles, Punishments, and Last Judgment: Visionary Past and Prophetic Future in Early Colonial Peru," *American Historical Review* 93 (1988): 995.

9. R. L. Roys, *The Book of Chilam Balam of Chumayel* (Washington, D.C., 1933): 20, 43.

10. R. V. Bricker, *The Indian Christ, the Indian King: The Historical Substrate of Maya Myth and Ritual* (Austin, Tex., 1981): 55–61, 332 n. 22.

11. J. M. Watanabe, "From Saints to Shibboleths: Image, Structure, and Identity in Maya Religious Symbolism," *American Ethnologist* 17 (1990): 135.

22: Holy Russia

1. D. Strémooukhoff, "Moscow the Third Rome: Sources of the Doctrine," in M. Cherniavsky, ed., *The Structure of Russian History: Interpretive Essays* (New York, 1970): 111, 110, 113.

2. D. Schakovskoy, "The Genesis and Permanence of 'Holy Russia,'" in Y. Hamant, ed., *The Christianization of Ancient Russia: A Millennium, 988–1988* (Paris, 1992): 82–84.

3. D. Obolensky, "Russia's Byzantine Heritage," in Cherniavsky, ed., *Structure of Russian History*, 6, 11; N. Lupinin, *Religious Revolt in the Seventeenth Century: The Schism of the Russian Church* (Princeton, 1984); P. Meyendorff, *Russia, Ritual, and Reform: The Liturgical Reforms of Nikon in the Seventeenth Century*

(Crestwood, N.Y., 1991); W. Palmer, *The Patriarch and the Tsar,* 6 vols. (London, 1871–76).

4. M. Cherniavsky, "The Old Believers and the New Religion," *Slavic Review* 25 (1966): 1–39.

5. M. Khodarkovsky, "'Not by Word Alone': Missionary Policies and Religious Conversion in Early Modern Russia," *Comparative Studies in Society and History* 38 (1996): 272–73.

6. Khodarkovsky, "'Not by Word Alone,'" 278.

7. Y. Slezkine, "Savage Christians or Unorthodox Russians: The Missionary Dilemma in Siberia," in G. Diment and Y. Slezkine, eds., *Between Heaven and Hell: The Myth of Siberia in Russian Culture* (New York, 1991): 15–31.

8. Khodarkovsky, "'Not by Word Alone,'" 289.

9. H. Chevigny, *Russian America: The Great Alaskan Venture, 1741–1867* (New York, 1965): 40.

10. Chevigny, *Russian America,* 200–201; D. Grigorieff, "Metropolitan Innocent: The Prophetic Missionary," *St. Vladimir's Theological Quarterly* 21 (1977): 22; V. Rocheau, "Innocent Veniaminov and the Russian Mission to Alaska, 1820–1840," *St. Vladimir's Theological Quarterly* 15 (1971): 105–20.

11. M. Oleska, ed., *Alaskan Missionary Spirituality* (New York, 1987): 132–35, 346–48.

12. Grigorieff, "Metropolitan Innocent," 23.

13. S. Kan, "Russian Orthodox Brotherhoods Among the Tlingit: Missionary Goals and Native Response," *Ethnohistory* 32, 3 (1985): 196–223; Chevigny, *Russian America,* 204.

14. Grigorieff, "Metropolitan Innocent," 29–30, 35; Oleska, *Alaskan Missionary Spirituality,* 251–52.

23: American Zion

1. R. Michaelsen, "Dirt in the Court Room: Indian Land Claims and American Property Rights," in D. Chidester and E. T. Linenthal, eds., *American Sacred Space* (Bloomington, 1995): 52; John Cotton, *God's Promise to His Plantations* (London, 1630): 4–5; Thomas Harriot, "Brief and True Report of the New Found Land of Virginia," in R. Hakluyt, ed., *Voyages to the Virginia Colonies* (London, 1986): 116.

2. J. Cohen, *"Be Fertile and Increase, Fill the Earth and Master It": The Ancient and Medieval Career of a Biblical Text* (Ithaca, N.Y., 1989): 307–11; P. Seed,

Ceremonies of Possession in Europe's Conquest of the New World 1492–1640 (Cambridge, 1995): 16–40.

3. F. Jennings, *The Founders of America* (New York, 1993): 191; J. Axtell, "The Invasion Within: The Contest of Cultures in Colonial North America," in H. Lamar and L. Thompson, eds., *The Frontier in History: North America and Southern Africa Compared* (New Haven, 1981): 248.

4. S. Bercovitch, *The Puritan Origins of the American Self* (New Haven, 1975): 103–4, 117–19.

5. John Winthrop, "A Modell of Christian Charity (1630)," in P. Miller and T. H. Johnson, eds., *The Puritans: A Sourcebook of Their Writings*, 2 vols. (New York, 1963): 1:198–99; Increase Mather, *The Times of Men* (Boston, 1675): 7.

6. Peter Bulkeley, "The Gospel Covenant: Or the Covenant of Grace Opened (1651)," in *The Annals of America*, vol. 1. (Chicago, 1968): 212.

7. E. S. Morgan, *The Puritan Dilemma: The Story of John Winthrop* (Boston, 1958): 11; John Cotton, "Copy of a Letter from Mr. Cotton to Lord Saye and Seal in the Year 1636," in Miller and Johnson, *The Puritans*, 1:320, 209–10; Winthrop, "A Modell of Christian Charity," 195; Winthrop, *Annals of America*, 169.

8. Nathaniel Ward, "The Simple Cobler of Aggwam (1647)," in Miller and Johnson, *The Puritans*, 1:222.

9. Roger Williams, *Complete Writings*, 7 vols. (New York, 1963): 7:37; Morgan, *Puritan Dilemma*, 117, 152.

10. George Fox, *The Journals of George Fox*, ed. J. L. Nickalls (Cambridge, 1952): 11, 34.

11. K. T. Erikson, *Wayward Puritans: A Study in the Sociology of Deviance* (New York, 1966): 120.

12. L. J. Cappon, ed., *The Adams-Jefferson Letters*, 2 vols. (Chapel Hill, N.C., 1959): 2:560.

13. H. W. Foote, *Thomas Jefferson: Champion of Religious Freedom, Advocate of Christian Morals* (Boston, 1947): 52; D. W. Adams, ed., *Jefferson's Extracts from the Gospels: "The Philosophy of Jesus" and "The Life and Morals of Jesus"* (Princeton, 1983).

14. A. W. Peach, *Selections from the Works of Thomas Paine* (New York, 1928): 232.

15. Charles Louis Montesquieu, *The Spirit of the Laws*, ed. D. W. Carrithers, trans. T. Nugent (Berkeley, 1977): 328; T. L. Hall, *The Religious Background of American Culture* (Boston, 1930): 172; S. K. Padover, ed., *The Complete Jefferson* (New York, 1943): 676.

16. W. W. Sweet, *The American Churches: An Interpretation* (New York, 1945): 46–47.

17. Peter Cartwright, *Autobiography* (New York, 1972): 37–38.

18. A. Koch and W. Peden, ed., *The Life and Selected Writings of Thomas Jefferson* (New York, 1944): 261.

19. G. M. Frederickson, *White Supremacy: A Comparative Study in American and South African History* (Oxford, 1981): 73; F. J. Klinberg, *Anglican Humanitarianism in Colonial New York* (Philadelphia, 1940): 223; J. C. Hurd, *The Law of Freedom and Bondage in the United States*, 2 vols. (New York, 1968): 1:232.

20. A. J. Raboteau, *Slave Religion: The "Invisible Institution" in the Antebellum South* (Oxford, 1978): 162–63; Charles Colcock Jones, *The Religious Instruction of Negroes in the United States* (Savannah, Ga., 1842): 126.

21. A. Bontemps and L. Hughes, *The Book of Negro Folklore* (New York, 1958): 292; T. L. Webber, *Deep Like the Rivers: Education in the Slave Quarter Community, 1831–1865* (New York, 1978): 128; J. Lovell, Jr., *Black Song: The Forge and the Flame* (New York, 1972): 234; J. M. Brewer, *American Negro Folklore* (Chicago, 1968): 149.

22. Raboteau, *Slave Religion*, 92.

23. N. O. Hatch, *The Democratization of American Christianity* (New Haven, 1989): 68, 230–31; J. O'Kelly, *A Vindication of the Author's Apology* (Raleigh, N.C., 1801): 60–61.

24. A. F. Tyler, *Freedom's Ferment: Phases of American Social History from the Colonial Period to the Outbreak of the Civil War* (New York, 1944): 73.

25. T. O'Dea, *The Mormons* (Chicago, 1957): 55.

26. D. L. Morgan, *The Great Salt Lake* (Indianapolis, 1947): 199; J. Bracht, "The Americanization of Adam," in G. W. Trompf, ed., *Cargo Cults and Millenarian Movements: Transoceanic Comparisons of New Religious Movements* (Berlin, 1990): 132.

24: African Prophets

1. P. Seed, *Ceremonies of Possession in Europe's Conquest of the New World 1492–1640* (Cambridge, 1995): 131–33; H. V. Livermore, *A New History of Portugal* (Cambridge, 1967): 129.

2. Hugo Grotius, *De iure praedae commentarius*, trans. G. L. Williams (Oxford, 1950): 242.

3. W. MacGaffey, "Dialogues of the Deaf: Europeans on the Atlantic Coast of Africa," in S. B. Schwartz, ed., *Implicit Understandings: Observing, Reporting,*

and Reflecting on the Encounters Between Europeans and Other Peoples in the Early Modern Era (Cambridge, 1994): 257.

4. R. Gray, *Black Christians and White Missionaries* (New Haven, 1990): 80.

5. D. W. Bebbington, *Evangelicalism in Modern Britain: A History from the 1730s to the 1980s* (London, 1989): 3.

6. J. Campbell, *Travels in South Africa* (London, 1815): 526; J. B. Peires, "Nxele, Ntsikana, and the Origins of the Xhosa Religious Reaction," *Journal of African History* 20 (1979): 51–62; W. H. I. Bleek, *Zulu Legends*, ed. J. A. Engelbrecht (Pretoria, 1952): 3–4.

7. P. B. Clarke, *West Africa and Christianity* (London, 1986): 159; E. W. Smith, *Robert Moffat, One of God's Gardeners* (London, 1925): 147.

8. R. Moffat, *Missionary Labors and Scenes in Southern Africa* (London, 1842): 268; J. Mackenzie, *Ten Years North of the Orange River: A Story of Everyday Life and Work Among the South African Tribes from 1859 to 1869* (Edinburgh, 1871): 134; H. A. Reyburn, "The Missionary as Rainmaker," *The Critic* 1 (1933): 146–53.

9. S. S. Walker, "The Message as the Medium: The Harrist Churches of the Ivory Coast and Ghana," in G. Bond, W. Johnson, and S. S. Walker, eds., *African Christianity: Patterns of Religious Continuity* (New York, 1979): 22–64; D. Shank, "The Taming of the Prophet Harris," *Journal of Religion in Africa* 27 (1997): 78.

10. J. D. Y. Peel, *Aladura: A Religious Movement Among the Yoruba* (London, 1968); B. C. Ray, "Aladura Christianity: A Yoruba Religion," *Journal of Religion in Africa* 23 (1993): 266–91.

11. M.-L. Martin, *An African Prophet and His Church,* trans. D. L. Moore (Oxford, 1975): 44.

12. M. Aquina, "The People of the Spirit: An Independent Church in Rhodesia," *Africa* 37 (1967): 203–19; E. Gunner, "The Word, the Book, and the Zulu Church of Nazareth," in R. Whitaker and E. Sienaert, eds., *Oral Tradition and Literacy: Changing Visions of the World* (Durban, 1988): 214–15.

13. R. I. Rotberg, *The Rise of Nationalism in Central Africa: The Making of Malawi and Zambia, 1873–1964* (Cambridge, Mass., 1965): 68.

14. K. E. Fields, *Revival and Rebellion in Colonial Central Africa* (Princeton, 1985): 108.

15. G. Shepperson and T. Price, *Independent African: John Chilembwe and the Origins, Setting, and Significance of the Nyasaland Native Rising of 1915* (Edinburgh, 1958).

16. Rotberg, *Rise of Nationalism,* 135.

17. E. L. Blumhofer, *Restoring the Faith: The Assemblies of God, Pentecostalism, and American Culture* (Urbana, Ill., 1993): 57; F. D. Goodman, *Speaking in Tongues* (Chicago, 1972); Fields, *Revival and Rebellion*, 156.

18. Fields, *Revival and Rebellion*, 165.

19. Blumhofer, *Restoring the Faith*, 22–23; G. Wacker, "Marching to Zion," *Church History* 54 (1885): 496–511.

20. J. P. Kiernan, "Where Zionists Draw the Line: A Study of Religious Exclusiveness in an African Township," *African Studies* 33, 3 (1974): 79–90.

21. G. C. Oosthuizen, *Post-Christianity in Africa: A Theological and Anthropological Study* (Stellenbosch, 1968); B. Sundkler, *Bantu Prophets in South Africa*, 2d ed. (Oxford, 1961); D. Chidester, J. Tobler, and D. Wratten, *Christianity in South Africa* (Westport, Conn., 1997): 323–451.

22. J. Mbiti, "Response to the Article by John Kinney," *Occasional Bulletin of Missionary Research* 3, 2 (1979): 68; D. Tutu, "Whither African Theology?" in E. Fasholé-Luke, ed., *Christianity in Independent Africa* (London, 1978): 369; N. Mandela, *Long Walk to Freedom: The Autobiography of Nelson Mandela* (Randburg, South Africa, 1995): 12, 25.

25: Asian Heavens

1. Matteo Ricci, *Opere storiche del P. Matteo Ricci*, 2 vols., ed. T. Venturi (Macerata, 1911–13): 2:215; J. Gernet, *China and the Christian Impact: A Conflict of Cultures*, trans. J. Lloyd (Cambridge, 1985): 16–17.

2. Li Zhi, *Hsü Fen-shu* (Peking, 1961): 36; A. Walter, "Demerits and Deadly Sins: Jesuit Moral Tracts in Late Ming China," in S. B. Schwartz, ed., *Implicit Understandings: Observing, Reporting, and Reflecting on the Encounters Between Europeans and Other Peoples in the Early Modern Era* (Cambridge, 1994): 422–23.

3. P. D'Elia, ed., *Fonti Ricciane: Documenti originali concernenti Matteo Ricci e la storia delle prime relazioni tra l'Europa e la Cina, 1579–1615*, 3 vols. (Rome, 1942–49): 108; Matteo Ricci, *China in the Sixteenth Century: The Journals of Matthew Ricci, 1583–1610*, trans. L. J. Gallagher (New York, 1953).

4. Matteo Ricci, *Opere storiche*, 2:225; Gernet, *China and the Christian Impact*, 22; Matteo Ricci, *The True Meaning of the Lord of Heaven (T'ien-chu Shih-i)*, ed. E. J. Malatesta, trans. D. Lancashire and P. H. Kuo-chen (St. Louis, 1985): 125.

5. Gernet, *China and the Christian Impact*, 44–45, 57.

6. Matteo Ricci, *True Meaning of the Lord of Heaven*, 447.

7. Gernet, *China and the Christian Impact*, 159.

8. Matteo Ricci, *True Meaning of the Lord of Heaven*, 335.

9. Gernet, *China and the Christian Impact*, 168–69.

10. G. Elison, *Deus Destroyed: The Image of Christianity in Early Modern Japan* (Cambridge, Mass., 1973): 283–84.

11. Robert Morrison, *Memoirs of the Life and Labors of Robert Morrison*, 2 vols. (London, 1839).

12. T. Hamberg, *The Visions of Hung-Siu-tshuen, and Origin of the Kuang-si Insurrection* (New York, 1969): 21; J. D. Spence, *God's Chinese Son: The Taiping Heavenly Kingdom of Hong Xiuquan* (New York, 1996): 119, 115, 173.

13. C. Y. Hsü, *The Rise of Modern China* (Oxford, 1970): 299.

14. Spence, *God's Chinese Son*, 292, 233, 322.

15. S. Murakami, *Japanese Religion in the Modern Century*, trans. H. B. Earhart (Tokyo, 1980): 35; G. Minamiki, *The Chinese Rites Controversy from Its Beginning to Modern Times* (Chicago, 1985): 112; Ishii Ryosuke, ed., *Japanese Legislation in the Meiji Era*, trans. W. J. Chambliss (Tokyo, 1958): 400, 727.

16. Kikuchi Dairoku, *Japanese Education* (London, 1909): 1–3.

17. J. M. Kitagawa, *Religion in Japanese History* (New York, 1990): 243.

18. E. Brunner, "The Unique Christian Mission: The Mukyokai ('Non-Church') Movement in Japan," in W. Leibrecht, ed., *Religion and Culture: Essays in Honor of Paul Tillich* (New York, 1959): 287–90; Ryusaku Tsunoda, W. T. de Bary, and D. Keene, eds. and trans., *Sources of Japanese Tradition* (New York, 1958): 342–43, 347–50.

26: Hindu Christians

1. I. G. Zupanov, "Aristocratic Analogies and Demotic Descriptions in the Seventeenth-Century Madurai Mission," *Representations* 41 (1993): 127, 130.

2. L. W. Brown, *The Indian Christians of St. Thomas* (Cambridge, 1956): 43–59.

3. S. Bayly, *Saints, Goddesses, and Kings: Muslims and Christians in South Indian Society, 1700–1900* (Cambridge, 1989): 252.

4. G. T. Mackenzie, "History of Christianity in Travancore," in V. N. Aiya, ed., *The Travancore State Manual*, 3 vols. (Trivandrum, 1906): 203.

5. H. D'souza, *In the Steps of St. Thomas* (Poona, 1964): 36–37.

6. W. S. Hunt, *The Anglican Church in Travancore and Cochin 1816–1916* (Kottayam, 1920): 103–4; Bayly, *Saints, Goddesses, and Kings*, 294.

7. M. M. Thomas, *The Acknowledged Christ of the Indian Renaissance* (London, 1969).

8. W. T. de Bary, ed., *Sources of the Indian Tradition* (New York, 1958): 575; Ram Mohan Roy, *English Works of Raja Rammohun Roy* (Alahabad, 1906): 74, 483ff.

9. Joshua Marshman, *A Defense of the Deity and Atonement of Jesus Christ in Reply to Rammohun Roy of Calcutta* (London, 1822): 34ff.

10. Marshman, *Defense of the Deity,* 34ff.; Roy, *English Works,* 700–775, 570–72.

11. De Bary, *Sources of Indian Tradition,* 68; M. C. Parekh, *Bramarshi Keshub Chunder Sen* (Rajkot, 1931): 101, 160; J. N. Farquhar, *Modern Religious Movements in India* (London, 1915): 57.

12. Ramakrishna, *The Gospel of Ramakrishna* (New York, 1942): 34; N. Devdas, *Sri Ramakrishna* (Bangalore, 1965): 32.

13. Vivekananda, *The Complete Works of Swami Vivekananda,* 8 vols., 5th ed. (Calcutta, 1931): 7:2.

14. M. K. Gandhi, *An Autobiography or The Story of My Experiments with Truth,* 2 vols., trans. M. Desai (Ahmedabad, 1927, 1929): 1:48.

15. Gandhi, *Autobiography,* 2:752.

16. M. K. Gandhi, *Christian Missions* (Ahmedabad, 1940): 28; M. K. Gandhi, *The Message of Jesus Christ,* comp. A. T. Hingorani (Bombay, 1963): 3.

17. Gandhi, *The Message of Jesus,* 36, 10, 19.

18. Gandhi, *The Message of Jesus,* preface, 79.

19. Gandhi, *The Message of Jesus,* 12, 23; Gandhi, *Collected Works,* 89 vols. (Delhi, 1958–83): 64:397.

20. Gandhi, *Autobiography,* 1:202; S. K. George, *Gandhi's Challenge to Christianity* (Ahmedabad, 1960); E. S. Jones, *Mahatma Gandhi: An Interpretation* (London 1948): 79.

21. R. Panikkar, *The Unknown Christ of Hinduism* (London, 1964); *The Trinity and World Religions* (Madras, 1970); *The Silence of God* (Maryknoll, N.Y., 1989).

27: Christian Cargo

1. R. Lovett, *The History of the London Missionary Society, 1795–1895,* 2 vols. (London, 1899): 1:120–21.

2. William Ellis, *Polynesian Researches, During a Residence of Nearly Six Years in the South Sea Islands,* 2 vols. (London, 1829): 2:225, 2:215, 1:329.

3. J. Garrett, *To Live Among the Stars: Christian Origins in Oceania* (Geneva, 1982): 16.

4. P. Lawrence, *Road Belong Cargo: A Study of the Cargo Movement in the Southern Madang District, New Guinea* (Manchester, 1964).

5. Nikolai Nikolaevich Mikloucho-Maclay, *New Guinea Diaries, 1871–1883,* trans. C. L. Sentinella (Madang, Papua New Guinea, 1975).

6. Lawrence, *Road Belong Cargo,* 80–81.

7. J. Guiart, "The Millenarian Aspect of Conversion to Christianity in the South Pacific," in S. L. Thrupp, ed., *Millennial Dreams in Action: Studies in Revolutionary Religious Movements* (New York, 1970): 124.

8. K. Burridge, *Mambu, A Melanesian Millennium* (New York, 1970): 184–85, 188–89.

9. A. Porter, "'Commerce and Christianity': The Rise and Fall of a Nineteenth-Century Missionary Slogan," *The Historical Journal* 28 (1985): 597–98.

10. Max Weber, *The Protestant Ethic and the Spirit of Capitalism,* trans. T. Parsons (New York, 1958).

11. J. Wells, *James Stewart of Lovedale: The Life of James Stewart* (London, 1908): 216.

12. John Wesley, *Sermons* 2:230–31; 2:286; Robert Southey, *The Life of Wesley and the Rise and Progress of Methodism,* 2 vols., ed. M. H. Fitzgerald (Oxford, 1925); E. P. Thompson, *The Making of the English Working Class* (London, 1963): 369.

13. Herbert Spencer, *The Study of Sociology* (London, 1873): 179–80, 388.

14. N. Armstrong, "The Rise of the Domestic Woman," in N. Armstrong and L. Tennenhouse, eds., *The Ideology of Conduct: Essays in Literature and the History of Sexuality* (London, 1987); A. De Riencourt, *Women and Power in History* (London, 1983): 306.

15. George Whitefield, *The Works of the Reverend George Whitefield, M.A.* (London, 1772): 5:183–85.

16. M. Douglas, *Purity and Danger: An Analysis of the Concepts of Pollution and Taboo* (London, 1966); A. McClintock, *Imperial Leather: Race, Gender, and Sexuality in the Colonial Contest* (London, 1995): 167–69.

17. A. Douglas, "Heaven Our Home: Consolation Literature in the Northern United States, 1830–1880," in D. E. Stannard, ed., *Death in America* (Philadelphia, 1974): 63, 66.

18. Karl Marx and Friedrich Engels, *On Religion* (New York, 1964): 316–17.

19. J. Husslein, ed., *Social Wellsprings: Fourteen Epochal Documents by Pope Leo XIII* (Milwaukee, Wis., 1940): 14–23, 168; Karl Kautsky, *Foundations of Christianity,* trans. H. Mins (New York, 1953).

20. Reinhold Niebuhr, *Moral Man and Immoral Society* (New York, 1960): 165;

D. B. Meyer, *The Protestant Search for Political Realism, 1919–1941* (Berkeley, 1960): 174–75.

21. V. I. Lenin, *Religion* (New York, 1959): 93; C. Lane, *Christian Religion in the Soviet Union* (London, 1978): 26–27.

22. M. Spinka, *The Church in Soviet Russia* (Oxford, 1956): 65–66; P. Walters, "A Survey of Soviet Religious Policy," in S. P. Ramet, ed., *Religious Policy in the Soviet Union* (Cambridge, 1993): 12.

28: Holocaust

1. Immanuel Kant, *Religion Within the Limits of Reason Alone,* trans. T. M. Greene and H. H. Hudson (New York, 1960): 116–18, 127–28, 156, 162; *Conflict of the Faculties,* trans. M. J. Gregor (New York, 1979): 94–95.

2. Friedrich Schleiermacher, *On Religion: Speeches to Its Cultured Despisers,* trans. R. Crouter (New York, 1988): 211–13; *The Christian Faith,* ed. H. R. Mackintosh and J. S. Stewart (Edinburgh, 1928): 38; M. A. Meyer, *The Origins of the Modern Jew: Jewish Identity and European Culture in Germany, 1749–1824* (Detroit, 1967): 77.

3. Martin Luther, "Lectures on Galatians," *LW* 26:101; "Lectures on Jonah," *LW* 19:102–4; H. A. Oberman, *The Roots of Anti-Semitism: In the Age of Renaissance and Reformation* (Philadelphia, 1984): 118–22.

4. J. S. Conway, *The Nazi Persecution of the Churches, 1933–45* (New York, 1968): 5, 15; Martin Bormann, "Circular on the Relationship of National Socialism and Christianity," in Conway, *Nazi Persecution of the Churches,* 383–86; G. Lewy, *The Catholic Church and Nazi Germany* (New York, 1964): 274–75.

5. R. Gutman, *Richard Wagner: The Man, His Mind, and His Music* (New York, 1968): 426; Richard Wagner, "Heroism and Christianity" (1903): 279.

6. M. Ryan, "Hitler's Challenge to the Churches: A Theological Political Analysis of *Mein Kampf,*" in F. H. Littell and H. G. Locke, eds., *The German Church Struggle and the Holocaust* (Detroit, 1974): 160; O. Kalbus, *Vom Werden deutscher Filmkunst. Part II: Der Tonfilm* (Altona, 1935): 121–23; G. Lease, *"Odd Fellows" in the Politics of Religion: Modernism, National Socialism, and German Judaism* (Berlin, 1995): 161–62.

7. D. L. Bergen, *Twisted Cross: The German Christian Movement in the Third Reich* (Chapel Hill, N.C., 1996): 23, 31, 23, 65, 63.

8. Joseph Lortz, "Katholischer Zugang zum Nationalsozialismus," *Reich und Kirche: Eine Schriftenreihe,* 2d ed. (Münster, 1934): 28, 4, 23; Karl Adam,

"Deutsches Volkstum und katholisches Christentum," *Theologische Quartal-schrift* 114 (1933): 40–41; Lease, *"Odd Fellows" in the Politics of Religion*, 145–49.

9. Bergen, *Twisted Cross*, 205.

10. Dietrich Bonhoeffer, *Gesammelte Schriften*, 6 vols., ed. E. Bethge (Munich, 1958): 1:39–40; F. H. Littell, "Church Struggle and the Holocaust," in Littell and Locke, *German Church Struggle and the Holocaust*, 15.

11. J. S. Conway, "The Churches," in H. Friedlander and S. Milton, eds., *The Holocaust: Ideology, Bureaucracy, and Genocide* (Millwood, N.Y., 1980): 204.

12. Karl Barth, *The Epistle to the Romans*, trans. E. C. Hoskyns (Oxford, 1933): 10; *Church Dogmatics*, 4 vols., ed. G. W. Bromiley and T. F. Torrance (Edinburgh, 1956–69); E. Busch, *Karl Barth: His Life from Letters and Autobiographical Texts* (London, 1975): 223, 228.

13. E. H. Robertson, *Christians Against Hitler* (London, 1962): 48–52.

14. Busch, *Karl Barth*, 248, 235; U. Tal, *Christians and Jews in Germany: Religion, Politics, and Ideology in the Second Reich, 1870–1914*, trans. N. J. Jacobs (Ithaca, N.Y., 1985): 204.

15. P. Mendes-Flohr, *Divided Passions: Jewish Intellectuals and the Experience of Modernity* (Detroit, 1991): 152–59.

16. Elie Wiesel, *Against Silence: The Voice and Vision of Elie Wiesel*, 3 vols., ed. I. Abrahamson (New York, 1985): 1:166; Johann-Baptist Metz, *The Emergent Church: The Future of Christianity in a Post-bourgeois World* (New York, 1981): 28.

17. F. H. Littell, *The Crucifixion of the Jews: The Failure of Christians to Understand the Jewish Experience* (Macon, Ga., 1986): 2; G. G. Baum, *Christian Theology After Auschwitz* (London, 1976): 8.

18. Jules Isaac, *Jesus and Israel*, ed. C. Huchet-Bishop, trans. S. Gran (New York, 1971): 489–95; A. P. Flannery, ed., *Documents of Vatican II* (Grand Rapids, Mich., 1984): 738.

19. Irving Greenberg, "Cloud of Smoke, Pillar of Fire: Judaism, Christianity, and Modernity After the Holocaust," in E. Fleischner, ed., *Auschwitz: Beginning of a New Era* (New York, 1977): 11.

20. Ignaz Maybaum, *The Face of God After Auschwitz* (Amsterdam, 1965): 36, 306.

21. Richard L. Rubenstein, *After Auschwitz: Radical Theology and Contemporary Judaism* (Indianapolis, 1966): 54–55.

22. Rubenstein, *After Auschwitz*, 153, 151–52.

23. Emil L. Fackenheim, "Transcendence in Contemporary Culture: Philosoph-

ical Reflections and a Jewish Theology," in H. W. Richardson and D. R. Cutler, eds., *Transcendence* (Boston, 1969): 150.

24. Paul M. Van Buren, *A Theology of the Jewish-Christian Reality. Part I: Discerning the Way* (New York, 1980): 116–17.

29: Cold War

1. T. Robbins, D. Anthony, M. Doucas, and T. Curtis, "The Last Civil Religion: Reverend Moon and the Unification Church," *Sociological Analysis* 37 (1976): 111–25; *Divine Principle*, 2d ed. (Washington, D.C., 1973): 523–24.

2. D. Chidester, *Salvation and Suicide: An Interpretation of Jim Jones, the Peoples Temple, and Jonestown* (Bloomington, 1988).

3. Hal Lindsey, *The Late Great Planet Earth* (New York, 1973): 54, 156–57, 175.

4. G. Halsell, *Prophecy and Politics: Militant Evangelists on the Road to Nuclear War* (Westport, Conn., 1986): 46; S. D. O'Leary, *Arguing the Apocalypse: A Theory of Millennial Rhetoric* (Oxford, 1994): 172–93.

5. R. Fried, *Men Against McCarthy* (New York, 1976): 213; J. Roty and M. Decter, *McCarthy and the Communists* (Boston, 1954): 154–56; R. E. Flanders, *Senator from Vermont* (Boston, 1961): 255.

6. W. Martin, *A Prophet with Honor: The Billy Graham Story* (New York, 1991): 165.

7. Bill Bright, *Revolution Now* (San Bernardino, Calif., 1969): 11–12; M. Sherwin, *The Extremists* (New York, 1963): 110.

8. Anonymous, "A Layman's Faith," *Christianity Today* 8 (July 1957): 33; Reinhold Niebuhr, "Literalism, Individualism, and Billy Graham," *Christian Century* (May 23, 1956): 640–41.

9. Reinhold Niebuhr, *The Irony of American History* (New York, 1952): 3–4.

10. Nicolas Berdyaev, *Dream and Reality* (New York, 1962): 178.

11. Paul Tillich, *The Courage to Be* (New Haven, 1953): 173.

12. R. S. Ellwood, *The Fifties Spiritual Marketplace: American Religion in a Decade of Conflict* (New Brunswick, N.J., 1997): 183.

13. Martin Luther King, Jr., *Stride Toward Freedom* (New York, 1958): 101; L. Bennett, Jr., *What Manner of Man?* (Chicago, 1962): 82, 66; R. A. Spivey, E. S. Gaustad, and R. F. Allen, eds., *Religious Issues in American Culture* (Menlo Park, Calif., 1972): 78; L. V. Baldwin, *To Make the Wounded Whole: The Cultural Legacy of Martin Luther King, Jr.* (Minneapolis, 1992): 203; W. Minter, *King Solomon's Mines Revisited: Western Interests and the Burdened History of Southern Africa* (New York, 1986): 137; Bennett, *What Manner of Man?* 240.

14. Malcolm X, *The Autobiography of Malcolm X* (New York, 1964): 200; A. Pinkney, *Red, Black, and Green: Black Nationalism in the United States* (Cambridge, 1976): 167; James H. Cone, *A Black Theology of Liberation* (Philadelphia, 1970): 23, 120–21, 125.

15. Gustavo Gutiérrez, *Theology of Liberation,* trans. C. Inda and J. Eagleson (Maryknoll, N.Y., 1973): 175–76; Gutiérrez and R. Shaull, *Liberation and Change* (Atlanta, 1977): 84.

16. F. Gray, *Divine Disobedience* (New York, 1971): 311–12; J. M. Kirk, *Between God and the Party: Religion and Politics in Revolutionary Cuba* (Tampa, Fla., 1989): 53, 96, 106–7; Fidel Castro Ruz, *Fidel and Religion: Castro Talks on Revolution and Religion with Frei Bretto* (New York, 1985).

17. W. R. Goodman, Jr., and J. J. H. Price, *Jerry Falwell: An Unauthorized Profile* (Lynchburg, Va., 1981): 91; F. Fitzgerald, "Reporter at Large: A Disciplined, Charging Army," *New Yorker* 57 (May 18, 1981): 106, 108; Jerry Falwell, *Listen America!* (Garden City, N.Y., 1980): 24, 13; *America Can Be Saved* (Murfreesboro, Tenn., 1979): 141.

18. P. Gifford, *The New Crusaders: Christianity and the New Right in Southern Africa* (London, 1991): 35; R. Hunsicker, "South Africa: Nation of Strong Religious Values," *Family Protection Scoreboard* (Costa Mesa, Calif., 1987): 13; L. Jones, "Right-Wing Evangelicals and South Africa," *Moto* 64 (April 1988): 12.

19. Concerned Evangelicals, *Evangelical Witness in South Africa: A Critique of Evangelical Theology and Practice by Evangelicals Themselves* (Dobsonville, South Africa, 1986): 4.

20. L. Thompson, *The Political Mythology of Apartheid* (New Haven, 1985): 43–44; J. A. Loubser, *The Apartheid Bible: A Critical Review of Racial Theology in South Africa* (Cape Town, 1987): 53.

21. J. W. de Gruchy, "A Short History of the Christian Institute," in C. Villa-Vicencio and J. W. de Gruchy, eds., *Resistance and Hope: South African Essays in Honor of Beyers Naudé* (Cape Town, 1985): 17; J. W. de Gruchy and C. Villa-Vicencio, eds., *Apartheid Is a Heresy* (Grand Rapids, Mich., 1983); C. Villa-Vicencio, *Trapped in Apartheid* (Maryknoll, N.Y., 1988): 147–48.

22. D. Chidester, *Religions of South Africa* (London, 1992): 213.

23. Steve Biko, *Steve Biko—I Write What I Like: A Selection of His Writings* (San Francisco, 1986): 92, 94, 98; P. Walshe, *Church Versus State in South Africa: The Case of the Christian Institute* (Maryknoll, N.Y., 1983): 221.

24. C. Villa-Vicencio, *Between Christ and Caesar: Classic and Contemporary Texts on Church and State* (Grand Rapids, Mich., 1986): 269, 268, 259.

25. Chidester, *Religions of South Africa,* 257.

26. D. Chidester, *Patterns of Power: Religion and Politics in American Culture* (Englewood Cliffs, N.J., 1988): 282.

30: New World Order

1. G. Kepel, *The Revenge of God: The Resurgence of Islam, Christianity, and Judaism in the Modern World,* trans. A. Braley (London, 1994): 47–99.

2. Francis Fukuyama, *The End of History and the Last Man* (New York, 1992).

3. R. L. Moore, *Selling God: American Religion in the Marketplace of Culture* (Oxford, 1994).

4. S. Head, *When Pirates Ruled the Waves* (London, 1985): 108; J. H. Ellens, *Models of Religious Broadcasting* (Grand Rapids, Mich., 1974): 16; J. K. Hadden, "The Globalization of American Televangelism," in R. Robertson and W. R. Garrett, eds., *Religion and Global Order* (New York, 1991): 221–44.

5. S. D. O'Leary, "Cyberspace as Sacred Space: Communicating Religion on Computer Networks," *Journal of the American Academy of Religion* 64 (1996): 783.

6. G. Davie, *Religion in Britain Since 1945: Believing Without Belonging* (Oxford, 1994): 47.

7. D. Groothuis, *The Soul in Cyberspace* (Grand Rapids, Mich., 1997); M. A. Kellner, "Losing Our Souls in Cyberspace: Douglas Groothuis on the Virtues and Vices of Virtual Reality," *Christianity Today* 41, 10 (1997): 54.

8. C. Campbell, *The Romantic Ethic and the Spirit of Modern Consumerism* (Oxford, 1987).

9. M. Pendergrast, *For God, Country, and Coca-Cola: The Unauthorized History of the World's Most Popular Soft Drink* (New York, 1993); D. Chidester, "The Church of Baseball, the Fetish of Coca-Cola, and the Potlatch of Rock 'n' Roll: Theoretical Models for the Study of Religion in American Popular Culture," *Journal of the American Academy of Religion* 54 (1996): 749–50.

10. C. McDannell, *Material Christianity: Religion and Popular Culture in America* (New Haven, 1995): 47.

11. T. Boswell, "The Church of Baseball," in G. C. Ward and K. Burns, eds., *Baseball: An Illustrated History* (New York, 1994): 189–93.

12. D. Marsh, *Louie, Louie* (New York, 1993): 73–74; M. Bayles, *Hole in Our Soul: The Loss of Beauty and Meaning in American Popular Music* (New York, 1994).

13. F. Bronson, *The Billboard Book of Number One Hits* (New York, 1985): 201.

14. J. Benson, *Transformative Getaways: For Spiritual Growth, Self-Discovery, and Holistic Healing* (New York, 1996); D. MacCannell, *The Tourist: A New Theory of the Leisure Class* (New York, 1976).

15. Hendrik Kraemer, *The Christian Message in a Non-Christian World* (London, 1938): 107; *Why Christianity of All Religions?* (London, 1962): 15; E. Percy, ed., *Facing the Unfinished Task: Messages Delivered at the Congress of World Mission* (Grand Rapids, Mich., 1961): 9; G. Lindbeck, *The Nature of Doctrine: Religion and Theology in a Postliberal Age* (London, 1974).

16. Karl Rahner, *Theological Investigations*, vol. 5 (London, 1961): 118, 133, 132; John Hick, *God Has Many Names: Britain's New Religious Pluralism* (London, 1980): 50.

17. John Hick, *God and the Universe of Faiths* (London, 1977): 122.

18. Hans Küng, *The Declaration of a Global Ethic* (London, 1993).

19. U. Hannerz, *Transnational Connections: Culture, People, Places* (London, 1996): 91–101.

Index